The Complete Slayer

By the same author:

SLAYER: AN EXPANDED AND UPDATED UNOFFICIAL AND
 UNAUTHORISED GUIDE TO BUFFY THE VAMPIRE SLAYER
SLAYER: THE NEXT GENERATION – AN UNOFFICIAL AND
 UNAUTHORISED GUIDE TO SEASON SIX OF BUFFY THE VAMPIRE
 SLAYER
SLAYER: THE LAST DAYS OF SUNNYDALE – AN UNOFFICIAL AND
 UNAUTHORISED GUIDE TO THE FINAL SEASON OF BUFFY THE
 VAMPIRE SLAYER
SLAYER: A TOTALLY AWESOME COLLECTION OF BUFFY TRIVIA
HOLLYWOOD VAMPIRE: AN EXPANDED AND UPDATED UNOFFICIAL
 AND UNAUTHORISED GUIDE TO ANGEL
INSIDE BARTLET'S WHITE HOUSE: AN UNOFFICIAL AND
 UNAUTHORISED GUIDE TO THE WEST WING
HIGH TIMES: AN UNOFFICIAL AND UNAUTHORISED GUIDE TO
 ROSWELL

By the same author with Paul Cornell and Martin Day:
THE NEW TREK PROGRAMME GUIDE
X-TREME POSSIBILITIES
THE AVENGERS DOSSIER

By the same author with Martin Day:
SHUT IT! A FAN'S GUIDE TO 70S COPS ON THE BOX

THE COMPLETE SLAYER

An Unofficial and Unauthorised Guide
to Every Episode of
Buffy the Vampire Slayer

Keith Topping

First published in Great Britain in 2004 by
Virgin Books Ltd
Thames Wharf Studios
Rainville Road
London
W6 9HA

A catalogue record for this book is available from the British Library.

ISBN 0 7535 0931 8

Typeset by TW Typesetting, Plymouth, Devon
Printed and bound in Great Britain by Mackays of Chatham PLC

Contents

The Complete Slayer
is dedicated to Joss Whedon
and the cast and crew of
Buffy the Vampire Slayer.

Thanks for the last seven years.

Acknowledgements

The author wishes to thank the following for their encouragement and contributions to what is now seven separate editions or spin-offs of *Slayer*: Ian and Janet Abrahams, Becki Ablett, David Alder, Jessica Allen, Marie Antoon, Rebecca Barber, Jeremy Bement, Robyn Bennett, Michael Billinghurst, Stephen Booth, Sean Brady, Jo Brooks, Anthony Brown, Suzie Campagna, Paul and Wendy Comeau (thanks for all the scones), Neil Connor (computer-related assistance above and beyond the call), Paul Cornell and Caroline Symcox, Allison Costa, Rob Crowther, Michael Cule, Peter Darvill-Evans (who started it all), Doug Dean, Keith RA DeCandido, Alexandre Deschampes, Dan Erenberg, Nicola Guess, Kathryn Fallon, Jeff Farrell, Irene Finn, Simona Fischer, Lisa Harrold, the Godlike Genius of Jeff Hart, Lea Hays, Claire Hennessy, Kathy Hill, Ralph Holland, David Howe, Alan Hufana, Alryssa Kelly, Kevin Lamke, Helen Lane, Sarah Lavelle, Di Lawson, Gary Lewis, Peter Linford, Michael Lee, Dave and Lesley McIntee, Ian McIntire, Paul McIntyre, Jackie Marshall, Scott Marshall, Alan Miller, David Miller at *Shivers*, Jon Miller, John Molyneux, the legendary Ian Mond, John Mosby, Ingrid Oliansky, Tara O'Shea, Eva Palmerton, Sarah Parker, Mark Phippen, Alex Popple, Ian Reid, Shaun Reid, Leslie Remencus, Justin Richards, Gary Russell, John Seavey, Jill Sherwin, Trina Short, Dan Smiczek, Jim Smith, Mick Snowden, Tom Spilsbury, Matt Springer, Paul Steib and Wendy Wiseman, Dave Stone, Jim Swallow and Mandy Mills, Ruth Thomas, Caroline Trevelyan, Iain Truskett, Yochanan and Veda Urias, (the real) Maggie Walsh, Bill and Jacque Watson, Christopher Weimer, Geoff Wessel, Alicia White, Kyle Whitehead, Thomas Whitney, Martin Wiggins and the Fat Dragon Ladies.

My gratitude is due to numerous website custodians who spared the time to answer my, no doubt annoying, emails. Also to Will Cameron, Tony Dryer, Beth Kiefner, Judy Pykala, Carol Stoneburner and Deb Walsh who helped to fill some vital gaps. Plus, everyone at Gallifrey One and CONvergence (including my fellow campaigners for a Tasteful-Lesbian-Shower-Scene, Anna Bliss, Stephanie Lindorff, Jody Wurl and Windy Merrill). Not forgetting David Bailey, Jason Boulter, Matt Broughton, Paul Condon,

Davy Darlington, Simon Guerrier, Scott Matthewman, Jim Sangster and all my pals on the *Buffy Watchers* mailing list.

A special thank you to my Scooby Gang: my long-suffering editor Kirstie Addis, Martin Day (*my* Watcher), Diana Dougherty, Clay Eichelberger, Rob Francis (who *again* went for the doughnuts), Robert Franks, Shaun Lyon and Jason Tucker (invaluable critique), Tony and Jane Kenealy, Paul Simpson (who provided unedited transcripts of his interviews with many of the cast and crew), Kathy Sullivan (without whom there would have been no *Slayer*), Susannah Tiller (significant contributions to the **Playing the Homophobia Card** section), Graeme Topping, Deborah Williams (for numerous contributions to both the book and my sanity) and Mark Wyman. All of who, time and again, loaned this ongoing project their boundless enthusiasm and considerable talents.

And, as always, to my family for their continuing support.

This book was written on location, in Newcastle upon Tyne, Van Nuys, North Hollywood, Minneapolis, London, Bath, Bristol, Paris and Madeira, and various airports and hotels in between.

Preface

Xander: '*He did a spell just to make us think he was cool?*'
Giles: '*Yes.*'
Xander: '*That is so cool!*'

– 'Superstar'

When I first proposed *Slayer* to Virgin Publishing late in 1998, my main reason for wanting to write the book was that there was no episode guide to *Buffy the Vampire Slayer* available in Britain. By the time the book was commissioned two months later, there were *three* in the shops. Such is the pace at which a cult can grow into a mainstream success. OK, so there *are* other *Buffy* books out there, and some of them are very good. (One or two are written by friends of mine!) *Slayer* is different to all of them, however. Certainly, it covers the same episodes, but it covers them in very different ways. The aim of *Slayer* is to offer a British perspective to this most Californian of subjects and to provide a touch of critical analysis where other books may fear to tread.

Buffy was, on one level, a quasi-fairy tale in which a group of young people were the focus of a battle between the forces of good (as represented by themselves) and evil (represented, mostly, by an older generation). In other words, it was 'The Brothers Grimm' with a rock'n'roll soundtrack and its own syntax. Yet there was always more to this series than sharp one-liners and eye-candy set pieces. Without getting too pretentious, *Buffy* shared more in common with *Hamlet* than a blond hero and death on a large scale. *Buffy* was about growing up and facing the totally mundane horrors of the adult world. About a time when the game of life was still being played by *our* rules but with the knowledge that this was changing. It concerned the point where childhood ends and the ordinary, everyday realities of career, relationships and responsibilities appear on the horizon. Thus, as the viewer explored Sunnydale, we saw a world that we could, hopefully, recognise and identify with. Because it was *our* world too. A world of hormone-charged teenagers with their own secret language. A world where educational establishments played host to the epic battle between the forces of light and darkness. A world where the body count (both physical *and* emotional) was astronomical. These themes were universal and timeless, not tied to a particular part of the United States in the dying days of the 20th century.

The story was simple: Buffy Summers and her mother move from Los Angeles to the small Californian town of Sunnydale after her expulsion from a previous school (there was that nasty business of the gym burning down). On her first day at Sunnydale High, Buffy befriended two local nerds, Xander Harris and Willow Rosenberg, which excluded her from the cool set, led by the formidable Cordelia Chase. Buffy also met her Watcher, Rupert Giles, because (as we discovered) she was a *Vampire Slayer*: A once-per-each-generation clan of stake-wielding super-babes who rid the world of the vampires, the demons and the forces of darkness. As *SFX* said, when placing the series in their 'Top Fifty SF TV Shows of All Time', '*Buffy* should be awful . . . In the land where the one-line pitch is king, *Buffy* rules . . .'

But *Buffy* was also a peek into a toy shop of magnificent conceit – a series fixated in equal measure by the claustrophobic 'outsider' constraints of the adolescent years and by a battle fought by a heroine, not because she *wants* to (indeed, she was initially a reluctant Slayer), but because she was good at it and because, like most dirty jobs, *someone* had to do it. Into this mix came elements of high (and sometimes extremely *low*) comedy and much confident and self-aware dialogue. *SFX* believed that the main reason for *Buffy*'s success was that it had 'the three cornerstones of quality TV: good writing, good characters and good acting. More to the point, *Buffy* is the perfect combination of both cynicism and quality; a well-written, well-acted series that just happens to star gorgeous teenagers in soap-style situations.' Heavyweight US critic Matt Roush also wrote of the series' genre-crossing appeal: 'A show as terrific as *Buffy*, with its kicky commingling of humour and horror, may be aimed at the youth market. But it deserves a following as wide as its buzz is loud. If only it could overcome the perception of its silly sounding title . . . I'd argue that it has a bigger emotional resonance than any youth soap on the air.'

Anthony Stewart Head who played the erudite Giles, told *DreamWatch* about his first impressions of the script: 'I was sitting in the Border Grill in Santa Monica . . . I laughed out loud and suddenly found myself having to stop because people were looking at me! As I was reading it, I couldn't wait to turn the page and find out what happened next. I thought this is an extraordinary combination. I'm no judge of what is going to be a success on TV but this *has* to be a success.' And so it proved.

Headings

Dreaming (As Blondie Once Said) is Free: Lots of TV series do cool dream sequences. *Buffy* did *magnificent*, surreal, scary, funny ones – as you'll find listed here.

Dudes and Babes: Who's hot and who's *not* among the beautiful people of Sunnydale. The author is grateful to a plethora of fans (of various sexualities) for gleefully adding suggestions and the odd secret fantasy to this section.

Authority Sucks!: Which aspect of square-conformity was trying to bring the kids under their thumb. A category for would-be anarchists everywhere.

Mom's Apple Pie: Aspects of traditional US family life either shown or subverted. We also keep an eye on Buffy's (often tempestuous) relationship with, firstly, her mother and then her younger sister Dawn and how, in the absence of Joyce, Buffy rapidly turned into a parent. With all of the horrors that such a metamorphosis entails. Brian Lowry, writing in the *Los Angeles Times*, noted that: 'Parents on most of WB's teen-orientated shows – *Dawson's Creek*, *Buffy*, *Felicity* and *Zoe, Duncan, Jack & Jane* – aren't just absent or inept; rather, in the few scenes they're given they are frequently clueless, bullying or dysfunctional, in need of a stern lecture from their kids regarding morality.'

Denial, Thy Name is Joyce: A category that details Joyce Summers's amazing propensity for self-delusion and how this trend subsequently started to rub off on other characters, specifically her daughters. Kristine Sutherland, who played Joyce, in a thoughtful, revealing interview with Paul Simpson, confessed: 'A parent of an adolescent has to walk a very fine line, and sometimes what's called for is a healthy dose of denial and looking the other way. I really believe in the power of denial.' We've noticed.

It's a Designer Label!: Fashion statements, tips and victims are detailed, along with the lengths of the skirts involved. *Buffy*'s costume designer Cynthia Bergstrom did, in fact, select clothes for the cast from fashionable L.A. stores such as Neiman-Marcus, Fred Siegel Flair, Tommy Hilfiger, Macy's, Contempo Casuals and Traffic. However, Sarah Michelle Gellar, according to *Entertainment Weekly*, 'put the kibosh on turtlenecks and microminis, which is why Buffy's criminally short skirts vanished after season one.'

References: Pop-culture, 'Generation X' and general homage to all things esoteric. In previous editions I've occasionally pointed out where characters 'misquote' from a text. It has been suggested, rightly, that more often than not such misquotations are actually deliberate allusions and that paraphrasing might be a more accurate way to describe these.

Geek-Speak: A section that tries to catch all of Warren, Jonathan and Andrew's media referencing and general *sadness*. And Xander's too.

Bitch!: Girls will be girls . . . All those moments that make the little boys twitch nervously.

Awesome!: The monsters that menace Sunnydale. The action-sequences. The 'funny bits'. All the things that make the average viewer go '*COOL!*'

Valley-Speak: From 'the netherworld known as the 818 area code' and for those who, *like*, don't understand what's, *you know*, being said. *Totally.* The series unique teen-speak described by Buffy's creator, Joss Whedon, as 'twisting the English language until it cries out in pain'.

Cigarettes and Alcohol: An occasional category dealing with teenage naughtiness of the nicotine-and-lager variety.

Logic, Let Me Introduce You to This Window: Goofs, plot-holes and continuity errors.

I Just *Love* Your Accent: Examples of *Buffy*'s charmingly Californian view of the British.

Quote/Unquote: The dialogue worth rewinding the video for.

Other categories appear occasionally. Most should be fairly self-explanatory. **Critique** details what the press and fan groups had to say while **Comments** from the production crew and cast have been added where appropriate. **Soundtrack** highlights the series' excellent use of music. Songs marked '*' appear on *Buffy the Vampire Slayer – The Album* (see **62**, 'Wild at Heart').

Preface to the Complete Edition

The Complete Slayer attempts to tell the unedited story of a remarkable television show.

On 20 May 2003, after six and a half years, 144 episodes, a highly regarded spin-off series and a merchandising line that stretches from shot-glasses to ladies underwear via designer-jewellery, *Buffy the Vampire Slayer* faded from our TV screens for the final time. It did so in a characteristically entertaining way with a highly enjoyable episode called 'Chosen', which brought many of the dramatic themes that the series had covered full-circle. *Buffy*, like all great stories, had a beginning, a middle and an end.

Except that *Buffy* will, frankly, *never* die. The characters have spun off into a popular series of novels and comics, the show has been sold on video and DVD to millions of households and it's now in the perpetual twilight world of syndication. Like *Star Trek* and *The X-Files* before it, you can guarantee that somewhere in the world at any given moment someone will be watching an episode of *Buffy*. Which is strangely comforting, and not a little ironic, given the series' humble origins and constant fights to find, and then maintain, any sort of audience.

More importantly, the series also ended with renewed hope, with many of the characters still alive – and available for a feature film or some other spin-off at some vague point in the future. What follows will, hopefully, explain why.

Keith Topping
Escaping by Canoe
Merrie Albion
August 2004

It's a Joss-thing

'I was there almost all the way through shooting. I eventually threw up my hands because I could not be around Donald Sutherland any longer. It didn't turn out to be the movie that I had written. They never do, but that was my first lesson. Not that the movie is without merit, but I just watched a lot of stupid wannabe-star behaviour . . .'

– Joss Whedon on *Buffy the Vampire Slayer* (1992)

Joe Whedon was born in New York on 23 June 1964, and was raised in uptown Manhattan where he grew up as a confirmed anglophile watching British PBS television series like *Masterpiece Theatre* and *Monty Python's Flying Circus*. His interest in super-hero comics seemed 'deeper, more consuming than in other children', he would later note. 'While they were outside playing, I was indoors, fascinated by a stack of comic books.'

Whedon attended the classy Riverdale High School in New York. It was the worst period of his life. He describes himself at this age as painfully shy and, to this day, doesn't admit to having a single happy memory of those awkward teenage years. 'I was one of those kids who no one pays attention to, so he makes a lot of noise and is wacky.' Though high school was akin to a horror movie for him, to make matters worse 'girls wouldn't so much as poke me with a stick'. So, as with many emotionally bruised and shy young people, rather than face these demons out in the open, Whedon spent much of his time isolated at home reading comics and novels by science fiction authors like Frank Herbert and Larry Niven. On one occasion in an art class, Whedon drew a self-portrait in which his hand disappeared, because he thought that he was becoming invisible to people and that no one would ever love him. This was to become a key element in an idea he was already formulating about a movie set during the teenage years in which traditional horror motifs of vampires and demons are subservient by the *real* problems of growing up as an isolated outsider. 'Basically, school is about alienation and horror,' Joss notes. 'I was very unhappy in high school all the time.' Asked, by *DreamWatch*, how much like his subsequent character Xander Harris he, himself, was as a teenager, Whedon is willing to admit:

'Less-and-less as he gets laid more-and-more.' His education also included a, slightly happier, period at Winchester Public School in England. ('My mother was a teacher,' he adds. 'She was on sabbatical in England so I had to go *somewhere*.')

On his return to the US, Whedon studied film at Connecticut's Wesleyan University in 1987. College turned out to be a much more pleasurable experience than high school. '[It] rocked. I was still miserable for most of the time, but in a party way,' he adds wryly. After graduating, Whedon decided to follow in the family tradition and became the world's first third-generation television writer. His grandfather, John, was a pioneering TV writer in the 1950s and scripted episodes of *The Dick Van Dyke Show*, *The Donna Reed Show* and *Leave it to Beaver*. Joe's father, Tom, was an award-winning auteur, producing *The Golden Girls* and writing for *The Dick Cavett Show*, *Alice* and *Benson*. Older brother, Zachery, is also a theatre playwright. Whedon's father urged him to try writing a TV script ('so I could make enough money to move out of the house', he alleges). Broke and without any job prospects, he moved to Los Angeles and decided to change his name to Joss, meaning 'lucky' in Chinese.

After writing many speculative movie scripts in his late teens, and working in a video store by day to pay the rent, Joss finally landed a writing job on the popular sitcom *Roseanne* (he would also subsequently produce the TV version of the hit movie *Parenthood*). 'My life was completely about film,' he told *teen movieline*. '[I] learned about filmmaking by analysing two particular movies, *Johnny Guitar* and *The Naked Kiss*.' However, with his encyclopaedic fanboy knowledge of horror movies and comics, Whedon had always wanted to write for that market (one of his favourite films remains Stanley Kubrick's *The Shining*) and he freely acknowledges the influence of two stylistically fascinating modernist vampire movies – *The Lost Boys* and *Near Dark* – on the concept of *Buffy*. ('Sometimes we have fruity European Anne Rice-type vampires,' notes Whedon. 'Sometimes we have the dusty, western *Near Dark*-type vampires. And sometimes we just have a bunch of stuntmen.') 'I watched a lot of horror movies as a child,' Whedon told *The Big Breakfast*. 'I saw all these blonde women going down alleys and getting killed and I felt really bad for them. I wanted one of them to kill a monster for a change. So I came up with *Buffy*.'

Whether *Buffy the Vampire Slayer* should be regarded as an example of Joss Whedon's incredible writing talent or as a triumph for his persuasive skills is (to this day) unclear, but the very fact that the concept ever made it beyond its initial one-line description more than suggests the latter. Joss's movie script for *Buffy*, written when he was just 21, suffered four years of rejection before finding a supporter in producer Howard Rosenman.

However, the eventual film, made in 1992, disappointed Whedon bitterly. But as a young writer at the very bottom of the Hollywood ladder he had little control over the finished product. Director Fran Kuzui increased the camp factor and downplayed the terror in the script. 'When you wink at the audience and say nothing matters, you can't have peril,' notes Joss. To him, that was the end of the project and, over the next four years, Whedon became one of Hollywood's hottest movie screenwriters. He worked primarily as a script doctor – sometimes uncredited, though for rapidly increasing salaries – on movies like *Twister*, *Speed*, *Alien: Resurrection* and *Toy Story* – for which he was Oscar nominated. 'Most of the dialogue in *Speed* is mine, and a bunch of the characters,' Joss told Tasha Robinson. 'I have the only poster left with my name still on it. Getting arbitrated off the credits of *Speed* was *not* fun.' *Waterworld* was an even more frustrating experience for Joss. 'I refer to myself as the world's highest-paid stenographer,' he says. 'People ask me, "What's the worst job you ever had?" [I say] "I once was a writer in Hollywood . . ." Talk about taking the glow off [the movie industry].' *Waterworld*, he notes, was a good idea, 'but the script was the classic "They write a generic script and don't care about the idea." When I was brought in, there was no water in the last 40 pages. It all took place on land, or on a ship. I was basically taking notes from Kevin Costner, who was very nice to work with, but he's not a writer. So I was there for seven weeks, and accomplished nothing. I wrote a few puns, and some scenes that I can't even sit through because they came out so bad. It was the same situation with *X-Men*.'

As he told *Entertainment Weekly* in 1997: 'I always look at my movie career as an abysmal failure,' and certainly most of his early original screenplays (including *Suspension*, which he described as '*Die Hard* on a bridge') were optioned but never produced. Then, out of the blue, in 1996 Joss was asked by Sandollar Productions to revive *Buffy* as a TV format. *Buffy*, and its highly charged Los Angeles spin-off *Angel*, have subsequently become two of *the* great TV success stories of the 90s and Whedon remains much in demand in Hollywood, writing *Titan AE* and *Atlantis: The Lost Empire*.

Producing a show like *Buffy*, one would assume that Joss is a great lover of gore, yet he isn't by any stretch of the imagination. 'I love horror movies. I also love science fiction and fantasy. I love any world that is different from the one I'm in right now. I think I mostly love the supernatural because I don't believe in it and, therefore, I love the escape of it.' Joss likes to listen to movie scores and praises the work of James Cameron, Sawnee Smith and Gene Colan. His horror genre influences include *Tomb of Dracula*, *Morbius* and numerous movies including *Blade* and the remake of *The Blob*. He thinks that *The Night of the Comet* is hugely underrated and adored the stage version of Frank Langella's *Dracula*.

What makes Joss an outsider in a cut-throat industry is his drive and his passion to work. Near the end of *Buffy*'s fourth season in early 2000, he was rushed to hospital for an emergency appendectomy. After his operation, within 48 hours he was back at the studio writing the season finales for *Buffy* and *Angel*.

Described by virtually everyone who has ever met him as down-to-earth and soft-spoken, with a wicked sense of humour, patience and thoughtfulness, Joss is married to Kai Cole, a textile and interior designer. They live with their son, Donavan, and four cats in Los Angeles. Still, at heart, a comics and TV fanboy like many of the people who watch his shows, Joss is alleged to have attended several conventions in 1998 and 1999 under the pseudonym of 'Mr Spratt', until he became instantly recognisable to fans. Something of a renaissance man, Joss has also written an acclaimed comic mini-series (*Fray*) for Dark Horse and turned his hand to songwriting for the musical *Buffy* episode **107**, 'Once More, With Feeling'. He achieved a lifetime ambition in September 2002 with the release of the 'original cast soundtrack' on CD. 'Very occasionally,' Joss wrote in the sleevenotes, 'life doesn't suck.' His next major project is a movie version of his 'Sci-Fi Western' *Firefly*, due for release in 2005.

Did You Know?: Interviewed in 1996, Hammer films chairman Roy Skeggs noted that Miramax films wanted to remake the camp-classic *Dracula A.D. 1972* as '*Dracula 1999* reset in Los Angeles, [with] the modern wizz-kids fighting vampires'. Hang on, that sounds familiar . . .

'Since the dawn of man, the Vampires have walked among us. Feeding. The only one with the strength or skill to stop their heinous evil is The Slayer. She who bears the birthmark, the mark of the coven. Trained by The Watcher, one Slayer dies and the next is chosen.'

M1
Buffy the Vampire Slayer – The Movie

A Kuzui Enterprises/Sandollar Production/20th Century Fox
Theatrical Release: September 1992; 86 minutes (rated PG-13)

Co-Producer: Dennis Stuart Murphy
Executive Producers: Sandy Gallin, Carol Baum, Fran Rubel Kuzui
Producers: Kaz Kuzui, Howard Rosenman
Writer: Joss Whedon
Director: Fran Rubel Kuzui
Cast:
Kristy Swanson (Buffy), Donald Sutherland (Merrick), Paul Reubens (Amilyn),
Rutger Hauer (Lothos), Luke Perry (Pike), Michele Abrams (Jennifer),
Hilary Swank (Kimberly), Paris Vaughan (Nicole), David Arquette (Benny),
Randall Bantinkoff (Jeffrey), Andrew Lowery (Andy), Sasha Jenson (Gueller),
Stephen Root (Gary Murray), Natasha Gregson Wagner (Cassandra),
Candy Clark (Buffy's Mom), Mark DeCarlo (Coach), Tom Janes (Zeph),
James Paradise (Buffy's Dad), David Sherrill (Knight), Liz Smith (Reporter),
Paul M. Lane (Robert Bowman), Toby Holguin (Vampire Fan),
Eurlyne Epper-Woldman (Graveyard Woman), Andre Warren (Newscaster),
Bob 'Swanie' Swanson (Referee), Erika Dittner (Cheerleader), JC Cole (Biker),
Michael S. Kopelow (Student), Ricky Dean Logan (Bloody Student),
Bobby Aldridge, Amanda Anka, Chino Binamo, Al Goto, Terry Jackson,
Mike Johnson, Sarah Lee Jones, Kim Robert Kosci, Clint Lilley, Chi-Muoi Lo,
Jimmy N. Roberts, David Rowden, Kenny Sacha, Ben R. Scott,
Kurtis Epper Sanders, Sharon Schaffer, Lincoln Simonds (Vampires)

Southern California – the 'Lite Ages': 'Killing time' takes on a new meaning at Hemery High when Buffy (a blonde-brained cheerleader) is told by the mysterious Merrick that she is the Chosen One – the Vampire Slayer. But when Lothos and his cackling sidekick Amilyn seek vengeance on the Slayer, Buffy finds herself up to her neck in trouble, battling against the undead and her rapidly dwindling popularity with her Valley-girlfriends, with only the help of a drifter and a pointed stick. *Totally.*

Dudes and Babes: For the girls, Luke Perry. Say no more.

Authority Spanks!: In Administrator Murray's office, a green spanking paddle is visible, even though corporal punishment is banned in California (see **9**, 'The Puppet Show').

A Little Learning is a Dangerous Thing: Buffy: 'Excuse me not knowing about El Salvador. Like I'm ever going to Spain anyway?' Cassandra's question about the ozone layer is met with Buffy's reply, 'Gotta get rid of that.'

Mom's Apple Pie: Buffy's mom (unnamed and clearly a *very* different character from Joyce) calls Jeffrey 'Bobby'. Buffy offers the sulky opinion that she probably thinks Buffy's name is Bobby too. One of the best scenes in the film occurs when Buffy comes home extremely late and her mother apprehends her at the door asking if she knows what time it is? Buffy replies it's 'around ten', which her mom wanted to know as her watch had stopped. (See **33**, 'Becoming' Part 1 for an interesting variation.)

It's a Designer Label!: Buffy's electric-blue cheerleader leggings and red flower-patterned miniskirt in the opening scenes are tame compared to her gym-wear during her first meeting with Merrick. Yellow sports bra, multicoloured pants and shocking-pink leggings. Is she *colourblind*? (Possibly, if her desire for that lemon-yellow jacket is anything to go by.) The Grace Kelly-style prom dress and hairdo don't suit her and when Pike stands on the end of the dress, ripping it, she's wearing jogging pants underneath. Which is *very* convenient.

References: 'It's time to put away such childish things' alludes to I Corinthians 13:11. 'The rest is silence' are the eponymous hero's dying words in *Hamlet*. Buffy sings a few lines from Louis Gost and Morris Albert's 1975 easy-listening standard 'Feelings'. Also, Sting's battle to save the rain forests, the 'Elvis Lives' myth, actor Christian Slater *(Heathers, Kuffs, Very Bad Things)*, *Kung Fu*, a misquote from *The Wizard of Oz* and an oblique reference to the circumstances surrounding Jimi Hendrix's death.

The Drugs Don't Work: Administrator Murray claims to have 'done acid' at a Doobie Brothers concert and believed he was a giant toaster before freaking-out when his friend Melissa's head turned into a party balloon.

'You May Remember Me From Such Films and TV Series As . . .': Kristy Swanson's movies include *Highway to Hell*, *Marshal Law*, *Flowers in the Attic*, *The Phantom*, *Bad to the Bone* and *The Chase*.

She played Erica Paget on *Early Edition*. Luke Perry was Dylan in *Beverly Hills 90210*, and 'Sideshow' Luke Perry in *The Simpsons*. Paul Reubens is best known as Pee-Wee Herman in *Pee-Wee Herman's Big Adventure*. Donald Sutherland's CV includes many of this author's favourite movies (*Dr Terror's House of Horror*, *The Dirty Dozen*, *M*A*S*H*, *Klute*, *Don't Look Now*, *The Eagle Has Landed*, *The First Great Train Robbery*, *Murder by Decree*, *Backdraft* and *JFK*). During the 60s, Sutherland was a British TV regular; he's the voodoo god Dwumbala in an episode of *The Champions*, for instance, and also appeared in *Man in a Suitcase*, *The Saint* and *The Avengers*. Dutch actor Rutger Hauer is a cult figure in Britain via his adverts for Guinness during the 80s and films like *Blade Runner*, *The Hitcher*, *The Osterman Weekend* and *Fatherland*. Hilary Swank played the lead in *The Next Karate Kid* and won an Oscar for her transsexual performance in *Boys Don't Cry*. David Arquette is a star of the *Scream* movies and also features in *Never Been Kissed* and *Muppets from Space*. Stephen Root's credits include *Crocodile Dundee II*, *Ghost* and *Robocop*, while he provides the voice of Bill Dauterive in *King of the Hill*. Candy Clark was Mary-Lou, Thomas Newton's girlfriend, in *The Man Who Fell to Earth*. She's also in *Cat's Eye*, *American Graffiti* and *Amityville 3-D*. Natasha Gregson Wagner was in *High Fidelity* and *Stranger Than Fiction*.

Don't Give Up The Day Job: Liz Smith is a famous gossip columnist in the US. JC Cole's brief appearance was in addition to his production role on the film, as 'Dolly Grip'. Stuntwoman Kim Koscki would later work on *The Flinstones* and *Apollo 13*, while the TV Announcer is played, uncredited, by Jeff Coopwood, a voice-artist who worked on *The Rock* and *Star Trek: First Contact* and was the voice of Captain Panaka in *Star Wars Episode 1: The Phantom Menace*.

Stun-Your-Friends Trivia!: The basketball player wearing No. 10 is a young Ben Affleck (before starring roles in *Chasing Amy*, *Good Will Hunting*, *Shakespeare in Love*, *Armageddon* and *Dogma*). And the small plump girl playing Charlotte the waitress . . .? Can that *really* be future talkshow diva Ricki Lake?

Valley-Speak: The movie as a celebration and a critique of Valley-girl culture is full of such contrivances as: 'Mr Howard is *so heinous*', 'This is *so lush*' and 'Does the word "*Duh!*" mean anything to you?'

Buffy and Jennifer on why they aren't going to a movie theatre: '*Bogus* corn.'

Kimberly's opinion of the jacket Buffy wants: 'Pur-leeze. It's *so* five minutes ago.'

Surfer-kid: 'This party sucks, man.'

Pike: 'Pity, you seem like such a *flink*.'

Cigarettes and Alcohol: 'You're *thrashed*,' Buffy tells Pike. 'That,' he says, 'would explain the slurred speech.'

Logic, Let Me Introduce You to This Window: When Pike fights the vampire wearing the Varsity jacket, Buffy leaps on the vampire's shoulders and wraps her legs around his head. The next shot has her falling on Pike with the vampire nowhere to be seen. The implication is she's killed him but how exactly? (An answer is given in **2**, 'The Harvest' and it's not pretty.)

Quote/Unquote: Andrew trying not to touch Buffy's bottom as she leans over him to kiss Jeffrey: 'I don't want to sound sexist or anything, but can I borrow her?'

Buffy's dad: 'Be good. Stay away from the Jag.'

Buffy, on Merrick's claims: 'Does Elvis talk to you?'

Amilyn, after Pike causes his arm to be severed: 'Kill him. A lot.'

Buffy's ambitions: 'All I wanna do is graduate from school, go to Europe, marry Christian Slater and die.'

Lothos, as Buffy stakes him: 'Now I'm *really* pissed-off.'

Notes: 'I'm in a graveyard with a strange man, hunting for vampires, on a school night.' Imagine a cross between *Beverly Hills 90210*, *Clueless* and *An Interview with a Vampire* and you're about a third of the way to how weird **M1**, *Buffy the Vampire Slayer* is. It's a badly plotted film (Whedon's script was extensively rewritten). Donald Sutherland is great but the movie dies on its feet the moment his character is written out with half an hour to go. It's also a very shallow tale; we care little about these people. This is particularly true of Buffy herself who in this incarnation is a selfish moron, hanging around with her sycophantic tittering girlfriends long after she realises that there are more important things in life. There *are* nice realistic moments like her discussion with Merrick about suffering from the cramps ('my secret weapon is PMS'). In places the film is actually quite (conceptually) dark. The bottom line is see it if you get the chance, but don't be surprised if it's not to your tastes.

Buffy owns a teddy-bear (see **5**, 'Never Kill a Boy on the First Date'; **10**, 'Nightmares'; **21**, 'What's My Line?' Part 1). She used to do gymnastics and still knows the moves. She wants a career as a 'buyer', even though she doesn't know what one does. She had the 'hairy mole' birthmark that identified her as the Slayer removed (an element that was, along with the PMS references, not picked up on during the series).

Differences between the movie and the series: Vampires can fly and don't turn to dust when staked. They can't enter a building unless invited, including public areas like the school gym (see **7**, 'Angel'; **30**, 'Killed By Death') and leave no image on film (see **21**, 'What's My Line?' Part 1; **46**, 'Helpless'). Merrick (in a confusing speech that suggests reincarnation, but also extreme longevity) says he has 'lived a hundred lifetimes' and that it's been the same life over and over with the knowledge to prepare the Slayer. But when he's killed by Lothos, there's no evidence of soul transference, so maybe he's simplifying things for Buffy by not telling her there are other Watchers. The implication of Buffy's dreams (the Slayer is reborn each generation), also suggests reincarnation. Among the previous Slayers mentioned are a Magyar peasant girl, an Indian Princess, a slave in Virginia and a serving girl (possibly in medieval England, certainly somewhere where there were knights). The Hemery High basketball team are called the Hogs. Much of the location filming took place in North Hollywood, Sherman Oaks and Pasadena. Marshall High School (also used in *Pretty in Pink*) was the location of Hemery High.

Soundtrack: 'Keep It Comin' (Dance Till You Can't Dance No More)' by C&C Music Factory, 'In The Wind' by War Babies, 'Man Smart, Woman Smarter' by Dream Warriors, 'I Fought The Law (And The Law Won)' by Mary's Danish, 'I Ain't Gonna Eat Out My Heart Anymore' by Divinyls, The Cult's 'Zap City', 'Silent City' by Matthew Sweet, 'Inner Mind' by Eon, Toad the Wet Sprocket's 'Little Haven', 'Party With The Animals' by Ozzy Osbourne, 'Light Comes Out Black' by Rob Holland and 'We Close Our Eyes' by Susannah Hoffs.

Did You Know?: One of the extras on the movie was Seth Green (playing a dorky teenage vampire). The scene in which he appeared was cut before release. However, his photo *can* be seen on the sleeve of the 1997 commercial video.

Joss Whedon's Comments: Concerning his now-legendary running battle with Donald Sutherland on the set of the *Buffy* movie, Joss told Tasha Robinson: '[Sutherland] was just a prick. People always make fun of Rutger Hauer. Even though he looked kind of goofy in the movie, I give him credit, because he was into it. Whereas Donald would rewrite all his dialogue, and the director let him. He was incredibly rude to everyone around him. Some people liked him in the movie because he's Donald Sutherland. He's a great actor. He could read the phone book and I'd be interested. But he acts well enough that you don't notice, with his little ideas about what his character should do, that he was actually destroying the movie.' On the other hand, Joss had nothing but praise for Paul Reubens: 'He is a God that walks among us. He's one of the sweetest, most professional and delightful people I've ever worked with. He was my beacon of hope in that whole experience.'

The Comic: In an attempt to marry the continuity of the movie with the many variations of these events described in the TV series, January 1999 saw the publication by Dark Horse of a three-part comic *Buffy the Vampire Slayer – The Origin*, adapted from Whedon's original screenplay by Daniel Brereton and Christopher Golden, pencilled by Joe Bennett and inked by Rick Ketcham. This drew heavily on the movie, but included elements subsequently changed by the series (such as Buffy's first meeting with Merrick, seen in 33, 'Becoming' Part 1) and parts of the screenplay not used but alluded to in *Buffy* folklore (the burning down of the Hemery High gym). Some of the story is told in the form of a (possibly unreliable) narrative by Buffy's former friends, while an intriguing coda has Buffy telling Willow and Xander about a trip to Las Vegas with Pike before she came to Sunnydale.

U1
The Untransmitted TV Pilot

*'In every generation there is a Chosen One. She will stand
against the vampires, the demons and the forces of darkness.
She is The Slayer.'*

The film wasn't what Joss had in mind (Robia LaMorte told
DreamWatch: 'I know Joss was really upset about the movie,
because he wasn't in the position to have the creative control over
it'). In 1996 Whedon was asked by Sandollar to revive *Buffy* as a
TV format. Whedon wrote and partly financed a 25-minute
'presentation' show-reel. The script (the first draft of which was
dated 26 January 1996) was a work-in-progress version of 1,
'Welcome to the Hellmouth'. Tony Head has indicated that
Whedon also directed the 'presentation', recalling 'he's now an
incredible director, but he had a fairly unhelpful crew'.

Head, along with Sarah Michelle Gellar, Nicholas Brendon,
Charisma Carpenter, Mercedes McNab, Julie Benz and Danny
Strong were all featured, although there was a different Willow, a
different Principal Flutie and no trace of Angel. Having chosen his
cast, Whedon invited them all to his home for a script read-
through. 'The chemistry was remarkably good,' Head told *Xposé*.
'I think one of the successes of the show is that Joss's casting is
bang on.' The editing was, according to *The Watcher's Guide*, the
work of future co-producer David Solomon. Head also remembers
that 'it wasn't as polished as the pilot became. The effects were
great but the end scene that I did was horrible.'

The Blonde Leading the Blonde: Here, Buffy is a brunette.

No Fat Chicks!: The script describes Willow as: *Bookish and very
possibly dressed by her mother. The intelligence in her eyes and the
sweetness of her smile belie a genuine charm that is lost on the
unsubtle highschool mind.* Casting her as a shy obese girl with a
very unflattering skirt length and then (when a series was
commissioned) dropping her in favour of someone thinner was,
perhaps, unfortunate. Who knows what a self-esteem-boost for
millions of fat kids an overweight character could have achieved?
(Given that the entire population of the USA will, according to
recent statistics, be clinically obese by the year 2032, how likely is
it that a group of misfits like the Scooby Gang would all be slim

to the point of anorexia?) Having said that, Riff Regan is clearly nervous and fluffs some of her lines badly. 'She was lovely,' Tony Head remembered. 'But there was no doubt about it, when I read the script that wasn't Willow at all.'

Thankfully, Alyson Hannigan was just a phone call away.

It's a Designer Label!: Darla's flowery dress and black leggings clash with the faded 80s soul-boy look of her male counterpart. Buffy's blue-suede shoes, ginger miniskirt and technicolour-yawn top show little sign of what we would come to expect, though in this incarnation, Willow *does* seem to have seen 'the softer side of Sears'. If the 'presentation' shows one thing that the series needed to get sorted, it's what they were trying to say about clothes. As Cordelia notes, 'I know flannel is *so* over, but I can never tell what's coming next.' Taste, seemingly.

References: Fashion guru Laura Ashley (see **11**, 'Out of Mind, Out of Sight'), Martha Stewart (see **37**, 'Faith Hope and Trick'), The Beach Boys' 'Surf's Up', *The Muppets Take Manhattan*, *Crossroads* and Lionel Ritchie, allusions to *Terminator II: Judgement Day* ('She's back, and this time it's personal'), *Bambi*, The Smiths' 'Meat is Murder' and *The Flinstones*. Giles quotes *Hamlet* ('there are more things in heaven and earth than are dreamt of in your philosophy'). A poster of FW Murnau's *Nosferatu* decorates the final scene.

Bitch!: Cordelia to Xander: 'Has any girl ever spoken to you of her own free will?'

Awesome!: Loads of cool images (like the close-up on a skull in the opening scene) and Buffy's fight with three vampires in the auditorium. Her gymnastic way of getting from the first floor of the library to the ground is a particular highlight. There's a terrific sequence (dropped from **1**, 'Welcome to the Hellmouth') in which Xander shows Buffy around school.

'You Might Remember Me From Such Films As . . .': Stephen Tobolowsky, who played Principal Flutie, appeared in *Thelma and Louise*, *Spaceballs*, *Single White Female* and *Basic Instinct*. Readers may know him as Ned, the Insurance Man, in *Groundhog Day*.

'Is The Band Any Good?': Long before their debut on the series (see **16**, 'Inca Mummy Girl') Dingoes Ate My Baby are mentioned. One of the Cordettes (see *Angel*: 'Rm w/a Vu') think 'They Rock!'

but Xander tells Buffy, 'They don't know any actual chords yet, but they have *really* big amps.' (See **50**, 'Doppelgängland', **62**, 'Wild At Heart'.)

Dust to Dust: Only one vampire death is seen in close-up and it's interesting to compare the rather slow and ordinary 'crumbling skeleton' effect seen here to the beautifully realised explosion of dust featured in the series itself.

Valley-Speak: Girl #2: 'Chatter in the caf is that she [Buffy] got kicked out and that's why her mom had to get a new job.' Girl #1: '*Neg!*' Girl #2: '*Pos!*'

Buffy: 'I was *totally* phasing.' And: 'I'm *way* sure'. And: 'I'm *totally jammin'* on your dress'. And: 'I've both been there, and done that . . .'

Logic, Let Me Introduce You to This Window: Why does Buffy immediately assume, when Xander tells her that Willow has a date, that it's with a vampire?

You Can See Why They Dropped *That* Idea: Flutie's habit of calling Buffy 'Bunny', 'Bambi', 'Betty' and 'Wilma'. They would have run out of pun-names by episode three.

What A Shame They Dropped . . .: This gem from the shooting script. Guy: 'My parents grounded me! It's *so* not fair.' Other Guy: 'You should sue.' Guy: '*No way*. My dad's lawyer is *way* better than mine.'

Quote/Unquote: Xander: 'Those guys are the Howzers. They'd be *total hardcore gangstas* except for the Upper-class White-Guy stigma. Total wannabes, but they're OK.'

Flutie's school rules: 'No gang-colours. No fur. No hanging from the rafters in the cafeteria screaming "Meat is Murder" during Sloppy Joe-day.' And: 'We *almost never* have dead kids stuffed in the locker.'

Buffy: 'What is it with vampires and clothes? You always think the march of fashion stopped dead the day you did.'

Notes: As Buffy says: 'Relax. The world's in beauty hands.' One has to agree with Tony Head's assessment of this oddity. That is, nice ideas (and clearly with potential) but *how* did they ever sell it as a series? It's unfair to apply the same criteria to something that was never intended for public consumption as to the actual series, but there was obviously still much to be done. The characterisation is odd too, although Cordelia and Xander are excellently played (*love* Nick Brendon's demonstration of Buffy's 'crane technique').

The school is Berryman High, whose football (or basketball) team are called the Bulls. Buffy chews gum (a habit we don't see her repeat until **58**, 'Living Conditions'). She is taking 'Euro-centric history' (it's not her best subject). She was thrown out of her last (unnamed) school for 'causing trouble' (there's no reference to burning down the gym). She was on the Student Council. She mentions the football team and Xander jokingly asks if she was on that too. She seems to be referring to her time as a cheerleader (see **M1, 3**, 'The Witch'). She implies that her last Watcher died (is it Merrick she's talking about?). The History teacher is Mr Bron, and Mr Worth teaches Math.

Of course, the series *was*, ultimately, picked up. As Tony Head told *DreamWatch*: 'Several people have said it's one of the few instances where a TV spin-off improves on what people originally knew as the project. It's basically what Joss originally envisaged. I'm just glad to be part of what he eventually got made.'

Did You Know?: 'Mutant Enemy', Joss Whedon's production company, takes its name from a line in 'And You, And I' by prog-rock dinosaurs Yes.

*'We can do this the hard way, or . . . Actually,
there's just the hard way.'*
— 'Welcome to the Hellmouth'

Season One (1997)

Mutant Enemy Inc/Kuzui Enterprises/Sandollar Television/20th Century Fox
Created by Joss Whedon
Producer: Gareth Davies
Co-Producer: David Solomon
Executive Producers: Sandy Gallin, Gail Berman, Fran Rubel Kuzui,
Kaz Kuzui, Joss Whedon
Co-Executive Producer: David Greenwalt

Regular Cast:
Sarah Michelle Gellar (Buffy Summers),
Nicholas Brendon (Xander Harris),
Alyson Hannigan (Willow Rosenberg),
Charisma Carpenter (Cordelia Chase, 1–5, 7, 9–12),
Anthony Stewart Head (Rupert Giles),
David Boreanaz (Angel, 1–2, 4–5, 7, 11–12),
Mark Metcalf (The Master, 1–2, 5, 7, 10, 12),
Ken Lerner (Principal Flutie, 1–2, 4, 6),
Kristine Sutherland (Joyce Summers, 1–3, 7, 9–10, 12),
Julie Benz (Darla, 1–2, 7),
Mercedes McNab (Harmony Kendall, 2, 11),
Elizabeth Anne Allen (Amy Madison, 3),
Amanda Wilmshurst (Cheerleader, 3[1]),
William Monaghan (Dr Gregory, 3–4),
Andrew J Ferchland (The Anointed One, 5,[2] 7, 10, 12),
Robia LaMorte (Jenny Calendar, 8, 12),
Dean Butler (Hank Summers, 10),
Armin Shimerman (Principal Snyder, 9, 11)

---

[1] Credited as 'Senior Cheerleader' in **3**, 'The Witch'.
[2] Credited as 'Boy' in **5**, 'Never Kill a Boy on the First Date' and as 'Collin' in **7**,
'Angel'.

1
Welcome to the Hellmouth

US Transmission Date: 10 Mar 1997[3]
UK Transmission Date: 3 Jan 1998[4]

Writer: Joss Whedon
Director: Charles Martin Smith
Cast: Brian Thompson (Luke), J Patrick Lawlor (Thomas), Eric Balfour (Jesse),
Natalie Strauss (Teacher), Amy Chance (Girl #1), Tupelo Jereme (Girl #2),
Persia White (Girl #3), Carmine D Giovinazzo (Boy)

On her first day at Sunnydale High, Vampire Slayer Buffy
Summers befriends Xander and Willow, to the chagrin of resident
snob Cordelia Chase. In the library, Buffy meets Mr Giles, who
reveals that he is her Watcher. A corpse is discovered and Buffy
ascertains that the victim was killed by a vampire. She argues with
Giles about her responsibilities, both being unaware that Xander
has overheard. On her way to the Bronze club Buffy encounters a
stranger who warns her that she is living at 'the Mouth of Hell'.
He gives Buffy a crucifix and tells her that 'the Harvest' is coming.
At the cemetery Willow is attacked by female vampire Darla, who
has also captured another offering to the Master, Xander's friend
Jesse.

Dudes and Babes: Angel's first appearance set many a female heart
aflutter (Buffy describes him as 'dark, gorgeous in an annoying
sort of way'). Darla is cute until she turns all vampiry, at which
point the attraction becomes somewhat obscure (see 7, 'Angel').
But Miss Summers in *that* skirt . . . Hubba. Xander's fumbling
attempts to chat her up are a highlight ('You forgot your . . .
stake').

Authority Sucks!: Principal Flutie ('All the kids here are free to call
me Bob. But they don't') seems prepared to let Buffy's past lie
until he reads about the gym burning down.

---

[3] All US transmission details refer to the WB network (seasons one to five) and,
subsequently, UPN (seasons six and seven). *Buffy* actually received its first airing
in New Zealand, where it began on 2 February 1997, a full six weeks ahead of the
series' US debut.
[4] All UK transmission details – unless otherwise stated – refer to the initial
broadcast of episodes on the Sky One Satellite/Digital/Cable channel. *Buffy*'s
terrestrial UK debut came on 30th December 1998 on BBC2 with an edited
compilation of 1, 'Welcome to the Hellmouth' and 2, 'The Harvest'.

A Little Learning is a Dangerous Thing: Xander tells Willow he has a problem with the math. When she asks which part, he replies 'the math'. She advises that he borrow *Theories in Trig* from the library. We're informed that 25 million people died in the Black Death and that it was an early form of germ warfare.

Mom's Apple Pie: Joyce's plea to Buffy before she starts her first day at Sunnydale High is, 'Try not to get kicked out.' Buffy says stakes are being used for self-defence in LA as pepper-sprays are passé.

It's a Designer Label!: Cordelia would kill to live in LA to be so close to so many shoes (see *Angel*: 'City Of'). Buffy recognises a vampire by his jacket, noting that only someone who has lived underground for 10 years would wear something so unfashionable. Willow's dress was one that her mom picked out (see **78**, 'Restless'). Buffy's red miniskirt and knee-length leather boots are smashing, but the two skirts she considers wearing to the Bronze make her look, she believes, either like a slut or a Jehovah's Witness.

References: Cordelia's coolness factor test includes what Buffy thinks of James Spader (*Pretty in Pink*, *Less than Zero*, *Sex, lies and videotape*, *Stargate* and *Crash*) and former TV host and musician John Tesh, and the opinion that vamp nail polish is *so* over. Also department stores Neiman-Marcus and Sears, coffee-house chain Starbucks, the Jehovah's Witness magazine *Watchtower* and 80s pop group De Barge.

Awesome!: The montage that forms Buffy's nightmare (many fans believe these to be scenes from the movie – they aren't). Buffy's fight with Luke in the mausoleum is impressive, though her first meeting with Angel tops it for emotional impact, *and* gymnastic stunts.

'You Might Remember Me From Such Films and TV Series As . . .': Sarah Michelle Gellar appeared in Burger King adverts as a four-year-old and had a starring role in *Swans Crossing*. She won a Daytime Emmy for her performance as Kendall Hart in the soap *All My Children*. Her movies include *I Know What You Did Last Summer* (as Helen Shivers), *Cruel Intentions* (as Kathryn Merteuil), *Scooby-Doo* (as Daphne) and *Scream 2*. Alyson Hannigan was also a child actress, making her debut in *My Stepmother is an Alien*. She has appeared in *Roseanne*, *Picket Fences* and *Touched*

By An Angel and her movies include several films that explore the dark – if sometimes comic – underbelly of the US high school system, *Indecent Seduction*, *Dead Man on Campus*, *Boys & Girls* and the *American Pie* trilogy. Tony Head is known to British audiences for his Gold Blend commercials opposite Sharon Maughan in the 1980s (the adverts were also popular in the US where the coffee is called 'Taster's Choice'). He played Adam Klaus in the pilot of *Jonathan Creek* and appeared in two *The Comic Strip Presents* ... along with series like *Secret Army*, *Bergerac*, *Howard's Way*, *Spooks*, *Manchild*, *Little Britain* and *New Tricks*. Fans of *The X-Files* will recognise Brian Thompson as the enigmatic Alien Pilot. He was also in *The Terminator* and *Star Trek: Generations* (playing a Klingon). J Patrick Lawlor had a small role in *Pleasantville*.

Don't Give Up The Day Job: Director Charles Martin Smith is also an actor who appeared in *Deep Impact*, *The Untouchables*, *Starman*, *American Graffiti*, *Pat Garrett and Billy the Kid*, *The X-Files*, *The Outer Limits* and *The Twilight Zone*. Producer Gareth Davies worked for the BBC in the 1960s on *The Wednesday Play* (including Dennis Potter's groundbreaking dramas *Vote, Vote, Vote For Nigel Barton*, *Alice*, *Where the Buffalo Roam*, *Message for Posterity*, *Angels are so Few* and the notorious *Son of Man*). He subsequently produced *Tales of the Unexpected* and *Boon* before moving to America to work on *Remington Steele*.

Valley-Speak: Buffy: 'OK? What's the sitch?' And: 'Gee, everyone wants to know about me. How *keen*.' 'The wiggins' is Buffy's personal version of 'the willies'. Many subsequent episodes feature it, or a variation.

Cordelia: '*Totally* dead. *Way* dead.' And: 'My mom doesn't even *get* out of bed anymore. The doctor says it's Epstein-Barr. I'm like, *pleeease*! It's chronic hepatitis, or at least chronic fatigue syndrome. I mean, *nobody* cool has Epstein-Barr anymore.'

Xander, on Buffy: 'Pretty much a *hottie*.' And, to Jesse: 'You're certainly a font of nothing.'

Logic, Let Me Introduce You to This Window: In the library, Giles piles several books into Buffy's arms, while telling her about all the mythical creatures that exist. The bindings are all facing Buffy, except in one shot when they're the other way around. When Buffy looks for Willow in the Bronze, she breaks a stool leg to use as a weapon. Next time we see her, it has become a stake.

I Just *Love* Your Accent: Asked by *The Watcher's Web* whether his time in England and exposure to British Telefantasy had scarred him for life, Joss Whedon noted: 'I saw *Blake's 7*, *Sapphire and Steel* and *Doctor Who* but I was at boarding school and didn't have much opportunity. What we watched were our heroes like *Starsky and Hutch*. I watched a huge amount of British TV while I lived in America. That's one of the reasons I was so anxious to come. I was an entire PBS kid. *Masterpiece Theatre*, *Monty Python*, BBC Shakespeare's.' 'You want the contrast,' Whedon told Rob Francis when asked if his time in Britain had helped to get characters like Giles right: 'At the same time I hope he's been a little more human than just stuffy. The great thing is there are dirty words that the American audience don't know.'

Giles was the curator at a British museum. Or, possibly *the* British Museum. His ideal night is staying home with a cup of Bovril (can you *get* Bovril in the US?) and a good book (see **8**, 'I Robot . . . You Jane').

Motors: Joyce Summers drives a Jeep Cherokee Sport (see **40**, 'Band Candy').

Quote/Unquote: Giles on zombies, werewolves, incubi and succubi: 'Everything you ever dreaded was under your bed but told yourself couldn't be in the light of day. *They're all real.*'

Buffy's reply to Giles's surprise that the vampire she's tracking isn't dead: 'No, but my social life is on the critical list.'

Notes: 'This is Sunnydale. How bad an evil can there be here?' A great debut, well paced, superbly characterised (we already feel as if we've known these people for *years*) and with a wicked sense of humour. 'Welcome to the Hellmouth' is an intricate doll's house of a plot, with many knowing winks to the audience. If you don't find something of interest in this, you're probably dead.

Buffy's previous school was Hemery High in Los Angeles (see **M1**). She burned down the gymnasium because it was full of vampires (real reason), or asbestos (official excuse). Xander's skateboarding skills leave much to be desired. Xander and Willow used to go out, but split up when he stole her Barbie doll (they were five). Willow says that when she's with a boy it's hard for her to say anything cool or witty. 'I can usually make a few vowel sounds and then I have to go away.' The book Giles shows Buffy to establish his Watcher credentials is an ancient volume called *Vampyr*. When Giles tells Buffy about all of the mythical creatures that exist, she asks if he sent away for the *Time Life* series. Giles confirms that he *did* and received the free calendar. Giles says, of Sunnydale: 'Dig a bit in the history of this place. You'll find a steady stream of fairly odd occurrences. I believe this area is a centre of mystical energy, that things gravitate towards it,' and 'The influx of the undead, the supernatural occurrences, it's been building for years. There's a reason why you're here and a reason why it's now,' (see **51**, 'Enemies'; **56**, 'Graduation Day' Part 2).

The Bronze ('they let anybody in, but it's still the scene') is in the bad part of town, which is half-a-block from the good part of town. It is said that the whole of Sunnydale can be seen from the top of the gym, which ties in with there not being a whole lot of town, (see **15**, 'School Hard') even if it has got an international airport (see **21**, 'What's My Line?' Part 1). If a vampire sucks someone's blood, this will usually kill the person being attacked. The victim will only turn into a vampire if they suck the vampire's blood in return (see **33**, 'Becoming' Part 1, though the series occasionally contradicts this. See **46**, 'Helpless'). The vampires refer to themselves as 'the Old Ones' (as does Giles in **2**, 'The Harvest'). The history teacher is called Mr Chopski. Female gym Coach Foster has chest hair according to Cordelia. The two girls discussing Buffy in the locker room are called Aphrodisia and Aura (they appear to belong to the Cordettes, see *Angel*: 'Rm w/a Vu'). Another of their friends, the one who reveals that Buffy was expelled from Hemery, is called Blue.

All initial US transmissions were accompanied by a pre-episode caption warning *tonight's presentation is rated TV-PG and contains action scenes which may be too intense for younger viewers* (or a variation). When the BBC purchased the series, they edited the episodes with a blunt hacksaw instead (notably any fight sequences). Overseas prints of this episode do not feature the voice-over concerning two previous Slayers – Lucy Hanover in Virginia in 1866 and a nameless woman in Chicago in 1927.

Nick Brendon told *Spectrum*: 'Being on a network like WB at the time was beneficial for both parties. I think that *Buffy* has helped to launch that network and make it the fastest-growing on TV.' The school used for location filming was Torrance High in Los Angeles. *Beverly Hills 90210* and *She's All That* were also filmed there.

Soundtrack: The theme music is by Nerf Herder [*] whose name was an insult Princess Leia hurled at Han Solo in *The Empire*

Strikes Back. Sprung Monkey perform 'Believe', 'Swirl' and 'Things Are Changing' in the Bronze. Another song, 'Saturated', is heard when Buffy tries to decide which dress to wear.

Did You Know?: David Boreanaz's audition scene was the sequence in which Angel warns Buffy about the coming Harvest. It was shot at two in the morning 'in some god awful street' according to Boreanaz.

2
The Harvest

US Transmission Date: 10 Mar 1997
UK Transmission Date: 10 Jan 1998

Writer: Joss Whedon
Director: John T Kretchmer
Cast: Brian Thompson (Luke), Eric Balfour (Jesse), Deborah Brown (Girl),
Teddy Lane Jr (Bouncer), Jeffrey Steven Smith (Guy in Comp Class),
Kerry Zook (Female Victim)[5]

Buffy saves Xander and Willow, but Jesse has been taken by the vampires. Luke and Darla tell the Master about Buffy. Suspecting she may be the Slayer, they use Jesse as bait. Buffy and Xander return to the cemetery and meet the stranger who warned Buffy about the Harvest. He introduces himself as Angel. They find Jesse, but he's now a vampire. Buffy and Xander escape through a ventilation duct. At the Bronze, Buffy tricks Luke into believing it is sunrise and, with his Vessel dead, the Master's Harvest is prevented.

Dudes and Babes: Xander's inadequacy when Buffy won't let him help is touching. Buffy complains about Angel's cryptic wise-man act. For the boys, there's Cordelia dancing.

Mom's Apple Pie: Buffy's mom grounds her for skipping class. 'If you don't go out it'll be the end of the world? *Everything*'s life or death to a sixteen-year-old girl.'

A Little Learning is a Dangerous Thing: Cordy discovers how to save a computer file. Not.

---

[5] Uncredited.

It's a Designer Label!: Willow's dungarees are horrible. *Love Angel's* disco-threads. Buffy's Raybans and her leather jacket give the final scenes a touch of class.

References: Luke burning himself on Buffy's cross mirrors a device used in many vampire films, notably Hammer's *Dracula: Prince of Darkness*. Buffy mentions Sam Peckinpah's notoriously violent *The Wild Bunch*.

Bitch!: Cordelia: 'Hello, Miss Motormouth, can I get a sentence finished?' And: 'Excuse me, who gave you permission to exist?' Cordelia and Harmony also discuss what a 'psycho loony' Buffy is.

'You Might Remember Me From Such Films and TV Series As . . .': Both Nick Brendon and David Boreanaz made guest appearances on the popular sitcom *Married: With Children*. Brendon also appeared in the movies *Children of the Corn III* and *Psycho Beach Party*. A former cheerleader for the San Diego Chargers, Charisma Carpenter began her acting career with a small part in *Baywatch*, playing Hobie's girlfriend Wendie (probably the only time you'll see the words *Baywatch* and 'small part' in the same sentence). Aaron Spelling auditioned her for the 'über-vixen-bitch' Ashley Green in NBC's *Malibu Shores*. She also played Beth Sullivan in the *Josh Kirby: Time Warrior* TV movies and appeared in an advert for Spree sweets ('It's a kick in the mouth').

Mark Metcalf played Doug Neidermeyer in the classic *National Lampoon's Animal House*. Kristine Sutherland was Matt Frewer's wife in *Honey I Shrunk the Kids* and appeared in *Legal Eagles*, *California Dream*, *Remington Steele* and *Providence*. Ken Lerner is in dozens of films including *Robocop 2* and *The Running Man* and was Fonzie's love rival Rocko in *Happy Days*. The daughter of former Arsenal and England left-back Bob McNab, Mercedes McNab played the young Sue Storm in *The Fantastic Four* and was in both *The Addams Family* and *Addams Family Values*. Former ice-skater Julie Benz (once ranked 12th in the US) was one of many actresses who auditioned for the role of Buffy. She played Kate Topolsky in *Roswell* and was in *As Good As It Gets, Jawbreaker, A Fate Totally Worse Than Death, Darkdrive, Shriek if You Know What I Did Last Friday the 13th* and *Satan's School for Girls*.

Don't Give Up The Day Job: John T Kretchmer was Assistant Director on the first two *Naked Gun* movies and *Jurassic Park*.

Valley-Speak: Buffy: 'We *so* don't have the time . . .' Her description of the Harvest is: 'A suck-fest.'

Logic, Let Me Introduce You to This Window: Why is that globe spinning in the library while Giles is talking about the Earth's ancient history? In the computer class, Harmony asks: 'Are we going to the Bronze tonight?' Cordelia replies that of course they are, this being Friday night and there's 'no cover'. If it's Friday, then why are they at school the next day? And, as we see, there clearly *is* a cover charge. When Xander and Buffy are climbing to the surface, watch Xander's left hand grabbing Buffy's breast after the vampire reaches out for her foot.

I Just *Love* Your Accent: Flutie refers to the British royal family and to 'all kinds of problems' in the UK. Oh really? Wish we had a crime rate as low as California, mate. Giles hates computers, an attitude he describes as 'a bit British', which is pretty insulting to perfectly respectable UK-based net-nerds like this author. And most of his friends. (See **8**, 'I Robot . . . You Jane'.)

Quote/Unquote: Buffy notes that the first time she saw a vampire, she tried to rationalise their existence: 'Once I'd done with the screaming part.' (See **33**, 'Becoming' Part 1.)

Luke on Jesse: 'I thought you were nothing more than a meal, boy. Congratulations, you've just been upgraded. To "bait".'

Buffy asks Giles what he can say that will make the day any worse. 'How about The End of the World?' '*Knew* I could rely on you.'

Notes: 'Yesterday, "Uh-oh Pop-Quiz". Today, it's "rain of toads".' Even better. Here we see the various strands that make *Buffy* work meshing perfectly. This concludes the series' opening with an apocalyptic storyline and lots of cool jokes and gets better every time you see it.

Giles indicates that the world is older than most people realise and is dismissive of Christianity, noting that, contrary to popular mythology, it did not begin with a paradise. (This doesn't explain how a crucifix and holy water are deadly to a vampire, nor tie in with the very Christian presentation of Hell in the series, the plethora of Biblical-lore either quoted or subverted and references to the crucifixion in **15**, 'School Hard'. See also **44**, 'Amends'; **45**, 'Gingerbread'.) Giles notes that for untold eons demons walked the Earth. They made it their home, but in time they lost their purchase on this reality (see **143**, 'End of Days'). The way was made for mortals. All that remained of the Old Ones are certain magicks. The last demon to leave this reality fed off a human, mixed their blood. He was a human form possessed, infected by the demon's soul. He bit another, and another, and so they walk the Earth, feeding.

Willow has 'accidentally' decrypted the city council's computer security system allowing her access to much classified material. Luke recounts the last time someone attacked him and survived: '1843, Madrid. He caught me sleeping.' Things that will kill a vampire (aside from a wooden stake) include garlic, fire, holy water, sunlight and beheading. Buffy has done a little of the latter, including the story she tells Xander about her hacking off a varsity footballer's head with a small penknife. (So *that* explains that garbled scene in **M1**?) She beheads a vampire, using a cymbal (unless you were watching on BBC2). There was an earthquake in Sunnydale in 1937 during the Master's last bid for freedom (see **12**, 'Prophecy Girl'; **67**, 'Doomed'; **122**, 'Grave'). Sunnydale was first settled by the Spanish who called it *Boca del Infierno*. It is a portal between this reality and the next ('other dimension' references crop up regularly too).

When the BBC broadcast this episode (as a double feature with **1**, 'Welcome to the Hellmouth'), several cuts were made including the almost-complete ruination of the 'Just say you're sorry' eye-poking sequence. Thankfully, Sky broadcast the episode uncut.

Soundtrack: Sprung Monkey's 'Right My Wrong' and the Dashboard Prophets' 'Ballad For A Dead Friend' and 'Wearing Me Down'.

3
The Witch

US Transmission Date: 17 Mar 1997
UK Transmission Date: 17 Jan 1998

Writer: Dana Reston
Director: Stephen Cragg
Cast: Robin Riker (Catherine), Jim Doughan (Mr Pole),
Nicole Prescott (Lishanne)

It's cheerleading tryouts, and Buffy hopes to make the squad. However, horrible things happen to leading contenders (including the blinding of Cordelia). Willow's friend Amy, whose mom was a great cheerleader, is an obvious suspect and when Buffy, Xander and Willow perform an experiment to confirm if Amy is a witch, the test proves positive. Amy concocts a spell to kill Buffy. Desperate to reverse it, Giles and Buffy meet Amy's mom, Catherine, and discover that she has switched bodies with her daughter so that she can relive her glorious past. While Giles prepares the reversal, Catherine realises what is happening. She attacks Buffy, but Giles completes the spell. Catherine, back in her own body, unleashes an energy bolt but Buffy uses a mirror to trap the witch in her own cheerleading trophy.

Dudes and Babes: 'You were pretending seeing scantily clad girls in revealing postures was a spiritual experience,' Willow tells Xander who spends the episode trying to date Buffy, including giving her a chain with *Yours Always* written on it. He says it came that way. Poor lad, he obviously has a lot on his plate once Buffy tells him he's *totally* one of the girls (a reversal of his informing Willow that she's like a guy). Let's not forget that Buffy has needs too, as we're reminded by her reaction to an African fertility statue: 'Jeepers!'

Authority Sucks!: Giles forbids Buffy to join the cheerleading squad to which she asks: 'And you'll be stopping me, how?' Saucy minx.

Mom's Apple Pie: The issue of parental pressure is central (with the implication of child abuse in Buffy's description of Catherine as 'Nazi-like'). Joyce (who is seemingly more concerned with her gallery's first exhibition than Buffy) doesn't come out of the episode too well, but the closing scenes are well done as she admits she doesn't understand her daughter. She says she wouldn't want to be sixteen again (judging by the uncool 'wannabe'-girl we see glimpses of in **40**, 'Band Candy', it's obvious why not).

It's a Designer Label!: Let's start with Buffy's cheerleading outfit (those red sports knickers they wear are *outstanding*). The discerning male viewer is also pointed in the direction of Cordelia's jogger shorts. Minus points for Amy's horrible sweatshirt, with a CND logo.

References: 'Count the ways' is a reference to Elizabeth Barrett Browning's *Sonnets from the Portuguese*. Also, the LA Lakers, *Sabrina the Teenage Witch*, *Mommie Dearest* (the biography of actress Joan Crawford), Marvel's *Fantastic Four* character Johnny

Storm the Human Torch and HG Wells's *The Invisible Man*. Buffy sings a couple of lines from the Village People's 'Macho Man'.

There's an oblique reference to Farrah Fawcett Majors (of *Charlie's Angels*) when Buffy looks at her mom's yearbook photo and notes that she's accepted Joyce had sex, but is not ready to know she had 'Farrah-hair'. Joyce says it was actually *Gidget*-hair, referring to the Sally Fields sitcom based on the *Gidget* novel by Frederick Kohner. Giles gives a precise little essay on Spontaneous Human Combustion.

Bitch!: Buffy believes Giles should 'get a girlfriend . . . If he wasn't so old.'

Cordelia's response to Willow saying Amber is on fire. 'Enough of the hyperbole.'

Willow, after Giles wonders why anyone would wish Cordelia harm: 'Maybe, they *met* her?'

Awesome!: Giles's reaction to Buffy enslaving herself 'to this cult', which turns out to be the cheerleading squad. Plus Amber's hands on fire and the girl with no mouth.

'You Might Remember Me From Such Films and TV Series As . . .': Robin Riker was the female lead in the seminal 1980 horror movie *Alligator*. She's also made guest appearances on *M*A*S*H*, *The A-Team* and *Murder She Wrote*. Elizabeth Anne Allen, like Julie Benz and Mercedes McNab, auditioned for the role of Buffy. She played Shelly in *Silent Lies*, Carri in *Green Sails* and appeared in *Illegal Blue*.

Don't Give Up The Day Job: Writer Dana Reston was story editor and producer on the Fran Drescher sitcom *The Nanny*. Jennifer Badger, Charisma Carpenter's stunt-double, was one of the stunt team on *Austin Powers: The Spy Who Shagged Me*. Sarah Michelle Gellar's stunt-double on the first four seasons was London-born Sophia Crawford who played Chameleon in *WMAC Masters* and Carmella in *Night Hunters*.

Valley-Speak: Buffy: 'He totally lost his water.' And: 'I need to get the skinny on Amber.' And: 'Get *down* with your bad self.'

Cordelia: 'You're going to be so very *beyond* sorry.'

Cigarettes and Alcohol: Willow says Amber only ever got detention once, for smoking. ('Regular smoking . . . With a cigarette.')

Logic, Let Me Introduce You to This Window: Sunnydale must have the most dangerous parcel delivery service in America. One would have expected the van driver to, at least, slow down after crashing into a parked car and nearly running a blind girl down. Maybe he was on a time bonus? Amber Grove's hair is significantly shorter when seen from behind as Buffy is putting out the fire on her hands. When Giles and Buffy arrive at the Madison home, Giles's car is missing its front licence plate. (This 'error' was spotted by lots of American fans, which is odd because in many states such plates are not required by law. The same thing crops up in **26**, 'Innocence' and **27**, 'Phases'.) When did Amy steal Buffy's bracelet? On overseas prints, the credits list the band that play the theme tune as Nerfherder (one word). The sign in the gym reads, 1996 CHEERLEADING TRYOUTS. It should be 1997. Joyce, born in 1958, would have been in High School circa 1974. *Gidget* was a sitcom from 1966. As with the subsequent reference to Dorothy Hamill being Buffy's heroine in **21**, 'What's My Line? Part 1 (Hamill was Olympic champion four years before Buffy was even born) this seems to be an example of writers sampling elements of their own childhood onto the characters without any thought as to whether they're chronologically appropriate.

Motors: A first look at Giles's 1963 Citröen DS Coupé. Unfortunately, it's fallen greatly into disrepair.

What a Shame They Dropped . . .: Giles repeats the mistakes of *Monty Python's Holy Grail*: 'The ducking stool. We throw her in the pond. If she floats, she's a witch. If she drowns, she's innocent . . . Some of my texts are a bit outdated.'

Quote/Unquote: Xander tells Buffy that he laughs in the face of danger. 'Then, I hide until it goes away.'

Giles, at the cynical looks the others give him as he talks enthusiastically about the cornucopia of fiends, devils and ghouls that inhabit the Hellmouth: 'Pardon me for finding the glass half full.'

Notes: 'This witch is casting horrible and disfiguring spells so that she can become a cheerleader?' *Major* revaluation time: Initially dismissed as one of the lesser episodes of the season 'The Witch' improves *hugely* with repeated viewing although half the episode *is* made up of non-sequiturs. Extreme eye-candy, certainly, but with a real depth and intelligence.

Xander has checked the books *Witches: Historic Roots to Modern Practice* and *The Pagan Rites* out of the library ('It's not what you think'), to look at the semi-nude engravings ('OK, maybe it *is* what you think'). Willow describes herself and Xander as the Slayerettes. Catherine led her team to be tri-county champions, still a unique achievement. She and Amy's father were Homecoming King and Queen. They got married immediately after graduation. Amy's father was a big loser who ran off with Miss Trailer Trash when Amy was twelve. But, since this is really Catherine speaking, it's difficult to know how much is true. Sunnydale's basketball team are the Razorbacks.

Soundtrack: 'Twilight Zone' by Dutch techno-duo 2 Unlimited.

What's In A Name?: Willow shares her unusual name with the character played by Britt Ekland in Robin Hardy's horror masterpiece *The Wicker Man*. Cordelia first appeared in the Holinshed's *Chronicles* and was used by Shakespeare in *King Lear*. It's also the name given to the smallest of Uranus's moons, discovered by *Voyager 2* in 1986. Variations on the surname Giles appear in England as far back as *The Domesday Book* in 1086. St Giles lived as a hermit in France and the name derives from the Celtic word for 'servant'. A large number of English churches were dedicated to him though the name itself was not popular, possibly because of St Giles's association with beggars and cripples of whom he is the patron saint.

4
Teacher's Pet

US Transmission Date: 25 Mar 1997
UK Transmission Date: 24 Jan 1998

Writer: David Greenwalt
Director: Bruce Seth Green
Cast: Musetta Vander (She-Mantis), Jackson Price (Blayne),
Jean Speegle Howard (Natalie French), Jack Knight (Homeless Guy),
Michael Robb Verona (Teacher), Karim Oliver (Bud #1)

When biology teacher Dr Gregory goes missing, the school assigns a substitute, the alluring Ms French. Gregory's body is found in the cafeteria, minus his head. Believing a clawed vampire who attacked Angel to be responsible, Buffy sees the creature about to attack Ms French, then flee in terror. Buffy concludes that Natalie French is a She-Mantis. Giles calls a friend who went mad hunting such a creature for details on how to kill it. At Natalie's home,

Xander is drugged and locked in a cage in the basement, next to another boy from school, Blayne, who says that the She-Mantis has already eaten the head of her mate.

Dudes and Babes: Xander is jealous of Angel. Mind you, anybody who has dreams like young Mr Harris (finding time to finish his solo and 'kiss you like you've never been kissed before') deserves what they get, frankly. He may have been distracted by the cheerleaders modelling their new short skirts (see **3**, 'The Witch'). Giles's description of Natalie is 'lovely, in a common, extremely well-proportioned way'. Her slinky black dress reveals *how* well proportioned. As Xander says: 'It's a beautiful chest . . . dress.'

A Little Learning is a Dangerous Thing: How ants communicate. With other ants. The sexually charged lesson on the Praying Mantis and its wily ways reveals that there are 1,800 plus species worldwide, in most of which the females are larger and more aggressive.

School Dinners: The following items are on a noticeboard in the cafeteria: salad bar, meat loaf, lasagna, sloppy joes, macaroni and cheese, fajitas, cheese burger, blueberry pie, orange Jell-O, brownies. Buffy and Willow are horrified to find out they're getting hot dog surprise for lunch. Cordelia has a medically prepared lunch, prescribed by her doctor (implication: it's to keep her weight steady), but finding Dr Gregory's body in the kitchen seems to put her off her food. Anyone eating while viewing this episode, beware of Natalie's insect sandwich.

It's a Designer Label!: Buffy's red dress in Xander's dream and her extremely short light blue skirt are impressive, but the episode highlight is her yellow stretchpants. Angel gives Buffy his leather jacket. The She-Mantis's fashion sense is described as predatory.

References: Xander's flashbacks bear similarity to techniques used in another seminal high school series, *Parker Lewis Can't Lose*. There are name-checks for *The Exorcist*, the legends of Virgin thieves (the Greek sirens and the Celtic maidens) and an oblique reference to *Godzilla* and its sequels ('We're on Monster Island').

Awesome!: Buffy's fight with the claw-handed vampire. Twenty seconds of unrestrained violence. Or, in the case of the BBC edit, *five* seconds of unrestrained violence.

'You Might Remember Me From Such Video Games, Films and TV Shows As . . .': Jean Speegle Howard was the mother of Ron

Howard and had a great role in his movie *Apollo 13* (as Jim Lovell's confused mom). Musette Vander had a starring role in the *Voyeur* computer game. She also played Munita in *Wild Wild West* and appeared in *Stargate SG-1*.

Don't Give Up The Day Job: One of writer David Greenwalt's first jobs was as Jeff Bridges' body-double before becoming a director on *The Wonder Years* and producer on *The X-Files* and *Doogie Howser MD*. His film scripts include *Class, American Dreamer* and *Secret Admirer* (which he also directed) and *one* acting role as 'Uniformed Cop' in a 1981 horror-spoof called *Wacko*. Director Bruce Seth Green's TV work includes series like *Knight Rider, Airwolf, MacGyver, She-Wolf of London, V, SeaQuest DSV, Xena: Warrior Princess, TJ Hooker, Hercules: The Legendary Journeys, American Gothic* and *Jack & Jill*.

Cigarettes and Alcohol: Xander drinks the martini that Ms French gives him.

Logic, Let Me Introduce You to This Window: Xander throws a chair leg into a vampire's chest during his dream. It goes into the right of the chest, as opposed to where the heart is. Since it's a dream, we can excuse this as Xander's naiveté in the ways of killing (though he's already staked one vampire: Jesse in **2**, 'The Harvest'). The door shouldn't be left open during a private session with a counsellor. Dr Gregory's narration on the ant features a slide of a beetle. As Natalie eats her insect sandwich, for most of the scene her sweater sleeves are pulled up to her elbows. However, for the close-up of her hands pouring the insects on to the bread, the cuffs cover her wrists. When Xander is tied up in Natalie's basement, he has a flashback to her first class with him. If Blayne was heading straight to biology when Buffy and friends were sitting outside, we can assume that it was the first class of the day. Certainly, the group are seen at lunch *afterwards*. However, as Natalie approaches Xander, the clock behind him says 1:45. After Buffy hacks the She-Mantis to death, she wipes the machete blade on the seat of her pants. Bet she caught it from her mom on the next washing day (see **34**, 'Becoming' Part 2). Angel's scar from his encounter with the clawed vampire: although vampires seem to heal quickly (Angel being shot in **7**, 'Angel', for instance), this doesn't always work (see **43**, 'The Wish'; **55**, 'Graduation Day' Part 1).

I Just *Love* Your Accent: Giles's former colleague, Carlysle, first discovered references to the She-Mantis in old German texts. He tried to hunt her after boys were murdered in the Cotswolds, but went insane. (Giles tells him in a telephone call that he *was* right about the She-Mantis, but probably wrong about his mother being reincarnated as a Pekinese.)

Quote/Unquote: Giles on bat sonar: 'Soothingly akin to having one's teeth drilled.'

Notes: 'A perfect end to a wonderful day.' Loads of fun with a dangerous, sexy villainess – a complete subversion of the pretty girl in peril form of horror fantasy. The She-Mantis is so over-the-top that it moves into areas of grand kitsch. Isn't the monster costume gloriously pants? Proof that in the best traditions of *Doctor Who* a witty, entertaining series can still do crap monsters on a budget and get away with it.

Xander's middle name is LaVelle (he's embarrassed by it). He says he likes cucumber. He's also a virgin (which we *all* knew anyway). The real Natalie French's address is 837 Weatherley Drive.

Soundtrack: Superfine perform 'Already Met You' [*] in the Bronze (the singer is less than impressed with Xander's dancing). Their song 'Stoner Love' is also featured.

Critique: *Buffy* received its first UK publicity with this episode, as *Today's Choice* in the Satellite section of *Radio Times* (though it had been previously mentioned in the magazine's John Peel column). It was described as 'a huge hit in the States', a 'supernatural drama' and 'a sort of *Beverly Hills 90210* meets *The X-Files*'.

Did You Know?: One of David Boreanaz's previous movie roles had been playing 'Vampire Victim' in a movie called *Macabre Pair of Shorts* (1996).

5
Never Kill a Boy on the First Date

US Transmission Date: 31 Mar 1997
UK Transmission Date: 31 Jan 1998

Writers: Rob Des Hotel, Dean Batali
Director: David Semel
Cast: Christopher Wiehl (Owen), Geoff Meed (Andrew Vorba),
Paul-Felix Montez (Mysterious Guy), Robert Mont (Van Driver)

Giles discovers a dead vampire's ring belongs to the Order of Aurelius, just as Buffy gets a date with Owen Thurman. Unfortunately, Buffy learns that an ancient prophecy, the rising of the Anointed, will be fulfilled tonight and, by the time she has finished her patrol, she finds Owen dancing with Cordelia at the Bronze. A shuttle bus crashes and all the passengers are killed by the vampires. Giles asks Buffy to check out the funeral home where the bodies were taken. She refuses, saying that she needs a break. Giles goes himself and encounters two vampires. Xander and Willow alert Buffy though she is unable to get rid of Owen. Buffy finds Giles in the storage room and she and Owen fight the vampire whom Giles believes to be the Anointed One. Enraged when Owen is hurt, Buffy tosses the vampire into the incinerator. Owen wants to go out with Buffy again, but only to relive the adrenaline rush. Buffy refuses. Meanwhile, the Master meets the *real* Anointed One.

Dudes and Babes: Owen seems a little bookish for Buffy (and Cordy for that matter), despite Buffy's brattish outburst to Giles ('Cute guy. Teenage post-pubescent fantasies').

Cordelia on Angel: '*Hello*, salty-goodness!'

A Little Learning is a Dangerous Thing: Owen's *Emily Dickinson for Beginners* gives a nice introduction to the works of the poet (1830–1886). It's certainly a more impressive overview than Giles stuffily noting that she was quite a good poet 'for an American'.

School Dinners: There's a discussion on what the green stuff served in the cafeteria actually is.

It's a Designer Label!: Buffy's green and white dress ('Does this make me look fat?'). Let's heave a sigh of delight for her tiger-skin anorak too.

References: Nick Brendon impersonates Jerry Seinfeld: 'Everyone forgets, Willow, that knowledge is the ultimate weapon.' Vorba sings the hymn 'Gather At The River'. Also, *Soylent Green*, *The Untouchables* and *Superman* ('even Clark Kent had a job'). Xander has a Tweety Pie wristwatch. There's a possible reference to Patrick McGoohan's 1960s series *Danger Man*, but as that show was called *Secret Agent* in the US, it's likely a coincidence.

Bitch!: Buffy: 'Boy, Cordelia's hips are wider than I thought.'

'You May Remember Me From Such Films and TV Series As . . .': Geoff Meed was in *Brother*, *Passions*, *ER* and *Enterprise*.

Valley-Speak: Buffy: 'I *totally* blew it.' And her legendary taunt to Vorba: 'Bite me.'

Logic, Let Me Introduce You to This Window: If a vampire's clothes turn to dust when they are destroyed, why does the ring remain intact? In the first shot of the shuttle bus, the interior lights are illuminated. When the scene cuts inside, all the lights are off. As Buffy tells Giles, 'If the Apocalypse comes, beep me,' she reaches forward, grabs her pager and holds it up. The next shot is from the side and there's no table on which the pager could have been resting.

Quote/Unquote: Buffy, when Giles shows an interest in the ring of the dead vampire: 'That's great. I kill 'em, you fence their stuff.'

Giles: 'I'll just jump into my time machine, go back to the twelfth century and ask the vampires to postpone their ancient prophecy for a few days while you take in dinner and a show?'

Notes: 'Prophecy. Anointed One. Yadda yadda yadda.' A solid, if rather uneventful episode, with not much to get excited about except for the usual array of one-liners. The climax, however, is clever as the identity of the Anointed One is revealed.

Giles was ten when his father told him he was destined to be a Watcher (as part of a tiresome speech about responsibility and sacrifice). Giles wanted to be a fighter pilot (or a grocer). At least two previous members of the Giles family were Watchers, Giles's father, and his paternal grandmother. He has volumes of prophecies and predictions, but says that he doesn't have an instruction book on how to be a Slayer (this is contradicted in **22**, 'What's My Line?' Part 2).

Soundtrack: Three Day Wheely's 'Rotten Apples', Rubber's 'Junkie Girl' and 'Let The Sun Fall Down' by Kim Richey. Velvet Chain perform the dramatic 'Strong' [*] and 'Treason' in the Bronze.

6
The Pack

US Transmission Date: 7 Apr 1997
UK Transmission Date: 7 Feb 1998

Writers: Matt Kiene, Joe Reinkemeyer
Director: Bruce Seth Green

Cast: Eion Bailey (Kyle), Michael McRaine (Rhonda), Brian Gross (Tor), Jennifer Sky (Heidi), Jeff Maynard (Lance), James Stephens (Zookeeper), Gregory White (Coach Herrold), Jeffrey Steven Smith (Adam), David Brisbin (Mr Anderson), Barbara K Whinnery (Mrs Anderson), Justin Jon Ross (Joey), Patrese Borem (Young Woman)

On a zoo trip, Kyle and his gang of bullies are confronted by Xander in the quarantined hyena house. All the teenagers leave with yellow eyes and changed personalities, with Xander acting cruelly, particularly to Willow. Buffy and Giles discover an African tribal legend concerning hyena spirits. The pack find Herbert, the school's pig mascot, and eat him. Buffy is attacked by Xander but she locks him in the book cage. The rest of the pack are sent to the Principal's office, where they eat Flutie. Buffy and Giles talk to the zookeeper, who describes a way of reversing the curse. Buffy leads the pack, including Xander, to the zoo, where the keeper plans to create a transfer to gain the hyena spirits himself. He is successful but is thrown into the hyena pit by Buffy and a recovered Xander.

Dudes and Babes: Willow tells Buffy that Xander makes her head all tingly. Xander seems similarly excited by the sight of zebras mating. He says he's been waiting for Buffy to jump on his bones.

A Little Learning is a Dangerous Thing: Willow's attempts to teach Xander basic geometry are hindered by his possession.

School Dinners: Xander's hunger isn't satisfied by Buffy's croissant or various hotdogs so he goes for a giant, uncooked bacon sandwich. Without the bread. Buffy asks: 'Didn't your mom teach you, don't play with your food?'

It's a Designer Label!: Ouch! The Rupert Bear-pants on the girl walking behind Buffy in the opening scene and Xander and Willow's near-matching Nerds-On-Tour gear. Buffy wears the jacket Angel gave her (see **4**, 'Teacher's Pet'). It goes with her shoes, she says. *It* may, but her pink miniskirt definitely doesn't go with the black ski-cap she's wearing in the final scene.

References: The signs in the zoo are in the same font as those in *Jurassic Park*. The line 'all shiny and new' may be a nod to Madonna's 'Like A Virgin'. Noah's Ark is referred to (cf. Giles's Christianity-baiting speech in **2**, 'The Harvest'). Also, *The X-Files* ('I can't believe you, of all people, is trying to Scully me'), *The Wizard of Oz* ('Oh great, it's the Winged Monkeys'), and *Silence* *of the Lambs* ('a bottle of Chianti'). Buffy makes a sarcastic comment about Yanni, the notorious US easy-listening synth-musak guy.

Bitch!: Rhonda and Heidi do their best to make Buffy's life a misery in the opening scene.

Awesome!: Buffy's practice session with Giles. His reaction to her aggression is priceless.

'You Might Remember Me From Such Films As . . .': David Brisbin was in *Twin Peaks: Fire Walk With Me* and *Forrest Gump* and played Nicholas Cage's landlord in *Leaving Las Vegas*. Jennifer Sky played Amarice in *Xena: Warrior Princess*.

Valley-Speak: Buffy: 'Xander has been acting *totally*-wiggy since that day at the zoo.'

Logic, Let Me Introduce You to This Window: When Xander is locked in the cage, Willow watches a documentary about hyenas; however, while the first clip shows a pack of hyenas, all subsequent ones depict African Wild Dogs. Why would Willow keep viewing this, especially with Xander caged behind her? Seems a touch masochistic.

Cruelty to Animals: Two words: bacon sandwich (see **School Dinners**).

Quote/Unquote: Giles, upon being told that Xander has been teasing the less fortunate, has a noticeable change in demeanour, and is spending his time lounging about: 'It's devastating. He's turned into a sixteen-year-old boy. Of course, you'll have to kill him.'

Willow: 'Why couldn't Xander be possessed by a puppy? Or some ducks?'

Notes: 'Once they separate them, the pack devours them.' The silliest episode of the season, though, in a lot of ways, the most disturbing. Xander makes an extremely credible bully (it's in the eyes). There's not enough plot to fill the screen-time requirements, however, and what there is, is often a bit inconsequential (an act closing with the implied death of a pig, for instance). But overall it's an effective and occasionally scary piece.

Buffy seems to have an affinity with pigs. Willow knows Xander's blood pressure is 130/80. There are references to Buffy rescuing Willow and Xander in **2**, 'The Harvest', and Xander's knowledge of guitar music (given his daydream in **4**, 'Teacher's

Pet', we presume he can play, but see **47**, 'The Zeppo'). The Razorbacks is not only the name of the Sunnydale High basketball team (see **3**, 'The Witch'), but also their football team (using the same name for all sports teams is not uncommon in US high schools). Wretched Refuse are a local rock band. The opening scenes were shot at San Diego Zoo.

Soundtrack: Sprung Monkey's 'Reluctant Man', Dashboard Prophets' 'All You Want' and Far's 'Job's Eyes'. The incidental music is some of the best of the season.

Around The World In 45 Minutes: Just to prove that *Buffy* wasn't purely an English-language phenomenon, the series was broadcast in a bewildering array of countries and dubbed-languages, including: Argentina, Australia, Brazil, China, Denmark, Finland (as *Buffy Vampyyrintappaja*), France (*Buffy Contre Les Vampires*), Germany *(Buffy Im Bann der Dämonen)*, Israel, Hungary (*Buffy, a Vámpirok Réme*), Italy, Japan, the Netherlands, Norway, Poland, Portugal *(Buffy A Caça Vampiros)*, Spain and Sweden *(Buffy Vampyrdödaren)*. The iron fist of American cultural imperialism inside the velvet glove of quality television.

7
Angel

US Transmission Date: 14 Apr 1997
UK Transmission Date: 14 Feb 1998

Writer: David Greenwalt
Director: Scott Brazil
Cast: Charles Wesley (Meanest Vamp)

The Master sends the Three (a trio of vampire super warriors) after Buffy, who is saved by Angel. However, when they kiss, Angel suddenly reveals that he is a vampire. Giles discovers that Angel's vampire name is Angelus, and he and Xander believe it's Buffy's duty to kill the vampire. Angel meets Darla who suggests that Angel tell Buffy about his curse. Darla goes to Buffy's house and attacks Joyce, leaving her for Buffy to find in Angel's arms. Buffy hunts down Angel, and finds him in the Bronze. They fight but Angel tells Buffy that this is a trap, just as Darla shoots Angel.

Dudes and Babes: Drool factor eleven, on a scale of one to ten as far as *everybody* is concerned. Xander dancing is a bit special . . .

in terms of comedy. Darla's Catholic schoolgirl look is disturbingly effective.

Denial, Thy Name is Joyce: Joyce believes her neck wounds were caused by her passing out and falling on a barbecue fork, despite the fact that she doesn't own one.

It's a Designer Label!: Xander's greeny-yellow shirt and Willow's horrible stripy top clash for the worst clothes of the season. Cordy is horrified that somebody has a carbon copy of her Todd Oldman one-of-a-kind dress: 'This is exactly what happens when we sign these free-trade agreements.' She tells Xander to get his extreme oafishness off her two hundred dollar shoes.

References: Friar Tuck of the Robin Hood legends. The Master's line 'out of the mouths of babes' is from Psalms 8:2. Also, *Spider-Man* ('with power comes responsibility'). The Darla/Angel reminiscences about their past may have been conceptually inspired by *Highlander* and *Forever Knight*. Watch out for a *Smoking Sucks* poster, and issues of the fanzine *Twisted* on the wall at the Bronze.

Bitch!: Xander tells Cordelia: 'I don't know what everybody's talking about. That outfit doesn't make you look like a hooker.'

Surprise!: End of act one: Angel turns towards Buffy with his face contorted and fangs bared. *Gasp.* One of the most shocking moments of 90s television that has every viewer shouting 'But . . .?' at their TV sets.

Logic, Let Me Introduce You to This Window: When Angel hears Joyce scream from inside the Summers' home, Sarah Michelle Gellar's scream from earlier in the episode is used on the soundtrack. Just before Buffy is attacked by the Three, she passes a green-lit window. After Angel saves her, the pair run off in the opposite direction to that which Buffy arrived, but pass the same window. When Buffy takes Angel dinner in her bedroom, she is wearing a shiny-red lipstick. After the discussion about her diary, she isn't. As noted in **4**, 'Teacher's Pet', vampires healing properties are sometimes spectacular. The cross-mark on Angel's chest is missing from future bare-chested scenes. At what point did Buffy tell Giles about the Three so that he could research them from midnight until six? How did Darla know when Angel would arrive at Buffy's home for her plan to work? Does Darla have an unlimited supply of ammunition during the climax?

Quote/Unquote: Willow on speaking up: 'That way lies madness, and sweaty palms.'

Darla: 'It's been a while.' Angel: 'A lifetime.' Darla: '. . . Or two, but who's counting?'

Willow: 'So he *is* a good vampire? I mean on a scale of one to ten. Ten being someone who's killing and maiming every night. One being someone who's . . . not.'

Notes: 'You're living overground. Like one of *them*.' *The* revelation of *Buffy*'s first season. *Everything* you know is wrong. Beautifully filmed and acted, easily the highlight of the first year and, as things would turn out, a pilot episode for a spin-off series three years later.

Buffy and Joyce live at 1630 Revello Drive. Giles is a master with the quarterstaff (except when fighting Buffy). Angel confirms the legend about a vampire being unable to enter a building unless invited (see **M1**), though this doesn't apply to public domain (see **15**, 'School Hard'; **30**, 'Killed By Death'). Angel says his family are dead, killed by vampires long ago. In fact, *he* killed them. And their friends. And their friends' children. Angelus is approximately 240 years old and was 'made' by Darla in Ireland (see **33**, 'Becoming' Part 1; *Angel*: 'The Prodigal'). He spent decades creating havoc in Europe (the Master regards him as 'the most vicious creature I ever met'). Eighty years ago (actually, 98, see **33**, 'Becoming' Part 1; **44**, 'Amends'; *Angel*: 'City Of'; 'Orpheus') he left Europe after killing a Romany gypsy girl whose clan cursed him and restored his soul, giving him a conscience. He came to America but shunned other vampires (see *Angel*: 'Are You Now, or Have You Ever Been?'; 'Why We Fight'). He drinks refrigerated blood, the implication being that it's not human (see **11**, 'Out of Mind, Out of Sight'; **21**, 'What's My Line?' Part 1; **54**, 'The Prom'). He has a tattoo on his back. Angel and Darla last met in Budapest, Hungary, at the turn of the century (see **85**, 'Fool for Love'; *Angel*: 'Darla'). Darla is approximately 400 years old (Buffy suggests she's been around 'since Columbus' but is clearly making a sarcastic 'ageist' comment. *Angel*: 'Darla' confirms the date of Darla's sireing by the Master as 1609 in Virginia). Bullets can't kill vampires, but they can hurt like hell.

Soundtrack: 'I'll Remember You' by Sophie Zelmani.

8
I Robot . . . You Jane

US Transmission Date: 28 Apr 1997
UK Transmission Date: 21 Feb 1998

Writers: Ashley Gable, Tom Swyden
Director: Stephen Posey
Cast: Chad Lindberg (Dave), Jamison Ryan (Fritz),
Pierrino Mascarino (Thelonius), Edith Fields (School Nurse),
Damon Sharp (Male Student), Mark Deakins (Voice of Moloch)

Cartona, Italy, 1418: Moloch the Corrupter is trapped in a book. Sunnydale 1997: computer teacher Jenny Calendar and her students are scanning books on to computer. Some time later Willow tells Buffy she has met a guy called Malcolm online. Buffy asks computer nerd Dave to find out more about Malcolm, but he warns her to stay away from Willow. Buffy follows Dave to a computer facility. After Buffy survives near-electrocution, and Dave apparently kills himself, Willow suspects that Malcolm is not all he seems. She is kidnapped by Moloch's human acolyte, Fritz. Willow discovers that Moloch has created a robotic body for himself as Buffy and Xander break into the facility. Giles informs Ms Calendar that a demon is loose on the Internet. She tells him that she was already aware of this. In an attempt to trap Moloch, they recant the spell, which traps Moloch in his robot body. Moloch attacks Buffy, but she electrocutes him.

Dudes and Babes: 'That dreadful Calendar woman' – a Technopagan-babe. How come we never had teachers like her at my school?

A Little Learning is a Dangerous Thing: Buffy: 'Woah! I *got* knowledge!' We are solemnly informed that Nazi Germany was a model of a well-ordered society, which is *technically* correct. It was only when it came to the murdering half of Europe-thing that it all went pear-shaped.

It's a Designer Label!: Buffy's white vest-type T-shirt and *tiny* skirt in the opening scene. If Giles is ever on the *Jerry Springer Show* episode *My Slayer Dresses Like A Hooker*, this will be Exhibit A. The skirt puts in another appearance later, accompanied by a black T-shirt that leaves little to the imagination. Her private investigator's dark glasses and trenchcoat are much more restrained.

References: Buffy's pop-culture reference to her spider-sense concerns *Spider-Man*. The title is a homage to *Tarzan* and Isaac Asimov. It could be coincidental, but there are lots of references to *Macbeth* ('I'll see you anon', 'we three', Malcolm.) Xander refers to 'With a little help from my friends', which seems a bit retro for him. Maybe his parents have a copy of *Sgt Pepper's Lonely Hearts Club Band* lying around? Or, given Xander's paraphrasing of 'I Am The Walrus' in **22**, 'What's My Line?' Part 2, more likely *The Beatles 1967–70*. His self-aware 'for those in our studio audience who are me' is homage to the many US sitcoms that were videotaped before a live studio audience (*Happy Days*, *Cheers* etc.). The voice-synthesiser that Moloch uses has more than a touch of *2001* about it.

Fritz cutting a message into his arm: while self-mutilation is by no means rare (Elizabeth Wurtzel's *Prozac Nation* contains a harrowing autobiographical account of the disorder), one cannot help but think of Manic Street Preachers guitarist Richie Edwards and his carving the slogan '4-Real' into his arm during an interview with *NME* in the early 90s. The notorious case of Internet couple Robert Glass and Sharon Lopatka who fantasised about Glass killing Lopatka, to the point where she allegedly knowingly went to her death at his hands, gained much publicity with Glass's arrest in October 1996, around the time this episode was being written. It's possible that Buffy and Xander's hysterical discussion about Willow's net-friend is a reference to this.

'You Might Remember Me From Such TV Series As . . .': Chad Lindberg was excellent as the moody teenager Bobby Rich in *The X-Files* episode 'Schizogyny'.

'You Might Remember Me From Such Pop Music Video's As . . .': Aside from a brief stint in *Beverly Hills 90210*, as Jill Fleming, Robia LaMorte was Pearl in Prince's videos 'Diamonds and Pearl' and 'Cream'.

Don't Give Up The Day Job: Stephen Posey was cinematographer on *Friday The 13th Part V: A New Beginning, The Slumber Party Massacre* and *Bloody Birthday*.

Valley-Speak: Buffy: 'Let's focus here, OK?'

Not Exactly A Haven For the Bruthas: Jenny's angry rant about knowledge being kept for a handful of white guys. Political correctness aside, there *is* an undercurrent of racial tension in *Buffy*. Has anyone else noticed how few non-Caucasian people there are in Sunnydale? (See **37**, 'Faith Hope and Trick'.)

Logic, Let Me Introduce You to This Window: Buffy's status changes from 'sophomore' to 'senior' between the records that Moloch accesses and those Fritz is looking at. Her date of birth also changes from 24 October 1980 to 6 May 1979 (see **10**, 'Nightmares'; **67**, 'Doomed'). It's also worth noting that her full name is Buffy Summers, with no mention of a middle name (see **35**, 'Anne'). Buffy attempts to delete Willow's file from the computer. However, when Buffy turns on the monitor, the folder is already open. Watch the hand-held scanner Willow is using – it doesn't cover more than two-thirds the page width, yet scans the entire text of Moloch. How did Buffy keep track of Dave if he drove off in his car? And why didn't she see Dave's hanging body as soon as she entered the lab? Buffy is focused-on through the PC camera. If such cameras have a focusing element, it would be manual. More significantly, the camera centres on her. Not possible. The cameras have no motors and if this was some Moloch magic, you'd think Willow would notice the movement of a non-moveable object. Malcolm Black? OK, it's close to Moloch but what kind of a name is that for a demon to choose? Malcolm is Gaelic – 'the followers of St Columbus'. Four kings of Scotland used it, and it's a character name in *Macbeth* (see **References**), but still . . .

Buffy telling Giles to call Willow at home seems dumb, when she's already talked to Willow earlier about her being inaccessible when she's on the net. If Willow *was* at home at this point (in fact, where *was* she?) then they wouldn't be able to talk to her. When Giles leaves the library following his discovery of the blank book, why don't we see him through the window of the room he goes into? 'I know the secrets of your kings' – what is Moloch on about? He's become modern enough to hold convincing conversations with Willow, but he's unaware of a lack of kings in the modern world? As in many TV shows, there is a naive correlation between the Internet and sources-of-all-knowledge. Confidential information isn't stored on the Internet *because* it is not a safe medium.

I Just *Love* Your Accent: 'How am I going to convince her there's a demon on the Internet?' is an amusing (if probably unintentional) reference to the UK-based Internet provider Demon.

Quote/Unquote: Jenny: 'I know our ways are strange to you, but soon you will join us in the twentieth century, with three whole years to spare.'

Giles: 'I'll be back in the middle ages.' Jenny: 'Did you ever leave?'

Moloch: 'Right now a man in Beijing is transferring money to a Swiss bank account for a contract on his mother's life. Good for him.'

Notes: 'He's gone all binary on us.' The funniest episode of the first season. *Buffy* proves it can do sitcom, taking a technophobe's view of the Internet and having fun with it. Intelligent characterisation (Giles's horror of a world without books) adds a dose of *realpolitik* to the fantasy elements.

Buffy's Grade Point Average is 2.8, according to her school record, which destroys the Buffy-is-doing-lousy-at-school idea. A 2.8 GPA, while not in Willow's league, still corresponds to C+ or B-level (see **42**, 'Lover's Walk'). Willow keeps a picture in her locker of Giles and herself. Xander has an uncle who worked at CRD, 'in a floor-sweeping capacity'. There are references to Buffy and Xander's disastrous crushes on non-humans in **7**, 'Angel' and **4**, 'Teacher's Pet', respectively. Giles says he has a child-like terror of computers and still prefers a good book (see **1**, 'Welcome to the Hellmouth').

Cool injoke: Fritz uses a program called 'Watcher Pro Security'. Elmwood, where Malcolm claims to live, is 80 miles from Sunnydale. The announcer's voice heard while Giles listens to the radio is, apparently, Joss Whedon. Among the news items reported are all FBI's serial-killer files being downloaded on to the net and a fragment concerning financial irregularities involving an Archbishop.

9
The Puppet Show

US Transmission Date: 5 May 1997
UK Transmission Date: 28 Feb 1998

Writers: Rob Des Hotel, Dean Batali
Director: Ellen S Pressman
Cast: Richard Werner (Morgan), Burke Roberts (Marc),
Lenora May (Mrs Jackson), Chasen Hampton (Elliott), Natasha Pearce (Lisa),
Tom Wyner (Voice of Sid), Krissy Carlson (Emily (Dancer)),
Michelle Miracle (Locker Girl)

Giles is assigned by Principal Snyder to produce the annual talent show. Snyder forces Buffy and friends to participate as punishment for their regular absences. They meet Morgan, who is doing a ventriloquist act with his puppet Sid. One of the dancers is killed in the changing room, and Morgan seems a likely killer. Buffy breaks into his locker, but finds his puppet is missing. Buffy discovers Morgan's dead body with its brain removed. In her bedroom, Buffy is attacked by the puppet, and he later tries to stab her. They realise both believed they were fighting a demon. Sid explains that he is a demon hunter who is cursed to live inside a puppet's body. Marc, the real demon, straps Giles into a guillotine. Buffy saves Giles's life, aided by Sid, who kills the demon, freeing himself from his wooden existence.

Authority Sucks!: The appointment of a new school principal gives plenty of opportunity for power-crazed megalomania. However, Snyder's dialogue suggests that he is less knowledgeable about the Hellmouth than he will subsequently become: his 'there's something going on here' seems genuine. At this point he may be on the outside of whatever conspiracy it is that he's most certainly on the inside of by **15**, 'School Hard'. (See also **31**, 'I Only Have Eyes for You'; **34**, 'Becoming' Part 2; **53**, 'Choices'.)

A Little Learning is a Dangerous Thing: Mrs Jackson's history class gets a minimal overview of the 'Monroe Doctrine', as well as a (somewhat simplistic) definition of the word eponymous. Willow knows the square root of 841 is 29.

Mom's Apple Pie: Buffy appeals to her mother *not* to attend the talent show.

It's a Designer Label!: Buffy's slip-on tortoiseshell dress is great, compared to Willow's duck T-shirt. But what *are* they all wearing at the end?

References: Cordelia sings 'The Greatest Love Of All' (*very* badly). Originally a hit for George Benson, it's more familiar via Whitney Houston's version. Xander's cries of 'Redrum' are from Stephen King's novel *The Shining* and Stanley Kubrick's film adaptation. 'Does anyone else feel like we've been Keyser Soze'd?' concerns the mysterious (and possibly fictitious) villain of *The Usual Suspects*. There's a reference to *The Sting*, while aspects of the plot may have been influenced by the 'Prey' segment of the 1975 TV movie *Trilogy of Terror*. After Willow flees during the *Oedipus Rex* sequence, Xander and Buffy move together in imitation of artist Grant Wood's *American Gothic* (see **10**, 'Nightmares', for Willow suffering stage-fright again).

Bitch!: Xander, replying to Cordelia's self-pitying whinge that the murdered Emily could have been her: 'We can *dream*.'

Awesome!: Xander's double-take when discovering Sid is missing. Pure *Tom and Jerry*.

'You Might Remember Me From Such Films and TV Series As . . .': Armin Shimerman played Pascal on *Beauty and the Beast* and then became a TV comedy icon as the Ferengi bar owner Quark in *Star Trek: Deep Space 9*. He also had a semi-regular role as a judge in *Ally McBeal*. His films include *Blind Date*, *The Hitcher* and *Stardust Memories*. Krissy Carlson was in *Sunset Beach*.

Valley-Speak: Buffy: 'However did you finagle such a premo assignment?'
   Willow: 'Creep factor is also heightened.'

Logic, Let Me Introduce You to This Window: While Buffy says 'I'm never going to stop washing my hands', you can hear Willow typing and the computer beeping. However, the monitor is visible and no program is running.
   Buffy lives a fair distance from school (her mom drives her there each day) and Sid only has little legs, so how did he manage to get all the way from school to Buffy's house and back in one night? After Sid stabs the demon, the knife is left sticking out of Marc's body. When Buffy picks up Sid, the knife has disappeared. Why would the teacher let Morgan keep his puppet on his desk during class? Where were the rest of the talent show participants when Buffy was fighting the demon just before the curtain opened?

Quote/Unquote: Snyder: 'There are things I will not tolerate. Students loitering on campus after school. Horrible murders with hearts being removed. And also smoking.'
   Giles advises a nervous Cordelia on overcoming stage fright by imagining all of the audience in their underwear. Cordelia: 'Eww. Even Mrs Franklin?' Giles: 'Perhaps not.'

Notes: 'I don't get it, what is it, avant garde?' Outrageously over-the-top, the impression of 'The Puppet Show' is of some sort of 'Plan B' in operation (did another script fall through?). It's very different from the surrounding episodes and nearly everyone is out-of-character; but it's a memorable debut for Armin Shimer-man, with good jokes and top quality direction.

Willow plays the piano, though not in public. Snyder is obviously well read on the events of previous episodes, making specific reference to the death of his predecessor in **6**, 'The Pack', and the case of spontaneous cheerleader combustion in **3**, 'The Witch'. Buffy doesn't like ventriloquist's dummies (there's no story behind it, she just doesn't). The day before these events Buffy, Willow and Xander left school to fight a demon. Since this doesn't sound like the events of **8**, 'I Robot . . . You Jane', we must presume there's at least one missing adventure in between.

Sid says he knew a Slayer in the 1930s who was Korean. There's a rivalry between the dancers and the school band.

Critique: Peter Fairly reviewed this episode in *The Journal*: 'Last night, they stretched the plot, in a series in which the credibility factor is rapidly approaching warp nine, to breaking point. Take a school play, another corpse – Buffy's school has already seen its headmaster eaten alive and various staff and pupils dispatched in unsavory ways – and a moody scholar with headaches whose best friend is a wooden ventriloquist's dummy, and you have a ready-made scenario for Buffy to strut her ghoul-slaying stuff.'

10
Nightmares

US Transmission Date: 12 May 1997
UK Transmission Date: 7 Mar 1998

Writer: David Greenwalt
Story: Joss Whedon
Director: Bruce Seth Green
Cast: Jeremy Foley (Billy Palmer), Justin Urich (Wendell), J Robin Miller (Laura),
Terry Cain (Ms Tishler), Scott Harlan (Aldo Gianfranco), Brian Pietro (Coach),
Johnny Green (Way Cool Guy), Patty Ross (Cool Guy's Mom),
Dom Magwili (Doctor), Sean Moran (Stage Manager)

Everyone is having nightmares, and some of them are starting to affect reality. But only Buffy can see the strange little boy hanging around school. A girl, smoking in the boiler room, is attacked and Buffy and Giles learn that the girl is the second victim of the same attacker. The first was a junior league baseball player, Billy Palmer, currently in a coma. Giles theorises that Buffy saw an astral projection of the comatose boy. Billy explains that he is trying to hide from 'the Ugly Man'. Buffy dreams that the Master is free and when Giles, Willow and Xander find Buffy she has become a vampire. They rush to the hospital to try to wake Billy.

Dreaming (As Blondie Once Said) is Free: Among the nightmares-made-flesh are Buffy walking into the Master's lair but being powerless against him. She also has fears concerning a history test she hasn't studied for, her father telling her that *she* was the reason for her parents' divorce and being turned into a vampire. Giles's two nightmares are losing his ability to read and Buffy's death. Xander faces twin fears – nakedness (except for his underwear) in class and a clown who terrorised him at his sixth birthday party (that this is a dream sequence is evidenced by the swastikas, echoing Xander's earlier comment about being more frightened of Nazis than spiders). Willow suffers from stage fright (see **9**, 'The Puppet Show'; **78**, 'Restless'), while Cordelia turns into a Chess-club geek. Wendell's arachnophobia is understandable once he explains the background and the 'Way-Cool Guy's fear of his mom embarrassing him in front of his friends is one we've all shared. But, *come on*, who dreamed about giant flies destroying Sunnydale?

A Little Learning is a Dangerous Thing: Xander didn't pay much attention in Ms Tilsher's active listening class, being more interested in the midnight blue angora sweater she was wearing. He is surprised to find that spiders are arachnids ('they come from the Middle East?'). Buffy shouldn't find this too amusing – she gets 'astral' and 'asteroid' mixed up. Giles can read five languages. On a normal day.

Mom's Apple Pie: Xander's birthday party sounds like the kind of nightmare many children suffer; but a darker side to the competitiveness of American life is highlighted in Billy being beaten by his coach for dropping a catch that lost the game. Joyce's attempts to convince Buffy that her father loves her, without weakening her own position, are hilarious, if a bit scary.

It's a Designer Label!: Buffy's T-shirt manages to take our attention away from Xander's horrible shirt, Cordy's pink pants and Willow's yellow tights.

References: Visual references to Poe's *The Premature Burial* and Hansel and Gretal (Xander following a trail of chocolate; see **45**, 'Gingerbread'), and dialogue samples from *The Wizard of Oz*

('You were there. And you'), *Star Trek* ('Red alert'), *Cinderella* ('a dream is a wish your heart makes') and *Rosemary's Baby* ('This isn't a dream'). *Evita* is mentioned concerning Cordelia's delusions of grandeur. The opera that Willow dreams herself into is Puccini's *Madame Butterfly* (as Cio-Cio-San).

Bitch!: Cordelia on Buffy's panic over how she'll be able to pass a test she hasn't studied for: 'Blind luck?'

'You Might Remember Me From Such TV Series As . . .': Dean Butler is best known as Almanzo in *Little House on the Prairie*. He was also in *The Final Goal*.

Don't Give Up The Day Job: Sean Moran was one of the dancers in *Grease*. Dom Magwili is also a writer; his credits include the movie *Bikini Hotel*.

Valley-Speak: Xander: 'Which is a fair wiggins, I admit . . .'

Logic, Let Me Introduce You to This Window: When Buffy is talking about her parents' separation, Willow slips her backpack off. In the next shot, it's on her shoulder again. How did Vampire-Buffy get to the hospital in daylight?

Quote/Unquote: Xander tells the clown how rotten he was: 'Your balloon animals were *PATHETIC*. Anyone can make a giraffe.'

Notes: 'Our nightmares are coming true.' A surreal, well-structured episode with some of the most memorable images of the season, 'Nightmares' highlights are in the area of characterisation, subtly playing with secret fears of the regulars. The climax is overdrawn, but scenes such as Xander overcoming his clown-terror more than make up for that.

Buffy has a red stuffed animal (see **M1**). Her parents divorced last year, although they were separated for some time before that (see **33**, 'Becoming' Part 1). Willow says *her* parents don't bicker though they do occasionally glare. Given that Buffy was born in both 1979 *and* 1980 in **8**, 'I Robot . . . You Jane', it's little surprise to see her gravestone read 'Buffy Summers 1981–1997' (see **100**, 'The Gift'). When Buffy sees the Master in the graveyard he says, 'You're prettier than the last one', indicating that he met the Slayer before Buffy. However, we have to ask ourselves if this is a *real* conversation or just Buffy's overactive imagination. Willow has a Nerf Herder sticker on the inside of her locker door. She attended Xander's sixth birthday party at which he ate a chocolate hurricane and was chased by the clown (we never find out exactly why, but the experience has scarred Xander's life).

11
Out of Mind, Out of Sight (aka: Invisible Girl)

US Transmission Date: 19 May 1999
UK Transmission Date: 14 Mar 1998

Writers: Ashley Gable, Tom Swyden
Story: Joss Whedon
Director: Reza Badiyi
Cast: Clea DuVall (Marcie Ross), Ryan Bittle (Mitch), Denise Dowse (Ms Miller), John Knight (Bud 1), Mark Phelan (Agent Doyle), Skip Stellrecht (Agent Manetti), Julie Fulton (FBI Teacher)

Cordelia's boyfriend Mitch and her friend Harmony fall victim to attacks while Cordy is running for May Queen. Willow and Buffy link the attacks to missing student Marcie Ross whom no one can remember. Buffy finds Marcie's yearbook, the entries in which suggest that Marcie had no friends. Cordelia, having worked out that she may be the next target, asks Buffy for help. Marcie sets a trap for Giles, Willow and Xander in a gas-filled basement. While Angel saves their lives, Buffy and Cordelia wake up in the Bronze, tied to chairs. Marcie has gone mad during her isolation, and wants to disfigure Cordelia, but Buffy overcomes the difficulties of fighting an opponent she cannot see. Two FBI agents take Marcie into custody, and tell Buffy and Cordelia to forget what happened.

Dudes and Babes: Naked guys alert. Plus Angel in leather-jacket-and-vest mode. Xander says he would use the power of invisibility to guard the girls' locker room.

Authority Sucks!: Snyder's hysterical reaction to Harmony breaking her ankle is to tell her not to sue the school.

A Little Learning is a Dangerous Thing: Ms Jackson's English class is doing *The Merchant of Venice*, focusing on the anger of the outcast, which is this episode and, indeed, this series all over. Xander's research leads him to note: 'Great myths speak of cloaks of invisibility, but they're usually for the gods.'

It's a Designer Label!: Cordelia says she's having her May Queen dress specially made as off-the-rack clothes give her 'the hives'.

Check out Harmony's kitten T-shirt, Willow's Tasmanian Devil T-shirt, Buffy's pink skirt and the peach skirt she wears in the final scene.

References: Writer and scholar Helen Keller (1880–1968), *Poltergeist*, *The Merchant of Venice*. 'Gee, it's fun, we're speaking in tongues,' says Buffy, referring to the spiritual gift of *glossolalia*. 'Crush! Kill! Destroy!' was the catchphrase of the robot in *Lost in Space*. On the blackboard, there's a reference to Irish playwright Samuel Beckett (1906–89).

Bitch!: Even when she's trying to be nice, Cordy asks Buffy: 'You were popular? In what alternate universe?' And, in response to Giles's comment that he doesn't recall seeing her in the library before: 'Oh no. I *have* a life.' And, when seeing a picture of Marcie: 'Oh my God. Is she *really* wearing Laura Ashley?'

'You Might Remember Me From Such Films As . . .': Clea DuVall's movies include a starring role in *The Faculty* and *Can't Hardly Wait* (with Seth Green).

Valley-Speak: Cordelia on Shylock: 'Colour me *totally* self-involved . . .'
Buffy: 'I think I speak for everyone here when I say, *"Huh?"* '

Logic, Let Me Introduce You to This Window: As Giles says, 'I've never actually heard of anyone attacked by a lone baseball bat before,' Xander puts a potato chip in his mouth. In the next shot from a slightly different angle Xander is holding a sandwich as he says: 'Maybe it's a vampire bat.' There is clearly something strange going on in the cafeteria, as Buffy's French fries change into a drink during the same scene. After Snyder announces Cordelia as May Queen, he steps to the left as Cordelia comes to the microphone. For the distance shots, Snyder is standing behind Cordelia's left shoulder, but in close-up Cordy is the only person in shot. The board at the Bronze reads: 'Closed for Fumigation' (stock footage from 7, 'Angel'). How does Angel get to the school during daylight? After Marcie slashes Cordelia's face, Buffy kicks the instrument table, knocking Marcie out of the way. Buffy rushes to Cordelia's chair and tries to loosen the rope. As Buffy is attacked by Marcie, the rope around Cordy's left hand comes free. For the rest of the scene, however, the rope is still tied. Why did Marcie's clothes become invisible as well as her body? If it's something to do with them being in contact with her body then why isn't the knife she holds also invisible? How did Marcie get

Cordelia and Buffy to the Bronze without anyone noticing? When Marcie goes into the classroom full of other invisible students, how does she know the chair she sits on isn't occupied?

Quote/Unquote: Angel's moment of Byronic anguish: 'Looking in the mirror everyday and seeing nothing there. It's an overrated pleasure.'

Giles: 'Once again, I teeter on the precipice of the generation gap.'

Notes: 'Being this popular is not just my right, it's a responsibility.' Conceptually the most extreme episode of *Buffy* yet, focusing on one of Joss Whedon's key elements – the anger of the outcast. An intriguing and mysterious opening gives way to a thoroughly slovenly middle section, before the episode comes to an excellent climax. Great direction, particularly during the flashbacks. The scene between Giles and Angel is particularly well written. (Giles notes that Angel and Buffy's affection is 'rather poetic, in a maudlin sort of way'.)

There's also the rehabilitation of Cordelia Chase and a first hint that, far from being a simpering bad girl with mush for brains, she is actually a tough cookie. Her eyes are hazel. She once 'sort of' ran over a girl on a bicycle in her car (she must, therefore, have passed her driving test sometime after **3**, 'The Witch'). Willow and Xander tell a (seemingly amusing) story about something that happened to Cordelia in sixth grade that involved antlers and a man in a hat. Cordelia refers to Buffy attacking her in **1**, 'Welcome to the Hellmouth'. Buffy was the equivalent of May Queen at Hemery. It's confirmed that Angel casts no reflection and that he hasn't fed from a human for a long while (see **7**, 'Angel'; **33**, 'Becoming' Part 1; *Angel*: 'Orpheus'). Xander invites Willow home for dinner, noting: 'Mom's making her famous "Phonecall to the Chinese place".' Willow doubts the Harrises even *have* a stove. *Entertainment Weekly* observed that Xander's family life 'beyond his parents fighting, his mother's [lack of] cooking and his dad's unemployment remain a mystery. "He was abused as a child," deadpans Brendon. "I've got two people in mind for his dad – George Hamilton and Steven Seagal".' (See **78**, 'Restless'; **116**, 'Hell's Bells'.)

Mitch's dad is Sunnydale's most powerful lawyer, assuming that Willow and Xander aren't lying to Snyder. Angel tells Giles that the Master is planning something big (see **12**, 'Prophecy Girl' for the climax to *that* story arc). Salient books of Slayer prophecy have mostly been lost, including *The Tiberius Manifesto* and *The*

Pergamum Codex (which Angel manages to acquire. Did he get it from the demon bookseller in **53**, 'Choices'?). Giles is currently reading a Hindi text, *Legends of Vishnu*. When Buffy shows Marcie's yearbook picture to Cordelia, Willow's photo is next to Marcie's, which makes the fact that Willow can't remember Marcie even sadder. Page 54 of the textbook at the end of the episode contains the heading: *Chapter 11: Infiltration and Assassination.* The subheading states *Case D: Radical Cult Leader as Intended Victim.* The paragraph begins 'August 2nd 19XX'. The rest of the page consists of lyrics from the Beatles' 'Happiness Is A Warm Gun'.

12
Prophecy Girl

US Transmission Date: 2 Jun 1997
UK Transmission Date: 21 Mar 1998

Writer: Joss Whedon
Director: Joss Whedon
Cast: Scott Gurney (Kevin)

Xander asks Buffy to the Spring Fling but is turned down. Giles translates an ancient Codex, and discovers a prophecy predicting the death of the Slayer as Jenny tells him that portents suggest the apocalypse is coming. As Giles and Angel discuss the prophecy Buffy overhears them. When Cordelia and Willow discover several murdered students, Buffy decides she must follow her destiny, entering the Master's lair alone. Xander and Angel find Buffy's drowned body but Xander performs mouth to mouth resuscitation and revives her. An army of vampires attack Giles, Cordelia, Willow and Jenny in the library as the Hellmouth is about to open. Buffy faces the Master again and pushes him through the library skylight where he is impaled on a beam of wood. With the Hellmouth closed, at Xander's suggestion they all leave for the Bronze.

Dudes and Babes: Poor Xander, he hasn't got a *clue* has he? Trying to get Willow on the bounce from Buffy is dumb. There's a fragile beauty to Buffy that can inspire exchanges like, Angel: 'You're in love with her', Xander: 'Aren't you?'

Mom's Apple Pie: The dress Joyce buys her daughter is, indeed, beautiful. Joyce tells Buffy that she attended Homecoming during her freshman year without a date (*with* Gidget-hair? See **3**, 'The

Witch'). It was horrible for an hour until she met Buffy's father (who *did* have a date). This fits with the uncool girl that Joyce describes herself as in **3**, 'The Witch' and whom we see in **40**, 'Band Candy'.

It's a Designer Label!: Buffy's grey T-shirt and blue skirt, plus Willow's green trainers and zigzag jumper.

References: Xander describes Country as the music of pain. The Master's 'where are your jibes now?' is a rhetorical question Hamlet asks Yorick's skull in *Hamlet*. A few seconds of a *Porky the Pig* cartoon are seen on the TV in the room where the vampires killed the boys. There's a quotation from Isaiah 11:6 ('The wolf shall lie with the lamb'). Xander refers to the *Star Trek: The Next Generation* episode 'The Best of Both Worlds': 'Calm may work for Locutus of the Borg'. The rising of the dead and their descending on the library owes much to Romero's *Night of the Living Dead*, while the Master's death may have been suggested by the climax to Hammer's *Dracula Has Risen from the Grave*, in which Dracula was impaled on a cross.

Awesome!: Buffy taking on a vampire mostly in slow motion. The scene of Xander asking Buffy out to the dance is heart-rending because you *know* what the answer is going to be. Cordelia being 'nice' to Willow (to gain her help in setting up the sound system for the dance).

***That* Scene:** Highlight of the episode is the stunning scene in which Cordelia and Willow discover the bodies of Kevin and friends. It's almost voyeuristic. In no other series would we be made to care so much about Cordelia's loss. Alyson Hannigan told *DreamWatch*: 'We did two different versions of the scene. We did the tame version for America and . . . a bloodier version that we thought we could get away with in Europe. We poured blood everywhere . . .'

Valley-Speak: Xander, on the results of asking Buffy on a date: 'On a scale of one to ten? It sucked.'

Logic, Let Me Introduce You to This Window: While Buffy is walking in the tunnels, the shadow of one of the production team can be seen on the wall. When Xander asks Buffy to the prom, keep an eye on his backpack. In distance shots it's resting on the bench beside his legs, in close-ups, the strap is on his right shoulder. When Buffy falls into the pool, her arms are under her body while her hair is tied up in a ponytail. But when Angel and

Xander find her, her arms are spread out and her hair is undone and floating in the water. Everyone leaves for the Bronze at the end of the episode. However, it's clearly daylight outside the library (Angel should burn to death from the sun coming through the broken skylight.) How does Angel pay his phone bills? Or his rent for that matter? How could Angel and Giles not notice Buffy coming into the library? Did Buffy *really* tell Xander where Angel lives? (How else would he know?)

What a Shame They Dropped . . .: After Buffy has rejected Xander, the original script called for a scene in which it rains pebbles. 'Check it out,' says a student, 'it's raining stones!' 'Figures,' notes a heartbroken Xander.

Quote/Unquote: Buffy: 'I'm 16 years old. I don't want to die.' And, after knocking Giles unconscious: 'When he wakes up, tell him . . . Think of something cool, tell him I said it.'

Willow, on finding the bodies: 'It wasn't our world any more. They [the vampires] made it theirs. And they had *fun*.'

Notes: 'By the way, I like your dress.' A staggering season finale. Once again the direction is stunning and the story features a circular feeling as elements from the initial episodes are again referred to. One of the finest aspects is the juxtaposition between Giles and Jenny talking about Armageddon, and Cordelia and Kevin discussing their trivial dance.

Willow checks with Xander that nerds are still 'in'. Xander doesn't handle rejection well, which, he notes, is odd since he's had a lot of practice at it. Giles finally realises that the vampire Buffy killed in 5, 'Never Kill a Boy on the First Date', *wasn't* the Anointed One. Among the portents of the end days are a cat giving birth to a litter of snakes, a boy being born with his eyes facing inward and blood pouring from the sink in the girls' bathroom. This was the first *Buffy* episode to be rated TV-14.

Soundtrack: 'I Fall To Pieces' by Patsy Cline, and 'Inconsolable' by Jonathan Brooke.

***Buffy the Vampire Slayer* Will Return . . .:** At this point the production team and cast didn't know whether *Buffy* would be picked up for a second season (indeed, the lateness of the renewal is why Anthony Stewart Head had to vacate his potentially recurring role *in Jonathan Creek*). Therefore, the final scenes have an added poignancy since – at the time of shooting – this may have been our last look at the characters. Fortunately, a second season *was* eventually commissioned.

Did You Know . . .?: Sarah Michelle Gellar originally screen-tested for Cordelia (we get a vague idea of how she may have played the role from her performance in *Cruel Intentions*). According to an *FHM* interview, Katie Holmes (*Dawson's Creek*, *Disturbing Behaviour*, *The Gift*) turned down the part of Buffy so that she could finish school.

'I wish dating was like Slaying.
Simple, direct, stake to the heart . . .'
— 'Bewitched, Bothered and Bewildered'

Season Two (1997–98)

Mutant Enemy Inc/Kuzui Enterprises/Sandollar Television/20th Century Fox
Created by Joss Whedon
Producer: Gareth Davies
Co-Producer: David Solomon, Gary Law (19–34)
Consulting Producer: Howard Gordon (13–25)
Executive Producers: Sandy Gallin, Gail Berman, Fran Rubel Kuzui,
Kaz Kuzui, Joss Whedon
Co-Executive Producer: David Greenwalt
Regular Cast:
Sarah Michelle Gellar (Buffy Summers), Nicholas Brendon (Xander Harris),
Alyson Hannigan (Willow Rosenberg), Charisma Carpenter (Cordelia Chase),
Anthony Stewart Head (Rupert Giles),
David Boreanaz (Angel/Angelus,[6] 13–15, 17–34),
Kristine Sutherland (Joyce Summers, 13, 15–16, 23–26, 28–30, 33–34),
Julie Benz (Darla, 33), Mercedes McNab (Harmony Kendall,[7] 25, 28),
Elizabeth Anne Allen (Amy Madison, 28), Amanda Wilmshurst (Cheerleader, 14),
Andrew J Ferchland (the Anointed One, 13, 15),
Robia LaMorte (Jenny Calendar, 13–15, 19, 23, 25–26, 28–29, 34),
Dean Butler (Hank Summers, 13),
Armin Shimerman (Principal Snyder, 13, 15, 18, 21, 31–34),
James Marsters (Spike, 15, 18–19, 21–22, 25–26, 28–29, 31, 33–34),
Juliet Landau (Drusilla, 15, 18–19, 21–22, 25–26, 28–29, 31, 33–34),
Brian Reddy (Bob, 15, 31),
Seth Green (Daniel 'Oz' Osborne, 16, 18, 21–22, 25–28, 33–34),
Jason Hall (Devon, 16, 28),
Danny Strong (Jonathan Levinson,[8] 16–17, 22, 24, 29, 32),
Larry Bagby III (Larry, 18, 27), Robin Sachs (Ethan Rayne, 18, 20),

---

[6] During episodes **26**, 'Innocence' to **34**, 'Becoming' Part 2, David Boreanaz plays
Angelus who, while occupying Angel's body, is a *very* different character.
[7] Credited on-screen as appearing in **25**, 'Surprise', but the scene was actually cut
before transmission.
[8] Credited as 'Hostage Kid' in **22**, 'What's My Line?' Part 2, and as 'Student' in **29**,
'Passion'.

Julia Lee ('Chanterelle'/'Lily'/Anne Steele, 19),
Bianca Lawson (Kendra, 21–22, 33), Eric Saiet (Dalton, 21, 25),
Saverio Guerra (Willy, 21–22), James G MacDonald (Detective Stein, 23, 34),
Jeremy Ratchford (Lyle Gorch, 24), James Lurie (Mr Miller,[9] 26, 31)

13
When She Was Bad

US Transmission Date: 15 Sep 1997
UK Transmission Date: 28 Mar 1998

Writer: Joss Whedon
Director: Joss Whedon
Cast: Brent Jennings (Absalom), Tamara Braun (Tara)

Buffy's back from summer vacation, but to Giles's surprise she recommences her training immediately. Buffy suffers a nightmare and awakens to find Angel in her room. He warns her that the Anointed One has been gathering vampires, but Buffy is dismissive. Cordelia and Jenny are kidnapped by vampires and Buffy is told to go to the Bronze. Assuming she is walking into a trap, Buffy realises too late that it is actually a diversion to allow the abduction of Giles and Willow, as the blood of the people closest to the Master when he died is needed for his revivification. With Angel and Xander's help, Buffy tracks the vampires to a warehouse and, in a whirlwind of violence, deals with the issues that Giles believes she still has outstanding.

Dreaming (As Blondie Once Said) is Free: Buffy's nightmare features the Master (wearing Giles's face) trying to strangle her.

Dudes and Babes: Buffy working out. Oh, sweet mother . . . Buffy and Xander dancing is erotic in all sorts of ways but is clearly designed to make Angel jealous. It's actually a nasty, cruel trick Buffy pulls since Willow doesn't look too pleased, while Xander is left completely baffled as to where he stands.

Authority Sucks!: Snyder: 'That Summers girl. I smell trouble. I smell expulsion and just the faintest aroma of jail.'

A Little Learning is a Dangerous Thing: Xander has trouble working out what B-I-T-C-H spells.

---

[9] Credited as 'Teacher' in **26**, 'Innocence', but this scene was cut before transmission.

Mom's Apple Pie: Joyce tells Hank that she hasn't been able to get through to Buffy for a long time and that she'll be happy if Buffy gets through the year without getting expelled (see **34**, 'Becoming' Part 2).

It's a Designer Label!: Cordy's trousers in the final scene. *Hot damn.* Willow sports yet another pair of *horrible* tights (these are yellowy-green).

References: The title alludes to nursery rhyme *Jemima*. Xander and Willow's 'dumb game' includes dialogue misquotes from *The Terminator, Planet of the Apes, Star Wars* and *Witness.* Xander refers to Giles as G-Man, a nickname given to the FBI, which was allegedly first used by bank robber Machine Gun Kelly in 1934. Cordy uses *The Three Musketeers* as an insult. After Willow points out that they were actually quite cool, Xander suggests 'Three Stooges' would have been more appropriate. Again, it's possible to spot the influence of Hammer's *Dracula, Prince of Darkness* (both contain a victim suspended above a vampire's corpse so that their blood can be used to reanimate it).

Bitch!: Buffy telling Cordelia: 'Your mouth is open, sound is coming from it. This is never good.' And: 'You won't tell anyone that I'm the Slayer. I won't tell anyone you're a moron.'
    Cordy considers that Buffy is 'campaigning for Bitch of the Year', to which Buffy replies, 'As defending champion, are you nervous?'

Awesome!: The opening: Buffy kicking the crap out of a vampire and throwing him against a tree with a conveniently placed stake-shaped branch with a cheeky, extremely postmodern nod to the audience: 'Hi guys. Miss me?' Subtext: the audience assumes that Buffy is addressing *them*, but the theme of the story is the fear of rejection and of finding that your friends don't need you any more. Buffy is actually targeting Willow and Xander.

Don't Give Up The Day Job: This episode marked the debut of Sophia Crawford's husband, Jeff Pruitt, as *Buffy*'s stunt coordinator. In addition to numerous stunt credits, Jeff has acted in movies like *The Bad Pack*, *Scanner Cops* and *Martial Law*.

Act Naturally?: When Xander is telling Cordelia not to mention Buffy's Slaying abilities in public, watch the extra in the blue shirt on the right of the screen. Is that the most dreadful piece of ham you've seen this side of a bacon commercial? He does another little cameo of scene-stealing a moment later, walking behind Willow as she says 'a little too good?'

Valley-Speak: Xander: 'Please, I'm *so* over her.'

Logic, Let Me Introduce You to This Window: Watch the tree with the conveniently stake-shaped branch. In the preceding scene the branch is missing. The morning after Angel's visit, Buffy rides to school with her mom. In the car, Buffy is wearing a pink camisole. However, in her next scene at the school, Buffy sports a white tank top. The pink camisole shows up again the next day. Nobody seems to notice Cordelia's or Jenny's absence for an entire day. As Buffy, Angel and Xander spy on the revivification ritual, the vampires gather around the Master's skeleton. The long-haired vampire moves into position, to his right stands the vampire wearing a tan jacket. Moments later, as Buffy stakes the long-haired vampire, all the other vampires turn towards her. Tan-jacket-vampire is now opposite to where he was earlier. As Giles hangs above the skeleton, his hand brushes it and the bones bend. Buffy's sledgehammer skills leave a bit to be desired. Her first blow destroys the skull. The second smashes the left side of the rib cage. The next nine occur off-screen. When we see the skeleton again, it still looks remarkably intact. Buffy tells Giles that she put her friends in danger on the second day of school. Willow later confirms that it's Wednesday. However, it should be Thursday. The Anointed One sees the remains of the Master's skull at the climax, but Buffy smashed it earlier.

Quote/Unquote: Snyder: 'There are some things I can just smell. It's like a sixth sense.' Giles: 'Actually, that would be one of the five.'

Cordy's advice: 'Whatever's causing the Joan Collins 'tude, deal with it. Embrace the pain. Spank your inner moppet. Whatever.'

Xander telling Buffy: 'If they hurt Willow, I'll kill you.'

Notes: 'At least when she was burning stuff down I knew what to say.' A slow, but alluring opener. Good fight sequences aside, the best bits are the Buffy/Cordelia scenes, which add depth to both characters. It's certainly the finest of what was to become an annual reinvention by Joss Whedon with the first episode of this and subsequent seasons becoming, in effect, pilots for a new series. It's just a pity that after some fine approach-play, several goal-scoring opportunities are missed until the exciting climax. And, is it just me or does this episode look *cheap*?

Buffy spent the summer in LA with her dad, partying and shopping. She says she never thanked Xander for saving her life (**12**, 'Prophecy Girl'). Xander always does 'scissors' in 'rock–scissors–paper'. He bets Willow that Giles will need to consult his books within ten minutes of the start of school. He wins, with over a minute to spare. Cordy spent the summer with her parents in Tuscany. Suffering, apparently. Jenny says she went to a couple of festivals (including naked mud dancers, which sounds like fun.)

Two pieces of stock footage are used across a scene-break. The first (the front of school with a bus passing in the foreground) crops up in many episodes. The second shows the water fountain in the plaza. The guy walking away in a purple shirt is Owen from **5**, 'Never Kill a Boy on the First Date'.

Soundtrack: 'It Doesn't Matter' by Alison Krauss and Union Station [*]. 'Spoon' and 'Sugar Water' by Cibo Matto, featuring Sean Lennon (who perform in the Bronze and get name-checked by both Xander and Willow).

Did You Know?: Sarah Michelle Gellar has a phobia about cemeteries. As she told *FHM* (in the issue in which readers voted her top of 1999's *100 Sexiest Women*), 'I used to cry if I went near one . . . The first series was a horrible nightmare, so for the second they had to build fake cemeteries.'

14
Some Assembly Required

US Transmission Date: 22 Sep 1997
UK Transmission Date: 4 Apr 1998

Writer: Ty King
Director: Bruce Seth Green
Cast: Angelo Spizzirri (Chris), Michael Bacall (Eric), Ingo Neuhaus (Daryl),
Melanie MacQueen (Mrs Epps)

After the discovery of the robbed graves of three cheerleaders, suspicion falls on two of Willow's acquaintances from science club, Chris and the ghoulish Eric. In their lab, the boys only require a head to perfect a mate for Chris's formerly dead brother, Daryl. Daryl kidnaps Cordelia during a football game, but Buffy defeats him and Xander rescues Cordelia from the burning lab.

Dudes and Babes: Eric's pornography collection is so huge it scares even Xander. Cordelia hangs on to Angel's arm when Buffy enters the library and gets him to take her home.

A Little Learning is a Dangerous Thing: Buffy is worried that Slaying is interfering with her trigonometry homework. As Cordelia notes, 'I don't think anyone should be made to do anything educational in school if they don't want to.'

It's a Designer Label!: Check out Eric's nasty shirt, Willow's multicoloured patterned blouse and Jenny's tight cream stretchpants. When Eric ties Cordelia up, he lifts her skirt and we get a look at those red cheerleader knickers again (see **3**, 'The Witch').

References: *The Effects of Gamma Ray Radiation on Man in the Moon Marigolds* is a possible influence (the school science fair, the embittered mother, the name of Willow's project). Giles refers to Cyrano de Bergerac while Buffy provides an oblique reference to film critics Gene Siskel and Roger Ebert. There's a homage to *Batman* ('it's the Bat-signal'). Eric sings a few lines from the Temptation's 'My Girl'.

Bitch!: Another episode full of glorious Cordy/Xander exchanges. Cordelia: 'Why are these terrible things always happening to me?' Xander: 'Karma?'

Awesome!: Buffy falling into the grave. Xander and Cordy's escape on the medical trolley through the burning lab.

Surprise!: The first appearance of Daryl.

'You Might Remember Me From Such Films As . . .': Michael Bacall played Perry in *Free Willy*.

Valley-Speak: Buffy's advice on dating to Giles: 'Just say, "Hey, I gotta *thing*, you have a *thing*. Maybe we could have a *thing*".'

Logic, Let Me Introduce You to This Window: The cheerleaders were students at Fondren High, so why have they the letter J on their uniforms? None of the pictures that Eric develops matches the shots he took. There was no boy in a striped-shirt walking behind Buffy, Willow was looking at her clipboard when she was photographed and Cordelia's eyes were aimed away from the camera for the first two shots, then her hand covered her face for the last. How did the keys roll that far under Cordelia's car? Look at the depressions in the earth caused by dragging the body from the grave? Either the ground was *immensely* soft, or the body was that of the world's first thirty-stone cheerleader.

I Just *Love* Your Accent: Buffy: 'Speak English, not whatever it is they speak in –' Giles: 'England?'

Quote/Unquote: Buffy refuses to dig graves: 'Sorry, but I'm an old-fashioned gal. I was raised to believe that men dig up the corpses and women have the babies.'

Cordelia: 'Hello, can we deal with my pain please?' Giles (uninterestedly patting her on the back): 'There, there.'

Giles on American football: 'I just think it's rather odd that a nation that prides itself on its virility should feel compelled to strap on forty pounds of protective gear just in order to play rugby.'

Notes: 'Love makes you do the wacky.' An overt homage to *Bride of Frankenstein*, which takes far longer to get to the point than it should (in a series as sharp as this, it's surprising that somebody doesn't say 'this is *just* like *Frankenstein*!'). Includes lots of enjoyable set pieces that transcend the obvious *denouement*. The episode has aged rather better than several around it and repeated viewing is recommended.

Buffy owns a yo-yo. There are references to Buffy's dance with Xander in **13**, 'When She Was Bad'. Jenny likes Mexican food (Buffy somehow guessed she would). Willow believes that she's the only girl in school who has the Coroner's office website bookmarked. Her science project is 'Effects of subviolet light spectrum deprivation on the development of fruit flies'. That sounds a more likely winner than Cordelia's 'The Tomato – fruit or vegetable?' 'It's a fruit,' Willow notes, helpfully. There's at least one issue of *Scientific American* that Willow hasn't read. Angel reveals that he is 241 years old (see **33**, 'Becoming' Part 1; *Angel*: 'City Of'). Giles assumed that Jenny spent her evenings downloading incantations and casting bones. In fact, she *does*, but she likes football too. Tony Head's voice replaced the original narrator on the opening monologue from this episode onwards.

15
School Hard

US Transmission Date: 29 Sep 1997
UK Transmission Date: 11 Apr 1998

Writer: David Greenwalt
Story: Joss Whedon, David Greenwalt
Director: John T Kretchmer
Cast: Alexandra Johnes (Sheila), Keith Mackechnie (Parent),
Alan Abelew (Brian Kirch), Joanie Pleasant (Helpless Girl)

Snyder assigns the organisation of Parent–Teacher Night to his two worst students, Sheila and Buffy. Vampire couple Spike and Drusilla arrive in town but are coldly received by the Anointed One. The Night of St Vigeous will occur on Saturday, the time when a vampire's strength is at its peak. Spike lures Sheila to his warehouse and feeds her to Drusilla. At Parent–Teacher Night Buffy is unable to keep Snyder and Joyce apart and is in trouble with her mom until Spike's vampires attack the school. Buffy herds the parents into a room, while Willow and Cordelia hide in a nearby closet, and Giles, Xander and Jenny barricade the library. Buffy takes on the vampires, including Sheila. After an angry confrontation with his former guru, Angel, Spike almost kills Buffy but Joyce smashes an axe over Spike's head. Joyce tells Buffy how proud she is of her daughter's bravery and says that those qualities are more important than Buffy's problems at school. Spike and Dru, however, are here to stay.

Dudes and Babes: Buffy worries about whether she has a split-end. Some people are just never satisfied. Xander, once again, dances like somebody trying to crush cockroaches.

Authority Sucks!: Snyder says he wants his students to think of him not as their pal but as their judge, jury and executioner.

A Little Learning is a Dangerous Thing: Xander learns a very important lesson in this episode: never rummage through a girl's handbag because you never know what you might find. It's a little mousie, right?

Mom's Apple Pie: Buffy and Joyce have a mini-argument about Parent–Teacher Night, including the explicit threat that Buffy will be stopped from going out with her friends. However, despite Snyder's attempts to paint Buffy as a troublemaker, Joyce comes to realise that Buffy is a resourceful girl who cares about other people (however, see **24**, 'Bad Eggs'). Snyder now has *two* problems called Summers, noting, 'I'm beginning to see a certain mother/daughter resemblance.'

It's a Designer Label!: What *is* Xander wearing? That shirt should carry a public health warning. Willow's dungarees also deserve attention. Buffy has a cute purple top. Sheila has one of the same colour, but several degrees sluttier, and an extremely short skirt to match.

References: Spike's bravado in front of the other vampires may be an oblique reference to the infamous 'Show us your yarbles' sequence in *A Clockwork Orange*. The title (and aspects of the plot) come from the classic action movie *Die Hard*. The works of novelist Anne Rice (*An Interview With a Vampire*, among others) are referred to in a derogatory way. Spike calls Angel 'my Yoda' (from *The Empire Strikes Back*) and 'an Uncle Tom', a cynical term normally applied to a black whose behaviour towards whites is regarded as servile after the character in HB Stowe's novel *Uncle Tom's Cabin* (1852). There are possible references to the Beatles' 'From Me To You' and *Jack and the Beanstalk*.

Bitch!: Xander: 'Does anybody remember when Saturday night meant date night?' Cordelia: '*You* sure don't.'

Awesome!: Giles swearing for the first time ('*bloody* right I will . . .'). Buffy's fight with the vampire behind the Bronze is so good it gets a round of applause from Spike. Cordy's hilarious prayer in the final scene.

The Drugs Don't Work: Spike says he was at Woodstock (presumably he had a tent and slept during daylight). He fed on a flower person and spent the next six hours watching his hand move. Snyder and Bob's 'official' explanation for the outbreak of violence at the school is: 'Gang-related. PCP' – a reference to the hallucinogenic narcotic phencyclidine, the street name of which is Angel Dust.

'You May Remember Me From Such Films and TV Series As . . .': Juliet Landau appeared in *The Grifters*, *Pump Up the Volume*, *Theodore Rex*, *Citizens of Perpetual Indulgence*, *Parker Lewis Can't Lose* and *La Femme Nikita*. She's best known for her performance as Loretta King opposite her father, Martin, in Tim Burton's *Ed Wood*. James Marsters isn't from London, though the accent is good enough to fool many UK fans. He's actually from California and he can been seen (using his real voice) in a guest slot on *Millennium* and, briefly, *The House on Haunted Hill*.

Valley-Speak: Spike: 'Any of you wanna test who's got the biggest wrinklies around here, step on up.'

Cigarettes and Alcohol: Willow notes Sheila was already smoking in fifth grade.

Logic, Let Me Introduce You to This Window: Buffy and Willow leave their books on the table as they dance at the Bronze. These have vanished when Xander returns to the table to fetch a stake from Buffy's bag. Someone may have stolen them but, why not take the bag too? Why doesn't Buffy confront Spike when he tells her that he's going to kill her? Willow and Cordelia run into a room next to a trophy cabinet to hide from the vampires. When we see them inside the closet, the cabinet is nowhere near the door. The vampires cut the power in the school, so why is the cabinet still illuminated? Why was Snyder turning off all the lights in the lounge while some of the parents were still there?

Much of the continuity in **15**, 'School Hard', concerning Spike's origins is contradicted (or, at least, greatly expanded upon) in **85**, 'Fool for Love', **139**, 'Lies My Parents Told Me' and the *Angel* episodes 'Darla', 'Destiny' and 'The Girl in Question'. In particular, Giles says that he can find no historical reference to a vampire named Spike, implying that, until recently, Spike was still using the name William. However, in 'Fool for Love' we discover that he took the name Spike almost immediately upon becoming a vampire, taking exception when Angel continued to call him by his human name.

Motors: Spike's 'deathmobile' is a 1963 DeSoto.

What a Shame They Dropped . . .: Buffy: 'I don't suppose this is something about happy squirrels?' Giles: 'No, vampires.' Buffy: 'That was my next guess!'

Quote/Unquote: Spike: 'If every vampire who said he was at the crucifixion was actually there, it would have been like Woodstock.'

Jenny tells Giles: 'You have *got* to read something that was published *after* 1066.'

Joyce's triumphant: 'Nobody lays a hand on my little girl.'

Notes: 'So, who do you kill for fun around here?' A *gorgeous* episode. Funny in all the right places, but with a real tension and menace. The introduction of the drop-dead-sexy Spike and Drusilla is the point at which *Buffy* went from being merely a very good show into being a *great* one.

In reply to Snyder referring to Buffy burning down a school building, Buffy says this was never proved (the Fire Marshal said it could have been mice). Given that she freely admitted to burning the Hemery gym in **1**, 'Welcome to the Hellmouth', and that she later tells Sheila she burned down more than one building, are we to assume that this refers to the destruction of the old science lab in **14**, 'Some Assembly Required'? Spike's reference to the crucifixion begs the question were the vampires who attended afraid of crosses? This is the first time that Mrs Summers is referred to as Joyce. Sheila stabbed a horticulture teacher with some pruning shears, which seems to put Buffy's anti-social activities into stark context. Spike, also known as 'William the Bloody' (he gained his nickname by torturing his victims with railroad spikes) is younger than his mentor Angelus, who sired him (a term that Angel is reticent to explain to Xander). Giles notes Spike is 'barely 200' (something flatly contradicted in **63**, 'The Initiative'. See also **85**, 'Fool for Love'; **139**, 'Lies My Parents Told Me'). He has killed two Slayers in the last century. One was during 'The Boxer Rebellion', which *just* fits into that timescale (this was an anti-foreigner uprising in China during the years 1898–1900). He says that the last Slayer he killed begged for her life (he's lying – see **85**, 'Fool for Love'). His lover, Drusilla, collects dolls. Before coming to Sunnydale they were in Prague. This episode includes the first hints that Snyder, in collaboration with others (in this case Bob), knows *something* odd is occurring in Sunnydale, but that they are actively engaged in a cover-up (see **31**, 'I Only Have Eyes for You'). According to the sign Spike's car knocks down, Sunnydale has a population of 38,500. And decreasing (see **42**, 'Lover's Walk'). The French teacher is called Mr Dujon.

Soundtrack: Nickel perform '1000 Nights' and 'Stupid Thing' in the Bronze.

16
Inca Mummy Girl

US Transmission Date: 6 Oct 1997
UK Transmission Date: 18 Apr 1998

Writer: Matt Kiene, Joe Reinkemeyer
Director: Ellen S. Pressman

Cast: Ara Celi (Ampata), Henrik Rosvall (Sven), Joey Crawford (Rodney), Kristen Winnicki (Gwen), Gil Birmingham (Peru Man), Samuel Jacobs (Peruvian Boy)

Sunnydale's student exchange program brings the beautiful Ampata to town. Unbeknown to her new friends, however, Ampata is a mummy-girl who escaped from her tomb when the seal was broken. While Xander and Ampata develop a mutual attachment, Giles asks Ampata to translate the pictograms on the seal, but she refuses. Buffy and Giles discover that the mummy has the ability to drain the life-force of its victims. Buffy finds a shrivelled corpse in Ampata's trunk. Giles begins to piece together the broken seal to send Ampata back to her mummified state. Ampata attacks him, also throwing Buffy into an open tomb. But Xander tells her that if she wants another life it must be his and Buffy pulls the disintegrating Ampata apart.

Dudes and Babes: A Xander-love story that lets us see his sensitive and vulnerable side. Ampata's gorgeous and Xander can't believe how lucky he is ('You're not a praying mantis?' he asks, referring to 4, 'Teacher's Pet').

A Little Learning is a Dangerous Thing: Willow helps the inordinately stupid Rodney with his chemistry. He has almost memorised the fourteen natural elements. Willow notes there are 103. However, since the discovery of the 103rd (Lawrencium in 1961), a further eight had been identified by 1998.

Mom's Apple Pie: Is Joyce's pleasure at how quickly Ampata is fitting into Sunnydale society a sly dig at her daughter's inability to do likewise?

No Fat Chicks!: Buffy is seen drinking a can of (non-Diet) Pepsi. She should have a look over her shoulder at the three girls with enormous bottoms who wobble through shot and reflect on America, the land of the pancake breakfast.

It's a Designer Label!: Good stuff: Buffy's very low-cut top in the scenes investigating Rodney's disappearance and her kick-boxing vest and stretchpants, Apmata's night-shorts, Cordelia's blue miniskirt. *Very* bad stuff: Buffy's white-trash look, Willow's bobble-hat. Willow's Eskimo costume could also be a contender but it seems to do something for Oz, so the jury's still out on that one. Xander says lederhosen make his calves look fat. There's also a delicious *double entendre* between Buffy and Giles over the word trunks.

References: Willow makes specific reference to the Mummy-film genre and the plot bears a similarity to Hammer's *Blood From the Mummy's Tomb*. Buffy makes a pun concerning *Mommie Dearest*. The name of Oz's band, Dingoes Ate My Baby, is a reference to the case of Australian mother Lindy Chamberlain wrongly imprisoned for murdering her infant daughter. Readers may know the film dramatisation *A Cry in the Dark*. Xander's 'Ay carumba' is a probable nod to *The Simpsons*, while 'I am from the country of Leone. It's in Italy pretending to be Montana' identifies someone as a fan of Sergio Leone's spaghetti westerns.

Bitch!: Cordelia on Willow's Eskimo suit: 'Near *faux pas*. I nearly wore the same thing.'

Awesome!: A big girly cat-fight. Encore. Xander's fight with the Bodyguard is rather good. He's beginning to be able to handle himself (in a Xander kind-of way . . .).

'You Might Remember Me From Such Films and TV Series As . . .': Seth Green's movies include *Stephen King's It*, *Radio Days*, *Can't Hardly Wait*, *Idle Hands*, *Enemy of the State*, *Knockabout Guys*, the *Austin Powers* trilogy (as Scott Evil) and *My Stepmother is an Alien* (as Alyson Hannigan's boyfriend). He played a very Oz-like character in *The X-Files* episode 'Deep Throat' and provided the voice for Chris Griffin in *Family Guy*. Seth's a great actor and his (often understated) contribution to *Buffy* can't be praised highly enough. 'He can *own* a scene he has no lines in,' noted Joss Whedon. Danny Strong, who originally screen-tested for the role of Xander, was Juke Box Boy in *Pleasantville* and appeared in *Saved By the Bell: The New Class*, the *Clueless* TV series, *New Suit* and *Spoof! An Insider's Guide to Short Film Success*. Jason Hall can be seen in *No Child of Mine* and *Play Dead* and was one of the voice-artists on *The 10th Kingdom*.

Valley-Speak: Buffy: 'It's the über-suck.'
Cordelia on her Swedish exchange student: 'Isn't he lunchable?'

Logic, Let Me Introduce You to This Window: When Buffy opens Ampata's trunk the head of the mummified corpse is on the right. Later, when she opens the trunk for a second time, it's moved to the left. With Rodney Munson attending, how could Buffy and Sheila (see 15, 'School Hard') be the two worst students in school? (With Snyder you get the feeling it's all about appearances.) Xander and Ampata sit on the bleachers with Xander's bag lying on the seat in front of them. When the Bodyguard attacks them the bag is knocked down several seats. When Xander runs off with Ampata, the bag has returned to its original position. Ampata tells Buffy that she doesn't have any lipstick. However, she applied some in the school restroom. In the museum Giles is about to reassemble the final piece of the seal when Ampata grabs it from him. In the next shot the seal appears whole, just before Ampata smashes it. Given that Cordelia has a book showing (presumably) all the exchange students, it's a surprise that nobody questions Ampata's credentials. How well could Xander drive so soon after almost having his life-force sucked out of him? Given that Xander can drive in this episode, why does he need Cordelia to give him a lift in **21**, 'What's My Line?' Part 1.

Quote/Unquote: Buffy's sarcastic impression of Giles: 'I'm so stuffy, give me a scone.'

What impresses Oz in a girl involves: 'A feather boa and "Theme from *A Summer Place*".'

Xander on Sunnydale bus depot: 'What a better way to welcome somebody to our country than the stench of urine?' And: 'We're in the Crime Club, which is kind of like the Chess Club. Only with Crime. And no Chess.'

Notes: 'I can translate salivating boy-talk.' Nobody ever sets out to make a deliberately bad hour of television, but sometimes nothing goes according to plan. This is one such instance. 'Inca Mummy Girl', a dreadfully uneven story, lacks explanations, a focus and a degree of rationality. The direction, on the other hand, is terrific so at least this hollow tale of unrequited love and betrayal isn't a complete loss.

Xander claims his dad once tried to give him to some Armenians. He knows approximately four words of Spanish. Buffy refers to how upset she was at the prophecy of her death in **12**, 'Prophecy Girl'. During the dance at the Bronze, a 'WP' sticker is seen representing the band Widespread Panic (these stickers crop up in many episodes, so it's fair to assume someone on the production team is a fan).

Soundtrack: The Dingoes Ate My Baby songs 'Shadows' and 'Fate' are by Four Star Mary.

17
Reptile Boy

US Transmission Date: 13 Oct 1997
UK Transmission Date: 25 Apr 1998

Writer: David Greenwalt
Director: David Greenwalt
Cast: Greg Vaughan (Richard), Todd Babcock (Tom), Jordana Spiro (Callie),
Robin Atkin-Downes (Machida), Christopher Dahlberg (Tackle),
Jason Posey (Linebacker), Coby Bell (Young Man)

Buffy accepts Cordelia's invitation to a fraternity house party.
While Buffy and Cordelia attend the party, Willow discovers that
the bracelet Buffy recently found belonged to a missing student
called Callie. When confronted by Giles and Angel, Willow tells
them where Buffy is. Xander gatecrashes the party but is humili-
ated and thrown out. Buffy is drugged, waking next to Cordelia
and Callie in the basement. The fraternity is a cult that worship a
snake-demon called Machida, to whom the girls are to be
sacrificed. Giles, Angel and Xander invade the ceremony just as
Buffy frees herself and kills Machida.

Dudes and Babes: Buffy says her dreams about Angel contain
surroundsound. You and every other female on the planet, girl.

Authority Sucks!: Giles's chastising Buffy ('... and don't think
sitting there pouting is going to get to me because it won't') is
worthy of Snyder.

A Little Learning is a Dangerous Thing: Willow explains the plot of
the Hindi movie she, Xander and Buffy are watching on Channel
59: 'She's sad because her lover gave her twelve gold coins, but
then the wizard cut open the bag of salt and now the dancing
minions have nowhere to put their big maypole fish thing ...'

It's a Designer Label!: A nice collection of miniskirts – Cordelia's
blue one we've seen before, Buffy's green effort also looks familiar,
but Willow's dark purple skirt is a beaut. Cordelia states that
Buffy shouldn't wear black, silk, chiffon or spandex to the frat
party as these are Cordelia's trademarks. She also tells Buffy not
to 'do that thing with your hair'.

References: Herman's Hermits 'There's A Kind Of Hush', Nancy
Sinatra's 'These Boots Are Made For Walkin' ', *The Incredible*

Hulk, Godzilla and the *Superman* comics ('You could go on to live among rich and powerful men . . . in Bizarro-World').

Bitch!: Cordelia: 'Buffy, it's like we're sisters. With *really different hair.*'

Awesome!: Buffy taking on the entire frat coven *and* the snake-demon while Xander, Angel and Giles muck about upstairs with the varsity footballers.

'You Might Remember Me From Such TV Series As . . .': Robin Atkin-Downes, hiding inside the snake costume, played the poetry-spouting telepath Byron in *Babylon 5*.

Valley-Speak: Tom: 'And you are?' Buffy: '*So* not interested.'

Cigarettes and Alcohol: Buffy and Cordelia both drink in this episode. The implication is that it's the first time Buffy has ever had alcohol (though after a summer of partying mentioned in **13**, 'When She Was Bad', you've got to wonder what sort of parties she gets invited to).

Logic, Let Me Introduce You to This Window: The student lounge seems to have the quickest coke machine in the world. Willow buys a can of Coca-Cola Classic, which is delivered almost before the coins have left her hand. What kind of glass was that balcony door made out of? Callie just runs through it. Greg Vaughan's name is misspelled as 'Vaughn' in the opening credits. Willow asks a question that most of us have been *dying* for *someone* to articulate for years. If Angel casts no reflection then how do vampires shave? Sadly, she doesn't get an answer. Why does Buffy wear black to the party when Cordelia specifically asked her not to?

Motors: Cordelia's car is a red Chrysler Sebring convertible with the license plate Queen C.

Quote/Unquote: Angel: 'This isn't some fairy tale. When I kiss you, you don't wake up and live happily ever after.' Buffy: 'When you kiss me, I want to die.'

Willow's rant at Giles and Angel: 'She's sixteen-going-on-forty. And *you* . . . You're gonna live forever, you don't have time for a cup of coffee?'

Xander's beating up the frat-boy who made him dance in women's clothes: '*That's* for the last sixteen and a half years.'

Notes: 'Party's over, jerkwater.' Two substandard episodes in a row is almost unique in a series as good as *Buffy*. A pity really, as a lot of the ideas in 'Reptile Boy' are very good and Greenwalt's script is quite well structured. But . . . it's just so *obvious*. And the acting from a lot of the non-regulars is really poor. If you're going to do *Animal House*-with-demons, at least make it funny.

The local paper is called *The Sunnydale Press*.

Soundtrack: 'Wolves' by Shawn Clement and Sean Murray, 'Bring Me On' by Act of Faith, and 'She' by Louie Says.

18
Halloween

US Transmission Date: 27 Oct 1997
UK Transmission Date: 2 May 1998

Writer: Carl Ellsworth
Director: Bruce Seth Green
Cast: Abigail Gershman (Girl)

Halloween, a traditionally quiet time in the supernatural community, is interrupted by the opening of a costume store owned by warlock Ethan Rayne. Forced by Snyder into accompanying groups of children on their trick-or-treating, Buffy, Xander and Willow find themselves in a clothes-created nightmare as Rayne's spell transforms people into the reality of their costumes. While the children turn into monsters and ghouls, Xander becomes a soldier, Willow emerges from her body as an intangible ghost and Buffy as a helpless noblewoman. Willow leaves Xander and Buffy with the unaffected Cordelia to get Giles's help. Angel arrives, but frightens Buffy who runs from the house and hides in a warehouse, pursued by Spike who is about to kill Buffy when Giles forces Ethan to reverse the spell.

Dudes and Babes: Buffy and Angel kissing at the climax. Buffy tells Giles that Ms Calendar thinks he is a babe and a 'hunk of burning . . . something'. Of course, it's a lie to allow Willow to steal the Watcher Diaries, but Giles doesn't seem displeased by it. Plus Cordelia in her pussycat costume.

Authority Sucks!: Snyder volunteers Xander, Buffy and Willow for Halloween chaperone patrol duty: 'Bring them back in one piece and I won't expel you.'

A Quiet Night In?: The subversion of Halloween being a festival for the undead by having them all stay home that night and let the children get on with it (see **60**, 'Fear Itself'; *Angel*: 'Life of the Party').

It's a Designer Label!: Xander likes his women in spandex but completely renounces this when he sees Buffy in the eighteenth-century dress. It's certainly preferable to the checky flares she wears. Willow's hooker look is effective but she's right – it, ultimately, isn't her (though, again, it gets Oz's attention).

References: Allusions to *Xena: Warrior Princess* (a compliment *Xena* subsequently returned by referring to 'Buffus the Bachae Slayer'), Catwoman, *Star Trek* (Cordy's description of Angel as a Care Bear with fangs is similar to how Mr Spock's pet Sehlat was described), US sitcoms clichés ('Hi honey, I'm home') and a misquote from *The Godfather*. 'Be seeing you' echoes the catchphrase of *The Prisoner* (Robin Sachs has confirmed that this *was* deliberate).

Bitch!: Cordelia on Buffy after a fight: '*Love* that hair. It screams "Street Urchin".'

Awesome!: The black and white camcorder footage of Buffy's fight with the vampire in the pumpkin patch. The best bit of the episode is Giles's reaction to Willow walking through the wall (*what* was that he almost said?).

Surprise!: Giles's entire conversation with Ethan ('Hello, Ripper!') despite being nothing more than innuendo screams back-story alert (see **20**, 'The Dark Age').

'You Might Remember Me from Such Films and TV Series As ...': Robin Sachs was in one of this author's favourite films, Hammer's notoriously sexy *Vampire Circus*. *Babylon 5* fans will recognise him as Hedronn. He has provided the voice for the Silver Surfer in *The Fantastic Four* and appeared as the villain Sarris in *Galaxy Quest*.

Logic, Let Me Introduce You to This Window: When Buffy slams Larry against the drinks machine, a Diet Dr Pepper falls out. However, this was not a choice according to the selection buttons (see **55**, 'Graduation Day' Part 1). While reviewing the video of Buffy's fight, Spike orders the vampire with the remote control to rewind. At this point both Buffy and the vampire are standing and fighting. However, after the tape is rewound, Buffy has the vampire on the ground and is about to kill him. Perhaps he hit fast forward by mistake? Vampires cast no reflection in a mirror (see **11**, 'Out of Mind, Out of Sight'), so how do they appear on videotape, which uses mirrors as part of the focusing/view-finding mechanism? (See **46**, 'Helpless'; **138**, 'Storyteller' and numerous *Angel* episodes.) After Giles tells Willow to leave when he confronts Ethan, Willow bumps into a curtain and then closes the door despite supposedly being intangible. Buffy and Angel are attacked in the Summers' kitchen by what appears to be a vampire (Angel even asks for a stake), so who invited this vampire in?

I Just *Love* Your Accent: Aside from the episode featuring two fine British actors, the van that Oz drives has its steering wheel on the right, which suggests it's also British.

Quote/Unquote: Xander: 'A black-eye heals, but cowardice has an unlimited shelf-life.'

Spike on the mayhem that Ethan has caused: 'This is just . . . neat!'

Cordelia's reaction to Willow telling her that she isn't a cat, she's in high school and that they are her friends, well sort of . . .: 'That's nice, Willow. And you went mental *when* . . .?'

Notes: 'This could be a situation.' One of the best of the season, showing that *Buffy* had recovered from the lethargy of the previous episodes. A story about perception with a subplot in which the clothes, literally, maketh the man (or the Slayer). Plus an icily witty performance from the excellent Robin Sachs. Willow gets to do all the groovy detection stuff, Xander becomes *macho* and Buffy faints a lot. What more could one ask for?

This episode answers the question of whether or not Cordelia knew about Angel's vampirism at this stage. Giles says he has many relaxing hobbies including cross-referencing. Cordelia is still dating Dingoes Ate My Baby's singer Devon (see **16**, 'Inca Mummy Girl'), although a break-up seems imminent given her conversation with Oz.

Soundtrack: 'Shy' by Epperley and 'How She Died' by Treble Charger.

Head On . . .: 'I think Giles likes Buffy, but she frustrates him,' Head told Paul Simpson. 'She represents everything he doesn't understand. Ultimately he becomes extremely fond of her. People have said, what is it? A father/daughter relationship? There's nothing like it on TV. It's difficult to pigeonhole. He becomes extremely fond of her and gets into all sorts of terrible trouble because of it . . . Xander is a complete anathema to him. A great annoyance because he never seems to take anything seriously. Cordelia is . . . who knows where she's coming from? Willow he respects greatly, but it's all a confusion to him. He's never really sure of anybody or anything. The only thing he is sure about is what he's supposed to do.'

19
Lie to Me

US Transmission Date: 3 Nov 1997
UK Transmission Date: 9 May 1998

Writer: Joss Whedon
Director: Joss Whedon
Cast: Jason Behr (Billy Fordham), Jarrad Paul (Marvin),
Will Rothhaar (James)

Billy 'Ford' Fordham, Buffy's boyfriend at Hemery, arrives in Sunnydale. At the Bronze, she introduces Angel to Ford but the situation is awkward. Outside, Buffy hears a scuffle and sends Ford back while she confronts a vampire. She makes up a story explaining her actions, but Ford says that he knows she's the Slayer. Later, Ford attends a club full of groupies who dream of joining the undead. Angel asks Willow to find out what she can about Ford. She discovers that he never registered at Sunnydale High, confirming Angel's suspicions. Ford meets Spike and offers him the Slayer in exchange for immortality. Buffy goes to the club and while they wait for Spike to arrive she tries to reason with Ford, who reveals he has incurable brain cancer. Spike and his cohorts arrive and begin to feed. Buffy grabs Drusilla and tells Spike to let the clubbers go. Later, Buffy returns to find Ford's body.

Dudes and Babes: The idea of a Goth club full of vampire worshippers would be *so* cool if only Ford's friends weren't such a bunch of dweebs. Especially Marvin in that cape.

Willow tells Xander why Angel was in her room: 'Ours is a forbidden love!'

A Little Learning is a Dangerous Thing: Cordelia says she can relate to Marie Antoinette (the executed wife of France's Louis XVI). Unfortunately, she gets oppressed and depressed mixed up.

It's a Designer Label!: Willow's high-collared blouse in the Bronze. Giles claims not to have any clothes other than those he wears to school (which, judging by the stripy tie he takes to his date with Jenny, seems to be true). Also, Xander's red Adidas top and Ford's orange shirt. Chanterelle's low-cut red dress is a definite highlight.

References: The TV movie that fascinates Ford is a 1973 adaptation of *Dracula* starring Jack Palance. Buffy notes that when Ford ignored her in fifth grade she sat in her room for months listening to Divinyls' 'I Touch Myself'. Before adding that, of course, she had no idea what it was about. For anybody who *doesn't* know, it's a celebration of masturbation. Joss Whedon seems to be a fan of the Doors judging by references to 'The End' ('This is the end') and a misquote from 'Five To One' ('No one gets out of here alive').

Awesome!: Angel and Drusilla in the playground is about as sinister as *Buffy* has ever got. I'm sure we've *all* got people we'd like to shout 'Lying Scumbag' to, as Buffy does to Ford.

Don't Give Up The Day Job: Make-up supervisor Todd McIntosh has a cameo in the club as the man dressed as a vampire standing in a coffin who says 'Hi' to Xander.

'You Might Remember Me from Such TV Series As . . .': Jason Behr would go on to deserved stardom as the alien schoolboy Max Evans in *Roswell*.

Valley-Speak: Buffy: 'Do we have to be in total share-mode?'

Logic, Let Me Introduce You to This Window: Before they left for the club, Spike gave orders to the vampires to make the Slayer their first priority. When they enter, however, they attack everybody *but* Buffy. When Buffy fights in the alley behind the Bronze as Ford watches, pay attention to the length of her hair. From behind it seems much longer than usual (it's obviously Sarah's stunt-double Sophia Crawford). Again we don't see Willow's parents, though we do hear her mom's voice. It's also worth asking exactly *when* (and *how*) Ford worked out Buffy is the Slayer? Remember, when he first tells her he knows, he hasn't met Spike at that point.

Quote/Unquote: Xander, upon learning that the vampires are known as the lonely ones: 'We usually call them "The nasty, pointy, bitey ones".'

Drusilla on Angel's infatuation with Buffy: 'Your heart *stinks* of her.'

Buffy on the stupidity of the club teenagers: 'Spike and his friends are going to be pigging out at the All You Can Eat Moron Bar.'

Buffy: 'Does it get easy?' Giles: 'What do you want me to say?' Buffy: 'Lie to me.' Giles: 'Yes, it's terribly simple. The good guys are always stalwart and true, the bad guys are easily distinguished by their pointy horns or black hats, and we always defeat them and save the day. No one ever dies, and everybody lives happily ever after.'

Notes: 'I know you're the Slayer.' A highly effective tear-jerker, 'Lie to Me' potters along for a while, seemingly concerned with jealousy, before becoming a pointed essay on betrayal and obsession (the juxtaposition of what Angel once did to Drusilla with Billy's attempted manipulation of Buffy is nicely realised) and ends up with one of the finest climaxes of the season. Highlights include Angel entering Willow's house for the first time and a philosophical finale.

Ford was Buffy's fifth grade crush (though he was a year older). Something embarrassing happened to Buffy during the swimsuit section of her ninth grade beauty contest. Willow has upgraded from a desktop computer to a laptop between **8**, 'I Robot . . . You Jane', and this episode. Angel was obsessed with Drusilla when she was still human. He sent her insane by killing everyone she loved and tortured her before following her to a convent where she sought refuge and sired her (see **33**, 'Becoming' Part 1; *Angel*: 'Dear Boy'). Angel is said to have cold hands, which fits in with the idea first presented in **12**, 'Prophecy Girl', that his body is, basically, dead (see **26**, 'Innocence'; **55**, 'Graduation Day' Part 1). Giles thought Drusilla had been killed by a mob in Prague (see **15**, 'School Hard'). Jenny takes Giles to a Monster Truck rally, at which he seems to have a *really* bad time. Coffee is said to make Willow jumpy (something she shares with Angel, see **54**, 'The Prom').

Soundtrack: On first US transmission, the episode included Sisters of Mercy's 'Never Land'. Due to unresolved copyright issues, all subsequent broadcasts and commercial releases remove this and replace it with 'Blood Of A Stranger' by Shawn Clement and Sean Murray. Also: 'Lois On The Brink' by Willoughby and 'Reptile' by Creaming Jesus.

20
The Dark Age

US Transmission Date: 10 Nov 1997
UK Transmission Date: 16 May 1998

Writer: Dean Batali, Rob Des Hotel
Director: Bruce Seth Green
Cast: Stuart McLean (Philip Henry), Wendy Way (Deirdre),
Michael Earl Reid (Custodian), Daniel Henry Murray (Creepy Cult Guy),
Carlease Burke (Detective Winslow), Tony Sears (Morgue Attendant),
John Bellucci (Man)

Giles identifies a body found at the school as Philip, an old friend
from London. Buffy prevents a vampire attack on the hospital
blood supplies with Angel's help, but is surprised that Giles didn't
turn up as planned. At his apartment, she finds him drinking.
Buffy finds Ethan Rayne, who tells her about the Mark of Eyghon
that both he and Giles wear. Buffy locks the resurrected Philip into
the book cage while Giles argues with Ethan, but they are
disrupted by Philip breaking open the doors. He dissolves into a
liquid puddle, which touches Jenny's unconscious body, trans-
forming her into Eyghon. Giles explains that in their youth he and
his friends conjured up the demon, who is trying to kill everyone
who wears his mark. Ethan knocks Buffy out and tattoos her,
burning off his own tattoo with acid. Eyghon enters Angel's body
but is destroyed by the demon within.

Dudes and Babes: Giles and Jenny's kiss. Is it any wonder Tony
Head has such a following among the ladies? Xander believes that
he could live without the thought of Giles and orgies in the same
sentence.

A Little Learning is a Dangerous Thing: Willow informs Xander
that hot lava is used to kill a heretic, not a demon.

It's a Designer Label!: Buffy's green training vest, Giles's blue
pyjamas and Willow's fluffy green jumper. Rather cruelly, Buffy
speculates that Giles's diapers were tweed.

References: A bizarre array include *Hamlet* ('The rest is silence'),
ER, *Lost Weekend*, *The Sound of Music*, Frank Sinatra's 'I've Got
You Under My Skin' and Bill Withers' 'Lean On Me'. 'Be seeing
you' crops up again (see **18**, 'Halloween').

'**Anywhere But Here . . .**': A game anyone can play: Buffy wants to be on a beach, having her feet massaged by Gavin Rossdale (singer with grunge band Bush). Willow's contribution is a dinner date in Florence with actor John Cusack (*True Colours*, *Gross Pointe Blank*, *Being John Malkovich*, *High Fidelity*, *Serendipity*). Xander implies that both have recently changed their fantasies, though his remains large-chested actress Amy Yip at the Waterslide Park.

Bitch!: Xander's moment of Premier League sarcasm: 'A bonus day at class, plus Cordelia? Mix in a little rectal-surgery and it's *my best day ever*.'

Awesome!: Willow's anger at Xander and Cordy bitching (and their reactions to it). Giles's nightmares (the first one, especially). Cordelia tripping Ethan.

Surprise!: The photograph of a much younger Rupert.

Never Mind the Warlocks!: Tony Head, interviewed on the BBC's *Fully Booked*, confirmed that the photo of Giles playing bass was actually his head superimposed on the body of Sid Vicious.

Valley-Speak: Cordelia: 'It's *totally* bogus.'

Cigarettes and Alcohol: A clearly drunk Giles answers the door to Buffy.

Logic, Let Me Introduce You to This Window: Cordelia says the police were asking Giles about a homicide. However, she entered the library after that was mentioned. After Giles learns of Deirdre's death and hangs up the phone, he removes his spectacles and puts them on the desk some inches away from his notebook. In the next shot, the glasses are on top of the notebook. After Philip bursts from his cage, Buffy lunges at him. When the camera angle switches, Buffy's kicking leg switches with it. It's midnight when Giles phones Britain where, he says, it's 5 a.m. The west coast of the US is *eight* hours behind UK time.

Quote/Unquote: Buffy: 'Have I ever let you down?' Giles: 'Do you want me to answer that, or shall I just glare?'

Eyghon: 'You're like a woman, Ripper. You cry at every funeral.'

Notes: 'You're back?' A direct sequel to **18**, 'Halloween', the only disappointment of this cracking episode is that the viewer expects the revelations about Giles's past to be bigger than a university dropout experimenting with Bad Magicks. Clever ending though, and some great stunts (notably Jenny crashing through the window).

This was the first episode since **12**, 'Prophecy Girl', to earn the TV-14 rating. Buffy thinks Giles counts tardiness as a deadly sin. Notice the look Willow gives Xander when he asks, 'When are we gonna need computers for real life?' Xander refers to having known Cordelia for 12 years. (In the prologue to *The Xander Years Vol. 1*, Keith RA DeCandido provides a lovely cameo of the five-year-old Xander dumping a bowl of ice cream on Cordelia's head.) Xander's uncle Rory was a stodgy taxidermist by day, while by night indulging in booze and whores (see **47**, 'The Zeppo'; **116**, 'Hell's Bells'). Giles studied history at Oxford. When he was 21, he dropped-out and lived in London. He played bass in a band (see **40**, 'Band Candy') and fell in with a crowd of occultists who included Ethan, Philip, Deirdrie Page, Thomas Sutton and Randall (whom Eyghon killed). Giles's approximate age, and his reference to the Bay City Rollers, place this in the early 70s (see **61**, 'Beer Bad'). But weren't the Rollers a bit tame for such badass mothers as Giles and his gang? Black Sabbath or Led Zeppelin would seem more their gig. Of course, this could be an example of British humour.

Soundtrack: The music Buffy uses for her callisthenics: The riff sounds like the KLF's 1991 hit '3 AM Eternal'; however, it's a common sample and it could be almost anything.

21
What's My Line? Part 1

US Transmission Date: 17 Nov 1997
UK Transmission Date: 23 May 1998

Writers: Howard Gordon, Marti Noxon
Director: David Solomon
Cast: Kelly Connell (Norman Pfister), Michael Rothhaar (Suitman),
PB Hutton (Mrs Kalish)

Buffy interrupts two vampires robbing a mausoleum. Frustrated with Buffy's thwarting of his schemes, Spike summons the Order of Taraka, a society of assassins, to deal with her. Several strangers arrive in Sunnydale, including a girl who stowed away in an aircraft cargo hold. That night, Buffy skates on the empty ice rink while waiting for Angel. A one-eyed man attacks her, but Angel helps Buffy to kill the assassin. Giles tells Buffy that the Order will not stop until they complete their mission. Distraught, Buffy goes to Angel's apartment. Angel asks his usual informant, Willy, for information but is attacked by the mysterious girl. She traps Angel in a cage, soon to be flooded with sunlight, and tells him that she is going after his girlfriend. Buffy wakes as an axe swings towards her. The girl tells Buffy that she is Kendra, the Vampire Slayer.

Dudes and Babes: Kendra the, seemingly Caribbean, *second* Slayer.

Authority Sucks!: Although Snyder's hardly seen, his shadow hangs over the episode. His hoop of the week for Buffy to jump through is the Career Fair. He tells Xander: 'Whatever comes out of your mouth is a meaningless waste of breath.'

A Little Learning is a Dangerous Thing: Willow checks with Giles that both slayed and slew are acceptable past tenses for slay.

It's a Designer Label!: Cordy and Buffy both have extremely cute black miniskirts. Check out Kendra's red satin pants.

References: The title is from a legendary 50s TV show in which members of the public mimed their jobs for a team of celebrities to guess their occupation. (That was the British version at least. The US game show of the same name was apparently quite different.) There are allusions to *The Simpsons* ('Have a cow!'), *Highlander* ('There can be only one'), *My Fair Lady* ('By George, I think he's got it') and *Scooby-Doo Where Are You?* (This is the first occasion where Buffy's friends, in this case Xander, refer to themselves as the Scooby Gang.) Plus, another Biblical reference, this time to King Solomon.

Bitch!: Cordelia asks if she's 'mass transportation'. Xander replies, 'That's what a lot of the guys say but it's just locker-room talk.'

Awesome!: The location filming of Buffy and Giles in the graveyard. Kendra's fight with Buffy and the triple-cliffhanger.

Surprise!: The last six words of the episode.

'You Might Remember Me From Such Films As . . .': Eric Saiet was in *Felicity*, *Roswell*, *Home Improvements*, *Ugly Naked People*, *Groundhog Day*, *Godzilla* and played Shermanite in *Ferris Bueller's Day Off*. Saverio Guerra was Benny in *Blue Streak*, Woodstock in *Summer of Sam* and Bob in *Becker*.

Don't Give Up The Day Job: Howard Gordon was previously co-producer on *The X-Files* (co-writing the episode 'Synchrony' with David Greenwalt) and, later, wrote for *24*. David Solomon was first editor, then producer on *Perry Mason*.

Logic, Let Me Introduce You to This Window: When the bus carrying the first bounty hunter arrives, look at the steps. The flooring is white and a 'Watch your step' sign is on each step. However, when the hunter steps down the flooring is now red and the signs have disappeared. In the sequence where Pfister's right arm is regenerated the cuff of his shirt sleeve is three or four inches above his elbow. However, subsequently the sleeve ends at elbow level. During the chick fight, Kendra slams Buffy on to Angel's table and it collapses. In the next shot, a dazed Buffy lies on the broken table. However, for the remainder of the fight the debris is nowhere to be seen. How does Kendra know where Angel's apartment is? It's possible that she followed him from the ice rink, but why didn't she attack him then? How does Dalton carry the cross of du Lac? Surely (like all crosses) it should be *deadly* to a vampire? Angel's reflection is briefly seen in the frame of a picture in Buffy's bedroom.

Quote/Unquote: Giles tells Buffy she'd be amazed at how numbingly pompous and long-winded some of the Watcher Diaries are. Buffy: 'Colour me stunned.'

Notes: 'She's a bloody thorn in my bloody side.' What a *great* episode this is, full of fine dialogue, terrific action sequences and a sense of impending horror. The Buffy/Angel scenes at the ice rink are a little undiscovered treasure, while the episode ends with the biggest *Ohmigod!* moment on the series since we discovered Angel's true nature.

Buffy owns a stuffed-pig called Mr Gordo (see **57**, 'The Freshman'). Buffy wanted to be an ice skater (her heroine was Dorothy Hamill, the 1976 Olympic figure skating champion). Willow suffers from a fear of frogs (see **30**, 'Killed By Death'). Angel is supplied his blood (pigs, seemingly) by Willy the Snitch (see **54**, 'The Prom'). Geographical note: Sunnydale is on Route 17.

Kendra's Voice: When Fox began their release of *Buffy* video box-sets in the UK in 1999 they hit some initial teething problems. One of these was a faulty batch of one of the tapes in the Season 2 set, many of which featured a lack of synch between the soundtrack and the picture on a portion of **16**, 'Inca Mummy Girl'. One concerned online retail outlet, which had delivered hundreds of sets, wrote to their customers, alerting them to the problem and asking if anyone who purchased the box had noticed other problems. 'Yes,' replied one joker, 'Kendra's voice is funny.' It was this author who informed the company that, actually, it was *supposed* to sound like that.

Soundtrack: 'Spring' from Vivaldi's *The Four Seasons*.

22
What's My Line? Part 2

US Transmission Date: 24 Nov 1997
UK Transmission Date: 30 May 1998

Writer: Marti Noxon
Director: David Semel
Cast: Kelly Connell (Norman Pfister), Spice Williams (Patrice)

Giles realises that Kendra must have been called when Buffy briefly died. Kendra informs the others of her encounter with Angel. They go to Willy's bar but Angel has been taken by Spike, who needs him as part of a ceremony to restore Drusilla's strength. Xander and Cordelia discover the perfume salesman is not human and take refuge in the basement. They argue, then passionately kiss, before escaping. There is an attempt on Buffy's life by the third assassin, during which Oz saves Willow and is shot in the arm. Buffy and Kendra force Willy to lead them to Spike. Kendra refuses to go with Buffy and reports back to Giles. At the church, Buffy discovers that she has walked into a trap. Kendra attacks the assassins who are holding Buffy. Giles and Willow take on a couple of vampires, while Xander tricks Pfister into becoming stuck in liquid adhesive and he and Cordelia stomp the worms to death. Spike takes Drusilla but Buffy knocks him out and everyone flees the burning church.

It's a Designer Label!: Cordy's wet dress. Kendra's best shirt is her *only* shirt, and she's naturally a bit peeved when it gets torn.

References: Disneyland is mentioned, along with John Wayne, Kate Douglas Wiggin's novel *Rebecca of Sunnybrooke Farm*, *Mighty Morphin Power Rangers*, brat-pack actress Molly Ringwald (*Pretty in Pink, The Breakfast Club*) and a sarcastic reference to Chevy Chase. Plus a misquote from the Beatles' 'I Am The Walrus'.

Bitch!: Buffy's Sigourney Weaver moment: '*Nobody* messes with my boyfriend.'

Awesome!: Every scene featuring Xander and Cordelia (particularly when he turns the hose on her).

Surprise!: Xander and Cordy in the basement. 'Coward!' 'Moron!' 'I hate you!' Dramatic music. *The kiss.* Now *who* guessed *that* was going to happen?

Valley-Speak: Willow notes that Oz is experiencing 'computer nerd solidarity'.

Xander discovers that Angel sired Drusilla: 'Man, that guy got some *major* neck in his day.'

Logic, Let Me Introduce You to This Window: As with the previous episode, how is Spike able to hold the cross without it burning him? Cordelia pulls a worm from her hair and drops it onto a book marked 'Biology', which Xander then slams shut. In later shots, it's a different book. Spike says that the full moon is required for the ritual. Giles reports the ritual must take place on the night of a new moon. You can't have both on the same night. If Kendra was sent to her Watcher at an early age, long before she was called to be the Slayer, then how many potential Slayers exist at any one time? In **M1**, Merrick suggests that Watchers are only given one Slayer and that it's up to them as to when they tell the girl of her destiny and begin training – although Merrick talking of getting a new Slayer if Buffy dies and Giles asking Gwendolyn – in **41**, 'Revelations' – if she's had a Slayer before seems to refute this. The suggestion from this episode, plus **37**, 'Faith Hope and Trick' (confirmed in season seven), is that there are always dozens of would-be Slayers awaiting the call.

I Just *Love* Your Accent: The only episode to feature the word flummoxed. Xander asks if the Career Day was sponsored by 'the British soccer fan association', which shows that he knows as much about the complexities of a serious social phenomenon as he does about everything else.

Quote/Unquote: Willy: 'I swear on my mother's grave . . . Should something fatal ever happen to her, God forbid.'

Notes: 'You've been a very bad daddy.' The series' first attempt at a two-part storyline is helped by the hilarious Xander/Cordelia subplot. The episode becomes a bit of a runaround in the middle, sagging under the weight of such a stretched storyline, but that is, surely, the best burning church climax you're likely to see anywhere.

Kendra's Watcher is called Sam Zebuto. Giles has never met him but knows him by reputation. There are continuity references to Buffy's death in **12**, 'Prophecy Girl', as well as the Praying Mantis-lady from **4**, 'Teacher's Pet'. There *is* a Slayer handbook (which Giles has never thought it necessary that Buffy read, directly contradicting what he said in **5**, 'Never Kill a Boy on the First Date'. See also **80**, 'Real Me'). There are 43 churches in Sunnydale. Drusilla and Spike have previously lived in Paris. Drusilla's mother (whom Angel killed, along with most of the rest of her family) ate raw lemons. Oz eats animal crackers. Despite being something of a computer expert and brilliant at tests, he doesn't want a career, instead describing his ambition as to be able to play E flat diminished 9th. That's actually a fancy name for a pretty bog-standard chord, telling us something about Oz's confidence in his own ability (see **47**, 'The Zeppo'; **52**, 'Earshot').

23
Ted

US Transmission Date: 8 Dec 1997
UK Transmission Date: 6 Jun 1998

Writers: David Greenwalt, Joss Whedon
Director: Bruce Seth Green
Cast: John Ritter (Ted Buchanan), Ken Thorley (Neal),
Jeff Pruitt (Vampire #1), Jeff Langton (Vampire #2)

Buffy finds her mother kissing a man. Joyce introduces Ted who makes an impression on Xander and Willow, but not Buffy. While playing mini-golf Ted takes exception to Buffy's sullenness and threatens her, but regains his pleasant personality when the others join them. Buffy tells her mother about Ted's threat but Joyce doesn't believe her. After patrol, Buffy finds Ted reading her diary. Buffy attempts to get it back but he throws her against the wall. Enraged, Buffy sends him tumbling down the stairs, killing him. Xander, Willow and Cordelia discover a drug in the cookies that

Ted baked. At Ted's home, they find the bodies of his previous four wives in a closet. Ted appears again in Buffy's room. Buffy stabs Ted with a nail file, revealing wires and circuits. The android Ted knocks Buffy unconscious and confronts Joyce. She believes his lies at first, but then grows suspicious. Buffy regains consciousness and smashes a frying pan over Ted's robotic skull.

Dudes and Babes: Xander and Cordelia's strange relationship continues to develop, if that's the right word. Xander asks Cordy if she'd like to accompany him to the utility closet to make out. Cordelia asks if *that's* all he ever thinks about (it is, see **52**, 'Earshot'). Before adding 'OK'. Jenny refers to Giles's puppy-dog-eyes and Xander talks about Buffy playing games of the naughty stewardess.

Authority Sucks!: Another walk along the tightrope of child abuse (see **3**, 'The Witch').

A Little Learning is a Dangerous Thing: There's very little in the way of classroom scenes, though news of Ted's death seems to have made it to school before Buffy did.

Mom's Sticky Buns: 'Seeing my mother Frenching a guy is definitely a ticket to therapy-land.' The secret of Ted's great mini-pizzas is after baking, fry it in herbs and olive oil in a cast-iron skillet. Joyce asks Buffy if she wants any sticky buns, which is a bit of innuendo crying out for a suitable reply.

Denial, Thy Name is Joyce: Even by her own standards some sort of award is due to Mrs Summers for *thinking* about believing Ted's story of *not* having died.

It's a Designer Label!: *What* is that on Willow's head? It looks like a tea-cosy. 'Hey, Cordy, nice outfit,' says Xander. That's a brazen lie. The yellow miniskirt is particularly unfortunate.

References: Xander, Willow and Buffy have a pointless argument about 70s popstars Captain and Tennille ('Love Will Keep Us Together'). There's a discussion on the psychology of Sigmund Freud (1856–1939). Both *Psycho* and *The Terminator* seem to be influences (the heroine cheating at golf may be a subtle *Goldfinger* reference) and *Thelma and Louise*, *Licence to Kill* and *Superman* get name-checked along with John Stanley's legendary Saturday night horror-movie slot *Creature Features*, which ran for several years on KTVU in Oakland. There's an allusion to *The Stepford Wives*. 'Good morning, sunshine' is a misquote from *Hair*.

Awesome!: A terrified Giles holding up a cross . . . to Jenny ('I get that reaction from men all the time'). Plus Buffy kicking the stuffing out of the vampire.

Surprise!: 'You killed him.' Not as surprising as Ted's return from the grave.

The Drugs Don't Work: Or, in this case, *do*. Willow identifies the drug Ted uses in his cookies as demotoran, which shares properties with Ecstasy, the street name for MDMA (methylenedioxymethamphetamine).

'You Might Remember Me From Such Films and TV Series As . . .': John Ritter was the star of the sitcom *Three's Company* (the American version of *Man About the House*). He also had the leading role in the *Problem Child* movies and *Stay Tuned*. Ken Thorley was the Bolian barber Mr Mott in *Star Trek: The Next Generation*.

Valley-Speak: Xander: 'You *rock*!'

Logic, Let Me Introduce You to This Window: When Buffy climbs into her room her nightstand is in darkness. However, in close-shots it's well illuminated. After Buffy punches Ted, he drops her diary and it can be seen on the floor. However, when Ted picks Buffy up the diary has vanished. Xander opens Ted's closet door with his left hand while holding a torch in his right, down by his side. As the door opens, the shot cuts to a different angle, and the torch is by his head. Where is the miniature golf course? In **13**, 'When She Was Bad', Willow says that there's no such course in Sunnydale. Silly explanations about layers of tweed aside, how did Giles not only survive a point-blank hit in the back with a crossbow bolt, but also have the strength to pull it out *and* stab the vampire with it? What was Willow looking *at* under the microscope when examining Ted's cookies? Analysing a foodstuff for its chemical make up requires lots of complicated tests, but magnifying wouldn't seem to be one of them.

Quote/Unquote: Giles: 'I believe the subtext here is rapidly becoming the text.'

Xander on his triumphant discovery that Buffy is having parental issues: 'Freud would have said the exact same thing. Except, he might not have done that little dance.'

Giles, after Cordelia mentions Eyghon in a conversation about facing responsibility for someone's death: '*Do* let's bring that up as often as possible.'

Stepford Dad: There are two schools of thought on this episode. One is that it's almost the definitive *Buffy*-as-teenage-horror tale in a series in which hyena-kids, vampires and witches are *de rigueur* as opposed to reality where we have bullies and step-fathers. The implication is that Joss Whedon uses the clichés of the horror genre to represent the terrors of being a teenager (Joyce's new boyfriend is a violent robot because, to a teenage girl, that's exactly how a prospective stepfather appears). Put simply, in *Buffy the Vampire Slayer* the obsessions and fears of teenagers are made flesh. All valid. But there is another, more logical critical analysis on 'Ted' that is nowhere near as positive. What ruins the episode, for many, is that this is not a *Buffy*verse story: it's straight SF. This is the *only* episode in the series in which there is *no* supernatural element whatsoever. There's no magic or demons at work; instead we are asked to believe (in a series that, for instance, takes its technology pretty seriously) that in the 1950s (with the compo-nents of the era) a convincing android/replicant could be made. Even Moloch in **8**, 'I Robot . . . You Jane', utilising the peak of research technology, could only come up with something like *Robocop* (see **93**, 'I Was Made to Love You').

Notes: 'I'm not wired that way'. A disturbingly uneven episode. 'Ted' contains one of *the* great performances in *Buffy*: John Ritter's chilling portrayal of a psychotic control-freak on the verge of screwing up two people's lives. Unfortunately, *Buffy*'s *raison d'être* required some form of demonisation of the central character and, in doing so, a huge opportunity to explore a relevant issue is lost. He's a robot – you can come out from behind the sofa and laugh at the risible final scenes. Otherwise, 'Ted' contains all you'd expect from two of *Buffy*'s best writers: pithy dialogue, intelligent characterisation and superb timing. What a pity it couldn't have contained more *soul*.

There are continuity references to the previous episode (Angel's absence for most of the episode is touched upon). According to Jenny it's been three weeks since the events of **20**, 'The Dark Age' (she is still having trouble sleeping). Buffy doesn't bruise easily, which suggests that Slayers have abnormally quick recuperative powers (see **30**, 'Killed by Death'; **56**, 'Graduation Day' Part 2).

24
Bad Eggs

US Transmission Date: 12 Jan 1998
UK Transmission Date: 13 Jun 1998

Writer: Marti Noxon
Director: David Greenwalt
Cast: James Parks (Tector Gorch), Rick Zieff (Mr Whitmore),
Brie McCaddin (Mall Girl), Eric Whitmore (Night Watchman)

Buffy encounters cowboy vampires Lyle Gorch and his brother Tector. Mr Whitmore gives eggs to his students for a parenting assignment. When Buffy goes to sleep a tentacle slithers from her egg and attaches itself to her face. Xander reveals he boiled his egg to prevent it from breaking. When Buffy notices her egg shaking, a purple insect-like creature bursts out and Buffy stabs it with a pair of scissors. At school, Buffy and Xander are knocked unconscious by Cordelia and Willow. Joyce arrives looking for Buffy. Giles places one of the creatures on her back, and they join the others in their effort to dig up Mother Bezoar, a pre-prehistoric parasite. While searching for a weapon, a recovered Buffy is faced with Lyle and Tector. They fight and both Tector and Buffy are pulled into the parasite creature, but seconds later Buffy emerges, having killed it. Giles invents a story involving a gas leak to prevent awkward questions.

Dudes and Babes: The opening shot of the legs of the Mall Girl suggests more than we actually get. Tector says that Sunnydale doesn't have a decent whore in the city limits, which doesn't fit in with what we know about the place.

A Little Learning is a Dangerous Thing: Mr Whitmore's sex education class descends into farce. 'That was a rhetorical question, Mr Harris, not a poll.'

Mom's Apple Pie: The nadir of Joyce and Buffy's relationship with Buffy getting about four levels of punishment as the episode progresses. (When Joyce told Buffy in **15**, 'School Hard', that it would be at least a week and a half before her pride in her daughter wore off, it seems she wasn't exaggerating. 'Bad Eggs' takes place in a weird parallel universe where the close relationship established in 'School Hard' never happened and where Joyce still thinks her daughter is an irresponsible tearaway.) Buffy says she never asked for back-seat parenting and notes she doesn't want to be a single parent (even a surrogate one to an egg) like her mother.

It's a Designer Label!: The dress that Buffy wanted made her look like a streetwalker according to Joyce. Cordy's little grey skirt and leather slit miniskirt, and a bear bag (she claims she started the nationwide craze for bags shaped like animals).

References: Lyle and Tector Gorch were the characters played by Ben Johnson and Warren Oates in *The Wild Bunch* (see **2**, 'The Harvest'). 'Bad Eggs' includes dialogue and textual references to *Die Hard* ('Yippie kai-aye'), the Beatles' 'Dig A Pony' ('All I want is you'), *Batman* ('Think about the future'), *Dial M For Murder* (the scissors scene) and William Castle's *The Tingler*.

Bitch!: Xander, kissing Cordelia: 'This would work a lot better for me if you didn't talk.'

Don't Give Up The Day Job: Both James Parks (a carpenter on *Reality Bites*) and Rick Zieff (the casting assistant on *Breakdown*) have film-industry jobs other than acting.

Valley-Speak: Buffy: 'I just feel all funky.'

Logic, Let Me Introduce You to This Window: The opening scenes are set during daylight. Therefore, how is Lyle not a pile of ash on the floor? In the arcade, the girl with Lyle plays the pinball machine. In the initial shot, her handbag is hanging from her right wrist. However, in the next shot the straps are further up her arm. During Buffy's fight with Lyle in the arcade, both of them collide with the same pinball machine that the girl was playing earlier and the machine is now off. How does the shell of Buffy's egg repair itself? Watch closely in the scene in the library where Buffy put her egg on the desk close to a chain. The respective positions of the chain and the egg change from shot to shot about four times. It's so obvious that one almost suspects it's been done deliberately to provide books like this with something to talk about. The walking around zombified cliché enables Giles to converse with some intricacy with Joyce, allows Cordelia to knock Buffy out with a single blow, but also renders its slaves incapable of attacking a concrete floor in anything more than slow motion. Isn't it lucky that a pre-prehistoric creature lays eggs *exactly* like hen's eggs? After she loses consciousness, the parasite falls from Willow's back. However, when everyone else collapses no parasites can be seen dropping from their backs.

Quote/Unquote: Giles on Xander boiling his egg: 'I suppose there is a sort of Machiavellian ingenuity to your transgression.' Xander: 'I resent that ... Or, possibly, thank you.'

Joyce on children: 'They're such a ... I don't want to say burden ... Actually, I kind of *do* want to say burden.'

Notes: 'Long story.' *And* a tall one. And not a very good one either. This is such a lopsided episode that it's surprising it doesn't collapse. The main-focus is the subplot about the parasitic eggs, while the two hick vampires serve absolutely no purpose – they're too stupid to be a threat to anyone. 'Bad Eggs' also seems to think it's really funny in places where it, clearly, isn't. That the episode has to resort to devices such as Xander's pratfall when he and Buffy enter the cave is an indication of just how desperate a production this is. My least favourite episode, because you *know* this series is capable of much more.

Buffy had a giga-pet, but she sat on it and it broke. Xander implies Cordelia has bad breath. Cordelia says she has a friend ('not me') who once had sex in a car at the top of a hill and accidentally kicked the handbrake. Angel cannot have children. Before they became vampires, Lyle and Tector massacred a Mexican village in 1886. The mall used at the beginning is the Sherman Oaks Galleria north of Los Angeles. After Willow enters the science lab and stands next to the dead hatchling, on the blackboard behind her is written 'Posting Board'. This was an acknowledgment (by Jeff Pruitt) to the regulars on the *BtVS Posting Board*. When Joyce enters the library, keep your eyes on the standing sign. Under 'Sunnydale HS Library', it says: 'Website Coming', and 'BVS Brats Talk,' more in-jokes for the series' Internet fans.

25
Surprise

US Transmission Date: 19 Jan 1998
UK Transmission Date: 20 Jun 1998

Writer: Marti Noxon
Director: Michael Lange
Cast: Brian Thompson (The Judge), Vincent Schiavelli (Uncle Enyos)

Buffy has a nightmare in which Drusilla kills Angel. Jenny is visited by her Uncle Enyos and reveals Angel's involvement with

Buffy. Enyos demands that she keep them apart. Due to his injuries, Spike is confined to a wheelchair while Drusilla takes delivery of mysterious boxes. A surprise birthday party is arranged for Buffy, but is ruined by a vampire attack. Angel realises that the vampires are collecting body parts of the Judge, a demon who, when assembled, can destroy humanity. Angel finally professes his love for Buffy and they consummate their relationship. With disastrous consequences . . .

Dreaming (As Blondie Once Said) is Free: Buffy's nightmare: Like all good dreams, it features a rock'n'roll soundtrack; Willow speaks French, accompanied by a small monkey, crockery smashes and, in a moment dripping with Freudian symbolism, Angel is staked by Drusilla. Buffy also mentions a dream she had in which she and Giles opened an office warehouse in Las Vegas, which sounds like a good series in itself.

Dudes and Babes: Oz says he's groupie free these days (see **55**, 'Graduation Day' Part 1). Xander tells Buffy he feels a 'pre-birthday spanking coming on'. Drusilla dancing is certainly provocative.

It's a Designer Label!: Drusilla's red dress, Buffy's short black skirt, green pants and white jacket, Giles's stripy tie, plus another tea-cosy for Willow. There's a lovely close up of Oz's Fender Stratocaster.

References: Xander mentions the diner chain Denny's. There are references to *Dead Poets Society* ('Seize the day') and *Jack and the Beanstalk* ('grind his bones to make your bread'). 'Discretion is the better part of valour' paraphrases *Henry IV, Part 1.*

Bitch!: Giles: 'A true creature of evil can survive the process. No one human ever has.' Xander: 'What's the problem? We send Cordy to fight this guy and go for pizza.'

Awesome!: The reassembly of the Judge, followed by Dalton's rather messy death. Buffy crashing into her own surprise party and killing a vampire with a drumstick. Plus the charming scene where Willow and Oz ask each other out.

'You Might Remember Me From Such Films and TV Series As . . .': Vincent Schiavelli's movies include *Ghost*, *One Flew Over the Cuckoo's Nest* and *Tomorrow Never Dies.*

Valley-Speak: Buffy: 'You can't spend the rest of your life waiting for Xander to wake up and smell the hottie.'

Xander to Giles: 'Are you ready to get down, you funky party weasel?'

Logic, Let Me Introduce You to This Window: When Buffy approaches Willow's table in her dream, the monkey is facing Buffy. In the next shot it's facing Willow, then it turns around to face Buffy as Willow waves. Why would Angel take the time to get dressed before running outside if he was in extreme pain? How do the boxes containing the body parts of the Judge fit together? When the panels open, inside is one big chamber instead of six small ones. The gypsy curse subplot is indescribably dumb. The punishment for Angelus is to give him a soul. Fine. But to take it away again if he gets happy, turning him *back* into Angelus, the vicious creature that has killed thousands . . .?

I Just *Love* Your Accent: Xander asks Giles: 'Are all you Brits such drama queens?'

Quote/Unquote: Enyos: 'Vengeance demands that his pain be eternal.'

Spike, on Dalton: 'He's a wanker, but he's the only one we've got with half a brain.'

Notes: 'The time for watching is past.' *This* is teen-drama? An astonishingly sensual, erotic episode. 'Surprise' is about as far removed from traditional horror clichés as it's possible to get. Buffy takes her first, faltering steps into the adult world . . . and the *real* horrors to come. Grown-up intelligent, beautiful television. And with barely a joke in sight.

Buffy loses her virginity (would it be too indelicate to ask whether the thought that she's committed what amounts to necrophilia occurred to anybody in Broadcast Standards and Practices?). Willow speaks to the monkey in French, saying: '*L'hippo a piqué ton pantalon*', which means 'The hippo stole your trousers', a reference to Oz's joke in **22**, 'What's My Line?' Part 2, that all of the monkeys (who are French) in Animal Crackers have pants and the hippos are jealous. Angel refers to the Irish as 'my people' when giving Buffy the claddagh ring. Jenny's real name is Janna. She is a Kalderash Romany gypsy and has been sent to America by her clan specifically to watch Angel. In addition to Prague and Paris, Spike and Drusilla also spent time in Vienna and Spain (see also *Angel*: 'The Girl in Question').

Soundtrack: 'Transylvanian Concubine' by Rasputina [*] and 'Anything' by Shawn Clement and Sean Murray, featuring Care Howe.

26
Innocence

US Transmission Date: 20 Jan 1998
UK Transmission Date: 27 Jun 1998

Writer: Joss Whedon
Director: Joss Whedon
Cast: Brian Thompson (The Judge), Ryan Francis (Soldier),
Vincent Schiavelli (Uncle Enyos), Carla Madden (Woman), Parry Shen (Student)

Angel reverts to his Angelus persona and visits Spike and Drusilla. The Judge attempts to disintegrate him, but there is no humanity left to kill. Drusilla tells Angelus they plan to bring forth Armageddon, but he asks for one night to punish the Slayer. Buffy goes to her lover's apartment but finds him cruel and dismissive. Angelus turns up at school, intending to kill those close to Buffy, starting with Willow. He is prevented by Xander and Jenny. Xander forms a plan to steal an army rocket launcher to defeat the Judge and with the help of Willow, Oz and Cordelia, he succeeds. Buffy and Giles discover Jenny's dark secret and that the curse cannot be reinvoked. Putting Xander's plan into action, they follow the Judge, Angelus and Drusilla to a shopping mall, where Buffy uses the weapon to destroy the Judge.

Dudes and Babes: The semi-pornographic flashback to Buffy and Angel interacting is, of course, all done in the best possible taste. Soft focus, unruffled sheets (without stains) and no sweating. Just like sex *isn't*.

Mom's Birthday Muffin: Mrs Summers doesn't notice that Buffy arrives home in different clothes to the ones she had on when she left the previous day. Very observant, Joyce. Her birthday muffin for Buffy is both affectionate and stupidly pointless.

It's a Designer Label!: Xander's palm-tree shirt and Cordelia's extremely short tartan skirt.

References: The Judge zapping everyone may be homage to the climactic scene in *Raiders of the Lost Ark*. The movie theatre where

Buffy and Angelus fight is lined with posters for Warner Bros'
animated feature *The Quest for Camelot*. At the end, Buffy and
Joyce are watching *Stowaway* (starring Shirley Temple). Also,
software giants IBM and the Smurfs.

Bitch!: Willow on Xander and Cordelia's attraction to each other:
'Weird? It's against *all laws of God and Man*!'

Awesome!: The scene where Angelus threatens Willow in front of
Jenny and Xander. The slow-motion killing of the Judge as
Angelus and Dru are thrown away from the explosion (yes, *just*
like that scene in *Die Hard*). Buffy fighting Angelus and kicking
his goolies.

Surprise!: The moment when we discover, along with Dru, Spike
and the Judge, that Angel is Angelus again. 'Yeah, baby, I'm
back.'

'You Might Remember Me From Such Films As . . .': Ryan Francis
played the young Peter in Spielberg's *Hook*.

Valley-Speak: Xander: 'Now, I'm having a wiggins.'

Logic, Let Me Introduce You to This Window: When Angel ran
outside in **25**, 'Surprise', it was raining heavily. At the beginning
of this episode, however, the rain has stopped. When Buffy dreams
about her intimate night with Angel, she is wearing silver nail
polish. But, in **25**, 'Surprise', she wasn't. The episode's time frame
is completely up the spout. Buffy runs home distressed, as Xander
tells Cordelia to meet him at Willow's house in half an hour.
Willow, meanwhile, is supposed to bring Oz and his van. The scene
then shifts to Buffy's bedroom, where she falls asleep. Buffy wakes
up the next day and goes to school to force the truth out of Jenny.
The following scene depicts Xander and Cordy stealing the rocket
launcher, events that happened the night before. Presumably, Giles
managed to keep Buffy's attack on Jenny from Snyder, otherwise
she'd be suspended on the spot. (One of the students even asks,
'Shall I get the Principal?') How many vans does Oz have? In **18**,
'Halloween', he drove a zebra-striped van with a steering wheel on
the right. Here he drives a dark-coloured left-hand-drive. In **12**,
'Prophecy Girl', Angel confirmed he had no breath, so how does
Angelus exhale all that smoke after feeding on the cigarette-
smoking prostitute? In **34**, 'Becoming' Part 2, we find out vampires
in general, and Spike in particular, are at pains *not* to see the end
of the world, so what's the deal with initiating Armageddon here?

Quote/Unquote: Willow, angry at discovering Xander and Cordelia kissing: 'I *knew* it. Well, knew it in the sense of not having the slightest idea, but I *knew* there was something I didn't know.'

Spike to Angelus: 'I know you haven't been in the game for a while, mate, but we *do* still kill people. Sort of our *raison d'être*, you know?'

Cordelia sums up the plot: 'There's an unkillable demon in town, Angel's joined his team, the Slayer's a basketcase, I'd say we've hit bottom.' Xander: 'I have a plan.' Cordelia: 'Oh no, here's a lower place.'

Cordelia asks Xander if looking at guns makes him want to have sex: 'I'm seventeen. Looking at *linoleum* makes me wanna have sex.'

Notes: 'Psst . . . We're gonna destroy the world. Wanna come?' Strangely, nowhere near as effective as **25**, 'Surprise', despite containing numerous impressive performances. Highlights include Alyson Hannigan's uncanny ability to be angry and funny at the same time (notably in the sequence where she can't think of a nasty word to call Giles). What holds the episode back is the unnecessary subplot about the rocket launcher that pushes the viewer away from the important relationship characterisation. And there's that odd, downbeat ending with Joyce and Buffy and the birthday muffin, which deserved better direction.

Buffy says she beat up Willy the Snitch to get information about Angel (see **21/22**, 'What's My Line?'). There are references to Xander's military expertise in **18**, 'Halloween'. He says he can still put together an M16 rifle in 57 seconds. Xander was the Treasurer of the 'We Hate Cordelia Club' of which Willow was also a founder member.

27
Phases

US Transmission Date: 27 Jan 1998
UK Transmission Date: 4 Jul 1998

Writers: Rob Des Hotel, Dean Batali
Director: Bruce Seth Green
Cast: Camila Griggs (Gym Teacher), Jack Conley (Cain),
Megahn Perry (Theresa Klusmeyer), Keith Campbell (Werewolf)

Xander and Cordelia make out in her car and are attacked by a werewolf. Giles is excited having never encountered a Lycanthrope before. One of Buffy's classmates, Theresa, walks home alone and meets Angelus. Buffy and Giles investigate the woods and discover a werewolf hunter named Cain. They drive to the Bronze, arriving as teens flee from the werewolf inside. It escapes before Buffy can capture it. Buffy and Giles hear on the radio that Theresa has been murdered. As the sun rises, the werewolf slowly transforms back into its human form. Oz. Willow invites Oz to help her do some research, but he refuses. Before he can lock himself up, Willow calls at his home. Oz tries to warn her of the danger as he begins to transform. A lengthy chase begins, climaxing in Willow shooting Oz with a tranquilliser. The next day, Oz tells Willow that he'll be fine as long as he locks himself up around the full moon every month. To his surprise, Willow is still interested in dating.

Dudes and Babes: As relationships become clearer (Oz and Willow, Xander and Cordy), poor Buffy is left to trail around with Giles for most of the episode. Theresa's cute, but something about her screams *Angelus-bait*.

A Little Learning is a Dangerous Thing: Willow helps Cordelia with her history homework (or, possibly, does it for her).

It's a Designer Label!: Willow has another of those tea-cosy bobble-hats, a Smiley-face backpack and a pair of sickly yellow overalls. Oz's *New York City Yoga* T-shirt, Theresa's red 'burial' miniskirt(!), Buffy's miniskirt (also red).

References: Visual and dialogue references to various classic werewolf films including *The Wolf Man, Curse of the Werewolf, Dr Terror's House of Horror, The Beast Must Die, The Howling* and *An American Werewolf in London*. Also, Kraven the Hunter from *Spider-Man*, Calvin Klein's Obsession aftershave, Robbie the Robot from *Forbidden Planet* and the exercise device Thigh Master. Larry's outing may be a nod to *Heathers* ('I *lurv* ma dead-gay son!'). Xander's sexuality-denial (just like Chandler in *Friends*) is completely in-character: he's witty, knows way-too-much about pop-culture and is lousy with women (even though all his best friends are girls). For Larry, the clichéd bully, to be revealed as gay – and subsequently transformed into a decent, likeable human being by the experience (see **52**, 'Earshot') – is significant for both the gay and straight audience.

Bitch!: Willow says she has never got a 'Mi-aow' before, but she's certainly awarded one for 'What's [Xander's] number? 1-800-I'm-dating-a-skanky-ho.'

Awesome!: Xander accidentally outing Larry. Oz's telephone conversation with his aunt concerning his cousin ('and *how long* has that been going on?') and his reassuring Willow that bunnies can really take care of themselves.

Surprise!: Who the werewolf changes into.

The Drugs Don't Work: Phenobarbitone (which Giles mispronounces as Phenabarbitol) is a powerful barbiturate used to treat insomnia, so it's a perfect tranquilliser.

'You Might Remember Me From Such Films As . . .': Jack Conley often gets meaty detective-type roles in movies like *Payback, Mercury Rising, LA Confidential* and *Get Shorty*.

Don't Give Up The Day Job: Keith Campbell was Tom Cruise's stunt-double in both *Mission: Impossible* movies and doubled Val Kilmer in *Batman Forever* and *The Saint*. He was on the stunt team for *Blaze, Analyze This, Face/Off, Patriot Games, Stargate* and *Deep Impact*. As an actor, readers may recognise him as Perp in *Men In Black*.

Valley-Speak: Willow: 'I want smoochies.'
  Oz: 'That's fairly freaksome.'

Logic, Let Me Introduce You to This Window: Two men push Giles's car as it arrives in front of the Bronze. Keen-eyed viewers can spot the tops of their heads through the rear window. While Buffy is trapped in the net her flashlight is off, but it's on again when the net lowers to the ground. After everyone evacuates the Bronze, Buffy runs inside while putting her backpack on. She bumps into someone and one of the straps falls from her left shoulder. As she walks inside, the camera angle switches and the strap is back in place. After Buffy senses the werewolf's movement, she slides off the left strap and walks upstairs and through a curtain. The angle switches again, and now the backpack is in her right hand. During the chase through the woods, Willow trips. As she gets up, notice the stains on her overalls. When she gets to the library, they're spotless. In the library scene, for several shots Giles is not wearing glasses but in others he is. After knocking the gun from Buffy's hands, the werewolf shoves her backwards but she falls face-first over Giles. What are Oz and Larry, two seniors, doing in a self-defence class full of juniors? If Oz didn't realise he was a werewolf until the morning after the full moon, then where did he wake up the previous morning? Shouldn't the bullet Cain makes be too hot to handle seconds after having been molten silver? Buffy says a Werewolf is human 28 days each month; it should be 25 days each lunar month.

I Just *Love* Your Accent: Giles, on Cain: 'Pillock!'

Cruelty to Animals: Cain: 'First they tell me I can't hunt an elephant for its ivory. Now I've got to deal with People for the Ethical Treatment of Werewolves.'

Quote/Unquote: Oz: 'That's great, Larry, you've really mastered the single entendre.'

Cordelia: 'We came here to do the thing I can never tell my father about because he still thinks I'm a good girl.'

Giles: 'You hunt werewolves for sport?' Cain: 'No, I'm in it purely for the money.'

Notes: 'Good doggy, now play dead.' A *really* funny episode, taking all the best bits of classic werewolf texts and playing with them in an amusingly postmodern way. Lovely direction more than makes up for the terrible werewolf make-up (which actually *adds* to the kitschy, sub-*Howling* homage that the episode is). Stellar performances from Seth Green and Alyson Hannigan. A template for how *Buffy* was changing and growing into something very different from the series when it began.

Giles's delight on discovering a werewolf case makes Buffy remark: 'He needs to get a pet.' Oz notes that the cheerleading statue has eyes that follow him around the room (see **3**, 'The Witch'). He doesn't smoke. He took Willow to the movies last night, and although he's forgotten the movie itself, he did enjoy the popcorn. He was bitten by his cousin Jordy, whose parents are called Maureen and Ken. There are references to Xander becoming dog-like in **6**, 'The Pack', and to his allegedly being unable to remember those events, and a very funny PMS reference – Willow noting that 'three days out of the month, *I'm* not much fun to be around either'. Cordelia has dated lots of guys in bands (see **16**, 'Inca Mummy Girl'). On patrol, Buffy sees Brittany Podell making out with Owen Stadeel, who is supposed to be going with Barrett Williams. Buffy's locker has a Velvet Chain (see **5**, 'Never Kill a Boy on the First Date') sticker on it.

Soundtrack: 'Blind For Now' by Lotion.

Did You Know?: Joss Whedon gave Seth Green a copy of the script for 'Phases' to persuade the actor to accept an offer to become a regular: 'It had all this metaphorical stuff and gave strong shades to the character,' says Seth. 'I said, "I want to be part of this"!'

28
Bewitched, Bothered and Bewildered

US Transmission Date: 10 Feb 1998
UK Transmission Date: 11 Jul 1998
Writer: Marti Noxon
Director: James A Contner
Cast: Lorna Scott (Miss Beakman), Jennie Chester (Kate),
Kristen Winnicki (Cordette), Tamara Braun (Frenzied Girl), Scott Hamm (Jock)

Harmony and her friends mock Cordelia for dating Xander. Giles warns Buffy that Angelus has a history of committing horrid acts on Valentine's Day. Buffy receives a box of roses and a card with the word 'soon' on it. At the Bronze, Xander gives Cordelia a gift. After admiring the necklace, Cordelia breaks up with him. Xander is furious and it only gets worse for him the next day, as everyone in school seems to know what happened. Xander tells Amy that he knows she's practising her mother's art of witchcraft. Xander blackmails Amy into casting a love spell on Cordelia, so that he can then dump *her*. Much to Xander's dismay, the spell has no effect on Cordy. However, every other female in Sunnydale seems attracted to him. Xander spends his time running away from all the women in his life while Giles and Amy try to reverse the spell. And also reverse a spell that's turned Buffy into a rat. While a mob of girls battle each other, Xander and Cordelia arrive at Buffy's house. Joyce starts seducing Xander, so he and Cordelia barricade themselves in the basement. Giles and Amy perform the reversal spells. Next day, Harmony mocks Xander, but Cordelia comes to his defence, telling her friends that she will date whom she wants to. However lame.

Dudes and Babes: In an episode all about the shallowness of relationships based purely on physical attraction, let's nail this one right away. Does anybody else wish there hadn't been a convenient object for Buffy to hide behind when she suffers from a slight case of nudity? A pig-out and a vid-fest are said to be the time-honoured tradition of the loveless.

A Little Learning is a Dangerous Thing: Or, no learning in Amy's case since she uses her mojo to con Ms Beakman into believing she handed in a test paper.

Mom's Apple Pie: Joyce coming on to Xander is a bit strong, even given the implications concerning what a raver she used to be (see **12**, 'Prophecy Girl'; **40**, 'Band Candy').

Denial, Thy Name is Joyce: How on *earth* could Joyce fall for Cordelia's lame scavenger hunt excuse in reply to the obvious question, 'What are you twenty girls and one boy doing in my basement and why am I holding a carving knife?' Since everybody seems to have retained their memories of these events (note Buffy's sudden need for cheese confession), it's reasonable to assume that Joyce has also, and that she's just (as Buffy suggests) repressing after 'hitting on one of my friends'.

It's a Designer Label!: Buffy's red coat and black gloves and Xander's overcoat (it can get pretty cold in California once the sun goes down in February). Harmony's gang have some *horrible* clothes, including the blonde girl with the fat bottom wearing a very unflattering navy-blue miniskirt, a scarlet PVC coat and a lime-green blouse. Buffy's light blue (sheep-motif) vest and leopardskin slit-miniskirt and Cordelia's red Valentine dress are better. And Xander's 'nice shirt' is actually rather good. Cordelia admires his clothes and he admits he allowed Buffy to dress him. Is Oz's hair going to remain the same colour two episodes running?

References: The title derives from Rodgers and Hart's 'Bewildered' (made famous by Frank Sinatra). Xander's reference to a 'parallel universe' takes us into a whole SF sub-genre. Elvis is namechecked. Oz's guitar is inscribed 'Sweet J', a possible reference to Lou Reed's Velvet Underground song 'Sweet Jane' (see **59**, 'The Harsh Light of Day'. This is also a subtle *Austin Powers* in-joke, Sweet J being the name of Scott Evil's best friend). The sequences of Joyce asking Xander to let her in and attacking the door with a carving knife was influenced by *The Shining*.

Bitch!: Xander, surprised that Cordelia hasn't been affected by the spell: 'Is this love? Cos, maybe on you it doesn't look any different.'
　　Cordelia to Joyce: '. . . And keep your mom-age mitts off my boyfriend. *Former*.'

Awesome!: Cordelia's sheep speech to Harmony.

The Drugs Don't Work: Midol is an over-the-counter medicine frequently used in the US as a treatment for PMS. Roofie is the street name for the date rape drug, Rohypnol.

Don't Give Up the Day Job: Director James Contner's previous work includes *Midnight Caller, 21 Jump Street, Wiseguy, The Equalizer, Miami Vice, The Flash, Lois and Clark: The New Adventures of Superman, SeaQuest DSV, Hercules: The Legendary Journeys, American Gothic, Dark Skies, The X-Files* and *Charmed.* He was cinematographer on movies such as *Heat, Monkey Shines, Jaws 3-D, The Wiz, Superman* and *Times Square.* It's his camera-work on the concert footage in *Rock Show: Wings Over the World.*

Valley-Speak: Guy in orange shirt: 'Dude, way to get dumped.'
. Xander: 'I made her put the love-whammy on Cordy.' And: 'Every woman in Sunnydale wants to make me her cuddle-monkey.'

Logic, Let Me Introduce You to This Window: Xander nails three boards to the basement's doorframe. When Joyce's knife pokes through, sending Xander and Cordy running down the stairs, we see one of the boards runs all the way from the bottom left corner to the upper right. However, when Willow and the others open the door, the board is much higher. The timescale of the end of the episode is impossible. Xander saves Cordelia from the mob of girls early in the day, yet when they arrive at Buffy's house to hide, it's evening.

Cruelty to Animals: Angel's past is littered with depraved displays of ultraviolence on Valentine's Day (including, on one occasion, nailing a puppy to something).

Quote/Unquote: Xander, after Cordelia has dropped her bomb-shell: 'Were you running low on dramatic irony?'
    Xander, when Buffy suggests they should comfort each other: 'Would lap-dancing enter into that scenario at all? Coz I find that *very* comforting.'

Notes: 'It's funny how you see someone every day, but not really *see* them.' Taking an old sitcom idea (loser-guy-becomes-babe-magnet-through-nefarious-skulduggery) and peppering it with many great one-liners, 'Bewitched' is easily the best episode of the season. A story in which comedy and characterisation work in perfect harmony.

Willow has been in Xander's bed before, but they were both (much) younger. We get our first decent look at Xander's room (it has a Hazardous Waste sticker on the door). Among the Marvel and pop-art posters (including one for Widespread Panic, see **16**, 'Inca Mummy Girl'), it's nice to spot an acoustic guitar (maybe the daydream in **4**, 'Teacher's Pet' wasn't all fantasy. However, see **47**, 'The Zeppo').

Two stickers for the band Lotion, which performed in **27**, 'Phases', are visible. The first on the locker behind Giles when we first see him. The second is on the locker next to Cordelia's, glimpsed when Harmony slaps her. Chris Beck's incidental music is some of the best in the series, wonderfully fitting the light tone of the episode. Sarah Michelle Gellar was missing for most of this episode as she was hosting *Saturday Night Live* that week.

Soundtrack: Four Star Mary's anthem 'Pain' [*] is the song Dingoes Ate My Baby mime to in the Bronze. Also 'Drift Away' by Naked and 'Got The Message' by 70s funksters the Average White Band. *Niiice.*

Sky Nil: After this episode, Sky pulled *Buffy* from its 8 p.m. Saturday slot, citing low viewing figures (it was replaced by *3rd Rock from the Sun*, which promptly drew *lower* ratings). It would be almost a year before *Buffy* was shown on Sky again, and then only after a long campaign by fans.

Did You Know?: This is producer Gareth Davies's favourite episode, but for very unusual reasons. As he told *Entertainment Weekly*, with Gellar off-set for five days, the writers turned Buffy into a rat. 'Nothing against Sarah, but that rat was *marvellous*. It was a real trouper!' In the same interview, London-born Davies confided that the character he most relates to is Giles, because 'I can understand every word he says'.

29
Passion

US Transmission Date: 24 Feb 1998
UK Transmission Date: 16 Jul 1999

Writer: Ty King
Director: Michael E Gershman
Cast: Richard Assad (Shopkeeper), Richard Hoyt Miller (Policeman)

Buffy awakens to discover a drawing from Angelus on her pillow. She pleads with Giles for a way of stopping Angelus entering her home. She tells her mother that Angel is stalking her and that Joyce should never invite him in. Jenny, hoping to restore Angel's soul, purchases an Orb of Thesulah. The shopkeeper warns her that the spell's translation has been lost, but Jenny replies that she's working on the text. With Jenny's help, Giles devises a spell to exclude Angelus from places he had previously been invited into. Angelus asks Joyce to help him get Buffy back and mentions that they made love, but he is unable to enter the Summers' house as Willow and Buffy perform the spell. Jenny completes her program, but Angelus knows what she is planning and kills her, leaving her body in Giles's bed. Giles attacks Angelus at the factory and Buffy arrives in time to prevent Angelus from killing her Watcher, but Angelus escapes. Willow takes over as substitute teacher and accidentally misplaces the computer disk that is the key to Angel's soul.

A Little Learning is a Dangerous Thing: Jenny asks Willow to take her computer class and, after Jenny's death, Snyder makes the same request.

Mom's Apple Pie: Joyce claims to have read all the parenting books as she shares dinner with Buffy. After Angelus tells Joyce that he and Buffy had sex, she and Buffy have the were-you-careful talk: Joyce regains a lot of plus points here with her sympathetic handling of the situation.

It's a Designer Label!: Features some really lousy clothes like Willow's orange sweater, Buffy's grey pants and Xander's red shirt and checky strides.

References: The mass-murdering dictator Joseph Stalin (1879–1953), US book chain Barnes & Noble, *A Charlie Brown Christmas* (see **81**, 'The Replacement') and Russ Meyer's notorious biker sex-movie *Faster, Pussycat! Kill! Kill!* are mentioned.

Ménage à Trois: Interviewed by *TV Guide*, David Boreanaz, James Marsters and Juliet Landau described the Angel/Spike/Dru relationship in detail. Boreanaz: 'Angel has a very sarcastic side and he knows how to torment Spike. Every time Spike pushes my buttons, I push his ... He's all talk.' Marsters: 'Angel was my mentor, [but] I'm grown up now and I don't need him any more.' When interviewer Tim Appelo described the relationship as 'the scariest romantic triangle since the *Archie* comics,' Landau replied: 'In a funny way [Drusilla and Spike] have a healthy relationship. We *do* go out and kill people, but we have a loving, giving relationship. But with Angel, it's almost like an incestuous, abusive relationship. That's why when I chained him to a bed and burned him with holy water, it was . . . a strange cross between sexuality and power.'

Bitch!: Cordelia: 'I'd do the same for you if you *had* a social life.'

Awesome!: Angelus killing Jenny against every dramatic convention that the viewer thinks they are party to, followed by the horribly voyeuristic sequence in which he watches Buffy and Willow's reaction to the phone call informing them of Jenny's death. Giles's murderous attack on Angelus and the moment when Buffy tells Giles that she won't let him kill himself because she can't do this alone.

Don't Give Up The Day Job: Michael Gershman began his career as a camera operator on movies such as *The Gauntlet*, *The Deer Hunter*, *Blow Out*, *The Golden Child* and *Die Hard 2*.

Logic, Let Me Introduce You to This Window: The object Willow is nailing to her wall is referred to as a crucifix. It isn't, it's a cross. Why didn't Willow notice that her aquarium was empty as she poured fish food into it? Who put Jenny in Giles's apartment? We must assume it was Angel although we've never seen him in Giles's apartment before.

Cruelty to Animals: Willow on her dead fish: 'We hadn't really had time to bond yet.'

A Death in the Family: According to Alyson Hannigan, 'Angel . . . had to kill somebody we loved; we were warned about that. Actually, I think it was supposed to be Oz that was killed, then they decided they'd keep Oz and killed Ms Calendar.' According to Robia LaMorte: '[The filming of] the confrontation in the classroom was one day in itself. That took probably four or five hours because of all the fire and explosions . . . On a separate day we did the rest . . . to the point of my death. A lot of running in high heels! The good thing about TV is, as soon as the camera goes to those tighter shots, put those sneakers on.'

Quote/Unquote: Giles: 'Yes, Xander, once again you've managed to boil a complex thought down to its simplest possible form.'

Angel's final words of wisdom: 'If we could live without passion, maybe we'd know some kind of peace. But we would be hollow. Empty rooms, shuttered and dank. Without passion, we'd be truly dead.'

Notes: 'Passion. It lies in all of us. Sleeping, waiting and though unwanted, unbidden, it will stir. Open its jaws and howl.' Not the masterpiece that it's often made out to be because it spends half the episode building towards a signposted climax, but containing a dramatic intensity that is frequently overpowering and with the performances to match (Tony Head has never been better). 'Passion' is another example of how adult a series *Buffy* can be. A note of praise for Michael Gershman's fluid direction.

Willow's parents would never let her have a puppy. Her father's name is Ira and the Rosenberg family are Jewish (as hinted in previous episodes). Once invited into a house, a vampire is always welcome (except if, as in this case, a reversal spell is performed). The sign on the front of the school says (in Latin) 'Enter All Ye Who Seek Knowledge', which Angelus claims is his invitation (but, see **30**, 'Killed By Death', concerning vampires and public places). The sites that Angelus can no longer visit include Buffy's house, Willow's house (which he entered in **19**, 'Lie to Me') and Cordelia's car (**14**, 'Some Assembly Required'). Joyce remembers Angel as 'the college boy' who was tutoring Buffy in history (**7**, 'Angel').

In the scene where Buffy and Joyce are eating dinner, look over Joyce's shoulder at the picture. It's a publicity photo of Sarah Michelle Gellar that appeared in the August 1997 issue of *Entertainment Weekly*.

Soundtrack: 'Never An Easy Way' by Morcheeba, Puccini's 'Acte 10 Soave Fanciulla' from *La Bohème*. During the graveyard scene, a choral voice can be heard. It belongs to Tony Head, who suggested to Christophe Beck that he provide the accompaniment.

30
Killed By Death

US Transmission Date: 3 Mar 1998
UK Transmission Date: 23 Jul 1999

Writers: Rob Des Hotel, Dean Batali
Director: Deran Sarafian

Cast: Richard Herd (Dr Stanley Backer), Willie Garson (Security Guard), Andrew Ducote (Ryan), Juanita Jennings (Dr Wilkinson), Robert Munic (Intern), Mimi Paley (Little Buffy), Denise Johnson (Celia), James Jude Courtney (Der Kindestod)

Buffy is in hospital with a dose of flu. Overcome with fever, she sees a demonic figure stalking the halls. A boy, Ryan, tells Buffy that Death is coming for them and that he is invisible to adults. Buffy tells her friends about Death. The prime suspect is one of the doctors, Backer, but Buffy sees him killed by an invisible force. Willow helps Buffy investigate Backer's office for clues, while Giles and Cordelia discover the legend of Der Kindestod, a demon who sucks the life from children. Buffy ingests some of the flu virus so that she will be able to see her enemy and (with Willow creating a diversion) she and Xander follow him to the basement, where the children are hiding. Buffy kills the demon.

Dudes and Babes: A sick Buffy in her fluffy bed-socks is so cuddlesome, you want to hug her till she pops.

A Little Learning is a Dangerous Thing: Willow has done Buffy's homework for her. All she has to do is sign it and the ruse will be complete.

It's a Designer Label!: There's some horrible stuff on display, including Buffy's white trainers, Willow's red tights and Cordy's green-lined parka. But Cordelia's short dark skirt and black booties are heavenly.

References: Gwyneth Paltrow, Mr Potatohead, Humphrey Bogart, Death-as-a-chess-player in Ingmar Bergman's *The Seventh Seal* and *Bill & Ted's Bogus Journey*, the DC superheroine Power Girl, Greek poet Homer. Angelus hums Beethoven's ninth symphony 'Ode to Joy' (see *Angel*: 'Rm w/a Vu'). Obliquely, Sherlock Holmes and *The Invisible Man* ('If I see a floating pipe and a smoking jacket, he's dropped'). Dare one mention how reminiscent of *Nightmare on Elm Street* the episode is (notably the third movie, *Dream Warriors*)?

Bitch!: Cordelia's inept sympathy for Buffy: 'We're all concerned about how *gross* you look.' As Giles notes: 'Cordelia, have you ever actually *heard* of tact?'

'You Might Remember Me From Such Films and TV Series As . . .': Richard Herd played James McCord in *All The President's Men,*

Henry Skerridge in *Midnight in the Garden of Good and Evil*, and Commander John in *V*, though readers may remember his performance as 'Captain Galaxy' in the 'Future Boy' episode of *Quantum Leap*. His TV credits include *Starsky and Hutch, The A-Team* and *Hart to Hart*. Willie Garson, in addition to small parts in *There's Something About Mary, Mars Attack! Groundhog Day* and *The Rock* and recurring roles in *NYPD Blue* and *Stargate SG-1*, has made something of a career out of playing Lee Oswald, appearing in both the movie *Ruby* and *Quantum Leap*. Denise Johnson was one of the voice artists on *A Bug's Life*.

Valley-Speak: Cordelia's attempt to articulate what Der Kindestod does consists of several repetitions of '*Eww!*'

Logic, Let Me Introduce You to This Window: When Buffy rants about killing vampires, Dr Wilkinson gives her a tranquilliser injection straight to her arm. The drug should have been administered intravenously. Before Buffy sees Der Kindestod, her bedside clock changes from 2:26 to 2:27. In the following shot, the clock reads 2:15. When Buffy looks into the children's ward for the first time, there is no blue 'Basement Access' plaque on the exit door. Why is there an unlocked, clearly labelled door that leads from the children's ward straight to the hospital basement? Reports differ on the actual number, but there are certainly very few Krispy Kreme donut takeaways in Southern California, so Cordelia must have driven *miles* to get Xander his donut breakfast. It *must* be love.

I Just *Love* Your Accent: Giles visits Buffy in hospital carrying a brown paper bag full of grapes. A ubiquitous gift for the invalid and a cultural stereotype that should be exterminated with extreme prejudice.

Quote/Unquote: Cordelia: 'I was using "watch her back" as a euphemism for "looking at her butt".'
    Buffy, on how she intends to stop Der Kindestod: 'Thought I might try violence.'

Notes: 'Fear is for the weak.' Again well directed (the weirdly angled corridors for instance) and, despite the obvious Freddie Kruger-riffs, for the most part a clear and simple story about the bogeyman. It gets a bit confusing towards the end, but the characterisation (particularly of Cordelia and Xander) is impressive. The plot is a bit like a jigsaw that has a couple of pieces missing, but it does (eventually) make sense.

When Buffy was eight her cousin Celia (to whom she was close) died in hospital while Buffy was alone with her. It is subsequently revealed that the invisible Kindestod sucked the life from her. This presumably means either there is more than one Kindestod, or that Buffy is victim of 'Jessica Fletcher's Syndrome', having *always* been a magnet for these kind of deadly events. Or it's just a huge coincidence and an excuse for a contrived plot device. Your choice. There's an oblique reference to Buffy's amazing self-healing power, as previously hinted (**23**, 'Ted'). Joyce tells Giles how sorry she was to hear about Ms Calendar's death (**29**, 'Passion'). Xander and Willow used to play 'Doctor' (literally, since Willow had lots of medical textbooks and Xander didn't have the heart to tell her she was playing it wrong). Buffy claims never to have played the game. Cordelia's raised eyebrows at this suggest (a) she doesn't believe Buffy and (b) she herself has. Frequently. There's another reference to Willow's frog-phobia (**21**, 'What's My Line?' Part 1). Buffy likes peanut-butter and jelly sandwiches without the crust, and drinks juice that is two-parts orange to one-part grapefruit. This episode explains how vampires can enter factories and school buildings. After Willow asks if Angelus can attack Buffy while she's in the hospital, Xander says: 'He can come in. It's a public building.'

31
I Only Have Eyes For You

US Transmission Date: 28 Apr 1998
UK Transmission Date: 30 Jul 1999

Writer: Marti Noxon
Director: James Whitmore
Cast: Meredith Salinger (Grace Newman), Christopher Gorham (James Stanley), John Hawkes (George), Miriam Flynn (Ms Frank), Brian Poth (Fighting Boy), Sarah Bibb (Fighting Girl), Ryan Taszreak (Ben), Anna Coman-Hidy (50s Girl #1), Vanessa Bodnar (50s Girl #2)

Buffy finds a boy and girl fighting in the school hallway. He holds a gun and shouts, 'Don't walk away from me, bitch.' Buffy stops the boy from shooting, but the couple are confused about why they are arguing and where the gun came from. Or went to, since it is nowhere to be seen. More weirdness occurs, including a teacher writing the same words on a blackboard as Buffy has a daydream about the school in the 50s. Xander is attacked by a rotting arm in his locker. Willow looks up shooting incidents at school and finds a case from 1955, where a student (James) shot his teacher (Grace), then himself. Buffy recognises their faces from her dream. In the cafeteria all the food turns into snakes. Willow plans to exorcise the spirit with Buffy, Xander and Cordelia chanting from different locations in the school at midnight. However, a swarm of wasps invades the hallways. Giles, after initially believing that the troubled spirit is Jenny, speculates that James's soul is haunting the school, seeking forgiveness from Grace. But this can never happen, since each time the scenario is re-enacted, Grace dies. Buffy returns to school and meets Angelus and the pair are possessed by the ghosts. Buffy (acting out James's role) 'kills' Angelus. Buffy prepares to shoot herself, when Angelus stops her, forgives her and they share a kiss before the souls depart, leaving Buffy and Angelus in an embrace. Angelus escapes, feeling violated. He takes Drusilla to find blood. After they leave, Spike rises from his wheelchair.

Authority Sucks!: Snyder tells Buffy he intends to carefully look over the details of the gun incident until he can work out how it's all her fault. He's interrupted, mid-rant, by a vegan chaining himself to the snack machine.

The Conspiracy Starts at Home Time: In one short exchange between Snyder and Bob, an entire back-story is created and the suspicions that viewers had from the scene featuring the same pair in **15**, 'School Hard', is confirmed. We learn that Snyder was given his job by the City Council. Snyder refers to 'you people', which suggests that whatever is taking place, it involves the Sunnydale PD (or perhaps he's talking in a wider context; see **33** 'Becoming' Part 1), and the little flinch he gives when Bob suggests that he talk to the mayor speaks volumes. But, when Snyder states 'we're on a Hellmouth', suddenly a lot of things become clear. They *know*.

A Little Learning is a Dangerous Thing: Buffy notes that she has repressed anything math-related (nice to know repression runs in the family). Willow wants her students to read the chapters on information grouping and binary coding. Xander doesn't know the difference between a scapular and a spatula. There's a short essay on the New Deal. Also, Giles's completely bonkers Fox Mulder-like leap to the wrong conclusion about the identity of the malevolent ghost.

School Dinners: Snakes in the spaghetti. If you have lunches, prepare to part with them.

It's a Designer Label!: A *big* round of applause for Cordelia's tight red sweater. Buffy's suede boots and impossibly short brown skirt (it's really a long vest, isn't it?) cop similar reactions. Also the red and gold dress worn by the singer with Splendid. On the minus side, Willow's rainbow jumper and pale green top.

References: Paraphrases from *Julius Caesar* ('you came, you saw, you rejected') and *The Merchant of Venice* ('the quality of mercy is not Buffy'), plus references to OJ Simpson, the Nazi's Final Solution, Ernest Hemmingway, the Loch Ness Monster, Alice Cooper's rebellion anthem 'School's Out' (see **144**, 'Chosen') and *The Exorcist* ('I saw that movie. Even the priest dies'). *Poltergeist* is mentioned and parts of the plot seem influenced by it (notably Cordelia's mirror-sequence). 'You've got to roll with the punches' is from Van Halen's 'Jump'. Snyder's line 'I'm no stranger to conspiracy. I saw *JFK*' describes this series in microcosm. The characters of James and Grace share their names with those of the lead actors in Hitchcock's *Rear Window* (Stewart and Kelly respectively). 'I'm dead-as-hell and I'm not gonna take it any more' alludes to Peter Finch's Oscar-winning dialogue in *Network*.

Awesome!: That incredibly touching scene between Giles and Willow at the start. And Buffy and Angelus playing out the James/Grace scenario.

'You Might Remember Me From Such Films and TV Series As . . .': Christopher Gorman played Walt in *A Life Less Ordinary*. John Hawkes was Pete Bottoms in *From Dusk Till Dawn* and was terrific in *The X-Files* episode 'Milagro'. Miriam Flynn was the voice of Maa in *Babe*.

Don't Give Up The Day Job: Although director James Whitmore's credits include *Melrose Place*, *Quantum Leap*, *The X-Files*, *Nowhere Man* and *The Pretender* he is also an actor, playing Bernie Terwilliger in *Hunter*.

Valley-Speak: Xander: 'Oh yeah, baby, it's snakealicious in here.' And: 'I don't want to *poo-poo* your wiggins.'

Logic, Let Me Introduce You to This Window: After Buffy re-enters the wasp-surrounded school, Giles and the others stand in front of the building. The shot of them staring at the wasps is the same one used after they had escaped. Look closely and you'll spot Buffy's legs. After Snyder leaves Buffy alone in his office, the 1955 yearbook falls from the bookshelf. When it hits the floor, the cover flips open. As Buffy bends down the book is closed. 'I Only Have Eyes For You' by the Flamingos is used during the flashbacks to 1955. However, the song wasn't released until 1959. Why is Cordelia, who had her own diet in **4**, 'Teacher's Pet', eating spaghetti in the school cafeteria?

Quote/Unquote: Giles: 'You should never be cowed by authority. Except, of course, in this instance where I am clearly right and you are clearly wrong.'

Xander: ' "Something weird is going on"? Isn't that our school motto?'

Notes: 'Love is forever.' Serious stuff. Marti Noxon's combination of ghost story and pop-culture-angst combines to produce an episode that flirts with saying something really profound, but never quite delivers. The redemption theme is wonderfully handled and there's a (genuinely) *great* last scene, but when you're dealing with a subject as horrific as teen-suicide, you need more than gestures. Like **13**, 'When She Was Bad', this focuses on what an intolerant character Buffy can be (there are narrative links between Buffy ranting at her friends' stupidity here and her rows with Angel in the season opener).

Willow gives Giles a rose quartz stone that belonged to Jenny. It's been suggested that Willow should be unable to retrieve any of Jenny's computer files, as her PC was destroyed in **29**, 'Passion'. In the former episode, when Angelus threw the computer from her desk, the monitor smashed and burst into flames. The hard drive, however, fell on the ground away from the monitor. It's perfectly possible that it suffered no significant damage. Of course, there may have been backup disks. (Indeed, if *anyone* is going to keep floppies it would be a computer teacher.) The original US broadcast was followed by a public service announcement by Sarah Michelle Gellar on behalf of the 'American Association of Suicideology'.

Soundtrack: Aside from the Flamingo's recording, 'Charge' by Splendid [*].

32
Go Fish

US Transmission Date: 5 May 1998
UK Transmission Date: 6 Aug 1999
Writers: David Fury, Elin Hampton
Director: David Semel
Cast: Charles Cyphers (Coach Marin), Jeremy Garrett (Cameron Walker),
Wentworth Miller (Gage Petronzi), Conchata Ferrell (Nurse Greenliegh),
Shane West (Sean), Jake Patellis (Dodd McAlvy)

A victory party for the school swim team sees everyone celebrating
except Buffy. But when two swimmers disappear, she and her
friends become involved. Snyder encourages Willow to raise the
failing grade of Gage Petronzi. Giles believes that as the victims
were the best swimmers in school, Gage is the next likely target.
While keeping Gage under surveillance, Buffy saves him from an
attack by Angelus. With some positions open, Xander makes the
swim team. Buffy sees Gage tear away his own skin, emerging as
a monster. Xander learns that steroids are passed to the team in
the steam room. Coach Marin tells Buffy about Russian experiments with fish DNA on their Olympic swimmers. He forces Buffy
into the sewer so his boys can satisfy their needs. Xander struggles
with Marin, as Buffy fends off the creatures and the Coach ends
up in the sewer.

Dudes and Babes: Xander in red Speedos ('I'm undercover', 'Not
under much'). The double-takes on the faces of Cordy, Buffy and
Willow are wonderful. It must be said, Xander's far too well-built
to be a total geek – it *must* be his personality.

Authority Sucks: Xander is outraged by Snyder's manipulation of
Willow to up Gage's grades, noting that it's a slap in the face to
everyone who studied hard to earn their Ds.

A Little Learning is a Dangerous Thing: Since Willow is still in
charge of the computer class, everybody's pie charts look like
they're supposed to. Except Gage's. Xander, seemingly, doesn't
know who wrote the Constitution. His take on history is little
better ('the discus throwers got the best seats at the crucifixions').
Cordelia's opinion on the 'all men are created equal thing':
'Propaganda spouted out by the ugly and less deserving.' And on
Abraham Lincoln: 'Disgusting mole and stupid hat.'

It's a Designer Label!: Cordelia's miniskirts take much of the viewers attention, but Buffy's stretchpants are practical *and* fun. She lets the side down, wearing leather trousers in the sewer scenes: just the sort of thing for chasing fish monsters. Willow's usual hippychick look is further emphasised by a pair of flared orange pants.

References: The title is from Rose Troche's 1994 lesbian movie. 'Go Fish' is also the name of a popular card game in the US. (It's the game, incidentally, that Dawn and Xander are playing in **112**, 'Doublemeat Palace'.) Xander's favourite teams include the New York Yankees, Abbot and Costello, and *The A-Team*. Also referenced: Gertrude Edderley, the first woman to swim the English Channel, Twisted Sister, the 80s glam-metal band, *The Creature from the Black Lagoon* and the Brooke Shields film *Blue Lagoon*. Willow celebrating the chocolatey goodness of Oreo cookies may be an in-joke (Alyson Hannigan had previously done commercials for Oreo). There are dialogue and visual allusions to *Jaws*. Xander paraphrases the Commodores' 'Three Times A Lady' and there's an oblique reference to Thomas Dolby's 'She Blinded Me With Science'. Magazines seen in the library include *Women's Sports and Fitness*, *Sports Illustrated*, *Vegetarian Times*, *National Geographic*, *PC World*, *Slam!*, *Smithsonian*, *Horseman*, *Skin Diver* and *Art News*.

Bitch!: Cordelia's suggestion after Xander asks what he can do to help the investigations: 'Go out into the parking lot and practice running like a man.'

Awesome!: Buffy taking on two monsters in the dressing room (interesting use of a lacrosse stick) and Buffy and Angelus battling ('Why, Ms Summers, you're beautiful'). Cordelia's pride in Xander when he becomes the hero (' . . . and you looked really hot in those Speedos!') is perfectly in-character. A highlight is Willow's interrogation of Jonathan and her reaction to his confession that he peed in the pool ('*Eww!*').

'You Might Remember Me From Such Films and TV Series As . . .': Charles Cyphers was one of John Carpenter's repertory company, appearing in *Assault on Precinct 13*, *Escape from New York*, *The Fog* and the first two *Halloween* movies. On TV he appeared in *The Dukes of Hazzard*, *Wonder Woman*, *Charlie's Angels* and *Starsky and Hutch*. Conchata Ferrell was Susan Bloom in *LA Law* and was in *True Romance*, *Edward Scissorhands* and *Network*.

Valley-Speak: Xander: 'Last month he's the freak with jicama breath who waxes his back. He wins a few meets and suddenly inherits the cool gene?'

Gage: 'Aw, dude, what *is* that foulness?'

Logic, Let Me Introduce You to This Window: The first shot of the Bronze features a blank chalkboard. However, when Buffy observes Gage with Angelus, it has gained an advert: DJ 2NITE, NO COVER. Coach Marin is concerned that the swim team will find out about the recent deaths. In the Bronze, Gage seems unaware of Cameron's death. When Buffy tells him of the killer, she doesn't mention Cameron by name. But Gage's question after Angelus's attack is, 'Was that the thing that killed Cameron?' In the final shot, we see three creatures in the ocean. Where's the fourth?

Quote/Unquote: Cordelia gets most of the best lines, including: 'Xander, I know you take pride in being the voice of the common wus.' And, when believing that Xander has become an aquatic monster: 'We can still date . . . or not. I'd understand if you want to see other fish.'

Buffy: 'I think we'd better find the rest of the swim team and lock them up before they get in touch with their inner halibut.'

Notes: 'Is steroid-abuse usually linked with "Hey, I'm a Fish"?' Another Xander-led episode and another comedy classic. Amid the hilarity of one of *Buffy*'s funniest conceits, however, is a very cynical little essay on drug-enhanced performance and the ceaseless search for winners that the US school system produces. Few other series, too, could have gotten away with the sexual overtones of this episode. Astonishingly, 'Go Fish' has a low reputation with some of the series' Internet fans, regularly appearing alongside **16**, 'Inca Mummy Girl', and **24**, 'Bad Eggs', in *Least Favourite Episode* polls. Seldom has an episode less-deserved such a fate.

The school board are having trouble finding a competent teacher this late in the term, so Willow is continuing to sub through finals (see **29**, 'Passion'). Although we had previously seen Sunnydale docks (**25**, 'Surprise'), this episode confirms that it's a coastal town with its own beach. Did the fish creatures eat Coach Marin, or did they have something else in mind? They leave at least half of Nurse Greenliegh intact and the coach specifically states that they've had their dinner and have other needs. Xander's smirk when Buffy says 'Those boys really loved their coach' suggests some horrible ideas.

Soundtrack: 'Mann's Chinese' by Naked, and 'If You'd Listen' by Nero's Rome.

33
Becoming Part 1

US Transmission Date: 12 May 1998
UK Transmission Date: 13 Aug 1999

Writer: Joss Whedon
Director: Joss Whedon
Cast: Max Perlich (Whistler), Jack McGee (Doug Perren),
Richard Riehle (Buffy's First Watcher),[10] Shannon Weller (Gypsy Woman),
Zitto Kazann (Gypsy Man), Ginger Williams (Girl), Nina Gervitz (Teacher)

Galway, 1753: Angel encounters Darla, who offers to show him her world. Sunnydale, 1998: Giles is asked by the museum to look at a stone artefact. London, 1860: Drusilla enters a church, and is told by Angelus that she is the spawn of Satan. Sunnydale, 1998: Buffy and Willow discover the disk on which Jenny stored the spell to restore Angel's soul. Rumania, 1898: the body of a gypsy girl lies on the ground, while a curse of restoration is cast. Angelus is told that he will be haunted by the souls of those he has killed. Sunnydale, 1998: Angelus tells Spike about the demon Acathla who possesses the power to swallow the Earth. Kendra arrives, having been sent by her Watcher because another dark force is threatening Sunnydale. Manhattan, 1996: Angel, living as a tramp, is approached by a demon, Whistler, who offers Angel the chance to regain his dignity. Los Angeles, 1996: Whistler shows Angel the Chosen One, observing Buffy's initial meeting with her first Watcher. Whistler says Buffy is just a child and will need Angel's help. Sunnydale, 1998: Angelus fails to revive Acathla. A girl vampire walks into an exam room, tells Buffy that she must meet Angelus that night, then bursts into flames. Buffy finds Angelus at the cemetery and they fight, but it is a trap to get the Slayer away from her friends. At the library the vampires attack. Drusilla kills

---

[10] There is considerable debate in the *Buffy* fan community as to whether this character is Merrick or not. Certainly, the scenes set in Hemery High are conceptually close enough to the movie to suggest that the film's events are canonical. Additionally, at least one 'official' book on the series lists the character as Merrick.

Kendra; Willow and Xander are left unconscious and Giles is taken away. Buffy arrives as a police officer orders her to freeze.

Dudes and Babes: This is the episode that gets all the girls banging on about how tragic (and, therefore, sexy) a figure Angel is. Mind you, the Irish accent could use a bit of work, David. *Begorrah.*

Authority Sucks!: Snyder asks Buffy to give him a reason to kick her out (see **34**, 'Becoming' Part 2).

A Little Learning is a Dangerous Thing: Willow is enjoying teaching and helps Buffy with some chemistry homework.

Mom's Apple Pie: A clever reversal of the 'Do you know what time it is?' scene from **M1**: Joyce catches Buffy coming in late from Slaying and has a blazing row with her.

School Dinners: Xander's re-enactment of Buffy's killing a vampire using two fish sticks is certainly worth seeing.

It's a Designer Label!: Watch out for Buffy's red dress and her brilliant trouser-suit and blue frock-coat. Cordy's red sweater from **31**, 'I Only Have Eyes for You', puts in another appearance. On the minus side, Buffy's hooded top, her yellow coat and horrible pants in the 1996 sequences and Whistler's green shirt.

References: Allusions to *The Sword in the Stone*. Buffy calls Acathla 'Alfalfa' from *The Little Rascals*. The sequence in which Darla cuts her chest with her fingernail and makes Angel drink from it is yet another moment that seems to have been inspired by *Dracula, Prince of Darkness* (see **2**, 'The Harvest'; **12**, 'Prophecy Girl'). Angel's mentor shares his name with one of the vampire killers in *Blade*.

Bitch!: Cordelia on Snyder: 'A tiny impotent Nazi with a bug up his butt the size of an emu.'

Xander: 'So, this spell might restore Angel's soul? Well, here's an interesting angle: Who cares?'

'You Might Remember Me From Such Films and TV Series As . . .': Max Perlich was Johnny Hardin in *Maverick* and was a regular on *Homicide: Life On the Streets* (as James Brodie). Jack McGee is one of those actors that seems to be in *everything*: He's in *Backdraft, Lethal Weapon 2* and *Showgirls,* plays a sheriff in *Basic Instinct* and is the cop who sprays Val Kilmer with mace in *The Doors*. Richard Riehle had lots of film credits including *Fear and*

Loathing in Las Vegas, *Casino*, *The Fugitive* and *Fried Green Tomatoes at the Whistle Stop Cafe*. Zitto Kazann is in *Waterworld*.

Valley-Speak: Buffy: 'Ready to rock.' Plus her *total* Valley-girl act: 'Call me!'

Logic, Let Me Introduce You to This Window: In **14**, 'Some Assembly Required', Angel is 241 years old. Assuming that episode took place in 1997, he would have been born in 1755 or 1756. According to **18**, 'Halloween', Angel was 18 years old in 1775 and still human. However, here Angel is bitten by Darla in 1753, three years before he was born (see **Angel's Age**). According to the flashbacks, Angel saw Buffy at least twice before they met in **1**, 'Welcome to the Hellmouth', despite him saying in the opening episode, 'I thought you'd be taller'.

What a Shame They Dropped . . .: A marvellous Whistler line: 'There are three kinds of people that no one understands. Geniuses, madmen and guys that mumble!'

Quote/Unquote: Drusilla: 'Met an old man. I didn't like him. He got stuck in my teeth.'
　　Spike: 'It's a big rock. Can't wait to tell my friends. *They* don't have a rock this big.'

Notes: 'So, what are we? Helpless puppets? No, the big moments are gonna come, you can't help that. It's what you do afterwards that counts.' 'Becoming' Part 1 explores the nature of destiny and does it *beautifully*. Sharing similarities with the *Highlander* TV series isn't the worst of crimes as this poetic exercise in controlled storytelling delves into two centuries of Angelus's past with a series of conceptually ingenious flashbacks. However, Kendra's arbitrary death (though well played) is a disappointment.
　　Giles has been using his Orb of Thesulah as a paperweight, which is a clever in-joke, referring to what The Magic Box owner told Jenny he'd sold the Orbs for in **29**, 'Passion'. Xander says that Buffy has killed five vampires over the previous three nights. Buffy's boyfriend when she first became the Slayer was called Tyler. Kendra calls the stake that she gives to Buffy 'Mr Pointy'. We see another copy of *The Sunnydale Press* (see **17**, 'Reptile Boy'; **55**, 'Graduation Day' Part 1). The episode includes flashbacks to events first mentioned in **7**, 'Angel': Darla's siring of Angel and his being cursed by the Romany people. The 1860 sequence shows that Drusilla was psychic before she became a vampire. She refers

to her mother in the present tense, which means this must have taken place at the beginning of Angelus's relationship with her, as **19**, 'Lie to Me', makes clear he killed all of those close to her before finally killing her. Indeed, this could be their first meeting (although Angelus is certainly taking risks to be close to her – entering a church, for example. See also *Angel*: 'Dear Boy'). Whistler's reference to Buffy as just a child seems to imply that the Slayer is normally older (see **46**, 'Helpless'). The Hemery High set is a façade on the Universal backlot in Studio City. It was also the Hill Valley Clock Tower in the first two *Back to the Future* films.

Angel's Age: *Angel*: 'The Prodigal' finally nails the problem of exactly how old Angel is. Liam, it states, was born in 1727 and became a vampire in 1753. Although the date of Liam's death confirms the on-screen information in **33**, 'Becoming' Part 1, it contradicts several other bits of dating in *Buffy* (notably Willow's observation, taken from *The Watcher's Diaries* in **18**, 'Halloween', that Angel was still human in 1775). It seems that vampires take their age from the time that they actually become a vampire (see, for instance, Spike's age as given in **63**, 'The Initiative') though in Angel's case this is *still* a couple of years away from the dates given in *Buffy* episodes during 1997–98 (that Angel was either 240 or 241). See also **85**, 'Fool for Love'; *Angel*: 'Dear Boy' and 'Darla' for further continuity.

34
Becoming Part 2

US Transmission Date: 19 May 1998
UK Transmission Date: 13 Aug 1999

Writer: Joss Whedon
Director: Joss Whedon
Cast: Max Perlich (Whistler), Susan Leslie (First Cop),
Thomas G Waites (Second Cop)

Buffy is arrested for murder, but escapes and visits the hospital in disguise. Xander tells her that Willow is in a coma and Giles has disappeared. At Giles's apartment, Buffy meets Whistler, who tells her that Angel was destined to stop Acathla, not revive him. A patrol cop recognises Buffy but Spike helps her escape, explaining that he wants to stop Angelus. Buffy takes him back to her house, where a vampire attacks her mother. Buffy kills it and explains to Joyce that she is a Vampire Slayer. Joyce is angry at having been kept in the dark and tells Buffy that if she leaves now, not to bother coming back. Giles refuses to divulge the information that Angelus needs, despite being tortured. Willow tells the others that she will try the curse again. Buffy returns to the library to retrieve Kendra's sword. Snyder finds her and gleefully expels her, calling someone to tell the mayor the good news. Drusilla tricks Giles by making herself look like Jenny. Giles says Angelus's blood is the key to the awakening. Xander frees Giles as Buffy sword-fights Angelus, leaving Spike to hustle Drusilla away. Willow restores the curse on Angelus's soul just as Buffy is about to deliver the final blow. However, Acathla is awakening and Buffy must send Angel to Hell. Homeless and expelled, Buffy boards a bus and leaves Sunnydale.

Dudes and Babes: Buffy's claim to be the drummer in a rock band with Spike as the singer is such a wonderful image we almost wish it were true.

Authority Sucks!: 'You stupid little troll, you have no *idea*.' But Snyder *does*, as Buffy discovers in the scene where he expels her.

Denial No More!: 'Mom, I'm a Vampire Slayer.' There's not much even Joyce can say to that, although 'Have you tried *not* being a Slayer' is an impressive comeback. Buffy rages at her mother's inability to see what's been staring her in the face for the last two years, asking how many times Joyce has washed blood out of Buffy's clothes (see **4**, 'Teacher's Pet').

It's a Designer Label!: Buffy's undercover hat. Xander's purple jumper crops up again. There's also Oz's yellow shirt and a pink one in the final scene. Cordelia's lemon dress is a highlight.

References: Snyder's 'Your point being?' echoes Homer Simpson's reply in *The Simpsons* episode 'Marge on the Lam', when asked if he's just holding on to the coke cans that have both his arms stuck in two drinks machines. 'A gay old time' refers to *The Flinstones*. 'Goodbye Piccadilly, farewell bloody Leicester Square' alludes to the song 'It's A Long Way To Tipperary'.

Bitch!: Buffy to Snyder: 'You never got a single date in High School, did you?' (See **40**, 'Band Candy'.)

Awesome!: Willow's 'resolve'-face. The lengthy Buffy/Angelus sword-fight. Plus the delightful comedy scene with Joyce and Spike sitting in formal silence on the sofa (see **42**, 'Lover's Walk').

'You Might Remember Me From Such Films As . . .': Thomas Waites appeared in two of this author's favourite movies, playing Windows in *The Thing* and Fox in *The Warriors*.

Logic, Let Me Introduce You to This Window: Why does Buffy invite Spike into her home? One would imagine she'd learned something from the events of **29**, 'Passion'? When did Xander show Buffy the funky-looking mansion on Crawford Street? Buffy couldn't have known that Drusilla was responsible for Kendra's death (Xander was unconscious before Drusilla entered the library) yet that's what she tells Spike. Principals cannot expel students without a school-board hearing. If Spike is so anti-the End of the World then what was all that business with the Judge in **26**, 'Innocence'? During the final battle scene, Buffy's hair changes from loose to pony-tailed several times. Spike drives out of the garage and turns the steering wheel hard to the left, keeping it in that position for several seconds (the car should, therefore, be going in circles). Angelus's sword-fighting double looks more like Xander than Angelus. Major logic flaw: the script implies that only Angel's blood could revive Acathla, even though it's supposed to be Angel's destiny to *stop* this happening.

I Just *Love* Your Accent: Spike says he likes dog racing and Manchester United (in that, he's typical – most of their supporters live *anywhere* but Manchester). Whistler says that raiding an Englishman's fridge is like dating a nun. You're never going to get to the good stuff.

Quote/Unquote: Buffy to Whistler: 'If you're gonna crack jokes, I'm gonna pull out your rib cage and wear it as a hat.'

Spike: 'I don't fancy spending the next month trying to get librarian out of the carpet.'

Go Straight to Hell: Angelus: 'You're going to Hell.' Buffy: 'Save me a seat.'

Notes: 'I've had a *really* bad day.' Initially more concerned with power-politics and characterisation than plot, for 20 minutes the episode stutters (despite the hospital scenes contrasted with the grotesque brutality of Angelus torturing Giles) before a magnificent recovery to its tragic conclusion. It is *impossible* to watch the final few moments of this episode without a lump in the throat.

Xander tells an unconscious Willow that she is his best friend and that he loves her. Significantly, the first word Willow says on coming out of her coma is 'Oz'. The last time Angelus tortured someone, the chainsaw hadn't been invented. Spike refers to Joyce hitting him with an axe in **15**, 'School Hard'. Snyder says the Sunnydale police are deeply stupid, which seems accurate on the evidence we've seen (see **48**, 'Bad Girls'). The road sign at the end of the episode reads 'Now leaving Sunnydale. Come back soon!'

Soundtrack: 'Full Of Grace' by Sarah McLachlan. Christophe Beck's magnificent score won a deserved Emmy. The epic love theme 'Close Your Eyes' [*] accompanies the final Buffy/Angel scenes.

'I Need A Hug': The Mutant Enemy vampire on the closing credits replaced his usual 'Grrr Arrrgh' with this touching sentiment. Most viewers probably agreed with him.

'I'm a blood-sucking fiend! Look at my outfit!'
                                            – 'Doppelgängland'

Season Three (1998–99)

Mutant Enemy Inc/Kuzui Enterprises/Sandollar Television/20th Century Fox
Created by Joss Whedon
Producer: Gareth Davies
Executive Producers: Sandy Gallin, Gail Berman, Fran Rubel Kuzui,
Kaz Kuzui, David Greenwalt,
Joss Whedon
Co-Producers: Marti Noxon, David Solomon, Kelly Manners
Regular Cast:
Sarah Michelle Gellar (Buffy Summers), Nicholas Brendon (Xander Harris),
Alyson Hannigan (Willow Rosenberg), Charisma Carpenter (Cordelia Chase),
Anthony Stewart Head (Rupert Giles), David Boreanaz (Angel),
Mark Metcalf (The Master, 43),
Kristine Sutherland (Joyce Summers, 35–37, 40, 42, 44–46, 48–49, 51–55),
Mercedes McNab (Harmony Kendall, 43, 55–56),
Elizabeth Anne Allen (Amy Madison, 45), Robia LaMorte (Jenny Calendar, 44),
Armin Shimerman (Principal Snyder, 36–37, 40, 45, 50, 53, 55–56),
James Marsters (Spike, 42), Seth Green (Daniel 'Oz' Osborne, 35–48, 50–56),
Jason Hall (Devon, 36, 39–41, 50),
Danny Strong (Jonathan Levinson, 36, 39, 43, 52, 54, 56),
Larry Bagby III (Larry, 35, 43, 52, 56), Robin Sachs (Ethan Rayne, 40),
Julia Lee ('Chanterelle'/'Lily'/Anne Steele, 35),
Saverio Guerra (Willy, 44, 47), James G MacDonald (Detective Stein, 49),
Jeremy Ratchford (Lyle Gorch, 39), James Lurie (Mr Miller,[11] 35, 55),
Fab Filippo (Scott Hope, 37–39),
Eliza Dushku (Faith, 37–39, 41, 44, 47–51, 53–56),
K Todd Freeman (Mr Trick, 37, 39–40, 48–49),
Harry Groener (Mayor Richard Wilkins III, 39–40, 42, 45, 48–51, 53–56),
Jack Plotnick (Deputy Mayor Allan Finch 39, 42, 48–49),
Emma Caulfield (Anya Jenkins, 43, 50, 54–55), Harris Yulin (Quentin Travers, 46),
Alexis Denisof (Wesley Wyndam-Price, 48–56),
Amy Powell (TV News Reporter, 49), Megan Gray (Sandy, 50),
Ethan Erickson (Percy West 50, 52, 55–56), Andy Umberger (D'Hoffryn, 50),
Bonita Friedericy (Mrs Finkle,[12] 53, 54)

---

[11] Credited as 'Teacher' in **35**, 'Anne'.
[12] Credited as 'Manager' in **53**, 'Choices'.

35

Anne

US Transmission Date: 29 Sep 1998
UK Transmission Date: 20 Aug 1999

Writer: Joss Whedon
Director: Joss Whedon
Cast: Carlos Jacott (Ken), Mary-Pat Green (Blood Bank Doctor), Chad Todhunter
(Rickie), Michael Leopard (Roughneck), Harley Zumbrum (Demon Guard),
Barbara Pilavin (Old Woman), Harrison Young (Old Man), Alex Toma (Aaron),
Dell Yount (Truck Guy)

The Scoobies try to carry on Buffy's work in her absence, but
they're not very good at it. Buffy, meanwhile, is working as a
waitress in an LA diner. There she meets Lily, whom she knew as
Chanterelle in Sunnydale. Lily tells Buffy that her boyfriend,
Ricky, is missing. Buffy reluctantly agrees to help and finds an old
man dead in the street whom she identifies as Ricky from his
unique tattoo. Lily is ensnared by Ken who runs the Family
Home, a refuge for homeless teenagers. Clues lead Buffy to the
Home where she finds Lily about to be initiated. Lily, Buffy and
Ken pass through a black pool into another-dimensional factory
where hundreds of missing teenagers are working as slave labour.
Ken says a day on Earth equates to 100 years in this dimension.
Buffy organises a rebellion among the slaves and helps them to
freedom. Buffy gives her apartment and job (along with her name)
to Lily and returns home.

Dreaming (As Blondie Once Said) is Free: Buffy and Angel on a
beach at sunset.

Dudes and Babes: Lily (see **19**, 'Lie to Me') is *still* as wet as a slap
in the face with a haddock and now has dead-boyfriend issues to
deal with. Subsequent to this episode, she changes her name to
Anne Steele and runs a shelter for the homeless (see *Angel*: 'Blood
Money'; 'The Thin Dead Line'; 'Not Fade Away').

Buffy's Peach Pie: Buffy tells Lily that she can't guarantee the
peach pie at the diner contains actual peaches.

Denial, Thy Name is Joyce: Joyce says she doesn't blame herself
for Buffy leaving; she blames Giles (which is pretty hypocritical
since it was she who threw Buffy out of the house).

It's a Designer Label!: The pink flowery dress that Buffy wears in her dream is the same one she wears in **36**, 'Dead Man's Party'. Cordelia wears a tasteful green skirt but Willow's at it again, with a short purple skirt and tea-cosy hat (this is, incidentally, the only episode in which a tea-cosy is mentioned; it's something Buffy says she's always wanted, even though she doesn't know what one is). There are some nice pants on display, including Cordelia's blue flares, the tight red pair worn by the lead singer of Belly Love and Lily's cream hipsters.

References: 'Duck and cover' was a 50s information campaign aimed largely at children on how to protect themselves in the event of a nuclear attack. Buffy beats up Ken, telling him it's her impression of Mahatma Gandhi (1869–1948) when he was really pissed-off. Buffy's assumed name, Anne Summers, raised a lot of smiles in Britain where this is the name of a leading erotica store.

Bitch!: Cordy notes that Xander has always been attracted to monsters (see **4**, 'Teacher's Pet') and refers, caustically, to the Inca Mummy Girl. Xander gets his own back with 'the vampire kills you, we watch, we rejoice'. Then there's a repeat of the **22**, 'What's My Line?' Part 2, kiss-sequence (with *that* music again).

'You Might Remember Me From Such Films As . . .': Harrison Young played the old Private Ryan in *Saving Private Ryan*. Carlos Jacott was tremendous as the agent in *Being John Malkovich* and also appears in *She's All That*, *The Last Days of Disco*, *Grosse Pointe Blank* and as Ramon the Pool Guy in *Seinfeld*.

Don't Give Up The Day Job: Stunt co-ordinator Jeff Pruitt has a cameo role as the Family Home doorman. He previously played a vampire in **23**, 'Ted'.

Logic, Let Me Introduce You to This Window: Willow's scream interrupts Xander and Cordelia's fight and we see Cordy run towards Willow with Xander behind her. In the following shot, Oz is running in the same direction while Xander and Cordy are standing still. For most of the episode Buffy wears a purple T-shirt under a black hooded sweatshirt. After she tells the other prisoners, 'Anyone who's not having fun here, follow me,' she's wearing a different top beneath her sweatshirt. Buffy wears a pair of white Nike trainers but after Lily pushes Ken off the balcony, watch Buffy's shoes as she climbs up. They're light grey deck shoes. How could Willow not have known that Oz didn't finish school? Larry was a senior last year, wasn't he? What were those slaves working on?

Quote/Unquote: Ken: 'You've got guts. I'd like to slice you open and play with them.'

Notes: 'I didn't ask for you to come to me with your problems. I just wanted to be left alone.' Clever opening (particularly Oz's incompetent attempt at throwing a stake) but this is a *real* disappointment. A downbeat story about the sick underbelly of LA and an exercise in reformatting; 'Anne' tries hard to say something about society, but it's uninvolving stuff and after a while the viewer simply wants the episode finished and Buffy back in Sunnydale. It's a *long* 40 minutes to sit through just to get to 'I'm Buffy the Vampire Slayer . . . And you are?'

Buffy's middle name is Anne. She has a fluffy toy duck in her rented apartment. Cordelia spent the summer in Mexico where, she says, they have cockroaches big enough to own property (see **13**, 'When She Was Bad'). Giles has a friend in Oakland who gives him a (false) lead on vampire activity.

Soundtrack: Belly Love perform 'Back To Freedom' in the Bronze.

Critique: The third season began with a glowing write-up in *TV Guide*: 'Can we tell you how great it is not to have to choose between *Buffy* and *Ally McBeal* any more? Kicking off a hot Tuesday line-up (followed by the much anticipated *Felicity*), this smart-sexy-funny-scary original is at the top of its game.'

36
Dead Man's Party

US Transmission Date: 6 Oct 1998
UK Transmission Date: 27 Aug 1999

Writer: Marti Noxon
Director: James Whitmore Jr
Cast: Nancy Lenehan (Pat), Paul Morgan Stetler (Young Doctor), Chris Garnant (Stoner #1)

A Nigerian mask from Joyce's gallery proves to be an even bigger headache for Mrs Summers than organising a homecoming that will please her (still confused) daughter. First, a cat is raised from the dead, then an elaborate party with all of Buffy's friends is ruined by the arrival of gatecrashing zombies. Buffy, whose uncommunicative, sulky demeanour proves trying even to Xander and Willow, manages to fight the demon of the mask, Ovu Mobani, the Evil Eye, which inhabits the body of Joyce's neighbour Pat. Killing the demon makes the zombies vanish and leaves Buffy alone with those closest to her, to come to her senses and start acting like herself again.

Dreaming (As Blondie Once Said) is Free: For the second episode running, Angel appears only in a dream sequence. And a very surreal one at that, set in a deserted school.

Authority Sucks!: Snyder's reply to Joyce, saying that Buffy was cleared of all charges surrounding Kendra's death: 'While she may live up to the "not a murderer" requirement for enrolment, she *is* a troublemaker.' He advises Buffy that 'Hot-Dog-on-a-Stick' are hiring. Joyce later describes Snyder as a nasty little horrid bigoted rodent-man.

The Conspiracy Starts at Home Time: The mayor is mentioned twice. When Joyce says she will discuss Buffy's expulsion with him, Snyder says *that* will be an interesting meeting.

Mom's Apple Pie: Joyce believes that Buffy has no appreciation of primitive art (this is a *bad* thing?). Buffy says she was starving until the four-course snack Joyce made her after dinner. The 'mom's not perfect' scene is a tremendously effective one – and for once, we're actually on Joyce's side.

It's a Designer Label!: Joyce's orange mom-pants. Giles wears a very tasteful three-piece suit in grey. Buffy's jogging pants. On the minus side, Devon's brown shirt.

References: Fashion designer Tommy Hilfiger, popular 70s toy the Weebles, *Rambo*, *The Bad Seed*, UK techno group Shut Up and Dance, *USA Today*, the sitcom *Mr Belvedere* and Jacquelyn Mitchard's novel *The Deep End of the Ocean*. The title comes from a song by Oingo Boingo. Aspects of the story may have been influenced by *Night of the Living Dead* and *Mask*.

Awesome!: Buffy's fight on (and off) the roof with the demon, especially the garden-spade ending.

'You Might Remember Me From Such Films As . . .': Both Nancy Lenehan and Paul Morgan Stetler were in *Pleasantville*.

Valley-Speak: Oz on the differences between a gathering, a shindig and a hootenanny.

Stoner, on whose party it is: 'Heard it was for some chick that got out of rehab.'

Logic, Let Me Introduce You to This Window: Buffy sets the table for six. However, Joyce invited seven (eight counting Pat). When Xander asks the group to vote on how Buffy's homecoming should be celebrated, Willow raises her right hand with a pencil in it. When the camera returns to Willow, her hand is still raised, but where's the pencil? When Buffy goes to her bedroom and starts to pack, she leaves the door slightly open. After the commercial break, when Willow finds Buffy, the door is fully open. (Despite a *major* party taking place downstairs, these scenes have virtually no background noise.) When Buffy stakes the zombie to see if it's a vampire, the zombie raises its left arm in reaction. Next shot, the arm is still on the floor. The wallpaper pattern changes between shots after Buffy and Pat fall out of the window. Will Dingoes Ate My Baby ever do their guitarist another personal favour after *this*? And, grabbing the principal like that could easily cost a librarian his job. (There *has* to be more to this scene than we see. Why does Giles believe he can get away with it? And why does Snyder give in?)

Quote/Unquote: Buffy: 'What about home-schooling? It's not just for scary religious people any more.'

Giles: ' "Do you like my mask? Isn't it pretty? It raises the dead!" *Americans!*'

Notes: 'So, this is a typical day at the office?' A long-winded way to get Buffy and her friends back together again, though it's much funnier than 35, 'Anne', and, consequently, more interesting. At least the effects are very good, but the party scenes of Buffy bitching the Scooby Gang are painful to watch.

Giles hot-wires his car (he says it's like riding a bicycle, which suggests he's done some of this during his dark past; see 45, 'Gingerbread'). Willow isn't a fully-fledged witch yet, that takes years (see 45, 'Gingerbread'; 50, 'Doppelgängland'). Xander's call-sign during the patrol is Night Hawk. The Summers have skis in their closet.

Critique: '*Buffy* works against atmospherics, going for the contrasts implicit in a horror story setting that looks like the subject of a Beach Boys song,' wrote Lloyd Rose in the *Washington Post*. 'Impossibly fit, gorgeous teens stroll the halls. Buffy, in the person of Sarah Michelle Gellar, is a major babe, way too good-looking to ever be the nerd she's portrayed as . . . The movies' response to feminism has been to create heroines who might be called "Boys With Breasts". But though Buffy batters bad guys with the best of them, she's all girl. She's emotional. She has bad hair days (which Cordelia is always quick to comment on). She worries about her boyfriend. And with Gellar in the role, she's the sexiest nerd in history. Whedon isn't above the more traditional S&M images: who can forget how Buffy looked after killing a snake-demon, her little black dress clinging to her lithe figure, broken manacles dangling from her wrists like saucy bracelets?'

Soundtrack: Dingoes Ate My Baby mime to 'Never Mind', 'Sway' and 'Pain' (see **28**, 'Bewitched, Bothered and Bewildered') by Four Star Mary.

37
Faith Hope and Trick

US Transmission Date: 13 Oct 1998
UK Transmission Date: 3 Sep 1999

Writer: David Greenwalt
Director: James A Contner
Cast: Jeremy Roberts (Kakistos), John Ennis (Manager)

At Sunnydale's Happy Burger, two vampires search for the Slayer. Principal Snyder readmits Buffy to school, under orders from the board. Giles tells Buffy he needs to perform a binding spell on Acathla to keep the demon dormant and asks for details of Angel being sent to Hell. At the Bronze, Cordelia points out a couple on the dance floor. Buffy follows and discovers the boy is a vampire. What takes her by surprise is the girl's ability to deal with him, stopping only to greet Buffy and introduce herself as Faith, the new Slayer, called after Kendra's death. Faith tells Buffy that her Watcher is at an annual retreat, but Giles discovers that the Watcher is dead. Buffy and Faith are attacked by Kakistos, Mr Trick and their acolytes. The Slayers defeat Kakistos. Unable to keep her secret any longer, Buffy tells Giles and Willow that Angel was cured before she killed him. Buffy revives plans for her weekend date with Scott Hope just as, unknown to her, Angel returns from Hell.

Dudes and Babes: Faith, the new Slayer, is personable, according to a green-eyed Buffy. Faith says that Slaying makes her hungry and horny (Buffy agrees about the hungry part). Willow notes that Buffy does 'that thing with your mouth that boys like. No not *that* thing . . .' What on earth is she talking about? Also debuting is Scott Hope, Buffy's nice normal non-boyfriend. Angel appears naked in the final scene.

Authority Sucks!: Joyce tells an outmanoeuvred Snyder: 'What I believe my daughter is trying to say is "Nyah-nyah-nyah".'

A Little Learning is a Dangerous Thing: The preconditions of Buffy becoming a schoolgirl again are that she takes make-up tests on all of the classes she skipped last year, along with providing a letter of recommendation from a member of the faculty who isn't an English librarian and seeing the school psychologist (see **38**, 'Beauty and the Beasts'). She eventually passes all of these, although her initial reaction to the English test ('They give you a credit for speaking it, right?') makes one wonder how, exactly.

Mom's Apple Pie: Faith greatly enjoys the fries that Joyce serves for dinner.

It's a Designer Label!: Willow's fluffy light-blue sweater sums up her personality. Ditto Cordelia's vampy Raybans. And Faith's impressive trouser wardrobe (tight multicoloured hipsters in her first scene, crimson leathers later on). She sometimes sleeps naked, unlike Buffy who's seen in a lime-green nightshirt. Oz's horrible dyed shirt puts in another appearance.

References: The episode title is derived from I Corinthians 13:11 (see **M1**). Martha Stewart (American home and garden guru) is mentioned (see **U1**). Mr Trick says that Sunnydale's death rate makes DC look like Mayberry (a reference to *The Andy Griffiths Show*). Seventies disco-kings KC & The Sunshine Band are name-checked and there are allusions to George Gershwin's 'Summertime' and *Single White Female*. Scott wants to take Buffy to a festival of films by silent comedy genius Buster Keaton (what a fabulous chat-up line *that* is). Angel's climactic return is a tribute to *The Terminator* with him falling from the sky, naked, in a blaze of light.

Bitch!: Buffy and Faith get their claws out (chiefly over what little the latter knows about Angel). As usual, though, neither can hold a candle to Cordy, particularly her assessment of Faith: 'Does anyone believe that's her *actual* hair colour?'

Awesome!: The pre-titles at the Happy Burger ('*now* I'm hungry') is a classic.

'You Might Remember Me From Such Films As . . .': Eliza Dushku made her film debut aged eleven in *That Night*. She played Emma in *Bye Bye Love*, Missy in *Bring It On*, Dana Tasker in *True Lies* and the title role in *Tru Calling* and was in *This Boy's Story*, *Jay and Silent Bob Strike Back* and *Soul Survivor*. K Todd Freeman was McCullers in *Grosse Point Blanke* and Muddy in *The Cider House Rules*.

Not Exactly A Haven For The Bruthas: Mr Trick notes that, admittedly, Sunnydale is strictly of the Caucasian Persuasion. 'But you just gotta stand up and salute that death rate.'

Logic, Let Me Introduce You to This Window: During the tour of Sunnydale High, Willow identifies one of the classrooms as the cafeteria. After Buffy tries to stake Kakistos the second time, she leaves the stake sticking out of his chest. When Faith drives the huge beam through Kakistos' chest, the smaller stake is gone.

Quote/Unquote: Buffy's idea of girly stuff is: 'Date and shop and hang out and go to school and save the world from unspeakable demons.'

Xander's reaction to Faith's semi-erotic Slaying tale: 'Wow, they should film that and show it every Christmas.'

Buffy's first rule of Slaying: 'Don't die.'

Notes: 'If doing violence to vampires upsets you, you're in the wrong line of work.' A great David Greenwalt script, with many fine moments (the uncoupling scene; Buffy's silent exasperation at her friends' sudden desire to be with Faith while she has to study). A subtle game played by Giles to get Buffy to confront her own demons leads to a shocking conclusion. A little gem.

Buffy doesn't believe in two things: coincidence and Leprechauns. Giles tells her the former *does* exist but, as far as he knows, the latter do not. In the final scenes Buffy is wearing a heart-shaped pendant instead of her usual crucifix. Willow says that when Giles is mad he makes a cluck-cluck sound with his tongue. Giles likes kayaking. A Watchers retreat is held in the Cotswolds each year (Giles had never been invited). In a hilarious exchange, Buffy tells Faith that Oz is a werewolf. 'It's a long story.' 'I got bit,' says Oz. 'Obviously not *that* long,' notes Buffy (see **27**, 'Phases'). Faith grew up in South Boston. She had a female Watcher (the second time a female Watcher has been alluded to; see **5**, 'Never Kill a Boy on the First Date'; **41**, 'Revelations'). Faith tells a vampire, 'My dead mother hits harder than that' (see **51**, 'Enemies'). Whatever Kakistos did to Faith's Watcher before killing her, it wasn't pleasant. Interesting Fan Theory: was Kakistos Faith's *Cruciamentum* (see **46**, 'Helpless')? A Watcher test that went wrong, causing the death of Faith's Watcher, may help to explain (almost) all of Faith's subsequent actions.

Soundtrack: 'Going To Hell' by the Brian Jonestone Massacre, 'The Background' by Third Eye Blind, and 'Cure' and 'Blue Sun' by Darling Violetta.

38
Beauty and the Beasts
(aka: All Men Are Beasts)

US Transmission Date: 20 Oct 1998
UK Transmission Date: 10 Sep 1999

Writer: Marti Noxon
Director: James Whitmore Jr
Cast: John Patrick White (Pete), Danielle Weeks (Debbie),
Phill Lewis (Mr Platt)

It's Oz's 'time of the month', but Xander sleeps during his watch and a brutal murder may mean that Oz escaped. Buffy meets her counsellor, Mr Platt, and discusses her relationship with Angel. At the morgue, Willow collects evidence that proves the victim was mauled by a savage animal. Buffy encounters someone running through the woods. To her horror, it's Angel. Confining him, Buffy is unable to tell her friends about her discovery. Buffy visits Mr Platt, ready to confess that she needs help, but finds him dead. Scott's friend Pete and his girlfriend Debbie are in a storage room. Pete transforms into a monstrous creature and strikes Debbie. Oz notices Debbie's bruised eye, but she says she walked into a door. While Buffy and Willow confront Debbie, Pete goes to the library and finds Oz ready for transformation. Insane with jealousy Pete attacks Oz. A chase follows in which Oz is tranquillised and Pete kills Debbie. He attacks Buffy but she is saved by Angel.

Dudes and Babes: Faith appears not to have been joking when telling Buffy that Slaying makes her horny. Their discussion about boys and Faith's observation about 'a good, down-low tickle' is only half-a-notch above *filthy* (cf. Buffy's handling of the phallic crystal in **46**, 'Helpless'). In an episode all about repressed male sexual aggression, it's interesting that the two most direct references to sex are both from girls. (Willow tells Xander she and Oz have done a half-monty though, tactfully, she refuses to reveal which half.) Angel appearing almost naked and Faith dancing to her Walkman in the library are highlights.

It's a Designer Label!: Willow's nasty crimson and green jumper and Scott's yellow shirt. Buffy's green top is great, but the last word goes to Willow's grey tights.

References: Willow seems to have an affinity for *Scooby-Doo, Where Are You?* We've seen her wearing a *Scooby* T-shirt in earlier episodes and now we see that she owns a *Scooby* lunchbox. Also, Jack London's *Call of the Wild*, *The Full Monty*, Monopoly, Barbie and Ken dolls, *Dr Jekyll and Mr Hyde*, *The Sound of Music*, *The English Patient* and *Manimal*. 'You shouldn't make me angry' is an allusion to *The Incredible Hulk*.

Awesome!: Willow, Xander and Cordelia in the morgue examining the first victim's body. Giles is shot in the back by one of his friends aiming for someone else *again* (see **23**, 'Ted').

'You Might Remember Me from Such Films As . . .': Phill Lewis was Steve Jessup in *City Slickers* and Dennis in *Heathers*.

Valley-Speak: Pete: 'Check out Scotty liking the manic-depressive chick.'

Xander: 'This guy is pretty barf-worthy. Can't we be elsewhere?'

Logic, Let Me Introduce You to This Window: When Oz transforms, he doesn't remove his clothes. During the transformation, there's no indication that Oz's clothes are ripping apart, but when we see Wolf-Oz, his clothes are gone. When Cordelia says, 'Now I'm gonna be stuck with serious thoughts all day,' a close-up of Xander reveals the strap of his bag is covering the right side of his collar. In the next shot, it's under his collar. Why is everybody sitting around in the library, waiting for Buffy to come in, at 5.25 p.m.?

Quote/Unquote: Mr Platt: 'Lots of people lose themselves in love, it's no shame. They write songs about it.'

Oz: 'You know that thing where you bail in the middle of an upsetting conversation? I have to do that.'

Notes: 'Pete's not like other guys, is he, Debbie?' The issue of domestic violence is dealt with in much the same way that **23**, 'Ted', did parental abuse – by avoiding and demonising it. The episode is disturbingly misanthropic (see Faith's 'all men are beasts' speech which I'm *very* uncomfortable with for all sorts of reasons, not least that the – female – writer has the same character talking about down-low tickles in the same scene). Not only that, but the way to stop male violence towards women seems, from the resolution, to be female violence back at them. Well, that's *one* solution, but it becomes even more suspect when Buffy (who, let's be honest, has taken out far more dangerous opponents than Pete) suddenly requires Angel to rescue her. There's an unpleasant, aggressive and thuggishly PC side to some of the points the episode makes. Too well written to be easily dismissed, but far too wrapped up in a handbag full of hate to be likeable.

Giles has dreams that he saved Jenny (see **29**, 'Passion'). He notes there is no record of anyone returning from the demon dimension, adding that time runs a very different course there. Buffy knows this (see **35**, 'Anne'). Sunnydale High has a marching jazz band in which Debbie and Jeff, the first victim, played.

Soundtrack: 'Teenage Hate Machine' by Marc Ferrari.

Joss Whedon's (Ironic) Comments: 'Someone mentioned that the show has developed a feminist subtext,' Joss told the *Posting Board*. 'Well, I never! I just wanted to show a quiet, obedient girl learning to attract men through cosmetics and physical weakness. (Probably a mistake to cast the off-puttingly plain Miss Gellar, in that case.) But sometimes we can't control our creations. Forgive me.'

39
Homecoming

US Transmission Date: 3 Nov 1998
UK Transmission Date: 17 Sep 1999

Writer: David Greenwalt
Director: David Greenwalt

Cast: Ian Abercrombie (Old Man), Billy Maddox (Frawley),
Joseph Daube (Hans Gruenshtahler), Jermyn Daube (Frederick Gruenshtahler),
Lee Everett (Candy Gorch), Tori McPetrie (Michelle Blake),
Jennifer Hetrick (Ms Mason), Chad Stahelski (Kulak)

While Cordelia plans her campaign for Homecoming Queen and
Buffy breaks up with Scott, Mr Trick assembles a team of
specialists to take part in Slayerfest '98 and rid himself of Buffy
and Faith. Buffy is furious that she missed the yearbook photo
session because of Cordelia's thoughtlessness and runs against her
friend for Queen, putting Xander, Willow and Oz in awkward
positions. They get Buffy and Cordelia together in a limo and tell
them to work out their problems. Unfortunately, the car is
hijacked by Trick's men and Buffy and Cordelia take refuge in a
cabin. Disposing of some of their enemies, they return to school
and defeat the rest just in time to attend the Homecoming
announcement, discovering that they have both lost. Mr Trick
arrives at City Hall, where Mayor Wilkins introduces himself.

Babes and Babes (Bring Your Own Subtext): Buffy tells Angel about
Scott ('a nice solid guy. He makes me happy'), at which point Scott
breaks up with Buffy and attends Homecoming with another girl.
Trick refers to Buffy's nubile flesh, which proves what we already
suspected: he's a vampire with *taste*. Xander notes that Buffy and
Faith are in the library getting all sweaty, which *presumably* means
they're training. Throw in Oz's reference to Buffy and Cordelia
mud wrestling and you have a slash-fiction fan's delight. In
response to an Internet question about a perceived lesbian
relationship between Slayers, Joss Whedon commented: 'I just read
the piece on Buffy and Faith . . . and by God, I think she's right! I
can't believe I never saw it! Actually, despite my facetious tone, it's
a pretty damn convincing argument. But then, I think that's part of
the attraction of the *Buffy*verse. It lends itself to polymorphously
perverse subtext. I, personally, find romance in every relationship. I
love all the characters, so I say Bring Your Own Subtext!'

The Conspiracy Starts at Home Time: We finally meet the
dirt-obsessed Mayor Wilkins. He reveals that he's aware Mr Trick
is a vampire and wants his help in eliminating a rebellious element
from Sunnydale. Wilkins says that he's been mayor for some time
and that this is an important year (see **48**, 'Bad Girls'; **49**,
'Consequences'; **51**, 'Enemies'; **53**, 'Choices' and **55/56**, 'Graduation Day').

It's a Designer Label!: Buffy's gym shorts. Willow asks Xander if he remembers an eighth grade cotillion when Xander wore a clip-on. It's worth noting that *everyone* looks great in their Homecoming clothes (Xander in a tux, Willow's long black dress, Buffy and Cordy's dresses). Watch out for Trick's crimson crushed-velvet jacket and orange tie. Candy Gorch's pink feather boa, and purple satin pants are equally desperate.

References: Oz's 'as Willow goes, so goes my nation' refers to a famous quote about General Motors. Cordelia says she's been doing the Vulcan Death-Grip since she was four. Of course, as all Trekkies know, the Vulcan Death-Grip doesn't exist. Mr Trick makes an ironic comment about American frontiersman Daniel Boone (1735–1820). Flying ace Amelia Earhart (1898–1937) and author Maya Angelou (born 1928) are name-checked alongside an allusion to English evangelist John Wesley (1703–91).

Bitch!: Faith's revenge on Scott over his break up with Buffy, telling him, in front of his date, that the doctor says the itching, swelling and burning should clear up but they have to keep using the ointment. Buffy's strategy board lists the strengths and weaknesses of her opponents. Cordelia's strengths are: 'Popular with boys', 'Makes friends easily', 'Expensive clothes' and 'Perfect teeth', while her weaknesses include 'Manipulative', 'Two-faced', 'Fake smile', 'Bad in sports', 'Superficial', 'No sense of humour' and 'Xander!' (Anyone else think the exclamation mark makes this *incredibly* mean?) Michelle's entries include (strengths): 'Nice', 'Friendly', 'Good cook' and 'Athletic'; (weaknesses): 'Bad skin', 'Wears polyester', 'PB Crazy', 'Dandruff' and 'Too much make-up'. Holly's list include (strengths): 'Debating skills', 'Straight A' and 'Sweet'; (weaknesses): 'Few friends', 'Introvert' and 'Always studying'. Cordelia's opinion of 'I laughingly use the phrase "competition"' is: 'Holly Charlston: Nice girl, brain dead, doesn't have a prayer. Michelle Blake: Open to all mankind, especially those with a letterman's jacket and a car. She could give me a run.' Once Buffy joins the race, it gets nasty.

Awesome!: One of the *great* sequences as Buffy battles the yellow-skinned demon while Cordelia hits it with a cooking spatula. 'Cor, the gun!' shouts Buffy. Cordelia picks up the gun and fires wildly. 'Cordelia,' says Buffy, in resignation, 'the spatula!' 'Homecoming' also contains fine characterisation as Willow and Xander remember old times, speculate on the future, dance and kiss. Wonderful stuff. But it's Buffy and Cordelia's episode with the scenes in the cabin, Cordy facing down Lyle Gorch and the disgusted looks on their faces at the end all highlights.

'You Might Remember Me From Such Films and TV Series As . . .': Three-time Tony-nominated German-born Harry Groener played Tam Elburn in the *Star Trek: The Next Generation* episode 'Tin Man'. He also appeared in *Amistad* and *Dance With Me*, the US version of *Dear John*, and *The West Wing*. Jack Plotnick was Edmond Kay in *Gods and Monsters* and had a recurring role as Barrett in *Ellen*. Ian Abercrombie was Justin Pitt in *Seinfeld*. Jennifer Hetrick played Jean Luc Picard's girlfriend Vash in *Star Trek: The Next Generation* and *Deep Space 9* and Walter Skinner's wife in *The X-Files*. She was also Corrine Hammond in *LA Law*.

Don't Give Up The Day Job: Chad Stahelski, in addition to being David Boreanaz's stunt double, also worked on such films as *The Matrix, 8mm* and *Alien: Resurrection.*

Logic, Let Me Introduce You to This Window: After Buffy and Faith finish their training session Faith lays the punching pads on the table. Next shot, she's still holding them. The position of the rifle in Frawley's hands as Mr Trick introduces the Slayerfest participants changes between shots.

Quote/Unquote: Mr Trick: 'We all have the desire to win. Whether we're human, vampire . . . whatever the hell you are, my brother. You got a spiny-looking head-thing, I never seen that before.'

Willow: 'I'm not a friend; I'm a rabid dog who should be shot. But there are forces at work here. Dark, incomprehensible forces.'

Cordelia: 'Listen up, needle-brain. Buffy and I have taken out four of your cronies, not to mention your girlfriend.' Lyle: 'Wife!' Cordelia: 'Whatever!'

Notes: 'You've awakened the Prom Queen within.' What an astonishing piece of work. *Buffy*-as-sitcom taking such an *obvious* idea (two friends fight over a beauty contest) and throwing in a bunch of misfit monsters for them to kill. This is what we probably all imagine American teenage life is like – if we've taken enough acid. One of two back-to-back jewels that illustrate everything that is *great* about this series.

Buffy refers to **36**, 'Dead Man's Party', saying that lots of people came to her Welcome Home party. Willow helpfully adds, 'They were killed by zombies.' Ms Moran was Buffy's favourite teacher in her class Contemporary American Heroes. Unfortunately, she doesn't remember Buffy at all. At Hemery, Buffy was Prom Princess, Fiesta Queen and was on the Cheerleading Squad (see **M1**; **3**, 'The Witch').

Soundtrack: 'Fell Into The Loneliness' by Lori Carson, 'Jodie Foster' by The Pinehurst Kids, 'How' by Lisa Loeb, 'Fire Escape' by Fastball and 'She Knows' by Four Star Mary (the song that Oz supposedly wrote for Willow).

40
Band Candy

US Transmission Date: 10 Nov 1998
UK Transmission Date: 24 Sep 1999

Writer: Jane Espenson
Director: Michael Lange
Cast: Peg Stewart (Ms Barton)

The mayor asks Mr Trick to help him collect a tribute to a demon and Trick subcontracts the sale of cursed chocolate to Ethan Rayne. Snyder makes the students sell the chocolate to raise money for the school band. Buffy sells her bars to Joyce and Giles and is surprised when Giles doesn't show up for school. She finds him at his home with Joyce, apparently working out a schedule to make it easier for Buffy to spend time with both of them. At the Bronze, Buffy and Willow notice lots of adults acting like rowdy teenagers. Buffy realises that something is wrong with the candy. At the factory, she discovers her mother and Giles making out. Inside, Buffy finds Ethan, whose job was to divert the adults from the main objective, paying tribute to the demon Lurconis who eats babies. In the sewers Buffy finds the babies, the demon and Mr Trick. While Buffy fights the vampires, Giles and Joyce move the babies out of harm's way. Buffy detaches a gas pipe and creates a blowtorch to defeat the demon.

Dreaming (As Blondie Once Said) is Free: One that we don't get to see. Buffy being chased by an improperly filled-in answer bubble screaming 'None of the above'.

Dudes and Babes: Joyce: 'So, why do they call you Ripper?' Giles: 'Wouldn't you like to know?' Oz imagines Giles was a pretty together teen. Buffy corrects him: 'Giles at 16? More "Bad-Magick-Hates-the-World-Ticking-Time-Bomb-Guy".' When Joyce gives Buffy her pair of handcuffs, Buffy orders her to '*Never* tell me.' In **52**, 'Earshot', we find out what interaction occurred between Giles and Joyce. There are more gratuitous bare-torso shots of Boreanaz and two plump miniskirted cheerleaders who walk behind Giles and Buffy in the final scene.

Authority Sucks!: Snyder says he got a commendation for being principal from the mayor, who shook his hand twice. (Knowing what we subsequently do about Wilkins, it's to be hoped that Snyder wore gloves.) But he still ends up getting the kids to clean up the graffiti off the lockers. Some things never change.

The Conspiracy Starts at Home Time: The mayor tells Mr Trick, 'I made certain deals to get where I am today,' adding, 'That's what separates me from other politicians. I keep my campaign promises.'

A Little Learning is a Dangerous Thing: Willow notes that Oz is the highest scoring person on SATs never to graduate. It's unclear whether she's talking about just Sunnydale High or the whole country. Xander is against a system that discriminates against the uninformed. Cordelia, on the other hand, is looking forward to the SATs, noting that she usually does well on standardised tests (see **42**, 'Lover's Walk'). Buffy says, 'We can study at the Bronze. A little dancing, a little cross-multiplying.'

Mom's Apple Pie: Buffy tells Joyce she's a good mom, but not the best as she won't let her daughter drive. While they eat Chinese food there is a lengthy discussion on responsibility. Once the cursed chocolate kicks in, we have something of a paradox.

Denial, Thy Names Are Joyce and Rupert: Buffy: 'At least I got to the two of you before you actually did something.' Joyce: 'Right.' Giles: 'Indeed.' (See **52**, 'Earshot'.)

It's a Designer Label!: 'Mom started borrowing my clothes. There should be an age limit on lycra pants,' notes Cordelia. One could say the same about Joyce and that miniskirt. On the plus side there's Buffy's red top and grey jogging pants, her green skirt, Willow's light-blue miniskirt and Cordy's tartan skirt. Minus points for Oz's yellow T-shirt, Willow's fluffy red jumper and orange trainers and Trick's purple shirt.

References: Cordy's dad takes copies of *Esquire* magazine and locks himself in the bathroom. Also, MTV's *The Real World*, *A Christmas Carol*, Willy Loman from Arthur Miller's play *Death of a Salesman*, TV show *Nightline*, '70s soft-rockers Seals & Crofts, *The Rocky Horror Picture Show* ('Let's do the time warp again'), Billy Joel, the sitcom *Welcome Back Kotter* (and the character Vinnie Barbarino played by John Travolta), country and western singer Juice Newton, Burt Reynolds, a paraphrase from *The Wild Ones* ('I just gotta see what you got') and Bow Wow Wow's 'I Want Candy'. 'Kiss Rocks!' refers to the American glam metal band. 'Louie Louie', a hit for the Kingsmen in 1963, is performed a-cappella by lots of old guys. 'Believe me when I say that a wrong answer *will* cost you all your points' is a general parody of game shows.

Bitch!: Giles and Joyce are at it this week: 'For God's sake, let your mum have a sodding candy bar' and 'You wanna slay stuff and I'm not allowed to do anything about it. Well, this is what I wanna do, so get off my back' respectively.

Awesome!: Buffy hitting Giles with the ball, blindfolded and her double-take when spotting her mother and Giles kissing. Top marks for the characterisation of Giles, Joyce and Snyder as teenagers with Tony Head's incredible cockney wide-boy ('Ooo, copper's got a *GUN*!') *just* outdoing Armin Shimerman's equally valid interpretation of Snyder as a cowardly nerd who desperately wants to be part of the cool kids' scene. Joyce, meanwhile, becomes what we always suspected she was: a totally uncool, over-talkative, rather sly wannabe hanging around with the coolest guy in town (note the disgusted look on Giles's face when she asks if he likes Seals & Crofts). Kristine Sutherland's view of this scene is interesting: 'I thought Joss captured it perfectly. [Giles] is ignoring me, he's completely into the music and I'm trying to figure out how to connect with him. It brought up a lot of those horribly painful adolescent feelings . . .'

Best moment: The '*YES*!' from Giles, punching the air as Buffy hits Ethan.

Don't Give Up The Day Job: Writer/Producer Jane Espenson is a sitcom veteran who has written for *Dinosaurs*, *Ellen* and *Star Trek: Deep Space 9*.

Valley-Speak: Buffy: 'Voila! Driveyness!' And: 'You guys are just wigging me out.'

Sex and Drugs and Rock'n'Roll and Cigarettes and Alcohol: Giles smokes and drinks red wine with Joyce while listening to Cream's 'Tales Of Brave Ulysses'. ('I gotta get a band together,' he says as Eric Clapton's guitar solo starts and he adds, 'listen to this bit.') 'You've got good albums,' notes Joyce (see **59**, 'The Harsh Light of Day'). LP covers glimpsed in Giles's apartment include the Who's *Face Dances*.

'Whoa, Summers. You Drive Like a Spaz!': Snyder's comments are echoed by Buffy: 'Look at that dent the size of New Brunswick. I did that.' Joyce: 'Oh my God. What was I thinking when I bought that geek machine?' Later Joyce notes, 'Buffy assures me that it happened battling evil, so I'm letting her pay for it on the instalment plan.'

Logic, Let Me Introduce You to This Window: When Buffy drives her mom's jeep, a pair of headlights can be seen behind. The car appears to be no more than a few feet away, but when Buffy makes the right turn, it's much further. When Buffy bends down to switch on the radio, you can still see the headlights through the jeep's rear window, but seconds later there's no sign of it. Although the boxes of candy say Milkbar, Giles says that Buffy convinced him to buy twenty Cocoariffic bars. Why do all of the spell-affected adults, regardless of their actual age, speak and act as though their teenage years were during the 1970s? Giles's white T-shirt has a hole in the chest in some scenes but this disappears in others. When he emerges after falling into the sewer, he seems remarkable dry and clean.

I Just *Love* Your Accent: Joyce says it must be cool being from England. Giles's reply is: 'Not particularly!'

Quote/Unquote: Giles on the SATs: 'It's a rite of passage.' Buffy: 'Is it too late to join a tribe where they just pierce something or cut something off?'

Ms Barton: 'Willow, that's a tree ... Are there any nachos in here, little tree?'

Mr Trick: 'That's the reason I love this country. You make a good product and the people will come to you. Of course, a lot of them are gonna die, but that's the *other* reason I love this country.'

Giles on Buffy's interrogation technique: 'You're *my* Slayer. Go knock his teeth down his throat.' And, to Snyder: 'You filthy little *ponce*. Are you afraid of a little demon?'

Notes: 'And *don't* do that.' It was going to take a work of *genius* to better **39**, 'Homecoming'. Here then, ladies and gentlemen, is 'Band Candy', a work of *genius*. Again, the central idea is not new – adults acting like children, to the chagrin of the *real* children. But there's a cleverness to the presentation here that charms the viewer while they are rolling on the floor laughing. *Still* one of my favourite episodes.

Buffy says Giles is allergic to being late. Cordelia refers to her life before Xander as BX. Snyder claims to have taken Tae Kwon Do at the Y. Scott Hope is mentioned by Angel (Buffy hasn't told him that she and Scott have broken up; see **39**, 'Homecoming').

Soundtrack: Aside from the Cream classic, 'Blasé' by Mad Cow, 'Violent' by Four Star Mary and 'Slip Jimmy' by Every Bit of Nothing.

Did You Know?: In Mike Hodges' 1987 film *A Prayer For The Dying*, Tony Head plays a cockney thug named Rupert. For his legion of female fans, it's a movie worth checking out as he removes most of his kit in the course of it.

Jane Espenson's Comments: Asked on the *Posting Board* how scripts are assigned, Jane noted: 'Usually it kind of rotates. Whoever has had the longest break writes the next one. But if one person pitched a specific idea, they usually get to write it (like "Band Candy"). Or if a specific story calls for a specific kind of writing strength – Marti [Noxon] tends to get the big love relationship stories. And then sometimes a writer's personal schedule will dictate which episodes they're available for . . .' Jane continues to cite 'Band Candy' as her favourite episode ('It was the first, and my original idea').

41
Revelations

US Transmission Date: 17 Nov 1998
UK Transmission Date: 1 Oct 1999

Writer: Douglas Petrie
Director: James A Contner
Cast: Serena Scott Thomas (Gwendolyn Post), Kate Rodger (Paramedic)

Faith's new Watcher, Gwendolyn Post (Mrs), sets the group a task, the recovery of the Glove of Myhnegon. Gwendolyn has little respect for Giles and his frustration grows as he is unable to find any information on the demon Lagos, also searching for the glove. Xander sees Angel and follows him back to the mansion where he observes Buffy and Angel kissing. Buffy is quizzed by her friends, Giles feeling that she has let him down. Faith finds an angry Xander at the Bronze and decides to kill Angel. Giles tells Gwendolyn he has recovered the Glove and she smashes a statue over his head. Xander alerts Buffy to Faith's intentions. Arriving at the mansion, Faith sees her new Watcher wrestling with Angel for the Glove and she attacks him but is stopped by Buffy. Gwendolyn puts on the Glove and gains the ability to fire lightning. Buffy severs the glove from Gwendolyn, leaving Faith feeling betrayed.

Dudes and Babes: Gwendolyn is a typically Hitchcock-style villainess. Faith refers to Buffy's liaison with Angel, asking what it was like boinking the undead (see **25**, 'Surprise'). Faith lists some of her ex-boyfriends as Ronnie (deadbeat), Steve (klepto) and Kenny (drunk). Her motto now is 'get some, get gone' (see **47**, 'The Zeppo'; **48**, 'Bad Girls').

A Little Learning is a Dangerous Thing: Books that Giles's library *doesn't* possess include Hulme's *Paranormal Encyclopaedia* and *The Labyrinth Maps of Malta* (which *is* on order). Giles *does* have a copy of Sir Robert Kane's *Twilight Compendium*.

It's a Designer Label!: Oz's gold-lamé waistcoat is rather rock'n'roll. So is Buffy's pink Bronze dress, though her bomb ski-cap isn't. Faith's crimson leathers appear again.

References: *Mary Poppins*, *Marathon Man*.

Bitch!: Gwendolyn: 'Faith, a word of advice. You're an idiot.'

Awesome!: An exercise in synchronised Slaying; about 10 minutes is taken up with one fight or another including Faith and Angel battling and the Buffy/Faith fight. Plus the effects as Gwendolyn is killed. Best bit: the series of facial expressions Willow gives as Buffy fights the demon.

'You May Remember Me From Such Films As . . .': Serena Scott Thomas was James Bond's doctor in *The World is Not Enough*, appeared in *Let Him Have It* and played the title role in *Diana: Her True Story*.

The Drugs Don't Work: Cold Turkey is a euphemism for heroin withdrawal and is used as a general term for quitting any form of addiction.

Don't Give Up The Day Job: Doug Petrie wrote the 1996 movie *Harriet The Spy* and episodes of *Clarissa Explains It All*.

Logic, Let Me Introduce You to This Window: While a frustrated Giles instructs Xander to find information on Lagos, Willow stands on the upper level of the library. As Xander ascends the stairs, Willow is some distance from where she was in the previous shot. In the scene at Willow's locker, she hoists her backpack on to her right shoulder, then starts to close the locker door with her right hand. In the reverse-angle shot, Willow's right hand is on her shoulder strap while she closes the locker with her left. Why is Faith's motel door unlocked in the last scene when Buffy enters?

I Just *Love* Your Accent: Giles gets flustered when Gwendolyn arrives. (Buffy asks, 'Interesting lady. Can I kill her?') Gwendolyn says there's talk within the Council that Giles has become too American. 'Him?' asks Buffy. Gwendolyn notes that she's completely knackered training with Faith, who refers to her as Mary Poppins. Gwen also uses lots of supposedly British expressions like 'everything's gone to Hell in a hand basket' and shares Giles's obsession with tea. Xander believes Giles needs a surgeon to remove the British flag from his butt.

Notes: 'Keeping secrets is a lot of work.' A case of 'after the Lord Mayor's Show'. There's little *wrong* with 'Revelations'; indeed, it's a Tasmanian Devil of an episode, a whirlwind of manic violence. Perhaps it's only subtlety that's missing, although the final scenes and Faith's growing cynicism at the world signal the way her character would subsequently develop.

Giles indicates that a Watcher may have more than one Slayer, which contradicts what we thought we knew about the Watcher/Slayer relationship (see **21/22**, 'What's My Line?'). There are 12 cemeteries in Sunnydale. Xander notes Buffy has been killing zombies and torching sewer monsters, references to **36**, 'Dead Man's Party', and **40**, 'Band Candy', respectively. Gwendolyn was sacked by the Watcher's Council for misuse of Dark Power.

Soundtrack: 'Run' is the Four Star Mary song that Dingoes Ate My Baby mime to. Also, 'West Of Here' by Lotion and 'Silver Dollar' by Lolly.

True Faith: 'The [script] said "Faith dancing wildly; a mix between Biker Chick and Trailer Trash",' Eliza Dushku told *Science Fiction World*. 'It's totally kinky, but fun, to play the animal instinct and get paid and have it called work.'

42
Lover's Walk

US Transmission Date: 24 Nov 1998
UK Transmission Date: 7 Oct 1999

Writer: David Vebber
Director: David Semel
Cast: Marc Burnham (Lenny), Suzanne Krull (Clerk)

Spike returns to Sunnydale after splitting with Drusilla. Desperate to win her back he kidnaps Willow and Xander and threatens to kill them unless Willow performs a love spell. Buffy arrives home to find Spike telling his sob-story to her mom, while a horrified Angel is unable to enter. They reluctantly agree to help him get what he needs and then get out of Sunnydale. Realising that their situation seems hopeless, Xander and Willow kiss, unaware that Oz and Cordelia have just arrived to rescue them. As Cordelia runs upstairs, she falls and is impaled on a steel rod. Spike, Buffy and Angel fight a group of vampires. Spike is reawakened by the battle and decides to win Drusilla back by good old-fashioned torture. Cordelia survives but won't forgive Xander's betrayal.

Dudes and Babes: Spike's arrival mirrors the opening scene of **15**, 'School Hard' (his car crashing into the WELCOME TO SUNNYDALE sign). Everyone has a bad time relationship-wise in this episode but it's hard not to feel for poor Xander. That final scene with Cordy is heartbreaking.

The Conspiracy Starts at Home Time: The mayor, practising his putting, says he would sell his soul for a decent short game before adding that it's a bit late for that now. He was aware of Spike's activities last year (and approved) but says this year is different and agrees with his deputy's suggestion to ask Mr Trick to send a welcome committee.

A Little Learning is a Dangerous Thing: Willow's SAT score for English verbal of 740 (which she is disappointed with) is more than all of Xander's scores added up. (The maximum score in one subject is 800.) Buffy's combined score, 1430, surprises everyone, including herself. Cordelia also seems to have done well (as she predicted she would in **40**, 'Band Candy').

Mom's Apple Pie: Spike's talk with Joyce over a cup of hot chocolate is hilarious (he asks if she has any little marshmallows). She suggests that Buffy belongs at a good college with keg parties and boys, not on the Hellmouths with vampires. So, replace Slaying with alcohol and sex? Interesting . . .

It's a Designer Label!: Horrible stuff first: Willow's red pants and stripy miniskirt, Xander's purple shirt. Buffy's green vest-type T-shirt and tight training pants make up for these. Willow's fluffy pink sweater appears (see **50**, 'Doppelgängland').

References: The title is an Elvis Costello song. Also, Cletus the Slack-Jawed Yokel (from *The Simpsons*), *The Exorcist* and *Scanners* ('Her head span around and exploded') and *Weird Science*. The book Angel's reading is *La Nausée* by French existentialist Jean-Paul Sartre (1905–80).

Bitch!: Spike on Drusilla after she gave him the we-can-still-be-friends nonsense: 'She didn't even care enough to cut off my head, or set me on fire. Is that too much to ask? Some little sign that she cared.'
   Buffy to Spike: 'I violently dislike you.'

Awesome!: Spike at the Magic Box, asking for a leprosy curse to make Angel's parts fall off. The brilliant action-sequence of Buffy, Angel and Spike taking on dozens of vampires. The excellently-timed funeral sight-gag.

Cigarettes and Alcohol: Spike spends half the episode wasted on Jack Daniels.

Logic, Let Me Introduce You to This Window: While Spike holds the broken bottle to Willow's face, the position of her hair changes from shot to shot. Something similar happens to Spike's shirt when he's pinned to the kitchen table by Buffy and Angel. Why did Joyce leave the back door unlocked? With all her concerns over her daughter's occupation (particularly after the events of **29**, 'Passion', and **36**, 'Dead Man's Party') one would think she'd be more protective of the sanctity of her home.

I Just *Love* Your Accent: With Spike around the insults get rather football-terrace, telling Buffy to 'shut your gob' and referring to Angel as a 'great *pouf*' (see **85**, 'Fool for Love').

Quote/Unquote: Spike on Buffy and Angel: 'You'll be in love till it kills you both. You'll fight and you'll shag and you'll hate each other till it makes you quake, but you'll never be friends. Love isn't brains, children, it's blood. Blood screaming inside you to work its will. I may be love's bitch, but at least I'm man enough to admit it.'

Notes: 'Love's a funny thing.' Yet another confident, articulate, amusing vehicle for a production at the very peak of its creativity. Little happens, but it's a pivotal reaffirming link to the past while pointing a way forward. It's *great* to see Spike back (his scenes with Joyce are a joy) and he's, by far, the most level-headed character in the episode. Simply gorgeous.

Xander wanted to be a fireman in sixth grade (see **81**, 'The Replacement'). Cordelia has pictures of Xander and herself (and some group shots, which were taken on the pier) inside her locker. Oz can smell Willow when she's nearby (Cordy speculates it's some residual werewolf thing; see **75**, 'New Moon Rising'). Spike says he used to bring Dru rats in bed along with the morning paper. After leaving Sunnydale, they went to Brazil but she never forgave him for his pact with Buffy. She flirted frequently, including a tryst with a Chaos Demon (who Spike describes as 'all slime and antlers', see **85**, 'Fool for Love'). The US broadcast was followed by an advert for the phone service 1-800-Collect featuring Sarah Michelle Gellar and David Boreanaz – in character – with a prize of a walk-on part in an upcoming *Buffy* episode (see **54**, 'The Prom').

Soundtrack: The version of 'My Way' heard at the end is *not* by Sid Vicious, but rather is a sound-alike cover by Gary Oldman from the soundtrack of *Sid and Nancy*.

Critique: *Shivers* reviewer Ian Atkins was fulsome in his praise: 'You would have to be undead if you did not think "Lover's Walk" was a classic episode of *Buffy*, and a beautiful piece of television too. After "Homecoming" and "Band Candy", it's good to see that the show does not need to rely on laughs for an episode to work ... The main reason is because the episode presents a situation most viewers have been in: of love going wrong when reality breaks through the violins and roses. Pretence and denial can only go so far. It's almost painful to watch ... The sad final montage of broken hearted, lost souls is remarkably powerful and needs no words.'

The Comic: In another continuity-knitting exercise, April 1999 saw Dark Horse's one-shot comic *Spike and Dru: Paint the Town Red*, co-written by James Marsters and Christopher Golden, which takes place between **34**, 'Becoming' Part 2 and **42**, 'Lover's Walk', with the couple living in Turkey.

43
The Wish

US Transmission Date: 8 Dec 1998
UK Transmission Date: 8 Oct 1999

Writer: Marti Noxon
Director: David Greenwalt
Cast: Nicole Bilderback (Cordette #1), Nathan Anderson (John Lee),
Mariah O'Brien (Nancy), Gary Imhoff (Teacher), Robert Covarrubias (Caretaker)

When new girl Anya asks Cordelia if she wishes things were different, Cordy wishes that Buffy had never come to Sunnydale. In the blink of an eye, Cordy finds herself in the world she wished for: a terrifying grey place of tiny classes, horrible clothes and rampant vampire activity; a world where Xander and Willow are still together, even in death; where the Master lives and is about to unleash the ultimate terror on mankind. Giles and his White Hats try to fight forces against which their weapons are useless, in a world made by Cordelia's wish. Buffy arrives but she dies at the hands of the Master just as Giles smashes Anyanka's amulet and puts the world to rights.

It's a Wonderful What?!: Lots of shows have done 'what if?' scenarios, *Moonlighting*'s 'It's a Wonderful Job' being a good example. The dark versions of the regulars may have been suggested by the Mirror Universe in *Star Trek*. (The characterisation of Evil-Willow owes much to the mirror-Major Kira in *Deep Space 9*.)

Dudes and Babes: Willow in leather, licking Angel. *Oh yes!*

It's a Designer Label!: Cordelia has a Prada bag, which Anya recognises (Cordy says most people in Sunnydale can't tell the difference between Prada and Payless – a discount shoe chain). She asks if Anya's amulet is a Gucci. There's a reference to *W* ('the fashion magazine for the discerning woman').

References: Buffy calls Giles Jeeves, referring to the butler in PG Wodehouse's Bertie Wooster novels. 'What's done is done' is from *Macbeth*, while there are allusions to Smokey Robinson and the Miracles' 'Tears Of A Clown', Sam and Dave's 'Soul Man', Aldous Huxley's *Brave New World*, *Superman* comics ('Bizarroland') and *Star Trek*.

Bitch!: Harmony suggests that Cordy date Jonathan: 'He won't cheat on you. At least for a week.'

Awesome!: The sequence in which Willow and Xander kill Cordelia (while Giles can only watch) is one of the most disturbing in the series, while the slow-motion deaths of Xander, Willow and Buffy are extraordinary.

Surprise!: The end of act one, Anya revealed as a demon. 'Done!'

'You May Remember me From Such TV Series As ...': Emma Caulfield played Lorraine Miller in *General Hospital* and Susan Keats in *Beverly Hills 90210*.

Valley-Speak: Xander: 'Slap my hand, soul man.'

Logic, Let Me Introduce You to This Window: The last cut that Cordelia makes to Xander's photograph is around chin level. However, when we see it burning the photo includes Xander's chest.

Quote/Unquote: Cordelia: 'Buffy changes it. It was better, I mean the clothes alone. The people were happy. Mostly.'
   Buffy: 'This is a "get in my pants thing"? You guys in Sunnydale talk like I'm the Second Coming.'
   Anya: 'How do you know the other world is any better than this?' Giles: 'Because it *has* to be.'

Those Prosthetics?: Alyson Hannigan confirmed: 'They're quite comfortable ... They're squishy. It was fun to be evil for a week, but if you had to do it week in and week out your face would fall off with all that glue.'

Notes: 'We fight. We die. Wishing doesn't change that.' Fanfiction-in-the-area. Such an *obvious* idea, so well done. The characterisation of the alternative-universe regulars is magnificent with Tony Head's anguished, out-of-his-league Giles just topping Sarah Michelle's portrayal of a scarred Buffy who has never experienced Giles's influence and, as a result, is hardened and cynical (like Faith), living only for Slaying. Plus the little things like the cloves of garlic on the school lockers to remind us that we've wandered into another world. And Willow in leather, mustn't forget *that*.

There are references to Cordelia being bitten by a snake in **31**, 'I Only Have Eyes for You', Angel having previously seen Buffy in 1996 (**33**, 'Becoming' Part 1) and Amy (see **3**, 'The Witch'; **28**, 'Bewitched, Bothered and Bewildered'; **45**, 'Gingerbread'). In the world in which Buffy never came to Sunnydale, Willow and Xander were turned into vampires and the Harvest happened. Giles runs a motley band of vampire hunters called White Hats (who include Oz and Larry). He speaks to Buffy's Watcher (is it Merrick?) who tells him that she is currently in Cleveland. Giles refers to Sunnydale as '*a* Hellmouth', which indicates there is more than one (see **144**, 'Chosen'). Nancy notes that vampires are attracted by bright colours.

Soundtrack: 'Tired Of Being Alone' by the Spies, 'Dedicated To Pain' by Plastic and 'Never Noticed' by Gingersol.

Critique: According to *SFX*, 'The Wish' was 'Another chance for the main cast to play against type ... It's a sign of a series that is supremely confident in its writers and actors, that they feel they can do this. The final scene is comic genius, with Cordelia making increasingly nasty wishes and Anya desperately but impotently trying to grant them.'

44
Amends (aka: A Buffy Christmas)

US Transmission Date: 15 Dec 1998
UK Transmission Date: 14 Oct 1999

Writer: Joss Whedon
Director: Joss Whedon
Cast: Shane Barach (Daniel), Edward Edwards (Male Ghost),
Cornelia Hayes O'Herlihy (Margaret), Mark Kriski (Weatherman),
Tom Michael Bailey (Tree Seller Guy)

Christmas is coming, but for Angel (reliving, in his dreams, his past massacres) it isn't a time of festive cheer. Angel visits Giles for help but is distracted by the ghost of Jenny Calendar. Buffy confides in Giles that she shared Angel's dream. Jenny tells Angel that he is losing his soul again and killing Buffy is the only act that will bring him peace. Giles links these manifestations to the Harbingers, a group of priests who can summon the First Evil. Angel contemplates suicide but is saved by a combination of Buffy's persuasion and a freak snowstorm.

Dreaming (As Blondie Once Said) is Free: Buffy's line about making guest spots in Angel's dreams may be a reference to the, then-planned, *Angel* spin-off. His dreams contain an interesting balance of historical fact (the murders of Daniel and Margaret), surrealist nightmares (Buffy appearing at the Victorian dinner party) and erotic stimulation of the moist variety (*that* night with Buffy – see **25**, 'Surprise').

Dudes and Babes: Nice hair and moustache combination in the 1838 sequences but Boreanaz's Irish accent is still woefully naff (see **33**, 'Becoming' Part 1). Margaret's description of Angel, before Darla got to him, is of a drunken, whoring layabout who was a disappointment to his parents and whose only success in life was to die before he got syphilis.

Mom's Apple Pie: Christmas in the Summers household seems nice and relaxed, despite Buffy suggesting that Joyce is 'still number one with the guilt-trip'.

Denial, Thy Name is Joyce: Watch Joyce's reaction to Buffy's suggestion that they invite Giles around to Christmas dinner.

It's a Designer Label!: Xander's trampy red sweatshirt is a definite black mark, but on the plus side we have Buffy's blue shirt and white overcoat, Willow's slinky red dress and Faith's extremely short miniskirt.

References: A cheesy version of 'Joy To The World' is heard when Buffy and Joyce visit the tree farm. Also, David Bowie's 'Scary Monsters (And Super Creeps)'. Giles quotes the Crystals' 'He's A Rebel'.

Bitch!: Cordy will spend Christmas skiing in Aspen, she gleefully tells her friends.

Awesome!: Two great sequences – Giles inviting Angel into his home at the point of a crossbow and Oz and Willow deciding *not* to have sex.

'You Might Remember Me From Such Films and TV Series As . . .': Cornelia Hayes O'Herlihy played the teenage Princess Margaret in *Gods and Monsters*. Before moving to America, she appeared in episodes of *Newman and Baddiel in Pieces*.

Don't Give Up The Day Job: Although Mark Kriski often plays news reporters (he's in *Speed*, for instance) he's a *real* weatherman for KTLA Morning News in Los Angeles.

Valley-Speak: Buffy: 'These are the guys working the mojo on Angel?'

Logic, Let Me Introduce You to This Window: The snowdrift seems to be the quickest in meteorological history. (Is it supposed to be magical and/or at the intervention of some higher power? If so, then we're getting frighteningly close to *Quantum Leap* territory. See **Joss Whedon's Comments**.)

I Just *Love* Your Accent: Buffy reads an ancient text about a child being born of a man and a goat, who had two heads the first of which shall speak only in riddles. 'No wonder you like this stuff,' she tells Giles, 'it's like reading *The Sun*.'

Quote/Unquote: Xander: 'That's the Christmas spirit.' Willow: 'Hello? Still Jewish. Hanukkah spirit, I believe that was.'

The First: 'I'm not a demon, little girl, I'm something you can't even conceive . . . I am the thing the darkness fears.'

Notes: 'I think we're losing him.' Redemption is the theme of this variant on *A Christmas Carol*. In places the ideas are far better than the execution. As with **35**, 'Anne', this deals with potentially massive subjects that then get pushed into the background. This is, theoretically, the most dangerous enemy that Buffy has ever encountered, but there's no real ending (however, see season seven). The good stuff on offer is mostly in the way of character-isation.

Angel says vampires aren't big on Christmas. Is it the commer-cialisation they object to, or just the Christianity? Xander always sleeps outdoors on Christmas Eve (he says it's so that he can look at the stars and feel the nature vibe, though, in reality, Cordelia reveals it's so he can avoid his family's drunken fights). What drink is chilling in the ice bucket on Willow's coffee table? It looks like a 2-litre bottle of either Sprite or 7-Up. Two (seemingly fictitious) films are playing at the Sunnydale cinema. *Abilene* (rated PG), and one that begins *Pray For* . . . The books Giles gives

Xander and Buffy for research purposes are *The Black Chronicles* and *The Diary of Lucius Temple*.

Joss Whedon's Comments: 'The snow was not evil! The snow was "hope",' Joss told the *Posting Board*. 'Was it a cheap *Deus Ex Machina*? Well, obviously I don't think so or I would avoid the question . . . I know some people here thought it was corny, but I didn't just pull it out of a hat. The whole episode was leading to that, it was the point, not just a way to end it . . . Was it God? Well, I'm an atheist, but it's hard to ignore the idea of a "Christmas miracle" here (though *Pray* on the marquee was a coincidence). The Christian mythos has a powerful fascination to me and it bleeds into my storytelling. Redemption, hope, purpose, Santa, these all are important to me, whether I believe in an afterlife or some universal structure or not. I certainly don't mind a strictly Christian interpretation being placed on this episode by those who believe – I just hope it's not limited to that.'

Soundtrack: Willow's attempt to seduce Oz is accompanied by 'Can't Get Enough Of Your Love, Babe' by the Walrus of Lurv himself, Barry White.

45
Gingerbread

US Transmission Date: 12 Jan 1999
UK Transmission Date: 15 Oct 1999

Teleplay Jane Espenson
Story: Thalia St John, Jane Espenson
Director: James Whitmore Jr
Cast: Jordan Baker (Sheila Rosenberg), Lindsay Taylor (Little Girl),
Shawn Pyfrom (Little Boy), Blake Swendson (Michael), Grant Garrison (Roy),
Roger Morrissey (Demon), Daniel Tamm (MOOster)

The discovery of two children's bodies by Joyce has a profound effect on Sunnydale. Apparently the work of occultists, it leads to a witch-hunt within the town. Willow, Amy and even Buffy are targeted while Giles's books are confiscated, leaving him to rely on the Internet. Oz sends a message to Willow, who discovers that these children have been repeatedly murdered every 50 years back to their origins in the Hansel and Gretel fairytale. Buffy, Willow and Amy are tied to stakes in City Hall to be burned. Giles and

Cordelia stop the ceremony and reveal the children to be a demon, which Buffy impales with the stake she is tied to.

Authority Sucks!: Snyder's glee at being given the power to search the lockers: 'This is a glorious day for Principals everywhere. No pathetic whining about students' rights. Just a long row of lockers and a man with a key.'

Mom's Milk of Human Bigotry: Joyce's bonding-visit to see what Buffy does (complete with thermos flask and sandwiches) goes disastrously wrong and she finds herself in her worst nightmare. She says that for too long she's been too afraid to speak out and that silence is the town's disease. Her setting up of Mothers Opposed to the Occult turns Sunnydale into Salem. Oh well, we all make mistakes.

Denial, Thy Names Are Joyce and Rupert: The awkwardness between them is really funny ('It's been a while', 'Not since . . . A while').

Denial, Thy Name is Sheila Rosenberg: Willow's mom is an academic, the co-author of a recent paper on *The Rise of Mysticism Among Adolescents*. The implication (of not noticing her daughter's five-month-old haircut and the last long chat they had being about a children's TV show) is that she and Willow don't talk much. She believes Willow's claim to be a witch is delusional and a cry for discipline, though she subsequently concludes that she's been rather closed-minded. Willow later tells Buffy that her mother is doing 'that selective memory-thing your mom used to be so good at'. Sheila *does* remember that Willow is dating a musician and Oz must attend the Rosenbergs for dinner.

It's a Designer Label!: Buffy's blue frock coat and pink jumper. Cordelia says her hairspray is imported and costs $45.

References: *My Friend Flicka,* the pre-school TV show *Mr Roger's Neighbourhood* and the puppet King Friday and *Apocalypse Now* ('I love the smell of desperate librarian in the morning') are referenced, along with the Salem witch trials. Xander says, 'Oh man, it's Nazi Germany and I've got *Playboy*s in my locker,' and refers to *Jack and the Beanstalk*. The writer of the article Willow finds is Howard Fine, the name of two of the Three Stooges.

Bitch!: Giles refers to Snyder as 'that twisted little homunculus'.

Awesome!: The shocking pre-title sequence (Joyce's horrified cry of 'It's Mr Sanderson from the bank' would be comical in other circumstances). The Giles, Xander, Oz and Buffy scenes in the library; an example of a minimalist setting helping with the development of a storyline. Oz and Xander's incompetent attempts to save Buffy and Willow.

It's *That* Idea Again: Willow's mother calls Buffy 'Bunny' (see U1).

Don't Give Up The Day Job: Co-writer Thalia St John would subsequently write for the WB's other great fantasy show of the era, *Roswell*. Grant Garrison worked as a carpenter and art labourer on films such as *Dreammaster: The Erotic Invader* and *Cyberella: Forbidden Passions*. Roger Morrisey started his career as a dolly grip on films such as *Access Denied* and *Silent Lies* before acting in *Dizzyland* and *Tale of the Mummy*.

Valley-Speak: Buffy on her mother: 'She's completely wigging.'

Logic, Let Me Introduce You to This Window: During the locker search, a cop is looking through a coin purse behind Snyder. Some time later he's still looking through the same purse (maybe Snyder was right about how stupid the Sunnydale police are). For the final scene, we first see an establishing shot revealing that it's nighttime. However, the rest of the scene appears to take place in daylight. Where did those pictures of Hans and Greta Strauss come from? It's strange that the residents of Sunnydale are holding a witch burning *indoors*. A more politically correct name for Joyce's group would be *Parents* Opposed to the Occult, but that would have made the acronym even more unfortunate.

I Just *Love* Your Accent: Giles believes the murders may be the work of European wiccan covens.

Quote/Unquote: Joyce: 'Good, honey! Kill him!'
Buffy: 'We need those books.' Giles: 'Believe me, I tried to tell that to the nice man with the big gun.'
Snyder: 'Just how is *Blood Rites and Sacrifices* appropriate material for a public school library? Chess Club branching out?' (As with a lot of questions asked in this episode, you've got to wonder why somebody hasn't asked it before.)
Buffy, on MOO: 'Who came up with that lame name?' Snyder: 'That would be the founder. I believe you call her "Mom".'
Willow: 'I'm a witch. I can make pencils float. And I can summon the four elements. OK two, but four soon. And I'm

dating a musician . . . I worship Beelzebub. I do his biddings. Do you see any goats around? No, because I sacrificed them . . . Prince of Night, I summon you. Come fill me with your black, naughty evil.'

Buffy: 'I'm like that kid in the story, the boy that stuck his finger in the duck.' Angel: 'Dyke. It's another word for dam.' Buffy: 'OK, that story makes a lot more sense now.'

Notes: 'How many of us have lost someone who just disappeared? Or got skinned?' There's a *lot* of anger in this episode. The *probable* targets were those people who use sudden violent incidents to pursue an agenda of censorship. How ironic it was that just months afterwards those same people would be out in force again, with *Buffy* on their hitlist (it was really disturbing watching this episode mere days after the Littleton High School massacre with news programmes full of similarly hysterical reactions from people in search of *anyone* to blame). The anger in witch-hunt stories is often blind, but I'll give any episode that rages against being judgmental in such a refreshingly honest manner ten out of ten for effort. And, astonishingly, considering the subject matter, 'Gingerbread' is also, in places, *really* funny.

Slayers are not supposed to kill people (see **23**, 'Ted'; **48**, 'Bad Girls'), though Buffy's horrified 'someone with a *soul* did this?' suggests breaking that rule is on her mind. It's Buffy's birthday next week (see **46**, 'Helpless'). Cordelia asks Giles how many times he's been knocked unconscious. As with Buffy constantly allowing herself to get distracted by diversionary tactics he does, indeed, seem to fall for that one rather a lot (see **39**, 'Homecoming'). He has the ability to pick locks with a hairpin (Cordelia notes, 'You really *were* the little youthful offender, weren't you?' see **36**, 'Dead Man's Party'; **40**, 'Band Candy'). Amy performs the same spell as she did on Buffy in **28**, 'Bewitched, Bothered and Bewildered', with similar results, turning *herself* into a rat. On the net, Giles somehow finds his way into the 'Frisky Watchers Chat Room'.

Should The Bible Be Banned?: Buffy tells her mother that maybe next time that the world is getting sucked into Hell, she won't be able to stop it because the anti-Hell-sucking book isn't on the Approved Reading List.

It was inevitable that this episode would happen sooner or later. The Christian Right in America never quite knew what to make of *Buffy* – the plethora of wiccan elements was an immediate cause for concern, but essentially the series concerned teenage-good-fighting-evil so they couldn't complain on that score without dragging *The Hardy Boys* and *Nancy Drew* into the equation and, despite never quite knowing if it took place in a Christian universe or not, *Buffy* seemed to achieve moral acceptability. That was until the magic 's' word (sex) started cropping up. When Buffy slept with Angel in **25**, 'Surprise', it was open target practice on the series for anybody with access to the Old Testament and a computer and the Net was swamped with warning articles emanating from the Bible Belt (real 'Watch *Buffy the Vampire Slayer* and be damned for eternity' nonsense). Whether 'Gingerbread' was a reaction to this – albeit brief – wave of hysteria is unknown (certainly the episode has, subsequently, been used by fans to rub in the face of any religious objector). Interestingly, however, there is little criticism of religion in either the series in general or 'Gingerbread' itself (that would be commercial suicide in a TV industry still dominated by advertising and network nervousness of offending *anyone*). Instead, what 'Gingerbread' *does* question, vocally and angrily, is a more disturbing saga. In America, many school and public libraries ban certain books. The website *http://www.cs.cmu.edu/People/spok/most-banned.html* lists the 50 most commonly suppressed, including works by William Shakespeare, John Steinbeck, JD Salinger, Mark Twain, Roald Dahl, Maya Angelou, William Golding, Kurt Vonnegut, Alice Walker and Margaret Atwood. It's sad that a nation which promotes freedom of speech, has within it elements that seek to limit this on their own people. (Joyce's line 'MOO just wants to weed out the offensive material' seems chillingly realistic.) Readers can find more information at *http://www.ala.org/bbooks/* the American Library Association's webpage.

Pagan Man Wasn't *Just* an Aftershave: Recognised by both the Home Office and the Church of England as a bona-fide religion, Paganism involves a wide body of beliefs, including wicca, druidry and shamanism, which have their roots in the world's pre-Christian nature religions. The Pagan Federation was set up in 1971 to help counter misconceptions about Satanism and the like. It is estimated that today there are over 50,000 Pagans in the UK alone. Federation spokesperson Andy Norfolk was quoted in *Alternative Metro* as saying that TV programmes such as *Buffy* and *Charmed* has greatly helped to increase the profile of Paganism: 'Stories of young women who use magic to battle bad guys could be seen as positive role models.'

Jane Espenson's Comments: Jane explained 'Gingerbread's creation on the *Posting Board*: 'Thalia St John and I never met. She pitched the "parent's group, witch-burning" idea a long time ago. I pitched a "book burning" idea. Joss meshed 'em, I added *Hansel and Gretel* and someone arranged the shared "story by" credit. I did talk with Thalia on the phone after the episode had aired.' In another interview with the *Raven's Realm* website, Jane explained, in detail, her interaction with the cast: 'I have the opportunity to see the actors every day. This morning I had a long talk with Tony Head. So far I really haven't had actors pitching story ideas at me. I think they know that has to go through Joss.'

46
Helpless

US Transmission Date: 19 Jan 1999
UK Transmission Date: 21 Oct 1999

Writer: David Fury
Director: James A Contner
Cast: Jeff Kober (Zackary Kralik), Dominic Keating (Blair),
David Hayon-Jones (Hobson), Nick Cornish (Guy),
Don Dowe (Construction Worker)

As her 18th birthday approaches, Buffy suffers dizzy spells and weakness, suggesting that she's losing her powers. In reality she is being drugged by Giles as part of *Cruciamentum*, a ritual that Slayers undergo to prove their resourcefulness. The weakened Slayer must survive an encounter with a vampire, in Buffy's case the insane Zackary Kralik. All does not go according to the plans of Chief Watcher Quentin Travers, Kralik escaping and abducting Joyce. Giles tells Buffy the truth, to her disgust. Buffy goes in search of Kralik, despite her lack of strength. She cleverly manipulates Kralik into drinking holy water. Travers commends Buffy on successfully passing the test. However, since Giles demonstrated a relationship with Buffy that the Council deems too close, he is relieved of his Watcher duties.

Dudes and Babes: There's an extremely gratuitous shot of Boreanaz's rippling biceps. If that had been one of the girls, everybody would be crying 'exploitation'.

Authority Sucks!: Quentin's treatment of Giles. This is the first hint that the Watcher's Council is a subdivision of a small fascist dictatorship (see **90**, 'Checkpoint').

A Little Learning is a Dangerous Thing: Cordelia has a paper to research on Bosnia.

Mom's For Dinner: Kralik killed and ate his own mother, something he takes great delight in telling Joyce.

It's a Designer Label!: Buffy's All Saints-style combat pants. Another triumph for Willow: a pair of suitably horrible hats (a red tea-cosy-bobble one and a yellow abomination), a nasty yellow jumper and pink miniskirt.

References: 1988 Olympic figure skating champion and *South Park*-icon Brian Boitano, Bizet's opera *Carmen*, and *Superman*. Angel's present for Buffy is *Sonnets from the Portuguese* by Elizabeth Barrett Browning (see **3**, 'The Witch') inscribed 'Always'.

Bitch!: Cordelia tells one potential suitor that he shouldn't take her flirting seriously as she is on the rebound from Xander.

Awesome!: Buffy and Angel working out, Kralik's death sequence and Xander and Oz's discussion on what sort of kryptonite is deadly to Superman (Oz is right – green is deadly, red mutates and gold drains power).

The Drugs Don't Work: The pills that Kralik so desperately needs get both Blair and Kralik himself killed.

'You Might Remember Me From Such Films, TV Series and Adverts As . . .': Jeff Kober played Bear in the *X-Files* episode 'Ice', was Dodger in *China Beach* and Booga in *Tank Girl* and appeared in *Coyote Moon* and *CSI*. Readers may recognise him as Ray, the voice of Reef Radio in those annoying Bacardi adverts. Harris Yulin is a character actor par-excellence, appearing in *Bean*, *Clear and Present Danger*, *Scarface*, *24* and *Ghostbusters II*. In one of those coincidences that only seem to crop up in the crazy world of unauthorised TV books, on the day that I viewed this episode, I stopped the video and playing on TV at that moment was an episode of *Ironside* featuring a much younger Mr Yulin. Dominic Keating plays Malcolm Reed in *Enterprise*.

Valley-Speak: Buffy, to Quentin: 'Bite me!'

Cordelia: 'First of all, *posse*? *Passé!* Second of all, anyone with a teaspoon of brains knows not to take my flirting seriously.'

Logic, Let Me Introduce You to This Window: The last knife that Buffy throws in the library breaks a glass object. However, whenever the camera focuses on the target, there's nothing made of glass nearby. Were Hobson and Blair's deaths part of Quentin's plan from the beginning? Kralik can be photographed (see **M1**) despite a camera using mirrors as part of its focusing mechanism (see **11**, 'Out of Mind, Out of Sight'; **21**, 'What's My Line?' Part 1; *Angel*: 'Are You Now or Have You Ever Been?'). Buffy says she and her dad go to the Ice Show every year for her birthday, but there was no mention of this last year during **25**, 'Surprise'. Buffy seems to push the bookcase on to Blair rather easily considering how weak she is. She must have switched Kralik's water with the holy water amazingly quickly.

I Just *Love* Your Accent: Exactly where is Quentin from? He certainly doesn't sound English. Giles says he doesn't give a rat's arse about the council's orders, and refers to the *Cruciamentum* as a dozen-century-old archaic exercise in cruelty.

Quote/Unquote: Angel on Buffy's heart: 'I could see that you held it before you for everyone to see and I worried that it would be bruised or torn. More than anything in my life, I wanted to keep it safe, to warm it with my own.' Buffy: 'That's beautiful. Or, taken literally, incredibly gross.'

Buffy: 'Hummers. Big turn-off. I like guys who can remember the lyrics.'

Notes: 'I don't *know* you.' A story that manages to rise above voyeurism just long enough to become a hymn to the power of intelligence over superstition. Betrayal is the key theme in a modern *Red Ridinghood*-variant that relies on an old fan-fiction standby, setting a character up to be hurt, so that they can then be comforted. An important piece of the developing story-arc, but 'Helpless' is hard work at times, and difficult to enjoy.

Willow went to see *Snoopy on Ice* when she was small (her father took her backstage and she got so scared she threw up on Woodstock.) Faith is on one of her unannounced walkabouts. There are numerous continuity references, including Giles saying Buffy may have a flu bug (see **30**, 'Killed By Death'), Angel telling Buffy he saw her before she became the Slayer (see **33**, 'Becoming' Part 1), references to the parties in **25**, 'Surprise', and **36**, 'Dead

The Complete Slayer

Man's Party', Buffy's love of skating (**25**, 'Surprise'), 'Mr Pointy' the stake from **33**, 'Becoming' Part 1, and Buffy's birthday present last year being a severed arm in a box. There is no evidence that Blair fed on Kralik to become a vampire (Kralik's dialogue with both Blair and Buffy suggests that the process has more to do with the quantity of blood the vampire takes rather than on cross-feeding as stated in **1**, 'Welcome to the Hellmouth'; see **33**, 'Becoming' Part 1; **56**, 'Graduation Day' Part 2). Blair also rises remarkably quickly and seems very focused for someone who has undergone such a radical change (see Angel's observation in **14**, 'Some Assembly Required', about how confusing it all is for a vampire at first). Quentin says the Slayer must undergo *Cruciamentum* '*If* she reaches her 18th birthday', which suggests that most Slayers are called before that age (Buffy herself was 15, see **67**, 'Doomed'). However, as both Kendra and Faith seem to prove, older girls *have* been called. This also suggests that the calling is not, necessarily, in any fixed order and that had Buffy not died in **12**, 'Prophecy Girl', and lived for several years thereafter, Kendra may not have automatically been the next Slayer.

Electra on Azalea Path: What's going on in the Buffy/Giles relationship? Quentin says Giles has a father's love for Buffy and the implication from Buffy's (unsubtle) attempt to get Giles to take her to the Ice Show in her dad's place indicates her (possibly subconscious) need for a father-substitute. She spends a lot of time trying to get Giles and Joyce together, only to be *horrified* when they *do* (see **40**, 'Band Candy'; **52**, 'Earshot'). Poet Sylvia Plath (1932–63) was a great exponent of Electra (the female equivalent of Oedipus Complex proposed by Freud, based on the Greek myth of Agamemnon's daughter). In such poems as 'Full Fathom Five', 'Electra on Azalea Path' and 'Daddy' she explored her own relationship with her father, and her search for a replacement figure in her life.

Who Watches the Watchers?: 'Joss and I had similar-but-differing backstories,' Tony Head has recalled. 'Joss had an idea of who the Watchers were and what their place in the world is. I had a slightly different picture which informed me better . . . Joss's vibe was that like some villages in England are famous for their cheese, there's a village in Cheshire or something that is famous for its Watchers!'

47
The Zeppo

US Transmission Date: 26 Jan 1999
UK Transmission Date: 22 Oct 1999

Writer: Dan Vebber
Director: James Whitmore Jr
Cast: Channon Roe (Jack O'Toole), Michael Cudlitz (Bob),
Darin Heames (Parker), Scott Torrence (Dickie), Whitney Dylan (Lysette),
Vaughn Armstrong (Cop)

Combining their talents, Giles, Willow, Faith and Buffy defeat the Sisterhood of Jhe. Xander, however, can only watch. Stung by Cordelia's jibes that he is a passenger in a team of superheroes, Xander attempts to find his own speciality and borrows his uncle's car, but succeeds only in coming to the attention of local psychopath Jack O'Toole. O'Toole, however, needs a wheels-man in his quest to resurrect three dead friends. This leads Xander into one of the strangest nights of his life. One during which he will lose his virginity and prove to himself that he's the equal of his friends. Unfortunately, they're too busy with the End of the World to notice.

Dreaming (As Blondie Once Said) is Free: Every nightmare Willow's had – that doesn't involve academic failure or public nudity – concerns the Hellmouth creature seen in **12**, 'Prophecy Girl'. Indeed, she once dreamed it attacked her while she was late for a test *and* naked.

Dudes and Babes: Lysette, the girl Xander takes out to the Bronze, seems to prove the old theory that it's a guy's car that impresses the ladies. The ridiculousness of his liaison with Faith is emphasised when he's pushed out of her room semi-clothed, with his pants in his hands and an inane grin on his face. Yeah, we've *all* had those sorts of nights . . .

It's a Designer Label!: What is up with Buffy's hair – it looks like a perm's gone wrong somewhere. Xander's pink jumper takes few prisoners.

References: *Superman*'s pal Jimmy Olsen is mentioned twice. Also, fast-food chain Taco Bell, the Beastie Boy's *Hello Nasty* and Michael Jackson's 'Wanna Be Startin' Something'. Bob's overriding concern after eight months dead is '*Walker, Texas Ranger*.

You been taping 'em?' The title, as alluded to by Cordelia, refers to Herbert Zeppo Marx (1901–79), the fourth Marx Brother and the one that everyone forgets alongside his illustrious siblings Groucho, Chico and Harpo. (Does this make Cordy herself Gummo, the fifth – even *more* obscure – member?)

Bitch!: Cordelia to Xander: 'Of all the humiliations you've had that I've witnessed, that was the latest.' And: ' "Cool." Look it up. It's something that a subliterate that's repeated twelfth grade three times has and you don't.'

Xander tells Cordy: 'Feel free to die of a wasting disease in the next twenty seconds.'

Awesome!: The Xander/Oz/essence of cool scene. Plus the sequence in the boiler room with some of Xander's dialogue seemingly inspired by *Dirty Harry*.

'You Might Remember Me From Such Films As . . .': Channon Roe played Surfer in *Boogie Nights*.

Don't Give Up The Day Job: Michael Cudlitz worked as construction coordinator on *American History X* and *Beverly Hills 90210*, a series he also acted in.

Valley-Speak: Faith: 'These babes were wicked rowdy.' (Wicked is an all-purpose New England slang adjective cementing Faith's Boston background; see **55**, 'Graduation Day' Part 1.)

Logic, Let Me Introduce You to This Window: The cafeteria scene begins with a shot of the lunch counter. The camera rises and we see Xander in the background along with Buffy and Willow, Oz is nowhere to be seen and Xander is wearing completely different clothes from the rest of this scene. (This is footage from **31**, 'I Only Have Eyes For You'. The episode also features that stock-shot from **5**, 'Never Kill a Boy on the First Date', with Owen.) Jack couldn't raise his dead friends earlier because, he says, he had to wait eight months for the stars to align. But he, himself, died three weeks ago and yet his grandpappy (presumably) raised him the same night. Throughout the scene in the boiler room, the bomb can be heard beeping as the seconds tick by. But the digital countdown jumps from 10 up to 13, then to 7 and takes many more than six beeps to reach 2, at which point Jack finally disarms the bomb.

Motors: Xander's green 1957 Chevrolet Bel Air.

Quote/Unquote: Willow: 'Occasionally, I'm callous and strange.'

Xander, on his car: 'It's my thing.' Buffy: 'Is this a penis metaphor?'

Cordelia: 'It must be really hard when all your friends have like superpowers. Slayer, werewolf, witches, vampires ... You must feel like Jimmy Olsen.'

Jack brandishes a knife: 'Are you scared?' Xander: 'Would that make you happy?'

Notes: 'Did I mention I'm having a very strange night?' I'm a sucker for Xander-led episodes and, as with **28**, 'Bewitched, Bothered and Bewildered', and **32**, 'Go Fish', the decision to use Nick Brendon's comic talents is an inspired one. 'The Zeppo' was *hated* by many online *Buffy* fans who completely missed the point and demanded to know why we kept cutting back to Xander and his trivial chase through the school when the fate of the world was at stake. I love the way everything keeps happening just out of Xander's reach and we see things for once through his eyes. (For instance, when Buffy and Angel kiss, the dialogue seems trite and melodramatic; are we seeing real events or Xander's over-the-top version of it?) True heroism isn't always about saving the world, sometimes it's about facing up to your own fears, as this episode demonstrates – showing that Alexander Harris is every bit the hero that his friends are. Great music too.

Giles says most of his sources have dried up since he was relieved of his duties by the Council. He tries to contact the Spirit Guides who live outside of time and have knowledge of the future, but he is unable to. Giles is always the one who asks for jellied donuts in the mix during research sessions and is horrified when Buffy eats the last one (*top* bit of snitching by Willow on Buffy). Xander asks Oz if learning the guitar is hard (Oz replies, 'Not the way I play', see **22**, 'What's My Line?' Part 2), which proves that Xander's dream in **4**, 'Teacher's Pet' *was* fantasy and the guitar we see in his bedroom *is* just for show. He reveals some musical talent, having played the flugelhorn in eighth grade. Xander tells Jack he is *not* retarded. 'I had to take that test when I was seven. A little slow in some stuff, mostly math and spatial relations, but certainly not challenged.' He mentions his Uncle Rory again (see **20**, 'The Dark Age').

Soundtrack: 'G-Song' by Supergrass and 'Easy' by Tricky Woo. The acoustic guitar riff played as Xander walks away from Cordelia at the end sounds like the opening chords of Oasis's 'Talk Tonight'. But it isn't.

Critique: In *Shivers*, Ian Atkins observed: 'That "The Zeppo" is an immensely clever episode can be seen by just how few fans originally got the joke: the story polarised opinion into hate it and love it and yet it's hard to understand the former: the story of Buffy and friends' experience is little more than a retread of **12**, "Prophecy Girl", with a bigger budget. What the viewer gets instead is a brave and playful experiment in the mechanics of point of view, and it's just as exciting, witty and dramatic as any of the surrounding stories . . . "The Zeppo" isn't just a comedy episode. But you've got to get the joke to see that.'

48
Bad Girls

US Transmission Date: 9 Feb 1999
UK Transmission Date: 28 Oct 1999

Writer: Douglas Petrie
Director: Michael Lange
Cast: Christian Clemenson (Balthazar), Alex Skuby (Vincent),
Wendy Clifford (Mrs Taggert)

While hunting the vampire sect El Eliminati, Buffy and Faith become reckless, despite Angel's warning that the demon Balthazar is not as dead as newly arrived Watcher, Wesley, believes. In need of weaponry, the Slayers break into a hunting equipment shop, but their shoplifting spree is cut short by their arrest. Though they escape, Buffy recognises the dangerous game she's playing and that the time she is spending with Faith has upset Willow and Xander. When Giles and Wesley are captured by Balthazar's vampires, Buffy helps them before she can deal with the consequences of Faith's most irresponsible act of all – the staking of the deputy mayor. Mayor Wilkins performs a ritual in his office and becomes invincible. Buffy visits Faith's motel to discuss their crime but is disturbed by Faith's lack of guilt.

Dudes and Babes: In the opening scene, Faith is astonished that Buffy and Xander have never . . . You know. ('Not even *once*?') Buffy says they are just friends, to which Faith replies, 'What else are friends for?' Faith is very descriptive about her need for sex ('A little after-hours [grunt]') and about how sweaty Slaying makes her (see **37**, 'Faith, Hope and Trick'; **38**, 'Beauty and the Beasts'). Xander's eye twitches whenever Buffy mentions Faith.

The Conspiracy Starts at Home Time: The strands of innuendo that have been building all season start to come together. The mayor, who again hints at a non-human longevity, says that it will be 100 days to his ascension during which time nothing can harm him (not even getting his head sliced in half). After this process earthly affairs will not concern him, as he will be on a higher plane. Balthazar seems to know what is coming, telling Buffy and her friends, 'When *He* rises, you'll wish I'd killed you all.'

A Little Learning is a Dangerous Thing: Having been accepted for early admission to university, Willow is being wooed by both Harvard and Yale (see **50** 'Doppelgängland'). She says Chemistry is a lot like witchcraft, only with less newt. Xander, meanwhile, is hoping to get into either appliance repair or motel management post-school, though he has yet to hear from the Hot-Dog Emporium.

Mom's Waffles: Joyce is on a diet, though she seems to be seeking an excuse to have some waffles. When Buffy says she doesn't want any, Joyce notes that they only don't have calories if she's making them for Buffy.

It's a Designer Label!: Is that underwear Faith is washing in her sink at the end? Why does Willow's jumper look like the Swiss national flag?

References: Wesley's middle name is a tribute to the king of British science fiction, John Wyndham (1903–69), author of *The Day of the Triffids*, *The Midwich Cuckoos*, *The Kraken Wakes* and *Random Quest*. There's a lengthy discussion on comic strips, *Family Circus* (by Bill Keane, a rather twee story of family life), *Marmaduke* (by Brad Anderson, about a trouble-making Great Dane) and *Cathy* (by Cathy Guisewite, concerning the trials of a single woman). Also *Sesame Street, Magnum Force*, Kipling's *Captains Courageous* and Hot Chocolate's 'Every One's A Winner'. Balthazar looks a lot like the vampire archivist Pearl in *Blade*.

Bitch!: Judging by a horrible comment Cordy makes to Xander, his father seems to have recently become unemployed (see **54**, 'The Prom'). Mind you, his suggestion that she start modelling her own line of hooker-wear is almost as bad.

Awesome!: Buffy and Faith shaking their funky stuff in the Bronze. Balthazar is the most disgusting villain we've had in a while, with the scariest face this side of Keith Richards. His scenes with Giles and Wesley ('Stay calm, Mr Giles', 'Thank God you're here, I was planning to panic') are funny, though the action sequence that follows seems to go on *forever*.

'You May Remember Me From Such Pop Videos, Films and TV Series As . . .': Alexis Denisof can be seen in the video for George Harrison's 'Got My Mind Set On You'. He subsequently played Richard Sharpe's love-rival, Johnny Rossendale, in *Sharpe* and appeared in *Rogue Trader*, *First Knight*, *True Blue* and the Reeves/Mortimer remake of *Randall and Hopkirk (Deceased)*. Christian Clemenson has a blink-and-you'll-miss-him part in *Armageddon* and more substantial roles in *Apollo 13* (as Dr Chuck), *The Big Lebowski*, *The Fisher King*, *Broadcast News* and *Hannah and Her Sisters*.

Valley-Speak: Faith, on dead vampires: 'They're toast.'
  Willow: 'I can *totally* handle myself.'

Not Exactly a Haven For the Bruthas: Mr Trick thinks El Eliminati should use Uzis instead of swords.

Cigarettes and Soft Drinks: The mayor and Mr Trick are about to share a root beer at the end.

Logic, Let Me Introduce You to This Window: When Buffy breaks into the display case, the dagger falls and she catches it between her index and middle fingers. In the next shot it's between her thumb and index finger. Why didn't Buffy bandage her wound before going to the Bronze with Faith? When telling Wesley about the three vampires she and Faith killed, Buffy says, 'One of them had swords. I don't think he was with the other two.' All three of the vampires were dressed in the same Eliminati uniform, so why would she think they weren't together?

I Just *Love* Your Accent: *Two* British Watchers. (Love the bit where Giles and Wesley simultaneously clean their spectacles). Giles uses the *very* British insult twerp to Wesley. The new Watcher's three most important words ('Preparation, preparation, preparation') could be a reference to Tony Blair's speech during the 1997 election campaign when he said that the three most important things in Britain were education, education, education.

The song that Faith and Buffy dance to is 'Chinese Burn' by British indie-band Curve.

Quote/Unquote: Buffy: 'Whenever Giles sends me on a mission, he always says "Please". And afterwards I get a cookie.'

Wesley says that El Eliminati were a 15th-century duellist cult whose numbers dwindled after, among other things, 'A lot of pointless duelling.'

Notes: 'Want. Take. Have.' An up-and-down trip. 'Bad Girls' has lots of good ideas that aren't followed up in the next episode so, sadly, it's a case of guilt-by-association. The introduction of Wesley allows Giles to get into the action more, which has both positive and negative aspects (attempting to turn him into Bruce-Willis-in-Tweed is a definite negative, as his OTT stunts in the warehouse prove). However, Alexis Denisof's performance is genuinely funny. It was amusing to see Internet fans getting annoyed at how 'irritating' Wesley was. That's the whole *point*, kids, he's *supposed* to be. Sadly, another inclusion in the growing family of characters means that Oz, Cordelia and Xander hardly appear.

There are continuity references to **41**, 'Revelations', and Gwendolyn Post and an oblique reference to Xander and Faith's liaison in **47**, 'The Zeppo'. Giles's first entry in the *Watcher Diary* noted that Buffy was wilful and insolent and that her abuse of the English language was such that he understood only every other sentence. Wesley says he has faced two vampires himself, under controlled conditions (was this, perhaps, a Watcher equivalent of *Cruciamentum*? See *Angel*: 'Spin the Bottle'). There seem to be girl-gangs in Sunnydale. Just how stupid *are* the police in Sunnydale? (See **33**, 'Becoming' Part 1.) The complete mayoral 'Things to Do' checklist is: 'meet scouts', 'Lumber Union reschedule', 'call temp agency', 'become invincible', 'meeting with PTA', 'haircut'. Mrs Haggard is the Chemistry teacher.

Alexis Sold: Although born in the US, Alexis Denisof had done most of his work in Britain and, seemingly, had an old friend to thank for the part of Wesley. 'They were looking for somebody "who thinks he's Pierce Brosnan but is actually George Lazenby",' Tony Head told Paul Simpson and Ruth Thomas. Head suggested Alexis, with whom he had worked in a 1993 theatre production of *Rope* in Chichester. 'He played one of the guys who did the murder and was fantastic, as indeed they've found on *Angel*.'

49
Consequences

US Transmission Date: 16 Feb 1999
UK Transmission Date: 4 Nov 1999

Writer: Marti Noxon
Director: Michael Gershman
Cast: Patricia Place (Woman)

The deputy mayor's murder is discovered. Buffy tries to convince
Faith to confess without success, but they break into his office and
spot the mayor and Mr Trick together. Buffy is concerned by
Faith's lack of conscience, though Faith says Slaying puts them
above the law. Buffy confesses to Willow, who advises that she see
Giles. When she gets to the library, she finds Faith has told Giles
that Buffy was responsible. Giles assures Buffy that he's aware of
Faith's lies and they ask Angel to help Faith face up to the horror
of what she has done. Unfortunately, Wesley overhears the
conversation and he and his men subdue Angel and capture Faith.
She escapes and seems to have gone rogue, but Buffy finds her at
the docks and Faith saves Buffy from an attack by Mr Trick,
whom she kills. However, the mayor gets a visit from Faith at his
office, asking for a job.

Dreaming (As Blondie Once Said) is Free: Buffy's nightmare has
her drowning, with Finch holding on to her foot. When she
struggles to the surface, Faith pushes her back under.

Dudes and Babes: Faith and Xander are (but for Angel's intervention) at it again, only with more strangulation involved. Presumably, this is the sequence that got the TV-14 rating. Faith and
Angel's use of the term 'safety words' suggests a knowledge of the
BDSM community (see **140**, 'Dirty Girls').

A Little Learning is a Dangerous Thing: Cordelia checks out books
from the library by Sigmund Freud (see **23**, 'Ted') and Carl Gustav
Jung (1875–1961) for her psychology class.

Mom's Apple Pie: The pained expression on Joyce's face when
Buffy arrives home to find a policeman waiting for her speaks
volumes. Joyce cuts a lonely figure watching TV alone in the early
hours of the morning.

Denial, Thy Name is Faith: Faith attempts to shift the blame for the murder on to Buffy (Giles notes that Faith may be good at a lot of things, but lying isn't one of them).

It's a Designer Label!: Faith's leather strides, previously seen, plus a pair of incredibly tight jeans, and her Motor City Baby T-shirt. Also, Buffy's pink overcoat.

References: Obliquely, *Star Trek: The Next Generation*. Also, MasterCard, The Troggs' 'Wild Thing', England's most underrated band the Kinks, Carolyn Crawford's Motown classic 'My Smile Is Just A Frown Turned Upside Down' and 'Zip A Dee Doo Dah' from *Song of the South*. 'We *are* The Law' alludes to *Judge Dredd*.

Bitch!: When Buffy says Cordelia is a friend, Cordy replies: 'Let's not exaggerate.'

Awesome!: Xander confessing that he slept with Faith to Giles, Buffy and Willow and their different reactions to it.

Surprise!: Faith turning up at the mayor's office at the end.

Don't Give Up The Day Job: A genuine TV news reporter, Amy Powell has also appeared in similar roles in *White Man's Burden* and *The Bird Cage*.

Valley-Speak: Faith: 'You'd *dig* that, wouldn't you? To get up in front of all your geek pals and go on record about how I made you my boy-toy for the night.'

Logic, Let Me Introduce You to This Window: The day after Finch's murder (see **48**, 'Bad Girls'), Buffy went to Faith's motel (in daylight and a clean outfit). 'Consequences' begins with Buffy waking up from a nightmare; then she goes to school. This means it's at least two days since the murder. But the detective questioning the witness at the scene of the crime says: 'You heard the man scream at about what time last night?' (Finch didn't scream.) Later, Buffy tells Faith: 'Less than twenty-four hours ago, you killed a man,' when it's closer to 48. When Angel watches the police at the crime scene, blood can be seen smeared down the dumpster where Finch was killed. However, in **48**, 'Bad Girls', Faith didn't stab Finch until he had already slumped to the ground. Is Detective Stein the only officer in the police department making house calls on a regular basis? (Or, more to the point, is he part of the ongoing police conspiracy?) How does Wesley know where Angel lives? The calendar in Giles's office is for April 1997.

I Just *Love* Your Accent: The Watcher's Council is referred to by Wesley as 'The Watcher's Council of Britain'. Is it just this author or did anyone else feel really sorry for Wesley when he's left alone in the library after Buffy's caustic put-down?

Quote/Unquote: Mr Trick's death-line: 'Oh no, this is no good at all.'

Notes: 'We're warriors, we're built to kill.' A really awful episode that attempts to look at what creates human weakness, but fudges it completely. Even the best bits of 'Consequences' feature heavy-handed moralising and bad characterisation that would be unacceptable from a series novice let alone one of its most accomplished writers. Top-heavy with a claustrophobic atmosphere that stifles creativity, 'Consequences' squats in a hole, afraid to actually *say* anything worthwhile.

Giles says this isn't the first time a Slayer has killed a human ('It's tragic, but accidents happen'). The Council, however, take a dim view of such events, suggesting that Faith will be locked up for a long time. (That would have been self-defeating if this was their approach to previous cases. Locking up your only Slayer.) Wesley speaks to Quentin on the telephone. Angel's entrance into Faith's room isn't the first time we've seen this phenomenon (in **26**, 'Innocence', Angel was able to enter Uncle Enyos's hotel room without an invitation). Presumably motels are public domain (see **30**, 'Killed By Death'). There's a reference to the Scooby Gang's confrontation with Buffy over her keeping Angel's return a secret in **41**, 'Revelations'. Michael is mentioned; he and Willow are still trying to 'de-rat' Amy (see **45**, 'Gingerbread').

Soundtrack: 'Wish We Never Met' by Kathleen Wilhoite.

50
Doppelgängland

US Transmission Date: 23 Feb 1999
UK Transmission Date: 5 Nov 1999

Writer: Joss Whedon
Director: Joss Whedon
Cast: Michael Nagy (Alfonse), Norma Michaels (Older Woman),
Corey Michael Blake (Waiter), Jennifer Nicole (Body-Double Willow)

Desperate to end her time as a mortal, Anyanka begs D'Hoffryn to create a temporal fold that would allow her to retrieve her amulet. He refuses, so she seeks Willow's help. The spell is broken before the necklace is returned, but it does have one unexpected side-effect: the calling into this dimension of the vampire Willow from the world created by Cordelia's wish. After various confusing meetings in which her friends believe that Willow has become a vampire, the truth is discovered. Evil-Willow convinces some vampires to work for her and restore chaos to Sunnydale and Anya promises to help in the hope of getting her necklace back. But their plans are defeated by Willow, who pretends to be her evil-self in a game of double-bluff.

Dreaming (As Blondie Once Said) is Free: Evil-Willow wakes up in a pink cardigan: 'Oh no, this is like a *nightmare*.'

Dudes and Babes: There are numerous references to sex (even more than **43**, 'The Wish'; 'Doppelgängland' is *full* of lesbian overtones). The mayor considers Faith's fleabag hotel has a very unsavoury reputation: 'There are immoral liaisons going on there.' Faith notes: 'Yeah, plus all the screwin'.' When Evil-Willow finds Xander in the Bronze, they embrace, much to Xander's discomfort: 'This is verging on *naughty touching* here. Don't want to fall back on bad habits. Hands! Hands in new places!' When Evil-Willow is discovered, a conversation ensues on how she is *exactly* like Willow except, as Buffy says: 'Your not being a dominatrix. As far as we know.' Willow replies: 'Oh, right. Me and Oz play Mistress of Pain every night.' Which leads Xander to ask: 'Did anyone else just go to a scary visual place?' Willow finds her other self 'So evil and skanky. And I think I'm kind of gay.' Buffy tells her to remember that a vampire's personality has nothing to do with the person it was. Angel says, 'Well, actually . . .' Then, thankfully, he shuts up (see **75**, 'New Moon Rising').

Authority Sucks!: Snyder, as in **32**, 'Go Fish', manipulates Willow, in this case to help Percy with his history paper on Roosevelt.

A Little Learning is a Dangerous Thing: Xander gets Willow's new nickname 'Old Reliable' mixed up with the film *Old Yeller* and the geyser Old Faithful.

It's a Designer Label!: Oz's yellow El Speedo shirt is a sight for sore eyes. Or a cause of them. Willow's pink fluffy jumper puts in another appearance, as do Evil-Willow's leathers.

References: *Vanity Fair* magazine, *Bill and Ted's Excellent Adventure* ('No way', 'Yes way'), *Old Yeller*, *The Creature from the Black Lagoon*, PlayStation, *Arts & Entertainment Channel*'s *Biography*, the psychiatry of Rorschach patterns, John Wayne.

Bitch!: Cordelia finds Evil-Willow in the book cage: 'It occurs to me that we've never really had the opportunity to talk. You know, woman to woman, with you locked up . . .'

Awesome!: Willow finding Giles, Xander and Buffy in the library mourning her death ('Oh God, who died?') and their reactions to, first, seeing her and then to discovering that she's not a vampire (Xander seems to think there's something wrong with the cross he's holding). And her reaction to *their* reaction. This is closely followed by a subsequent scene as Angel tries to give them the bad news about Willow and the facial expressions of Buffy, Giles and Xander at his double-take. Xander's 'We're right there with you, buddy' sums up the whole thing. In an episode full of such gems, there's also Willow, pretending to be Evil-Willow, asking Anya and Alfonse, 'Could a human do this?' and then screaming loudly. Xander's joy that in Evil-Willow's world he's a bad-ass vampire, the special effects as Willow and Anya attempt to bring forth the amulet ('Have you tried looking behind the sofa? *In Hell*?'), Willow's discovery of her breasts, her control of a pencil (see **45**, 'Gingerbread') and Percy's apple-for-teacher bit.

'You May Remember Me From Such TV Series As . . .': Andy Umberger was in *The West Wing*, *NYPD Blue* and *Angel*. Ethan Erickson played Dane Sanders in *Jawbreaker* (alongside Julie Benz) and appears, uncredited, in *Scream 3*.

The Drugs Don't Work: Willow on Xander, Buffy and Giles acting strangely: 'You all didn't happen to do a bunch of drugs, did you?'

Valley-Speak: Willow: 'Aren't you sort of naturally buff, Buff?'

Cigarettes and Alcohol: Anya, despite being 1,120 years old, still can't get a beer in the Bronze without ID and has to settle for a coke instead.

Logic, Let Me Introduce You to This Window: When Evil-Willow throws Willow over the library counter, Willow lands on her right side when she rolls off the edge. In the following shot, Willow is on her left. The entire episode is based on a *HUGE* logic flaw: **43**,

'The Wish', created Dark Sunnydale not as an alternative dimension but to *replace* normal Sunnydale. With the destruction of the amulet, things snap back into place and version two of reality never existed. Either one Sunnydale can exist or the other, but not both. So, at the end of 'The Wish', Evil-Willow and all the other Dark Sunnydale characters never existed. How did Wesley get into the bathroom before Cordelia and Evil-Willow? He was running towards them in the hallway, but somehow got in there first and came from behind Cordelia.

I Just *Love* Your Accent: Faith sarcastically refers to Wesley as Princess Margaret.

Quote/Unquote: Anya: 'For a thousand years I wielded the power of the Wish. I brought . . . forth destruction and chaos for the pleasure of the lower beings. I was feared and worshipped across the mortal globe. And now I'm stuck at Sunnydale High. Mortal. A child. And I'm flunking math.'

A bewildered Willow as Buffy and Xander, realising she's not a vampire, hug her: 'Oxygen becoming an issue.'

Oz: 'Professional bands can play up to six, sometimes seven completely different chords.' Devon: 'That's just like fruity jazz bands.'

Evil-Willow: 'This is a dumb world. In my world, there are people in chains and we can ride them like ponies.'

Notes: 'Aren't you gonna introduce me to your . . . *Holy God*, you're Willow.' Odd, isn't it, that it's the 'funny' episodes that contain the best characterisation? 'Doppelgängland' is a superb example. It's a story about loss on several levels (Anya's lost her power, Cordelia her boyfriend and Evil-Willow her world) and also about how reality is sometimes less real than fantasy ('This world's no fun,' says Evil-Willow. 'You noticed that too?' replies Willow). This is a genuinely groundbreaking piece of work and a particular favourite of many of the *Buffy* cast and crew.

Buffy has been undertaking sessions with the Watcher's Council psychiatrist after the events of **49**, 'Consequences'. Willow wanted to be a florist. Evil-Willow remembers Oz was a White Hat in her world. Dingoes Ate My Baby had a gig in Monterey on Sunday. They don't have a roadie. Snyder refers to the swim team debacle of last year (see **32**, 'Go Fish') and notes that Willow has a letter of acceptance from every university with a stamp. The mayor tells Faith he's a family man. The movies playing at the Sunnydale cinema are an 'R' rated film, the last word of which is *Hotel*, and one which begins *The Goose Ran* . . .

Soundtrack: 'Virgin State Of Mind' by K's Choice [*], Spectator Pump's 'Priced 2 Move'.

51
Enemies

US Transmission Date: 16 Mar 1999
UK Transmission Date: 11 Nov 1999

Writer: Douglas Petrie
Director: David Grossman
Cast: Michael Manasseri (Demon), Gary Bullock (Shrouded Man)

Buffy and Faith encounter a demon who offers to sell them the Books of Ascension. Faith reports to the mayor, who orders her to retrieve the books and kill the demon. Faith and the mayor plan to banish Angel's soul and, with the aid of a mysterious Shrouded Man, succeed. Angelus and Faith plan to torture Buffy. Buffy taunts Faith, but when an angry Faith blurts out more information about the coming events Angel tells her that his Angelus role is an act. Faith escapes and is comforted by the mayor, who reminds her that when the Ascension takes place, her broken friendship with Buffy will be irrelevant.

Dudes and Babes: The movie that Buffy and Angel see is *Le Banquet D'Amelia*, which seems to be a sexy arthouse affair ('I thought it'd be about food,' notes Buffy. Angel remarks that there was some food involved). 'Check out the lust-bunny,' says Faith when she sees Angel and the episode sees the pair almost becoming entangled (it gets explicit when Faith is astride Angel and he notes, 'I should have known you'd like it on top,' before asking her to wriggle). There are also numerous bondage allusions.

The Conspiracy Starts at Home Time: The Ascension will happen on Graduation Day (see **56**, 'Graduation Day' Part 2). Faith notes that the mayor built Sunnydale for demons to feed on. Oz discovers that Mayor Wilkins is over 100 years old and Wesley guesses that he isn't human. The implication is that, far from being a recent phenomenon, demonic activity has been rife in Sunnydale for decades, hence it *is* possible to rationalise people turning a blind-eye to the town's mortality rate (see **37**, 'Faith, Hope and Trick'; **45**, 'Gingerbread'). They've never known any different (see, for example, Oz's 'it all makes sense' comments concerning vampires in **25**, 'Surprise').

A Little Learning is a Dangerous Thing: Cordelia is doing an English paper and wants Wesley's help . . . because he's English.

Mom's Apple Pie: Joyce seems to have reduced every aspect of Buffy's life into two categories: Vampire problem, and non-Vampire problem. When Angel flirts with her, we find that she's recently had highlights added to her hair.

It's a Designer Label!: Some disastrous stuff like the demon's orange shirt and Willow's sheepskin coat (see **53**, 'Choices'). Buffy's blue dress and Faith's tarty jacket are better.

References: *Reader's Digest*, the Hanna-Barbera cartoon *Super Friends*, the final words of murderer Gary Gilmore before his execution ('Let's do it'), another allusion to *Scooby Doo, Where Are You?* and to Samuel Beckett's *Waiting for Godot*. The music is reminiscent of *The Omen*.

Awesome!: Angel punching Xander ('that guy just *bugs* me'). Most of the best bits involve Giles, particularly the scene with the Shrouded Man where he informs everyone that the debt settled was over the introduction of the Shrouded Man to his wife.

Surprise!: Faith: 'What can I say? I'm the world's best actor.' Angel: 'Second best!'

Valley-Speak: Faith: 'Sure. Fine. Whatever'.

'You Might Remember Me From Such Films As . . .': Gary Bullock was in *Robocop 2* and *3* and also appeared in *Species* and *The Handmaid's Tale*.

Logic, Let Me Introduce You to This Window: When Cordelia enters the library to ask Wesley to dinner, the sound of her shoes on the floor doesn't match the action on screen. When Angel slides the mayor's letter opener across the desk, the reflection of his hand on the nameplate can be seen. After Faith runs from the mansion, we cut to a nighttime exterior shot of the school. However, the following scene – in which Giles thanks the Shrouded Man – takes place during the day (sunlight pours through the windows). Exactly how much of Buffy, Angel and Giles's scheme was preplanned and how much was improvised? For instance, did Angel know about the mayor's invincibility, or was he aiming to kill him?

I Just *Love* Your Accent: Buffy wears a Union Jack-print shirt. Xander refers to Wesley as a limey bastard.

Cruelty to Animals: The mayor knows that 'There's more than one way to skin a cat' is a factually accurate statement.

Quote/Unquote: 'Giles: 'Demons after money? Whatever happened to "The still-beating heart of a virgin"?'
     Mayor Wilkins's two words that will make all of Faith's pain go away: 'Miniature golf!' (What is it with *Buffy* villains and miniature golf? See **23**, 'Ted'.)

Notes: 'You had to tie me up to beat me. There's a word for people like you, Faith. Loser.' The story of a Slayer going rogue should have been the crowning jewel in this often brilliant season. Sadly, 'Enemies' never begins to hit the mark – the ideas are good, but the script is slow moving. There are some serious problems with the narrative viewpoint of the episode too, a lot of which makes no sense once Angel's deception is revealed (even *with* hindsight and some artistic licence). This is a long-winded one-trick story that runs out of steam well before the climax.

It's been a while since Angel went to the movies. Buffy doesn't own a kimono. Xander says he applied some pressure to Willy the Snitch (who *did* survive **47**, 'The Zeppo') for information on the demon. Xander subsequently reveals that he bribed Willy with $28. The Watcher's Council won't reimburse without a receipt. Faith's mother was a drunk who never loved her and wouldn't let her have a puppy (see **37**, 'Faith, Hope and Trick').

52
Earshot

Original Scheduled Transmission Date: 27 Apr 1999[13]
US Transmission Date: 21 Sep 1999
Australian Transmission Date: 14 Sep 1999
UK Transmission Date: 12 Nov 1999

[13] Postponed due to the Columbine school shootings. Some Internet sources list **52**, 'Earshot', as initially advertised for transmission on 13 Apr 1999 in the trade press. Confirmation of this has proved impossible.

Writer: Jane Espenson
Director: Regis B Kimble
Cast: Keram Malicki-Sanchez (Freddy), Justin Doran (Hogan),
Lauren Roman (Nancy), Wendy Worthington (Lunch Lady),
Robert Arce (Mr Beach), Molly Bryant (Ms Murray), Rick Miller (Student),
Jay Michael Ferguson (Another Student)

While battling a demon, Buffy is infected by its blood, making her telepathic. At first it seems the only drawback for the Slayer is that she knows exactly what her friends are thinking. However, as the horror of being able to read *everyone*'s thoughts threatens to overwhelm her, Buffy overhears someone in the school cafeteria planning a killing spree. Angel, Giles and Wesley battle to find a cure, while the rest of the gang try to discover who would be alienated enough to commit such an atrocity.

The Caption: 'Mindful of the tragic events last week at Columbine High School, the originally scheduled episode of *Buffy the Vampire Slayer* will air at a later date.'

Dudes and Babes: Buffy says the boys of Sunnydale are seriously disturbed. The thoughts of the lad who wants to shove her against a locker suggest that she's right.

A Little Learning is a Dangerous Thing: 'Maybe I'll take French. How hard can it be? French babies learn it!' *Othello* is used as a metaphor in the same way that *The Merchant of Venice* was in **11**, 'Out of Mind, Out of Sight'. Buffy uses her power to read both Nancy Doyle and Ms Murray's minds in English class (Ms Murray: 'Jealousy's merely the tool that Iago uses to undo Othello. But what is his motivation? What reason does Iago give for destroying his superior officer?' Buffy: 'He was passed over for promotion. Cassio was picked instead, and people were saying that Othello slept with his wife.') Xander thinks that four times five is thirty and six times five is thirty-two (see **1**, 'Welcome to the Hellmouth'; **47**, 'The Zeppo').

Mom's Apple Pie: Buffy notices that her mother seems nervous about spending any time with a telepath. Then . . . 'You had *sex* with *Giles*?' (See **40**, 'Band Candy'.)

Denial, Thy Names Are Joyce and Rupert: Which leads to . . . Buffy: 'On the hood of a police car? . . . *TWICE*!' As she later informs Giles: 'We can work out after school. If you're not too busy having *sex with my mother*!' (See **72**, 'Who Are You?'; **94**, 'The Body'.)

It's a Designer Label!: Buffy tells Giles: 'When I walked in a few minutes ago, you thought, "Look at her shoes. If a fashion magazine told her to, she'd wear cats strapped to her feet."' Willow's pussycat T-shirt and sun hat, Oz's Eater T-shirt, Xander's tasteful yellow sweater and Buffy's white miniskirt. Buffy tells Giles she has a hard time finding jeans that fit her.

References: Principal Snyder has the Bangles' 'Walk Like An Egyptian' stuck in his head. Oz misquotes Rene Descartes, while there are references to *Othello* and Pierce Brosnan. The clock tower finale shares conceptual and visual links with Hitchcock's *Vertigo*, *The X-Files* episode 'Blood' and the 1966 Charles Whitman murders. Mr Beach's history class is studying Henry VIII judging from the blackboard.

Bitch!: Giles: 'I was just filling Buffy in on my progress regarding the research of the Ascension.' Wesley: 'What took up the rest of the minute?'

Oz, on the Sunnydale cheerleaders: 'Their spelling's improved.'

Awesome!: *All* of the Scooby Gang's thought sequences are wonderful and Oz's are extremely Zen. (Xander's are the funniest, naturally, though Cordelia's are a bit disturbing – can she *really* be that shallow?) Best bit of a clever climax (full of red herrings) is Nancy's unimpressed reaction to Buffy's astounding gymnastic feat ('*I* could have done that'). *Love* the box of rat poison with RAT POISON! written on it. And Giles walking into the tree.

'You Might Remember Me From Such Films And TV series As . . .': Lauren Roman was Laura English on *All My Children*. Keram Malicki-Sanchez appeared in *American History X*.

Don't Give Up The Day Job: Director Regis Kimble began as *Buffy*'s film editor (a role he also filled on *Matlock*). On *Angel*, he designed the series' stunning title-sequence.

Valley-Speak: Student: 'Wait till I'm a software *jillionaire* and you're all flipping burgers. Who's the loser then?'

Not Exactly a Haven For the Bruthas: Nancy says race is an issue. In *Othello*.

Logic, Let Me Introduce You to This Window: If the demons are telepathic, why don't they anticipate Buffy's attack? What's all that rubbish Angel spouts about vampire's thoughts being unreadable for the same reason that their reflections can't be seen? Isn't a high-velocity rifle a bit of an ostentatious suicide weapon? Couldn't Jonathan find a handgun?

I Just *Love* Your Accent: A jealous Xander refers to Wesley's Pierce Brosney-eyes being all over Cordelia. When we hear what Wesley actually *thinks* about Cordelia, we're forced to agree. Giles calls Wesley a berk.

Quote/Unquote: Willow: 'According to Freddy's latest editorial, "The pep rally is a place for pseudo prostitutes to provoke men into a sexual frenzy which, when thwarted, results in pointless athletic competition."' Xander: 'And the downside being?'
Buffy: 'I'm suddenly gonna grow this demon part ... It could be claws, or scales ...' Willow: 'Was it a *boy* demon?'
Buffy: 'God Xander! Is that *all* you think about?'
Cordelia tries to discover if Mr Beech is the would-be murderer: 'I was just wondering, were you planning on killing a bunch of people tomorrow?'
Jonathan: 'Stop saying my name like we're friends ... You all think I'm an idiot. A *short* idiot.'

Notes: 'You read my mind.' In 'Earshot', Jane Espenson taps into something dark and nasty at the core of the American psyche. Fear. The episode is marbled with the hidden terrors at the heart of the teenage years. Each character must face their own fears in an isolated environment because no one has time to help them; they're too busy dealing with fears of their own. That's the point of Buffy's little speech at the end – like the song says, 'Everybody Hurts'. But where Espenson's study of these social misfits *really* scores is characterised by the points in the episode where she allows us to actually *see* how confused and alone everyone feels. 'Earshot' is a glorious meditation on isolation, regret, the belief that knowledge is power, paranoia and self-loathing. And, magnificently, redemption. The episode takes events like those that it (with horrible irony) predicted and gives them contextualisation – a face, rather than merely a number. That such an epic, lyrical episode fell victim to its own prophecy merely adds to its greatness. In 20 years' time there'll be *legends* about 'Earshot'.
Willow is still tutoring Percy (see **50**, 'Doppelgängland'). Giles says that Angel's charade in **51**, 'Enemies', was important in bringing Faith's treachery into the open. When Oz reads the school newspaper he goes straight to the obituaries. Angel says

he's been with dozens of bad girls like Faith but that in 243 years he's loved one person. Larry is much happier since Xander helped out him (**27**, 'Phases'). These days even his grandma is fixing him dates with guys. The demon Azareth was ritually flayed. The headlines of various issues of *Sunnydale High Sentinel* are: 'Teachers Fail Competency Exam; Dropouts Find Happiness'; 'Apathy on the Rise – No One Cares' and 'Big Game Draws Mindless Brain Dead Mob'. Freddy also writes that 'Dingoes Ate My Baby play their instruments as if they have plump Polish sausages taped to their fingers.' Oz agrees this is fair. The Sunnydale basketball team is in the divisional championships.

Despite the best intentions of all concerned, WB still managed to put their foot in it when replacing the postponed episode with, of all things, **48**, 'Bad Girls'. As the *St. Paul Pioneer Press* noted: 'Tonight's regularly scheduled new episode . . . has been pulled by the WB Network in the wake of the Littleton High-School shootings. The episode centred on Buffy's clairvoyant ability in which she read the thoughts of someone who was contemplating killing other students . . . Instead, WB airs a repeat, 'Bad Girls', in which Buffy craves a taste of the wild side and follows Faith into her reckless world. *The repeat seems about as bad as the scrapped one*' [my italics]. The first *legal* broadcast of 'Earshot' actually occurred in some regions of Australia a week before the US eventually got to see it in September 1999.

Jane Espenson's Comments: Jane fascinatingly spelled out on the *Posting Board* what happens to an average *Buffy* script: 'Joss and the whole staff work out the story for each episode together and in detail. In theory. In actuality, we all sit and pretend we're being helpful while Joss works out the story. Then the writer for that episode writes a "beat sheet", then a "full outline", based on that work in which each scene is described [as per] what Joss worked out. What the writer has added at this point is an indication of the shape of the scene – the order the information comes out in, some more specifics about what each character thinks and expresses during the scene, how it transitions into the next scenes, a few sample jokes. Joss gives the writer notes on the outline. He nixes bad things, adds good things, makes sure it's on track. Then the writer writes the first draft. It may sound like this doesn't leave much room for individual creativity, after all, the writer knows exactly what will happen in each scene, but in fact, there are many ways to write each scene and the writer has to pick the best way.

Then Joss gives notes on the first draft. These can be minor or enormously detailed, or "This scene? Make it better." It takes several days usually, for the writer to implement the changes he asks for, because it [can] require rethinking in a big way. There may be further drafts after that, time permitting. Eventually, Joss takes the script away and does his own rewrite. Again, [it can be] minor or enormous. I laugh when people say that one of us has better "plotting" than another or that Joss wouldn't have let a character say that if he'd written the episode. It *all* goes through the big guy . . . When Joss writes an episode, Joss writes an episode *himself*. It's a beautiful process of aloneness.'

Reality Bites: The reaction of some online *Buffy* fans to the postponement of 'Earshot', in light of the terrible events that took place in Colorado, says much about TV fans' occasional lack of priorities. WB's decision to delay broadcast was supported by Joss Whedon, who told the *Posting Board*: 'We're taking it out of the order. It's about how lonely everybody is . . . and how somebody just snaps.' (Whedon also noted: 'Oddly enough, when we were shooting it I thought it felt like the final High School episode. The last three are very personal, but "Earshot" sort of contains the show's *thesis statement* in a way, though I wish it could have aired in order.') Seth Green added: '[it was] the right decision to postpone . . . It would have seemed really callous and inappropriate. But the actual episode has nothing to do with school violence.' WB's main concern was one exchange: Xander: 'I'm still having problems with the fact that one of us is just gonna gun everyone down for no reason.' Cordelia: 'Yeah, because that *never* happens at American high schools?' Oz: 'It's bordering on trendy.' Plus Xander's: 'Who hasn't just idly thought about taking out the whole place with a semi-automatic?' 'I don't think I have ever been suicidal at the point that Jonathan was at in "Earshot", so I can't really say that I could relate to that emotional state,' Danny Strong told *The Watcher's Web*. 'As far as the decision to pull it, I agreed with it. I thought it would have been totally insensitive to air the episode in the same week as Columbine.' A study of the *Buffy* newsgroups following the decision showed some posters allowing their disappointment to cloud both judgement and taste. The sad fact is that 15 unfortunate people in Colorado were unable to watch 'Earshot' when it was eventually transmitted, whether they were fans or not. At the end of the day, *Buffy* is still *just* a TV series.

Demonising America

'This is not gonna be pretty. We're talking violence,
strong language, adult content.'
– 'Welcome to the Hellmouth'

Shortly after *Buffy*'s BBC debut, the media critic AA Gill wrote a hysterically overblown review of the series in *The Sunday Times*:

'This is a High School where even the plain girls are models . . . And they're all remorselessly Anglo-white. If I were writing a communication studies thesis on *Buffy* . . . I might go so far as to say the allegory of vampirism has been subtly shifted from sex to outsiders. The monsters have the look of the underclass, the leather-jacketed, dangerous drifting denizens of street corners and recreation areas, the gangs of lost youth that prey on middle-class America.'

Opinionated stuff but not without an element of truth. In Sunnydale there are not only no drug dealers but also no homeless people (Spike mentions one in **42**, 'Lover's Walk', but we never see him) and frequently no ethnic diversity – something Mr Trick spotted immediately in **37**, 'Faith, Hope and Trick'. Instead, these pariahs of society have been replaced by the forces of darkness – a new underclass of demonised nightmares. When we *do* see the underbelly of Sunnydale (the prostitute in **26**, 'Innocence', for example) it's the cosiest underbelly imaginable. This is a small town with no sleaze, no junkies and no dog shit. In any sort of real-world-type scenario, Cordelia should be doing five lines of cocaine a day, Xander would be asking serious questions about his sexuality and Buffy would be living on the street selling her body to finance her smack addiction. 'Buffy's school,' added Gill, 'is an embattled fortress of learning and the old Eisenhower American way of life, full of beautiful, rich middle-American kids. It doesn't take a huge stretch of the imagination to see that this is how a lot of Americans view their current predicament, and there's no doubt where the real power lies.'

In other words, American small-town-*gothica* in the dying days of the millennium, and America is *scared*. If you tolerate this, your children will be next. 'Pre-wedlock humping isn't the fate worse than death that keeps American mothers awake worrying about their daughters,' Gill continued, and concluded:

'It's crack and gun control and the waves of ethnic visigoths that are sucking the blood right out of the nation. It's no great stretch of the imagination to set *Buffy* in the long line of separatist white xenophobia that is a continuing riff in American films and television. In fact, she has a lot more in common with John Wayne than she does with Peter Cushing.'

In many ways this view of contemporary America is *de rigeur*. One doesn't have to be a genius to spot the link between series that use science fiction and horror as an audience grabber while simultaneously pointing the finger at politicians and the media and the paranoia of many of the people who are vocal in their admiration of such series. Some people may watch *The X-Files* for revelation. More watch it as, they believe, an act of rebellion. In the words of one of the true philosophers of the age, Bruce Willis: 'You're either part of the solution or you're part of the problem.' *Buffy* was part of the solution, even if this was sometimes *in spite* of itself. Its agenda was always specific, measurable, achievable, realistic and timebound. 'It's a very ambitious show,' said Charisma Carpenter and she was correct. Put simply, *Buffy the Vampire Slayer* may (just) have been a series about post-millennium neuroses but, unlike *First Wave*, *Dark Skies*, *Millennium*, *Brimstone* and *The X-Files*, it *knew* that. In this regard, *Buffy* was always closer to the spirit of Homer Simpson, *Friends* and *Ally McBeal* than to Mulder and Scully or the kids of its WB network neighbours *Dawson's Creek*, *Felicity* and *Popular*.

Self-awareness is not, in itself, something to shout about too loudly. Being self-aware simply means that when you're bad, you *know* you're bad. Where *Buffy* scored again, and more tellingly, was that in addition to the knowing glances it gave to viewers and critics alike it seemed to have an uncanny knack of hitting weak spots at the heart of the intellectual demonisation process of American youth culture, the era's great trio of evil – television, rock music and the Internet. All of the elements, in other words, that *Buffy* itself satirised as 'evil' in **37**, 'Faith, Hope and Trick', and **45**, 'Gingerbread'. But sometimes we must pay the price for being ahead of the game.

In April 1999, two students from Littleton High School in Denver took guns into their school cafeteria and opened fire. It wasn't the first such incident to shock America in recent years, nor was it the last (indeed, within weeks, a similar if less fatal event had taken place in Georgia). That evening on *Newsnight*, the BBC's America correspondent Gavin Esler gave a critical summation of the mood of the country when he reported that, as with previous incidents of this kind, America was in a collective state of shock but with an equally collective determination that such a thing should never, ever be allowed to happen again. However, when it came to the actual apportioning of *blame*, this consensus had quickly evaporated. Each time something like this happens, noted Esler, within hours the TV screens are filled with people with easy answers and equally easy solutions. Blame the violence on TV or the cinema. Blame the power and lack of control of the Internet. Blame satanic messages in rock music. (In the particular case of Littleton, all three were combined by a media desperate to make some *sense* out of the tragedy, though it's noticeable that the Marilyn Manson angle was quickly pushed to one side when the controversial rock star actually stood up and defended his right to freedom of speech under the first amendment of the constitution.) Sadly, noted the reporter, this deflects the argument away from the *real* causes and, after much wringing of hands, everybody quietly forgets about such events until the next one happens. As Elizabeth Wurzel wrote in *Bitch*, discussing the case of Amy Fisher, a 16-year-old schoolgirl who, in 1992, shot her lover's wife: 'Bad people and bad parenting are what made Amy bad, not rock music or the Internet.'

None of this stopped **52**, 'Earshot', from being postponed a few days after the Littleton incident. By a horrible irony, the episode concerned just such a scenario. The decision to pull the episode by WB executives *was* understandable; indeed, given the circumstances, it was probably the only thing to do. Sometimes we do the right things for the wrong reasons. Sometimes, we can't even manage that. WB's subsequent decision to also postpone the *Buffy* season finale, **56**, 'Graduation Day' Part 2, four weeks later was a knee-jerk reaction which probably did more harm than good. By initiating headline-making cancellations, one tends to draw media attention *to* such episodes that may otherwise have passed by unnoticed. When Associated Press's Ted Anthony called *Buffy* 'a vivid piece of hip TV splatterpunk, a hybrid of *Fast Times at Ridgemont High*, gothic romance and one of the video games you might think was favoured by Columbine's "Trench Coat Mafia"', at least he tempered this with an interesting observation: 'While peppered with cartoonish violence – choreographed kung-fu, blood-rites and the occasional stabbing – *Buffy* is actually pacifist in many ways.'

That *Buffy* touched a raw nerve in the American psyche with these episodes – and others – is evidenced by the very nature of the episode cancellations themselves. They were pulled because they had *predicted* events rather than reacted to them. One should, perhaps, be grateful that **52**, 'Earshot', wasn't shown a week earlier as there would be those who would have used such a coincidence to suggest that *Buffy* had actually *caused* Littleton. Appearing on CNN, Sarah Michelle Gellar was asked whether she thought the violence in *Buffy* and programmes like it was, in any way, responsible for such acts. She responded: 'Our show is broadcast in England, throughout Europe and throughout the world. And apparently only in America do we have this problem. Why?' Why indeed?

Seth Green also expressed anger at the suggestion that controversy should be avoided just for the sake of it: 'This is a topical issue,' Green told *Entertainment Weekly*. 'It's a growing problem and Colorado isn't the only place it's happened. We just don't want to think these things happen, but they happen all the time.' The actor was bothered that the shootings had *again* made violence in entertainment a target for criticism. 'Instead of focusing on the fact that guns are so easily and readily available to kids and that people aren't watching their kids carefully enough or monitoring the emotions of their students, they'd rather say, "Oh, that guy's got a Mohawk," or, "That guy's got a leather jacket on, and *Natural Born Killers* is a film I don't like, and Marilyn Manson scares me, so all that shit should be put on a funeral pyre." I think that's wrong.'

Ultimately, we need television series and films that tackle issues that concern society. Sometimes the medium genuinely *is* the message and, if only briefly, a well-written teenage horror-comedy-soap-drama can have its finger so on the pulse of a nation that it hurts. In the spring of 1999 *Buffy* for one brief moment got to the absolute heart of what currently makes America tick. What it found was *fear*.

In the preface I said that *Buffy* shares more in common with *Hamlet* than a blonde hero and death on a large scale. Shakespeare, too, was writing his stories at a time of great change and his audiences were presented with plays that dealt with things that they could recognise in their own lives. In *Hamlet* [Act III, Scene II], the Prince tells the First Player that the purpose of drama is: 'To hold, as t'were, the mirror up to nature.'

Sometimes we need that mirror *very badly*.

53
Choices

US Transmission Date: 4 May 1999
UK Transmission Date: 18 Nov 1999

Writer: David Fury
Director: James A Contner
Cast: Keith Brunsmann (Vamp Lackey), Jimmie F Skaggs (Courier),
Michael Schoenfield (Security Guard #1), Seth Coltan (Security Guard #),
Jason Reed (Vamp Guard), Brett Moses (Student)

The final preparations for the mayor's Ascension are underway but the last piece of the jigsaw, the Box of Gavrok, comes to the attention of Buffy and her friends. An attempt to capture the Box from the mayor's office succeeds, but Willow is taken hostage by Faith and a swap is arranged in the school cafeteria. Snyder unwittingly interferes and the Box is briefly opened, revealing its deadly contents. Meanwhile, Buffy and Willow have some choices to make about where they will go to college and Cordelia faces an uncertain future.

Authority Sucks!: Wesley gives a little Masonic-type crossed-fingers sign when he starts his by-the-power-invested-in-me-by-the-Council bit.

The Conspiracy Starts at Home Time: The mayor receives the Box of Gavrok from Central America. It contains 50 billion of the spider-crab creatures. He finally meets Buffy (although they were in the same room in **45**, 'Gingerbread', and almost met in the sewers in **40**, 'Band Candy').

A Little Learning is a Dangerous Thing: Buffy has received acceptances from Northwestern University in Illinois and UC Sunnydale. Willow, inevitably, has the pick of every school in the country (Harvard, Yale and MIT are mentioned) and four or five in Europe (including Oxford). Cordelia's include USC, Colorado State and Columbia.

Mom's Apple Pie: Joyce's pride in Buffy's university acceptances is touching.

Denial, Thy Name is Joyce: Willow: 'Sounds like your mom's in a state of denial.' Buffy: 'More like a continent.'

Denial, Thy Name is Willow: When Buffy says her mother has to realise that she can't leave Sunnydale, Willow says, 'Maybe not now, but soon . . . Or maybe I, too, hail from Denial Land.'

It's a Designer Label!: *What* is Willow wearing? (a pink dress-thing with non-matching sheepskin coat and Doctor Martens). Also, Xander's Bean Sprout T-shirt and Giles's kipper tie, Buffy's green dress and Faith's *incredibly* revealing top.

References: Faith, turning to the dark side of the Force, refers to Darth Vader in the *Star Wars* movies. Also, the Duck and Cover campaign (see **35**, 'Anne'), *Batman* ('Think about the future', see **24**, 'Bad Eggs') and Nancy Drew. Xander is reading Jack Kerouac's *On the Road*, preparing for his sojourn as a bohemian. Willow refers to Friedrich W Moller's song 'The Happy Wanderer'. 'Raise 'em up my inner flagpole, see which one I salute,' paraphrases *Twelve Angry Men*. 'I made him an offer he couldn't survive,' alludes to *The Godfather*.

Bitch!: Xander: 'I think it'll be good for me, help me to find myself.' Cordelia: 'And help us to lose you. Everyone's a winner.' Xander: 'Look who just popped open a fresh can of venom!' When Buffy tries to intervene with: 'You guys, don't forget to breathe between insults,' Cordy's comeback is: 'I'm sorry, Buffy, this conversation is reserved for those who actually *have* a future.' 'She was just being Cordelia, only more so,' notes a conciliatory Willow. Later, Cordelia and Xander have another go. Xander: 'Ten minutes with you and the admissions department decided that they'd already reached their mean-spirited, superficial princess quota.' Cordelia: 'And once again, the gold medal in the Being Wrong event goes to Xander "*I'm-as-stupid-as-I-look*" Harris.'

Awesome!: Willow leaves Oz and Xander a diagram on how to mix the ingredients for her spell – Xander: 'How can you tell which is which? They both kind of look stick-figurey.' Oz: 'This one's me. See the little guitar?' Oz's violent outburst, Angel and Buffy taking on two vampires in the mayor's office and Snyder with the chair clamped to his chest. The mayor telling Angel and Buffy their relationship is doomed is a defining moment in the series. Given that so much of the show is about denial, it's interesting that it needs the series' most heinous villain to make the point . . .

Denial, Thy Names Are Buffy and Angel: . . . But, of course, they don't take any notice. It'll all end in tears (see **54**, 'The Prom').

Surprise!: The revelation that Cordelia is *working* in that dress shop (see **54**, 'The Prom').

The Drugs Don't Work: Snyder: 'What's in the bag?' Student: 'My lunch.' Snyder: 'Is that the new drug lingo?' Snyder's new quest seems to be a single-handed campaign to stamp out drugs even where they don't exist. As he asks the Scooby Gang: 'Why couldn't you be dealing drugs like *normal* people?'

Valley-Speak: Buffy: 'I gotta have a plan? Really? I can't just be proactive with pep?'

Logic, Let Me Introduce You to This Window: Did David Boreanaz dye his hair? It looks a lot darker than normal. When Cordelia shows Xander her acceptance letters, she hands him three envelopes and says, 'USC, Colorado State, Duke.' She then produces two more, one with a USC logo and says, 'And Columbia.' After the Gavrok spider-crab-thing is killed by Buffy, Angel helps her up, but where has the dead creature gone?

I Just *Love* Your Accent: Buffy: 'I can't believe you got into Oxford.' Oz: 'There's some deep academia there.' Buffy: 'That's where they make Gileses!' Willow: 'I could learn and have scones.' If *Inspector Morse* is to be believed, of course, Oxford has a mortality rate even higher than Sunnydale.

Quote/Unquote: Mayor Wilkins on his present to Faith: 'You be careful not to put somebody's eye out with that thing. Till I tell you to.'

Buffy, when Wesley reminds her that she's the Slayer: 'I'm also a person. You can't just define me by my Slayerness. That's . . . "Something-ism".'

Willow, to Vampire: 'Did you get permission to eat the hostage?'

Mayor Wilkins: 'This is exciting, isn't it? Clandestine meetings by dark of night, exchange of prisoners . . . I feel like we should all be wearing trenchcoats.'

Notes: 'Now we're supposed to decide what to do with our lives.' A pleasant way to snuggle into the Ascension story-arc. 'Choices' isn't the greatest of episodes (there's not much plot while there *is* a lot of capture-escape-capture), but it has much energy and humour. And, in Willow's confrontation with Faith, a key moment in the series.

Buffy's Aunt Arlene lives in Illinois. She and Angel recently found a Fire-Demon nest in a cave by the beach (which Angel considered a nice change of pace). There's a reference to 'Mr Pointy' (see **33**, 'Becoming' Part 1). It's established that Buffy will live in at college next season. The mayor had an Irish setter called Rusty. He married his wife, Edna Mae, in 1903 and was with her until she died, wrinkled and senile and cursing him for his youth, which indicates that she, at least, was human.

54
The Prom

US Transmission Date: 11 May 1999
UK Transmission Date: 19 Nov 1999

Writer: Marti Noxon
Director: David Solomon
Cast: Brad Kane (Tucker Wells), Andrea E Taylor (Sales Girl),
Mike Kimmel (Butcher), Tove Kingsbury (Tux Boy),
Michael Zlabinger (Student at Mic), Monica Serene Garnich (Pretty Girl),
Joe Howard (Priest), Damien Eckhardt (Jack Mayhew),
Stephanie Denise Griffin (Tux Girl)

The Senior Prom is coming and Xander has an interesting date. Anya. By chance he discovers Cordelia's part-time job and is shocked to learn that her family have lost all their money. But they are interrupted by an attack from a creature Giles describes as a Hell Hound. A bitter ex-classman, Tucker, has captured and trained the creatures to attack anyone wearing a tuxedo, after his failure to get a date to the prom. Buffy, angry after a breakup with Angel, averts the creatures' attack and arrives in time to receive a award from her classmates. And to enjoy a dance with her former lover.

Dreaming (As Blondie Once Said) is Free: The king of *all* dream sequences: Angel dreams that he and Buffy marry in church, walk down the aisle and out into a beautiful sunny day – at which point she, rather than Angel, bursts into flames. A photo of the pair in their wedding attire appeared in *TV Guide*, leading to all sorts of weird fan-rumours.

Dudes and Babes: Anya says she has witnessed a millennium of treachery and oppression by males and she has nothing but contempt for the gender. But she'd like Xander to go to the prom with her. (Anya: 'I have all these feelings ... I know you find me attractive; I've seen you looking at my breasts.' Xander: 'Nothing personal, but when a guy does that, it just means his eyes are open.') Buffy writes 'Buffy and Angel 4ever' on one of her schoolbooks.

Mom's Apple Pie: Joyce finally has a heart-to-heart with Angel (probably half-a-season too late), which, along with much of the rest of this episode, sets up the parameters for *Angel*. As with Mayor Wilkins in the previous episode, and Spike in **42**, 'Lover's Walk', Joyce tells Angel that there *can't* be a future for him and Buffy as a couple. The crucial difference, of course, is that she puts the onus on Angel, saying that if he *really* loves Buffy he must make the hardest choice of all.

It's a Designer Label!: Willow's pussy-cat T-shirt. All the cast look gorgeous in their prom outfits (especially Buffy's Pamela Dennis dress). When everyone gets obsessed with what they'll be going to the prom in, Giles says: 'I shall be wearing pink taffeta, as chenille will not go with my complexion. Now can we *please* talk about the Ascension!'

References: 'Miles to go before we sleep' refers to Robert Frost's 'Stopping By Woods On A Snowy Evening'. Also, *Psycho*, Prince's '1999' and Sister Sledge's 'We Are Family'. The videos that Tucker has forced the Hell Hounds to watch are *Prom Night* (1 and 4!), *Pump Up the Volume, Pretty in Pink, The Club* and *Carrie* (most of which concern disastrous events on prom nights). Many mythologies have Hell Hounds, the most famous being the three-headed dog Cerebus in Greek myth, which stood guard over the entrance to the Underworld. The creatures in this episode, however, seem more like werewolves, dog-like demon foot-soldiers left over from the Makhesh War.

Awesome!: Xander's disgust when someone else wins the Class Clown award. Oz's reaction to Xander's prom partner ('Interesting choice').

Don't Give Up The Day Job: In addition to playing Larry in *Starship Troopers*, Brad Kane was the singing voice for Aladdin in Disney's *Aladdin*.

Cigarettes and Alcohol: Buffy describes the prom to Angel as 'a cotillion with spiked punch and Electric Slide'. (A cotillion is a formal ball, usually given for debutantes to be introduced to society. The Electric Slide is a line-dance, often performed at weddings.)

Logic, Let Me Introduce You to This Window: The positioning of Angel's bed – facing a panoramic window – is majorly stupid. True, the window is covered by a thick drape, but all it needs is for Buffy or Angel himself to get a bit careless with opening the curtain at the wrong time (as here), or to come in a bit drunk the night before and forget to close it (we've all done that) and it's a question of how they'll get the ash stains from the bedsheets. Similarly, when Joyce calls at Angel's during the day why does he answer the door in clear sunlight? It could have been anybody asking him to step outside. In **52**, 'Earshot', the entrance to Angel's place was covered by a black drape (as the windows are), so when did he have the doors installed? When the Hell Hound bursts through the store window, the boy it attacks remains calmly adjusting his tuxedo. When Buffy takes her prom dress out of her bag she leaves the bag (full of lethal weapons) outside the school. We never saw Buffy put a knife in her jacket, yet she stabs one of the Hell Hounds with one. Does she carry it around all the time? (It looks like the knife she got at the library, but she put that one in her bag, not her jacket.) Blueberry scones, though very common in California, are rare (and virtually unknown) in England. Derby or fruit scones are a more likely object of a conversation between Giles and Wesley. Where did Angel get his tuxedo from? (Is there an all-night tux-hiring shop in Sunnydale?)

I Just *Love* Your Accent: Aside from half the songs being by British artists (Fatboy Slim, the Sundays), there's Giles's rant at Wesley (see **Quote/Unquote**). Cordy thinks that Wesley will look 'way-007 in a tux'.

Cruelty to Animals: Buffy says she killed her goldfish (presumably accidentally) when Angel talks about her possibly wanting to have children one day.

Quote/Unquote: Anya, asking Xander to the prom: 'You're not quite as obnoxious as most of the alpha males around here.'

Giles, on Buffy's break-up with Angel: 'I understand this sort of thing requires ice cream of some kind.'

Wesley asks Giles's opinion on whether he should ask Cordelia to dance: 'For God's sake man, she's eighteen. And you have the emotional maturity of a blueberry scone.'

Notes: 'Once again, the Hellmouth puts the special into special occasion.' Simply beautiful, a story about hidden feelings in which Buffy loses Angel but learns how appreciated she is, even if it's usually unspoken, Cordelia discovers how much Xander cares for her and where love ultimately triumphs. Interestingly, two weeks before this episode, **52**, 'Earshot' (which concerned a student apparently planning a spree-killing), was withdrawn and yet this episode (which *does* concern a student planning a spree-killing) escaped completely unchallenged. Maybe it was the *modus operandi* (Hell Hounds are acceptable, guns aren't)?

There are references to the weird stuff that goes on around Sunnydale including zombies (see **36**, 'Dead Man's Party'), hyena people (see **6**, 'The Pack') and Snyder (student humour, seemingly). Jonathan says that the Class of '99 has the lowest mortality rate of any class in Sunnydale High's history, which fits in with supernatural nastiness having gone on for decades rather than starting when Buffy arrived (see **51**, 'Enemies'). Given the events of **52**, 'Earshot', Jonathan's personal endorsement of Buffy's award is both sweet and touching. Buffy is given the title of Class Protector. The clothing store where Cordelia works is called April Fools (see **53**, 'Choices'). Her family have lost all their money after her father made a 'mistake' on his taxes (for 12 years). One fan theory is that Cordelia's medical bills from her injury in **42**, 'Lover's Walk', didn't help and this may explain her continued blaming of all of her problems on Buffy (see **43**, 'The Wish'). Xander pays for Cordy's prom dress with money from his road-trip fund (see **53**, 'Choices'), a selfless act that makes this author want to grow up to be Xander Harris. Giles states that there are thousands of species of demons (see **55**, 'Graduation Day' Part 1; **84**, 'Family'). Angel has no mirrors at home (which stands to reason despite Buffy's surprise). He gets his blood from a local meat factory (see **21**, 'What's My Line?' Part 1). He doesn't drink coffee as it makes him jittery. Wesley went to an all-male preparatory (see *Angel*: 'Spin the Bottle').

An unconfirmed rumour is that the winner of the 1-800-Collect competition (see **42**, 'Lover's Walk'), Jessica Johnson of Maryland, appears in this episode. The prize was a three-day trip for two to participate in the taping of an upcoming episode and $2,000 cash.

Soundtrack: One of the best: 'Praise You' by Fatboy Slim, 'The Good Life' by Cracker, 'El Rey' by The Lassie Foundation and the Sundays' beautiful version of 'Wild Horses' [*]. A ten-second snatch of Kool & The Gang's 'Celebration' brings a less than enthusiastic response from Buffy ('that song *sucks*!').

Did You Know?: A highlight of the *1999 MTV Movie Awards* was the appearance of Alyson Hannigan in a series of spoofs used to introduce the various categories. Among the films parodied were *I Know What You Did Last Summer, The Breakfast Club, Varsity Blues, She's All That, Say Anything* and (brilliantly) *Cruel Intentions*. The show, hosted by Lisa Kudrow, also saw Seth Green reprise his role as Scott Evil in an *Austin Powers* sketch. Around this time Seth also appeared on the *Conan O'Brien* chatshow and revealed that, although he is seldom pestered by fans, he *is* continually asked by shady characters if he would like some of their drugs. Two weeks later Sarah Michelle Gellar hosted the season finale of *Saturday Night Live*, going (almost) topless for a Holding Your Own Boobs sketch.

55
Graduation Day Part 1

US Transmission Date: 18 May 1999
UK Transmission Date: 26 Nov 1999

Writer: Joss Whedon
Director: Joss Whedon
Cast: Hal Robinson (Professor Lester Worth), John Rosenfeld (Vamp Lackey #2), Adrian Neil (Vamp Lackey #1)

With the mayor's transformation at hand, the Scooby Gang prepare for what they believe may be their last day on Earth. Angel walks into a trap and is shot with a poisoned arrow by Faith. Buffy is told that only the blood of a Slayer will save his life. Buffy goes to Faith's apartment and the Slayers fight to the death on the rooftop. Buffy stabs Faith with Faith's own knife, but as a final desperate act, Faith topples on to a passing truck.

The Conspiracy Starts at Home Time: The mayor tells Snyder that his help in maintaining order at Sunnydale High will be rewarded. He's dead meat, right?

A Little Learning is a Dangerous Thing: Mr Miller's class is playing Hangman instead of studying (a last-day-of-school tradition the world over).

Mom's Apple Pie: 'Looking back,' notes Joyce, 'maybe I should have sent you to a different school.' There's a great scene as Buffy tells Joyce she wants her to leave town until after the graduation as she won't be able to concentrate on fighting the demon if she's also worrying about Joyce.

It's a Designer Label!: Cordelia: 'I can't believe this loser look. I lobbied so hard for the teal. No one ever listens to me. Lone fashionable wolf.' There are, however, a whole bunch of cool clothes: Faith's pink dress, Buffy's red leather pants, Wesley's mauve shirt and the reappearance of Buffy's blue frockcoat.

References: 'Big Sister's Clothes' is an Elvis Costello song (see **42**, 'Lover's Walk'). Willow asks if the commencement speaker will be 'Siegfried? Roy? One of the tigers?' referring to the Masters of the Impossible. 'This is mutiny' is from *Mutiny on the Bounty*. Xander quotes *Jaws* ('We're gonna need a bigger boat'). The motto on the school yearbook is THE FUTURE IS OURS, a possible reference to lyrics in the Stone Roses song 'She Bangs A Drum'.

Bitch!: Cordelia to Xander: 'Dignity? You? In relation to clothes? I'm awash in a sea of confusion.' Willow says she'll miss Harmony. Buffy: 'Don't you hate her?' Willow: 'Yes, with a fiery vengeance. She picked on me for ten years. Vacuous tramp' (see **59**, 'The Harsh Light of Day'; *Angel*: 'Disharmony', 'Harm's Way').

Awesome!: Giles and Wesley fencing is hilarious, while Oz and Willow's final surrendering to intimacy is worth waiting for. Buffy and Faith's five-minute fight in Faith's apartment is a Hong Kong action-movie in miniature.

Valley-Speak: Faith: 'I feel *wicked* stupid in this.'
    Xander to Anya: 'That humanity thing's still a "Work in Progress", isn't it?'

Logic, Let Me Introduce You to This Window: Anya mentions her car. Where did she get the money? Indeed, where does she live? As Angel and Buffy argue in the street, he's holding a cardboard box with two hands. The camera moves to Buffy, but you can still see Angel at the edge of the shot and he doesn't move. When it cuts back to him, he has the box in only one hand. When Buffy tends to Angel in the library, the shots from the front show sweat on his face, but from the side he looks dry. Buffy says that the mayor will have a hundred helpless kids to feed on at graduation. That's a pretty small graduating class for a city with a population of 38,500 (see **15**, 'School Hard'; **42**, 'Lover's Walk') and a university. (There are, of course, other high schools in Sunnydale – see **14**, 'Some

Assembly Required' – and this *is* a place where teenage mortality is on the high side.) When Angel is shot with Faith's arrow, Giles notes that he is bleeding. If Angel is a walking corpse (in **54**, 'The Prom', Buffy confirms that his heart doesn't beat; see also **12**, 'Prophecy Girl'; **26**, 'Innocence'), this is impossible.

I Just *Love* Your Accent: Xander refers to Wesley as Monarchy Boy. Wow, *top* insult. When Wesley says Buffy can't turn her back on the Council she replies: 'They're in England. I don't think they can tell which way my back is facing.'

Cruelty to Animals: The mayor eats some of the Gavrok spider-crab-things.

Quote/Unquote: Xander on Anya's perception of men: 'Yes, men like sports. Men watch the action movie. They eat of the beef and enjoy to look at the bosoms. A thousand years of avenging our wrongs and that's all you've learned?'

Anya: 'I've seen some horrible things in my time. I've been the cause of most of them actually.'

Mayor Wilkins after Giles stabs him: '*That* was a little thoughtless. Violent outbursts like that in front of the children. You know, Mr Giles, they look to you to see how to behave.'

Anya: 'When I think that something could happen to you, it feels bad inside, like I might vomit.' Xander: 'Welcome to the world of romance.'

Mayor Wilkins to Vampire: 'We don't knock during dark rituals?'

Notes: 'That's one spunky little girl you've raised. I'm gonna eat her.' A fine example of how to move pieces into position without losing narrative cohesion. There *are* contrived elements (why turn Buffy into a murderer so pointlessly?) but as a series of mini-climaxes, the episode works brilliantly. The characterisation of the mayor is interesting. The trouble is he's so *sympathetic* – it's a bold thing for a series to have its most dangerous character *not* going around eye-gouging subordinates or doing OTT baddy-things that undermine credibility. Wilkins is someone who one feels *would* kill without a second thought if he felt it necessary, rather than spend time boasting like a hackneyed Bond-villain. He gets two glorious scenes with the Scooby Gang in **53**, 'Choices', and this episode that give the impression of a slightly eccentric, but basically decent, family man who just has a hobby of wanting to rule the world. Well, it's more sane than stamp collecting, isn't it?

Willow says she'll miss PE, though this seems to be a touch of temporary insanity. Her scene with the trusty soda machine – which gives her coke instead of root beer – could be a reference to the mistake with the Dr Pepper can in **18**, 'Halloween'. Percy thanks Willow for helping him with his history and for not kicking his ass like she did in the Bronze (see **50**, 'Doppelgängland'). The implication of the Willow/Oz/bed scene could be that both were previously virgins (though Oz's post-coital 'Everything feels different' may simply mean that Willow is the best he's ever had. He's certainly mentioned having groupies before and claimed in **44**, 'Amends', to have previously 'done it'). When Oz and Willow get intimate they do so without covering Amy's cage (*this* could be considered cruelty to animals), which is an incentive to keep Amy rat-like if *ever* there was one. Faith's childhood in Boston is mentioned (see **37**, 'Faith, Hope and Trick'; **47**, 'The Zeppo'). About 800 years ago in the Urals, a sorcerer achieved Ascension, becoming the embodiment of the demon Lohesh (a four-winged soul-killer). Anya witnessed this while cursing a local shepherd. All the demons that walk the Earth are tainted, human hybrids, like vampires. Those demons not of this realm are different. They're certainly *bigger*.

Soundtrack: Spectator Pump's 'Sunday Mail'.

Did You Know . . .?: The first – four-second – trailer for *Angel* appeared during the initial US broadcast of this episode. Against a red background, David Boreanaz turns towards camera with the words '*Angel*. This Fall' superimposed.

56
Graduation Day Part 2

Original Scheduled US Transmission Date: 25 May 1999
US Transmission Date: 13 July 1999
Canadian Transmission Date: 23 May 1999
UK Transmission Date: 26 Nov 1999

Writer: Joss Whedon
Director: Joss Whedon
Cast: Paolo Andres (Dr Powell), Susan Chuang (Nurse), Tom Bellin (Dr Gold),
Samuel Bliss Cooper (Vamp Lackey)

Buffy saves Angel's life by offering herself for him to feed on. Surviving (with the subconscious help of the comatose Faith),

Buffy, the Scoobies and the students of Sunnydale High surreptitiously arm themselves against the mayor's coming Ascension. The mayor begins to transform during his speech and kills Principal Snyder. The students attack using what weapons they have and, ultimately, Buffy destroys the demon, though at the cost of many lives. As she and her friends prepare for college, Angel leaves Sunnydale and Buffy behind.

The Caption (Slight Return): 'Mindful of recent tragic events affecting America's schools, the conclusion to *Buffy the Vampire Slayer*: Graduation Day, originally scheduled for tonight's broadcast, will air at a later date.'

Dreaming (As Blondie Once Said) is Free: Buffy: 'Is this your mind or mine?' Faith: 'Beats me.' The shared coma/dream/whatever-it-is takes on the dream in **54**, 'The Prom' for weirdness and beats it hollow. The sequence's climax is among Whedon's most beautifully realised scenes: Faith places her hand on Buffy's cheek; in a flash of light Buffy wakes up in her hospital bed. She slowly gets up and walks across the room to Faith, still in a coma and kisses her.

Question: Was this a psychic transference of Slayer powers from one Slayer to the next (or, in this case, previous)? Some of the dialogue (Buffy: 'How are you going to fit all this stuff?' Faith: 'Not gonna, it's yours') suggests as much. However, in an interview with *DreamWatch*, Joss denied this: 'It's more, emotionally, I wanted to take Buffy and Faith to a place where their relationship *could have been* rather than play them as arch enemies. There was a great deal of love between them and that would manifest itself when Faith was no longer in a position to be attacking.'

As for what 'Little Miss Muffet, counting down from 7-3-0' means . . . (see **71**, 'This Year's Girl'; **78**, 'Restless'; **79**, 'Buffy vs Dracula'; **100**, 'The Gift') . . .

Dudes and Babes: One final moment of greatness for Cordelia. In many ways she was at the core of why *Buffy* was so special. In *any other series* Cordy would have been a cardboard cipher. A hollow archetypal bad girl, laughed at and given her comeuppance once per episode. That's probably how the character was devised, but in the hands of a gifted actress and sympathetic writers, she blossomed. Angel drinking Buffy's blood is the clearest link in *Buffy* between vampirism and sexual awakening. Joss Whedon has suggested that he was unsure if he'd get away with this scene but that, in the furore over the students attacking the mayor, WB missed it completely.

Authority Spanks!: Mayor Wilkins to his minions: 'No snacking. I see blood on your lips, it's a visit to the woodshed for you.'

Authority Sucks!: Snyder, begrudgingly: 'Congratulations to the class of 1999. You all proved more or less adequate. This is a time of celebration so sit still and be quiet. Spit out that gum!' When the Mayor ascends: 'This is not disciplined. You're on my campus, buddy, and when I say I want quiet . . .' Followed, inevitably, by death.

A Little Learning is a Dangerous Thing: Giles saves Buffy's diploma from the flames. As Oz notes, they survived not just the battle but also high school, leading Buffy to ask if someone will wake her up when it's time to go to college.

It's a Designer Label: Difficult to work out which is worst, Buffy's leather pants or Jonathan's red anorak.

References: The mayor's suggesting Angel eat his spinach refers to Popeye the Sailor and another reference to 'Stopping By Woods On A Snowy Evening' (see **54**, 'The Prom').

Bitch!: Xander: 'I need to talk to you . . .' Harmony: 'You mean in front of other people?'

Awesome!: Angel feeding on Buffy. Wilkins changing into a 60-foot snake. The following battle sequences are breathtaking. Xander's sarcastic line about how much he'll miss Angel.

'You Might Remember Me From Such TV Series As . . .': Tom Bellin's impressive CV includes appearances on *The Monkees, Alias Smith and Jones, The Streets of San Francisco, The Rockford Files, The Bionic Woman, Charlie's Angels, Matlock* and *Beverly Hills 90210*.

The Drugs Don't Work: When Angel takes Buffy to hospital, Doctor Powell asks: 'You two been doing drugs?'

Valley-Speak: Cordelia: 'My point, however, is, crazy or not, it's pretty much the only plan. Besides, it's Buffy's. Slay gal, you know, little Miss likes-to-fight?' Xander: 'I think there was a "yay" vote buried in there somewhere.'

Xander: 'Angel, in his "Non-Key Guy" capacity, can work with me.' Angel: 'What fun.' Xander: 'Hey, "Key Guy" still talking.'

Surrealism Rules – Fish: Cordelia: 'I personally don't think it's possible to come up with a crazier plan.' Oz: 'We could attack the mayor with hummus.' Cordelia: 'I stand corrected.'

Logic, Let Me Introduce You To This Window: Sunnydale is said to have been founded 100 years ago by Wilkins (the WELCOME TO SUNNYDALE sign in **15**, 'School Hard', and **42**, 'Lover's Walk', says FOUNDED IN 1900). This doesn't square with **2**, 'The Harvest', which suggests that the town is much older, originally settled by the Spanish in the 1700s (see **64**, 'Pangs'). If the mayor set up Sunnydale as demon-feeding ground, is *he* also behind Buffy being there? Consider the numerous occasions when world-threatening stuff has only been averted because Buffy is on hand. The Master, the Judge, Acathla, the Hellmouth creature in **47**, 'The Zeppo', the First Evil in **44**, 'Amends', all Armageddon scenarios; **39**, 'Homecoming', and **42**, 'Lover's Walk', both indicate that the mayor had full knowledge of what was going on in Sunnydale during the two years prior to his introduction, so one has to wonder if there is something in how he's set the town up that means they will always fail, or if he's been depending on Buffy all along.

I Just *Love* Your Accent: Xander, after his discussion with Giles on tea ('you're destroying a perfectly good cultural stereotype'), makes reference to cricket batting averages. Cordelia demands an explanation for Wesley. 'In-breeding?' suggests Xander.

Quote/Unquote: Willow on Angel: 'He's delirious. He thought I was Buffy.' Oz: 'You too?'

Cordelia to Giles concerning Wesley: 'Does he have to leave the country? I mean, you got fired and you still hang around like a big loser . . .'

Wilkins: 'I'd get ready for some weeping if I were you. I'd get set for a world of pain. Misery loves company, young man, and I'm looking to share that with you and your whore.'

Cordelia: 'We'll attack him with germs . . . We'll get a container of Ebola virus . . . It doesn't have to be real, we can just get a box that says Ebola on it and chase him. With the box.' Xander: 'I'm starting to lean towards the hummus offensive.'

Wesley: 'It's rather a lot of pain actually. Aspirin anyone . . . Perhaps I could just be knocked unconscious?'

Giles: 'There's a certain dramatic irony attached to all of this. A synchronicity that borders on predestination one might say.' Buffy: 'Fire bad, tree pretty.'

Notes: 'The show's not over but there will be a short intermission. Don't want to miss the second act, all kinds of excitement.' A suitably intense finish to a remarkable six months of television. The build up is well handled though the effects-overload finale lacks some finesse. Of the three major semi-regular school age characters – Harmony, Larry and Jonathan – Larry dies in the graduation melee (see **109**, 'Smashed'). The other two survive to appear again – though in Harmony's case, as a vampire. Angel says that Buffy has no allergies (how does he know?) Buffy's amazing healing properties are again demonstrated (see **30**, 'Killed By Death'). The doctor's astonishment that Faith is still alive after her ordeal suggests that this is something all Slayers share. Buffy also notes that Angel heals fast (see **4**, 'Teacher's Pet'). Angel confirms that Buffy will not become a vampire as she did not feed from him (see **46**, 'Helpless'). Xander believes that Giles's coffee is brewed from the finest Colombian lighter fluid. There's another reference to Xander's military knowledge (see **18**, 'Halloween'; **26**, 'Innocence'). Wesley says a solar eclipse is standard procedure for an Ascension. Cuts were made to the episode before its first scheduled transmission, including Xander loudly celebrating the blowing up of school and some effects footage.

Soundtrack: Elgar's *Pomp & Circumstance March No. 1*.

What the Papers Said: Many newspapers sprang to the defence of *Buffy* when WB's postponement was announced. Robert Bianco, influential TV critic for *USA Today*, named *Buffy* as one of the best shows of 1998–9: 'This consistently surprising and enormously entertaining comic morality play from the incredibly talented Joss Whedon is one of the wittiest, smartest series on TV. Too smart for WB, maybe, which insulted the audience's intelligence and the show's integrity by shelving the season finale because of sensitivity concerns, even though no series has been more adept at teaching teens about responsibility and consequences. Never fear: Buffy will triumph, as she always does.' *Entertainment Weekly* also attacked WB: 'This post-Columbine squeamishness is not just idiotic (not airing one of the few programs that portray teens in powerful, responsible positions is being "respectful" of the tragedy?); it also gives strength to the notion that TV shows should be censored to fit whatever is politically prominent at the moment.' *Chicago Sun Times'* Richard Roeper added: 'Cloaking itself in a veil of disingenuous good intentions while combining cowardice with stupidity, WB squelched Tuesday's *Buffy* because of fears that impressionable young minds might be influenced by watching teenagers doing battle in the hallways of their high school with the town mayor, transformed into a 60-foot, serpentlike creature . . . Here's a thought. If you lose a child or a friend or a loved one in a school shooting, I would imagine your grief would be so overwhelmingly complete that you really wouldn't give a rat's behind about what they're doing on *Buffy* . . . Most American TV shows and movies, including stuff like *Buffy* and *The Matrix*, also play in dozens of foreign countries, including places where they have strict gun-control laws. And guess what? It turns out that the lack of access to handguns actually translates to fewer killings, regardless of what's playing on TV or at the local multiplex.' *The Newark Star-Ledger*'s Alan Sepinwall added: 'Virtually every episode of *Buffy* features some plot or another to kill students, their parents, their dogs, etc. If you start pulling every episode in which a massacre either happens or is planned, you won't have a show left. But if anything in television is an unwitting culprit, it's not the likes of *Buffy*, but TV news. Kids aren't stupid; they see the way CNN, MSNBC, *Dateline, 20/20*, etc. descend on these tragedies and cover them wall-to-wall for weeks at a time. If some troubled teenager decides he wants to go out in a blaze of glory, the cable news channels and news magazines have clearly established that they will make him famous.'

Mark Wyman, in a superbly balanced piece in *Shivers*, concentrated on the leaking of the episode on to the Internet: 'Something unprecedented happened this spring, after a major real-life horror incident prompted the postponement of two crucial episodes of *Buffy*. The novelty wasn't the cancellation, but how that temporary censorship was evaded, which puts in doubt the ability of censors at any level to prevent material from reaching public circulation.' When the episode finally aired, Matt Roush wrote an impassioned *TV Guide* article, concluding with his assessment that: 'If Emmy voters weren't such snobs about fantasy and youth genres, *Buffy* and its gifted creator Joss Whedon . . . would merit recognition. The writing is *that* sharp, the performances *that* good, the tone *that* consistent – a unique blend of ironic whimsy and tumultuous passion amid the carnage.'

Finally, Sarah Michelle Gellar, in a dignified statement, noted: 'I share WB's concern and compassion for the recent tragic events . . . I am, however, disappointed that the year-long culmination of our efforts will not be seen by our audience. *Buffy* has always been extremely responsible in its depiction of action sequences, fantasy and mythological situations. Our diverse and positive role models battle the horror of adolescence through intelligence and integrity and we endeavor to offer a moral lesson with each new episode. There is probably no greater societal question we face then how to stop violence among our youth. By cancelling intelligent programming like *Buffy*, corporate entertainment is not addressing the problem.'

Joss Whedon's Comments: On 27 May, Joss Whedon told the *Posting Board*: 'How about that season finale, eh? Although, looking at it objectively, it WAS a little like "Band Candy".' ('Graduation Day' Part 2 was replaced by a repeat of **40**, 'Band Candy'.) Whedon continued: 'For the record, I don't think the WB had to pre-empt the episode, but I understand why they did. When those of you who haven't seen it do, you'll wonder what all the fuss was about. But one violent graduation incident and the WB and I would feel like collective @$%. So, July. At least we won't be up against the final *Home Improvement*.' Whedon also noted: 'It's nice to see how much people care about seeing the episode – although there were threats made against WB execs which is most creepy. Look to poor Britain who get it [the series] in clumps, out of order, on different networks or not at all.'

This was a hectic period for Joss; as he explained: 'Today's schedule, an example of a typical day: Watch filming. Edit. Production meeting re the next episode. Prep next director, explain tone and meaning in script. Pick song for the Bronze. Casting. Drink huge amount of tea. Talk to Sarah about the script. Discuss directors for next season. Panic. More tea. Work on *Angel*.' And then he went online for an hour to talk about it. On the future of *Buffy*, in the wake of the furore over **56**, 'Graduation Day' Part 2, Joss told concerned fans: 'I made a couple of trims in the final episodes, but I was on board for that – they just seemed tasteless (by pure coincidence). But nothing will change in the creative process. If someone tries to start interfering with the show, I'll not make it anymore. Very simple.' But then Joss Whedon is a remarkable man. When told by *USA Today* that there was a flourishing black-market in videotapes and computer downloads of the withheld episodes, his advice to fans was simple: 'I'm having a Grateful Dead moment here . . . Bootleg the puppy!'

The Comic: Issue 20 of Dark Horse's, by now hugely popular, *Buffy* comic series (April 2000) was a Doug Petrie story entitled 'Double Cross' (pencilled by Jason Minor and inked by Curtis

Arnold) set in the aftermath of **56**, 'Graduation Day' Part 2, and featuring Angel and Buffy fighting one last foe together in their dreams.

City of Angel: Crawling from the apocalyptic emotional wreckage of *Buffy*'s third season, *Angel* was a chance for Joss Whedon and David Greenwalt to escape the world that they had fashioned in Sunnydale and step into the adult morass of Los Angeles. If one element defined the fundamental differences between the two series then it was *Angel*'s ability to get down into the gutter of the Big City while *Buffy* was stuck in the confines of small-town America. Creators of cult shows often fail to strike lucky with their second projects (*Crusade* and *Millennium* are recent examples). In a revealing interview with Rob Francis, Joss was asked the secret of getting a spin-off up and running while simultaneously maintaining the standards on the parent-show: 'We were very careful to learn while we were doing *Angel* not to set a formula until we had seen the results. What they meant, how people responded to them. I was determined not to have a second show that brought down the quality of the first.' It was during the *Buffy* episode **31**, 'I Only Have Eyes For You', that Whedon began thinking about a spin-off: 'Seeing David open himself up to playing this really emotional female role and doing it excellently – without overdoing it or being silly, without shying away from it as a lot of male action stars might have – was extraordinary. That was the moment when I thought, "This guy could carry his own show".'

Xander: 'College not so scary after all?'
Buffy: *'It's turning out to be a lot like high school,*
which I can handle.'

– 'The Freshman'

Season Four (1999–2000)

Mutant Enemy Inc/Kuzui Enterprises/Sandollar Television/20th Century Fox
Created by Joss Whedon
Producers: Gareth Davies, David Fury
Co-Producers: Jane Espenson, David Solomon,
James A Contner (59, 63, 69, 75, 77)
Consulting Producer: David Greenwalt
Supervising Producer: Marti Noxon
Executive Producers: Sandy Gallin, Gail Berman, Fran Rubel Kuzui,
Kaz Kuzui, Joss Whedon
Regular Cast:
Sarah Michelle Gellar (Buffy Summers), Nicholas Brendon (Xander Harris),
Alyson Hannigan (Willow Rosenberg), Anthony Stewart Head (Rupert Giles),
David Boreanaz (Angel, 64, 76),
Kristine Sutherland (Joyce Summers, 57, 60, 71-72, 78),
Mercedes McNab (Harmony Kendall, 59, 63–64, 78),
Elizabeth Anne Allen (Amy Madison, 65),
Armin Shimerman (Principal Snyder, 78), James Marsters (Spike, 59, 62–78),
Seth Green (Daniel 'Oz' Osborne, 57–62, 75, 78), Jason Hall (Devon, 59),
Danny Strong (Jonathan Levinson, 73), Robin Sachs (Ethan Rayne, 68),
Saverio Guerra (Willy, 70), Eliza Dushku (Faith,[14] 71–72),
Harry Groener (Mayor Richard Wilkins III, 71),
Emma Caulfield (Anya Jenkins, 59–60, 64–66, 68–70, 72–78),
Amy Powell (TV News Reporter,[15] 70, 72), Andy Umberger (D'Hoffryn, 65),
Ethan Erickson (Percy West, 67), Marc Blucas (Riley Finn, 57, 60–78),
Mace Lombard (Tom, 57, 63), Dagney Kerr (Kathy Newman, 57–58),
Lindsay Crouse (Professor Maggie Walsh, 57, 60–63, 66, 68–69, 77),
Phina Oruche (Olivia, 57, 66, 78), Paige Moss (Veruca,[16] 58, 61–62),
Adam Kaufman (Parker Abrams, 58–61, 63),
Bailey Chase (Graham Miller, 63–64, 67, 69–71, 73–75, 77),
Leonard Roberts (Forrest Gates, 63–64, 66–67, 69–72, 76–77),

---

[14] Credited onscreen as 'Buffy' in **72**, 'Who Are You?'.
[15] Credited as 'Reporter' in **70**, 'Goodbye Iowa'.
[16] Uncredited in **58**, 'Living Conditions'.

Amber Benson (Tara Maclay, 66, 68–78),
George Hertzberg (Adam, 69–70, 72–73, 75–78),
Jack Stehlin (Doctor Angleman, 69–70, 77), Neil Daly (Mason 69, 74),
Robert Patrick Benedict (Jape,[17] 73, 75),
James Michael Connor (Scientist #1,[18] 74, 75),
Conor O'Farrell (Colonel McNamara 75–77), Bob Fimiani (Mr Ward 76–77),
Sharon Ferguson (Primitive,[19] 78)

57
The Freshman

US Transmission Date: 5 Oct 1999
UK Transmission Date: 7 Jan 2000[20]

Writer: Joss Whedon
Director: Joss Whedon
Cast: Pedro Balmaceda (Eddie), Katharine Towne (Sunday), Mike Rad (Rookie),
Shannon Hillary (Dav), Robert Catrini (Professor Riegert), Scott Rinker (RA),
Denice J Sealy (Student Volunteer), Evie Peck (Angry Girl),
Jason Christopher (Non-Serious Guy), Jane Silvia (Conservative Woman),
Mark Silverberg (Passing Student), Walt Borchert (New Vampire)

On the first day of term Buffy wanders disorientated around
college – unlike Willow and Oz who seem completely at home.
Buffy meets her roommate, Kathy, and has a horrible first day,
kicked out of one class by an overzealous tutor, while another
professor, Maggie Walsh, refers to herself as 'the evil bitch-
monster of death'. Buffy meets a kindred lost soul, Eddie, but he
goes missing soon afterwards and she's further shocked by Giles's
refusal to help her. Eddie subsequently turns up as a vampire and
Buffy is forced to kill him, watched by a vampire gang led by the
sarcastic Sunday, who realises that Buffy is the Slayer. Buffy then
has her ass kicked. At the Bronze, Buffy meets Xander who raises

---

[17] Credited as 'Adam's Lackey' in **73**, 'Superstar'. Although appearing in the credits
for **75**, 'New Moon Rising', these scenes were cut before broadcast.

[18] Credited as 'Scientist' in **74**, 'Where The Wild Things Are'.

[19] Character referred to in dialogue, in this and other episodes, as 'the First Slayer'
(see **96**, 'Intervention').

[20] The BBC's transmission of season four – starting with this episode on 28 Sep
2000 – was the first ever broadcast of *Buffy* in widescreen/stereo. Although not
filmed as such, Mutant Enemy were able to offer widescreen prints for overseas
sales as a by-product of using bigger and better film-stock from season three
onwards. Joss Whedon has noted that as the episodes weren't framed with 16:9
transmission in mind, occasionally lights and microphones intrude into the
picture.

her spirits. While Xander goes for help, Buffy attacks Sunday's gang alone. Sunday breaks Buffy's Class Protector award, which finally gets the Slayer angry enough to kill them. Elsewhere on campus, a vampire is captured by men in military gear.

The Trailer: For the start of the season, a highly charged trailer of clips from the first four new episodes was broadcast, accompanied by flash-captions: 'From the darkness ... of a new beginning ... shines the light ... of a new challenge ...'

Dudes and Babes: Eddie: '*Of Human Bondage*. Have you ever read it?' Buffy: 'I'm not really into porn ...' So, Riley Finn ... Lots of fans *hated* him with a passion. I rather liked him, although it was obvious that, at this stage, the writers weren't sure of what to do with the character. What a shame, on the other hand, that they couldn't have found some way of keeping Sunday alive – her pissed-off hands-on-hips pose as she was killed was particularly impressive.

A Little Learning is a Dangerous Thing: Willow says that Buffy waited until the last minute before making her course selection, unlike Willow who, Buffy notes, chose her major in playgroup. Classes Buffy considers include Introduction to the Modern Novel ('I'm guessing I'd probably have to *read* the modern novel ... Do they have an introduction to the modern blurb?') and Images of Pop Culture. Maggie Walsh notes: 'If you're looking to coast, I recommend "Geology 101". That's where the football players are.' Buffy manages to confuse reconnaissance with the renaissance. Her excuse, to Xander, is that she's had a *really* long week.

Mom's Cardiac Arrest: 'Can't wait till Mom gets the bill for these books,' notes Buffy. 'I hope it's a funny aneurysm.'

Denial, Thy Name is Buffy: The episode concerns Buffy's inability to adapt to the changes taking place in her life. Until pushed.

Work is a Four-Letter Word: Xander spent the summer working in the kitchen (and, it is implied, the stage) of Oxnard's *The Fabulous Ladies Night Club*.

It's a Designer Label!: Sunday, on Buffy's clothes: 'I think you had a lot of misconceptions about college. Like that anyone would be caught dead wearing *that*.' Rookie adds: 'The best part was when you ragged on her clothes. She was like, *No! Not the ensemble!*' Sunday hates those jeans with little patches and refutes the idea that they're coming back into fashion by saying she intends to kill every person who wears them. Willow's orange pants and yellow hooded top are garish, though they're matched by Kathy's blue mottled miniskirt and Buffy's pink dress and jacket. Was the idea of sticking Buffy in pink for most of the episode to emphasise her girly femininity?

References: 'Remember, before you became Hugh Hefner, when you used to be a Watcher?' refers to the *Playboy* billionaire. Also, *Planet of the Apes* ('pretty much a madhouse. A madhouse'), Randy Newman's 'Short People', the Nuremberg rallies, Dietrich von Freiberg's *Treatise of the Intellect and the Intelligible*, W Somerset Maugham's *Of Human Bondage*, Lay's crisps advertising slogan 'You can never eat just one', *Grand Canyon*, French impressionist Claude Monet (1840–1926) and the founder of the Vienna Sezession Gustav Klimt (1862–1918). Kathy hangs a Celine Dion poster on her wall. *Must* be evil, then (see **58**, 'Living Conditions'). Xander misquotes 'America, The Beautiful' ('There's some purple mountains majesty'), Joan Armatrading's 'Love And Affection' and *Scarface*, namechecks the Marvel superhero team *The Avengers* and produces a hilariously mangled version of Yoda's advice to Anakin Skywalker in *Star Wars Episode 1: The Phantom Menace* (' "Fear leads to anger. Anger leads to hate. Hate leads to anger." No wait, hold on. "Fear leads to hate. Hate leads to the dark side . . . First you get the women, then you get the money" ').

Bitch!: Rookie: 'Are we gonna fight? Or is there just gonna be a monster-sarcasm-rally?'

Buffy, to Sunday: 'That's *my* skirt. You're never going to fit in it with those hips.'

Awesome!: Willow and Buffy too engrossed in choosing courses to notice the vampire emerging behind them. Willow's enthusiastic reaction to university ('I can feel my mind opening up and letting this place thrust into and spurt knowledge . . . That sentence ended up in a different place than it started . . .'). Sunday and her hapless gang of vampire misfits are *hilarious*. But the best bit is Xander and Buffy at the Bronze.

'You May Remember Me From Such Films and TV Series As . . .': A former professional basketball player with the Manchester Giants, Marc Blucas played the basketball hero in *Pleasantville*. His other movies include *Jay and Silent Bob Strike Back*, *We Were*

Soldiers, Prey for Rock & Roll and *A View From the Top*. He was Buddy Wells in *The 60s* and Billy in *Undressed*, a series that also featured Pedro Balmaceda. Katharine Towne, the daughter of Hollywood screenwriter Robert Towne, can be seen in *Mulholland Drive, The In-Crowd, But I'm a Cheerleader* and *She's All That*. Lindsay Crouse has a huge CV that includes *Out of Darkness, Chantilly Lace, House of Games, The Verdict, Slap Shot, All The President's Men, LA Law* and *The Outer Limits*. Readers may remember her as Kate McBride in *Hill Street Blues*. Robert Catrini's movies include *The Lottery* and *A Kiss So Deadly* while Phina Oruche was in *If Looks Could Kill, How Stella Got Her Groove Back, Punks* and *The Sky is Falling*. Denise J Sealy played Betty in *The Ditchdigger's Daughters*.

Valley-Speak: Buffy: 'I didn't mean to . . . suck.'
   Xander: 'The point is, you're Buffy'. Buffy: 'Maybe in high school.' Xander: 'Now, in college, you're Betty Louise?'

It's Snore Joke for the Afflicted: Kathy's snoring may be caused by sleep apnoea, a sleeping disorder in which breathing is restricted.

Cigarettes and Alcohol: During Buffy's visit Giles drinks scotch on the rocks. However, he later hands it to Olivia, so presumably it's *her* drink rather than his.

This Season's Obligatory Religious Joke: Girl: 'Have you accepted Jesus Christ as your personal saviour?' Buffy: 'You know, I meant to and then I just got really busy.'

The Drugs Don't Work: 'Slayer's blood's gotta be like Thai-stick' refers to particularly potent marijuana usually laced with another drug such as speed.

Logic, Let Me Introduce You to This Window: When Buffy is lost on campus, she is carrying a bag. Its stripes are slightly different on either side in different shots. In the scene in which Buffy tries to sleep while Kathy snores, Buffy's bedclothes are at chin level during close-ups, but several inches lower in the long shots. When the vampires clean out Eddie's room, they can be seen in the mirror above the sink. It appears that Rookie is involved in packing Eddie's stuff, but after a cut to the stereo that Dev is stealing, Rookie is now sitting at a desk, finishing the forged goodbye note. Several fans have noted that the vampires live in a building with a skylight, which doesn't seem very sensible.

I Just *Love* Your Accent: Buffy: 'Gentleman of leisure? Isn't that British for *unemployed*?'

Cruelty to Animals: Xander tells Buffy that she's sitting alone looking like she just got diagnosed with 'cancer of the puppy.'

Quote/Unquote: Willow on Xander's road trip: 'He wasn't coming back until he'd driven to all 50 states.' Buffy: 'Did you explain about Hawaii?' Willow: 'He seemed so determined.'

Dav: 'Does this sweater make me look fat?' Sunday: 'No. The fact that you're fat makes you look fat. That sweater just makes you look purple.'

Giles, after Buffy has met Olivia: 'I'm not supposed to have a private life?' Buffy: 'No. Because you're very, very old. And it's *gross*.'

Buffy: 'Thanks for the Dadaist pep talk, I feel much more abstract now.'

Xander saves the episode: 'When it's dark and I'm all alone and I'm scared or freaked out ... I always think, "What would Buffy do?" *You're my hero*.'

Notes: 'Freshmen. They're so predictable.' For the third season running *Buffy* gets off to a slow start, 'The Freshman' beginning like an episode of *Felicity, the Vampire Slayer*. You get the feeling that Joss Whedon, great writer that he is, just hasn't got the hang of these season openers *at all*. The episode takes a long time to make its points and wastes Giles completely. Two major points in its favour, however – a marvellous performance by Katharine Towne and one of the series' finest scenes, as Buffy is reunited with Xander.

Buffy notes it has been a slay-heavy summer. UC Sunnydale is five miles from the centre of town. Buffy, Willow and Oz are taking *Introduction to Psychology 105* with Professor Walsh. Willow is also taking Ethnomusicology (instead of Modern Poetry). Dingoes Ate My Baby have played at UCS on numerous occasions (and are playing again on Thursday night). Campus buildings include: Richmond Hall, Weisman Hall and Fischer Hall (site of Buffy's dorm here but, see **58**, 'Living Conditions'). In 1982, the Psi Theta fraternity house was abandoned and it's been dormant while zoning issues have dragged on. When Buffy answers the phone and no one speaks, it's Angel on the other end (we see him make the call during *Angel*: 'City Of'). Oxnard, where Xander spent most of his summer, is about 40 miles southeast of

Sunnydale. He tells Buffy that the engine fell out of his car, so he ended up washing dishes at *The Fabulous Ladies Night Club* for about a month and a half while paying for repairs. One night one of the male strippers called in sick but no power on this earth will make him tell Buffy the rest of that story. Then he traded in his car for one that wasn't entirely made of rust, came back home and is now sleeping in his parent's basement and paying them rent. Oz and his bandmates are living in a house off-campus.

Xander mentioned his proposed road trip in **53**, 'Choices'. Buffy tells Eddie that she doesn't have a security blanket, unless one counts Mr Pointy (see **33**, 'Becoming' Part 1). Interestingly, Buffy told Owen in **5**, 'Never Kill a Boy on the First Date', that she *had* a security blanket. Buffy sees that Sunday and friends have Mr Gordo, her stuffed pig (see **21**, 'What's My Line?' Part 1). Willow mentions the time Buffy disappeared for several months and changed her name (see **34**, 'Becoming' Part 2; **35**, 'Anne'). Sunday breaks the staff of the gold parasol presented to Buffy as Class Protector in **54**, 'The Prom'. Buffy's diary has been seen on two previous occasions – when she thought Angel had read it in **7**, 'Angel', and when Ted actually *did* in **23**, 'Ted'.

Soundtrack: 'Universe' by Stretch Princess, 'Freaky Soul' by Paul Riordan and 'I Wish I Could Be You' by the Muffs, along with another example of Giles's impressive record collection, David Bowie's 'Memory Of A Free Festival' (see **20**, 'The Dark Age'; **40**, 'Band Candy'; **59**, 'The Harsh Light of Day'). Splendid perform 'You And Me' at the Bronze, having previously appeared in **31**, 'I Only Have Eyes For You'.

Ad Break, Part 1 – 'Maybe She's Born With It': The initial US broadcast coincided with the debut of Sarah Michelle Gellar as *The Maybelline Girl* advertising '3-in-1 express make-up.'

Ad Break, Part 2 – 'Barq's *Does* Have Bite': Also during early October 1999, Barq's ran a TV advertising campaign featuring Nick Brendon in a graveyard accidentally staking a vampire and saying that a lucky viewer who bought a can or bottle with a gamepiece matching the name of a cast member announced during the 12 October episode (see **58**, 'Living Conditions') would have the chance to 'party with members of the *Buffy* cast'.

Critique: By the beginning of season four, *Buffy*'s critical standing among genre-sections of the media was at a zenith. A relative latecomer to *Buffy*, *SFX* columnist and TV writer Paul Cornell used an issue of his *Sound and Vision* diary to praise *Buffy*, along with *Ally McBeal*, contrasting these series with the kind of fantasy programmes that many genre fans seem to want: '*Buffy*'s metaphors are character-based rather than visual. "My boyfriend turned into an animal", "Be careful what you wish for", "Nobody seems to notice me". When you're a kid, the world seems a place of melodrama, of heroes and monsters. In *Buffy*, these concepts are made flesh. Sunnydale is the hypocrisy capital of adulthood, nice on the surface, run by demonic authorities, infested by creatures who are literally too old to care about the needs of those new to this world they never made. The characters are complex enough to grapple with the gap between being archetypes and individuals, like we all do at that age. Willow, for instance, is turning into an insecure, nervy, Jewish witchy wise-woman. Do you embrace being what your peers want you to be, like Cordelia does, or do you settle for not quite knowing who you are, like Buffy? Creator Joss Whedon is so good at real world interaction that he's even letting his characters grow up.'

Joss Whedon's Comments: The inspiration for Buffy's media professor, Joss Whedon told the *Posting Board*: 'I freely confess that he's based on an old professor of mine, Joe Reed, who kicked my friend David out of the class one day in front of two hundred kids. Joe is cool, by the way.'

58
Living Conditions

US Transmission Date: 12 Oct 1999
UK Transmission Date: 14 Jan 2000

Writer: Marti Noxon
Director: David Grossman
Cast: Clayton Barber (Demon 1), Walt Borchert (Demon 2),
Roger Morrissey (Tapparich), David Tuckman (Freshman)

Buffy encounters cohabitation problems with Kathy, a girl who irons her jeans, listens to Cher and labels her food. But these idiosyncrasies are nothing compared to the horrifying demon-riddled dreams that the girls are sharing. Buffy is encouraged to tolerate Kathy's ways but decides that Kathy is evil and intends to kill her. Giles, Xander and Oz confine Buffy, Giles believing that demons have possessed her. However, research proves that Buffy was right all along, just as an escaped Buffy finds Kathy, a demon's runaway daughter, attempting to procure Buffy's soul so that when her father comes for her, he will take the wrong girl. While Giles and Willow perform a spell to right the damage, Kathy's dad arrives. The demon opens a portal in the floor and takes Kathy home. Willow becomes Buffy's new roommate.

Dreaming (As Blondie Once Said) is Free: Buffy's dreams are terrifying. A demon pours blood into her mouth, puts a scorpion on her and sucks out her soul.

Dudes and Babes: We also get a glimpse of Parker Abrams who will become significant over the next few episodes. Initial impression? Smooth git.

A Little Learning is a Dangerous Thing: Buffy confuses two proverbs, a stitch in time saves nine and the early bird catches the worm.

Denial, Thy Names Are Giles, Oz, Willow and Xander: After all the weird stuff they've seen, one would expect the Scoobies to be willing to trust Buffy's instincts.

It's a Designer Label!: Lots of interesting clothes, starting with a yellow miniskirt worn by an extra in the opening scene. Kathy's various brightly coloured T-shirts and red shorts, Buffy's grey hooded top and red boob-tube, Willow's *strange* woollen shawl and rich blue top and Oz's peach Libertyville and green The Wheel T-shirts and sheepskin coat (a literal *wolf in sheeps clothing*).

References: Kathy's musical taste provokes references to chronically unhip VH-1 and the 90s trends of trip-hop and riot grrl. In a similar, diva, vein Parker notes: 'There's lots of popular artists who don't get their dues: Madonna, Whitney . . .' Also, German printer Johann Gutenberg, oblique references to *The Terminator*, *Really Bad Things*, *Austin Powers: The Spy Who Shagged Me* ('Mini-Mom of Momdonia'), Detroit ice-hockey team the Red Wings, *Titanic* and *The Exorcist* ('doing a Linda Blair on us'). Buffy's dreams may have been influenced by *Rosemary's Baby*, while the bit where Kathy plays with her hard-boiled egg is similar to a sequence in *Angel Heart*.

Bitch!: Kathy, on discovering that someone has used her milk: 'I just wanted to make sure that we didn't have a thief.' Buffy: 'Sid the Wily Dairy Gnome?' Buffy tells Giles: 'It's probably just me having a bitch attack.' Kathy feels that Buffy's problem is she's spoiled and that the world revolved around her at home.

Awesome!: Oz's amused reaction after Buffy has reduced a park bench to matchwood. The Buffy/Kathy fight is hugely impressive (Sophia Crawford really earning her money, being thrown around the room like a rag doll). But it's the scenes of Buffy trying to convince her friends that Kathy is evil that impress most.

Surprise!: Kathy's human face coming off in Buffy's hands, revealing her green eyes and orange skin.

'You May Remember Me From Such Films and TV Series As . . .': Adam Kaufman plays Ethan in *Dawson's Creek* while Paige Moss was Tara Marks in *Beverly Hills 90210*. Her movies include *Can't Hardly Wait*, *Murder Live!* and *Killer Instinct*.

Don't Give Up The Day Job: Clayton Barber, one-time Angel stunt-double, also worked on *Blade*, doubled for Chris O'Donnell in *Batman and Robin* and played a punk in *Summer of Sam*.

Valley-Speak: Buffy, to Giles: 'I'm still going *ick* from the last time you tried to recapture your youth' (see **40**, 'Band Candy').
Willow: 'So, spill. What was that all about, with the *cutie patootie*?'
Buffy: 'Listening to *The Best of VH-1* all day sort of put me on edge.' Willow: 'Kathy's still spinnin' the divas?' Buffy: ' "Coz it's *the fun-est*!" No big.'

Cigarettes and Alcohol: Oz refers to a Bloody Mary (vodka and tomato juice). Without the Mary.

Logic, Let Me Introduce You to This Window: Kathy shows Buffy her phone-call-logging system and points at a pad of paper. In one shot, the uncapped end of the pen is pointing at the paper, but in the next the pen is the other way round. As Buffy and Willow are walking away from Buffy's dorm, Willow carries a bag, the straps of which are solid colour on one side and camouflage print on the other. The straps flip back and forth between shots. When Kathy joins Buffy on patrol, Buffy's ponytail is in a different position subsequent shots. Giles tosses a towel over his shoulder when he sits down. When he stands up later, the towel is in his hand, but it returns to his shoulder seconds later. When Oz and Xander walk toward the tied-up Buffy, Oz is on Xander's right. Buffy knocks their heads together and they fall down, but in the shot of them on the floor, they've switched sides. During the Buffy/Kathy fight, the phone ends up between their nightstands. When the portal is opened, the phone is nowhere to be seen. Contrary to the implication of **57**, 'The Freshman', Buffy's dorm is Stevenson, not Fischer Hall.

Quote/Unquote: Buffy: '*Motorbike and Scooter* magazine?' Giles: 'Congratulations you've found me out. I'm a mod-jogger.'

Willow, concerning Giles: 'He's our *grown-up friend*. Not in a creepy way.'

Oz: 'So either you hit her or you did your wacky mime routine for her?' Buffy: 'I didn't do either, actually. But she deserved it, don't ya think?' Oz: '*Nobody* deserves mime.'

Willow, on the telephone: 'Giles, I just talked to Buffy and I think she's feeling a little insane. Not *bitchy-crazy*, more like *homicidal-maniac-crazy*. So I told her to come to you.'

Taparrich: 'Do you have any idea how much trouble you're in, young lady?' Kathy: 'I'm 3000 years old. When are you going to stop treating me like I'm 900?'

Notes: 'Kathy's evil . . . I'm gonna have to kill her.' Better. An interesting premise (the, literal, roommate-from-Hell) and some lovely directional touches, but the pacing is hopeless with a crammed last five minutes and a convenient *denouement* spoiling earlier good dialogue and characterisation.

Buffy and Kathy (and, later, Willow's) room is number 214. Both Buffy and Willow chew gum (see **U1**, the untransmitted pilot). Willow suggests that Buffy has become almost Cordeliaesque, the first reference to Cordy since **56**, 'Graduation Day' Part 2. Another of the courses Willow is taking is English. Her roommate seems to be a party animal. Willow hangs a Dingoes Ate My Baby poster at the end of the episode. Buffy refers to the Grotto, presumably a coffee shop on campus. The dining hall at UCS is called Rocket Cafe. Kathy tells the Scoobies that she's originally from Nebraska. The ritual of Mok'tagar, a race of trans-dimensional demons, involves the forced ingestion of animal blood while the victim sleeps. But while the Mok'tagar can assume many forms, including human, they can always recognise their kind due to the lack of a soul.

Further to Barq's Buffy Halloween Bash (see **57**, 'The Freshman'), the winning character gamepiece was revealed to be Riley Finn.

Soundtrack: Cher's 'Believe'. Over and over . . . Willow listens to Four Star Mary's 'Pain' [*] on the stereo. This highlight of their 1999 CD *Thrown to the Wolves* previously featured in both **28**, 'Bewitched, Bothered and Bewildered', and **36**, 'Dead Man's Party'. The Dingoes seem to have been in a studio and recorded at some stage (see **63**, 'The Initiative').

Joss Whedon Comments: 'Reaction seems mixed but OK. I can live with that,' Joss told the *Posting Board*. 'At least it's a *totally* accurate portrayal of roomies – I almost hired a man to kill mine when he straightened his rug. And he hated me even more. Marti wrote a script that I hardly had to touch, it was so tight. Taking/giving credit is a strange thing in TV. Sometimes you rewrite an episode completely, top to bottom, and no one ever knows. Sometimes five of us end up working on one script. Marti has done uncredited work on tons of *Buffy* and *Angel* scripts. Everyone compliments me on the crane-game scene in *Toy Story*, which I didn't write. Fact is, I've built an extraordinary staff. Wait till you see Jane Espenson's work next week.'

59
The Harsh Light of Day

US Transmission Date: 19 Oct 1999
UK Transmission Date: 21 Jan 2000

Writer: Jane Espenson
Director: James A Contner
Cast: Melix (Bryan)

Harmony returns to Sunnydale as a vampire. She attacks Willow but Oz saves her. Harmony, meanwhile, heads underground to her new boyfriend, Spike, who is trying to dig into a crypt. Buffy and Parker Abrams go to a frat party and run into Spike and Harmony, who mentions the Gem of Amara, much to Spike's annoyance. Giles always believed the Gem (which renders the wearer invincible) was a myth. Xander, meanwhile, has to deal with the return of Anya and her suggestion that they have sex so she can get Xander off her mind. Buffy spends the night with Parker, but is hurt by his casualness afterwards. Spike finds the crypt and, eventually, the gem and heads into the daylight. He attacks Buffy but she manages to wrestle the ring from his finger.

He starts to burn, but makes it into a sewer. Buffy tells her friends that she wants Angel to have the ring.

Dudes and Babes: Buffy: 'Does this always happen? Sleep with a guy and he goes all evil?' There's *loads* of sexual tension in Harmony and Spike's relationship, which veers perilously close to sadomasochistic. Harmony suggests that Drusilla also shared an abusive relationship with Spike.

A Little Learning is a Dangerous Thing: Harmony is surprised that they have museums in France.

Denial, Thy Name is Anya: 'We went to the prom,' Anya notes. Xander replies that this was their one and only date, the second being cancelled 'on account of snake'. And, Anya's previous life as a man-killing demon-thing. Which, he admits, is as much his issue as anything.

Denial, Thy Name is Xander: Xander: 'So, the crux of this plan is . . .?' Anya: 'Sexual intercourse. I've said it like a dozen times.' Xander: 'Just working through a little hysterical deafness here.'

It's a Designer Label!: Oz (see **58**, 'Living Conditions') and Willow (see **51**, 'Enemies') wear simultaneous sheepskins. There's *some* cool clothes – Buffy's dress and leather skirt, Oz's Dragon Inn T-shirt, Anya's red dress. Also Willow's totally impractical ankle-length dress (a forerunner of several she'll wear this season), Anya's chunky sandals and Harmony's shiny blue pants and lace-up mauve top.

References: Giles refers to the Gem as the vampire equivalent of the Holy Grail. Discount store Wal-Mart, Antonio Banderas (*An Interview With a Vampire*, *The Mask of Zorro*, *Evita*, *Desperado*), his wife Melanie Griffith (*The Drowning Pool*, *Body Double*, *Something Wild*, *Stormy Monday Working Girl* and *Tart*) and Cher's 'Love Hurts' are mentioned. *Indiana Jones and the Last Crusade* seems to have been an influence.

Bitch!: Buffy: 'Harmony. A vampire? She must be dying without a reflection.' Willow: 'She just made me so mad. "*My boyfriend's gonna beat you up*" . . . *If* you believe her. She always lied about stuff like that. "*He goes to another school. You wouldn't know him*".'
    Harmony: 'Hi. What a cute outfit. *Last year*.'
    Buffy to Spike: '*You* with Harmony? What'd you do? Lose a bet?'

Awesome!: Xander squirting his cran-apple skyward as Anya strips naked. Who said the single entendre was dead? Buffy's casual lying about how she got the scar on her neck ('angry puppy') and Willow's delightfully wimpy 'band-aid, now?'

Valley-Speak: Willow: 'Buffy's looking at Parker. Who, it turns out, has a reflection, so *big plus* there. Buffy's having *lusty wrong* feelings.'

Cigarettes and Alcohol: A guy juggles beer bottles at the party. Most other guests drink it.

Act Naturally: The girl walking down the corridor of Buffy's dorm as she and Parker stand outside her door on whom the camera lingers . . . Whose relative is *she*?

Logic, Let Me Introduce You to This Window: In *Angel*: 'In the Dark', Oz says he only knows sixth-grade first aid; here he seems remarkably proficient in bandaging a wound. When Harmony tells Buffy that Drusilla left Spike for a fungus demon, her hair changes between shots. Spike rips off the necklace that *isn't* the Gem, but a moment later it's back around his neck. Giles notes that there was a great deal of vampiric interest in locating the Gem during the 10th century. Questing vampires combed the earth, but no one ever found anything. It was concluded that it never existed. Hardly surprising since it was buried in Sunnydale, part of a continent not discovered by Westerners until the 15th century.

I Just *Love* Your Accent: 'I *love* writing both Spike and Giles,' Jane Espenson told the *Posting Board*, although she confessed: 'I find that I've exhausted my supply of British slang. I better read more *Professionals* fanfic, that's where I find the words.' Presumably that's where she picked up 'stupid bint' as used by Spike – an extremely derogatory (and borderline racist) term. Spike also notes: 'I would be insanely happy if I heard *bugger-all* about sodding France.' Spoken like a true Englishman.

Quote/Unquote: Anya, to Xander: 'I have condoms. Some are black . . . I like you. You're funny and you're nicely shaped and frankly it's ludicrous to have these interlocking bodies and not interlock. Please remove your clothing now.'

Harmony: 'You love that tunnel more than me.' Spike: 'I love *syphilis* more than you.'

Oz on Giles's record collection: 'OK, either I'm borrowing all your albums or I'm moving in.' Giles: 'There are more important things than records right now.' Oz holds up *Loaded*: 'More important than *this*?'

Notes: 'Sun beaming down in a nice, non-fatal way. It's very exciting.' Four returning characters signal the most *Buffy*-like episode of the season thus far. Xander's decidedly odd relationship with Anya is an obvious source of laughs, but inevitably most attention focuses on the return of Spike. A schizophrenic romp follows. The Spike subplot is great, the Buffy-gets-shoddily-treated-by-guy one isn't. Fortunately, the former (eventually) gets more screen time.

Buffy tells Parker that she once drowned (**12**, 'Prophecy Girl'). Xander says the last time he saw Anya, she was fleeing in terror (**55**, 'Graduation Day' Part 1) and refers to his and Anya's only date (**54**, 'The Prom'). He notes that Anya's brutally matter-of-fact invitation to sex is still more romantic than Faith (**47**, 'The Zeppo'; **49**, 'Consequences'). Harmony reminds Spike that he almost killed Willow last year (**42**, 'Lover's Walk') and, from the same episode, there are references to Spike's inability to win back Drusilla (who left him for a fungus demon). Buffy has a scar from Angel feeding off her (**56**, 'Graduation Day' Part 2). The Willow/Harmony exchange 'I haven't seen you since . . .' 'Graduation. Big snake huh?' also refers to this episode. When Xander turns on Giles's TV, it's tuned to Channel 14, the same channel that Joyce and Buffy watched in **49**, 'Consequences'. Spike says Sunnydale has witnessed some truly spectacular kickings of his ass – which include **15**, 'School Hard'; **18** 'Halloween'; **22** 'What's My Line?' Part 2 and **34**, 'Becoming' Part 2. Buffy has a copy of the Sunnydale High 1999 yearbook seen in **56**, 'Graduation Day' Part 2. Giles cleans his foil, which we last saw in **55**, 'Graduation Day' Part 1.

Buffy and Willow's answering machine message has Buffy saying: '*Hey, this is Buffy and Willow. We're not in right now, so please leave a message.*' Willow seems to have a new computer; the last one was a laptop, but she has a desktop in the dorm. Xander's basement flat has a fridge and a washing machine, as well as less practical adornments like a framed map of the US and a glitter-ball. The frat house seems to belong to Gamma Alpha Pi, judging from the Greek letters on the wall. The house across the street is Tau Omega Alpha. Parker says he switched from Pre-Med to History as his major and that all of his scars are psychological. His father died last year, which made Parker develop a live for now philosophy. All bollocks to get inside Buffy's knickers, of course.

Sunnydale is sometimes referred to by demons as the Valley of the Sun. At some point, the gang (except, perhaps unsurprisingly, Xander) found out that Angel was in Los Angeles. They seem to know where he's living since Oz goes to Angel Investigations in *Angel*: 'In The Dark'. Devon used to date Harmony (presumably *after* he split up with Cordelia in **18**, 'Halloween'. It's difficult to imagine Cordy accepting one of *Harmony*'s cast-offs). Giles owns a TV set (he's shallow like the rest of us, notes a relieved Xander). Giles claims he only watches public access television.

Soundtrack: The album Oz finds at Giles's home is *Loaded*, by the Velvet Underground. Oz is a fan, but we already knew this (see **28**, 'Bewitched, Bothered and Bewildered'). Songs include Four Star Mary's 'Dilate' (which Dingoes Ate My Baby mime to), Psychic Rain's 'Take Me Down', Dollshead's 'It's Over, It's Under', 'Faith In Love' by Devil Doll and three at the party by the splendid Bif Naked, 'Moment Of Weakness', 'Anything' and the epic 'Lucky' [*] (the song to which Buffy and Parker dance and then have sex in one of the series' best uses of music and visuals).

Head On ... Rupert's Record Collection: 'In one episode I had a wind-up gramophone,' Tony Head told Paul Simpson and Ruth Thomas. 'Now I've got a proper system. Still vinyl, though, and quite right too! Digital is all right but you miss a lot of ambient sound. I'd love Giles to open a record shop. If he ever has a shop it'll probably be a bookshop, but I'd love him to have a corner with all those old James Brown albums.'

Younger fans may be interested to know there was a UK psych/prog band in the late 60s called Rupert's Children. Never had a hit.

Jane Espenson's Comments: 'Harmony and Spike? Clearly not a love relationship like he had with Dru, but I think you can see that he considers her worth a dalliance,' Jane told the *Posting Board*. 'She's a pretty girl and seems to be up for a good time. I'm sorry that people found Buffy too naive in her reaction to Parker, but I will remind you that she was taken very much by surprise by his rejection and that even though she was, to a certain extent, using him to try to get over Angel, she still *genuinely* liked the guy. We all know [how] hard it is when you like someone who doesn't like you back. Even once you learn that they're scum, you still wonder why . . .'

Subsequently On *Angel*: 'In The Dark': In LA, Oz gives Angel the Gem, but Spike, together with a vampire torturer, Marcus, kidnap

Angel, demanding the ring as ransom. Angel is eventually rescued by his partner Doyle, Cordelia and Oz but not before Marcus has double-crossed Spike to obtain the ring. Angel kills Marcus, enjoys his first daylight in two hundred years then destroys the ring so that it cannot fall into the wrong hands again.

60
Fear Itself

US Transmission Date: 26 Oct 1999
UK Transmission Date: 28 Jan 2000

Writer: David Fury
Director: Tucker Gates
Cast: Marc Rose (Josh), Sulo Williams (Chaz), Walter Emanuel Jones (Edward),
Adam Bitterman (Gachnar), Aldis Hodge (Masked Teen), Darris Love (Hallmate),
Michele Nordin (Rachel), Adam Grimes (Lobster Boy),
Larissa Reynolds (Present Girl)

Buffy, still suffering from Parker-withdrawl, reluctantly joins Oz, Xander and Willow at a Halloween frat party. But, after an accident involving a demonic symbol, the gang find themselves in a House of Horrors, in which a demon feeds on their hidden terrors. Anya realises that something is wrong and goes to Giles for help. In the house, each of the gang faces their terrors but with the arrival of Giles, they are able to defeat the demon and discover that there is, literally, nothing to fear but fear itself.

Dudes and Babes: Frat Guy: 'Halloween isn't about thrills, chills and funny costumes, it's about getting laid.' Well, we know *that* ...

A Little Learning is a Dangerous Thing: Xander: 'I tend to hear the actual words people say and accept them at face value.' Anya: 'That's stupid.' Xander: 'I accept that.'

Riley says that Halloween isn't a night for responsibility. It's when the ghosts and goblins come out. Buffy replies: 'That's actually a misnomer.' It isn't. A misnomer is when something is incorrectly named; what she means is it's a fallacy.

Mom's Apple Pie: Joyce's alters the length of Buffy's red riding hood cape.

Denial, Thy Name is The Scooby Gang: The Scoobies' greatest fears are: Buffy, of being abandoned by her friends; Willow, that

Buffy doesn't need her help or take her magic seriously; Oz, of being unable to control the wolf within and, Xander, of being superfluous and invisible to his friends (which had already been dealt with in **47**, 'The Zeppo'). Anya tells Xander that he doesn't fit in with the gang.

Work is a Four-Letter Word: Xander helps Giles catalogue his books.

It's a Designer Label!: Riley's white shoes with black trousers. Oz's La Farge T-shirt and his Louisville 1988 basketball shirt. Buffy's flowery top and Xander's yellow and black sportshirt.

References: The title alludes to Franklin Roosevelt's 1938 inauguration speech. The video store gave Xander the Disney classic *Fantasia* instead of the 1979 SF/horror movie *Phantasm*. Oz notes: 'Maybe it's because of all the horrific things we've seen, but hippos wearing tutus just don't unnerve me the way they used to.' Willow describes *Julius Caesar* in seven words: 'Brutus. Caesar. Betrayal. Trusted friend? Back stabby?' There's a mention of Arbor Day, a little-celebrated US public holiday on the last Friday in April. Oz's reference to his Casio amplifier, 'Mi casio es su casio', is a clever pun on the Spanish phrase *Mi casa es su casa* (my home is your home). Giles owns a Frankenstein's monster doll and quotes from James Whale's *Frankenstein* ('It's alive!'). Buffy refers to *Abbott and Costello Meet Frankenstein*. Gachnar is reminiscent of the Wizard in *The Wizard of Oz*, who pretends to be powerful, but proves to be harmless. Xander quotes *Star Wars Episode 1: The Phantom Menace* ('Sensing a disturbance in the Force, Master?'). Possible influences: *Kiss of the Vampire* (the bat attack), Polanski's *Repulsion*, *Night of the Living Dead*. The Halloween costumes are: Red Riding Hood (Buffy), Joan of Arc (Willow), James Bond (Xander) and God (Oz).

Bitch!: Oz: 'Xander's a civilian.' Frat Guy: 'Townie, huh? He looked so normal.'

Awesome!: Oz's God-costume (his normal clothes with a sticker saying God), Giles's hilarious comedy-sombrero (and chainsaw!), Anya's rabbit outfit. Buffy and Joyce share a touching scene concerning regret. Scariest moment: the girl that Anya sees hammering on the window before the building swallows her. Funniest bit: the last line.

'You May Remember Me From Such Films and TV Series As . . .': Marc Rose played Perryman in *Clockwork Mice*. Sulo Williams was Manny in *Playing Mona Lisa*. Walter Emanuel Jones was the Black Ranger in *Mighty Morphin Power Rangers*, starred in *Malibu Shores* with Charisma Carpenter and appeared in *Talisman* and *Malcolm X*. Adam Bitterman's movies include *Denial* and *Homicide*. Aldis Hodge was Raymond in *Die Hard: With a Vengeance* and featured in *Big Momma's House*. Darris Love appeared in *Passing Glory* and *Shrunken Heads*.

Don't Give Up The Day Job: Tucker Gates directed episodes of *Angel*, *The X-Files*, *Roswell*, *Space: Above and Beyond*, *Nash Bridges* and *Cracker*.

Valley-Speak: Joyce: 'Your father *loved* to take you out.' Buffy: 'He was such a pain. Twelve years old and I can't go trick-or-treating by myself?' Joyce: 'He just wanted to keep you safe.' Buffy: 'No, he wanted the candy. I was *the beard*.'

Buffy: 'That just paved right over memory lane, huh?'

Cigarettes and Alcohol: Bottles of beer are in evidence at the party.

Logic, Let Me Introduce You to This Window: The Frankenstein's monster doll is swinging throughout Giles and Buffy's conversation, but in one shot it's stationary. The area on which the Mark of Gachnar is painted is obviously different from the rest of the floor. In the scene in which Oz and Xander bring over the sound system, the hair dangling on Xander's forehead moves around in different shots. When Willow is checking Buffy's wound, her left braid is behind her. The camera then switches angles, and it's resting on her shoulder. Giles's bag seems far too small for a chainsaw to fit into, let alone pull out so easily.

Quote/Unquote: Buffy: 'I was just thinking about the life of a pumpkin. Grow up in the sun, happily entwined with others. And then someone comes along, cuts you open and rips your guts out.'

Willow on the camouflaged guys: 'What are they supposed to be?' Oz: 'NATO?'

Xander on Oz's costume: 'I wish I'd thought of that before I put down my deposit. I could have been God.' Oz: 'Blasphemer.'

Giles: 'Don't taunt the fear demon.' Xander: 'Why? Can he hurt me?' Giles: 'No, it's just *tacky*.'

Xander: '*That's* your scary costume?' Anya: 'Bunnies frighten me.' (See **100**, 'The Gift'.)

Notes: 'If we're close our eyes and say it's a dream it'll stab us to death. These things are real.' Straight-comedy-horror of the kind that *Buffy* excels in. There's much to laugh at but also lots of subtle characterisation and a clever ending.

Only one person dies and that's an accident. Buffy remembers when Ethan turned everyone into their costumes (see **18**, 'Halloween'). That's why Xander wears the James Bond outfit (so if it happens again, he'll turn into someone cool). Giles repeats what he said in **18**, 'Halloween': Creatures of the night hate Halloween. They find it much too crass. Xander refers to Uncle Rory (see **20**, 'The Dark Age'; **47**, 'The Zeppo'; **116**, 'Hell's Bells') who likes his schnapps. Willow says she has much in common with Joan of Arc: being almost burned at the stake (see **45**, 'Gingerbread') and having a close relationship with God. She claims to be proficient in wicca-basics such as levitations, charms and glamours. She calls on Aradia, goddess of the lost, for her guiding spell. She is aracnophobic. Anya and Xander copulated in **59**, 'The Harsh Light of Day', which was a week ago. Joyce mentions that her last boyfriend was a homicidal robot (see **23**, 'Ted'). She didn't make any new friends the year she came to Sunnydale, largely through fear. 'I didn't believe I could trust anyone again. It's taken time and a lot of effort, but I've got a nice circle of friends now.'

Soundtrack: 'Kool' by 28 Days, 'Ow Ow Ow' by Third Grade Teacher and Verbena's 'Pretty Please'.

61
Beer Bad

US Transmission Date: 2 Nov 1999
UK Transmission Date: 4 Feb 2000

Writer: Tracey Forbes
Director: David Solomon
Cast: Eric Matheny (Main Cave Guy), Stephen M Porter (Jack, the Pub Manager), Kal Penn (Hunt), Jake Phillips (Kip), Bryan Cuprill (Roy), Lisa Johnson (Paula), Joshua Wheeler (Driver), Patrick Belton (College Kid #1), Kaycee Shank (College Kid #2), Steven Jang (College Kid #3), Cameron Bender (Stoner), Kate Luhr (Young Woman)

Xander gets a job bartending while Buffy drowns her sorrows over Parker Abrams by drinking with a bunch of snooty upperclassmen. This, at the very moment that the bar manager has spiked the beer causing the drinkers to revert to a caveman mentality. Buffy is affected too, but when the cavemen start a fire, Cave-

Slayer Buffy's instincts reactivate and she saves Willow's life. And batters Parker over the head with a stick.

Dreaming (As Blondie Once Said) is Free: Xander asks how Buffy's *fugue state* is coming along, referring to a state of altered consciousness that may last days. Buffy's daydream, saving Parker from the vampires, is hilariously over-the-top, including ice cream and flowers.

Dudes and Babes: Willow tells Parker: 'I got your number, *id-boy*. Only thing you're thinking about is how long before you can jump on my bones.'

Giles's description of Buffy is: 'Blonde. About this tall. Walks with a sort of a sideways limp.'

Authority Sucks!: Oz missed two classes of Psychology (and perhaps more when he went to LA). This is interesting, since Professor Walsh told Buffy in **60**, 'Fear Itself', that if she missed a second class, she'd be kicked out. Perhaps Walsh simply didn't notice Oz's absences.

Denial, Thy Name is Buffy: Concerning Parker, Buffy suggests that maybe he's just having trouble dealing. She asks Willow if guys sometimes put the girl they really like inside these deep little brain fantasy bubbles where everything's perfect. Maybe, Buffy suggests, she's in his bubble and soon he's going to realise that he wants more than just bubble-Buffy 'and he'll pop me out and we'll go to dinner'.

Work is a Four-Letter Word: Xander is the new barman at the college pub which, needless to say, he's hopeless at. His fake ID features a photo with an obviously stuck-on moustache.

It's a Designer Label!: Emmy nominated for 'Outstanding Hair-styling for a Series'. That's a joke category, right? Buffy's leather dream-pants are fantastic but there are some crappy clothes, like Buffy's orange top, yellow skirt and butterfly pyjamas and Xander's Hawaiian shirt. Keep your eye open for the very tight red dress worn by a girl Oz passes in the Bronze.

References: Xander refers to *Cocktail* and Chan Romero's 'The Hippy Hippy Shake'. Also, St Thomas Aquinas (1225–74; Italian philosopher and theologian) and, obliquely, Tom Wolfe's *The Electric Kool-Aid Acid Test*.

Bitch!: Guy, to Xander: 'I think we have a perfect venue here for conducting a little sociometry. A bipolar continuum of attraction and rejection. Given your sociological statuses I foresee a B-rejects-A dyad. I'm sorry, lemme clarify. You see, *we* are the future of this country and *you* keep our bowl of peanuts full.'

Willow: 'You heard of this Veruca chick? Dresses like Faith, voice like an albatross?'

Awesome!: Xander's incompetent bar-keeping. And that's about it . . . Giles is completely wasted and hardly anybody other than Xander gets any decent lines. Very poor.

'You May Remember Me From Such Films and TV Series As . . .': Eric Matheny was Chuck Britz in *The Beach Boys: An American Family* and Adam Beam in *Time of Your Life*. Steven M Potter has been in *Mad About You* and *Friends*, and the movie *Favourite Deadly Sins*. Lisa Johnson featured in *The Next Step*, while Patrick Belton appears in *Under the Bus*. Steven Jang was Sushi in *Mystery Men* and Vincent Wang in *One Fine Day*.

The Drugs Don't Work: Xander refers to Giles as '*Mister I spent the 60s in an electric-kool-aid-funky-satan-groove.*' Apart from correcting the era (it was the early 70s), Giles doesn't disagree (see **20**, 'The Dark Age'; **40**, 'Band Candy'). What, exactly, Jack puts in the beer is never revealed except that he learned its secrets from his warlock brother-in-law.

Valley-Speak: Buffy: 'Even if I had a pretend cigarette I couldn't tell you my pretend problems. The real ones have clogged up my headspace.' And: 'I'm suffering the afterness of a bad night of *badness*.'

Cigarettes and Alcohol: Willow refers to Wild Turkey, a brand of whisky. In California, you have to be 21 to work behind a bar, which is why Xander needs a fake ID. The two types of beer seen are Poker's Light and Black Frost. Buffy notes that her mother always said beer was evil.

Logic, Let Me Introduce You to This Window: As Xander tries to practice his bartending skills on Willow and Buffy, the coffee cups on the table move twice. When Xander holds up his fake ID, the shots from behind show that he's holding the licence with his thumb and middle finger, but in shots facing him, it's between with his thumb and index finger. When Willow drinks from the cup that Oz brought her, she holds it at the top, but as the camera changes angle, her hand is lower. The second time Buffy is drinking with the guys, the pitcher of beer gets fuller between shots. There's a real logic problem with the end of the episode. It's established that the cave-people fear fire (Buffy even says, when smelling the smoke, 'fire bad'). Yet she still goes inside the burning building. Now *that*'s sloppy.

I Just *Love* Your Accent: There's a Welsh flag on the wall of the pub.

Quote/Unquote: Xander: '*Nothing* can defeat *The Penis*.' And: 'You're a bad, *bad* man.'

Buffy: 'I went to see Xander. Then I saw Parker. Then came beer.' Willow: '. . . And then group sex?'

Giles: 'I can't believe you served Buffy that beer.' Xander: 'I didn't know it was evil.' Giles: 'But you knew it was *beer*.'

Notes: 'It's all about the sex . . . Men haven't changed since the dawn of time.' A thoroughly *rotten* episode. The comedy is lame and the lack of rationality in the plot is embarrassing. The ending suggests that the solution to betrayal and rejection is to clunk somebody over the head with a large piece of wood. Well, *thanks* Tracey, that *really* helps. One would have expected a debut writer could have produced something more adventurous or involving than this.

Buffy speaks a little French (more than Xander, anyway). Buffy likes open-shirted guys, pink roses and ice cream. One of the sororities at UC Sunnydale is Beta Delta Gamma. Oz knows the drummer of Shy.

Soundtrack: Lauren Christy's 'Perfect Again', 'I'm Gonna Fall' by Ash, Smile's 'The Best Years', 'Nothing But You' by Kim Ferron [*], 'Wonderland' by Collapsis and instrumental pieces 'It Feels Like I'm Dying', 'I Can't Wait' and 'People Will Talk' by Paul Trudeau. The music of Veruca's band, Shy, is by THC ('Overfire' features here). George Sarah, the group's composer/programmer appears as Shy's keyboard player in both **61**, 'Beer Bad', and **62**, 'Wild At Heart'. The video Buffy watches on TV is Luscious Jackson's 'Ladyfingers'. Jill Cunniff, the band's vocalist, was a childhood friend of Joss Whedon.

Critique: Tom Mayo in *SFX* didn't like the episode either: 'The Parker plot-thread feels artificially stretched out and the fact that his apology to Buffy is triggered by her hitting him with a stick is a strange message to send out ... It doesn't help that the usual clever dialogue is largely replaced by wanky sociological technobabble and grunts.'

62
Wild At Heart

US Transmission Date: 9 Nov 1999
UK Transmission Date: 11 Feb 2000

Writer: Marti Noxon
Director: David Grossman

Spike returns to Sunnydale but is immediately captured by the mysterious Commandos. It's full moon and Oz escapes from his cage and wakes naked next to another werewolf. Veruca. She scoffs at his cage-living habits and tells him that the wolf is part of him. Oz attempts to help Veruca by locking her up with him, but Willow finds them together next morning. Veruca tries to kill Willow but Wolf-Oz kills Veruca. Buffy then stops him from attacking Willow. Oz realises that he doesn't have control of the wolf and decides he must leave Willow with whom he shares a heartbreaking farewell.

Dreaming (As Blondie Once Said) is Free: Wish we could have actually *seen* Willow's dream instead of just hearing the edited highlights ('It's in the sandblaster ... All Geminis to the raspberry hats').

No Fat Chicks!: Veruca says she likes eating: 'I hate chicks who are like, "*does it have dressing on it?*" '

Dudes and Babes: Willow: 'I need a translator from the *Y* side-of-things.' Xander's view of sex fall into the categories: '*Wild-Monkey-Lurv*' and '*Tender-Sarah-McLachlan-Lurv*'.
   Veruca appears in bra and pants in one scene.

A Little Learning is a Dangerous Thing: Buffy seems to be doing really well in Psych, Maggie Walsh giving her a discussion group to lead. It's got to the point where she has Willow academically jealous.

Denial, Thy Names are Oz and Willow: You name it, they're denying it: the wolf inside him, the fear of losing Oz in her ...

Rent is a Four-Letter Word: Willow notes Xander's mom is cranky. Xander replies: 'We're having a little landlord-tenant dispute, so I'm withholding rent. An effective and, might I add, thrifty tactic. She won't let me put a lock on my door. She's afraid I'll start having *the sex*.'

It's a Designer Label!: Willow's shirt makes her look like a crazy birthday cake. Oz wears some ace T-shirts including a red Lou Reed one, and a mustard Clash design. Willow's sexy-Veruca look doesn't work at all. Check out Shy's bass player's boots.

References: The title comes from a David Lynch movie. Buffy suggests that Giles owns an Eight-Track (a chunky-cartridge audio format of the 70s), but she's probably being sarcastic. Also, the Rolling Stones, *wild-child* singer Fiona Apple, the late Jerry Garcia of the Grateful Dead, Elvis's 'Hound Dog', Sarah McLachlan and Habitrail (makers of pet environments, see **55**, 'Graduation Day' Part 1). In his room, Oz has posters for Cibo Matto (see **13**, 'When She Was Bad'), Widespread Panic (whose stickers have appeared in numerous episodes), Greg Gunn and Red Meat. Giles appears to be watching *Jeopardy* (knowing that the 30 Years War ended with the Peace of Westphalia, and not Yalta and bemoaning 'You moron. That dinette-set should be mine'). Oz and Veruca enjoy an intense discussion on amplifiers, name-checking several brands.

Bitch!: Willow's spell: 'I conjure thee, by Borabis, by Satanis, and the Devil. As thou art burning, let Oz and Veruca's deceitful hearts be broken. I conjure thee, by the Saracen Queen, in the name of Hell. Let them find no love or solace. Let them find no peace as well. Let this image seal this fate, not to love, only hate . . .'

Awesome!: Spike's 20-second appearance, ranting about the Big Bad being back just as he's captured by the Commandos.

Surprise!: The identity of the second werewolf.

Valley-Speak: Buffy: 'Yeah, she's *quelle-Fiona*. Colour me bored.'
Willow: 'I don't speak musicianese.' And: 'I felt all *spazzy*.'
Giles: 'It's ages since I've been to a gig. Don't look that way. I'm *down* with the new music. And I have the albums to prove it.'
Oz: 'You're a . . .' Veruca: 'Werewolf groupie. Nobody else gets it done for me.'

Logic, Let Me Introduce You to This Window: When Professor Walsh hands Buffy her paper, Buffy accepts it in her left hand, the next shot shows it in both hands. When Oz approaches Veruca in the café, she's holding her cup and about to take a drink, but as the camera switches away, she's just picking it up. During the Willow/Xander scene, Xander's hands change position on several occasions.

Cruelty To Animals: Call *People for Ethical Treatment of Were-wolves*. Veruca suggests that werewolves eventually retain the memories of their time in wolf form, though Oz hasn't reached that stage yet.

Quote/Unquote: Buffy: 'I'm sure Oz is flogging and punishing himself . . . This is sounding wrong before I even finish.'

Veruca: 'God, somebody's domesticated-the-hell out of you.'

Buffy to Oz: 'If it's possible, you seem more monosyllabic than usual.' And: 'Now might be a good time for your trademark stoicism.'

Willow: 'Don't you love me?' Oz: 'My whole life. I've never loved anything else.'

Notes: 'The wolf is inside me all the time, and I don't know where that line is any more between me and it.' From the ridiculous to the sublime. A brutal love story shot through with as much emotional impact as most series can manage in an entire season. Top marks to Seth and Alyson and to Paige Moss for an exercise in disturbing sexuality. If you don't cry at the end of this, you're a lost cause.

Buffy mentions running into the commando guys at Halloween (see **60**, 'Fear Itself'). She reminds Giles that she ran away and went to Hell, before she got over killing Angel (see **34**, 'Becoming' Part 2; **35**, 'Anne'; seemingly the demon-dimension seen in 'Anne' *was* Hell, unless she's speaking metaphorically). Giles says he made a very interesting moussaka last night. Though it's rare, this isn't the first time Giles has been to the Bronze (see **1**, 'Welcome to the Hellmouth'; **25**, 'Surprise'). Oz again refers to how cool Giles's record collection is (see **59**, 'The Harsh Light of Day'). Items seen in Xander's flat: a globe, a food blender, a CD rack (without many CDs) and a psychedelic Paris poster.

Willow mentions that there's a Wicca group on campus which she is joining (see **66**, 'Hush'). Oz's cage is in an underground crypt in one of the local cemeteries. He seems a dab hand at welding. When Oz says he knows how Willow feels seeing him with Veruca, he's bluntly referring to finding her with Xander in **42**, 'Lover's

Walk'. Willow says Oz gets a blushy thing behind his ears when he's attracted to someone. Shy have a Wednesday night residency at the Bronze. The Dingoes were supposed to be playing there next Friday but, presumably, that was cancelled unless they got a replacement guitarist quickly. Spike appears to believe in fate (which seems an odd attitude for a vampire).

Unconfirmed fan reports suggest that the building used for exterior shots of Giles's apartment is one previously used in *Melrose Place*. It certainly has the same number, 4616.

Soundtrack: 'Good Enough' by Eight Stops Seven, 'Dip' and 'Need To Destroy' by THC.

The Album: Released in November 1999, *Buffy the Vampire Slayer – The Album* (Columbia 496633 2) was a superbly put-together CD of music from the show (Nerf Herder's theme, Velvet Chain's 'Strong', Bif Naked's 'Lucky', a censored 'Slayer Mix' of Four Star Mary's 'Pain' and 'Transylvanian Concubine' by Rasputina) along with songs inspired by the series, including heavyweight acts like Garbage. It was an odd, but very effective, mixture containing tiny nuggets of Britpop (Hepburn's 'I Quit', the Sundays' 'Wild Horses') and the shimmering beauty of Splendid's 'Charge' amid the more expected grunge bands such as Guided By Voices (whose 'Teenage FBI' is the best thing on the CD) and Superfine's thrashy 'Already Met You'. The CD also included Chris Beck's Emmy-winning 'Close Your Eyes' theme from **34**, 'Becoming' Part 2. Produced by Patricia Joseph, with Joss Whedon credited as Executive Soundtrack Producer, the CD, helped by some judicious advertising, sold by the bucketload.

63
The Initiative

US Transmission Date: 16 Nov 1999
UK Transmission Date: 18 Feb 2000

Writer: Douglas Petrie
Director: James A Contner
Cast: Scott Becker (Lost Freshman)

Spike is being held in a hi-tech facility underneath the university. Riley, who has a crush on Buffy, is revealed to be a member of a military demon-hunting group – the Initiative – run by Professor

Walsh. They perform experiments on captured demons. Spike manages to escape and finds Willow, but is unable to bite her – the Initiative having put a chip in his head that renders him impotent. Buffy rescues Willow, and the Initiative and Buffy narrowly avoid discovering each other's secret identities.

Dudes and Babes: Three sex-babes walk through shot in the opening seconds as a salivating Forrest notes: 'Women. Young, nubile, exciting. Each one a mystery, waiting to be unlocked.' When Riley tells Forrest that the next hot girl he is looking at is Buffy, Forrest thinks it's a bit of Valley-Speak. Riley thinks Buffy is peculiar and prefers girls he can get a grip on. The fact that she went out with Parker Abrams (for about 30 seconds) seems common knowledge on campus. Parker says that Buffy is definitely a bunny in the sack but that later on, 'You know the difference between a freshman girl and a toilet seat? A toilet seat doesn't follow you around after you use it.'

Authority Sucks!: 'Since I'm neither a freshman nor a narcissist,' Walsh tells Willow, 'I have to consider the whole class. If your friend can't respect my schedule, I think it's best he not come back.'

A Little Learning is a Dangerous Thing: Harmony doesn't know the difference between French and Italian.

The Conspiracy Starts at Home Time: Special Agent Riley Finn, identity number 75329, and his colleagues Forrest Gates and Graham Miller form part of a government project known as the Initiative and run by Professor Walsh. Spike (Hostile 17) has been implanted with a chip that means he can't harm any living creature without intense neurological pain.

It's a Designer Label!: Buffy: 'I need to go find something slutty to wear.' Yet at the party, as Willow notes, she's sporting a halter top with sensible shoes. Riley, Forrest and Graham wear tastefully relaxed gear throughout. Minus points for Parker's horrible red sweatshirt, Harmony's tight scarlet pants and Buffy's gold dress.

References: Ouija-boards, the US Marine Corp's motto *semper fidelis*, the Denver Broncos, the Sex Pistols, *Star Trek: First Contact* and John Wayne. On the blackboard in Walsh's class are references to psychologists Ivan Pavlov (1849–1936) and BF Skinner (1904–90).

Bitch!: Willow: 'You spend time together, feelings grow deeper and one day, without even realising it, you find you're in love. Time stops and it feels like the whole world's made for you two alone, until the day one of you leaves and rips the still-beating heart from the other, who's now a broken, hollow mockery of the human condition.' Riley, after Buffy has left the party with Xander: 'It's not like she blew me off. She just left with another guy, that's all . . .' Forrest: 'I hate to say it, but they're probably on their way to make crazy-naked-sex.'

Awesome!: Xander and Harmony's side-splittingly girly fight (made all the funnier by the dramatic music and slow motion). Riley punching Parker after he makes lewd comments about Buffy. Plus the entire sequence where Spike is unable to bite Willow, filled with impotence metaphors ('Maybe you're trying too hard. Doesn't this happen to every vampire?'). The Initiative set must have cost a fortune.

'You May Remember Me From Such Films and TV Series As . . .': Bailey Chase was Flicker in *Cosmo's Tale*. Leonard Roberts played Emmet Taylor in *The 60s* and Tyrone in *Hoodlum* and also appeared in *Due South*.

The Drugs Don't Work: According to Tom, the Initiative drug the blood they give to captured vampires.

Valley-Speak: Forrest: 'She's a major-league *hottie*.'
 Spike: 'Your blondie-bear is here to stay.'
 Willow: 'I'll scream.' Spike: '*Bonus!*'

Cigarettes and Alcohol: Spike calls Harmony his little mentholated pack of smokes.

Logic, Let Me Introduce You to This Window: Spike wakes up on the cell floor with his shirt completely open. When the camera switches, the shirt is buttoned to his midriff. When Harmony strikes the match it seems to burn out, but next shot it's a large flame again. Walsh says Spike escaped at 2.47 p.m. This would be daylight and would also mean that she waited several hours before notifying Riley. Graham refers to Spike's 62.3-degree body heat as room temperature. Standard room temperature is between 68 and 77 degrees Fahrenheit. Spike says that he is only 126, but in **15**, 'School Hard,' Giles said that Spike was barely 200. Given that *Angel*: 'The Prodigal' finally answered the question of Angel's age and suggested that vampires take their age from the day they became a vampire, this dating means that Spike would have been sired around 1873 (however, see **85**, 'Fool for Love', and various subsequent episodes which dates his sireing to 1880). Lying about one's age – that's not very clever. Do vampires need to be invited into rooms in the dorm? Here it's a bit ambiguous, but in **76**, 'The Yoko Factor', Angel definitely does. Yet in **57**, 'The Freshman', Sunday's crew appear to be able to walk into any room.

I Just *Love* Your Accent: Spike uses the exclamation 'piffle'.

Quote/Unquote: Spike assumes that the Initiative is Buffy's work: 'I always worried what would happen when that bitch got some funding.'
Buffy: 'You know for someone who teaches human behaviour, you might try showing some.' Walsh: 'It's not my job to coddle my students.' Buffy: 'You're right. A human being in pain has nothing to do with your job.' Walsh to Riley: 'I like her.'

Notes: 'Remember, if you hurt her, I'll beat you to death with a shovel.' Six episodes of subplots begin to come together in this epic example of continuous narrative. There are key scenes involving Spike and Willow and Xander and Harmony take part in one of the most deliberately ridiculous fight sequences in TV history.
Willow says that Buffy likes cheese (see **28**, 'Bewitched, Bothered and Bewildered'; **78**, 'Restless') and ice-capades without the irony (see **21**, 'What's My Line?' Part 1; **46**, 'Helpless'). Oz's full name is Daniel Osborne. Willow has been in a black hole of despair since Oz left. Mr Gordo is mentioned again (see **21**, 'What's My Line?' Part 1). Giles likes raspberry fruit punch. Harmony berates Spike for trying to stake her (see **59**, 'The Harsh Light of Day') and has a unicorn poster in her lair (see **80**, 'Real Me'). Spike notes he wanted to bite Willow last year when she was wearing the fuzzy pink number with the lilac underneath (see **42**, 'Lover's Walk'). He speaks French. Buffy and Willow kept Kathy's stereo (see **58**, 'Living Conditions'). The Initiative HQ is under Lowell House where Riley lives. Riley says that Dingoes Ate My Baby played at a Lowell House party last year. **63**, 'The Initiative', was deliberately short on Buffy scenes to allow Sarah Michelle Gellar to film her part in *Angel*: 'I Will Remember You'. Production on *Angel* was, generally, one week ahead of *Buffy*. James Marsters's name was added to the opening credits on this episode in place of Seth Green. The voice of Xander's mother was heard for the first time.

Soundtrack: Jake Lee Rau's 'Welcome', Nikki Gregaroff's 'Like We Never Said Goodbye', Moby's 'Bodyrock', 'Never Say Never' by That Dog, Deadstar's 'Lights Go Down' and Four Star Mary's 'Fate' (also heard in **16**, 'Inca Mummy Girl').

Did You Know?: The list of Stevenson Hall residents which Spike looks at includes Jeff Pruitt (Stunt Coordinator), David Solomon (Co-Producer), and Lisa Rosenberg (Hair Stylist). Other names seen include: Cindy Rosenthal, Tim Speed and Brooks Tomb.

64
Pangs

US Transmission Date: 23 Nov 1999
UK Transmission Date: 25 Feb 2000

Writer: Jane Espenson
Director: Michael Lange
Cast: Tod Thawley (Hus), Margaret Easley (Curator/Anthropology Professor), William Vogt (Jamie), Mark Ankeny (Dean Guerrero)

At the groundbreaking ceremony for a new cultural centre Xander accidentally releases Hus, an Indian spirit, looking for vengeance on the white settlers who took his people's land. Meanwhile, Buffy wants to have a Thanksgiving with the people she loves, but must try to work out whom Hus will attack next. She and the Scooby Gang also have to deal with Spike, who arrives at Giles's home seeking help. When Angel – secretly in town to watch Buffy's back – tells Willow, Xander and Anya that Hus will target Buffy, they rush into a war between Buffy and a band of Native American spirits. With the battle over, everyone sits down to enjoy the meal and Xander reveals Angel's presence.

Dudes and Babes: Anya loves watching Xander perform sweaty manual labour and imagines having sex with him while doing so.

Pompous, Thy Name is Willow: Thanksgiving isn't about the blending of two cultures, says Willow: it's about one culture wiping out another. And then they make animated specials about the part with the maize and the big belt buckles. They don't show the next scene, where all the bison die and Squanto takes a musket ball in the stomach, which is all more-or-less historically accurate if, as with much of what Willow says in this episode, somewhat hysterically PC.

Work is a Four-Letter Word: Xander's current job is as a construction worker digging the foundation for the new cultural centre. Anya thinks that his workclothes are so much sexier than the outfit from his last job. Willow, however, misses the free hot dogs on sticks.

It's a Designer Label!: Buffy's Stetson. Willow wears a garish pink Sal's Surf Shop T-shirt and a peace symbol sweater. Her fluffy orange jumper puts in another appearance, as does Angel's blood-red shirt. Anya's multi-coloured pants and red top. Harmony wears a horrible blue and red sleeveless pullover.

References: The Village People are mentioned, along with Dutch post-impressionist Vincent Van Gogh (1853–90), the Californian supermarket chain Ralphs, *Superman* ('*soon-my-electro-ray-will-destroy-Metropolis*-bad'), misquotes of Robert Frost's *The Death of the Hired Man* (Riley's line is wrong, Buffy's reply is correct) and Mighty Mighty's 'Is There Anyone Out There?' Iowa landscape artist Grant Wood (1891–1942), *Gentle Ben*, *Julius Caesar* and General George Custer (1839–76). Buffy points out that many Indian reservations now have casinos.

Bitch!: Buffy to Spike: 'So, you haven't murdered anybody lately? Let's be best pals.'
  Spike: 'You know what happens to vampires who don't get to feed?' Giles: 'I always wondered that.' Spike: 'Living skeletons, mate. Like famine pictures from those dusty countries, only not half as funny.'

Awesome!: The scene between Giles and Angel (one of Tony Head's favourites). And the Giles/Willow confrontations (Willow: 'Angel? I saw him too.' Giles: 'That's not terribly stealthy of him.' Willow: 'I think he's lost his edge'). Sparkling dialogue in just about every scene (*love* the five-way argument about how to deal with Hus). The running joke about Angel being evil. Plus the *Scooby Gang-bicycle-challenge* and Giles's hilarious phone call while under attack.

'You May Remember Me From Such Films and TV Series As . . .': Tod Thawley was Eddie in *Roswell* and the voice of Nightwolf in *Mortal Kombat: The Animated Series*. Margaret Easley appeared in *Slackers* and *Introducing Dorothy Dandridge*. William Vogt was in *Murdercycle*.

Valley-Speak: Buffy: 'It's *so* not fair.'

Cigarettes and Alcohol: Giles has brandy, which he keeps in the bookcase.

Logic, Let Me Introduce You to This Window: During the Anthropology professor's speech, a car alarm goes and then abruptly stops. Anya acts as if she's never seen Angel before ('So this is Angel? He's large and glowery, isn't he?'), but they previously met in **50**, 'Doppelgängland'. As the Chumash spirits disappear, Spike is lying on the floor with the arrows still in him. One is missing from a previous shot. At dinner, Spike's shirt has no arrow holes in it. Spike complains that throughout an entire siege you'd think one of the gang would bleed. Buffy bled twice (she was shot with an arrow and cut with a knife).

I Just *Love* Your Accent: Buffy: 'Native American. We don't say "Indian".' Giles: 'Always behind on the terms. Still trying not to refer to you lot as "bloody colonials".' Giles says he likes mushy peas.

Cruelty To Vampires: Spike on his implant: 'I'm saying that Spike had a little trip to the vet, and now he doesn't chase the other puppies any more.'

Cruelty to Animals: Anya: 'To commemorate a past event, you kill and eat an animal. It's a ritual sacrifice. With pie.' Xander throws bread rolls at the bear that Hus turns into, while Buffy stabs it.

Quote/Unquote: Xander: 'Can we come rocketing back to the part about me and my new syphilis?' Anya: 'It'll make you blind and insane, but it won't kill you. The smallpox *will*.'

Spike: 'I can't take all this namby-pamby boo-hooing about the bloody Indians . . . *You won*. All right? You came in and you killed them and you took their land. That's what conquering nations do. It's what Caesar did and he's not going around saying, "I came, I conquered, I felt really bad about it." The history of the world isn't people making friends. You had better weapons, and you massacred them. End of story.' Xander: 'Maybe it's the syphilis talking, but some of that made sense.'

Willow: 'At least we all worked together. It was like old times.' Xander: 'Especially with Angel being here and everything . . . Ooops.'

Notes: 'You exterminated his race. What could you possibly say that would make him feel better?' One of Epsenson's best scripts, a comedy that takes time to examine ideological dogma (and, literally, *slays* it), the nature of custom and with wonderful lines for all of the regulars, especially fan-favourites Marsters and Caulfield. Every inch a gem, every scene a classic.

Buffy seems able to sense when Angel is nearby. Willow's mother does not celebrate Thanksgiving or Columbus Day because they concern the destruction of the indigenous peoples. Buffy says that Joyce is spending Thanksgiving with Aunt Arlene in Illinois (see **53**, 'Choices'; this is the first explicit acknowledgement that Kristine Sutherland would be missing for most of the rest of this season. The actress was, in reality, spending several months house-sitting for a friend in Italy). Willow mentions the church the Master was in (see **1**, 'Welcome to the Hellmouth'). Reference is made to Xander trying to avoid his family gatherings (see **44**, 'Amends'). Angel notes that his friend had a vision in which Buffy was in trouble, referring to Doyle at the climax of *Angel*: 'The Bachelor Party'. Willow asks Angel if it's true that Cordelia is working for him. Anya inflicted a lot of putrefying diseases when she was an avenging demon and tells Xander that it looks as though he is getting *all* of them. There was an earthquake in 1812 that buried the Sunnydale mission. Riley is from Iowa and his grandparents live in Huxley. Harmony has been doing a lot of reading and says that she is in control of her own power now and doesn't need Spike to complete her. The dean of UC Sunnydale is Matthew Guerrero. His house is near the gym.

Head On: 29, 'Passion' remains Anthony Stewart Head's favourite *Buffy* episode, telling Paul Simpson and Ruth Thomas, 'I think it had fantastic performances.' However, he also rates 'Pangs' highly: 'I thought Alyson in "Pangs" was just extraordinary – you don't see such an emotional performance on television. "Hush" was fantastic too. It's the one episode we can't show the kids cos it's so scary . . . Joss has some wonderful ideas. "Let's do two-thirds of the show in silence . . .! Just to see if we can . . ." Then [he] gives himself the task of writing it. I love that Joss plays with the medium. He's not content to say, "We've got something good, let's milk it dry." He wants to see where we can go with it . . . You've got "Doppelgängland" in which Alyson is brilliant as her alterego. I respect Joss hugely for taking risks, not sitting back turning out the same old stuff.'

Subsequently On *Angel*: **'I Will Remember You'**: Discovering Angel's secret visit, Buffy follows him to LA for a confrontation. But, as they prepare to go their separate ways, a demon attacks Angel. They pursue the demon and Angel kills it, but a mingling of blood restores Angel's humanity. The Oracles, Doyle's link to the Powers That Be, confirm Angel's new status and he and Buffy share a perfect day together. But Angel's new humanity has made him weak in a fight. After hearing that Buffy would perish if he were to remain human, he begs the Oracles to fold back time. They do, and despite Buffy's certainty that she will remember what they shared together, when time is reversed only Angel has the knowledge of what might have been.

65
Something Blue

US Transmission Date: 30 Nov 1999
UK Transmission Date: 3 Mar 2000
Writer: Tracey Forbes
Director: Nick Marck

One of Willow's spells goes awry, causing Giles to go blind, Xander to become attractive to demons and Buffy and Spike to get engaged. As the new couple plan their wedding, the demon D'Hoffryn notices Willow's abilities and offers to make her a vengeance demon just as he once did with Anya. Riley runs into a starry-eyed Buffy, who tells him that she is betrothed to a much older man (although not as old as her last boyfriend). Willow sticks with humanity and reverses the spell. Buffy tells a baffled Riley that she made the whole thing up to tease him.

Dudes and Babes: The banner that Riley helps to hang says 'UC SUNNYDALE LESBIAN ALLIANCE'.

Demonity Sucks!: Something that fans had suspected is established: some demons have the power to turn humans into demons. D'Hoffryn (who created Anyanka, see **127**, 'Selfless') seems disposed to getting the human's permission first.

It's a Designer Label!: An interesting mixture: Buffy's leopardskin skirt and the fluffy orange slip-on that Spike holds up. Willow's multicoloured poncho, tartan pyjamas and Speak No Evil shirt.

Xander's orange and white flower sweatshirt. Best of all, Anya's tight red top (which goes beautifully with her short haircut).

References: The title is a reference to the wedding rhyme: 'Something old, something new, something borrowed, something blue.' 'Doesn't rate huge in *The Zagat's Guide*' refers to a popular US guidebook. *The English Patient*, the daily TV soap *Passions* ('Timmy's down the bloody well'),[21] KC and the Sunshine Band's 'Boogie Shoes', the media creation girl-power, *One Million Years BC*, *The Brave Little Toaster*, Bette Midler's 'Wind Beneath My Wings', *Steel Magnolias* and Fruit Roll-Ups. Buffy hums *The Wedding March*. Willow misquotes Stevie Smith's 'Not Waving but Drowning'.

Bitch!: Spike: 'You are one step away, missy.' Buffy: 'Help. He's going to scold me.'

Buffy: 'My mother gave me that name.' Spike: 'Your mother? Yeah, *she's* a genius.'

Anya on how she became a demon: 'I'd been dumped, I was miserable, doing a few vengeance spells – boils on the penis, nothing fancy' (see **89**, 'Triangle'; **127** 'Selfless').

Awesome!: Giles's novelty Kiss the Librarian coffee mug. A continuation of the excellent multi-handed dialogue scenes that impressed so much in **64**, 'Pangs'. (Buffy: 'Spike and I are getting married.' Xander: 'How? What? How?' Giles: 'Three excellent questions.')

Don't Give Up The Day Job: Nick Marck began as an assistant director on *10*, *Battlestar Galactica*, *The Postman Always Rings Twice* and *Rehearsal for Murder* before becoming a director on *The Wonder Years*, *The X-Files*, *Dawson's Creek* and *Malcolm in the Middle*.

Valley-Speak: Buffy: 'Cars and Buffy are, like, un-mixy things' (see **40**, 'Band Candy').

Cigarettes and Alcohol: Willow gets extremely drunk in the Bronze on Miller Lite. Giles is drinking the hard stuff again (see **20**, 'The Dark Age'). In Giles's home we can see a decanter of whisky and a bottle of champagne.

---

[21] Many fans believe this to be a reference to the *Lassie* movies – in which Timmy *was* frequently down a well, or something similar. Since *Passions* does include a character called Timmy, the matter remains unresolved.

Logic, Let Me Introduce You to This Window: Buffy's hair changes from crimped to straight throughout the episode. Willow tosses her bag on to her desk, hitting a hanging star. The star swings, but after a cut from Giles to Willow, it has stopped. Spike's reflection can be seen several times in Giles's glass bookcase. When the demon breaks through the door into Xander's basement, some wood falls to the floor. A moment later, it's leaning up against the door. As the demon throws Xander on to the tool bench, a piece of paper falls to the floor. When Xander gets up, the paper is back on the bench. According to some eagle-eyed fans, the rat used to portray Amy is male (this also occurs in **67**, 'Doomed').

I Just *Love* Your Accent: The first use of the word ninny in the series.

Quote/Unquote: Spike: 'I won't have you doing mojo on me if you can't read properly. You might turn me into a stink beetle.' Giles: 'It would be a generous ending for you.'

Spike: 'I don't like him. He's insipid. Clearly human.' Buffy: 'Red paint. We could smear a little on his mouth; blood of the innocent.' Spike: 'That's my girl.'

Willow: 'No offence intended. I mean, you've been super-nice and everything, but I don't want to be a demon. I just wanna go back and help my friends.' D'Hoffren: 'That is your answer? I'm sorry to hear that. Oh well, here's my talisman. Change your mind, give us a chant.'

Notes: 'Just say yes and make me the happiest man on earth.' Another cracker that proves that Forbes's talent lies with satire rather than slapstick. Willow's disastrous attempts to rid herself of grief send the Scooby Gang into some of their worst nightmares (*nothing* could be more horrible for Buffy and Spike than what happens to them). It's a smart script with clever characterisation and a willingness to try something different.

Buffy mentions having seen Angel in LA for five minutes (see *Angel*: 'I Will Remember You'). Giles refers to Oz's departure in **62**, 'Wild at Heart', Willow remembers the spell that she almost cursed on Veruca. Buffy reminds Willow of her own beer fest, when she became Cave-Buffy (see **61**, 'Beer Bad'). Willow mentions Amy turning herself into a rat (see **45**, 'Gingerbread') and all the demons who've been attracted to Xander: Insect Lady (see **4**, 'Teacher's Pet'), Mummy Girl (**16**, 'Inca Mummy Girl') and Anya. D'Hoffryn was first seen in **50**, 'Doppelgängland', when Anya asked him to give back her powers and he refused. Anya was originally human; D'Hoffryn made her a demon 1120 years ago (see **127**, 'Selfless').

Devon is mentioned. Oz has been in touch with him and asked for his stuff to be sent on. UC Sunnydale has a park called Rugg's Field. Drowning is the only way to kill a Pargo demon. Spotted in Xander's flat: a dartboard, a portable TV, a basketball hoop and a poster for the band Red Meat (see **62**, 'Wild at Heart').

Soundtrack: Blink 182's 'All The Small Things' and 'Night Time Company' by Sue Willett. Excellent wacky Chris Beck score.

Tracey Frobes's Comments: 'We spend a lot of time in the writers' room discussing real emotions [and] things that have gone on in our own lives,' Frobes told *Cinescape Online*. 'What we can remember from college and exactly how we felt. You become very close to the people who you work with. You really *do* end up talking about all the pain that you've ever been through in very open and honest ways so that we can best portray that on the show.'

66
Hush

US Transmission Date: 14 Dec 1999
UK Transmission Date: 10 Mar 2000

Writer: Joss Whedon
Director: Joss Whedon
Cast: Brooke Bloom (Wanna-Blessed-Be), Jessica Townsend (Wanna-Blessed-Be),
Camden Toy (Gentleman), Charlie Brumbly (Gentleman),
Doug Jones (Gentleman), Don W Lewis (Gentleman),
Carlos Amezcua (Newscaster), Elizabeth Truax (Little Girl),
Wayne Sable (Freshman)

A group of skeletal demons – the Gentlemen – come to Sunnydale and steal everyone's voices. This is to enable them to take the hearts of seven chosen victims without them being able to scream. The Scooby Gang (as well as the Initiative) try to devise a means of defeating the sinister villains while deprived of the power of speech. Willow befriends a fellow wiccan, Tara, while Buffy and Riley fight the Gentlemen together, thereby revealing their secrets identities to each other.

The Trailer: The WB promoted this special episode with a series of unique trailers: 'Some fairy tales should not be told. This one will come true,' and 'Not a single word will be spoken for 29 minutes'.

Dreaming (As Blondie Once Said) is Free: Riley: 'Tell me about your dream. As a Psych major, I'm qualified to go "hmm".' The opening – Buffy and Riley making out in front of the class, before the little girl appears chanting her sinister rhyme – almost seems to belong in a different episode. Is the girl supposed to represent Buffy as a child?

Dudes and Babes: Anya: 'All you care about is lots of orgasms.' Xander: 'Remember how we talked about private conversations? How they're less private when they're in front of my friends?' Spike: 'We're not your friends. Go on.'

Anya, after Xander has bravely fought Spike, makes a circle with her thumb and forefinger and sticks another finger through it repeatedly. Yes, we get the message . . . as, indeed, does Xander. Tara makes her first appearance. There are hints that she and Willow may become more than just friends as they hold hands to create a spell. An interesting fan theory at the time of Tara's arrival was subsequently proved to be accurate: the way Tara both dresses and speaks bear all the hallmarks of someone from a repressive, possibly abusive, home environment (see **84**, 'Family').

The Conspiracy Starts at Home Time: Manipulation of the media: the TV reports that the entire town of Sunnydale has been quarantined due to an epidemic of laryngitis. This has to be an Initiative tactic, surely?

It's a Designer Label!: Some horrible skirts: Buffy's cream model, Tara's very unflattering brown number and Willow's disgusting pink one. Xander wears a couple of remarkably tasteless shirts. He also sleeps in his vest.

References: Seemingly influenced by the dreamlike horror films of Tim Burton (*Batman*, *Edward Scissorshands*, *Sleepy Hollow*) and Stephen King's 'Insomnia'. References to the Earth Goddess Gaia, the festival of Bacchanal, Superman's alter-ego Clark Kent, Revelations 15:1 and Pink Floyd. Buffy quotes Greek philosopher Terence: 'Fortune favours the brave.'

Bitch!: Willow on the wicca group: 'Bunch of *Wanna-Blessed-Be*'s. Nowadays every girl with a henna tattoo and a spice rack thinks she's a sister to the Dark Ones.'

Spike: 'Like I'd bite you anyway . . . Not bloody likely.' Xander: 'I happen to be very biteable, pal. I'm moist and delicious.'

Awesome!: Has *any* series shown a tenth of the wit and imagination of, for instance, the scene in which Giles silently tells Buffy, Willow, Xander and Anya the plot (*everything* in this sequence is perfect, from Anya casually eating popcorn while graphic murder drawings are shown, to the horrified look on Buffy's face at Giles having sketched an unflattering cartoon of her with big hips and a miniskirt). Xander and Spike continue to bicker brilliantly (just love Spike's impression of Anya). How ironic that, in a series about total female empowerment, it's a scream by the heroine that saves the day.

'You May Remember Me From Such Films and TV Series As . . .': Amber Benson played Meg in *Bye Bye Love*, Stoned Girl in *Can't Hardly Wait* and also appeared in *The Prime Gig* and *Imaginary Cries*. Don W Lewis was Major Keena in *Warrior of Virtue*. Camden Toy appeared in *My Chorus*.

Don't Give Up The Day Job: Doug Jones had behind-the-scenes roles on *Smooth Talk* (as set constructor) and *Untamed Heart* and *Equinox* (as a member of the swing gang). Carlos Amezcua is a newscaster on KTLA's *Morning News*. KTLA is the WB affiliate in Los Angeles. The weatherman from the same show, Mark Kriski, appeared in **44**, 'Amends'.

Valley-Speak: Wanna-Blessed-Be: 'One person's energy can suck the power from an entire circle. No offence.'
Willow: '*Blah blah Gaia. Blah blah moon.* Menstrual-lifeforce-power thingy . . .'
Buffy: 'I start babbling. And he starts babbling and it's a babblefest.'

Cigarettes and Alcohol: Olivia seems to be on the whisky again (see **57**, 'The Freshman'). Later she and Giles share a bottle of red wine.

Logic, Let Me Introduce You to This Window: When we first see the clock tower, it's one o'clock. The camera cuts to the interior, looking out at the clock and the minute hand is pointing to the 40-minute mark. As the scene in the lecture hall starts, Anya is empty handed. A moment later, she's eating microwave popcorn. In the same scene, Buffy holds her message board up to ask how she gets her voice back. The marker pen is in her right hand. After a quick cut away, it's in a slot on the board. As Spike opens the fridge, the cup of blood is full to the brim. He takes it out, but, despite tipping it, doesn't spill any blood. When Riley smashes the bottle, a chunk of glass lands on top of the box. When he starts to swing at the box, the glass is gone. When the Gentlemen's heads begin exploding, the shot of one of them is used twice. The list of Stevenson Hall residents that Tara prints out is not the same list that Spike looked at in **63**, 'The Initiative'. Some names are missing, they are in a different order, some students have moved to different rooms and this list includes phone numbers. The 'Yes, We Are Open' sign seems to move location. First, it's seen on a building beside the Espresso Pump, later it's on a premises close to the Sun Cinema. Spike is shown eating biscuits even though it's been long established that vampires don't eat.

I Just *Love* Your Accent: Spike mentions the British breakfast cereal Weetabix. The two-fingered reply that Spike gives to Xander is also *very* British. Amusingly, this gesture has turned up on a list of Obscure Cultural References on a *Buffy* Internet newsgroup. What an odd idea of culture.[22]

Quote/Unquote: Spike: 'Sometimes I like to crumble up the Weetabix in the blood. Give it a little texture.' Giles: 'Since the picture you just painted means I will never touch food of any kind again, you'll just have to pick it up yourself.' Spike: 'Sissy.'

Giles: 'I have a friend who's coming to town, and I'd like us to be alone.' Anya: 'You mean an *orgasm-friend*?' Giles: 'Yes, that's *exactly* the most appalling thing you could've said.'

Olivia: 'All the time you used to talk about witchcraft and darkness. I just thought you were being pretentious.' Giles: 'I was. I was also right.' Olivia: 'So everything you told me was true.' Giles: 'Well no, I wasn't actually one of the original members of Pink Floyd. But the monster stuff, yes.'

Notes: 'Talking about communication, talking about language. Not the same thing.' One of the bravest, most experimental pieces of modern TV pulled off in spectacular and confident fashion. A story about how people talk without actually communicating, 'Hush' is the first of several *Buffy* episodes that take the audience

---

[22] The rationale for this is, seemingly, that the first historical use of the gesture was by British – mostly Welsh – longbowmen as an insult to French archers during the battle of Agincourt (1415), although some sources suggest that's, actually, an urban myth.

on a guided tour of theoretical McLuhanism[23] (see, for example, **107**, 'Once More, With Feeling'). It's easily the scariest *Buffy* ever. And, also, one of the funniest (Giles's projector-screen lecture for the Scooby Gang in particular). A work of almost unparalleled imagination and style.

Willow says that she wants to float something bigger than a pencil (see **45**, 'Gingerbread'; **50**, 'Doppelgängland'; **53**, 'Choices'). Giles takes delivery of *The Sunnydale Press*, the same newspaper seen in **48**, 'Bad Girls' (see **73**, 'Superstar'). Willow asks Tara how long she has been a practicing witch. Since she was little, replies Tara, revealing that her mom had a lot of power (see **84**, 'Family'). At the front of Giles's stack of LPs is the unmistakable cover of *ChangesOneBowie*. There's another Red Meat poster (see **65**, 'Something Blue'). Xander has a novelty clear-plastic phone in his flat.

The call letters of the TV station the Scooby Gang are watching are KOUS. Sunnydale has a liquor store called *Hank's Jr. Mart*. The full nursery rhyme is: 'Can't even shout, can't even cry, the Gentlemen are coming by. Looking in windows, knocking on doors, they need to take seven and they might take yours. Can't call to mom, can't say a word, you're gonna die screaming but you won't be heard . . .'

Soundtrack: The music that Giles plays during the lecture is Camille Saint-Saëns's *Danse Macabre*, also the theme music for *Jonathan Creek*. Both Tony Head and Joss Whedon have confirmed that this was a coincidence.

Did You Know?: Joss told *Ultimate TV* that he had planned for Buffy and Riley to have sex in this episode, but 'it became clear that it was too early for that.' Among the extras at Maggie Walsh's dream-lecture in the opening scene is future *Angel* star Andy Hallett. Many of the exterior sequences were filmed on the backlots at Universal Studios.

Critique: *TV Guide* were fulsome in their praise, calling 'Hush': 'A masterpiece of suffering in silence and one of the season's best episodes of *any* series . . . 'Hush' was a largely wordless nightmare,

---

[23] McLuhanism: the philosophy contained in the writings of Canadian media-guru Marshall McLuhan (1911–80), author of *The Medium is the Message*, which states that the *way* people communicate with each other is far more important than *what* they actually communicate.

thanks to some voice-stealing demons. Whedon devised any number of ingenious ways to propel the plot without dialogue, proving that the unsaid can be scarier than all the screams in Hollywood.'

The cover of *The Hollywood Reporter* from 19 June featured an ad encouraging Emmy voters to nominate 'Hush', accompanied by quotes from TV reviewers including: 'If *Buffy the Vampire Slayer*'s Joss Whedon doesn't get at least an Emmy nomination for "Hush", a horror masterpiece that played out its last half hour in silence, there shouldn't be any Emmys at all' – Robert Bianco, *USA Today*. Plus: '*Buffy*'s the best show on the air: brainy, good-hearted, gloriously expressive TV poetry' – Tom Carson, *Esquire*.

Joss Whedon's Comments: 'The idea came from a few different places,' Joss told Kate O'Hare. 'One of them being, I just wish everyone would shut up. I'm tried of writing dialogue. There was a nugget of that. It's easy in TV to devolve into what I call "radio with faces".' To achieve the Gentlemen's particular mode of above-the-ground transport required suspending the actors from overhead cranes or strapping them on to a dolly kept out of camera range. 'They were expensive and time-consuming,' continued Joss. 'I had a very specific idea about what these guys would look like, and the make-up guys just nailed it.' On the *Posting Board* Joss confirmed that 'inspiration for the Gentlemen came from: *Nosferatu* (both the Max Shreck and Klaus Kinski versions), *Dark City*, *Hellraiser*, Grimm's Fairy Tales, *The Seventh Seal* and much Victorian influence. They came from many storybooks and silent movies, horror movies and nightmares. And Mr Burns (from *The Simpsons*).' When asked what actually scares *him*, Joss confessed: 'It's hard to describe. But I know the guys in "Hush" are as close to it as anything I've ever filmed. It was a monster to film and pulled the best (and most exhausted) work out of everyone. And it is, by the by, a Chris Beckathon. Give him an Emmy to go with his Emmy.'

When Emmy-time rolled around and Joss was, himself, nominated, he told *Variety*: 'It doesn't suck . . . I've had a steady diet of nothing, so I didn't expect a change. I wanted to make things harder on myself. It's easy to fall back on funny jokes and witty lines.' Sadly, though not unexpectedly, 'Hush' didn't win.

67
Doomed

US Transmission Date: 18 Jan 2000
UK Transmission Date: 17 Mar 2000

Writers: Marti Noxon, David Fury, Jane Espenson
Director: James A Contner
Cast: Anastasia Horne (Laurie), Anthony Anselmi (Partier)

Buffy and Riley argue about each having kept secrets from the other, but an earthquake interrupts them. Buffy worries that this may signify an apocalypse and she is correct – yet another ancient prophecy about to manifest itself. The Scoobies return to high school to stop the Hellmouth from opening, while Riley tries to convince a wary Buffy that a relationship between them is viable.

Babes and Babes (Bring Your Own Subtext): As it became clear that the relationship between Willow and Tara was something far more intimate than fans had initially believed, Joss Whedon told the *Posting Board*: 'We meant it to be *subtext*, but you guys have obviously worked it out. Yes, Willow is becoming a *Monkey-owner*. I just hope we don't get a lot of protest from Christian Right Groups over this. Marginally more seriously, Willow and Tara's relationship is definitely romantic. Thorny subject: the writers and I have had long topics about how to deal with the subject responsibly, without writing a story that sounds like people spent a long time discussing how to deal with it responsibly. To me it feels just right. *All* the relationships on the show are sort of romantic (hence the *Bring Your Own Subtext* principle) and this feels like the natural next step for her. I can only promise you two things: we're not going to do *Ally* or *Party of Five* in which we promote-the-hell out of a same-sex relationship for exploitation value that we take back by the end of the episode, and we will never have a *Buffy* where someone gets on a soapbox. I know there's a sweet story, which would become very complicated if Oz were to show up again. Which he will.'

A Little Learning is a Dangerous Thing: Buffy notes that Riley is part of some military monster squad which captures demons and probably has some official-sounding euphemisms for them, like 'unfriendlies' or 'non-sapiens'.' Riley notes that, actually, it's 'Hostile Sub-Terrestrials'. Buffy: 'So you deliver these HSTs to a bunch of lab-coats, who perform experiments on them, which among other things turn some into harmless little bunnies. How am I doing so far?' Riley: 'A little too well.'

The Conspiracy Starts at Home Time: Riley says that the Vahrall demon is not a capture, it's a kill, suggesting that the Initiative don't take all their specimens alive. Forrest believes that the Slayer is a bogeyman that Sub-Terrestrials tell their spawn about to make them eat their vegetables and clean up their slime pits.

Work is a Four-Letter Word: Xander's new job is as a pizza delivery boy.

It's a Designer Label!: Spike wearing a pair of Xander's knee-length shorts and a Hawaiian shirt is a comedy zenith. Also, Buffy's orange top and red trousers, Laurie's slutty red blouse (*very* Faith) and Willow's Bunny's Dog Walking Service T-shirt.

References: The title is a song by Julian Cope. When asked if he's heard of the Slayer, Forrest replies: 'Thrash band. Anvil-heavy guitar rock with delusions of Black Sabbath,' a joke that's four years overdue, frankly. References to *Superman* (Smallville), the Easter Bunny, *Bad Omens*, Morley Safer of CBS's *60 Minutes*, US Navy recruitment commercials ('it's not just a job, it's an adventure'), the video game Donkey Kong, paintball, WB Yates's 'The Second Coming' ('Things fall apart'), *End of Days*, *Survivors* ('what if the end of the world's coming in the form of a plague?'), GI Joe dolls and an oblique reference to Kentucky Fried Chicken. Porter, the hall where the party is taking place, is a college at UC Santa Cruz, which Marti Noxon attended. Both Kresge and Stevenson are also Santa Cruz colleges. Forrest tells Riley that he 'don't got game,' an allusion to the movie *He Got Game* in which Leonard Roberts appeared. Xander misquotes Smokey Robinson's 'I Second That Emotion'. Riley's room has a poster showing various sorts of balls.

Bitch!: Xander: 'You look like a big mooch that doesn't lift a finger around here. But I have to get to work.' Spike: 'Delivering melted cheese on bread, doing your part to keep America constipated.'

Spike on Xander and Willow: 'I should think you would be glad to greet the end of days. Neither one of you is making much of a go at it. Kids your age are going off to university; you've made it as far as the basement. And Red here, you couldn't even keep dog-boy happy. You can take the loser out of high school, but . . .'

Awesome!: Spike's fake American accent (think about this: James Marsters, an American, playing a British vampire doing a *bad* American accent – that takes some doing). Plus his closing rant about making the world safe for 'puppies and Christmas'.

'You May Remember Me From Such TV series As . . .': Anastasia Horne was Lori in *Undressed* and Ana in *Kids Incorporated*.

Valley-Speak: Willow: 'I haven't been a nerd for a long time. *Hello*, dating a guitarist. Or I was.'

Cigarettes & Alcohol: Willow says that Porter dorm is completely blacked out. So, naturally, they're dealing with this crisis in the only way they know how: *Aftershock Party*. Buffy replies that this is the dorm that once had a *Somebody Sneezed* party and the *Day That Ends in Y* party.

The murdered guy is mixing cocktails for a naked limbo contest before he gets killed.

Logic, Let Me Introduce You to This Window: In the continuation from **66**, 'Hush', Buffy's hair changes between episodes. After Riley knocks out the demon, it looks as though the right horn is missing. When Willow finds the dead boy, his eyes are open. Close-up shows them closed. As the gang research the Vahrall demons and Willow reads about the ritual, Xander's pizza shirt is open over a white T-shirt. For one shot, though, it's buttoned up. Willow wears the same clothes to the Aftershock Party as she does in the rest of the episode (covering at least two days). Was everything else in the wash? When Spike attempts to stake himself, the stake flies off and cannot be seen when Spike is lying on the floor. Xander steps in front of him and picks the stake up.

I Just *Love* Your Accent: Spike: 'You want me to tear this place apart, you bloody *pouf*?' Plus almost-English expressions (i.e. not very English at all) like: bloody rot, fag off and, 'Stuck in this basement washing *skivvies* for a *blighter* I wouldn't have bothered to bite a few months ago.'

Cruelty To Demons: Forrest tells Riley that demons are just animals.

Quote/Unquote: Buffy: 'I really thought that you were a nice, normal guy.' Riley: 'I *am* . . .' Buffy: 'Maybe by this town's standards, but I'm not grading on a curve.'

Giles: 'It's the end of the world.' Buffy: 'I *told you*. I said "end of the world" and you're like *poo-poo*. *Southern California*. *Poo-poo*.' Giles: 'My contrition completely dwarfs the impending apocalypse.' (See **2**, 'The Harvest'; **12**, 'Prophecy Girl'; **34**, 'Becoming' Part 2; **47**, 'The Zeppo'.)

Buffy: 'Do you know what a Hellmouth is? Do you have a fancy term for it? Because I went to high school on it for three years.'

Notes: 'I'm the Slayer. Chosen One. She who hangs out a lot in cemeteries . . . Look it up.' 'Doomed' can't quite overcome the written-by-committee-feel that inevitably comes from having three writers involved. Nevertheless, it's frequently amusing, a continuity-fest (including a look at what Sunnydale High is like post-graduation) and the double act of Xander and Spike continues to work incredibly well.

Buffy says that she's 'Capricorn, on the cusp of Aquarius,' which confirms that her birthdate is somewhere between 17 and 20 January 1981. This corresponds with episodes featuring Buffy's birthday (**25**, 'Surprise'; **46**, 'Helpless') airing during the third week of January. She mentions that the last time there was an earthquake in Sunnydale she died (**12**, 'Prophecy Girl'). She tells Riley that the last person who had fun slaying is currently in a coma. This is the first time we've seen Basketball Percy since **56**, 'Graduation Day' Part 2. Willow and he haven't kept in touch although she was aware that he got a football scholarship to USC. Buffy says that Riley is a Psychology graduate student, which would mean that he already has a Bachelor's degree.

Marcus Blucas becomes a series regular and part of the title sequence with this episode.

Soundtrack: 'Hey' by Hellacopters and Echobelly's 'Mouth Almighty'.

68
A New Man

US Transmission Date: 25 Jan 2000[24]
UK Transmission Date: 24 Mar 2000

---

[24] 'A New Man' was originally announced to air on 18 January but was rescheduled to 25 January.

Writer: Jane Espenson
Director: Michael Gershman
Cast: Elizabeth Penn Payne (Waitress), Michelle Ferrara (Mother)

Giles feels disgruntled when Buffy introduces Riley, and Maggie Walsh tells him that Buffy lacks a father figure in her life. Giles subsequently learns of the Initiative (and Riley's involvement in it). Ethan Rayne turns up and convinces Giles to go for a beer so that Ethan can warn him of some impending doom involving '314'. Giles gets drunk and wakes to find that Ethan has turned him into a Fyarl demon. Unable to speak English, he can't communicate with the gang, so he turns to Spike for help (which he gets, for $300 in cash) while Buffy hunts him down, thinking that the demon harmed Giles. Buffy almost kills him, but recognises his eyes. Back at the Initiative, Professor Walsh steps into a high-security room . . . 314.

Dudes and Babes: Anya hopes that Giles's story about a public school prank will involve treacle and a headmaster. Meanwhile, Willow and Tara practice more magick, floating a rose with interesting results.

Denial, Thy Name is Giles: Poor Giles, his feelings of rejection that have been simmering all year finally burst to the surface. He has been fighting demons for 20 years. 'Maggie Walsh and her nancy-ninja-boys come along and six months later demons are pissing themselves with fear.'

The Conspiracy Starts at Home Time: The Initiative is a US military operation. They are able to tap into the 911 emergency call system. Riley says that Ethan will be taken to a detention facility in the Nevada desert. Riley has killed 17 hostiles (11 vampires and six demons).

It's a Designer Label!: Giles's cool black shirt, sadly, gets ripped when he's a demon. Love his suede jacket, though. Willow's *As Seen on TV* T-shirt, Buffy's gold dress, Xander's orange trousers, Giles wearing Ethan's hideous silver satin shirt, and Spike, back-in-black.

References: Giles alludes to the legend of Theseus and the Minotaur. Also, I Spy, Spiderman, Paul Weller's 'Broken Stones' and the Beatles' 'Run For Your Life'. A Widespread Panic sticker can be seen on the rec-room noticeboard.

Bitch!: Walsh, to Buffy: 'We use the latest in scientific technology and state-of-the-art weaponry. You, if I understand correctly, poke them with a sharp stick.'

Spike on Xander's home: 'I've known corpses with a fresher smell. In fact, I've been one.'

Giles to Ethan: 'We've changed. Well not you. You're still sadistic and self-centered.'

Awesome!: The scenes of Ethan and Giles in the bar are a great mixture of comedy and pathos. Demon-Giles waking up Xander is hilarious, but it's Giles and Spike in the car that gives the episode its greatness (Giles: 'Do I have special powers? Like setting things on fire with my sizzling eye beams?' Spike: 'You got ... paralysing mucous.').

Surprise!: Yet *another* surprise birthday party for Buffy.

Don't Give Up The Day Job: Elizabeth Penn Payne was on the craft team of *Mid Summer*.

Cigarettes and Alcohol: Ethan and Giles get drunk on beer and whisky. Spike spends most of the episode smoking.

Logic, Let Me Introduce You to This Window: As Ethan tells Giles that he has poisoned Giles's drink, the head on the beer increases and then decreases. There are a variety of strange things going on with the glasses in this scene, including an empty one that appears and disappears a few times. When Buffy and Willow are having breakfast, Willow picks up her orange juice while the camera is facing her. When the camera switches to Buffy, the glass is still on the table. When Demon-Giles wakes Xander, there are clothes hanging on a line. On the left is a pair of briefs dangling by one peg. A moment later, they're on two pegs. Then one. Then two ... Xander doesn't even go halfway up the stairs before coming back down and stating that Giles isn't upstairs. When Spike and Giles talk in the cemetery, Spike puts a cigarette in his mouth. Next shot, he's still holding it. Ethan is supposedly staying at the Sunnydale Motor Inn, but the shot outside his motel is of a place called the Downtowner Apartments. This is the same shot used in 37, 'Faith, Hope and Trick'.

I Just *Love* Your Accent: Spike refers to a few bob, which was no doubt understood by all of four people in the US, and all of zero in Britain under the age of 35. Giles called Maggie Walsh a harridan and a fishwife.

Ethan: 'Oh, bugger. I thought you'd gone.'

Spike asking the waitress about Ethan and Giles: 'Two of them. English like me. But older. Less attractive.'

Motors: We finally get a car chase in *Buffy*. Granted it's between two Humvees and a Citröen . . .

What A Shame They Dropped . . .: Jane Espenson was asked during an online interview what happened to Spike after he crashed the car: 'That was cut . . . He got out of the car and said, "I can kill demons. I can crash cars. Things are looking up".' Both Robin Sachs and Tony Head have both confirmed that the confrontation between Buffy and Ethan went on far longer than broadcast, that it was a scene both enjoyed and that they were sad that it got cut so much.

Quote/Unquote: Ethan: 'We used to be friends, Ripper. When did all that fall apart?' Giles: 'The same time you started to worship chaos.'

Anya finding Giles's ripped shirt: 'I think it ate him up . . .'

Ethan: 'I really got to learn to just do the damage and get out of town. It's the "stay and gloat" that gets me every time.'

Notes: 'The world has past us by. Someone snuck in and left us a couple of has-beens in our place.' Yet another comedy-diamond from Ms Espenson; a trio of outstanding performances from Head, Sachs and Marsters and the funniest moment of the season (Giles scaring Walsh for no other reason than he doesn't like her).

Buffy jokes that having her toes smashed would be better than her previous birthday surprises (see **25**, 'Surprise'; **46**, 'Helpless'). She tells Riley about the Mayor (see **56**, 'Graduation Day' Part 2). It's confirmed that Buffy was 15 when she became the Slayer in 1996 (see **33**, 'Becoming' Part 1). She likes pancakes and waffles. She has been getting B- grades in Psych. Giles's tendency to get knocked on the head have included severe cranial trauma seen in **29**, 'Passion', **12**, 'Prophecy Girl', **41**, 'Revelations', **33**, 'Becoming' Part 1, **45**, 'Gingerbread', **64**, 'Pangs', and **52**, 'Earshot', among others. Giles went to a public school. Riley owns a master key that opens every shop on Main Street.

Soundtrack: 'Over Drive' by 12 Volt Sex, Other Star People's 'Then There's More', Scott Ellison's 'Down, Down Baby'.

Joss Whedon's Comments: '[Giles's] breakdown's been really funny,' Joss told *Ultimate TV*. 'And it's going to get worse. He's feeling obsolete and gets turned into a demon for an episode and Buffy's hunting him. It's the perfect "I've been replaced, and now they want to get rid of me" metaphor. He's cute as a demon. He's scary-looking, but he's Tony.'

Jane Espenson's Comments: During an Internet convention interview in July 2000, Jane noted: 'Some days you come in at nine, and you're immediately in the room with Joss all day breaking stories. Some days Joss is busy with *Angel*, or busy doing any of a million other things that he has to. And some days you don't even go to work because you're out on script. Some people come in and write their scripts in the office; I write mine at home or in the Beverly Hills Library. I pack up my computer and spend a day there.' Interestingly, Jane added that: 'Usually, nothing of great value is done without Joss in the room. Although, more and more, Marti is running it.' Both Jane and David Fury used time on the *Posting Board* to address comments from fans regarding the lower profiles of Xander and Giles during season four: 'Xander hasn't had a lot to do this year, I agree, but that will change. This year we had our first Giles-centric episode since **20**, "The Dark Age". The character is more peripheral in Buffy's life at the moment, but the actor is doing quite a lot.' Fury added: 'Perhaps it's not clear that Giles does not need to be near Buffy. Giles is the father figure going through an empty-nest syndrome. It's a phase he's slowly making his way out of. Xander's current character arc will play out next season. The dynamics of a post-high school experience is that there is bound to be some splintering. It's natural. Any contrivance like making Giles the campus librarian and Xander his assistant [a widespread fan rumour] is forced and redundant.'

69
The I in Team

US Transmission Date: 8 Feb 2000
UK Transmission Date: 31 Mar 2000

Writer: David Fury
Director: James A Contner

Walsh and Riley familiarise Buffy with the Initiative, but Willow worries that Buffy is getting involved with something she knows little about and that she's also not making enough time for her friends. On patrol with Riley, Buffy helps to capture a Polgara demon. Afterwards, Buffy and Riley spend their first night together and, unbeknownst to them, are watched by Walsh. Concerned that Buffy is becoming a threat to her plans, Walsh sets a trap to have the Slayer killed. Assuming that Buffy is dead, she tries to explain this to Riley, just as Buffy appears on video behind them, telling Walsh that her plan failed. Walsh goes to room 314 to check on her pet project, Adam, who wakes and stabs his creator to death.

Everybody Spanks!: Willow says Buffy is out with Riley: 'You know what it's like with a spanking new boyfriend?' 'Yes,' notes Anya, much to Xander's obvious discomfort. 'We've enjoyed spanking.' Later, Buffy finds that Riley's lunch is a Twinkie bar. 'He's *so* gonna be punished,' she notes. 'Everyone's getting spanked but me,' says a disappointed Willow.

The Conspiracy Starts at Home Time: The research area of the Initiative HQ is called the Pit. Walsh has surveillance cameras in the bedrooms of her boys.

Work is a Four-Letter Word: Xander's new job is selling Boost Bars.

It's a Designer Label!: Buffy's very silly ankle-length skirt, Tara's electric-blue hooded top and Willow's star jumper.

References: The obvious inspiration for Adam is *Frankenstein*. The title is a reference to the adage 'There is *no* "i" in "team",' often used by sports coaches. Also, Twinkies, *Sabrina, the Teenage Witch*, the Discovery Channel, Lightning Seeds' 'The Life Of Riley', David and Leigh Eddings's novel *Polgara the Sorceress*, the Wal-Mart chain, *The Avengers* and the character of Mother, *Private Benjamin* and the Clash's 'Rock The Casbah'. Also an oblique reference to *A Hard Day's Night* ('it's very . . . clean'). The dialogue when Riley, Forrest and Graham track the tracer is similar to a sequence in *Aliens*.

Awesome!: The intercutting of Riley and Buffy fighting the demon with them *performing the act* in bed later – all done like a combination of slow-motion Hong Kong action movie and sultry music video (with Delerium as the soundtrack). *Outstanding*. Xander spilling the cards when Anya talks about enjoying spanking is another highlight, though the slapstick ionisation-scene is a letdown.

'You May Remember Me From Such TV Series As . . .': Jack Stehlin played David Reese in *General Hospital*.

Don't Give Up The Day Job: George Hertzberg wrote and starred in the movie *Too Much Magic*. He also played Tom in *The Pornographer*.

The Drugs Don't Work: Willow: 'Wha'cha got in the boxes, drugs?'

Valley-Speak: Buffy: 'My *total* bad.'

Cigarettes and Alcohol: Giles has a bottle of cognac in the cabinet next to the sink.

Logic, Let Me Introduce You to This Window: When Walsh hands Buffy a stack of papers in the IHQ, Buffy holds them at chest height. But in some shots she's holding them much lower. Walsh goes into room 314 and the door shuts behind her. Then we cut to a frontal shot of her coming in and the door shutting again. When Buffy and Riley have sex, the pillowcases are green and white, but afterwards they're dark red, like the sheets. There's a hole in Spike's T-shirt from where he was shot with the tracer, but his jacket is intact. Buffy's clothes change between scenes. While Buffy is crouched over the map of the sewer system, her arms are crossed. In the next shot, her hands are clasped together. When the demon in the sewer knocks Buffy down, she falls in front of the gun, with her head towards it. Next shot, she and the gun are in different positions. The con-cam picks up audio, so when Buffy threw it down, Walsh should still have heard the fighting going on. The con-cam lands showing a sideways shot of the sewers. A few minutes later, the camera is shown flat on the ground, in a way that would result in a picture of the roof.

I Just *Love* Your Accent: Spike: 'You *right bastard*. That's all that's left. I spent the rest on blood and smokes.'

Cruelty to Animals: Walsh: 'They barely show up on the scanner and occasionally turn out to be raccoons.' She then hands Buffy a weapon, to which Buffy replies, 'You're not crazy about raccoons, huh?'

Quote/Unquote: Anya: 'You haven't been paying any attention to me tonight. Just peddling those process food breaks.' Xander: 'Let me put it in a way you'll understand. Sell bars. Make money. Take Anya nice places.' Anya: 'That *does* make sense. I support you. Go sell more.'

Giles on the tracer: 'It's blinking.' Spike: 'I don't care if it's playing "Rockin' The Casbah" on the bloody Jew's harp, just get it out of me.'

Notes: 'She's becoming a liability.' A game of two halves. Some *great* stuff and the final scene is a real surprise, but there does seem to be something of a sense of treading water for at least half of the episode.

Giles.pays Spike for his help during his recent metamorphosis, but he gets most of it back later. Riley tells Buffy that Walsh liked her before he did and told him so (see **63**, 'The Initiative'). Xander refers to his pseudo-soldier memory bank (see **18**, 'Halloween'). Riley takes vitamins at regular intervals (see **70**, 'Goodbye Iowa'). The government pulled him out of special operations training for this assignment.

Soundtrack: Lavish's 'Trashed', Black Lab's 'Keep Myself Awake' [*]. The song that plays throughout the Buffy/Riley fight/sex sequence is 'Window To Your Soul' by one of this author's favourite artists, Delerium.

70
Goodbye Iowa

US Transmission Date: 15 Feb 2000
UK Transmission Date: 7 Apr 2000

Writer: Marti Noxon
Director: David Solomon
Cast: JB Gaynor (Little Boy), Andy Marshall (Scientist #1),
Paul Leighton (Rough-Looking Demon), Karen Charnell (Shady Lady)

Riley is shocked that Walsh tried to have Buffy killed, but now that the professor herself is dead, the Initiative is falling into disarray. Riley goes into withdrawal from missing the drugs he was, unknowingly, fed and begins to doubt everything he once thought he believed in, including Buffy. Meanwhile, Adam reveals information about himself, while trying to learn about people by investigating their insides.

Cyber-Dudes and Babes: Adam describes himself as a kinematically redundant, bio-mechanical demonoid, designed by Maggie Walsh. In addition to organic material, he is equipped with GP2D-11 infrared detectors, a harmonic decelerator, plus DC servo.

The Conspiracy Starts at Home Time: The project, Adam, was designed by Walsh and Angleman to be the ultimate warrior, pieced together from parts of demons, men and machines. Unfortunately, he has a design flaw. He's completely *insane*.

Why does Tara sabotage Willow's spell to conjure the goddess Thespia? (See **84**, 'Family'.)

It's a Designer Label!: Buffy's crimson turtleneck and strawberry sweater and Giles's fleece jacket.

References: Adam's murder of the little boy is reminiscent of the monster killing a child in *Frankenstein*. Willow, Buffy and Anya watch the *Road Runner* cartoon *Wild About Hurry*. Also, the Weather Girls' 'It's Raining Men' (Buffy: 'It's raining monsters.' Xander: 'Hallelujah!'), *Goldilocks*, *Shazam* ('Holy moley'), Richard Wagner, GI Joe and *The Prisoner* ('I cannot be programmed. I'm a man').

Bitch!: Spike, to Buffy: 'Gotta hand it to ya, Goldilocks. You *do* have bleedin' tragic taste in men.'

Awesome!: Spike's two-thumbs-up encouragement to the Initiative to kill Buffy. The scene of Riley cracking up in Willy's bar is dramatically intense, though it goes on a little long.

'You May Remember Me From Such Films and TV Series As . . .': JB Gaynor was Jeremy Gelbwaks in *Come On, Get Happy: The Partridge Family Story*. Andy Marshall played Alphonse in *Hoods*.

The Drugs Don't Work: Riley and others in the Initiative have been fed drugs to increase their strength. When they stop, he suffers serious withdrawal symptoms.

Cigarettes and Alcohol: There are several scenes in Willy's Place where the distinctive bottles for Malibu, Blue Sapphire gin and Absolut Vodka can all be seen behind the bar.

Logic, Let Me Introduce You to This Window: When Buffy describes what happened in the sewers, she says that the gate slammed down and then she tried to use the gun. However, she actually used the gun first and the gate dropped later. Buffy tells Giles that Walsh sent her on a one-way recon, followed by a shot of Giles looking concerned. A few moments later, after Spike implies that Riley was in on it, the same shot of Giles is used. Spike no longer has a hole in his shirt where he was shot with the tracer in the last episode. Angleman slips in Walsh's blood and lands some way from Walsh's body. However, in the shot from above, the blood appears to stop much closer to her body. It's odd that Spike would have a TV in his mausoleum where one wouldn't normally expect electricity. There are a couple of continuity errors. The Polgara demon was captured the night before this episode starts. However, the second day into the episode, Riley suggests that 'the Polgara demon [we] captured last week' must have killed Walsh. Later, Willy says that he heard a Polgara demon was in town and taken off the streets 'a week or two ago'. Buffy takes the bandana from her hair and wraps it around Riley's hand. Moments later, she's wearing it again. Adam puts a second disk in his drive without having taken out the first. Riley doesn't have a tear in his shirt from being skewered by Adam. Angleman also doesn't have one in his lab coat, nor is he even bleeding (though there is blood on Adam's skewer). When the commandos burst in, Forrest doesn't believe that there was a demon in the room, even though Adam should have been visible through the window.

Quote/Unquote: Xander: 'Storm the Initiative? Yeah, let's take on those suckers.' Buffy: 'I was thinking more that we'd hide.' Xander: '*Oh thank God.*'

Riley: 'That's Hostile 17.' Spike: 'No. I'm just a friend of Xander's . . . Bugger it. I'm your guy.'

Anya: 'You should get yourself a boring boyfriend. Like Xander . . . You *can't have* Xander.'

Buffy: 'I'm the only one that can pass the retinal scan.' Xander: 'Eww. I don't wanna see *that*.' Buffy: '*Retinal.* Scan. Xander.'

Notes: 'I don't generally like to kill humans. But I've learned it pays to be flexible in life.' Marti Noxon's dialogue is sharp, as usual, but there doesn't seem to be a lot of sparkle here. The episode drifts along for far too long without much happening.

Giles's tattoo, the Mark of Eyghon, is shown when he turns off the TV (see **20**, 'The Dark Age'). Willy the Snitch mentions the Apocalypse demons (i.e. the Jhe) who beat the crap out of him in **47**, 'The Zeppo'. The Scooby Gang watch the news on Channel 14 again (see **49**, 'Consequences'; **59**, 'The Harsh Light of Day'). Spike has a cousin who is married to a regurgitating Phrivlops demon.

Soundtrack: Lou Reed's 'Romeo Had Juliet', 'My Last Romance' by Paul Singerman, Mark Cherrie's 'Big Ed'.

71
This Year's Girl

US Transmission Date: 22 Feb 2000
UK Transmission Date: 14 Apr 2000

Writer: Douglas Petrie
Director: Michael Gershman
Cast: Chet Grissom (Detective), Alastair Duncan (Collins),
Jeff Ricketts (Weatherby), Kevin Owers (Smith), Mark Gantt (Demon),
Kimberly McRae (Visitor), Sara Van Horn (Older Nurse), Brian Hawley (Orderly),
Jack Esformes (Doctor)

Faith awakens from her eight-month, Buffy-induced coma seeking revenge. After finding Buffy and the gang, she confronts her ex-friend on campus. The two Slayers fight but Faith escapes. Meanwhile, three mysterious men arrive in Sunnydale by helicopter. Faith, having received a final gift from the mayor, goes to Buffy's home and attacks Joyce, telling her that Buffy doesn't care about either of them. Buffy arrives and the pair again do battle, but Faith uses her gift to switch bodies with Buffy. As an unconscious 'Faith' lies on the floor, Joyce asks 'Buffy' if she is OK. 'Five by five,' she replies.[25]

Dreaming (As Blondie Once Said) is Free: 'So that's my dream,' Faith tells Buffy. '. . . And some stuff about cigars and a tunnel.' Initially, this takes place in the same setting as **56**, 'Graduation Day' Part 2, with Buffy and Faith *still* making the bed. Faith says: 'Little sis is coming' (a reference to Dawn, see **79**, 'Buffy vs Dracula'). The knife is still in Faith's stomach from **55**, 'Graduation Day' Part 1. Subsequently, Buffy is portrayed as a ruthless monster, who murders the mayor and then pursues Faith, literally, to the grave. The grass snake that the mayor picks up is an allusion to what he became in **56**, 'Graduation Day' Part 2.

Authority Sucks!: Willow: 'What about the Council?' Xander: 'Been there. Tried that. Not unlike smothering a forest fire with napalm as I recall.'

Denial, Thy Name is Joyce: Faith: 'Don't tell me you don't see it, Joyce. You've served your purpose. Squirted out the kid, raised

---

[25] The Buffy/Faith body-swap in 'This Year's Girl'/'Who Are You?': 'Buffy' refers to Faith inhabiting Buffy's body and 'Faith' refers to Buffy inhabiting Faith's body. Confused? You will be . . .

her up and now you might as well be dead. Nobody cares, nobody remembers, especially not *Buffy fabulous superhero*.'

It's a Designer Label!: Faith's multicoloured top, Xander's stripy tank-top and anorak. It's been a while since we've seen Willow in a stupid hat, though not in a horrible skirt like the one seen here. Giles sorts the washing, including a pair of spotty boxer shorts.

References: The title is a song by Elvis Costello (see **42**, 'Lover's Walk'). Faith climbing from the grave and standing in the rain may have been inspired by the prison escape in *The Shawshank Redemption*. Also, *Star Trek*, Talking Heads' 'Psycho Killer', Trey Parker's *Orgazmo* and Woody Allen's *Sleeper*, *The Terminator*, *Top Gun*, *The Patty Duke Show* and *Gunsmoke* ('I'd get out of Dodge post-hasty'). Yet another Widespread Panic sticker can be seen. Faith calls Riley the clean Marine, the nickname given to John Glenn by the other Mercury astronauts in *The Right Stuff*.

Bitch!: Xander on Adam and Faith: 'I'd hate to see the pursuit of a homicidal lunatic get in the way of pursuing a homicidal lunatic.'
  Willow on what they should do with Faith: 'Beat the crap out of her?'

Awesome!: Faith, generally.

'You May Remember Me From Such Films and TV Series As . . .': Alastair Duncan appeared in TV shows as diverse as *Blossom*, *Sabrina the Teenage Witch*, *Babylon 5* and *Highlander*. Kevin Owers played a steward in *Titanic*. Sara Van Horn was in *Great Balls of Fire!* and *Devil in the Flesh*.

Don't Give Up The Day Job: Mark Gantt was assistant property manager on *The Siege* and *Barb Wire*.

Valley-Speak: Willow on Faith: 'She's like this *cleavagey-slutbomb* walking around going "Ooh. Check me out, I'm *wicked cool*. I'm five by five".' Tara: 'Five what by five what?' Willow: 'See, that's the thing, no one knows.'

Cigarettes and Alcohol: Spike smokes when he meets Xander and Giles. It's interesting that the Watcher's Council have their own cigarette smoking man, Collins.

Logic, Let Me Introduce You to This Window: Before Buffy finds the demon hanging from the trees, someone is in the bushes to her right. Willow and Xander should have noticed Riley coming down the stairs behind Buffy. Faith rips off her monitor and nothing happens. It should flat-line at least. In Faith's dream, she climbs out of the grave and takes two steps forward. We then have a bird's-eye view of Faith where she's several feet from the grave. When Faith is watching the gang through Giles's window, Buffy has her arm around Riley. Between cuts, her arm goes back and forth from being draped around him to playing with his hair. As Buffy and Willow are talking, an extra in a striped sweater walks by on Buffy's left. Twice. When Faith is rummaging through Joyce's make-up, it's clear that she doesn't have a tattoo. The nurse only dials four numbers when she calls to tell the Watcher's Council that Faith has escaped, which suggests an internal call – yet they arrive in a helicopter. When Buffy unknowingly approaches Faith, she stops about a foot away. After the commercial break, she's much further back. As Faith climbs the wall, it moves a fraction. When Buffy looks over the wall, there are students sitting (without blankets) on the grass, which appears to be dry, even though on Buffy's side it has clearly just rained. As Tara and Willow come down the stairs, the pendant on Tara's necklace continually moves from side to side between shots. Buffy throws Faith across the dining table, knocking everything off. A moment later, the tablecloth and pieces of fruit are back where they were.

Who rings Buffy at Giles's to tell her that Faith has woken up? Not Joyce since Buffy doesn't react like it's her mother on the phone. The very brisk nature of her replies suggest that she's talking to someone whom she doesn't know. The police seem the obvious answer but why would *they* ring Buffy with this news? Buffy, after a very brief call, knows lots of details about Faith's escape (that she knocked out someone at the hospital and stole their clothes). Do the words ludicrous-plot-device seem applicable?

I Just *Love* Your Accent: Willow asks Buffy what she told Riley about Faith. 'That she's my wacky identical cousin from England, and whenever she visits, hijinks ensue.'

Quote/Unquote: Xander: 'I'd say this qualifies for a *Worst Timing Ever* award.'

Buffy: 'I've been looking for you.' Faith: 'Been standing still for eight months, B. How hard did you look?'

Spike: 'I'll head out, find this girl, tell her exactly where you are and then watch as she kills you. Can't any one of your damn little

Scooby Club at least try to remember that I hate you all? Just because I can't do the damage myself doesn't stop me from aiming a loose cannon your way.'

Faith: 'How do I look?' Joyce: 'Psychotic.'

Notes: 'It's like the whole world is moving and you're stuck ... like those animals in the tar pits. It's like you just keep sinking a little deeper everyday and no one even sees.' Some people may try to convince you that season four of *Buffy* failed to capture the heights of previous years. 'This Year's Girl' gives complete lie to this. Isn't it wonderful to see Harry Groener back, even if it's only for two scenes?

Xander refers to his history with Faith (see **47**, 'The Zeppo'). Faith is told about the events of **56**, 'Graduation Day' Part 2: 'Sunnydale High School isn't even there any more ... It was a tragedy. Lots of students died. The principal, the mayor.' Buffy tells Riley: 'Giles used to be part of this Council. For years all they ever did was give me orders.' Riley: 'Ever obey them?' Buffy: 'Sure. The ones I was going to do anyway.'

The detective says that Faith is wanted for questioning for a series of murders, which suggests that the Sunnydale police have worked out a connection between the killings of Alan Finch and Professor Worth. Presumably stabbings aren't *that* common, even in Sunnydale.

72
Who Are You?

US Transmission Date: 29 Feb 2000
UK Transmission Date: 21 Apr 2000

Writer: Joss Whedon
Director: Joss Whedon
Cast: Alastair Duncan (Collins), Chet Grissom (Detective), Rick Stear (Booke), Jeff Ricketts (Weatherby), Kevin Owers (Smith), Rick Scarry (Sergeant), Jennifer S Albright (Date)

'Buffy' eases herself into her new life, flirting with Spike, sleeping with Riley and insulting Tara behind Willow's back. Meanwhile, 'Faith' is kidnapped by the Watcher's Council to be taken to England. Living as 'Buffy', however, opens Faith's eyes to the realities of being a Slayer and she heroically saves the day when a group of Adam's vampire protégés take hostages in a local church.

'Faith' uses Willow and Tara's magic to reverse the switch and an anguished Faith leaves town.

Dreaming (As Blondie Once Said) is Free: 'Buffy' daydreams about stabbing Willow. That girl really has got some nasty stuff floating around in her head.

Dudes and Babes: 'Buffy' on 'Faith': 'A little stint in the *pokey*, show her the error of her ways. I'm sure there's some big-old-Bertha just waiting to shower her *ripe-little-self* with affection.' The lipstick shade Faith picks is called Harlot. 'Buffy' asks Riley: 'What do you wanna do with this body? What nasty little desire have you been itching to try out? Am I a bad girl? Do you wanna hurt me?' When Riley says that he loves her and doesn't want to play games, 'Buffy' is angry: 'Who are you? What do you want from her?' 'Faith', escaping from the Council, tells them that she don't have time for bondage-fun.

Babes and Babes (No Subtext Required): Tara: 'I am, you know.' Willow: 'What?' Tara: '*Yours.*' 'Buffy' is the first to spot the developing relationship.

A Little Learning is a Dangerous Thing: Willow: 'What's wetworks?' Xander: 'Scuba-type stuff.' Anya: 'I thought it was murder.' Xander: 'There could be underwater-murder, with snorkels.'

Mom's Apple Pie: Joyce suggests that she and Buffy spend some time together, some night when she's not being held hostage by a raving psychotic.

Denial, Thy Name is Faith: The first cracks begin to appear in Faith's facade. She hates what she is and this self-loathing explains why *becoming* Buffy had such an attraction for her. The final sequence features Faith, in Buffy's body, beating *herself* and screaming how 'disgusting' she is. This element would be taken further in the subsequent *Angel* sequels, 'Five By Five' and 'Sanctuary'.

It's a Designer Label!: Buffy's leather pants. Hot damn. Also, Willow's pink Peace T-shirt and Tara's chunky white sweater.

References: The title is a song by the Who. Spike misquotes Johnny Burke's jazz-standard 'Misty' ('I'm just as helpless as a kitten up a tree'). In the Bronze, a sticker is visible for the band Split.

Bitch!: 'Buffy': 'I forgot how much you don't like Faith.' Willow: 'After what she's done to you? I wish those Council guys would let me have an hour alone in the room with her. If I was larger and had grenades.'

Anya says she and Xander were going to light some candles and have sex. 'Buffy' replies 'We certainly don't want to cut into *that* seven minutes.'

Awesome!: 'Buffy' in front of the bathroom mirror, practising her moves ('You can't do that. It's *wrong*'). Giles creating a diversion. The reverse-body-swap.

'You May Remember Me From Such Films As . . .': Rick Stear played Stan in *Went to Coney Island on a Mission for God . . . Be Back by Five.* Rick Scarry's movie CV includes *Wag the Dog*, *Naked Gun 33⅓: The Final Insult*, *Us*, *Big Man on Campus* and *Fear* (which he also co-wrote).

The Drugs Don't Work: Riley mentions the drugs that Professor Walsh gave him seem to have made him stronger and increased his healing abilities (see **70**, 'Goodbye Iowa'; **82**, 'Out of My Mind'). 'Faith' is injected with a sedative.

Valley-Speak: 'Buffy': '*Wicked* obvious.'

Cigarettes & Alcohol: Spike drinks beer in the Bronze.

Logic, Let Me Introduce You to This Window: 'Buffy's hair changes between the reprise from the previous episode and the next scene. When Joyce and 'Buffy' go into the house, the door that Buffy smashed in **71**, 'This Year's Girl', appears to be intact. When the Watcher's Council squad jump from the truck, they initially open the door on their left. However, when they close the doors, this one also *shuts* first. Not possible: for doors to latch-close correctly, whichever one opens first should close last. After 'Buffy' imagines stabbing Willow, there's a knife next to her on the desk that wasn't in the previous shot.

I Just *Love* Your Accent: Weatherby: 'We're taking you back to the mother country . . . You've been a naughty girl.' And: 'Stop her, you *ponce*.'

Motors: The Council's big red armoured truck is stolen by Buffy and driven by Giles.

Quote/Unquote: Spike: 'You know why I really hate you, Sum-mers?' 'Buffy': 'Coz I'm a stuck-up tight-ass with no sense of fun?' Spike: 'Yeah, that covers a lot of it.' 'Buffy': 'Coz I can do anything I want and instead I choose to pout and whine and feel the burden of Slayerness? I could be rich. I could be famous. I could have anyone. Even you, Spike. I could ride you at a gallop until your legs buckled and your eyes rolled up. I've got muscles you've never even dreamed of. I could squeeze you until you popped like warm champagne and you'd beg me to hurt you just a little bit more. And you know why I don't? Because it's *wrong*.'

Giles: 'I know what you're going to say.' 'Faith': 'I'm Buffy.' Giles: 'All right, I *didn't* know what you were going to say.'

'Faith': 'What's a stevedore?'

Notes: 'Do you think I'm afraid of you? You're nothing. Disgust-ing, murderous *bitch*.' An extraordinary performance-of-a-lifetime from Sarah as Faith-in-Buffy's-body (she even slips into the Bostonian accent occasionally: listen to her pronunciation of 'about') and Eliza is only half-a-heartbeat behind. A story about fear, self-loathing, trust and redemption, handled sympathetically. This is the best *Buffy* two-parter, taking on a *massive* challenge and doing it coherently, without resorting to melodramatic exposition.

'Buffy' makes a sarcastic comment about Wesley's attempt to capture Faith in **49**, 'Consequences'. Faith uses a credit card that she finds in Joyce's house to ring the airport and book a ticket out of Sunnydale. It most probably belongs to Joyce but it could, just, be Buffy's. The expiry date, she notes, is May 2001. Can it be a coincidence that this was the exact month – just over a year later – in which Buffy did, indeed, expire (**100**, 'The Gift')? The card's number ends 6447.

Willow worries that Buffy has been possessed by a hyena and tells Tara that such possessions are unpleasant (see **6**, 'The Pack'). 'Faith' wants Giles to question her to prove she is Buffy. Giles asks who is the president. 'Faith' replies that they're checking for Buffy, not a concussion. Giles, she contines, turned into a demon and she knew it was him. Can't he just look in her eyes and be intuitive? Giles asks how this happened. 'Faith' responds: 'Ethan Rayne. And you have a girlfriend named Olivia. And you haven't had a job since we blew up the school, which is valid lifestyle-wise . . . When I had psychic power, I heard my mom think that you were like a stevedore during sex. Do you want me to continue?' Giles:

'Actually, I beg you to stop' (see **68**, 'A New Man'; **57**, 'The Freshman'; **56**, 'Graduation Day' Part 2; **52**, 'Earshot'; **40**, 'Band Candy'). Willow says the Bronze is the coolest place in Sunnydale. There isn't a lot of competition, however. The vending machine at Bergen's, apparently, came in second (see **1**, 'Welcome to the Hellmouth').

Willow notes that Buffy and Faith switched bodies, probably through a Draconian Katra spell. Riley says that he doesn't want a bunch of Marines staring in at him during sex, which implies that some of the Initiative are Marines rather than regular army like Riley. He is a suit-wearing churchgoer and is able, in military situations, to get the local police to defer command to him. Giles's TV is again tuned to Channel 14. The Watcher's Council squad are described as a retrieval team and a special operations unit – they handle the council's trickier jobs, e.g. smuggling, interrogation, wetworks, and are known to both Giles and, subsequently, Wesley (see *Angel*: 'Sanctuary'). Collins says that when they go on a job, they always put their affairs in order, in case of accidents. The Council can order a kill if necessary including, seemingly, a Slayer.

Soundtrack: Nerf Herder's 'Vivian', the Cure's 'Watching Me Fall', Headland's 'Sweet Charlotte Rose'.

73
Superstar

US Transmission Date: 4 Apr 2000
UK Transmission Date: 28 Apr 2000

Writer: Jane Espenson
Director: David Grossman
Cast: John Saint Ryan (Colonel George Haviland), Erica Luttrell (Karen), Adam Clark (Cop), Chanie Costello (Inga), Julie Costello (Ilsa)

Suave, cool, successful – Jonathan Levinson is everyone's hero, living in his mansion with gorgeous blonde twins: among other things, he's a movie star, a singer/musician, a basketball player and a better fighter than Buffy the Vampire Slayer, who takes orders from and looks up to him. However, Buffy begins to think that he's a little too perfect. How, for instance, did he star in *The Matrix* without ever leaving Sunnydale? His behaviour regarding a new monster is suspicious. Buffy concludes that he's altered the world to change how people perceive him and the Scooby Gang's research, much to their disappointment, confirms this. Jonathan admits to performing an augmentation spell that created a balancing force, a monster currently terrorising Sunnydale. With Buffy's help, Jonathan destroys the monster to break the spell and return everything to reality.

Dudes and Babes: Buffy has been pushing Riley away, resentful about his having slept with Faith (in **72**, 'Who Are You?'). Jonathan advises Buffy to forgive him, and Riley to let Buffy know that she's the only one for him. And it works.

Marc Blucas removes his shirt to reveal his torso in *exactly* the way that they used to get Boreanaz to every three or four episodes.

Denial, Thy Name is Anya: Anya on alternate realities: 'You could even make like a freaky world where Jonathan's some kind of not-perfect mouth-breather if that's what's blowing up your skirt these days. Just don't ask me to live there.'

The Conspiracy Starts at Home Time: Haviland says that recovery of Adam is the Initiative's most important job. To this end he has asked a 'tactical consultant to address us today'. Graham notes that it's about time they brought out the big guns. Jonathan says that before they can locate Adam they need to understand him better. Adam doesn't eat. Investigating Professor Walsh's original design schematics, Jonathan discovers that his power source is not biological at all. Rather, it's a small reservoir of uranium 235.

It's a Designer Label!: Jonathan wears a dapper mohair suit with a lime-green shirt, together with his black poloneck, and a white tux. Anya's the one with the leather trousers this week, plus a yucky blue and yellow blouse. Also, Willow's fur coat and Buffy's fringy suede jacket.

References: Jonathan spots Giles's chess opening is the Nimzowitsch defence, named after Aron Nimzowitsch (1886–1935). Also, *Batman* (Jonathan crashing through the skylight of the vampire nest), *Wonder Woman*, *He-Man: Masters of the Universe*, vice-president Al Gore's assertion that he invented the Internet, President McKinley (1843–1901), *The Matrix*, the US woman's soccer team and their victory in the 1999 World Cup and *Superman* ('he's like your Kryptonite'). The music is very James Bond-like. The movie playing at the Sun Cinema is *Being Jonathan*

Levinson (a variation on *Being John Malkovich*, presumably). The opening credits were redone to include shots of Jonathan interspersed with those of the regulars: the final shot, of Jonathan walking away, coat billowing behind him, is an *obvious* nod to *Angel*.

Awesome!: The title sequence. What a star that Danny Strong is. Buffy and Anya's conversation is not only pivotal, it's pure-dead-funny too.

'You May Remember Me From Such Films and TV Series As . . .': Robert Patrick Benedict was Richard Coad in *Felicity*. Eric Luttrell played Jody in *Honey, We Shrunk Ourselves*.

Don't Give Up The Day Job: Brad Kane (see **54**, 'The Prom') is the voice behind Jonathan's performance at the Bronze.

Logic, Let Me Introduce You to This Window: A parallel universe was previously seen in **43**, 'The Wish', and **50**, 'Doppelgängland', but that universe was completely alternate, wished into existence in the manner that Anya describes with her shrimp example. In this case, however, only Jonathan is actually altered. Everyone else's *perceptions* have been affected, but the rest of the world is still, essentially, the same. The only person, apart from Jonathan, who realises is Adam . . . How? The explanation given is a load of waffle. As they dance at the Bronze, Buffy puts her hand on Riley's shoulder. A moment later, the same shot is used again.

I Just *Love* Your Accent: One for all *Coronation Street* fans. John Saint Ryan spent a year in Weatherfield playing Charlie Whelan.

Quote/Unquote: Buffy: 'He starred in *The Matrix* but he never left town. And how'd he graduate from med school? He's only eighteen years old.' Xander: 'Effective time management?'
Anya: 'Say you really like shrimp a lot. Or we could say you don't like shrimp at all. "Blah, I wish there weren't any shrimp," you'd say to yourself . . .' Buffy: '. . . I think that Jonathan may be doing something so that he's manipulating the world, and we're all like his pawns.' Anya: 'Or prawns.' Buffy: '*Stop* with the shrimp . . .'
Xander: 'You can't just go *librum incendere* and expect . . .' [Xander's book bursts into flames.] Giles: 'Xander, don't speak Latin in front of the books.'
Anya: 'Who really did star in *The Matrix*?' Riley: 'That wasn't real *either*?'

Notes: 'Sounds like you could use my help.' How many other series take the mickey out of themselves as successfully as this? What **47**, 'The Zeppo', did for Xander, this does for an even more unlikely hero. One of the best *Buffy* episodes because it scores on just about every level – comedy, 'what if?' scenario *and* drama.

Buffy takes sugar in her coffee. In this reality, anyway. Jonathan mentions going to therapy after the thing with the bell tower and the gun (see **52**, 'Earshot'). Xander has problems opening milk cartons.

The *Sunnydale Times*'s website is at www.sunnydaletimes.com.

Alternate Continuity: In the Jonathan-universe, he seems to have taken over Buffy's role. Xander says that Jonathan crushed the bones of the Master and blew up the mayor. Willow mentions that Buffy gave Jonathan the Class Protector award at their prom. He calls Giles Rupert, and regularly beats him at chess. Jonathan has his own website, Jonathan.com. The *Jonathan* comic books (*Target: Jonathan*) are published by Dark Horse. Other officially endorsed products include: Jonathan-O's cereal, a basketball poster, an I ♥ Jonathan T-shirt, an autobiography called *Oh, Jonathan*, shoe advertisements, trading cards, a swimsuit calendar (Giles has one; a gift, allegedly) and at least two CDs (Tara notes at the Bronze that he's performing a song 'off the new album').

Soundtrack: Four songs by Royal Crown Revue (the band on stage at the Bronze who back Jonathan): 'Trapped (In A Web of Love)', 'Jonathan's Fanfare', 'Serenade In Blue' (the song that Danny Strong mimes to) and 'Hey Sonny'.

Danny Strong's Comments: When asked by Rob Francis whether the cast and crew played along with his 'Superstar' status during filming, Danny confirmed: 'Unfortunately, no. That would have been great. However, everyone has always treated me fantastically on the show. I was hoping that being the "Superstar" meant that I could get a date with Emma. Unfortunately, anytime I got near her, nerd-Jonathan would come out and screw everything up. It's probably for the best; I don't think my girlfriend would've approved.'

74
Where The Wild Things Are

US Transmission Date: 25 Apr 2000
UK Transmission Date: 5 May 2000

Writer: Tracey Forbes
Director: David Solomon
Cast: Kathryn Joosten (Mrs Holt), Casey McCarthy (Julie), Jeff Wilson (Evan),
Bryan Cuprill (Roy), Jeffrey Sharmay (Drowning Boy), Jeri Austin (Running Girl),
Danielle Pessis (Christie), David Engler (Initiative Guy)

While Buffy and Riley have reached a passionate stage of their
relationship, Anya believes that she and Xander are on the verge
of breaking up, and bonds with Spike while Xander flirts with a
girl named Julie at a Lowell House party. The party loses its fun
when the sexually repressed spirits of abused children who once
lived there begin to assert themselves, prompted by Buffy and
Riley's crazy-monkey-love. The gang go to Giles for help and they
battle against the poltergeists, finally reaching a blissfully unaware
Buffy and Riley with Xander and Anya rediscovering their passion
in the process.

Dudes and Babes *and* Authority Sucks!: '. . . You want sex? Let's
have sex. Hot, sweaty, big sex.' The pent-up sexual tension from
the children who where repressed at Lowell by religious maniac
Genevieve Holt manifests itself in what would usually be classified
as poltergeist activity. It is thought that, more often than not, the
owner of the poltergeist is a woman going through puberty,
beginning to grapple with the stress of womanhood – a metaphor
that this episode takes astonishingly literally.

Anya tells Xander: 'We have nothing in common besides both
of us liking your penis.' Xander's chat-up technique seems to be
improving (compare, for instance, some of his inept attempts
during season one with his confident swagger here).

A Little Learning is a Dangerous Thing: Graham got a D in Covert
Operations.

Work is a Four-Letter Word: Xander's new job is driving an ice
cream van.

It's a Designer Label!: Lots of short skirts seen at the party. Watch
out for Buffy's silvery shiny pants and thick sweater, Forrest's

orange jumper and Julie's pink top. A student at the party is wearing a UC⊙D sweatshirt.

References: This episode shares its title (and some of its themes) with a book by Maurice Sendak. Buffy's 'who says we can't all get along?' may be an oblique reference to Rodney King's much quoted plea for tolerance in 1992. Also, Martin Luther King (1929–68), Grace Jones's 'Slave To The Rhythm', the US series *Felicity* and the public furore over its star, Keri Russell, cutting her hair, 1 Kings: 16:21 (Jezebel) and *The Evil Dead*. Some of the condoms in the drawer appear to be the brand Durex. This is the first time condoms were shown on *Buffy*, though Anya did mention them in **59**, 'The Harsh Light of Day'. Xander's ice cream van has a giant insects poster.

Bitch!: Willow on Riley and Buffy: 'They're probably going to . . .' Giles: 'Thank you, Willow, I *did* attend university in the Mesozoic era, I do remember what it's like.'

Awesome!: Xander and Anya in the ice cream truck ('There's nothing wrong with my body.' Anya: 'There must be. I saw that wrinkled man on TV talking about erectile dysfunction . . .'). Giles produces a memorable double-entendre: 'In the midst of all that, do you really think they were keeping it up?'

'You May Remember Me From Such TV Series As . . .': Kathryn Joosten played Dolores Landingham in *The West Wing*.

There's a Ghost in My House: Xander: 'There's ghosts and shaking and people are going all *Felicity* with their hair.'

Cigarettes and Alcohol and Rock'n'Roll: Giles: 'Much as I long for a good-kegger, I have other plans. The Espresso Pump . . . It's a meeting of grown-ups. It couldn't possibly be of any interest to you lot.' When the gang *see* Rupert Giles *God of acoustic-rock*, it actually turns out to be of *great* interest to Willow, Tara and Anya. Everybody, in fact, except Xander ('Could we go back to the haunted house? Coz this is creeping me out'). Spike and Anya drink whisky and beer (respectively) at the bronze. Everybody's drinking at the party. Spike has taken to robbing people to keep himself in blood and beer.

Logic, Let Me Introduce You to This Window: Considering that a vine shoots through Anya's hand, there seems a remarkable lack of blood. Spike's reflection can be seen first in the Lowell House window and then, even more clearly, on the glass door.

Quote/Unquote: Xander: 'We're fresh out of superpeople and somebody's gotta go back in there. Who's with me?' Spike: 'I am . . . I know I'm not the first choice for heroics, and Buffy's tried to kill me more than once. And I don't fancy a single one of you. Actually, all that sounds pretty convincing.'

Xander: 'What do you feel?' Anya: 'Sad, afraid of being without you and a little hungry.' Xander: 'I meant about the house.' Anya: 'Oh. Still haunted.'

Notes: 'Seen a thousand relationships. First there's the love and sex and then there's nothing left but the vengeance. That's how it works.' Serious subject matter; child abuse. The episode tries hard not to get on its soapbox, but occasionally can't help itself. To be fair, there are some good lines, and the erotic symbolism works quite well. Giles's little cameo as a folk-rock sensation is a bright spot in an otherwise pedestrian tale.

Xander wonders if every UC◯D frat house is haunted (see **60**, 'Fear Itself') and, if so, why people keep coming to these parties (it's certainly not for the snacks). Anya mentions that she and Xander have only *not* had sex on two nights since they started going out. (Possibly when Spike stayed at Xander's in **64**, 'Hush', and when all the gang hid there in **70**, 'Goodbye Iowa'.) Willow had a bad-birthday-party-pony-thing when she was four years old, leaving her fearful of horses. Tara learned to ride when she was young.

Lowell House used to be the Lowell Home for Children, from 1949 to 1960, and housed upwards of 40 adolescents: runaways, juvenile delinquents and emotionally disturbed teenagers from the Sunnydale area.

Soundtrack: 'Parker Posey' by Crooner, Opus 1's 'Brit Pop Junkie', Caviar's 'I Thought I Was Found', 'The Devil You Know (God Is A Man)' by Face to Face [*], Lumirova's 'Philo' and 'One Of A Kind' by Fonda. Anthony Stewart Head sings a beautiful version of the Who's 'Behind Blue Eyes' at the Espresso Pump (the singing really *is* Tony, although the guitar is played by John King).

75
New Moon Rising

US Transmission Date: 2 May 2000
UK Transmission Date: 12 May 2000

Writer: Marti Noxon
Director: James A Contner
Cast: Mark Daneri (Scientist #2)

Oz's return to Sunnydale poses all sorts of complications in Willow's life, particularly as he has learned to control his wolf side. At least until he discovers Willow's scent on Tara and draws the logical conclusion. As the wolf emerges, he's captured by the Initiative. The Scooby Gang work out an infiltration plan with Spike's help. But Spike is in cahoots with Adam, who has promised to remove Spike's chip in return for help with his plan. Inside the Initiative, Riley tries to free Oz but is locked up. Buffy holds Colonel McNamara hostage, rescuing both Oz and Riley – now considered a traitor and a fugitive. Willow and Oz realise that they can't be together, as Willow is the one thing that can activate the wolf in Oz. Willow reveals that she is happy with Tara, and Oz leaves again. When Tara tells Willow that she should be with the one she loves, Willow replies, 'I am.'

No Thin Chicks: On 4 May 2000, in response to several very unkind postings about her, Amber Benson went online with an emotional message: 'I've been thinking a lot about what people said about Tara after the last episode. At first, I was very hurt. I tried to disassociate myself from feeling bad by saying: This is Tara that they are talking about, not me. But I couldn't. I guess it hurts when someone calls you ugly or makes nasty comments about your weight whether or not it is really *you* they are referring to. I am just a human being and I feel like I deserve to be treated as such. I also feel that Tara deserves a little more kindness and compassion . . . A body is a beautiful thing to waste. Believe me, I have seen enough of my friends and peers waste away to *nothing* so that they could work in this industry. So that they could perpetuate the *lie* that *anorexia* is beautiful. Love yourself for who you are, not what others think you should look like. It's more important in this life to love each other despite our imperfections.'

Dudes and Babes: Willow tells Buffy about herself and Tara, much to Buffy's obvious discomfort.

Authority Sucks!: McNamara says that he will institute a court-martial to investigate the extent of Riley's involvement with the Slayer. 'They're anarchists, Finn, too backwards for the real world. Help us take them down and you just might save your military career. Otherwise, you'll go to your grave labelled a traitor. No woman is worth that.'

A Little Learning is a Dangerous Thing: Buffy: 'Stay back, or I'll pull a William Burroughs on your leader.' Xander: 'You'll bore him to death with free prose?' Buffy: 'Was I the only one awake in English that day?'

Denial, Thy Name is Riley: Buffy on Riley's concern about Willow dating a werewolf: 'God, I never knew you were such a bigot.' Riley: 'I'm just saying it's a little weird to date someone who tries to eat you once a month.'

It's a Designer Label!: Return of the sheepskins (see **62**, 'Wild at Heart'). Anya is a vision in pink, while Buffy's light-blue roll-neck and bobble hat and Spike in combat green take some getting used to.

References: Radiohead, William Burroughs, the Jam's 'All Around The World', *The Fugitive* and Wheaties. The title is a reference to Credence Clearwater Revival's 'Bad Moon Rising', used to spectacular effect in *An American Werewolf in London* and now forever associated with werewolves. Riley quotes from the Sex Pistols' 'Anarchy In The UK' ('I am an anarchist'). Posters for the bands the String Cheese Incident and Devil Doll can be seen.

'You May Remember Me From Such Films and TV Series As . . .': Conor O'Farrell played James McDivitt in *From the Earth to the Moon*, was Detective Morrisey in *NYPD Blue* and appeared in *Eye of the Stalker*. Mark Daneri had a role in *When the Bough Breaks*.

The Drugs Don't Work: The Initiative scientists give Oz the drug Haldol to keep him quiet.

Logic, Let Me Introduce You to This Window: Oz's pendant keeps jumping in and out of visibility, even when he's not moving. When Oz is chasing Tara, he begins to run down a row of seats before the camera cuts to Tara. Next shot, Oz is at the beginning of the row again. When Tara throws the chair at Oz, Riley nails him with a tranquiliser dart at the same time. Oz falls to the floor, with no dart in his back. Riley steps over him and the dart is now in his back.

Cruelty to Animals: The imminent arrival of Miss Kitty Fantastico provokes a discussion on Witches' Familiars. Those cruel lesbians are planning to make their new kitty go bonkers with string and catnip.

Quote/Unquote: Spike: '*You* were a Boy Scout?' Adam: 'Parts of me.'

Giles: 'How did you get in?' Spike: 'The door was unlocked. You might want to watch that, Rupert. Someone dangerous could get in.' Buffy: 'Or, someone formerly dangerous and currently annoying.'

Oz: 'It was stupid to think that you'd just be waiting.' Willow: 'I *was* waiting. I feel like some part of me will always be waiting for you. Like if I'm old and blue-haired and I turn the corner in Istanbul and there you are, I won't be surprised.'

Notes: 'I always suspected that stuff about werewolf transform-ations being based on a lunar cycle was campfire talk.' A rambling exercise in one-step-forward-and-eight-sideways. Oz's return gets mixed up in the ongoing plotline and the whole thing is ultimately unsatisfying.

Buffy still hasn't told Riley about her relationship with Angel, but that will soon change. Devon is mentioned. Oz has been to Mexico (where his van broke down and he traded his bass to have it fixed), Rumania (where a warlock sent him to monks to learn some meditation techniques) and spent a long time in Tibet (where he got a lot of mileage out of the barter system). Riley ends the episode hiding in the ruins of Sunnydale High.

Critique: The *New York Daily News* declared that: 'Something really significant happens at the end of tonight's *Buffy the Vampire Slayer*. We don't see it, because the scene plunges into darkness and ends at that precise moment – but the dialogue leading up to that moment makes the episode a landmark in TV history. What happens is the shift from subtext to text of a very long-running, compelling and credible character development involving Alyson Hannigan's Willow . . . A declaration of love between two women may not sound like a big deal, especially on a series so grounded in fantasy . . . Beneath the literally monstrous surface of *Buffy the Vampire Slayer*, though, is a churning turmoil of metaphors about love, death, commitment and fear. Sex, on *Buffy*, is anything but casual; it can unleash demonic forces and change characters temporarily or permanently. Despite the silly-sounding fantasy elements, *Buffy* serves up more real angst, and more mature explorations of what it means to be a young person with emotions and responsibilities and insecurities and torn loyalties, than any of the more "realistic" youth dramas, such as *Beverly Hills 90210* or the WB's own *Dawson's Creek*, and *Felicity* . . . This is, in fact, unlike anything else I can recall on regular prime-time television: a character evolving naturally over four seasons of stories and arriving at a place of sexual rediscovery. Once again, *Buffy* quietly, but assuredly, impresses and amazes.'

Jane Espenson's Comments: Jane fanned the flames on the *Posting Board*: 'Willow and Tara? Are you asking what they do in private? We don't write those scenes, so I guess you could say we don't know either. What you see is what there is.'

Joss Whedon's Comments: On 4 May, Joss told the *Posting Board*: 'Tuesday's episode was pretty controversial and a real eye-opener for me. Despite my fervent hatred of criticism, I do understand when I've made a mistake. I thought the Willow-arc made sense for her character, but the fact is, most people *aren't* like that, and it's hard for normal people to understand a lifestyle that less than ten per cent of the population embrace. I don't want to be about issues – I just want to tell a story I think will engage and challenge, and this time I think I missed the mark. So I'm just hoping people understand we're feeling our way along here. We *are* listening. So we're going to shift away from this whole lifestyle choice Willow has made. Just wipe the slate. From now on, Willow will no longer be a Jew.' Nice to see that satire lives.

A couple of days later, Joss added: 'I may push the envelope a tad, I may make fun of the Standards and Practices guys, but I'm not out to stick it to them. We've had a pretty good relationship over the years. They have a family viewing audience to think about, I have a commitment to porn and between the two . . . I just want to say officially that I do know the difference between bigotry and someone just not liking the episode. And I have never spanked my creations. And by never I mean seldom . . .'

Subsequently On *Angel*: 'Five By Five', 'Sanctuary': Faith arrives in Los Angeles and is immediately recruited by Wolfram & Hart to assassinate Angel. To get Angel interested, she attacks Cordelia, and kidnaps and tortures her former Watcher, Wesley. Angel refuses to kill Faith despite having the opportunity to do so, and attempts to help her instead. But this is hindered by the arrival not only of the Watcher's Council squad lead by Collins, but also by Buffy, outraged to find her enemy in the arms of her former lover. Eventually, Faith gives herself up to the police, in the hope of finding redemption, but Buffy and Angel part on very bad terms.

76
The Yoko Factor

US Transmission Date: 9 May 2000
UK Transmission Date: 19 May 2000

Writer: Douglas Petrie
Director: David Grossman
Cast: Jade Carter (Lieutenant)

McNamara is ordered to get Riley back, while Spike plays each of the gang against each other, resulting in a drunk Giles and a big argument between Willow, Xander and Buffy. Angel follows Buffy from Los Angeles to apologise, but gets into a fight with Riley before he and Buffy settle their differences. Buffy sees Adam kill Forrest and has to tell Riley. Buffy walks out on the gang after their Spike-induced falling-out to fight on her own. A distraught Riley pays a visit to Adam.

Dudes and Babes: Willow on Buffy: 'I used to assume that we'd be roomies through grad school, well into little old ladyhood, you know, cheating at bingo together and forgetting to take our pills.' Anya says Xander is a Viking in the sack.

The Conspiracy Starts at Home Time: McNamara tells his government contact, Ward, that morale is a problem and that controlling the HSTs is getting harder. He suggests that Riley fell in with a bad crowd and that he doesn't think that Riley was ever the soldier that the government hoped he was. 'Boy thinks too much.' Nevertheless, Ward says, they want him back. Their data banks, however, don't have much on Buffy. 'She's just a girl,' says McNamara.

Work is a Four-Letter Word: Xander has worked for, and been fired from, Starbucks coffeehouse and a telephone sex line.

It's a Designer Label!: 'It's the pants, isn't it? It's OK, I couldn't take me seriously in these things either,' says Riley concerning the trousers he borrowed from Xander. Buffy's chunky sweater reappears.

References: Spike describes his plan to split up the Scoobies as the Yoko Factor and asks if Adam knows the Beatles. Adam does, noting that he likes 'Helter Skelter'. Spike explains that they were once a really powerful group – it's not a stretch to say that they ruled the world. When they broke up, everyone blamed Yoko Ono. But, Spike concludes, the fact is that the group split itself up; she just happened to be there. Spike says that Adam is like Tony Robbins . . . 'if he was a big, scary, *Frankenstein*-looking . . .' Also, the Doors' 'LA Woman', GI Joe, US Army adverts ('Be all you can be'), the New Jersey army base Fort Dix, *The Godfather* trilogy ('What kind of family are you, the Corleones?') and *The Wizard of Oz* (Spike: 'You're not exactly the whiz these days.' Willow: 'I *am* a whiz . . . If ever a whiz there was'). *Batman* (Xander: 'I'll stay behind and putt around the Batcave with crusty old Alfred'). The cup Anya holds appears to be from the burger-chain In-N-Out. Another WP sticker can be seen in Buffy's room.

Bitch!: Spike: 'For someone who's got *Watcher* on his résumé, you might want to cast an eye to the front door every now and again.' Anya: 'They look down on you.' Xander: 'And they hate *you*.' Anya: 'But they don't look down on me.'
Buffy: 'You've got to be kidding me. This is why you came?' Angel: 'No. This was an accident.' Buffy: 'Running a car into a tree is an accident. Running your fist into somebody's face is a plan.'
Angel on Riley: 'You actually *sleep* with this guy?' And: '. . . I don't like him!'

Awesome!: The Buffy–Xander–Willow–Giles argument. A defining moment as the Scooby Gang discover how far they have drifted apart. Also, Giles's girly squeal when Spike interrupts 'Freebird'. Angel kicking Riley's ass and the beautiful scene between Angel and Buffy.

Valley-Speak: Xander: 'Give it up for a American chipmanship.'

Cigarettes and Alcohol: Buffy: 'Are you drunk?' Giles: 'Yes, quite a bit actually.' Spike owns a zippo lighter and drinks a can of lager.

Logic, Let Me Introduce You to This Window: When Spike rushes into Giles's home his reflection can be seen in a mirror behind Tara and Willow. Angel says that he needs an invitation to enter Buffy's dorm, but Sunday and her buddies didn't need one in **57**, 'The Freshman' (see also **63**, 'The Initiative'). When Tara and Anya are in the bathroom, some of the muffled arguments heard from the front room seem to be from the soundtrack of **64**, 'Pangs'.

Cruelty To Demons: McNamara: 'They're animals, lieutenant. We pack them in until we're out of room and then we pack them in some more.'

Pussy Galore: The author shares Willow's appreciation of Miss Kitty Fantastico's cuteness.

Quote/Unquote: Riley on Angel: 'Sometimes things happen between exes and when I saw that he was bad . . .' Buffy: 'He's not bad.' Riley: 'Seriously? That's a *good day*?'

Giles: 'Whatever happened to Latin? At least when that made no sense, the church approved.'

Willow: 'You can't handle Tara being my girlfriend.' Xander: 'No. It was bad before that. Since you two went off to college and forgot about me. Just left me in the basement to . . . Tara's your *girlfriend*?' Giles (from upstairs): '*Bloody hell*.'

Notes: 'At this point a cynical person might think that you're offering just what we need when we need it most.' Everything comes to a head in this marvellous drawing together of the various subplots that have been battling for prominence. Some of it works beautifully (the Buffy and the Scooby Gang stuff, especially), some of it seems contrived (Forrest's needless death), but at least we're heading *somewhere*.

Buffy *has* now told Riley about her relationship with Angel. She just edited out what actually *sends* Angel bad. So, Xander tells him instead. Willow is thinking about taking Drama next year (see **80**, 'Real Me'). Spike tells Adam that he's previously killed two Slayers (see **15**, 'School Hard'; **85**, Fool for Love'). In his crypt, Spike has a VCR, a Nintendo and a TV to replace the one Forrest destroyed in **70**, 'Goodbye Iowa'.

Soundtrack: Tony Head sings a solo-acoustic version of Lynard Skynard's hippy anthem 'Freebird' until Spike, blissfully, interrupts him.

Critique: In their 11 May 2000 issue, *Rolling Stone* ran a gushing five-page cover-story on *Buffy*, going 'Behind the scenes at *the coolest show on TV*', with soundbites from many of the actors and production staff.

77
Primeval[26]

US Transmission Date: 16 May 2000
UK Transmission Date: 26 May 2000

Writer: David Fury
Director: James A Contner
Cast: Jordi Vilasuso (Dixon)

Adam has activated a chip in Riley's chest and he is now under Adam's control. Riley finds that Forrest has been reanimated, along with Walsh and Angleman. Buffy guesses that Spike was behind the gang's strained relations and she manages to convince her friends of this. They realise that Spike is working for Adam, who is preparing to start a war inside the Initiative. To stop him, Giles, Willow and Xander perform a spell, combining themselves within Buffy's body. This creates a SuperSlayer who fights and destroys Adam by ripping out his uranium core. With the demons loose in the Initiative, Riley overcomes his programming to fight Forrest. In the aftermath, the shadowy men in Washington realise that the Initiative has failed and decide to cancel the project.

The Conspiracy Starts at Home Time: Ward says that the Initiative represented the Government's interests in not only controlling the otherworldly menace, but also harnessing its power for their own military purposes. An experiment that has failed. 'Once the prototype took control of the complex, our soldiers suffered a 40 per cent casualty rate' and it was only through the actions of the deserter and a group of civilian insurrectionists that their losses were not total. Maggie Walsh's vision was brilliant, but ultimately unsupportable. The demons cannot be harnessed, or controlled. It is, therefore, 'our recommendation that this project be terminated and all records concerning it expunged. Our soldiers will be debriefed. Standard confidentiality clause. We will monitor the civilians and usual measures prepared should they try to go public. I don't think they will. The Initiative itself will be filled in with concrete. Burn it down, gentlemen . . . and salt the Earth.'

---

[26] Confusion once surrounded the title of this episode with at least one 'official' book referring to it as 'Primevil', a mistake that a previous edition of this guide repeated. The matter was finally settled with the release of the Season Four video-box, which confirmed the spelling as 'Primeval'.

Unemployment is a Twelve-Letter Word: Anya: 'You said you wanted to check the board at the unemployment office this morning. You can't go like that. They won't even interview you if you're naked.'

It's a Designer Label!: Giles's dressing gown and Buffy's see-through top and huge boots.

References: Influenced by *The Matrix* (especially Buffy's fight with Adam), *The Terminator* (Adam's gun-arm) and *Jaws* (the death of Forrest). *Alice in Wonderland* is referenced, along with Nancy Drew, the Trojan Horse and *Must-See TV*. Spike paraphrases Apollo 11's first words on the moon. *Manus, the Hands of Fate* was a B-movie made famous by *Mystery Science Theater 3000*.

Awesome!: Anya telling Xander that she loves him. Xander's reaction to Buffy and Willow hugging him ('Oh God, we're going to die, aren't we?'). The battle at the end.

Valley-Speak: Willow: 'Why do you think Spike made with the head games?' Xander: 'He's all dressed up with no one to bite. He's gotta get his ya-ya's somehow.'

Cigarettes and Alcohol: Spike uses his cigarette as a weapon, stubbing it out in Forrest's eye.

Logic, Let Me Introduce You to This Window: Xander's blanket repositions itself several times. When Buffy pulls Adam's uranium core out, she holds it horizontally. In the next shot, it's vertical. Giles's line, 'The enjoining spell is extremely touchy. It's volatile. We can't risk being interrupted,' seems to have been overdubbed on to the soundtrack in post-production.

I Just *Love* Your Accent: Spike says it warms the cockles of his non-beating heart seeing Riley and Adam together. He also uses cripes and blighters and Giles adds piffle.

Quote/Unquote: Giles: 'Xander, just because this is never gonna work, there's no need to be negative.'

Xander being hugged by the girls: 'Giles, hurry up. You *definitely* wanna get down here for this.'

Adam: 'You can't last much longer.' Buffy: '*We* can. *We* are forever.'

Notes: 'I've got to shut him down. His final phase is about to start.' Cometh the hour, cometh the men. A huge engine of destruction that manages the impossible and ties virtually every-thing up. Top quality direction helps.

The photo of Buffy, Willow and Xander that Buffy looks at is the same one she found in the basement in **36**, 'Dead Man's Party'. It also featured in **18**, 'Halloween'. Xander wonders if anyone misses the mayor. Giles speaks Sumerian. During the enjoining spell Xander takes the role of *Animus*, the heart, Giles is *Sophus*, the mind, and Willow becomes *Spiritus*, the sprit. Buffy is *Manus*, the hand.

At some point immediately after this episode, Willow spends an hour on the phone to Cordelia in Los Angeles helping her old friend to decrypt the Wolfram & Hart files stolen by Angel in *Angel*: 'Blind Date'. Willow says 'hey' to Wesley – a cute wink by Alyson to her real-life boyfriend, Alexis Denisof.

78
Restless

US Transmission Date: 23 May 2000
UK Transmission Date: 28 May 2000

Writer: Joss Whedon
Director: Joss Whedon
Cast: David Wells (The Cheese Guy), Michael Harney (Xander's Dad),
Rob Boltin (Soldier)

While Riley attends an Initiative debriefing, the Scooby Gang gather at Buffy's for a video night. Soon, they're asleep and dreaming, their dreams exploring fears, fantasies and speculation about the past, the present and the future. But they all have something in common (besides a non-sequitur Cheese Man): the first Slayer, a wild primeval girl from the dawn of time, awoken by having her power invoked by the enjoining spell. Buffy, a hero even in dreams, puts a stop to the first Slayer's terrors, but is left with Tara's enigmatic statement: 'You think you know what's to come. What you are. You haven't even begun.'

Dreaming (As Blondie Never Said) is Forty-Five Minutes of Cheese: Dealing entirely with dreamscapes, 'Restless' is about secrets. Hidden laughter behind half-closed doors and shuttered windows. Abuse monsters, public nudity, what the future holds . . . These are the dreams that make us. And the cheese will not protect us.

Willow dreams that she is attending drama class, a surreal adaptation of *Death of a Salesman*, starring her friends ('Your family's in the front row. And they look really angry') and in which she doesn't know her lines. Afterwards she finds herself back in class, wearing the clothes that she wore on the day she first met Buffy, while everyone laughs at her ('It's exactly like a Greek tragedy') and Tara and Oz whisper behind her back.

Xander's labyrinthine dream contains images of Joyce Summers's sexuality and Giles, Spike and Buffy playing like children while Xander ponders his future. Driving his ice cream truck with Anya, who is thinking about getting back into vengeance, Xander finds himself attracted to Willow and Tara and unable to understand Giles and Anya, but all of his escape attempts lead him back to his basement where he meets Snyder and a brutish representation of his father who asks, 'Are you ashamed of us? Your mother's crying her guts out. The line ends here with us and you're not gonna change that.'

Giles dreams of himself, Olivia (pushing a pram) and a childlike Buffy at a funfair, where Spike has hired himself out as a crass attraction. At the Bronze Giles meets Willow and Xander and, while Anya performs a terrible stand-up routine, he works out what is going on, telling his friends in song. All of the dreams end with a savage black girl attacking Willow, pulling out Xander's heart and scalping Giles. (The spirit, the heart, the mind … Remember that, it *might* be important.)

Buffy tells Tara she needs to find the others. 'Be back in time for Dawn,' she is told (see **80**, 'Real Me'; **100**, 'The Gift'). Buffy, abandons her mother to a life of living in the walls, finds Riley (who's been made surgeon general) and a humanised Adam drawing up a plan for world domination. Finally she finds herself in the desert with Tara and the first Slayer.

Buffy: 'At least you all didn't dream about that guy with the cheese. I don't know *where* the hell that came from.'

Dudes and Babes and Cheese: Xander's dream-image of Willow and Tara features Willow in a very short black leather dress and Tara in a short black skirt and revealing blouse.

Authority Sucks!: Giles notes: 'Somehow our joining with Buffy and invoking the essence of the Slayer's power was an affront to the source of that power.' Meaning that the first Slayer was able to hunt them in their dreams.

Riley on his world domination plan: 'Baby, we're the government. It's what we do.' (Concerning Riley and Adam sitting opposite each other at that table during Buffy's dream, Joss Whedon intriguingly notes: 'She was seeing that they were *two sides of the same coin*.')

A Little Cheese is a Dangerous Thing: In Xander's dream both Giles and Anya speak French, which Xander doesn't understand. As Joss Whedon told the Posting Board: 'At the last minute I dragged my assistant Diego in to read it. He's Mexican, speaks a little French (yeah, he's *trilingual*, which for someone as barely unilingual as myself is both annoying and annoying) and he was reading off a script so it may not have sounded perfect to some but the effect was just great for the dream.'

Denial, Thy Name is Cheese: Cheese Man: 'I wear the cheese. It does not wear me.'

Denial, Thy Name is Joyce: Buffy dreams of Joyce living in the college walls. 'I made some lemonade and I'm learning how to play mahjong.' Buffy doesn't think that Joyce should live there and Joyce notes: 'You could probably break through the wall.' But Buffy is already following Xander up the stairs.

The Conspiracy Starts at Cheese Time: Riley says that he has Graham among others testifying in his favour at the Initiative debriefing and that he may get out with an honorable discharge. 'Having the inside scoop on the administration's own Bay of Mutated Pigs is definitely an advantage,' he notes. 'You're blackmailing the government. In a patriotic way,' adds Willow.

It's a Designer Cheese!: The outfit Willow wears in her dream, after Buffy rips off her alleged costume, is the softer side of Sears clothes she wore in **1**, 'Welcome to the Hellmouth'. Also, Giles's black sweater, Willow's sun T-shirt, Joyce's red negligee, Spike in tweed, Xander's Sal's Surf Shop T-shirt (see **64**, 'Pangs') and Riley wearing the loudest chaps since James Stewart in *Destry Rides Again*.

References: *Apocalypse Now*. Willow asks for something less *Heart of Darkness*-y. Giles feels the film is overrated, then realises that its theme is Willard's journey to Kurtz rather than the Vietnam War. Riley alludes to the Bay of Pigs. The Greek writing on Tara's back is the beginning of a poem by Sappho. Xander's 'it's a gay romp' is a probable allusion to *The Producers*. 'This isn't *Madame*

Butterfly, is it? Because I have a whole problem with opera' (see **10**, 'Nightmares'). Also, *Death of a Salesman* (though I've never seen a version with a cowboy either) and CS Lewis's *The Lion, The Witch and the Wardrobe*. Visually influenced by *Lawrence of Arabia* and conceptually by *An American Werewolf in London* (a-dream-within-a-dream-within . . .).

Bitch!: Buffy: 'I'm going to ignore you, and you're going to go away. You're really gonna have to get over the whole primal power thing. You're *not* the source of me. Also, in terms of hair care, you really wanna say, what kind of impression am I making in the workplace?'

Awesome!: Giles *sings* the plot. ('Xander, help Willow. And try not to bleed on my couch. I've just had it steam-cleaned.') Buffy with dark hair. The stunning recreation of *Apocalypse Now* (even the music sounds like the Doors). Oz's 'I've been here forever'. The monochrome sequence of Spike as a sideshow freak ('at least it's showbiz'). The lighters.

'You May Remember Me From Such Films As . . .': David Wells's movie CV includes *Beverly Hills Cops*, *Basic Instinct*, *Doorways*, *Crackin Up* and *The Progeny*. Michael Harney is in *Erin Brockovich* and *Turbulence*. Sharon Ferguson features in *Malcolm X*.

Valley-Speak: Xander: 'Got the sucking chest wound swingin'. I promised Anya I'd be there for her big night. Now I'll probably be pushing up daisies, in the sense of being in the ground underneath them and fertilizing the soil with decomposition.' And: 'Don't get linear on me now, man.'

Logic, Let Me Introduce You to This Cheese: *Logic?!*

It's Not Easy Being Cheesey: Joss Whedon: 'The Cheese Man is the only thing in the show that means nothing. I needed something like that, that *couldn't* be explained, because dreams always have that one element that is just *ridiculous*.' Having said that, many fans have come up with various extraordinary (and some quite convincing) theories on what he *might* represent.

Pussy Galore: The kitten stalks towards the camera, in slow motion.

Quote/Unquote: Xander: 'She does *spells* with Tara . . . Sometimes I think about two women doing *a spell*. And then I do a spell *by myself*.'

Buffy: 'What else could I expect from a bunch of low-rent, no-account hoodlums like you? Your whole sex, throw 'em in the sea ... and wait for the bubbles. Men, with your groping-and-spitting all-groin-no-brain, three billion of you passing around the same worn-out urge.'

Snyder: 'I walked by your guidance counsellor's office one time. A bunch of you were sitting there waiting to be shepherded. I remember it smelled like dead flowers. Like decay. Then it hit me. The hope of our nation's future is a bunch of mulch.' Xander: 'I never got the chance to tell you how glad I was you were eaten by a snake.'

Anya: '. . . And then the duck tells the doctor that there's a man that's attached to my ass. You see, it was the duck and not the man that spoke.'

Notes: 'There's trees in the desert since you moved out, and I don't sleep on a bed of bones.' *Major weird.* Completely inexplicable and yet, at the same time, utterly compelling to watch. With the benefit of hindsight, 'Restless' is loaded with allusions to the themes of the following season – the arrival of Dawn, Xander's maturing, Willow and Tara's relationship – and to its eventual, fateful climax.

The clock in Buffy's dream reads 7:30, a likely reference to **56**, 'Graduation Day' Part 2, in which Faith mentioned counting down from 7–3–0. ('That clock's completely wrong,' replies Tara. See **100**, 'The Gift'.) Unlike every other episode the 'Previously on *Buffy the Vampire Slayer*' montage was immediately followed by the title credits.

Soundtrack: Anthony Stewart Head (vocals), Christophe Beck (piano) and Four Star Mary (all other instruments) perform Joss Whedon's 'The Exposition Song'.

Did You Spot?: Xander dead at a weeping Harmony's feet during the *Death of a Salesman* sequence. The sheep graffiti as Xander crawls from the back of the truck into his basement.

Joss Whedon's Comments: Asked by *DreamWatch* about the more experimental episodes of *Buffy* and how they compare to those done by other series, Joss confessed: 'I don't want to do things that are just a wink to the audience. I thought the *X-Files/Cops* thing ['X-COPS'] made sense, it actually worked in a weird way. But *Felicity* did *The Twilight Zone*, *Chicago Hope* did a musical show and I don't want to be one of those shows that is self-indulgent

. . . The episode that I did at the end of this season is all dreams and it is unbelievably bizarre, but it's in a world where it makes sense. As long as we don't start getting cutesy [or] stupid, we have opportunities to go to new places.'

'Death is your gift'

– 'Intervention'

Season Five (2000–01)

Mutant Enemy Inc/Kuzui Enterprises/Sandollar Television/20th Century Fox
Created by Joss Whedon
Co-Producers: Douglas Petrie, John F Perry, Marc David Alpert,
James A Contner (81, 93, 98)
Producers: Jane Espenson, David Solomon, Gareth Davies
Consulting Producer: David Greenwalt
Supervising Producer: David Fury
Co-Executive Producer: Marti Noxon
Executive Producers: Sandy Gallin, Gail Berman, Fran Rubel Kuzui,
Kaz Kuzui, Joss Whedon
Regular Cast:
Sarah Michelle Gellar (Buffy Summers), Nicholas Brendon (Xander Harris),
Alyson Hannigan (Willow Rosenberg), Anthony Stewart Head (Rupert Giles),
David Boreanaz (Angel 85, 95),
Kristine Sutherland (Joyce Summers, 79–83, 85–94, 99), Julie Benz (Darla, 85),
Mercedes McNab (Harmony Kendall, 80, 82, 84–85, 92),
Dean Butler (Hank Summers, 99), James Marsters (Spike 79–93, 95–100),
Juliet Landau (Drusilla, 85, 92), Emma Caulfield (Anya Jenkins),
Harris Yulin (Quentin Travers, 90), Megan Gray (Sandy, 84, 86),
Marc Blucas (Riley Finn 79–88), Bailey Chase (Graham Miller 82, 87–88),
Amber Benson (Tara Maclay 79–80, 82–84, 86–87, 89–100),
Sharon Ferguson (Primitive,[27] 96, 99), Michelle Trachtenberg (Dawn Summers),
Bob Morrisey (Crazy #1,[28] 80, 98–99),
Kelly Donovan (Xander Double, 81, 96),
Charlie Weber (Ben, 82–84, 86–87, 90, 92, 95, 97–100),
Clare Kramer (Glory, 83–84, 86, 90–91, 93, 95–100),
Paul Hayes (Older Night Watchman, 83, 87), Kali Rocha (Cecily Addams, 85),
Kevin Weisman (Dreg, 86–87, 90), Nick Chinlund (Major Ellis, 87–88),
Randy Thompson (Doctor Kriegel, 87–88, 94),
Abraham Benrubi (Olaf the Troll, 89), Cynthia LaMontagne (Lydia,[29] 90),
Oliver Muirhead (Philip, 90), Kris Iyer (Nigel, 90),
Troy T Blendell (Jinx, 90–91, 93, 95–97), Justin Gorence (Orlando 90–91, 98),

---

[27] Uncredited in **99**, 'The Weight of the World'.
[28] Credited as 'Crazy Guy' in **80**, 'Real Me'.
[29] Credited as 'Female Council Member' in **90**, 'Checkpoint'.

Paul Bates (Crazy #2,[30] 91, 98–99), Carl J Johnson (Crazy #3,[31] 91, 98–99),
Adam Busch (Warren Meers, 93, 96), Amelinda Embry (Katrina, 93),
Joel Grey (Doc, 95, 99–100), Todd Duffey (Murk, 95–100),
Lily Knight (Gronx, 98–99)

79
Buffy vs Dracula

US Transmission Date: 26 Sep 2000
UK Transmission Date: 5 Jan 2001

Writer: Marti Noxon
Director: David Solomon
Cast: Rudolf Martin (Dracula), EJ Gage (Mover #1), Scott Berman (Mover #2),
Marita Schaub (Vampire Girl #1), Leslee Jean Matta (Vampire Girl #2),
Jennifer Slimko (Vampire Girl #3)

Buffy comes face-to-face with the greatest vampire of all, Dracula.
While Buffy is powerless under the Count's influence – much to
the chagrin of Riley – Xander becomes the Dark One's emissary
and leads his friends into peril. Meanwhile, Giles contemplates
returning to England, feeling that he is no longer needed.

Denial, Thy Name is Riley: Jealous of Buffy's fascination with
Dracula, to the extent that he seeks out Spike for information, this
sees the start of Riley's realisation that Buffy and he are walking
different roads (see **81**, 'The Replacement'; **88**, 'Into the Woods').

Desperate, Thy Name is Joyce: She seemingly invites Dracula into
the house for coffee because she's lonely. Joyce tells Willow and
Tara that she sometimes feels like giving up on men altogether.

It's a Designer Label!: Willow's Wild Cherry Soda Pop T-shirt.
Buffy's two pairs of leather pants (scarlet and lurid-pink). Xander's Hawaiian shirt.

References: Although based on a real-life Transylvannian warlord,
Vlad Tepes, Count Dracula as a character first appeared in Bram
Stoker's eponymous 1897 classic. Several aspects of the episode are
drawn from this (the 'weird sisters' who menace Giles haunt
Jonathan Harker in the book) and also from Tod Browning's 1931

---

[30] Credited as 'Crazie #1' [sic] in **91**, 'Blood Ties'.
[31] Credited as 'Crazie #2' [sic] in **91**, 'Blood Ties'.

film adaptation (Xander's possession mirrors the character of Renfield. Nick Brendon's performance owes much to that of Dwight Frye in the movie). Also *Seseme Street*, *The Horse Whisperer*, Lestat from Anne Rice's vampire novels, *Creature Feature* (see **23**, 'Ted'), the Clash's 'Complete Control', Chicago serial-killer John Gacy (a reference to painting clowns), *Frankenstein* and *Eurotrash*. Willow paraphrases *Bull Durham* ('long, slow neckbites that last for days').

Bitch!: Riley thinks that Buffy throws like a girl.

Awesome!: Giles and Dracula's sisters. Dracula possessing Xander ('you are strange and off-putting'). Spike, on the Count: 'That gloryhound's done more harm to vampires than any Slayer. His story gets out and, suddenly, everybody knows how to kill us.'

'You May Remember Me From Such Films and TV Series As . . .': German-born Rudolf Martin played Vlad the Impaler in *Dark Prince: The True Story of Dracula*. He was Raoul in *Bedazzled*, the assassin in *24*, Gilbert in *Punks* and Anton Lang in *All My Children* opposite Sarah Michelle Gellar. Another co-star was the preteen Michelle Trachtenberg who played Lilly Montgomery. She was also Penny in *Inspector Gadget* and the eponymous *Harriet the Spy*. Martia Schaub appeared in *Southside*.

Don't Give Up The Day Job: Following the departures of Jeff Pruitt and Sophia Crawford, another key member of the *Buffy* crew, Chris Beck, left to pursue a career in film scoring. His replacement was *Thirteenth Floor* orchestrator Thomas Wanker. Jeff Pruitt reassured fans that *his* replacement was also a top choice: 'His name is John Medlen and he's great.' Sophia Crawford's replacement as Buffy's stunt-double was Melissa Barker who subsequently also doubled for Sarah on *Scooby-Doo*. Post-Production Supervisor Brian Wankum played Roger in *True Crime*.

Valley-Speak: Xander, to Dracula: 'I will serve you, your excellent spookiness.'
Buffy: 'Am I *Repeato-Girl*?'

Sex and Drugs and Rock'n'Roll: Although Xander tells Willow that everyone knows about her relationship with Tara, this apparently doesn't include Joyce. (The appearance of Dawn seems to change this. See **80**, 'Real Me'.)

Logic, Let Me Introduce You to This Window: After Buffy and Joyce have eaten dinner, Joyce has a plate in front of her which disappears and is replaced by a bowl. How come *everybody* (not just Riley) failed to notice the big honking castle in the middle of Sunnydale?

I Just *Love* Your Accent: 'I patterned Spike's accent after a guy I was in a play with three years ago. Now I'm listening to Tony Head who sounds kind-of like Spike in real life,' James Marsters told an online interview. 'His accent is just as fake as mine.'

Cruelty To Animals: Xander eats a spider and a fly.

Quote/Unquote: Buffy: 'Do you *know* what a Slayer is?' Dracula: 'Do *you*?'

Xander: 'Like any of that's enough to fight the dark master . . . bator.' And: 'I'm sick of this crap. I'm sick of being the guy who eats insects and gets the funny-syphilis.'

Notes: 'You're sure this isn't just some fanboy thing? Cos I've fought more than a couple of pimply, overweight vamps that called themselves Lestat!' Another sedate season opener in which the actors ease themselves back into their characters. But, with hindsight, there's a lot of setting up of the season's themes and some pointers towards its eventual *denouement*.

Dracula, seeing the scar on Buffy's neck, concludes that she has been tasted (see **56**, 'Graduation Day' Part 2). Dracula tells Buffy, 'You think you know what you are, what's to come. You haven't even begun,' similar to Tara's dialogue in **78**, 'Restless'. Giles owns an Apple Mac laptop and a scanner that he is using to create a database of his library. He's spent the summer labelling amulets and indexing his diaries. Anya met Dracula during her demon days. Since she was a silly young thing of 700, this would have been around the mid-16th century. Spike saw Dracula as a rival (who still owes Spike £11). Dracula is different from other vampires – he metamorphasises into a bat or a wolf, can control minds, appear in dreams and dissolve into mist. 'Party tricks' according to Riley; 'showy gypsy stuff' adds an unimpressed Spike. He can, however, be killed just like other vampires. Or not. Jury's still out on that. This episode also sees the – brief – debut of Buffy's feisty younger sister, Dawn.

Hang on . . . Buffy hasn't *got* a sister . . . Has she?

Soundtrack: Vertical Horizon's 'Finding Me'.

Did You Know?: The role of Dracula was originally intended for Sarah Michelle Gellar's boyfriend, Freddie Prinze Jr until his movie schedule clashed with production.

Criminal Connections: Eliza Dushku feared that her role as Faith may be a little too convincing as she became an icon for some of America's worst criminals, being inundated with letters from prisoners. 'I get mail from maximum security penitentiaries,' she told *Entertainment Weekly*. 'What are the authorities thinking, playing a show with teenage girls to Death Row inmates? They send me photos: "Here's a picture of me before I was incarcerated!" It's way-more creepy than *Buffy*.' When *Mean* magazine asked if it was true that Eliza was a spoiled child-star, she replied: 'I still am. The only time I [pull a star-fit] is with my brothers or my friends, and they know it's all bullshit. But I was the biggest brat on the planet. When you're 10 and have people waiting on you hand and foot and then all of a sudden you go back to the real-world, it's a smack in the face.' She also discussed her Mormon upbringing and her feminist mother who Eliza considers 'a tough-ass. She's really liberal. She raised four kids by herself and kept a job as a professor. She's really into, like, sisterhood and bonding. She's amazing.'

Tributes: Other TV series seem keen to name-check *Buffy* these days. *Xena*, for instance, mentioned their own Slayer, Buffus. *Friends* had Phoebe's porn-actress sister appearing in *Bouffet the Vampire Layer*, while *Malcolm in the Middle*, *Popular* and *Will & Grace* have all featured characters watching *Buffy* on TV. In the WB comedy series *Grosse Point*, Sarah Michelle Gellar appeared to indulge in an on-screen lesbian kiss and win herself an Emmy nomination – something, she says, that she'd never achieve on *Buffy*!

David Fury Comments: Speaking at the Writers' Guild of America West party and quoted in *The Richmond Times Dispatch*, Fury revealed: 'For all intents and purposes there is a Dawn Summers [who has] always shared a house and parents with Buffy. This creates a mystery that is not always the focus of the episodes but will leave the audience wondering, who *is* she? We don't really learn anything until episode five but Dawn will be a major part of what happens on *Buffy* . . .'

80
Real Me

US Transmission Date: 3 Oct 2000
UK Transmission Date: 12 Jan 2001

Writer: David Fury
Director: David Grossman
Cast: Brian Turk (Mort), Chaney Kley Minnis (Brad),
Faith S Abrahams (Peaches), Tom Lenk (Cyrus)

Buffy is forced to take Dawn with her when she and Giles visit the
Magic Box. They find the owner dead. Evidence points to a
vampire gang although when they learn that its leader is Harmony,
nobody takes them very seriously. Until, that is, Dawn is
kidnapped.

Dudes and Babes: Harmony's bonehead gang of incompetent
vampires are hilarious, particularly when they vote to kill her
(except for Brad, who abstained).

A Little Learning is a Dangerous Thing: Buffy has had to drop
Drama, which she was planning to take with Willow, due to
training pressures.

Work is a Four-Letter Word: Xander, Dawn believes, is much cuter
than anyone. And smarter too: skipping college and getting a job
working construction. And he's brave: 'Last week he went
undercover to stop that Dracula guy.'

It's a Designer Label!: Buffy's tie-around grey top. Harmony's
shiny gold pants. Dawn's minxy blue dress.

References: The title is a song by the Who. Also, JK Rowling's
Harry Potter novels ('I'm not going to Hogwarts'), *The Longest
Day* ('it's not the Invasion of Normandy'), 'Little Miss Muffet' ('I
know what you are. Curds and whey'; see **56**, 'Graduation Day'
Part 2; **71**, 'This Year's Girl'), *Monopoly*®, *Clue*® and *Game of
Life*®, Ruffles potato chips, George Clooney, the *For Dummies*
computer books, *This is Spinal Tap* (and the band's many
drummers who all die in bizarre gardening accidents or from
spontaneous human combustion), *Superman* ('the Fortress of
Solitude'), 'Time's Up' by the Buzzcocks, *The Banana Splits* and
Rowan and Martin's Laugh-In ('Here come de judge'). Giles admits
that when Spike lived with him, they watched *Passions* together

(see **65**, 'Something Blue'; **90**, 'Checkpoint'). The technique of having a character speak the punctuation of their dialogue ('Underline. Exclamation point') was used to devastating effect in Dennis Potter's *The Singing Detective*. Among the items seen in Dawn's bedroom are a lava-lamp, a Betty Boop doll, various fluffy toys and an REM poster. Outside the Magic Box, posters for the band Leftover and a performance at the Bronze by Todd Snider can be seen. A print by Dutch surrealist Maurits Cornelis Escher (1898–1972) is visible on Buffy's bedroom wall.

Bitch!: Harmony, to Xander: 'You're the hair-puller, you big girl.'
Buffy says she wouldn't allow Harmony into her house even when she was alive.

Awesome!: Breakfast at the Summers' house. Xander and Harmony's bitching session. Harmony: 'So, Slayer, at last we meet.' Buffy: 'We've met, Harmony, you halfwit!'

'You May Remember Me From Such Films As . . .': Bob Morrisey was in *The Book of Stars* and *Total Reality*. Tom Lenk appeared in *Boogie Nights* and *Popular*. Brian Turk's movies include *A Civil Action* and *The Lost World: Jurassic Park*.

Valley-Speak: Buffy, to Harmony: 'When you try to be bad, you *suck*.'

Sex and Drugs and Rock'n'Roll: As Dawn notes: 'Riley, my sister's boyfriend, is *so* into her. They're always kissing and groping. I bet they have sex.' Riley, himself, is more delicate, flattering Joyce before telling Buffy that 'I'm here to violate your firstborn' never goes over particularly well with parents.

Logic, Let Me Introduce You to This Window: At the Magic Box, Dawn's hair length changes between shots. There's a book called *A Treatise on the Mythology and Methodology of the Vampire Slayer*, which directly contradicts Giles's statement in **5**, 'Never Kill a Boy on the First Date' (see also **22**, 'What's My Line' Part 2). When did Harmony try to be head cheerleader? Or chair the homecoming committee for that matter? (see **3**, 'The Witch'; **39**, 'Homecoming').

I Just *Love* Your Accent: Dawn has heard Giles use the word newfangled. Willow tells Tara that Giles is British so he doesn't understand about stuff. Spike says 'bollocks' (see **85**, 'Fool for Love').

Motors: Giles has a new red and sporty BMW 328 iC. He doesn't like the fact that it has automatic transmission.

Quote/Unquote: Dawn, on Willow and Tara: 'They do spells and stuff, which is so much cooler than slaying. I told Mom one time I wished they'd teach me some of the things they do together. Then she got really quiet and made me go upstairs.'

Notes: 'Most magic shop owners in Sunnydale have the life expectancy of a Spinal Tap drummer.' An excellent episode, instantly allaying fears that Michelle Trachtenburg wouldn't be up to the task of making Dawn work. She's *brilliant* here, as are all of the regulars (particularly James Marsters who does so much with his few scenes).

Dawn, like her sister, has a diary. She is 14 and has a crush on Xander (see **92**, 'Crush'). Willow is Dawn's chess partner. Mr Bogerty is the most recent former-owner of the Magic Box. One previous owner also died on screen (see **42**, 'Lover's Walk'). Giles says that he had no idea the profit margins on the shop were so high (due, seemingly, to low overheads, out-of-state and international orders). It's no wonder, therefore, that there's never any trouble attracting new owners. The latest of which is Giles himself. Brad Konig once stood Harmony up in 10th Grade. She repaid this by sireing him. Brad also beat up kids (possibly including Xander) in gym class. Spike has a new TV in his crypt (still no word on where his electricity supply comes from, see **70**, 'Goodbye Iowa'). He intends to steal a satellite dish to go with it.

Soundtrack: 'Prelude from Holberg Suite' plays on the radio in Glies's car.

Did You Know?: Asked by *E! Online* about her relationship with former *Buffy* co-star Alexis Denisof, Alyson Hannigan noted: 'I had a crush on him the moment he showed up onset. He was the good one who said, 'Not while we're working together.' We became friends, and I was dating somebody else [Marilyn Manson drummer Ginger Fish]. When that didn't work out, he was on *Angel* and we started dating.'

Alyson Hannigan's Comments: The Willow/Tara relationship was discussed during the same interview: 'At first it was a little awkward,' noted Alyson. 'But I never had a problem with it, because it was handled with such grace. I would trust Joss with my life. I'd never doubt his ability to tell a story and make it romantic.'

Critique: 'The most innovative drama on any non-cable network (yes, I'm counting *The West Wing*),' wrote *Time* magazine's James Poniewozik. 'A hilarious allegorical story of independence, relationships and mortality, told through scary stories (just as *The Twilight Zone* did), that has got ever more touching and audacious in its fifth season.' Poniewozik drew particular attention to the storyline surrounding the introduction of Dawn: 'We'd never seen her before but the cast acted like she'd been there all along. What first seemed like a clumsy way of adding someone to the cast turned out to be both a great spoof on how aging TV shows meddle with their casts and a deft exploration of identity.'

Fame, Fame, Fatal Fame: 'I love being in a cult hit,' Sarah Michelle Gellar told Australian magazine *Dolly*. 'You feel less pressure and you don't get typecast, because you've not become "Rachel from *Friends*".' Bet Jennifer Aniston *loved* that.

81
The Replacement

US Transmission Date: 10 Oct 2000
UK Transmission Date: 19 Jan 2001
Writer: Jane Espenson
Director: James A Contner
Cast: Michael Bailey Smith (Toth), Cathy Cohen (Building Manager),
David Reivers (Foreman), Fritz Greve (Construction Worker)

A demon attacks Buffy but accidentally zaps Xander instead, splitting him into two bodies (one with Xander's strongest qualities, the other with his weakest). Meanwhile, Anya is confronted with her own mortality and Riley realises that Buffy doesn't return his love for her.

Dudes and Babes: A major episode for Xander with his sudden realisation (in both Cool and Uncool bodies) that he must grow up, get out of the basement and assure Anya that he is serious about their relationship. Which he does despite, as Giles notes, him being a bad influence upon himself.

A Little Learning is a Dangerous Thing: Buffy reads a book on the Crusades, the eight Christian military-expeditions (1099–1291) to recapture the Holy Land from the Muslims. Xander knows what the word olfactory means.

Work is a Four-Letter Word: Xander has been working for a construction firm for three months and, despite Uncool-Xander's reservations, he actually seems quite good at it. The foreman asks him to head the interior carpentry crew on a new job in Carlton.

It's a Designer Label!: Willow's red jumper. Riley's burgundy leather jacket. Buffy's spangly multicoloured top.

References: Allusions to *Star Trek*, Xander noting that there comes a point when you either have to move on or buy yourself a Klingon costume, plus direct allusions to the episode 'The Enemy Within' in which Captain Kirk is split in two ('kill us both, Spock'). Also *A Charlie Brown Christmas* (see **29**, 'Passion'. Here Xander *does* the Snoopy dance), BMW's slogan 'The Ultimate Driving Machine', Samuel Coleridge's *Rime of the Ancient Mariner* ('shiny things'), George Washington (1732–97) and Thomas Jefferson (1743–1809). Xander owns a collection of *Babylon 5* commemorative plates. At Xander's, the gang watch a badly dubbed kung-fu movie. Another Widespread Panic sticker can be seen on the phone booth. Giles hits Toth with a fertility statue of Oofdar, the goddess of childbirth.

Awesome!: Anya, on why Xander's hot-plate is on the blink: 'We think the cat peed on it'. Toth's fight with Buffy. Every scene featuring the two Xanders.

'You May Remember Me From Such Films and TV Series As . . .': Michael Bailey Smith played Belthazor in *Charmed* and was in *Purpo$e*. Fritz Greve appeared in *To Protect and Serve*. David Reivers can be seen in *Malcolm X*.

Don't Give Up The Day Job: Kelly Donovan is Nick Brendon's identical twin. He's a set decorator on *Buffy* and played Jacob in *Undressed*. Special effects coordinator Bruce Minkus previously worked on *The Terminator 2: Judgment Day*, *Schindler's List* and *Jurassic Park*.

Cigarettes & Alcohol: Cool-Xander and Anya share champagne at his new apartment.

Sex and Drugs and Rock'n'Roll: Dawn's friend Sharon's older brother knew a girl who choked on her boyfriend's tongue. Allegedly. Anya asks the others to delay reintegrating the Xanders so that she can take them home and have sex with them. One Xander is *appalled* at the prospect: 'It would be *very* confusing.'

They should all continue to pretend that they heard none of the disturbing sex talk, suggests Giles, wisely.

Logic, Let Me Introduce You to This Window: In the scene with the mannequin, Spike has a noticeable tan-line on his arms. Where can one get an answer machine like Anya's? When you hit play it knows exactly the bit of the message you want. In **80**, 'Real Me', Riley implied Anya had sustained a serious head wound when attacked by Mort; however, her only injury is a dislocated shoulder.

I Just *Love* Your Accent: Buffy, to Riley: 'He called you a toth. It's a British expression. It means, like, "moron".' Xander can do a reasonable upper-class British accent when pretending to be Albert, his reference for the apartment (see **90**, 'Checkpoint').

Quote/Unquote: Spike, when asked what he's doing at the garbage dump: 'There's a nice lady vampire who set up a charming tea room over the next pile of crap.'

Riley, on the Xanders: 'Psychologically, this is fascinating. Doesn't it make everyone wanna lock them in separate rooms and do experiments on them? Just me then?'

Notes: 'A demon has taken my life from me, and he's living it better than I do.' A very good episode with a different take on the evil-duplicate cliché to **50**, 'Doppelgängland', though a no less valid one. ('Wait till *you* have an evil twin,' Xander tells Willow. 'See how you handle it.' 'I handled it *fine*,' Willow pouts.) Plus, in one throwaway-line about Joyce having a headache, an entire season-long story-arc is set up.

On Xander's seventh birthday he wanted a toy firetruck but didn't get one. Then the house next door burnt down and real firetrucks came. For years afterwards Xander thought Willow had committed arson especially for him. Last year Xander believed he was lactose-intolerant, but it was just some bad Brie. When Xander is leaving his parents basement he points out to Riley where Spike slept (see **66**, 'Hush'), Anya and he drowned the Sepavro demon (**65**, 'Something Blue') and he had his heart ripped out (**78**, 'Restless', though technically that was only a dream). Buffy has what Riley terms a bad ice-skating movie obsession (see **21**, 'What's My Line?' Part 1). Anya has a list of what she wants from life. It includes a car, a puppy, a child and (possibly) a boat. She owns a handgun. Xander's parents are heard arguing upstairs. He notes that Buffy has been to Hell (probably a reference to **35**,

'Anne'). Spike uses a mannequin in a blonde wig to simulate Buffy when he needs to release some pent-up aggression (see **92**, 'Crush'; **96**, 'Intervention').

Did You Know?: Nick Brendon plays both Xanders. Kelly was used as a double, but did have some dialogue when the two were in the same shot (he mostly plays Cool-Xander).

Joss Whedon's Comments: Interviewed by *TV Guide*, Joss explained the thought processes behind creating recurring characters: 'It's not something that we take lightly. It's a question of how they fit into the group dynamic.' Whedon revealed that he felt the character of Anya could fill the smart-alecky void left by Charisma Carpenter. Regarding Anya, Joss noted: 'She speaks her mind rather bluntly and feels a bit on the outs with people, so makes perfect sense. Emma's extremely funny. You don't usually get that much funny in a girl that pretty.'

82
Out of My Mind

US Transmission Date: 17 Oct 2001
UK Transmission Date: 26 Jan 2001

Writer: Rebecca Rand Kirshner
Director: David Grossman
Cast: Time Winters (Initiative Doctor), Dierdre Holder (Hospital Doctor)

Joyce has a fainting spell. At the hospital Dawn discovers that Riley's heartbeat is irregular. When Buffy enlists the Initiative's help, Riley fights Graham rather than allow the government near his body again. Buffy manages to get Riley to an Initiative doctor, only to find that Spike is forcing the doctor to remove his chip.

Dreaming (As Blondie Once Said) is Free: We don't see Buffy's Hollywood-style *montage* of her college life (in which she wears glasses) but, thankfully, Spike's obsession provides one of the episode's few moments of class when Buffy bursts into his crypt; he asks her to end his torment and then they kiss. 'Oh God, no!' cried Spike, waking up.

Dudes and Babes: The debut of hunky young intern, Ben. At this stage, there's no hint that he's anything more than that.

A Little Learning is a Dangerous Thing: Buffy and Willow discuss aspects of the French Revolution including Jean-Paul Marat (1743–93, author of *The Chains of Slavery*), Charlotte Corday (a Girondin supporter who murdered Marat in his bath) and Maximilien-François Robespierre (1758–94, the Jacobin leader and instigator of the Reign of Terror).

The Conspiracy Starts at Home Time: The Initiative are monitoring Riley's phonecalls.

Work is a Four-Letter Word: Xander's carpentry skills are being put to good use in the Magic Box.

It's a Designer Label!: Buffy's blue top and red leather pants appear again. Anya's fawn skirt.

References: Buffy says Xander, Giles and Riley are her fairy-godmother, Santa Claus and Q wrapped into one ('Q from Bond, not *Star Trek*'). Spike seems to be watching *Dawson's Creek* on TV ('Pacey, you blind idiot. Can't you see she doesn't love you?'). Also, *1984* (an allusion to Big Brother), the CIA's abortive attempts to assassinate Cuban dictator Fidel Castro, the Confucius proverb 'better to light a candle than to curse the damn darkness' and Tinkerbell from *Peter Pan*. There's a Widespread Panic poster on the college wall. Spike plays 20 Questions with Harmony. In *The South Park* movie, Cartman, like Spike, had a chip inserted in his brain. Only, in Eric's case, it stopped him swearing.

Awesome!: Spike's sinister threat to Buffy just before he falls into an open grave. The brilliant dream sequence at the end.

'You May Remember Me From Such Films and TV Series As . . .': Time Winters appeared in *Gremlins 2: The New Batch*, *LA Story* and *True Vinyl*. Charlie Weber was Dillon Johnson in *Director's Cut*. Dierdre Holder was in *Jesus 2000* and *Code Blue*.

Don't Give Up The Day Job: Rebecca Rand Kirshner was a writer on *Freaks and Geeks*. One of the hospital paramedics was played by Dan Smiczek, an extra on many TV series. Dan's website (www.adventuresofdan.com/) details his experiences working on shows like *Roswell*, *The West Wing* and *The X-Files*. 'I'm about three feet from the [hospital] door when Sarah and Marc bust [in],' noted Dan. 'Marc was hilarious. He did this thing where he puts his hand on my shoulder like "thanks man for getting out of the way". In the meantime this guy came around with cookies for the crew and Sarah stocked-up. The crew were asking him "did you find Sarah to give her some". I'm guessing she's a little bit of a cookie-monster.'

The Drugs Don't Work: Whatever the Initiative stopped giving Riley last season, the result have been disastrous (his pulse is 150 per minute).

Valley-Speak: Harmony: 'I'm *totally* her arch-nemesis.'

Cigarettes & Alcohol: Harmony has taken up smoking (justifying this because she is evil).

Logic, Let Me Introduce You to This Window: After Riley's basketball game, the front of his shirt is drenched in sweat, but his back is completely dry. When he hits Graham, however, the back is wet too. One of the shots of Buffy in the opening fight scene is clearly Sarah's stunt double.

I Just *Love* Your Accent: Spike calls Harmony a silly bint (see **59**, 'The Harsh Light of Day').

Cruelty To Animals: Giles won't sell newt-eyes in the Magic Box. Instead he stocks Salamander-eyes, the cataracts on which give them a newt-like appearance.

Quote/Unquote: Harmony: 'I'll do anything.' Spike: 'Anything, will you?' Harmony: 'I said I'll do anything. Oh, you mean will I have sex with you? Well, yeah.'

Notes: 'You're going to die over some macho-pissing contest?' After such a great start to the season, this episode is a real disappointment, and something of a rehash of **70**, 'Goodbye Iowa'. It's difficult to work up much sympathy for Riley who acts like a jerk throughout, nor for Buffy whose sadistic treatment of Spike threatens to come back and haunt her. Best bit: the Doctor telling Harmony not to smoke while he's operating. And her reaction.

Buffy says she has the endurance of ten men. Dawn likes her omelettes with ketchup (urgh) and chicken fingers with mustard when she's ill. She prefers the free gifts you get in Sugar Bombs cereal than the actual cereal itself.

Soundtrack: Nickelback's 'Breathe'.

Did You Know?: 'I've pitched a couple of story ideas,' Tony Head told *DreamWatch*. 'Joss smiled and said, "No." But he did tell me why on both occasions.'

Marti Noxon's Comments: Nervous WB execs gave the *Buffy* production strong directions on the Willow/Tara relationship. As Marti Noxon told *TV Guide Online:* 'They draw the line at any physical intimacy, so we had to be crafty in the way we showed it. One of the points that we tried to make is that while the relationship is sexual, we didn't want to play it for titillation. A lot of shows have done "Come and watch the kiss" and then it never amounts to anything,' Noxon noted (referring specifically to *Ally McBeal*). 'In some ways the concerns that the network has about them being intimate doesn't feel like it's hindering us.'

83
No Place Like Home

US Transmission Date: 24 Oct 2000
UK Transmission Date: 2 Feb 2001

Writer: Douglas Petrie
Director: David Solomom
Cast: Ravil Isyanov (Monk), James Wellington (Night Watchman),
Staci Lawrence (Customer), John Sarkisian (Old Monk)

Buffy investigates a possible supernatural cause behind her mother's illness. Her search leads her to a woman called Glory who battles, and easily beats, the Slayer. Buffy discovers that she doesn't really have a sister. Dawn is the Key, sent to Buffy for protection.

Dudes and Babes: An introduction to Glory, a disturbingly alluring young woman. She is incredibly strong, seemingly needs (for reasons that will become apparent later) to suck the sanity from humans in order to maintain her own and desperately wants the Key.

A Little Learning is a Dangerous Thing: Dawn is writing a report on the rain forests.

The Conspiracy (Monastic Chant Mix): The Monk tells Buffy that many will die if she doesn't protect the Key. 'The Key is energy,' he notes. 'It's a portal. It opens the door . . .' For centuries it had no form. The Monk's brethren were its keepers. Then Glory ('the abomination') found them. They performed a spell that made the Key flesh and sent it to Buffy, as a sister, knowing that only the Slayer had the power to protect it. Buffy's memories and those of everyone else were rebuilt, confesses the Monk. However, he adds that Dawn is human and helpless. Buffy insists that Dawn is not her sister. '*She doesn't know that*,' replies the Monk, dying.

Work is a Four-Letter Word: Anya reveals a natural talent for shopwork and becomes Giles's assistant at the Magic Box.

It's a Designer Label!: Giles in a silly costume *always* gets a laugh (see **60**, 'Fear Itself'). Here, he wears a purple robe and pointed warlock's cap. And looks *ridiculous*. Also, Buffy's fur coat and tight mustard pants. Anya's leopardskin top. Willow's flowery blue jumper and Glory's awesome red dress.

References: The title is Dorothy's wish in *The Wizard of Oz*. Also, *The Oprah Winfrey Show*, *Iron Chef* (a Japanese cookery show), *The Uncanny X-Men* ('the danger room') and *The Amazing Spider-Man*. Glory makes another oblique reference to 'Little Miss Muffet', 'someone's gonna sit down on their tuffet and make this birthing stop' (see **56**, 'Graduation Day' Part 2; **71**, 'This Year's Girl'; **80**, 'Real Me'). The concept of Dawn has similarities to a series of stories in *Doctor Who* known as 'The Key to Time' in which the Black and White Guardians split the Key into six pieces, which the Doctor must reassemble to restore the balance of the universe (the final segment being a person). A sign in the Magic Box says: SHOPLIFTERS WILL BE TRANSFIGURED.

Bitch!: Anya: 'I've never had to afford things before and it's making me bitter.' Giles (sarcastically): 'The change is palpable.'
   Glory: 'I could crap a better existence than this.'
   When Buffy asks Spike for an explanation of what he's doing outside her house in five words or less, he replies: 'Out. For. A. Walk. Bitch.'

Awesome!: Xander teaching Anya the joys of raging insincerity in retail. The stunningly directed trance scene, with its sinister music and lighting as Buffy wanders around the house and, in one of the series' great moments, sees a photo of herself, Joyce and Dawn, with Dawn fading in and out. Buffy's epic (and losing) battle with Glory.

'You May Remember Me From Such Films and TV Series As . . .': Clare Kramer was Courtney Egbert in *Bring It On* and Heather in

Vig. Ravil Issyanov was in *The Saint* and *Hackers*. James Wellington appeared in *Roundabout*. John Sarkisian's movies include *Six-String Samurai*. Paul Hayes can be seen in *Chaplin* and *The X-Files*.

The Drugs Don't Work: The doctor's advice to Joyce concerning her fainting is to 'take four of some-pills a-day.' Ben gives the nightwatchman 9cc of Phenobarbitone to calm him. 'Have a nice trip,' Riley tells Buffy as she prepares for her trance.

Valley-Speak: Joyce: 'I can't be retro?'

Cigarettes & Alcohol: A multitude of Spike's cigarette butts indicate that his obsession with Buffy has transferred into stalking.

Logic, Let Me Introduce You to This Window: General one: If the Key has only recently become human, how come blood is the key to the ritual? Glory specifically says in **91**, 'Blood Ties', that the Key could be anything from a bicycle pump to a log, yet when the details of the ritual are revealed later in the season, it's obvious that the Key must be human since blood is the key to the Key. Bicycle pumps don't, generally, bleed.

I Just *Love* Your Accent: When Giles starts to panic about the number of people in the shop Xander's advice is: 'Stay British.'

Quote/Unquote: Joyce, after Buffy and Dawn have made her breakfast: 'So neither of you is pregnant, failing or under indictment? Just checking.'

Giles, on the Dagon-sphere: 'It appears to be paranormal in origin.' Buffy: 'How can you tell?' Giles: 'It's so shiny.'

Glory, beating Buffy: 'You know that thing with worms where if you have one, you rip it in half, you get two worms? Do you think that'll work with you?'

Notes: 'You're not my sister ... What *are* you?' The Dawn-revelation episode, and it's a *beaut* on all levels. The *Giles-opens-a-shop* subplot is really funny (especially Anya) but the real meat here is the introduction of Glory and the discovery that Dawn isn't a demon, which everyone had expected.

This episode takes place two months after the final scene of **79**, 'Buffy vs Dracula', and Dawn's arrival. Buffy always wanted piano lessons. Joyce's nickname for Dawn was little punkin' belly. Anya believes that the conjuring powder Giles sells is grossly overpriced and offers to hook him up with the Troll that sheds it (see **89**,

'Triangle'). Anya knew a legendary 16th-century French sorcerer, Cloutier, who perfected a spell to reveal demons, *tirer la couture*. The Magi enters a trance and is able to see a signature manifestation of the affliction. The Dagon-sphere has a history going back many centuries. It's a protective device, used to ward off primordial evil (specifically something referred to in the ancient texts as 'that which cannot be named').

Did You Know?: In late 2000, an American pressure group called 'The Parents Television Council' posted an Internet guide to *Buffy*: 'Buffy has earned red-lights for its sexual content, foul language and violence. Last season, sex was either shown or implied between Buffy and Parker, Buffy and Riley, Xander and Anya, Spike and Harmony and Oz and Veruca. In addition, homosexual undercurrents manifested between Willow and a fellow Wicca practitioner. Sexual content was at times graphic. In one episode a boy at a fraternity party became sexually aroused simply by touching a wall and grabbed his crotch. Other episodes have contained implied nudity, homosexual fantasies, masturbation, anatomical references, and references to orgasms and kinky sexual practices.' Don't know about other readers, but if I hadn't seen the series before hearing this I'd be tuning in straight afterwards.

Did You Spot?: When Buffy is in her trance and enters Dawn's room, reality is fractured and she sees flashes of the room as it should be – empty, dark and full of boxes. The room is the same one that Buffy walked into at the end of **78**, 'Restless', to be told by Tara, 'You think you know what's to come.' A piece of foreshadowing that impressed the hell out of this author.

Head On: In an interview with *E! Online*, long before the suggestion of a Giles spin-off was raised, Tony Head was asked about the possibility of *Buffy* taking a trip to London. 'In season three Joss wanted to shoot in Ireland,' noted the actor. 'The studio wouldn't let him. He was going to do three or four shows there, going back to find Angel's roots, which would have been nice.'

84
Family

US Transmission Date: 7 Nov 2000
UK Transmission Date: 9 Feb 2001

Writer: Joss Whedon
Director: Joss Whedon
Cast: Amy Adams (Cousin Beth), Steve Rankin (Mr Maclay),
Kevin O Rankin (Donny), Ezra Buzzington (Bartender),
Torry Pendergrass (Demon), Brian Tee (Intern), Peggy Goss (Crazy Person)

Members of Tara's family arrive on her 20th birthday. They announce that they want to take her home before she turns into a demon like her mother did at the same age. When Glory sends demons to kill the Slayer, Tara inadvertently helps them while attempting to prevent her friends from discovering what she believes lies within her.

Dudes and Babes: Cousin Beth is outraged that Tara has chosen education over her family, noting that Tara's brother Donny and her dad are having to 'do for themselves' while she is in Sunnydale living God-knows-what kind of lifestyle.

Denial, Thy Name is the Maclay Family: 'I hoped maybe you'd gotten over the whole witchcraft thing,' Mr Maclay tells Tara. 'You've been lying to these people for a year,' adds Beth. 'You've put a spell on them. Is that a human thing to do?' Maclay says that the women of their family have a demon in them. It's implied that Tara's mother stopped practising witchcraft at the age of 20 (see **Logic, Let Me Introduce You to This Window**). Interested in specifics, Anya asks what kind of demon she is, noting that there are a lot of different kinds and that while some are *very* evil, others have been considered useful members of society. Spike makes things simple by punching Tara in the nose and then collapsing in pain, proving that there is no demon in her. 'Just a family legend?' he asks Maclay. 'A bit of spin to keep the ladies in line?'

A Vastly Important Moment Which No One Spotted At The Time: Ben enters the hospital locker room, opens his locker and begins taking his clothes off. The camera pans back across the rows of lockers. A Lei-Ach demon comes into view, followed from behind, a few seconds later, by Glory. Ben and Glory are *never* in the same shot. Remember this for future reference.

It's a Designer Label!: Concerning Tara's present, Buffy has seen a cute sweater at Bloomy's. But, she wants it for herself. Also, Willow's purple dress. Glory's leather skirt and everyone's excellent party clothes in the Bronze.

References: *Miss Congeniality*, French-farce, an allusion to Sir Walter Scott's *Marmion* ('that was a tangled web of lies, sweetie') and Bob Marley and the Wailers' 'Rat Race'.

Bitch!: Buffy describes Glory as 'like Cordelia'. She is pretty sure that Glory dyes her hair.

Xander and Riley wrestle over whether Riley called Xander a bad name or something Latin. When Tara cracks an obscure joke she notes that it was funny if you studied Taglarin mythic rites. And you are a complete dork. Riley asks why Xander didn't laugh.

Awesome!: Dawn saying that she is going to her friend Melinda's house across the street. Buffy, fearing that Glory might attack her, uses the excuse that Melinda is a bad influence. 'I don't like you hanging out with someone that . . . short.' Spike's way of proving that Tara isn't a demon. The beautiful ending with Willow and Tara literally dancing on air.

'You May Remember Me From Such Films and TV Series As . . .': Amy Adams took over a role made famous by Sarah Michelle Gellar, as Katherine Merteuil in *Cruel Intentions 2*. She's also in *Psycho Beach Party*, *Drop Dead Gorgeous* and *Pumpkin*. Steve Rankin was in *Mercury Rising*, *LA Confidential*, *Apollo 13* and *The West Wing*. Ezra Buzzington's movies include *Fight Club*, *Magnolia* and *Me Myself & Irene*. Kevin O Rankin was in *After Diff'rent Strokes: When the Laughter Stopped*.

Valley-Speak: Willow: 'There's Scoobyage-afoot.'

Cigarettes & Alcohol: Riley has become a regular at Willy's Bar where he drinks whisky and buys Sandy (see **50**, 'Doppelgängland') vodka tonic, but tells her: 'My heart belongs to another. I don't go out with vampires. Never interested in my intellect.' Dawn is allowed to attend Tara's party at the Bronze and is provided with a stamp on her hand to prevent her from purchasing any booze. Only losers drink alcohol she tells Riley, Xander, Giles and Buffy, who all give each other worried looks.

Sex and Drug and Rock'n'Roll: This is the first time we see Willow and Tara in bed together. Spike's daydream of him fighting the Slayer in the most erotic way imaginable occurs while he's in bed with Harmony and about to climax (just as Buffy says, 'I'm coming right now').

Logic, Let Me Introduce You to This Window: In the last scene, Tara rests her head on Willow's shoulder. The camera cuts to a different angle and Tara has a large chunk of hair over her face. The angle switches back and it's gone. Much of this episode's revelations about Tara's mother don't really fit in with what Tara implies in **66**, 'Hush'.

Motors: The Maclays have a camper van.

Pussy Galore: The return of Miss Kitty-Fantastico. Tara and Willow devise a rather upsetting story about a lost cat.

Quote/Unquote: Giles: 'You're in a magic shop and you can't think what Tara would like.' Xander: 'What, are we gonna get her some cheesy crystal ball?' Giles: 'Bloody well better not. I've got mine already wrapped.'

Glory: 'Pay attention. I am great and I am beautiful. And when I walk into a room all eyes turn to me, because my name is a *holy* name.'

Xander, to the Maclays: 'You're dealing with all of us.' Spike: 'Except me . . . I don't care what happens.'

Notes: 'We are her blood kin. Who the hell are you?' 'We're *family*.' So, the great revelation concerning Tara is that she's . . . a perfectly normal non-demon girl. Fine. Bit of an anticlimax there, but the episode's outrage at small-minded bigotry and blind tradition is worth the effort of wading through several *very* long-winded exposition sequences.

Buffy and Giles decide not to tell the others about Dawn's real status (see **83**, 'No Place Like Home'). Buffy's father (see **9**, 'Nightmares') is currently living the cliché in Spain with his secretary and not returning Buffy's calls. Buffy says that when Hank left, Dawn cried for a week. 'Except she didn't. She wasn't there, but I can still feel what it was like.' At some point (before the events of **83**, 'No Place Like Home', presumably), Buffy moved into a single corner-suite at the university dorms. She has now decided to move back home to protect Dawn, telling the others it's to save money. Willow refers to the spell she and Tara attempted to reveal demons (which Tara secretly sabotaged, see **70**, 'Goodbye Iowa'). Xander, Anya, Willow and Tara play pool in the Bronze. Harmony shops at April Fools, the store where Cordelia worked (see **53**, 'Choices'). Anya exclaims during the demon attack that she's already been injured this month (see **80**, 'Real Me'). Riley mentions Graham and the government boys (see **82**, 'Out of My

Mind'). Harmony says she met Carol Beets (who sired Brandon from the sewer gang) who told her that the Lei-Ach demon is recruiting his brethren to kill the Slayer for some Big-Nether-Wig.

Soundtrack: Yo La Tengo's 'Tears Are In Your Eyes', Motorace's 'American Shoes', My Vitriol's 'Cemented Shoes' and Melanie Doane's 'I Can't Take My Eyes Off You'.

Critique: 'Wisely perhaps, "Family" doesn't attempt to go the whole distance by turning Tara into a fully sympathetic and likeable character,' John Binns noted in *Xposé*. 'The unspoken subtext of all this is arguably homophobia, personified by the irrational but clearly persuasive contention of Tara's father that his daughters become demons when they come-of-age.'

Did You Know?: Interviewed by Rob Francis, Amber Benson admitted she had no idea how much of a phenomenon *Buffy* was: 'I was actually in England. I truly believe that you guys are even more into *Buffy* than we are in the States. As an actor, the big hope is that you are able to eke out a living doing what you love and maybe if you're unbelievably, supremely lucky you get to actually become somewhat well known. *Buffy* puts you on the map faster than you can say.'

Joss Whedon's Comments: 'I've always believed that a family is the people who love and respect you. That you create your own family,' Joss told *scifi_ign.com*. 'When we created the show, they said "Do you want [Buffy's] family?" I said, "Basically, she *has* a family. Her father is Giles, her sister is Willow. It's already in place." I really wanted to get this message out, that it's not about blood. Tara was the perfect vehicle for that.' Joss also mentioned in several interviews how real-world disasters can create plotlines, revealing that Spike and Drusilla were supposed to return to Sunnydale together in **42**, 'Lover's Walk'. The Spike/Dru break-up was initially simply to cover for Juliet Landau doing a movie and thus being unavailable for one episode.

85
Fool for Love

US Transmission Date: 14 Nov 2000
UK Transmission Date: 16 Feb 2001

Writer: Douglas Petrie
Director: Nick Marck
Cast: Edward Fletcher (Male Partygoer), Katharine Leonard (Female Partygoer), Matthew Lang (2nd Male Partygoer), Chris Daniels (Stabbing Vampire), Kenneth Feinberg (Chaos Demon), Steve Heinze (Vampire #1), Ming Liu (Chinese Slayer), April Wheedon-Washington (Subway Slayer)

When a vampire stabs Buffy, she seeks information on the final battles of past Slayers from the only person she knows who has witnessed a Slayer's death: Spike. He not only details why his victims lost their lives, but his own history as a vampire. Meanwhile, Joyce's condition becomes worse.

Dudes and Babes: William was a very different character when he was alive, although there are all sorts of interesting psychological reasons why he may have turned into the animal that he did (see **139**, 'Lies My Parents Told Me'). Awkward and bookish with none of the confident swagger that we're used to from Spike, he was seemingly shaped by the pain of unrequited love. 'I know I'm a bad poet,' he tells Cecily, his muse. 'But I'm a good man.' She is horrified, telling William, 'You're beneath me'. When Buffy uses the same phrase to Spike 120 years later and he weeps in the gutter, it's impossible not to feel astonishing pity for this poor creature.

Once Angel told Spike about the legend of the Slayer he was, he confesses, obsessed. To most vampires the Slayer was the subject of cold sweat and frightened whispers, but Spike sought her out. He gives Buffy some valuable lessons, like the fact that the Slayer must always reach for her weapons, while a vampire's are all in-built. The first Slayer he killed was business, but the second, a black girl in New York in 1977, Spike says had a touch of Buffy's style ('I could have danced all night with that one').

A Little Learning is a Dangerous Thing: The second lesson Spike teaches is to ask the right questions. Buffy wants to know how Spike beat them. The real question, Spike says, should be why did *they* lose?

Denial, Thy Name is The Slayer: 'You got-off on it?' Buffy asks. She's talking about Spike killing the Slayers but his reply can be seen in a wider context: 'You're telling me *you don't*?' he asks. 'How many of my kind [have] you've done? We just keep coming. You can kill a hundred, a thousand, a thousand-thousand and all the enemies of Hell besides. And all we need is for one of us – *just* *one* – to have the thing we're all hoping for. One good day.' Every day, Spike continues, the Slayer wakes up with a question haunting her: 'Is today the day I die?' Part of Buffy wants death, he suggests, to stop the fear and uncertainty. '*That's* the secret,' concludes Spike. 'Not the punch you didn't throw or the kicks you didn't land. Every Slayer has a death wish.' Spike also believes that the only reason Buffy has lasted so long is because she has ties to the world. 'Your mum, your brat sister, the Scoobies. But you're just putting off the inevitable' (see **100**, 'The Gift').

It's a Designer Label!: Spike's leather coat originally belonged to the 1977 Slayer. The stabbing vampire's anarchy-symbol leather jacket and Clash T-shirt are excellent, but several minus points for his *extremely* 1974-Afro haircut. Also, the horrible clothes worn by Willow (woolly hat and baggy sweater), Xander (orange sweatshirt) and Anya (impractical shoes and *Doctor Who*-style scarf) when patrolling.

References: The Boxer Rebellion (1898–1900) was an officially supported peasant uprising to drive foreigners (particularly Christian missionaries) from China. Boxer was the name given to a Chinese society known as the *I-Ho Ch'üan* ('Righteous and Harmonious Fists'). They practised callisthenics in the belief that this gave them supernatural powers and made them impervious to bullets. Also, Cheetos (the cheesy snack produced by Frito-Lay), the Discovery Channel, misquotes from the Bee Gees' 'Words', the Clash's 'Death or Glory' and *The Untouchables* ('Here endeth the lesson'). Xander eats Tito's potato chips. There's a possible oblique reference to 'Frankly, Mr Shankly' by the Smiths.

Bitch!: Even in the 1880s, Spike knew just how to push Angelus's buttons, replying to his mentors poetic rhetoric about the artistry of a kill with a succinct: '*Poofter!*'

Awesome!: From the moment that Buffy and Spike begin talking it's full-steam-ahead for one of the finest 15 minutes in *Buffy*'s history. Particularly impressive is the inter-cutting between Buffy and Spike trading blows in the alley and Spike's memories of his battle with the Slayer on the New York subway. At times the two become one, with a 1977-Spike talking directly to Buffy. It's a quite astonishing sequence, worthy of multiple viewing to catch little glances and lines that you miss in the heart-stopping suspense of the fight itself. Also, Giles telling Buffy that Watchers find the death of a Slayer too painful to talk about, the tiny Kung Fu movie that is Spike's battle with the 1900 Slayer, the girl's dying request that Spike tell her mother that she is sorry and Spike's (seemingly genuine) regret that he doesn't speak Chinese. Plus the touching scene in South America of Drusilla and Spike breaking up after her tryst with a Chaos Demon (who is *exactly* as described in **42**, 'Lover's Walk'), the Scooby's incompetent idea of patrolling stealthily and the shot (reused in *Angel*: 'Darla') of the gang of four striding arrogantly amidst the chaos of the Boxer Rebellion as if they owned the world. *Magnificent*.

'You May Remember Me From Such Films and TV Series As . . .': Kenneth Feinberg was in *Hard Hunted*. Edward Fletcher appeared in *Titanic*. Steve Heinze can be seen in *The Limey* and *Double Deception*. Kali Rocha was in *Meet the Parents*, *When Billie Beat Bobby* and *Autumn in New York*. Matthew Lang appeared in *We Were Soldiers*.

Don't Give Up The Day Job: April Wheedon-Washington was Halle Berry's stunt-double in *Swordfish*. She also played Faith in *General Hospital*.

Valley-Speak: Dawn: 'Come on, who's *The Man*?'

Cigarettes & Alcohol: Spike notes that there are a few American beers that are underrated. Unfortunately, the one he's drinking isn't one of them. He also wants Buffy to order him spicy buffalo wings as part of his payment.

Logic, Let Me Introduce You to This Window: A retrospective one. In **15**, 'School Hard', Giles reads the details of Spike killing two previous Slayers from an ancient volume. But here, we find that the second of them was as recently as 1977. It's confirmed that Spike was sired by Drusilla, despite him having said on two previous occasions (**15**, 'School Hard'; *Angel*: 'In the Dark') that it was Angel who made him. To be fair, Joss Whedon has said several times that Dru was always intended to be Spike's sire (on 2 Jan 1998 he told the *Posting Board*: 'Angel was Dru's sire. *She* made Spike. But sire doesn't just mean [the] guy who made you, it means you come from their line. Angel is like a grandfather to Spike'). In **15**, 'School Hard', Giles said Spike was 'barely 200 years old.' In **63**, 'The Initiative', Spike says he is 126. Here, the year he became a vampire is confirmed as 1880, making him approximately 120. Spike's reflection can be seen periodically in the subway during the fight. The word 'poofter' is anachronistic for 1880 (in the *Oxford Dictionary of Slang* its first recorded usage is 1903). The New York Slayer moves her hand fractionally after Spike has killed her.

I Just *Love* Your Accent: Buffy says Watchers are prigs, a term referring to someone who displays an exaggerated sense of propriety. With his new name and Cock-er-nee accent, Spike was using 'bollocks' as an insult to Angel back in 1880. The English accents (Marsters and Landau's usual faultless delivery aside) are pretty woeful.

Quote/Unquote: William's poetry: 'My heart expands, 'tis grown a bulge in it. Inspired by your beauty, effulgent' (see *Angel*: 'Not Fade Away').

Spike, on killing his first Slayer: 'The best night of my life. And I've had some sweet ones.'

Drusilla, to William: 'You walk in worlds the others can't begin to imagine.'

Buffy: 'You think we're dancing?' Spike: 'That's all we've ever done.'

Notes: 'It wouldn't be you, Spike. It would *never* be you. You're beneath me.' Together with its *Angel* sequel, 'Darla' (shown immediately after this episode), this epic, extraordinary, lyrical, painful exercise in storytelling, crossing 200 years and as many emotions, should be studied (long and hard) by anyone who still thinks *Buffy* is just kids' stuff. That this series can get into the kind of philosophical and psychological areas that it does here, that it can make the audience genuinely *care* about a monster like Spike, speaks volumes for the intelligence and depth to the writing and the performance.

Buffy mentions the Slayers' accelerated healing powers. Spike and Buffy play pool in the Bronze (see **84**, 'Family'). Spike had the nickname William the Bloody when he was still human, as a result of his bloody awful poetry. Spike was sired by Drusilla on the night he met her in 1880. Angel and Darla were unhappy with Spike's addition to their group, as he drew attention to them and forced them into hiding. Spike says that if he doesn't intend to hurt someone (if, for instance, he throws a punch intended to miss), his chip won't activate. He also indicates that there are varying levels of pain, that it sometimes lasts longer, depending on what he does. Harmony refers to Spike staking her (see **59**, 'The Harsh Light of Day'). Giles refers to an 18th-century Slayer who forged her own weapons. Joyce announces that she is going into hospital overnight for a CAT scan.

Timeline Revisited: So much new information is revealed in this episode (and in *Angel*: 'Darla') that it's worth giving some praise to the writers as, the identity of Spike's sire aside, the continuity is spot-on.

Born as Liam in 1725 (*Angel*: 'The Prodigal'), Angelus was sired by Darla, one of the Order of Aurelius (see **12** 'Prophecy Girl') in 1753 (**33**, 'Becoming' Part 1). According to Darla, '[Angelus's] name would already be legend in his home village, if he had left anyone alive.' In 1760, the pair travelled to London ('we cut a bloody swath through South Wales and Northern England') and Darla's sire, the Master. (Darla had been sired in Virginia in 1609; *Angel*: 'Darla'.) Although Angelus insulted the Master and the pair left as enemies, at some stage there may have been a reconciliation as the Master remembers Angelus fondly in **7**, 'Angel'. Thereafter, Darla and Angelus travelled across Europe (they planned to go to Naples, though ended up in France in 1765; *Angel*: 'The Trial'; 'Heartthrob') creating mayhem and death wherever they went. On some occasions they operated alone, as when Angelus sired Penn (*Angel*: 'Somnambulist') in the late 1700s, or when he was in Dublin in 1838 (**44**, 'Amends'). They were together in 1860 in London when Darla found Drusilla, a girl with frightening psychic ability, and Angelus stalked her, killed her family, sent her mad and finally sired her (**19**, 'Lie to Me'; **33**, 'Becoming' Part I; *Angel*: 'Dear Boy'). And they were in the same city in 1880, when a sensitive young poet named William was sired by Dru. The gang then hid in Yorkshire, fleeing London barely ahead of an angry mob, due to William (now renamed Spike because of his habit of torturing his victims with railway spikes; **15**, 'School Hard'; *Angel*: 'Desinty') and his outrageous exploits.

In Borsa, Romania, in 1898, after killing a Kalderash Romany gypsy, Angelus was cursed to regain his soul (**33**, 'Becoming' Part 1) and, although Darla's initial reaction was to attempt to destroy him (*Angel*: 'Five By Five'), Angel, with his soul intact, rejoined the gang in China in 1900 (**15**, 'School Hard'), where Spike killed the then current Slayer. However, when Angel saved a missionary family from Darla, she once again rejected him. It's possible they met on at least one further occasion (in **7**, 'Angel', he says that he last saw Darla in Budapest at the turn of the century). Around the same time, he was supposed to meet Penn in Italy, but missed the appointment. Instead he travelled to America and was there during the depression (*Angel*: 'City Of'). He lived in LA in 1952 (*Angel*: 'Are You Now or Have You Ever Been?') and New York in 1996 (**33**, 'Becoming' Part 1) before travelling to Sunnydale in the same year.

Soundtrack: Crushing Velvet's 'XXX', 'Heal Yourself' by Elephant Ride, Avenue A's 'Run Cold', The Killington's 'Balladovie', Johann Sebastian Bach's 'Patita #3 in E Major' and Felix Mendelssohn's 'A Midsummer Night's Dream'.

Critique: 'An amazing episode,' wrote *SFX*'s Ed Gross, 'made even more astounding by the fact that this is the show's fifth season and the producers continually manage to pull the veritable rabbit out of the hat. It's fascinating to see Spike as a human in 1880s London, being rebuffed by the woman he has fallen in love with and heading outside to the darkness to seek solace. Instead, he literally bumps into Drusilla, Darla and Angelus.'

Did You Know?: 'It's just me and a guitar; I'm not going to be doing a lot of Smashing Pumpkins,' James Marsters told the press, concerning his debut performance as Acoustic-Rock God at 14 Below in Santa Monica, opening for Barry Williams (from *The Brady Bunch*). 'I do Tom Waits, Neil Young, Bob Dylan. All the good stuff, when they had songs written for voice and guitar. I wish I could do Johnny Lee Hooker, but I'm not that good.' James was also a huge hit at the N2K convention in London when he entertained a sizeable audience with a set of covers and original material.

Joss Whedon's Comments: 'If I could write for any show, it would be *The Simpsons* or *Twin Peaks*,' Joss told the *Buffy* magazine. 'As much as you could say that *Buffy* is a cross between *90210* and *The X-Files*, you could also say it's a cross between *The Simpsons* and *Twin Peaks*. Also, I want to kill Aaron Sorkin, eat his brains and gain his knowledge because I love *The West Wing* so much. His stuff is just amazing.'

Subsequently On *Angel*: 'Darla': A now-human Darla begins to feel guilt and confusion about her past. Wesley worries that Wolfram & Hart have planned all this to keep Angel busy. Darla tries to contact Angel for help and then, with Lindsey McDonald's aid, attempts to escape. Lindsey gives Angel information as to where Darla is being kept and Angel saves her. Darla begs her former lover to sire her so she won't be plagued by her soul, but Angel refuses.

86
Shadow

US Transmission Date: 21 Nov 2000
UK Transmission Date: 23 Feb 2001

Writer: David Fury
Director: Daniel Attias
Cast: William Forward (Dr Isaacs)

Joyce's scan reveals a shadow. A biopsy confirms that it's a brain tumour. Glory conjures up a supernatural snake to find the Key. The snake *does* find Dawn, but Buffy destroys it before it can report back. Riley, meanwhile, feels abandoned and begins to experiment with dark sexual games.

Dudes and Babes: The debut of Glory's spacious luxury apartment, her Imelda Marcos-style shoe fetish and her non-human minions (in this case Dreg and his outrageous grovelling).

Denial, Thy Name is Riley: Tired of waiting for Buffy to confide in him, wounded by constant reminders of Angel's presence and unsure of his position within the group, Riley goes to Willy's Bar again, gets drunk and accepts Sandy's offer (see **84**, 'Family'). As she lovingly bites his neck, he stakes her.

It's a Designer Label!: Buffy's leather jacket and silver boots. The long-haired shopper's spider-web shirt. Glory's crimson leather dress. Spike steals a pair of Buffy's pink knickers as Riley throws him out of her room.

References: Allusions to *Destroy All Monsters*, Marvel's *Captain America*, Starkist tuna's slogan 'Sorry Charlie', *The Usual Suspects*, *The Simpsons* (Giles uses Apu's catchphrase, 'Thank you, call again') and the Beach Boys' 'Fun, Fun, Fun'. Xander mentions 'Bipperty, Bopperty, Boo' (from *Cinderella*). The Canadian comedy series *SCTV* featured a regular skit called 'Farm Film Celebrity Blowup' where two hicks (John Flaherty and John Candy) reviewed movies and then exploded them (and often their creators) with the catchphrase 'They blowed up *real* good' (see **Valley-Speak**).

Bitch!: Spike, to Riley: 'Face it, white bread. Buffy's got a type, and you're not it.'

Awesome!: Dawn, telling Riley that Buffy cries a lot less with him than she did with Angel. Buffy's fight with Glory in the zoo's reptile house. The lengthy chase and battle between Buffy and the snake.

'You May Remember Me From Such Films and TV Series As . . .': Kevin Weisman was in *Robbers*, *Gone in Sixty Seconds*, *Man of the Century*, *Felicity*, *Just Shoot Me* and played Larry in *Roswell*. William Forward appeared in *Thirst*, *DOA*, *Chiller* and was Lord Refa in *Babylon 5*.

Don't Give Up The Day Job: Daniel Attias was producer on *Party of Five*, assistant director on *ET the Extra-Terrestrial* and helmed episodes of *The Sopranos*, *Ally McBeal* and *Sledge Hammer!* Just weeks after his second *Buffy* episode aired, Attias was involved in a family tragedy when his son David was charged with murdering four pedestrians with his car in Santa Barbara.

The Spell *Will* Work: Giles, unknowingly, sells Glory a Khul's amulet and a Sobekian bloodstone. The Sobekites were an ancient Egyptian reptile cult and the amulet is a transmogrification conduit. When Buffy finds out that Glory has been to the shop, she asks how did she get away with the bad-mojo stuff. Giles sold it to her, snitches Anya. 'If it's any consolation,' says a crestfallen Giles, 'I may have overcharged.'

Valley-Speak: Xander: 'Captain America blowed it up real good. All by his lone-wolf lonesome.'

Devil Worship and Rock'n'Roll: A customer asks if Giles stocks the LP *Aleister Crowley Sings*. Giles, sadly, notes that they don't but says he *does* have some very nice whale sounds. The advert for the Magic Box includes mention of 'Crystals!' 'Potions!' and 'Death Charms!'

Logic, Let Me Introduce You to This Window: Joyce's hair is different when she goes into the CAT scan from when she comes out. Glory hurts Buffy's right shoulder, but when Buffy is at the hospital she puts ice on the left. Watch out for the very obvious rubber snake that Clare Kramer handles when Glory pulls the cobra from the glass case. The Sunnydale area telephone code, 803, is a real code for South Carolina.

I Just *Love* Your Accent: Giles's slogan for the Magic Box is 'Your one-stop spot to shop for all your occult needs'.

Cruelty To Animals: Dawn asks what a CAT Scan is. It's actually an acronym for Computed Axial Tomography, so she can rest assured that they don't test it on cats.

Quote/Unquote: Xander: 'Am I right?' Giles: 'I'm almost certain you're not, but to be fair, I wasn't listening.'

Riley finds Spike in Buffy's room: 'Were you just smelling her sweater?' Spike: 'No. Yeah, all right, I did. It's a predator thing, nothing wrong with it.'

Notes: 'Your mother has ... low-grade glycoma. It's a brain tumour.' Welcome to the beginning of a very grim couple of weeks. Blowing about the next half-a-seasons' SFX budget on, let's face it, a pretty poor CGI-snake was a questionable decision, but 'Shadow' is basically sound (if hardly laugh-a-minute stuff), with excellent performances from Sutherland, Trachtenberg and Gellar in particular.

This episode begins the day after the events of **85**, 'Fool for Love'. Buffy learns that Glory's name is Glorificus (see **84**, 'Family'). The Magic Box is located at 5124 Maple Court in downtown Sunnydale. The phone number is 803-555-8966.[32] Spike says Willow has recently performed two uninvitation spells on Buffy's home, locking out Dracula (**79**, 'Buffy vs Dracula') and Harmony (**80**, 'Real Me'). The Sunnydale Zoo was last seen in **6**, 'The Pack'. Buffy says that the snake demon isn't mayor-size (see **56**, 'Graduation Day' Part 2). Dawn mentions celebrating her 10th birthday at the amusement park and notes that this was shortly after the family moved to Sunnydale. Anya refers to her fear of bunnies (see **60**, 'Fear Itself').

---

[32] Ever wondered why 555 is used as a telephone prefix in many US TV series? When exchange names were part of phone numbers, digits also corresponded to letters, the first three signifying the exchange that the caller was dialling. Unfortunately '5' was J, K and L and there aren't many American place-names using a combination of only those letters. Due to the low number of 555 codes, Hollywood was encouraged to quote them in their productions to prevent real telephone subscribers being harassed by people trying out numbers they'd heard in the movies. Now the 555 code *is* used by various Internet service providers. Only 555-0100 to 555-0199 are specifically set aside by Bellcore for the entertainment industry. As several of the numbers used in *Buffy* are not among those, presumably, the producers visited the website *www.home.earthlink.net/mthyen/* which lists other 555 numbers available.

Soundtrack: Thomas Wanker's beautiful piano score that accompanies the sad montage of characters at the end.

Did You Know?: 'The woman who owned the snake [said], "It's OK, we fed him a few days ago, he shouldn't be hungry",' Clare Kramer told *FHM*. 'To be honest, I'd much prefer to hold a snake than a hamster.'

87
Listening to Fear

US Transmission Date: 28 Nov 2000
UK Transmission Date: 2 Mar 2001
Writer: Rebecca Rand Kirshner
Director: David Solomon
Cast: Keith Allan (Skinny Mental Patient), Erin Leigh Price (Vampire Chick),
April Adams (Nurse Lampkin), Barbara C Adside (Creature),
Debbie Lee Carrington (Creature)

The gang investigate a suspicious death in the woods near a meteor crash site and discover that the killer is a Queller demon, summoned to silence madmen. Riley secretly calls the military for help. Joyce – whose condition causes her flashes of incoherence – goes home rather than wait in the hospital for her surgery. The Queller follows.

Dudes and Babes: It was Ben who brought the Queller demon to clean up Glory's mess, 'Just like I've done my whole damn life'. He is known to Dreg. Riley, meanwhile, is getting more hot-vampire-lurv (see **86**, 'Shadow'; **88**, 'Into the Woods').

Denial, Thy Name is Joyce . . .: Joyce remembers the events of **82**, 'Out of My Mind', where, before fainting, she momentarily didn't know who Dawn was. In her less lucid moments, she describes Dawn as 'nothing. You're a shadow.' She's not mine, is she? Joyce asks Buffy, 'She *does* belong to us, though?' Buffy confirms that Dawn does.

A Little Learning is a Dangerous Thing: The belief that the moon causes insanity is the origin of the term lunacy. Friends of the afflicted would pray to the moon to send a shooting star to quell the madmen (due to the Queller demon inside them). Such meteoric anomalies go back to an incident in 12th century Reykjavik. In the Middle Ages there were plagues of madness, but the insanity would always subside after a meteor event.

Willow is studying the First World War in history (underlying causes *and* trench-foot). She buys Dawn a book called *Spells* and Buffy a large book called *World History*. At the university library, Xander is reading a volume called *Meteors and You!* Tara notes that she and Anya have been reading international periodicals for meteorite landings.

It's a Designer Label!: The leather-pants vampire-gang in the opening scenes. Buffy's hooded top. Tara's tasteful poloneck.

References: Tara says that Japanese commercials are weird. Spike mentions the fast-food chain Burger Barn. There's a sign in dawn's bedroom saying PARENTAL ADVISORY LYRICS. Among Willow's presents are a yo-yo for Buffy and a beer-hat for Joyce.

Naming All the Stars: Willow identifies Canis Minor, a small constellation with two stars, Procyon and Gomeisa (in astronomy, it represents one of Orion's dogs). Cassiopeia is the W-shaped figure beneath Polaris. In Greek mythology, Cassiopeia was Andromeda's mother, chained to her throne for eternity as a punishment for her boastfulness. Both are visible in North America between November and March. Willow says that some of the stars we look at don't exist any more. In the time that it takes for their light to reach Earth, they've exploded. She continues that she loved to look at the stars when she was little. They're supposed to make one feel insignificant, but they made Willow feel like she was in space. Tara describes various constellations that she has made up because she doesn't understand the real ones: The Big Pineapple, Short-Man-Looking-Uncomfortable, Moose Getting a Sponge Bath and Little Pile o'Crackers.

Bitch!: Joyce, to Buffy: 'You shouldn't eat any more, you're disgustingly fat.'

Awesome!: The finding of the meteor. When Anya says 'If there's radiation you could go sterile,' watch Riley looking alarmed and Xander jumping hurriedly backward. Willow says that something evil crashed to Earth in the meteor and then slithered away to do badness. Giles replies that, in all fairness, they don't know about the slithered part. 'No. I'm sure it frisked about like a fluffy lamb,' adds Anya.

'You May Remember Me From Such Films and TV Series As . . .': Nick Chinlund was Billy Bedlam in *Con Air*, Donnie Pfaster in *The X-Files* and Detective Tancredi in *Third Watch*. He also featured in *Amy's Orgasm*, *Reform School Girl* and *Joshua Tree*. April Adams appeared in *Mission: Africa*. Debbie Lee Carrington played Felicity in *She's All That* and was in *Total Recall*, *Howard the Duck*, *Spaced Invaders* and *Return of the Jedi* (playing an Ewok).

Don't Give Up The Day Job: Keith Allan's usual industry job is title designer on *Hard* and *Zero Tolerance*. Barbara C Adside did stunts on *Bordello of Blood* while appearing in *Feds* and *Nemesis*. Randy Thompson directed the movie *Stages*.

The Drugs Don't Work: The doctor gives Buffy three bottles of pills for Joyce including sedatives and painkillers.

Valley-Speak: Willow, after killing two vampires: '*Yay* on me.'

Logic, Let Me Introduce You to This Window: It's unusual for a doctor to respond to a call button – that would normally be a nurse's job. The nurse can hear a crazy guy screaming but, seemingly, not the demon. Buffy doesn't drive (she does, but really badly, see **40**, 'Band Candy') and Joyce almost certainly can't in her condition, but one of them had to have driven home, as no other explanation is given for how they got there. Dawn says the crazy guy told her she wasn't real (see **80**, 'Real Me'). He didn't, merely telling her that she didn't belong here. Willow mentions the Tunguska explosion in Russia and gives the date as 1917. It was actually 1908.

Motors: Xander, looking at a representation of the planets, observes how small Mercury is compared to Saturn. Whereas, in contrast, the cars of the same name . . . Saturn is famous for popular S-Series (compact sedans). Mercury is a subsidiary of Ford and makes mid-size sedans and SUVs.

Cruelty To Animals: Dawn says a girl at school told her that gelatin is made from ground-up cows feet and that if you eat Jell-O, there's a cow somewhere, limping.

Quote/Unquote: Willow: 'We're experienced.' Anya: 'Yes, it seems like we're always dealing with creatures from outer space. Except that we don't ever do that!'

Willow says she feels like Santa Claus: 'Except thinner and younger. And female. And Jewish.'

Giles: 'It would appear that the world is not being invaded.' Tara: 'I'm pretty pleased about that.'

Notes: 'It's a killer snot monster from outer space.' One of the most unremittingly grim hours of television you'll ever see. Yet it's as darkly compelling as even the series' lightest moments.

The patient released from the hospital is the nightwatchman whom Glory attacked in **83**, 'No Place Like Home'. Previously, he mentioned his wife and two daughters, who we see with him in this episode. Willow says she doesn't want to be the one who finds the bodies any more (see **12**, 'Prophecy Girl'; **67**, 'Doomed'; **80**, 'Real Me').

Did You Know?: Although he was surrounded by men like Giles during his time at Winchester, Joss actually got the name from his housematron, Barbara Giles. 'Mostly I knew people like the Watcher's Council. There were some harsh old men teaching there.' Asked which of his characters he can most identify with, Joss noted: 'Sometimes it's Giles, because I'm so appalled by everything around me.'

88
Into the Woods

US Transmission Date: 19 Dec 2000
UK Transmission Date: 9 Mar 2001

Writer: Marti Noxon
Director: Marti Noxon
Cast: Rainy Jo Stout (Junkie Vampire Girl), Emmanuel Xuereb (Whip),
Adam G (Tough Vamp)

Joyce's surgery is successful. Buffy and Riley go home for celebaratory sex but Riley sneaks out in the middle of the night. Spike follows him to a vampire brothel, where Riley pays to have his blood sucked. Spike takes Buffy to the building to see for herself. Riley is approached by the military to return to the fold. He tells Buffy that he will leave if she doesn't give him a reason to stay, and a lecture from Xander makes Buffy realise how wrong she has been.

Dudes and Babes: Dawn says that when she was younger she used to put chopsticks in her mouth and pretend to be a vampire. Buffy would chase her, yelling, 'I'm the Slayer, I'm going to get you.' That's *disturbing*, notes Anya. 'You're emotionally scarred and will end up badly.'

A Little Learning is a Dangerous Thing: Buffy has been missing lots of school recently and says that she may have to take a few incompletes, but that she'll make it through the semester (see **97**, 'Tough Love').

Denial, Thy Name is Buffy: Xander perceptively notes that Buffy got burned with Angel and has been treating Riley like rebound-guy ever since when he's actually the kind that comes along once in a lifetime. He has never held back from Buffy, Xander continues. He's risked everything. Buffy is letting him leave because she doesn't like ultimatums. If he's not the guy, Xander continues, let him go. But if she really thinks she can love him then think about what she's about to lose. Buffy begins to cry. 'Run,' Xander tells her. But it's too late. Just as in **57**, 'The Freshman', Xander is the only person who seems able to say honest things to Buffy when she most needs it.

The Conspiracy Starts at Home Time: Though the Initiative is dead (see **77**, 'Primeval'), there is still a branch of the army that hunts demons, led by Major Ellis (see **87**, 'Listening to Fear') of which Graham is a member. They, apparently, make their services available around the world (this job is in Belize; a demon tribe is killing missionaries in the rain forest).

It's a Designer Label!: Buffy's *With the Beatles*-style black poloneck. Xander's tan jacket.

References: The title may refer to Stephen Sondheim and James Lapine's stage musical of the same name: a darkly amusing take on fairy tales, in which various characters ultimately find that there's no such thing as happily ever after. Xander mentions Moo Goo Gai Pan, a Cantonese dish of chicken, mushrooms, vegetables and sautéed spices. 'The chimp playing hockey? Is that based on the Chekhov?' alludes to the movie *MVP* and Anton Chekhov (1860–1904), Russian dramatist and author of *Uncle Vanya* and *The Cherry Orchard*. Also, *Game of Life* (see **80**, 'Real Me'), *The Graduate* ('Are you planning to seduce me, Mr Finn?'), *Rambo*, the State Farm insurance agency and *Penthouse*. The title is shared with an episode of *Buffy*'s WB-stablemate *Roswell* (presumably a compliment for the other series using 'Surprise' as one of *its* titles). Posters for the bands String Cheese Incident and Mentor can be seen outside the brothel.

Bitch!: Buffy, on Spike's sudden arrival: 'Every time you show up like this, you risk *all* of your parts.'

Awesome!: Xander and Giles *not* hugging at the hospital. Riley stabbing Spike with a plastic stake and then the pair getting drunk and maudlin afterwards. Buffy taking out seven vampires including the junkie she saw biting Riley with a javelin throw that would probably get her on the medal rostrum at the Olympics.

'You May Remember Me From Such Films and TV Series As . . .': Rainy Jo Stout was Nancy in *One*. Emmanuel Xuereb was in *Jerks*, *Natural Born Killers* and *Stonewall*. Adam G appeared in *The President's Man*.

Fun with Wigs: Joyce doesn't like the idea of wearing a wig and believes it will make her look like she has a cat on her head.

Valley-Speak: Dawn: 'I'm only sleeping here so Buffy and Riley can *boink*.'

Cigarettes & Alcohol: Anya thinks strawberry schnapps tastes like ice cream. Riley and Spike share a bottle of wine while discussing how much love *sucks*.

Vampire Sex and Drugs and Rock'n'Roll: Giles says he hasn't seen a vampire brothel since his Ripper days (see **20**, 'The Dark Age'). Such places have been in existence for centuries. Humans pay vampires to suck some of their blood because they find it arousing. The vampires get cash and blood but it can be dangerous for the humans involved. People can die accidentally, or meet a vampire who only pretends to play by the rules.

Anya is desperate to tell Riley about some of her and Xander's sexcapades involving the vaulting horse in Buffy's training area.

Logic, Let Me Introduce You to This Window: After Spike is staked by Riley, when he removes his hand from his chest there's no hole in his shirt. Spike reaches for the wine bottle and starts to open it. After a change of angle, he's got his hand on his chest; then starts to open the bottle again. Anya's hairstyle twice changes between scenes. When Buffy is hitting the punch-bag, both of her hands are taped. When Riley gets there, her left hand is taped but the right isn't. Riley didn't tell Buffy what time he would be leaving (he just said tonight), yet she somehow knew it would be at midnight. She also knows that he'd be leaving by helicopter when he didn't tell her that either. Several of the Scoobies have different clothes on to those that they wore in the final scene of **87**, 'Listening to Fear', despite the fact that these scenes take place just a couple of hours later.

I Just *Love* Your Accent: Giles notes that he's no longer a victim of crass holiday commercialisation but rather a purveyor of it as he hangs up a sign: DON'T FORGET! WINTER SOLSTICE, HANUKKAH, CHRISTMAS, KWANZAA & GURNENTHAR'S ASCENDANCE ARE COMING!

Cruelty To Animals: Anya's excitement at a film with a chimp playing hockey: 'That's hilarious. The ice is so slippery and monkeys are all irrational. We *have* to see this.'
    Anya: 'Who ordered more chickens' feet? The ones we have aren't moving at all.' Xander: 'That's generally what happens when you cut them off the chicken.'

Quote/Unquote: Anya, to Willow: 'I can just hear you in private. "I dislike that Anya. She's newly human and strangely literal".'
    Spike, to Riley: 'Sometimes I envy you so much it chokes me. And sometimes I think I got the better deal. To be that close to her and not have her. To be all alone even when you're holding her. Feeling her beneath you. Surrounding you . . . No, *you* got the better deal.'
    Xander, to Anya: 'I've gotta say something, cos I don't think I've made it clear. I'm in love with you. Powerfully, painfully in love. The things you do, the way you think, the way you move. I get excited every time I'm about to see you. You make me feel like I've never felt before in my life. Like a man. I just thought you might wanna know.'

Notes: 'What else do you want from me, Riley? I've given you everything that I have. My heart, my body and soul.' The end of a trilogy of *desperately* depressing episodes. 'Into the Woods', like the two immediately before it, abandons one of the series' great strengths – its humour – in favour of deep, dark and bitter truths. That these episodes work *at all* is a tribute to the writing. That they work as outstandingly well as they do is down to the cast, who play it like they mean it. I defy even the world's greatest Riley-hater not to be moved by the final shots of this episode.
    During her demon days Anya once made a man spontaneously combust, setting his village on fire in the process.

Soundtrack: Emilana Torrini's 'Summer Breeze'.

Did You Know?: According to *Soap Opera Weekly*, the 'In Memory of DC Gustafson' caption refers to Gustav Gustafson, a member of the *Buffy* crew and a close friend of Sarah who died in November 2000.

Joss Whedon's Comments: 'I love Marc and I loved Riley as a character,' Joss told the *Posting Board*. 'Some people responded to him and some didn't. Basically, it came down to nobody getting over Buffy and Angel. Because I'd done the tortured *Romeo and Juliet*, "This is the wrong guy, he's gonna make me miserable" romance, I wanted to see Buffy have a relationship with a nice guy. America doesn't want to see that. So it became instead a scenario where people thought, "She has a nice guy. She's going to walk all over him." I think Marc really came into his own, particularly this season. He has a Gary Cooper quality. But Gary Cooper can't live in the Buffyverse.' Joss also acknowledged, bravely, some of the less than successful aspects of season four: 'We didn't have the money to make [the Initiative] look good, so they kept patrolling past the same bush. Spike was hiding behind that shrub and I was like, "Why don't you look in the shrub? It's the only shrub there is!" We wanted to bring a James Bondian world to the show but, quite frankly, it was too expensive.'

89
Triangle

US Transmission Date: 9 Jan 2001
UK Transmission Date: 16 Mar 2001

Writer: Jane Espenson
Director: Christopher Hibler
Cast: Ranjani Brow (Young Nun)

With Giles in England, meeting the Watcher's Council, a squabble over who was left in charge of the Magic Box – Anya or Willow – leads to a spell going wrong and the arrival of a vengeful troll. Spike, meanwhile, tries to show Buffy his softer side.

Dudes and Babes: Anya observes that humans make the same mistakes over and over. Some guy dumps a girl, who calls on Anyanka to exact vengeance. The next year, same girl, different guy. 'After you smite a few you start going "My goodness, young lady. Maybe you're doing something wrong here too".' Buffy, meanwhile, saves a nun from a vampire and asks: 'The whole abjuring the company of men? How's that working for you?' She has taken down the Riley pictures in her bedroom.

A Little Learning is a Dangerous Thing: Willow says that she uses the time between classes to copy over her notes with a system of different coloured pens. It has been pointed out to her that this is insane. 'I said *quirky*,' notes Tara defensively. Tara likes Greek Art, which touches on mythology, history and philosophy. Buffy, however, says the professor spits too much when talking. Buffy has considered taking Central American Geopolitics but every time she hears the word jungle she thinks of Riley.

There's more on alternative universes (see **43**, 'The Wish'; **50**, 'Doppelgängland') with Willow noting that trying to send someone to a specific place is like trying to hit a puppy by throwing a bee at it. She and Anya mention several such universes including the land of trolls, the land of perpetual Wednesday, the crazy-melty-land and the now-legendary world without shrimp (see **73**, 'Superstar'; *Angel*: 'Underneath').

Denial, Thy Name is Buffy: A definite case of guilt-transference here as she gets really upset over the possibility of Xander and Anya's miraculous love being broken.

It's a Designer Label!: Buffy tells the others that the nun she saved let her try on her wimple. Buffy's fabulous pink silk blouse, Giles's grey tie, Willow's Rolling Stones T-shirt.

References: Willow describes Anya being like as the fish in the bowl, from Dr Seuss's *The Cat in the Hat*. Willow says, 'I wish Buffy was here,' and Buffy immediately walks in. Willow then adds, 'I wish I had a million dollars,' and looks around hopefully, a joke of Chandler's in the first episode of *Friends*. Also, Sea World and *Lord of the Rings*. Magazines seen in the Magic Box racks include *Massage*, *UFO Tesla*, *Green Egg*, *Sharmans & Drums* and *Nexus*. A sign in the Magic Box says: MAGIC HAPPENS.

Bitch!: Dawn: 'Whatcha doin'?' Buffy, sarcastically: 'Playing soccer.'

Willow, impersonating Anya: 'I like money better than people. People can so rarely be exchanged for goods and/or services.' And, when Anya says there are humans stranger than her: 'Unless I'm really wrong about Crazy Larry at the bus stop, he's probably not gonna turn Xander into a troll.'

Awesome!: Spike practising giving Buffy chocolates on his mannequin and ending up having a violent argument with it. Buffy's
dealing nicely with her own break-up but becoming distraught and
sobbing on Tara's shoulder at the suggestion that Xander and
Anya are having difficulties. Olaf breaking Xander's arm, and
calling him a tiny man. Plus one of the best bits of comedy on the
show: Buffy finds Spike tending an injured woman. Spike says,
defensively, that he isn't sampling. 'You want credit for *not* feeding
on bleeding-disaster-victims?' asks Buffy, walking away in disgust.
Spike: 'What's it *take*?!'

'You May Remember Me From Such Films and TV Series As . . .':
Abraham Benrubi played Larry Kubiac in the 90s cult classic
Parker Lewis Can't Lose, Jerry Markovic in *ER* and appeared in
Twister and *War Story*. Ranjani Brow was in *East of Hope Street*.

Don't Give Up the Day Job: Chris Hibler previously worked on
Matlock, *Quantum Leap* and *Moonlighting*. He was assistant
director on *Bedknobs and Broomsticks*.

Valley-Speak: Willow, on why she wouldn't try to have sex with
Xander: 'Hello! *Gay now?*'

Cigarettes & Alcohol: Anya realises that Willow is exerting peer
pressure. 'Any second you're gonna make me smoke tobacco and
have drugs.' Olaf drinks beer straight from the keg. Xander and
Spike share a beer while they play pool in the Bronze. (What's with
all this pool? That's three times in five episodes it's been used as a
dramatic tool.)

Logic, Let Me Introduce You to This Window: The Magic Box, in
an exterior shot, is next to a bookshop. This looks nothing like the
location seen in **80**, 'Real Me'. Anya's hairstyle changes dramatically between shots while she and Xander are in bed, along with
the level on his chest at which Nick Brendon has the bedclothes
positioned. Xander gets hit in the face with a huge hammer. Twice.
And *doesn't* have his skull crushed? (Look at the effect it had on
Glory in **100**, 'The Gift'.) Buffy was nowhere near the falling
gantry in the Bronze but still ends up beneath it when it lands.
Xander and Anya's position in relation to Buffy, Willow and Tara
changes several times between shots in the Bronze when confronted by Olaf. How does Buffy know so much about Riley's
mission? He certainly didn't tell her where he was going. When
Buffy and Dawn are talking in Buffy's room, Buffy is reading a

magazine. Later, it disappears and Buffy is holding a teddy bear. Anya says that she's never driven. In **55**, 'Graduation Day' Part 1, she told Xander she had a car outside, and suggested that they leave Sunnydale.

I Just *Love* Your Accent: Tara is envious of Giles. A trip to England sounds so exciting and exotic. 'Unless you're English.'

Cruelty To Animals: Willow used Hellebore to de-rat Amy (see **45**, 'Gingerbread'). It didn't work but, Willow believes, it might have made Amy really smart. 'She keeps giving me these looks like she's planning something.' Willow tried to emulate the Cat in the Hat's balancing feats when she was six and, as a consequence, wasn't allowed to have pet fish for five years (see **29**, 'Passion').

Quote/Unquote: Anya: 'I have finesse coming out of my bottom!'

Buffy: 'I killed something in a convent last night.' Xander: 'In any other room, a frightening declaration. Here, a welcome distraction.'

Willow: 'I'm not stealing. I'm just taking things without paying for them. In what twisted dictionary is *that* stealing?'

Olaf: 'Do you know where there are babies?' Spike, to Xander: 'What do you think, the hospital?'

Notes: 'You told the witch to do that, Anyanka. You seem determined to put an end to all my fun. Just like you did when we were dating.' Maybe I'm just a sucker for Jane Espenson's deliciously less-than-serious take on *Buffy*, but this episode (which was *loathed* by many Internet fans and journalists – 'Shockingly bad' according to the review in *DreamWatch*) is one of my favourites of the season. The jokes are good, Abraham Benrubi is terrific and the music is a particular delight.

Anya dated Olaf when he was a big dumb guy. He cheated on her so she made him into a troll, which is how she got the job as a vengeance demon (see **65**, 'Something Blue'; **127**, 'Selfless'). Then some witches trapped him in a crystal for centuries before Willow's spell released him. Giles returns to England to ask the Watcher's Council for help in finding out more about Glory. They have no record of her, but will look into the matter (see **90**, 'Checkpoint'). Buffy says that she trusts the Watchers as far as Giles could throw them. Spike likes the food in the Bronze, not just the chicken wings (see **85**, 'Fool for Love') but also Texas Tumbleweed (a flower-shaped-thing they make from an onion). Anya mentions the circumstances that saw Xander and Cordelia split (see **42**, 'Lover's

Walk'). She notes that Willow has known Xander since they were squalling infants and that Willow will always know him better than Anya. Tara is allergic to shrimp. Buffy gets a souvenir from the fight with Olaf: his hammer (see **100**, 'The Gift').

Soundtrack: Blur's Madchester classic 'There's No Other Way' and 'Bohemian Like You' by the Dandy Warhols.

Critique: 'There are a lot of pluses to the episode,' noted *SFX*'s Ed Gross. 'Notably, Spike's growing obsession over Buffy which at times seems fairly psychotic.'

Did You Know?: 'In Santa Monica I'm anonymous,' James Marsters told Paul Simpson and Ruth Thomas. 'People notice me, but I'm not Leonardo DiCaprio. But when I come [to England], there's a hype. It's like *A Hard Day's Night* or something. In Britain they're better at expressing it. You guys know how to break the ice like nobody else. It's really nice, because it takes some of the pressure off meeting people.'

Joss Whedon's Comments: 'Every season has a unifying theme,' Joss told *E! Online*. 'Last year it was the liberation of college and how it fractures you as a group and as a person. This year was about family and identity and Buffy being a Slayer. And next year I refer to as "Oh, Grow Up". It's about realising that we're young adults, and now we're making choices like our parents did, and we're just as bad at it as they were.'

90
Checkpoint

US Transmission Date: 23 Jan 2001
UK Transmission Date: 23 Mar 2001

Writers: Jane Espenson, Douglas Petrie
Director: Nick Marck
Cast: Peter Husmann (Mailman), Wesley Mask (Professor Roberts),
Jack Thomas (Council Member #4), John O'Leary (Council Member #5)

Buffy is visited by the Council of Watchers. They refuse to give Buffy any information on Glory until she passes their tests. Glory stalks Buffy and threatens her family. Then, the Knights of Byzantium attack the Slayer, declare themselves her enemy and promise that legions will follow. Finally, Buffy realises why everyone is targeting her. She tells the Watchers that she is in charge and orders Quentin to reveal what he knows about Glory.

Dudes and Babes: Members of an ancient order, the Knights of Byzantium, have a tattoo on their foreheads. They appear medieval in their speech and armaments, using swords and chain mail. They believe that the Key and its protector should be destroyed to prevent it from falling into the Beast's hands.

Authority Sucks!: Buffy's argument with Professor Roberts tackles such weighty topics as whether Rasputin was a vampire, did Columbus or the Vikings first discover America and the sleeping patterns of Prussian generals. 'You'd prefer I step aside?' asks the Professor wearily. 'You can teach your own course. Speculation 101?'

A Little Learning is a Dangerous Thing: Lydia notes that the removal from Burma of one of Giles's statues is a criminal offence. When triggered, it has the power to melt human eyeballs. Nigel adds that most of the merchandise in the Magic Box couldn't harm anyone, but there *are* some potent elements including focusing crystals, runic artefacts and an amulet of Caldis.

Deportation is an Eleven-Letter Word: If Buffy fights the Council, Quentin threatens, they will have Giles deported and make sure he never sets foot in the US again. Buffy asks Giles if they could really kick him out the country. In a heartbeat, he replies. The rough stuff, they're adequate at – a bit ham-handed, at times, but they get it done. But bureaucracy and pulling of political strings, they're the best in the world. They can kill with the stroke of a pen.

Denial, Thy Name is Everyone: In a breathtaking speech, Buffy says that she's had people lining up to tell her how unimportant she is. But now she understands why. Power. She has it. They don't and this bothers *them*. She notes that Glory considered Buffy a flea whom she could squash in a second. But she didn't. Glory had what in her warped brain probably passed for a civilised conversation. Why? Because she needs something from Buffy. Information. The Council, Buffy continues, haven't come all the way from England to determine whether or not she is good enough to be let back in. Rather, they've come to beg her to give their lives some semblance of meaning. It is suggested that the Scooby Gang are mere children. Buffy replies: 'We're talking about two very powerful witches and a thousand-year-old ex-demon.' And Xander? 'The boy has clocked more field time than all of you combined.'

The Conspiracy Starts at Home Time: Jinx notes that the signs of the alignment are moving faster than expected and that if Glory is to use the Key, she must act quickly.

It's a Designer Label!: Glory's red towel. Dawn's pyjamas and *Pink Panther* T-shirt. Giles's leather jacket and Willow's lilac shirt. Buffy wears the first woolly hat seen in almost a year.

References: Grigori Efimovich Rasputin (1871–1916), a Siberian peasant monk, notorious for his debauchery, who wielded influence over the Tsarina, Alexandra, and the Romanov court. Also, *Born on the Fourth of July*, *Masterpiece Theater*, *The Young Ones* ('Fascists!'), Christopher Columbus, the Japanese martial arts Aikido and Jujitsu, obliquely *The Ladies Home Journal* and Snap's 'The Power'. Spike is still watching *Passions* (see **65**, 'Something Blue'), a one-hour daily soap that began in July 1999 and is known for its supernatural storylines. The Knights of Byzantium take their name from the ancient free city in Thrace at the mouth of the Bosphorus, founded circa 660 BC by the Greeks. Roman occupied from AD 73, the city subsequently changed its name to Constantinople in 330, and became the centre of the Eastern Holy Roman Empire, which lasted until 1453 when the Ottoman Turks conquered it. The city is now Istanbul in Turkey.

Bitch!: Glory: 'I bet Mousy the Vampire Slayer has an idea where it is.'

Awesome!: Anya's terror that the Council may view her as a potential target leads to all sorts of hilarious panic. When Buffy says her group contains an ex-demon, Anya is horrified: 'Willow's a *demon*?!' Nigel asking Willow and Tara a simple question about their relationship with the Slayer turns into a fab rant of lesbian pride, while Lydia's giggly interrogation/flirtation with Spike is a season highlight (especially her revelation that she did her thesis on him. Spike seems *delighted*). Buffy's fight with the Knights. Plus yet another glorious Spike/Joyce scene (see **34**, 'Becoming' Part 2; **42**, 'Lover's Walk').

'You May Remember Me From Such Films and TV Series As . . .': Troy Blendell's movies include *Larceny* and *Love & Sex*. Kris Iyver was in *Some Girl* and *High Freakquency*. Wesley Mask can be seen in *Not of this Earth* and *Victim of Desire*. Oliver Muirhead

appeared in *Friends* and *Austin Powers: The Spy Who Shagged Me*.
John O'Leary was in *The Haunted*, *Airplane!*, *Demon Seed* and
Gene Pool.

Don't Give Up The Day Job: Cynthia Lamontague appeared in
American Virgin and *The Cable Guy*, and was Brian DePalma's
assistant on *Carlito's Way*.

Valley-Speak: Glory: 'I've been cooling my heels in this crappy
little town long enough.'

Cigarettes & Alcohol: Travers notes that when the Council
inventoried the Magic Box they found a bottle of single malt
scotch behind the incense holders. He says he could use a glass
after Buffy's triumphant demolition of their scheme.

Logic, Let Me Introduce You to This Window: Buffy mentions that
the Vikings discovered an America-shaped continent in the 1400s.
In fact it's believed that they discovered North America as early
as 1000. In the first scene, the sleeves on Buffy's shirt continually
change position.

I Just *Love* Your Accent: A further example of Xander's mastery
of a British accent. Dick Van Dyke's British accent, that is. Tara
thought English people were gentle. Xander says if the Council
deport Giles, they're not just destroying his career, but also
condemning him to a lifetime diet of blood sausage and bangers
and mash. Giles calls the Council poncy sods. Lots of tea is drunk.
Love the way when the Council throw everyone out of the Magic
Box, they're terribly English about it ('sorry for the inconven-
ience').

Quote/Unquote: Nigel: 'Magical proficiency level?' Willow: 'High.
Very high. One of those top levels.' Tara, panicking: 'Five!'
   Buffy: 'You're Watchers. Without a Slayer you're pretty much
watching *Masterpiece Theater*. You can't stop Glory. You can't do
anything with the information you have, except maybe publish it
in the *Everyone Thinks We're Insanos Home Journal*. So here's how
it's gonna work. You're gonna tell me everything you know. Then
you're gonna go away. You'll contact me if-and-when you have
any further information about Glory. The magic shop will remain
open. Mr Giles will stay here as my official Watcher, reinstated at
full salary.' Giles (pretending to cough): 'Retroactive!'
   Travers: 'Glory isn't a demon . . . She's a god.'

Notes: 'That was *excellent*!' Another cracking episode, clearing up many of the questions about the Council of Watchers posed in **46**, 'Helpless', and bringing Buffy and Giles back into the fold. But completely on *her* terms. Lots of great little moments, and a stunning climax.

Buffy refers to the life-endangering *Cruciamentum* that the Watchers Council put her through on her 18th birthday (see **46**, 'Helpless') and to when she and Faith switched bodies, resulting in her being kidnapped (see **72**, 'Who Are You?'). Buffy mentions the two instances when she was within slaying distance of Glory (**83**, 'No Place Like Home'; **86**, 'Shadow'). Xander tells the Council about the Scoobies' spell to create Super-Buffy (see **77**, 'Primeval'). His arm is still in a cast after Olaf's vicious pummelling in **89**, 'Triangle'. Reference is made to Riley. Willow and Tara are still working on the ball of sunshine spell (see **89**, 'Triangle'). Dawn is in Junior High. Since she's 14, she's likely in 8th grade. Anya's full name is Anya Christina Emmanuella Jenkins and she was born 4 July 1980 in Indiana. Technically, of course, none of that is *true*, since this is merely a persona that Anyanka created for herself when she tried to grant Cordelia's wish (see **43**, 'The Wish'). Nigel says there is an accredited institution for witches, which he presumes that Willow and Tara should be registered with (they're not). Joyce shares Spike's passion for *Passions*. Dawn, seemingly, does not.

Did You Know?: As reported in several UK newspapers, 14-year-old schoolgirl Heidi Rogan from Middlesbrough bravely fought off an attack by five teenage male thugs using martial arts moves she learned from watching *Buffy*. Finding herself surrounded, Heidi pole-axed one assailant and followed this with a jump-kick to the groin of another. The other three cowards promptly fled. 'Buffy's my hero and I think she would have been proud,' Heidi was quoted as saying.

91
Blood Ties

US Transmission Date: 6 Feb 2001
UK Transmission Date: 30 Mar 2001

Writer: Steven S DeKnight
Director: Michael Gersham

Cast: Michael Emanuel (Burly Guard), Candice Nicole (Young Buffy),
Joe Ochman (Janitor), Elyssa D Vito (Young Dawn)

It's Buffy's 20th birthday but, having told the Scooby Gang at last
about Dawn's true purpose, she finds little time to celebrate.
Particularly after Dawn, with Spike's help, breaks into the Magic
Box and discovers the truth about the Key.

Dreaming (As Blondie Once Said) is Free: Dawn has a flashback to
herself playing on the swings with Buffy when she was younger.

Dudes and Babes: A first direct hint about Ben's relationship with
Glory, Jinx telling Ben that his fate is directly linked to 'her
magnificently scented Glorificus'. Glory can't lay a finger on me
and you know it, Ben replies. Ben tells Dawn that he has a sister
too, and that he often wishes that she didn't exist. And just when
everybody in the audience is lulled into thinking, 'Ah, so Ben is
Glory's brother . . .', see **Surprise!**

A Little Learning is a Dangerous Thing: Dawn's homework is to
imagine what she will be like 10 years from now and write a letter
to her future self. When she finds out that she's the Key, Dawn
announces that she isn't going to school as blobs of energy don't
need an education. When she finally does go, she's suspended for
yelling obscenities at a teacher.

Denial, Thy Name is Buffy: Spike suggests that if Buffy had been
more honest with Dawn in the first place, she wouldn't be trying
to make herself feel better by blaming him.

The Conspiracy Starts at Home Time: Using *The Book of Tarnis*
(written by a 12th-century monk, one of the founders of the Order
of Dagon, who built the Dagon-sphere), the Council has discovered that Glory and two of her fellow gods ruled over one of
the more unpleasant demon dimensions. Anya and Giles confirm
there are thousands of such dimensions, all different and all
pushing on the edges of our reality. Glory, in human form, has
severely limited godlike powers. All the gang have to worry about
is that she's immortal, invulnerable, and insane, as living in this
world is affecting her mental state. She's only able to keep her
mind intact by extracting energy from the human brain. Giles adds
that she absorbs the energies that bind the human mind into a
cohesive whole. Once drained, all that's left behind is crazy people,
which explains the increase in the mentally unstable in Sunnydale.
The Key isn't described in any known literature, but research

indicates an energy matrix vibrating at a dimensional frequency beyond normal human perception. Only those outside reality can see the Key's true nature (see **80**, 'Real Me'). The Key is also susceptible to necromanced animal detection, particularly those of canine or serpent construct (see **86**, 'Shadow').

It's a Designer Label!: Glory's gold dress. Buffy's red blouse and fur coat. Willow's Cowboy City sweater. There's a fantastic bit of continuity to **84**, 'Family', as we see that Ben keeps Glory's red dress in his locker should he/she require a quick change. Willow and Tara's present for Buffy is a frilly dress that Anya takes a shine to.

References: Dawn's present to Buffy, a photo surrounded by shells, may be an oblique allusion to *Dark City*, a movie about reality and false memories in which one character remembers a place called Shell Beach, which never really existed. Also, the series' first reference to *Teletubbies*, *Little Red Riding Hood*, allusions to Sly and the Family Stone's 'It's A Family Affair', the Beatles' 'Get Back' and Bob Dylan's 'Don't Think Twice (It's Alright)' ('this doesn't have to be a complete waste of my precious time'), *Movie of the Week*, *The Simpsons* ('Your point being?'), *Wheel of Fortune*, REM's 'What's The Frequency, Kenneth', the get-out-of-jail-free card from Monopoly, Uncle Ben (the rice producer) and *Gentle Ben*.

Bitch!: Glory: 'Is that the best you little crap-gnats can muster?'

Awesome!: Dawn's confrontation with Orlando in the hospital.

Surprise!: Ben *is* Glory. Didn't see *that* one coming at all.

'You May Remember Me From Such Films and TV Series As . . .': Joe Ochman was in *Never Been Kissed* and *That's My Bush!* Justin Gorence appeared in *Puzzled*, *Melrose Place* and *The Sexperiment*

Don't Give Up The Day Job: Paul Bates was an electrician on *The Princess Stallion*, a generator operator on *The Winter Guest* and appeared in *Coming to America*. Carl Johnson was a puppeteer on *Men in Black*. Two of the stuntmen in this episode are W Glenn Malmskog, stunt coordinator on *Rumble in the Streets* and *The Protector*, and Scott Rhodes, a second unit director on *Citizen Toxie: The Toxic Avenger Part 4*, stuntman on *Vampire Vixens from Venus* and technical advisor on *Dogma*.

The Spell *Will* Work: Willow and Tara perform an early warning incantation at the Magic Box and around Buffy's house. If anything hellgodishly powerful comes within a hundred feet, screechy-siren-things will then screech.

Valley-Speak: Buffy: 'What's the homework *sitch*?'
Dawn, to Spike: 'Geez! Lurk much?'

Cigarettes & Alcohol: When he breaks into the Magic Box, Spike uses the Urn of Ishtar as an ashtray.

Sex and Drugs and Rock'n'Roll: Anya tells Dawn that she and Xander were talking about sex and adds that, sometimes, they like to pretend stuff. Which, seemingly, involves Xander dressing as a fireman, or a shepherd.

Logic, Let Me Introduce You to This Window: When Willow mentions that Dawn has been keeping her diaries for years and Buffy replies 'since she was seven. I remember too, Will,' Willow shouldn't *remember* this since even in the new timeline Dawn was approximately 10 when they met. Glory doesn't remember anything that Dawn said when she was Ben (presumably this also means that Ben knows nothing from the times when Glory inhabits his body, although later episodes fail to entirely clear this question up, and it doesn't explain how he knows who the Knights of Byzantium are. See, **98**, 'Spiral'; **99**, 'The Weight of the World'). When Dawn goes to her room and slams the door, part of the 'Parental Advisory Lyrics' poster on the opposite wall can be seen shaking in the mirror, indicating that the wall isn't real. When Dawn rips her diaries there's a magazine on the chest at the end of her bed that subsequently disappears. When Buffy enters Spike's crypt, whenever the camera shows Buffy from Spike's point of view, it's bright enough that she creates a shadow on the stone coffin. However, whenever the camera is behind Buffy, it's much darker.

Quote/Unquote: Willow: 'You know what they say. The bigger they are . . .' Anya: '. . . The faster they stomp you into nothing?'
Orlando, to Dawn: 'Cracked bones. The sun bleeding into the sky. The Key is the link. The link must be severed. Such is the will of God. Such is the will of God. SUCH IS THE WILL OF GOD!'

Notes: 'She probably feels like she can say or do anything right now. She's not real. We're not her family, we don't even know what she is.' Given that the Dawn/Glory arc has been so smoothly mixed in with other storylines, this episode is the first time this season where it's felt like the show is running on the spot. Having said that, there's a great central performance by Michelle Tra-chtenberg.

Both Willow and Tara used to be scared by candles that don't blow out. Dawn and Buffy visited Hank in San Diego one summer (probably in 1999, between season three and four) where they picked shells on the beach. Dawn doesn't like marshmallows (when she was five, Buffy told her they were made from monkey brains), though she does like hot chocolate. Willow performs a teleportation spell on Glory, which gives Willow a nosebleed and materialises Glory high above Sunnydale. After the fight in the hospital, Dawn is unable to remember that Glory and Ben are one and the same (see **98**, 'Spiral'). The playground was last seen in **45**, 'Gingerbread'. Xander refers to Dawn's crush on him (see **92**, 'Crush') and calls himself the Xan-Man, much to Giles's disgust.

Soundtrack: Star Ghost Dog's 'Holiday'.

Joss Whedon's Comments: The reaction to Willow's lesbian storyline had been, Joss told *E! Online*: 'Overwhelmingly positive, except for some extremely vocal people who are like, "I will no longer watch the show. You've made Willow a fag." It's not like I want to drive people away; I want to be inclusive. But it felt like the right step for Willow and Seth wanted to go make movies, so it all fell into place. We thought why not have two people fall in love?'

92
Crush

US Transmission Date: 13 Feb 2001
UK Transmission Date: 6 Apr 2001

Writer: David Fury
Director: Daniel Attias
Cast: Walter Borchert (Jeff), Frederick Dawson (Porter),
Joseph Diciandomenico (Matt), Asher Glaser (Boy in Bronze),
Jennifer Bergman (Girl in Bronze), Nell Shanahan (Waitress),
Greg Wayne (Student)

To Buffy's horror, she discovers that Spike has a crush on her. She's dealing with it pretty well until Drusilla returns to Sunnydale, kills a trainload of passengers and tries to return Spike to his former glory.

Dudes and Babes: Drusilla returns from her deranged rampage with Darla in Los Angeles. She leaves Sunnydale at the climax, as does Harmony, who is next seen seeking out her old friend Cordelia in LA in *Angel*: 'Disharmony'.

A Little Learning is a Dangerous Thing: Willow and Tara discuss Quasimodo's unrequited love for Esmaralda in Victor Hugo's *The Hunchback of Notre Dame*.

Denial, Thy Name is Spike: 'The only chance you had with me was when I was unconscious,' Buffy tells him and, of course, she's right. Poor Spike, he loses every smidgen of dignity that he ever almost had in his relentless obsession with the Slayer. He even seems to know, telling Buffy: '*This*, with you, is wrong. I know it. I'm not a complete idiot.'

It's a Designer Label!: Spike has stolen Buffy's tasteful blue cashmere sweater. Harmony's sexy negligee, the Bronze waitresses silver pants, Buffy's leather trousers. Dawn thinks Spike's hair and leather coat are 'cool and stuff'.

References: Xander calls Spike 'Un-*Evil Dead*'. The porter at Sunnydale station has a copy of *The Amazing Spider-Man*. Instead of reading *The Hunchback of Notre Dame*, Buffy rented the movie. Not the Charles Laughton classic either, but rather the Disney version with singing gargoyles. Plus, obliquely the Beatles' 'Help!', *Quantum Leap* ('Oh boy'), *Family Fortunes* ('Survey says vampires'), the Small Faces' 'Tin Soldier', Anne Rice's *Queen of the Damned*, actress Charlize Theron (*2 Days in the Valley*, *The Devil's Advocate*, *The Astronaut's Wife*, *Monster*) and Morticia from *The Addams Family*.

In one of the documentaries on the *Buffy* Season 2 DVDs, Marti Noxon describes the inspiration for Spike and Drusilla – and their loving-yet-self-destructive relationship – as being the notorious Sex Pistols bassist Sid Vicious and his girlfriend Nancy Spungen (as played in Alex Cox's controversial *Sid and Nancy* by Gary Oldman and Chloe Webb). When Vicious was arrested for Spungen's murder, in New York in 1978, his reported confession to the police was: 'I done it. I'm a dirty dog.' Here, Dru compares Spike to a bad dog on several occasions.

Bitch!: Spike, on his women troubles: 'Why do you bitches torture me?'

Awesome!: Anya dancing. Sexy. Buffy sitting down in the train carriage in the exact (tape-marked) position of one of Dru's victims. Dru's amused expression when Harmony calls Spike boo-boo. Spike telling Dawn a horror story of his murdering a family and, just as he gets to the most gruesome part (finding the little girl), Buffy enters the crypt and demands that he finish: 'So I rip it open, very violent, haul her out of there . . . And then I give her to a good family in a nice home, where they're never ever mean to her, and didn't lock her in the coal bin!' As Dawn says: 'That's *so* lame!' Buffy and Dawn's subsequent soul-versus-chip debate continues when Buffy tells Spike that he cannot love without a soul. Drusilla notes that vampires *can* love quite well. If not, always, wisely. Spike says that if Buffy doesn't admit that there's something between them, he'll untie Dru and let her kill Buffy instead. Drusilla adds: 'Yes please. I like that game much more!'

Don't Give Up The Day Job: Jennifer Bergman was a visual effects producer on *Blade* and *Firestorm*.

Valley-Speak: Buffy: 'Hanging out with Spike is not cool, Dawn, OK? It's dangerous, and icky.'

Cigarettes & Alcohol: Spike drinks bourbon from a hip flask and Budweiser in the Bronze.

Sex and Drugs and Rock'n'Roll: The Bronze is having a Grand Reopening, having been extensively remodelled following its demolition by Olaf in **89**, 'Triangle'. Xander is horrified when he is told that Dawn may have a crush on Spike. Because she's always had one on *him* (see **91**, 'Blood Ties').

When Harmony suggests that she and Spike play a game, to spice-up their love life, the next shot is of Harmony wearing Buffy's blue sweater and a pair of stretchpants and holding a stake. Spike, shirtless, then lunges from the darkness, aroused. Harmony says she isn't interested in threesomes unless it's boy-boy-girl, or Charlize Theron is involved. When Buffy is asked, by Joyce, if she may have innocently encouraged Spike, she notes: 'I *do* beat him up a lot. For Spike that's like third base.'

The Base System: For readers unfamiliar with baseball or contact with the opposite sex (or both) it goes like this. First base is kissing, second base is groping, third base is oral sex ('Ah, *third base*,' remembers Chandler, fondly, in *Friends*; see also *American Pie*) and home run is actual intercourse itself.

'West Hollywood': Buffy notes that the two vampires have nested. Spike asks: 'You're saying they're a couple of *poofters*?'

Logic, Let Me Introduce You to This Window: When Spike and Buffy attack the vampires, one is making popcorn over a lantern. They run away and Spike moves to follow, by which time the popcorn has disappeared, only to reappear a moment later. Why doesn't Spike's victim in the Bronze struggle or scream? Is she already dead? That seems to be the suggestion since Spike can drink from her. But *how*? Dru didn't appear to snap her neck or do anything other than push her gently in Spike's direction. There's no date on the issue of *The Sunnydale Press* that Buffy reads.

I Just *Love* Your Accent: Spike: 'Bleedin' crime, is what it is. Jackin' up the bar-price to pay for fixin' up this sinkhole. Not my fault insurance doesn't cover *Act of Troll*.' He tells Buffy not to get her knickers twisted and uses both bint and cock-up in casual conversation. One of Drusilla's victims on the train is wearing a cricket sweater.

Motors: Spike has a car in which he and Buffy stake out the vampires. Spike hums the Ramones' 'I Wanna Be Sedated' although, as Buffy noted in **46**, 'Helpless', she can't stand guys who hum.

Quote/Unquote: Joyce, when Buffy returns from the Bronze: 'I wasn't feeling all that safe with you gone. At first. Then I remembered that Rupert was here and I felt much, much safer.'

Buffy: 'You're like a serial killer in prison.' Spike: 'Women marry 'em all the time!'

Drusilla: 'Electricity lies, Spike. It tells you you're not a bad dog. But you are.'

Spike, telling Buffy he will kill Drusilla to prove his love: 'You have the slightest idea what she means to me? It's the face of my salvation. She delivered me from mediocrity. For over a century we cut a swath through continents. A hundred years, she never stopped surprising me. Never stopped taking me to new depths. I was a lucky bloke just to touch such a black beauty.'

Notes: 'Even if I did have a crush, he wouldn't notice in a million years. Spike's totally into you.' A compelling look at unrequited love and obsession that begins by showing Spike as sympathetic and ends with him as simply pathetic. One of the best scripts of the season, with a ton of clever set pieces and acebric wordplay.

Willow is still experiencing headaches and nosebleeds after her teleportation spell in **91**, 'Blood Ties'. Dawn says that she was not originally human. 'I was,' notes Spike. 'I got over it.' (See **85**, 'Fool for Love'.) Spike and Drusilla have a conversation concerning recent events in LA involving Angel and Darla, which summarise the *Angel* episodes 'To Shanshu in LA', 'Dear Boy', 'The Trial', 'Reunion' and 'Redefinition'. Dru still carries the burn scars from the latter. Drusilla wants Spike to return with her so that they can be a family again. Spike says he has done the LA scene and that it didn't agree with him. He mentions Dru leaving him for a chaos-demon (see **42**, 'Lover's Walk'; **85**, 'Fool for Love'). *The Sunnydale Press* headline is: METROTRAIN MURDER. SIX FOUND MURDERED ON TRAIN AT SUNNYDALE STATION. The newspaper costs 35¢ daily. The article was written by Jeannie Lozammo.

Soundtrack: 'Key' by Devics, and two songs by Summercamp, 'Play It By Ear' and 'Happy'.

Critique: 'A deliciously twisted, funny valentine, just missing the jugular by a crucial inch,' wrote Mark Wyman in *TV Zone*. 'The Bronze nightclub's reopening mirrors the series revivification. Harmony role-plays as Buffy to arouse Spike, while a railway massacre points to a rarity: a dangerous vampire at large in Sunnydale ... James Marsters' brilliantly shaded performance [makes] Buffy (whose response to him is morally accurate) seem the cruel-hearted one.'

Did You Know?: Sarah Michelle Gellar used an interview with *Cosmopolitan* to pay tribute to her mother: 'Everything I am is because of my mom,' Gellar says of the woman who guided her between auditions and school. She was much less effusive about her father, who divorced her mother when Gellar was seven, describing him as non-existent in her life. Pressed to elaborate, she borrowed Keanu Reeves's famous line from *Parenthood*: 'You need a licence to go fishing, you need a licence to drive, but any butt-reaming asshole can be a father.'

93
I Was Made to Love You

US Transmission Date: 20 Feb 2001
UK Transmission Date: 13 Apr 2001

Writer: Jane Espenson
Director: James A Contner
Cast: Gil Christner (Resident), Paul Darrigo (Driver), Shonda Farr (April), Kelly Felix (Teenager), Paul Walia (Friend)

A pretty girl arrives in Sunnydale looking for her boyfriend, Warren. After proving herself to be extraordinarily strong, the gang deduce that she is a robot, built by a lonely teenager who couldn't get dates. Buffy eventually tracks down Warren and his creation and stays with the android until her power runs out. Arriving home, Buffy finds Joyce motionless on the couch.

Dudes and Babes: April arrives at the Spring Break party and makes many heads turn. Anya graciously allows Xander a moment's distraction, although Tara is surprisingly jealous by Willow's sudden loss of concentration. When Spike tries to chat up April, she throws him through a window. 'She's a sexbot,' notes Xander, asking what guy doesn't dream about such a concept. Looking up, he finds Anya, Willow, Tara and Buffy scowling at him. Too many girls, he continues. 'I miss Oz. He'd get it. He wouldn't say anything, but he'd get it.'

At the party, Buffy and Ben cautiously arrange to go for a coffee, with the hope that it won't lead to anything further (like Ben having to leave town, for instance). Joyce has a date with Brian, a nice normal guy who works for a publishing house and sends her flowers, thanking her for a lovely evening. After her date, Joyce teases Buffy that she may have left her bra in Brian's car.

Instant Karma: Anya is familiar with the Hindu philosophy of Karma (the law of cause and effect, rebirth and spiritual release) and expects an instantaneous reward for allowing Xander to dance with a depressed Buffy.

Babysitting: Giles's evening with Dawn consisted of listening to aggressively cheerful music sung by people chosen for their ability to dance, then eating cookie dough and talking about boys.

Denial, Thy Name is Buffy: Despite Giles and Xander's assurances that Buffy can't be held responsible for what Spike feels, Buffy stills considers that 'something about me had to make him feel . . . "that's the one for me!" '

Denial, Thy Name is Spike: Spike goes to the Magic Box and talks to the Scoobies about misrepresentations, misunderstandings, slurs and allegations, claiming that he and Buffy were working together to get rid of Dru (see **92**, 'Crush'). We are not your friends, Giles tells him. 'This thing. Get over it.' Unfortunately, Spike's idea of moving on is to commission Warren to create a Buffybot for him (see **96**, 'Intervention').

Denial, Thy Name is Warren: 'So you have girl troubles?' Buffy asks. Warren confirms this is accurate. He couldn't get a date, so he created April to love him. But Warren found April too predictable and she became boring. Then he met Katrina in his engineering seminar. She was funny and built model monorails that run with magnets. Warren fell in love with *her*. Left with the complex issue of what to do with April, Warren simply abandoned her in his dorm room, believing that while he was away her batteries would run out.

The Conspiracy Starts at Home Time: Buffy tells Warren, 'We were at Sunnydale High together. *Do you know who I am?*' Warren replies 'Yes, I know.' It's clear that they're talking about the knowledge among Buffy's contemporaries about her status as Class Protector and that she is the girl who fights the monsters that terrorised their childhood (see **54**, 'The Prom').

Technophobia!: Anya says computers were once confusing to her. 'I'm eleven hundred years old. I had trouble adjusting to the idea of Lutherans.' Tara admits that she goes online occasionally but that everyone's spelling is really bad. Anya, however, has become addicted to online trading. The secret, she says, is to avoid tech companies, and go with smaller firms that supply basic components. Her initial investment tripled and she is now thinking of buying something expensive. Maybe an antelope. She designed a website for the Magic Box with a huge photo of herself on it. Anya is also the first to spot something odd about April, noting that the girl speaks with a strange evenness and selects her words too precisely.

Among the programs Warren installed in April are kissing_01.gfd, kissing_02.gfd, lstn sympthtc.gfd, gv_h_prsnts.gfd, *four* sex files, praise.gfd, neckrubs.gfd, three fetish files and at least *six* 'positions' files. Underneath *Warren* and *Boyfriend* appear other identifiers: really smart, handsome, best lover, snappy dresser and good dancer. She is also programmed to fight, with disciplines including kung fu and karate.

Work is a Four-Letter Word: When Tara notes at least April didn't do much damage, Xander looks at the broken window and replies:

'Double-glazed windows ain't cheap. The jamb needs to be completely repaired. Dear God, I'm the grown-up who sees the world through my job. I'm like my uncle Dave, the plumber.' When fixing the damage later, Buffy asks if he really understands the terminology he's using. Xander confirms that he does.

It's a Designer Label!: Buffy thinks Joyce's dress is not mom-ish at all. 'It's sexy. It screams, "Randy-sex-kitten, buy me one drink and I'll . . ."' Buffy's purple hooded top appears again. April's pink flowery dress and Buffy's sparkly gold top.

References: The title is from Lorraine Cato's 1996 hit. There's a possible oblique reference to the Who's 'The Kids Are Alright' and a direct one to the Beach Boys' 'Do You Wanna Dance?' Also, actor Warren Beatty, President Warren Harding (1865–1923), Prince Charming from *Cinderella*. The plot may have been influenced by *Weird Science*, *Westworld*, *Wonder Woman* and *Mannequin*.

Bitch!: Buffy, after April has thrown her across the room: 'I've had it with super-strong little women who aren't me.'

Awesome!: Buffy taking out her revulsion at Spike's attraction on a hugely padded Puffy Xander ('I'm alive,' he tells her when the assault is over. 'I can tell cos of the pain.'). Also, the shot of Ben standing in the middle of the apartment wearing Glory's red dress after getting off the phone and Buffy's fight with a growling April. There's also the first presentation of a harder Giles (see **100**, 'The Gift') in his confrontation with Spike. And, of course, the final scene (see **94**, 'The Body').

'You May Remember Me From Such Films and TV Series As . . .': Adam Busch was Kyle in *Magic Rock* and Manolo in *Léon*. He's also a member of the band Common Rotation. Shonda Farr appeared in *What Friends Are For* and *Jack Frost 2: Revenge of the Mutant Killer Snowman*. Kelly Felix was in *Sally and Johnny* and *AI Artificial Intelligence*. Gil Christner played Ed the Hippy in *More American Graffiti* and can also be seen in *Mystery Men* and *Masque of the Red Death*. Amelinda Embry was in *Romy and Michele's High School Reunion*, *Scrubs* and *Two Girls, a Guy, and a Pizza Place*.

Don't Give Up The Day Job: Paul Darrigo was a casting apprentice on *Piranha*.

Valley-Speak: Buffy: 'You're one creepy little *dweeb*.'

Logic, Let Me Introduce You to This Window: Who invited Ben to the Spring Break party? Come to that, who invited Warren and Katrina, both of whom attend another college altogether? When April throws Spike through the window, it's obviously a dummy. When Katrina walks out on Warren, she leaves wearing a green T-shirt and with no bags. Next time we see her, she's acquired a thick ginger cardigan.

Cruelty To Vampires: 'That's my secret to attracting men,' Buffy tells Xander. 'You slap 'em around a bit, torture 'em, make their lives a living hell . . . Sure, the nice guys, they'll run away, but every now and then you meet a real prince-of-a-guy like Spike who gets off on it.'

Quote/Unquote: Buffy: 'I'm very sorry, but if it makes you feel any better, my "funtime- Buffy-party night" involved watching a robot throw Spike through a window, so if you wanna trade . . . No, wait, I wouldn't give *that* memory up for anything.'

Notes: 'This is something that you can't possibly know. She's a robot.' Another episode that got a generally less-than-favourable review from the *cognoscenti* but, again, it's hard to see why. A serious study about male obsession (almost all of the male characters have something to be ashamed of) and its mirror image, female denial. But, with enough laughs to cheer up even a professional misanthrope if you don't step on the cracks. I love it. Magic Jane *again*, doing the seemingly impossible and gently debunking a standard media cliché, in this case the image men have in their search for the perfect woman. A nice juxtaposition with the *Angel* episode 'Happy Anniversary' shown two weeks previously and dealing with broadly similar subjects but in a very different way.

Warren went to Sunnydale High with Buffy for a semester, then graduated to technical college in Dutton. Dawn refers to the events of **23**, 'Ted' – a further example of the way in which *Buffy*'s past now, seemingly, includes Dawn as part of it (see **91**, 'Blood Ties').

Soundtrack: Mellonova's 'Hideeho', 'Kawanga!' by Los Strait-jackets and Caviar's 'OK Nightmare'.

Did You Know?: A popular contemporary fan rumour was that the robot-girl, April, was written specifically with Sarah Michelle Gellar's then-friend, teen-pop sensation Britney Spears in mind. Subsequently, Jane Espenson confirmed that this was true.

Jane Espenson's Comments: 'I love Giles making a joke,' Jane told *Xposé*. 'It's nice to let him have some fun.' Jane's first comic, *Jonathan*, was based in the alternative universe she created in 73, 'Superstar', and she was also author of the one-shot *The Lone Gunmen* comic for Dark Horse based on the popular characters of Byers, Langly and Frohike created by Chris Carter in *The X-Files*.

94
The Body

US Transmission Date: 27 Feb 2001
UK Transmission Date: 20 Apr 2001

Writer: Joss Whedon
Director: Joss Whedon
Cast: Tia Matza (Teacher), J Evan Bonifant (Kevin),
Rae'ven Larrymore Kelly (Lisa), Kelli Garner (Kristie),
Kevin Cristalon (First Paramedic), Stefan Umstead (Second Paramedic),
Loanne Bishop (911 Operator), John Michael Herndon (Vampire)

Joyce is dead, despite Buffy's frantic efforts to save her. Buffy, Dawn and their friends must each deal with the loss as best they can. But on the Hellmouth, despite everything, life goes on.

Dreaming (As Blondie Once Said) is Free: The Christmas-flashback that opens the episode. Plus the extraordinary use of imaginary sequences of Joyce recovering, slipping in and out the narrative.

Dudes and Babes: Tara says that Willow likes it when she rubs Willow's tummy.

A Little Learning is a Dangerous Thing: Concerning Santa, Anya says it's a myth that *he's* a myth. He's been around since the 1500s. He wasn't always called Santa, but Christmas night, flying-reindeer, coming down chimneys is all true. Of course, he doesn't traditionally bring presents so much as disembowelled children.

Work is a Four-Letter Word: When Xander punches a hole in Willow's wall, he notes: 'In my defence, some crappy wallmanship.'

It's a Designer Label!: 'The first person I ever lost,' Joss told an online interview, 'I had to find a black tie, because I thought you *had* to wear one to a funeral. Of course, it was California, so people showed up in Hawaiian shirts, but I didn't know that. I couldn't find one anywhere in LA. I was sweating, like, "If I don't find this, it'll be *sacrilege*." That's where the Willow-thing came from.'

References: Allusions to *Xena: Warrior Princess* ('strong like an Amazon') and Marvel's *The Avengers* ('gotta get with the assembling', see **57**, 'The Freshman'). There's a SMOKING SUCKS poster on the school corridor wall. Willow and Tara's room has a poster for String Cheese Incident. 'The Body' is the title of a Steven King novella (filmed as *Stand By Me*), which is thematically very similar to this – young people's reactions to death as a rite of passage.

Awesome!: The Christmas memories. That awful moment where Buffy, administering CRP, snaps one of Joyce's ribs. Buffy straightening Joyce's skirt as the paramedics arrive. The first imaginary sequence ('It's a beautiful miracle') and the relief that the audience feels, which is suddenly crushed when you realise that this is all going on in Buffy's head. The strange camera angles reflecting Buffy's dislocation and inability to look the paramedic in the face as he tells her that her mother is dead. The incredibly voyeuristic moments of Buffy, alone, wandering around the house in a state of shock, sinking to her knees and vomiting. Dawn's school life: how clever and yet obvious that she should have her own versions of Willow, Xander and Cordelia. Dawn's drawing. Willow's frustration at her inability to find appropriate clothes. *The kiss.* Xander's impotent anger at the unfairness of it all. Anya's confusion on how she should act leading to one of the finest moments in the series as she tearfully remembers the things that Joyce liked to do. Tara's numb empathy with the pain of others. Dr Kriegel lying to Buffy in voice-over. Tara telling Buffy about her own mother's death. The vampire waking up in the morgue as Dawn looks at Joyce's body. The final extraordinary lines.

'You May Remember Me From Such Films and TV Series As . . .': J Evan Bonifant was Buster in *Blues Brothers 2000*, Steven in *Dottie Gets Spanked* and Tum Tum in *3 Ninja's Kick Back*. Kelli Garner was in *Bully* and *Hometown Legends*. Tia Matza played Vicky in *Jackpot*. Loanne Bishop appeared in *Kiss the Girls*, *Kalifonia* and *Hill Street Blues*. Stefan Umstead was in *The Ice Cream Man*. Rae'ven Larrymore Kelly was Wanda in *Maximum Bob*, provided voices on *The Dead Presidents* and appeared in *The Ditchdigger's Daughter* and *A Time to Kill*.

Valley-Speak: Kevin: 'Kirstie, man. It's like she thinks, "I'm so hot, everybody should just bow down before me." And I'm, like, *whatever*.'

Cigarettes & Alcohol: Dawn says her nog tastes funny. She thinks she got one with rum in it. Giles opens a bottle of red wine.

Logic, Let Me Introduce You to This Window: As several fans with medical backgrounds pointed out (loudly) on the Net, some of the paramedics actions are inaccurate. They shouldn't have called time of death (in most states, including California, only a doctor can do that). Joyce should have been taken to hospital where she would have been declared DOA. Once CRP has been started by paramedics, it cannot be stopped until the patient is transferred to someone with a higher degree of medical training, and certainly not for the reason that the paramedics has another call to go to. It's also unlikely (although not inconceivable) that Buffy would have been left alone with the body. Chest compressions should be done with straight arms, at a 90-degree angle to the ground, slower than depicted by either Buffy or the medic and much deeper. For Buffy, this is to be expected, but for trained medical staff, it's inexcusable (although, to be fair, doing compressions 'properly' on an actor is probably not good for their health). The police should also have been called to conduct a preliminary interview and determine cause of death (although there's nothing to indicate that this wasn't done off-screen). Why is Dr Kriegel, Joyce's surgeon, doing her autopsy? Shouldn't a pathologist do that? It seems churlish to mention this but Kristine Sutherland does, briefly, appear to breathe during Buffy's frantic attempts to revive her.

Motors: Xander now owns a car.

Quote/Unquote: Willow: 'Why can't I be a grown-up?'

Anya: 'I don't understand how this all happens. How we go through this. I knew her, and then she's just a body, and I don't understand why she just can't get back in it and not be dead any more. It's mortal and stupid. And Xander's crying and not talking, and I was having fruit punch, and I thought, well, Joyce will never have any more fruit punch ever. And she'll never have eggs, or yawn or brush her hair, not ever, and no one will explain to me *why*.'

Dawn, poised to touch Joyce's body: 'Is she cold?' Buffy: 'It's not her . . . She's gone.'

Notes: 'We're not supposed to move the body.' A bittersweet symphony. A thing of grace, power and immense beauty, 'The Body' is like an act of flagellism, painful but necessary. It asks some hard questions about *Buffy*'s traditionally blasé attitude to mortality by making the death of a much-loved character, itself, almost a throwaway-prelude to the *real* horror that follows. The horror of coping with death. The characters move around the subject, circling it, avoiding dealing with it. Death depersonalises Joyce, stripping her of an identity until she is merely 'the body'. But, the vampire in the morgue is the body too. Everything is reduced to incidentals – particularly the vampire attack on Dawn, which takes on an operatic quality of side-theatre dismissed by an outraged Buffy with a smile on her face as she decapitates the series' most extreme presentation of a vampire-as-non-human (deathly pale, naked, autopsy scar still visible) while her sister shows no interest in the event. The story develops in an impressively non-linear fashion without traditional signposts that tell the viewer what a dream sequence is trying to say. There's also Tara and Willow's kiss – not erotic or out-of-place but genuine and loving in a moment of abject defeat. The performances are breathtaking: Amber Benson's anguished silence; Alyson Hannigan's portrayal of Willow facing up to the realisation that the world will not allow you to remain a child forever; Emma Caulfield's finest hour. Sarah Michelle gives a stunning turn, full of tiny details. But let's have a brief word about Michelle Trachtenberg. Her performance is worthy of a very experienced and mature actress. Which, of course, she was. She was also *fifteen*. And the fact that this lyrical piece didn't even earn a *nomination* for an Emmy is one of the most shameful disgraces in the history of those most arbitrary of awards.

Buffy asks Joyce and Giles to stay away from the candy (see **40**, 'Band Candy'). 1630 Revello Drive is near Hadley. Dawn's best friend is called Lisa. Last week Kevin Berman said she was freaky, though he turns out to be sympathetic and likes Dawn a lot. Her nemesis is a bitchy girl called Kirstie. Tara's mother died when she was 17.

Soundtrack: The only music heard is a brief snatch of the Christmas Carol 'The First Noel'.

Critique: 'Emmy voters take note,' wrote *TV Guide*'s Michael Ausiello, 'last week's haunting episode of *Buffy* in which the Scooby Gang mourned the death of Buffy's mother instantly earned a place as one of the finest hours of television ever produced.' 'There was a lot of integrity in this,' added Matt Roush, 'not just in how it played, but in how it wasn't oversold.' *The Guardian*'s Gareth McLean was moved to write: 'Again the allegation that *Buffy* is just another schmaltzy American teenshow (*Dawson's Creek*-with-fangs) is refuted. This episode was a brave, honest and wrenching portrayal of death and loss. This is a world in which death is commonplace, but *this* death moved away from cartoonish vanquishing of vampires and was all the more devastating for it. Joyce died on her couch looking as surprised as the rest of us at her passing. She died as *people* do.' Mark Wyman in *TV Zone* described the episode as 'a painful, grief-stricken drama played out in four-acts, largely in real-time – with no music, precious little fantasy, and a numbing sadness throughout. Quite rightly, it's been hailed as one of *Buffy*'s finest hours.' In *SFX*, Paul Cornell added that the episode is concerned with reality: 'Whedon directs our attention to the oddness of real life ... The acting honours go to Kristine Sutherland. Here's a woman who's willing to abandon dignity altogether for her craft, and play a corpse in an unflattering, knocked-about, utterly real way.' An editorial on the website *teevee.org* considered 'the fact that this episode was not nominated for any Emmy awards is all the proof you need that the Academy is comprised of a half-dozen drooling, comatose octogenarians. In what may be the best single hour of network drama in the past five years, Gellar's performance was positively searing, especially the opening ten minutes when the Slayer finds her mom splayed out on the couch. Buffy aged twenty years before the hour was over and Gellar pulled off a minor miracle in turning her snappy-but-weary-twentysomething into a crushed soul.' 'One of the toughest hours of television I've ever weathered,' noted Susan Kuhn at *scifi_ign.com*. Praising the episode's occasionally claustrophobic camerawork, lack of soundtrack and almost no supernatural influences, she drew particular attention to Emma Caulfield's performance. 'Anya has her purest expression of emotion. When she starts to cry and express those feelings of a being who has never dealt with death or loss before, it's a beautiful thing, a manifestation of the deepest of human aches.'

Did You Know?: At the *Angel* seminar at the Museum of Television and Radio's 18th annual William S Paley Television Festival in Los Angeles, Charisma Carpenter asked a question that many fans wanted the answer to: 'Why didn't you close [Joyce's] eyes?' Joss replied: 'To make it worse'. He also confirmed a long-held fan-suspicion, that the production purposely tries to pair a dark *Buffy* episode with a lighter *Angel*, and vice-versa.

Nick Brendon's Comments: 'I thought it was going to be much more sombre,' Nick told *E! Online*. 'It did really affect people. It was a lot warmer on the set than I'd anticipated. People were reminiscing. It was a blessing.'

Kristine Sutherland's Comments: 'Joss wanted to make it clear that this was *real* death. This wasn't about vampires. Our society doesn't grapple with death at all,' Kristine told *SFX*'s Paul Simpson and Ruth Thomas. 'I thought that in closing a person's eyes, it's a way of telling ourselves that they're asleep, and not really dead. We make up dead bodies so they look like they're still alive, and shove them off to funeral homes and pretend they don't exist. Europeans don't have that same "let's clean death up" attitude. Their reaction to death is not quite as antiseptic as ours. At an Irish wake you lay the body out on the kitchen table and everybody comes to look at it and have a big party. So, not closing Joyce's eyes was definitely scripted that way. The make-up was scripted as well. Todd [McIntosh] structured it so that it was a gradual progression until, in the morgue, I was literally grey-blue.' Asked when she knew that Joyce was going to suffer an illness, and die, Kristine's answer will amaze many: 'Before I went to Italy [at the beginning of season four]. I probably wouldn't have known that early but, when I told Joss that I was planning on going away for a year, he said, "But you have to come back. I need to kill you! And it's really important!"'

'My mother had an aneurysm,' Kristine continued, before explaining that, at one stage in the planning of the arc, Joss's idea was that Joyce had 'adopted a young girl, maybe five or six years old, so it was interesting how the adoption became [Dawn]. I knew that Joyce was going to get ill, then get better, then suddenly be gone. After I had the surgery, people had the idea that I would have my head shaved and wear a wig. I said, "You can't do that", because I knew from my mother that would not happen.' She also revealed that in most of the episode, she is playing Joyce's body. 'There might have been some times during the fight in the morgue where it was so in the background that they put in a mannequin, but for most of it I did an awful lot of laying around dead.' Another revelation was that the Christmas scenes were filmed first. 'All the stuff where [Joyce was alive] was shot the first day. We did the Christmas scene and then did the waking up in the ambulance stuff, and by the time that we started to do that, the mood on the set really changed. It was a very sombre set.'

The death of a much-loved character can be hard on the viewers, but Joyce's many fans took comfort from the fact that there were plans for the character to return. But only in flashbacks and dream sequences. 'There will be no real return for sure, because I *am* dead.' As for regrets: 'I always wished to do more of Joyce at work. Have a chance to explore her as a working woman. She had a job and provided the money for herself and the house and her daughter. Her capabilities as a single mother – they often explored her at home. I would've liked to have ventured into that area a bit more.'

Joss Whedon's Comments: Explaining the purpose of the Christmas-flashback to *TV Guide*, Joss noted: 'I wanted to get the credits over with. I knew that I had to have opening credits and I knew that there was no way that I was going to put them over the 911 sequence.' Hence, the Christmas gathering: 'It gave me a great transition from happy-to-dead,' he continued, adding that: 'Music would have been too easy. It would [tell you] to feel sad. I wanted to not have that safety net.' On Willow and Tara's overdue kiss: 'They are living together so they're probably already kissing. To make a big deal of it would've been wrong,' he noted and said that he waited for the right moment to script the scene. 'It belongs somewhere you least expect it.' WB execs, however, asked Whedon to cut the kiss, a request he flatly refused. 'I said, "The kiss is in, or I'm walking." This belongs in the show . . . There was one discussion and only one.' A WB representative responded: 'We had questions, but after reviewing the final cut, we chose to air it.' The brutal realism of the episode was interrupted by the vampire in the final act. 'I stayed away from unnatural things as much as possible,' Joss admits. 'I didn't have Glory or even Spike in the episode because I wanted everything to be very real. But because the show is *Buffy*, vampires are part of that world. So I wanted to have the vampire fight, but put it in the context of this occasion, because life is still going on . . . This tragedy has occurred and the world is supposed to stop. Some people thought that at the beginning of the next episode, Dawn was going to touch Joyce and heal her. I'm like, "Missing the point!" '

'This is a rite of passage that people go through. That I went through myself,' Joss told *scifi_ign.com*. 'I lost my mother several years ago. I wanted to capture something much more abstract. A morbidly physical reality of death and grief, of that first few hours. Just the incomprehensibleness of it, and the different ways everybody deals with it. My whole cast was extraordinary. But I really thought people were going to hate it, because the whole point was, there's no catharsis. It was just, "My mother is a dead body. And that's all." But people actually *did* get a catharsis from it. A lot of people who have experienced loss said it helped them to deal with it or that it moved them. I was surprised by that.'

Body Rock: Unsurprisingly, **94**, 'The Body', is a firm favourite among many of the *Buffy* cast and crew: 'It was so sad,' Amber Benson told Rob Francis. 'Kristine was fantastic, walking around the set in her death make-up. And Emma did that amazing scene. They must have done it twenty times . . . Everybody on the set was crying.'

'It was an experiment,' Whedon told Francis. 'I thought everyone would hate [it]. I thought they'd go glassy-eyed and wish it was over. It wasn't supposed to be cathartic. Or helpful. It was just supposed to show what it's like in that situation for the first few hours [after death]. There's almost an element of boredom to grief that I wanted to show. But lots of people got something from it and that really moved me.' Joss went on to admit that the directional style had been hugely influenced by the films of PT Anderson (*Magnolia, Boogie Nights*). 'It's embarrassing how much,' he noted.

95
Forever

US Transmission Date: 17 Apr 2001
UK Transmission Date: 27 Apr 2001

Writer: Marti Noxon
Director: Marti Noxon
Cast: Andrea Gall (Customer), Alan Henry Brown (Funeral Director),
Darius Dudley (Minister), Annie Talbot (Lady with Baby),
Noor Shic (Lady with Rosary)

Joyce's funeral is held and Angel returns to comfort Buffy. Dawn, with Spike's help, visits Doc, an expert in resurrection in an attempt to bring Joyce back. Despite being warned of potentially dire consequences, she casts the spell, only to change her mind at the last moment.

Dudes and Babes and Those of Indeterminate Origin: When Jinx tells Ben 'every moment you fight Glory, you're only fighting yourself', he's talking literally. Ben attempts to kill Jinx to protect Dawn's secret. But the minion survives and Glory now knows that the Key has human form. Whatever Doc is, he isn't human. He has a tail and his eyes turn black when he tells Dawn to keep in touch (see **99**, 'The Weight of the World').

A Little Learning is a Dangerous Thing: Giles keeps most of his potent texts and potions away from the public on the first floor of the Magic Box.

What is Willow playing at? Here we see the basic difference between being a witch and being Wiccan. Tara understands her relationship to the universe and has no intention of messing with it. For Willow, magic is still a game. She can see, intellectually, why some things shouldn't be attempted but, underscored by her grief and her desire to make Dawn less miserable once her platitudes have failed, this leads her to do an *extraordinarily stupid* thing, giving Dawn access to the resurrection spell.

Denial, Thy Name is Summers: Buffy's reaction to Joyce's death sees her bear a terrible guilt for not having arrived home earlier. She becomes morose and obsessive before the funeral, through which she is able to avoid reality for a few more days, before (as she tells Angel) she is required to face a future that she isn't prepared for. Dawn, due to immaturity possibly, can't see that her sister is clinging to mundane details by her fingertips to avoid dealing with larger issues (several of which involve her). Dawn is in pain and (not entirely unreasonably) wants everyone else to share. It's unfortunate that, given where she lives, dark forces are such a temptation. Which is where Willow comes in . . . It's to her credit that Dawn realises her mistake.

It's a Designer Label!: Dawn's 'panther' T-shirt. Tara's red leather funeral coat. Glory's black and white figure-hugging dress.

References: The episode is a variant of the traditional short-story *The Monkey's Paw*. And of Stephen King's *Pet Sematary* (though the former was an influence on the latter so we're into wheels-within-wheels territory). Doc hums Prokofiev's *Peter and the Wolf*. Anya asks Dawn: 'Don't you watch television? I thought all children despise effort and enjoy cartoons.' Also, the Prodigy's 'Breathe'. Dawn's spell is to the Egyptian God of the dead, Osiris (see **101**, 'Bargaining' Part 1).

Awesome!: Giles playing 'Tales of Brave Ulysses' in tribute to an almost-perfect day he once spent with Joyce (see **40**, 'Band Candy'). Spike arriving with flowers. Xander and Willow assume they're for Buffy but find, after Spike has left, that there's no greetings card. Angel and Buffy reunited, briefly, in tragedy. Anya and Xander's existential post-coital ruminations on the purpose of sex. The introduction of the dryly sinister Doc (Joel Grey is *fabulous*). The tearful climax. Not a lot of laughs, but many memorable moments.

'You May Remember Me From Such Films and TV Series As . . .': A cinema legend for his Oscar-winning performance as the Emcee in *Cabaret*, Joel Grey's career stretches back to 1952s *About Face*. He can also be seen in *Venus Rising*, *The Player* and *Man on a Swing*. He played the Devil in the final episode of *Dallas* and appeared in *Maverick* (as Billy the Kid) and *77 Sunset Strip*. Todd Duffey was in *Don't Try This At Home* and *Office Space*. Annie Talbot appeared in *Down Periscope*. Andrea Gall played Tracy Ullman in the spoof *Allyn McBeal*.

Valley-Speak: Xander, to Spike: 'We're all hip to your doomed obsession.'

Glory: 'Jinx, you robed-stud, you're my man! I'm even gonna let you slide on the lame toadying on account of your dying and stuff.'

Logic, Let Me Introduce You to This Window: At some point Wiccans took an oath never to perform resurrections. What, *all* of them?

Cruelty To Stuffed Animals: Trying to cheer Dawn up, Willow says that she could do a spell to make a stuffed animal dance.

Quote/Unquote: Spike, on Joyce: 'I liked the lady . . . She was decent. She didn't put on airs. She always had a nice cuppa for me. And she never treated me like a freak.'

Angel: 'I can stay in town as long as you want me.' Buffy: 'How's forever? Does forever work for you?'

Notes: 'I wanna bring Mom back.' Hard work, though Noxon writes Dawn better than any of the other staffers. But there's a sense of everything standing still for a week – the ongoing plot doesn't advance an inch (except for the introduction of Doc, and even that is handled in an oddly dispassionate way). Ultimately, 'Forever' is flawed by its own inertia, despite many moments of gut-wrenching beauty.

Buffy has been unable to contact her father in Spain to inform him of Joyce's death. Willow says she intends to visit her mother before going home (see **45**, 'Gingerbread') and that she has been doing this a lot since Joyce's death. Xander notes that *he* called to see Willow's mom (with whom he has always got on well) too, though he certainly isn't going to his own parents. The book Willow makes sure that Dawn has access to is *History of Witchcraft* (she considers it merely a history book, although Tara feels it's much more than that). Among its chapters are 'Age of Levitation', 'War of the Warlocks' and 'Resurrection: A Controversy Born'. Willow has started to keep a journal. The Ghora demon that Spike has to steal an egg from to aid Dawn's spell has its nest in the sewer near Tracey Street.

Soundtrack: In addition to the Cream song, 'Tomorrow We'll Awake' by Splendid.

Critique: *The National Review* called *Buffy* 'one of television's most morally serious shows. One of the show's most powerful themes is that the vampires often seem to have the better deal. An eternity of leather, sex, and will-to-power can seem very attractive to your average schoolkid. Vampires are not hobbled by conscience and seem to be masters of adult indulgences. One minute, a high-school guy is nervously babbling as he tries to ask Cordelia out; the next he's confident, sexy, mysterious. You just don't see him much during the day. But again and again, *Buffy* shows that this rock-star life is empty and brutal compared to the more difficult and more rewarding business of becoming a responsible adult, soul intact.'

Did You Know?: In Britain during early 2001, the Broadcasting Standards Commission criticised an early-evening broadcast of *Buffy* as being too sexually explicit for it's pre-watershed timeslot. Viewers (no numbers were given) objected to sex and violence in **59**, 'The Harsh Light Of Day', shown on BBC2 at 6.45 p.m. in October 2000. The BSC ruled: 'In relation to the sex scene, it considered that it had exceeded acceptable boundaries for broadcast at a time when young children could be watching.' The BBC said the show's time-slot was specifically to appeal to a teenage audience. In a statement to the commission, it added: 'There was a sexual aspect to scenes in this episode but, in all these sequences, sexual activity was implied rather than depicted and more comic than erotic.' Complaints over offensive language were not upheld.

The incident provoked utter hilarity in the US media and a dignified 'no comment' from Mutant Enemy and Fox.

96
Intervention

US Transmission Date: 24 Apr 2001
UK Transmission Date: 4 May 2001

Writer: Jane Espenson
Director: Michael Gersham

Spike's Buffybot is completed just as the real Buffy goes out of town on an enlightenment quest. Spike is captured by Glory's minions and tortured to reveal the identity of the Key but he refuses to betray Dawn, a noble gesture that even Buffy appreciates.

Dudes and Babes: Willow loans a fellow student a book containing last week's notes and says that she wants it back by Thursday. And not to write in it. Or put a coffee mug down on it. Or fold the page corners.

Authority Sucks!: Buffy tells Dawn if there are plates in her room, they should be cleaned before they get furry and have to be named. 'I was, like, five then,' replies her sister.

Denial, Thy Name is Spike: 'I feel kinda bad for the guy,' notes Xander. 'Gets all whupped and his best toy taken away.' Spike's refusal to betray Dawn despite being horribly tortured by Glory does bring the reward of a kiss from the real Slayer.

The Conspiracy Starts at Home Time: Glory says that Ben is getting stronger and she is losing control of him. When it's pointed out that she is a god, she replies: 'A god in *exile*. Sharing my body with an enemy.' She deduces that the Key is someone known to the Slayer. She orders her minions to find out who is new in the Slayer's circle. Glory cannot brain-suck vampires (possibly because they are impure).

Technophobia!: Warren says the Buffybot has everything Spike requested including real-world knowledge, family and friends' profiles, scenario responses and special skills. The robot tells Spike that she wants to hurt him but can't resist the sinister attraction of his cold, muscular body. Among her program folders are *Slaying*, *Locate Spike* and *Make Spike Happy*. The program files include two kissing and at least five positions options (see **93**, 'I Was Made to Love You'). Xander's listed attributes include: friend, carpenter, dates Anya. Anya's state: dates Xander, likes money, ex-demon. Willow's list is: best friend, gay (1999–Present), witch, good with computers. The robot cannot pronounce Giles's name properly. Although broken in the fight with Glory's minions, Willow believes she can fix it (see **100**, 'The Gift').

It's a Designer Label!: The Buffybot's girly-pink skirt and sweater. Buffy's suede jacket. Glory's green negligee.

References: Spike quotes U2's 'Even Better Than The Real Thing'. Willow wants to see a History Channel documentary on the Salem witch trials (this proves upsetting and she and Tara watch something about koala bears on Discovery instead). Also, Plasticine⒯, the Four Tops' 'I Can't Help Myself', Xander quotes from 'For he's a jolly good fellow'. Spike tells Glory that the Key is *The Price is Right* host Bob Barker. Visual references to the *Star Trek* episode 'What Are Little Girls Made Of?'

Bitch!: Glory, on Spike: 'What the hell is *that*, and why is his hair that colour?'
   Xander: 'No one is judging you. It's understandable. Spike is strong and mysterious and sort-of compact but well muscled.' Buffy: 'I am *not* having sex with Spike. But I'm starting to think *you* might be.'
   Spike, to Glory: 'The god of what, bad home perms?' And: 'The Slayer is going to kick your skanky, lopsided ass back to whatever place would take a cheap, whorish, fashion victim ex-god like you.'

Awesome!: Everything the Buffybot says is hilarious (it's a *wonderful* performance by Sarah) from her cheery discussion with Willow about making love to Spike in lots of different ways to her Spike-influenced description of Angel, as: 'lame. His hair grows straight up and he's *bloody stupid*.' The finale, Buffy impersonating the robot to give Spike a reward, is incredibly touching.

Valley-Speak: Glory: 'That's *fantabulous*!'

Logic, Let Me Introduce You to This Window: After Spike agrees to tell Glory who the Key is, we next see him drinking water. His face is much more lacerated than it was a moment earlier. It's possible that Glory tortured him a bit more in the interim just because she felt like it. Some of Spike's wounds disappear when he's in the elevator, only to reappear later. During the subsequent fight, Xander's hairstyle changes (probably these are the scenes that saw Kelly doubling for Nick). Willow began her relationship with Tara in 2000 rather than 1999.

Quote/Unquote: Buffy, on the ritual: 'How's it start?' Giles: 'I jump out of the circle and then jump back in it. Then I shake my gourd.' Buffy: 'I know this. The ancient shamans were next called upon to do the hokey-pokey and turn themselves around!'

Tara: 'When I lost my mother, I did some pretty dumb stuff, like lying to my family and staying out all night.' Anya: 'Buffy's *boinking* Spike.' Willow: 'Tara's right. Grief can be powerful. We shouldn't judge . . .' Tara: 'Are you kidding? She's nuts.'

Buffy, to Spike: 'The robot was gross and obscene . . . It wasn't even real. What you did, for me and Dawn, *that* was real.'

Notes: 'You look just like me. We're very pretty.' After two episodes with barely a laugh in sight, we all probably needed this more than we realised and Magic Jane comes up with the goods. A delightful slab of slapstick amid a story about trust and destiny. Yet another superb episode from this gifted writer.

Some Slayers before Buffy found it helpful to regain their focus and learn more about their role by visiting a sacred place and undergoing a quest. The (mental) location is a secret and Giles is unable to take Buffy there, so he has to perform a transference of his guardianship to a guide. A mountain lion leads Buffy into the dreamscape of **78**, 'Restless', and to a meeting with the guide, in the form of the First Slayer. Buffy believes she is losing her ability to love and her humanity. The Slayer forges strength from pain, she is told. 'Love will bring you to your gift'. Which is death (see **100**, 'The Gift'). Anya was in Salem during the witch trials.

Did You Know?: In January 2001, *Associated Press* announced *Buffy* had been nominated at the 12th annual Gay and Lesbian Media Awards, which honour accurate and inclusive representations of the lesbian, gay, bisexual and transgender community. Other nominees included *Queer as Folk*, *Dawson's Creek*, *Popular* and *The West Wing*.

Jane Espenson's Comments: Asked on the *Posting Board* about the kiss Buffy gave Spike, Jane noted that 'it was [in] gratitude and forgiveness'. Answering another question about how she began writing, Jane replied: 'I watched a lot of TV and then wrote sample

scripts that I sent to *Star Trek: Next Generation*. So all you kids
out there, watch TV! It's good for you.'

97
Tough Love

US Transmission Date: 1 May 2001
UK Transmission Date: 11 May 2001

Writer: Rebecca Rand Kirshner
Director: David Grossman
Cast: Anne Betancourt (Principal Stevens), Leland Crooke (Professor Lillian),
Alan Ketz (Slook)

Threatened with the possibility of having Dawn taken in care,
Buffy tries to become a parent. Glory comes to the conclusion that
Tara is the Key. Realising her error, she brain-sucks Tara. Willow
stages a revenge attack and, with Buffy's help, survives. But Tara,
in her deluded state, reveals Dawn's true identity to Glory.

Dudes and Babes: Ben hasn't been to work at the hospital for two
weeks (which seems to surprise him – presumably neither he nor
Glory are aware of the passage of time when they're not occupying
the body) and is thus fired. Tara tells Willow that it frightens her
how powerful a witch Willow is becoming. The discussion moves
on to other matters. 'I'm really sorry I didn't establish my
lesbo-street-cred before I got into this relationship,' Willow says
angrily. Willow adds that Tara has been out longer than her,
indicating that Tara was already describing herself as lesbian when
they met in **66**, 'Hush'.

Authority Sucks!: Dawn has missed lots of school without telling
Buffy. When Giles refuses Buffy's request to be the authority
figure, Buffy realises that she will have to do the strong guiding
hand and stompy-foot stuff herself. She then finds Dawn apparently messing about with Xander, Willow and Anya. In vain,
Willow protests that they were acting out a geometry problem.
Buffy looks unamused, despite some nice obtuse and acute puns.
After a huge argument about homework and chores, Buffy tells
her sister that if Dawn continues to miss school, Buffy will be
declared unfit to be her legal guardian.

A Little Learning is a Dangerous Thing: Buffy has decided to drop
out of college for the semester. She tells Lillian that she really

enjoyed his poetry class but doesn't have time for poetry now. Not even short ones like Haiku. Willow says she took Psych 101 from an evil government scientist who was skewered by her *Frankenstein*-like creation before the finals (see **69**, 'The I in Team'). The book that Willow uses is called *Darkest Magick*.

The Conspiracy Starts at Home Time: Glory says that her brain-suck feels like the victim is in a noisy little dark room, naked and ashamed. And there are things in the dark that need to hurt you because you're bad. Pinching things that go in your ears and crawl on the inside of your skull. And you know that if the noise and the crawling stop that you could remember how to get out. But you never, ever will.

Capitalism is a Ten-Letter Word: Anya has been reading about the USA and embracing the extraordinarily precious ideology that's helped to shape and define it. She proudly explains that the free market depends on the profitable exchange of goods-for-currency. 'It's a system of symbiotic beauty.'

It's a Designer Label!: Buffy's leather skirt. Anya's green dress. The reappearance of Glory's red dress and the debut of Tara's silly stars-and-moons pants.

References: Xander alludes to Wolfgang Amadeus Mozart's opera *Don Giovanni* (1797). Giles misquotes George Harrison's 'All Things Must Pass'. There's a John Lennon poster on Lillian's wall. Xander seems to be reading a copy of *The Incredible Hulk*. Also, Freudianism (see **23**, 'Ted'), Frances Hodgson's *The Little Princess* ('Miss Minchin's Select Seminary For Girls').

Awesome!: The blindfolded minions. Glory's hand-crushing and brain-sucking attack on Tara. Giles getting Slook to talk by doing something while Willow and Anya's backs are turned. A black-eyed, floating Willow's revenge attack on Glory – the first indication that Tara is right, she's becoming frighteningly powerful. Buffy's confrontation with Glory: 'They used to bow down to gods. Things change.'

'You May Remember Me From Such Films and TV Series As . . .': Anne Betancourt was in *Code Blue*, *Sliver*, *Life Stinks* and *Passions*. Leland Crooke appeared in *Dead Man Walking* and *The Lone Gunmen*.

Don't Give Up The Day Job: *Buffy*'s three Casting Directors, Anya Collof, Jennifer Fishman and Amy McIntyre Britt, worked together on *Bones*, *The Hollywood Sign* and *Class Warfare*.

The Drugs Don't Work: Willow is given medicine to keep Tara calm.

Cigarettes & Alcohol: Glory drinks a mimosa in her bubble bath.

Logic, Let Me Introduce You to This Window: Willow's definition of a Freudian slip isn't, strictly speaking, accurate (it's usually regarded as a subconscious substitution of one word with another which reveals a repressed emotion rather than, as Tara does here, merely a slip of the tongue revealing a repressed fear) though Freudian scholars themselves sometimes don't seem able to make up their mind what the term means. Glory says witches used to be crucified. Although there were a few isolated incidents of this in the Middle Ages, the practice certainly wasn't widespread. What sorts of slides are being used in a poetry lesson? Willow and Tara's dorm-room is on the second floor (see **94**, 'The Body'). But when Glory bursts through the wall, it's clearly on the ground floor. Why doesn't Tara react like all the other brain-sucked people who encounter Dawn until the moment that Glory appears?

Quote/Unquote: Anya tries to comfort Willow by saying she can sleep with her tonight: 'That came out a lot more lesbian than it sounded in my head.'

Notes: 'It's not like I don't have a life. I have Dawn's life.' A powerful episode, dealing with raw, bloodied emotions. Little fun for the viewer, but lots of intense frustration and anger that (after a while) become strangely compelling.

Tara mentions having to deal with her brother's problems after their mother's death (probably Donny, see **84**, 'Family'). Willow likes chicken salad sandwiches. Buffy prefers eggplant and Dawn goes for salami and peanut butter.

Critique: In an amateur publication *TV24* (associated with the website *www.offthetelly.co.uk*), someone called Robin Carmody noted that: '*Buffy* – well it's trash ... Parts of it are absolutely hilarious and, if they had a sense of irony, they'd be wonderfully camp. But I got the disturbing feeling that they mean it ... You want to kick their straight faces in.'

Did You Know?: 24-year-old Bath student Ian Stratton planned to spend the next six years watching *Buffy* videos, all in the name of research. Ian's PhD thesis, as widely reported in the UK press, was on the psychology behind monsters and why civilised 21st-century society still had a need to be scared. Nice work if you can get it.

David Fury's Comments: 'To the few of you who don't [think] this season's been as strong as any year of *Buffy*: "The Body," "Fool For Love," "Blood Ties," "Family," etc., all I can say is go watch some reality programming. This stuff's wasted on you,' Fury told the *Posting Board* on 18 April. 'Anyone who doesn't know that Marti Noxon is one of the prime reasons for the greatness of this show is a complete and utter moron.'

98
Spiral

US Transmission Date: 8 May 2001
UK Transmission Date: 18 May 2001

Writer: Steven S DeKnight
Director: James A Contner
Cast: Wade Andrew Williams (General Gregor), Karim Prince (Dante), Jack Donner (Cleric #1), Mary Sheldon (Nurse)

Fleeing from Glory, the Scoobies find themselves also pursued by the Knights of Byzantium, who are determined to destroy the Key to prevent Glory from using it. Hiding at a disused gas station, Buffy telephone's Ben to give medical attention to the injured Giles. Little does she know that she is bringing Glory closer to Dawn.

Dudes and Babes: Glory, not unexpectedly, can run at superhuman speed. Gronx tells Ben that he exists only because of Glory.

A Little Learning is a Dangerous Thing: Dawn is pleased to be skipping town because it means she won't have to study for a geometry test.

Denial, Thy Name is Buffy: Stubborn, to a point beyond sense, Buffy abandons strategy in favour of retreat and compromise for dictatorship. The Scoobies follow her without question, saying much for their trust in Buffy. She's never let them down before. But there's always a first time (see **99**, 'The Weight of the World').

The Conspiracy Starts at Home Time: Gregor says that Glory is from a demon dimension of unspeakable torment. She ruled as part of a triumvirate, but her power grew beyond that of her fellow gods. They feared Glory would attempt to seize their dimension and Glory was banished to a lower plane of existence, and forced to live and eventually die trapped within the body of a newborn male, created as her prison. That's her only weakness: kill the human and she dies too (but, see **100**, 'The Gift'). You have seen a glimpse of the true Beast, Gregor tells Buffy. Her power was too great to be completely contained. She found a way to escape her mortal prison for brief periods, until her energies are exhausted and she's forced back into her living cell. The Key, Gregor continues, is almost as old as Glory herself (see **91**, 'Blood Ties'). Where it came from and how it was created are mysteries. Countless generations of the Knights have sacrificed their lives in search of it, to destroy it before its wrath could be unleashed. But the monks found it first. Buffy asks why the monks didn't destroy the Key, if it's as dangerous as Gregor suggests. Because they were fools, he replies. They thought they could harness its power for the forces of light. Dawn asks why she was created. Gregor says her purpose is to open the gates that separate dimensions. Glory will use Dawn's power to return home and seize control of the Hell she was banished from. But, once the Key is activated, it will not merely open the gates to Glory's dimension. The walls separating realities will crumble, dimensions will bleed into each other, order will be overthrown and the universe will tumble into chaos. Gregor tells Ben that if the Key is not destroyed, unimaginable legions will perish, including everyone here.

It's a Designer Label!: The Knights' baseball caps! Willow's orange pants.

References: *Indiana Jones and the Last Crusade* (visually and the Knights' *raison d'être*). Inspired by probably every road-trip movie ever made. Allusion to *Bring It On* and *Dead Man Walking*. Anya suggests dropping a piano on Glory because it always works for that creepy cartoon rabbit when he's running from that nice man with the speech impediment. Also, *Monty Python's Holy Grail* ('Run away!') and *Monty Python's Flying Circus* (Anya's tin of spam), *Batman* (Xander refers to his car as the Xandermobile), *Sergeant Rock*, obliquely to Italian poet Dante Alighieri (1265–1321), author of *Inferno* and *La Vita Nuova* and 'Ozymandias' by Percy Bysshe Shelley (1792–1822), *The Simpsons* ('shouldn't someone be saying "Are we there yet?"'), Crimean war heroine Florence Nightingale (1820–1910), *Scarface*, *Julius Caesar* ('honourable men'), *The Outer Limits* and the Animals' 'It's My Life'. Spike calls the Knights role-playing rejects. Xander has a poster in his apartment of the cover of a pulp novel seemingly called *Tough Love*.

Bitch!: Gronx: 'No one can stand against her blindingly scrumptious luminescence.'

Awesome!: The truck hitting Glory. The chase and Buffy fighting the Knights on top of the Winnebago. Willow's energy barrier spell and the Knights flying backwards as it takes effect. The injured Giles's admission that he is proud of Buffy. Gregor explaining, sanely, to Buffy and Dawn what will happen if Glory gets the Key.

'You May Remember Me From Such Films and TV Series As . . .': Mary Sheldon was in *The Young and the Restless*. Karim Prince played Cestro in *Mighty Morphin Power Rangers* and Stanley in *Malcolm in the Middle*. Jack Donner was in *Stigmata*, *Soulkeepers*, *Star Trek* and *The Monkees*. He played Commander Kinwon in *Power Rangers in Space*. Wade Andrew Williams was Ted Daniels in *Erin Brokovich* and can also be seen in *Terror Tract*, *24*, *CSI* and *Star Trek: Voyager*. Lily Knight appeared in *Little Girls in Pretty Boxes* and *Static*.

The Knights Who Say 'Key': 'The Knights' sole purpose has always been to destroy the Key, *not* the Beast,' Steven DeKnight told the *Posting Board* on 11th May. 'Gregor says that if the Key is destroyed, the will of the Beast will be broken and she will fade. He also says that the Key is almost as old as the Beast (Glory says the same in **91**, "Blood Ties"). So, the Knights are an ancient order bent on destroying the Key before someone (NOT just Glory) screws the universe.' He added: 'As for Buffy killing the Knights . . . Buffy would never kill a *defenceless* person, even if they had the potential to do great harm (i.e. Spike). But guys trying to kill her and everyone she loves with pointy weapons? Sometimes you just don't have a choice. Also, you might have noticed that Buffy wasn't exactly her normal self, as witnessed by the catatonia at the end of **98**, "Spiral". I'm sure this explanation won't please everyone, but we're really pressing for the *Buffyverse* to become less black-and-white.'

The Drugs Don't Work: Ben says that one of the reasons he wanted to be a doctor was the drugs and the possibility of finding the right combination to keep Glory buried.

Valley-Speak: Spike: 'Buckle up, kids. Daddy's puttin' the hammer down.'

Xander: 'How're your feelers?' Spike: 'Nothing compared to the little bits we're gonna get chopped into when the Renaissance Faire kicks the door in.'

Cigarettes & Alcohol: Xander helps Spike to light a cigarette after the vampire injures his hands.

Logic, Let Me Introduce You to This Window: Gregor specifically says that the identity of the human vessel has never been discovered. Yet a scene later, he seems to recognise Ben. Presumably they have met (which would also explain how Glory knows Gregor's name). All the Knights of Byzantium appear to be American. When Glory runs at speed after Buffy and Dawn, one of the people she rushes close to looks in completely the wrong direction after she passes him. During Buffy's battle on the Winnebago, the face of Sarah's stunt double can be seen twice. The number of Knights involved in the chase fluctuates wildly from shot to shot.

Motors: Spike steals a decrepit Winnebago as the Scoobies getaway vehicle. Giles says he's driven tricycles with more power. Spike wanted to obtain a Porsche.

Cruelty to Animals: When the Knights attack the Winnebago and Giles asks for weapons, Spike suggests that he's driving one. 'Don't hit the horsies,' asks Willow rather pathetically. '*Aim* for the horsies,' Buffy orders.

Quote/Unquote: Ben: 'I didn't ask for any of this. I just want to be normal. Nothing's mine, is it? This life, this body, it's all infected. The only thing I ever cared about she's taken away from me.'

Xander, when the Knights discover the Scoobies' location: 'We got company. And they brought a crusade.'

Buffy, to Gregor: 'She doesn't remember anything about being this Key you're all looking for. The only thing that she remembers is growing up with a mother and a sister that love her. What kind of God would demand her life for something she has no control over?'

Notes: 'At least things can't get any crazier.' Who would have thought that such a talky episode with the information-overload that this one has would have been so entertaining? Base-under-siege-type drama needs a lot of suspense and good acting to keep it from collapsing under its own weight and 'Spiral' succeeds on both counts.

Xander mentions using the rocket-launcher to kill the Judge in **26**, 'Innocence'. Buffy tells Giles: 'We're not gonna win this with stakes or spells or pulling out some uranium power core' (references to **12**, 'Prophecy Girl'; **34**, 'Becoming' Part 2 and **77**, 'Primeval' respectively). Xander often gets travelsick. Glory's brain-sucked victims appear to share a mental link.

Critique: In another glowing piece in *TV Guide*, Matt Roush noted that: '*Buffy* layers its violent allegories with emotional empathy, nimble wit and barbed humour,' and described the likely pairing of *Buffy* with *Roswell* on UPN as: 'like displaying a Picasso alongside an *Archie* comic.'

Joss Whedon's Comments: Quizzed by *Horror Online*, Joss revealed some of his plans for *Buffy*'s future: 'I don't have an end of the show in my head,' he noted, 'because at the end we'll start making expensive movies every four years, not unlike *Star Trek*, only with somewhat younger and more compelling people in them. *Buffy* is not a show I feel I can wrap up neatly with a ribbon.'

99
The Weight of the World

US Transmission Date: 15 May 2001
UK Transmission Date: 25 May 2001

Writer: Douglas Petrie
Director: David Solomon
Cast: Alexandra Lee (Young Buffy), Matthew Lang (High Priest Minion)

Buffy's friends search for Glory without Buffy's help as the shocked Slayer lapses into a catatonic state. Willow goes into Buffy's mind to get her back. But on their return to reality, Giles had some unpleasant news.

Catatonia is Free: Entering Buffy's mind, Willow finds a six-year-old Buffy on the day that Joyce and Hank brought Dawn home. Buffy is frightened that her parents will pay more attention to the baby. Joyce tells Buffy that she can be the one to take care of Dawn. Next, Willow encounters Buffy filing a book in the Magic Box. Then Buffy's meeting with the First Slayer from **96**,

'Intervention', and finally another Buffy who stands by Joyce's grave and tells Willow that she understands the First Slayer's prophecy: death is your gift. It's what I do, she notes, picking up a pillow and smothering Dawn. Willow is particularly interested to know why Buffy keeps on returning to the tiny fragment in the Magic Box. What happened there? 'This was when I quit,' Buffy tells her. 'Just for a second ... I put a book back for Giles. Then it hit me. I can't beat Glory. And in that second of knowing it, I wanted it to happen.' If Glory wins then Dawn dies, Buffy continues. She would grieve and people would feel sorry for her. 'I imagined what a relief it would be.' Her belief that she condemned Dawn to death is what has sent Buffy into the trance. Willow realises that Buffy is simply suffering from guilt. 'You've carried the weight of the world on your shoulders since high school. I know you didn't ask for this, but you do it every day.'

Dudes and Babes: Spike confirms that Doc is a demon. When he and Xander visit Doc they discover that he is also in league with Glory. 'You think only underworld bottom-feeders worship the Beast?' he asks. Doc's blood is blue, he has a lizard-like tongue and is not killed when stabbed by Xander's sword in the chest.

The Conspiracy Starts at Home Time: Dawn's blood is 'the key to the Key'. Glory must bleed Dawn for the portal to open. Spike is the only one able to remember that Ben and Glory share the same body (see **98**, 'Spiral'). Glory has, he speculates, worked some magic where anyone who sees the change instantly forgets (see **91**, 'Blood Ties'). Spike, being non-human, is immune. Later, Glory complains that the cloak between her and Ben is fading, that she can remember what happened when Ben was in control of the body. When Dawn confirms that she too has these memories, Glory says: 'She's not supposed to remember that. Nobody should.' Significantly, when Xander is in Doc's presence, the fog clears and he also remembers.

When Buffy returns to the Magic Box she asks Giles if he has checked the ritual texts and found a way to stop Glory. He confirms that he has. Once Dawn's blood is shed, the fabric that separates realities will rip apart. The portal will close once the blood stops, Giles tells her. The only way is to kill Dawn.

It's a Designer Label!: Glory's ceremonial gown. Buffy's tight black jeans and matching top.

References: Spike compares Ben and Glory sharing a body to apartment-sharing sitcoms. Also Kewpie dolls, Armageddon (the final battle between good and evil as predicted in the Book of Revelation), *The Prisoner* ('we need information'), a *There's MONEY in arc welding!* poster, Glory alludes to a maxim first used by Desiderius Erasmus (1466–1536) and later popularised by English writer and humanist HG Wells (1866–1946): 'In the country of the blind the one-eyed man is king'. Spike uses the finger-on-the-nose correct answer sign from Charades.

Awesome!: Spike's discovery of Ben's rather pathetic little room in Glory's palace, and his smacking Xander on the head to get him to remember the Ben/Glory link. Glory's rant to Dawn on the madness of humanity (which actually makes a lot of sense). Spike and Xander's confrontation with Doc.

'You May Remember Me From Such Films As . . .': Alexandra Lee was in *Alone With a Stranger*.

The Drugs Don't Work: When Spike tries to convince the Scoobies that Glory and Ben share the same body and they look blank, in exasperation he asks: 'Is everyone here very stoned?'

Valley-Speak: Glory: 'Why am I not popping your head like a zit right now?'
   Xander: 'I'm so *large* with not knowing.'
   Willow: 'I think we already *deja*'d this *vu*.'

Logic, Let Me Introduce You to This Window: 'The Knights weren't formed to fight Glory. They were formed to find and destroy the Key, which has existed in our dimension for just this side of forever. Glory was cast-out from her dimension and into baby-Ben 25 years ago. She only recently gained the strength to emerge from her "prison",' Steven DeKnight told the *Posting Board*. 'Hope that clears it up.' Yeh, it pretty much does, actually. On the other hand, why, if the alignment takes place now and it's only at this time that Glory can use the Key, has she been so desperate to get her hands on it for, what, four months? Murk says that the big event will be tonight, but Glory tells Dawn she will be bled tomorrow. If what Willow sees are really Buffy's memories, and not her imagination, then it seems that Hank left a six-year-old girl on her own while he went to pick up Joyce and Dawn at the hospital. Of course, this could be Buffy's subconscious view of her father as an abandoner. Giles was severely injured in **98**, 'Spiral', yet after some minor hospital attention he's able to discharge himself. Willow changes clothes between her bringing Buffy out of her catatonia (which took place at Xander's apartment) and the final scene in the Magic Box. Ben says Glory can't die, that she's immortal, completely contradicting what was said in **98**, 'Spiral' (see **100**, 'The Gift'). The young Buffy is a lot blonder than the young Buffy seen in **30**, 'Killed by Death'.

I Just *Love* Your Accent: Spike's attempt to get through to Buffy: 'Oi, rise-and-shine, love!'

Motors: Spike hotwires Ben's car, noting that a better part of a century spent in delinquency just paid off.

Quote/Unquote: Glory, on humanity: 'How do they function like this in the world with all this bile running through them? You have no control. They're not even animals, they're just these meatbaggy slaves to hormones and pheromones and their *feelings. Hate 'em* ... Is this what the poets go on about? Call me crazy, but as hard-core drugs go, human emotion is just useless. People are puppets.'

Notes: 'I look around at this world you're so eager to be a part of and all I see is six billion lunatics looking for the fastest ride out. Everyone's drinking, smoking, shooting-up, shooting each other, or just plain screwing their brains out cos they don't want 'em any more. *I'm* crazy? Honey, I'm the original one-eyed chicklet in the Kingdom of the Blind.' A fragmented story, trying to tie-up many strands for the big finale. It just about works although the viewer really has to concentrate to catch a lot of the explanations. Don't blink, or you might miss two or three. Clare Kramer is fabulous, as she was all season.

Joyce's gravestone reads: Joyce Summers 1958–2001. Buffy once told Willow in Chemistry class that she talks funny.

Did You Know?: Early 2002 saw the release of Amber Benson's independently produced (and, subsequently, critically acclaimed) movie *Chance*. Directed, written by and starring the actress and featuring her *Buffy* colleague James Marsters along with David Fury, *Angel*'s Andy Hallett and Nick Brendon's fiancée Tressa DiFiglia, the film was described as 'a black comedy about how hard it is to find "the one"'.

100
The Gift

US Transmission Date: 22 May 2001
UK Transmission Date: 1 Jun 2001

Writer: Joss Whedon
Director: Joss Whedon
Cast: Craig Zimmerman (Minion #1), Josh Jacobson (Teen),
Tom Kiesche (Vampire)

Buffy and her friends prepare for the final battle with Glory. Giles's common-sense approach suggests killing Dawn, but Buffy will not consider it. Meanwhile, Xander proposes to Anya, Spike's rehabilitation into humanity continues and Willow attempts to reverse Glory's brain-suck on Tara. Glory is defeated when Giles kills Ben, but not before Doc makes Dawn bleed to open the portal. This leaves Buffy to makes the ultimate sacrifice.

Dudes and Babes: Glory tells Dawn that Ben is probably the reason Buffy and her friends are still alive. 'That little nagging pinch of humanity that makes me go for the hurt instead of the kill. Lowering myself to trade blows with the Slayer when I should have just put my fist through her heart.' Willow's powers seem to be growing daily. She produces spells that pull Tara back from Glory's influence and parts the crowd of Glory's minions to allow Spike to climb the tower. She also displays telepathic ability.

Work is a Four-Letter Word: Spike describes Xander as a glorified bricklayer.

References: The tower construction is reminiscent of one in the *Doctor Who* story 'Genesis of the Daleks'. *X-Men* (not only does the climax resemble the movie – bound-girl on a tower – but Willow has *become* Marvel Girl – telekinesis and now telepathy, see **101**, 'Bargaining' Part 1), *The Omen*, *Monty Python* ('a pointy stick?'), *Scanners* ('it might make all our heads explode') and Badfinger's 'Come And Get It'.

Murder: It's Xander who first suggests the alternative to killing Dawn might be to kill Ben, though he's clearly disgusted with himself for even voicing the idea. Giles, however, coldly and clinically does the deed to end the insanity of Glory's plans. This is a very different Giles from the one that we're used to. He does what has to be done, knowing it's a dirty job but that, ultimately, *someone* has to do it.

Awesome!: Buffy's surprise at finding a vampire who doesn't know her reputation. Giles's anger at Buffy's refusal to consider the possibility of killing Dawn to prevent the ritual. Dawn telling Ben to become Glory. They're both monsters, but at least Glory is open about it. Xander and Anya in the basement, from the ridiculous (the discovery of the toy bunny) to the sublime (Xander's proposal). Anya's decision to accept, but wait for the world not to end, indicates her faith in his belief of their mutual survival. She had been sure they would die, reinforced by the bunny-omen, but now, she says, their love will see them through. Spike telling Buffy that he will protect Dawn until the end of the world. Tara calling Giles a killer and Giles fulfilling this prophecy by clinically smothering Ben. Buffy disinterestedly pushing Doc out of the way as she reaches the top of the tower. Buffy diving from the platform. Spike weeping as Buffy lies dead before him.

'You May Remember Me From Such Films and TV Series As . . .': Tom Kiesche was in *The Animal* and *3rd Rock from the Sun*. Craig Zimmerman appeared in *Sabrina, the Teenage Witch* and *In the Light of the Moon*. Josh Jacobson was in *Not Another Teen Movie*.

Anya's Ideas Work: Despite Giles's withering sarcasm, Anya comes up with several ways of stopping Glory, including the Dagon-sphere (see **83**, 'No Place Like Home') and Olaf the Troll's enchanted hammer (see **89**, 'Triangle'). While the others seem immobilised by fear, Anya's self-preservation instincts re-emerge. But, unlike **55**, 'Graduation Day' Part 1, her love for Xander means that she is part of the battle rather than fleeing from it. It was, possibly, also Anya's idea to use the Buffybot (you can certainly hear Buffy thanking Xander and Anya for *something* when they emerge from the basement).

Valley-Speak: Xander: 'Smart chicks are *SO* hot!'
  Murk: 'Take mine, oh *groovetastic* one.'

Logic, Let Me Introduce You to This Window: 'We set up in "Blood Ties" that Buffy and Dawn were true blood relations, that their blood was the same, so the portal would be sated when EITHER stopped flowing,' Joss told the *Posting Board*. 'Nobody ever took orders from the Buffybot. Buffy gave the gang the speech in the magic shop then went down to change clothes with the bot.

At the tower you hear Buffy give Willow an order and then see the bot,' he continued, explaining the rationale behind two often-quoted errors. Joss also revealed, to *TV Guide*, the meaning of the mysterious '7–3–0' references that first surfaced in Buffy's dream-encounter with Faith in **56**, 'Graduation Day' Part 2. As many fans had suspected, this was a reference to the number of days in two years. Of course, the year 2000 was a leap year, so technically . . . Doc's shallow cuts to Dawn don't seem to pierce her flesh. In the next shot, the blood is gushing out. Given the location of the cuts, the blood should drip down the front of Dawn's dress, rather than running down her legs. As with Dracula's castle in **79**, 'Buffy vs Dracula', didn't anyone notice the construction of a massive tower of scaffolding in the middle of Sunnydale? Maybe we can let them off with that one – this *is* Sunnydale after all, and denial is rife.

I Just *Love* Your Accent: Giles and Spike hilariously misquote the St Crispin's Day speech from *Henry V* (Giles: 'We few. We happy few.' Spike: 'We band of buggered.').

Quote/Unquote: Teen: 'You're just a girl.' Buffy: 'That's what *I* keep saying.'

Anya: 'Usually when there's an apocalypse, I skedaddle. But now I love you so much, instead I have inappropriately timed sex and try to think of ways to fight a god . . . I honestly don't think that I could be more nervous than I am right now.' Xander, holding out a diamond engagement ring: 'Care to wager on that?'

Spike, to Buffy: 'I know you'll never love me. I know that I'm a monster. But you treat me like a man.'

Ben: 'She could've killed me.' Giles: 'No she couldn't. And sooner or later Glory will re-emerge and make Buffy pay for that mercy. And the world with her. Buffy even knows that and still she couldn't take a human life. She's a hero, you see. She's not like us.'

Notes: 'Dawn, listen to me. I will *always* love you. But this is the work that I have to do. Tell Giles I figured it out. And I'm OK. Give my love to my friends. You have to take care of them now . . .' You have to be strong. The hardest thing in this world is to live in it. Be brave. Live for me.' An episode about sacrifice. Xander refers to Ben as an innocent but not innocent in the way that Dawn is. He's closer to the truth than he knows. Dawn is ready to sacrifice herself for others to save the world. Buffy *does*. Anya and Xander have sex while looking for the sphere, a very human moment in a time of inhumanity. 'The Gift' is about choices. About priorities in a world where the only escape from the delicious ironies of life is through love. Willow has been busy working to help Tara and believes that she has let Buffy down. Buffy tells her that Tara should come first. Spike again shows himself ready to die because of a promise to a lady. This is a story about life's little victories. About how we are born to die but are redeemed through our fear of that death (the new dawn that rises as Buffy throws herself from the tower is a literal and a metaphorical acknowledgement of this). It's a life-affirming message that, even in death, the memories we leave behind guarantee us a kind of immortality.

The Apocalypse Will Not Be Televised: 'This is how many apocalypses for us?' Buffy asks. 'Six at least,' replies Giles, referring to **12**, 'Prophecy Girl'; **26**, Innocence'; **34**, 'Becoming' Part 2; **47**, 'The Zeppo'; **54**, 'Graduation Day' Part 2 and **77**, 'Primeval'. 'Feels like a hundred,' he continues. Buffy mentions sacrificing Angel to save the world (see **34**, 'Becoming' Part 2).

Spoiled Rotten: In America, despite the presence of accurate rumours on the Internet, the secret surrounding the season's shocking climax was pretty well kept from those who didn't go looking for it. In Britain, however, where 'The Gift' was shown ten days later, it was virtually impossible to avoid hearing about it. The *Evening Standard*, for instance, ran a *Buffy Dies* exclusive a few days before the final episode. Prize for the most banal action, however, went to the normally reliable Sky One which, after its broadcast of **99**, 'The Weight of the World', showed a trailer for 'The Gift' that included the final lingering shot of Buffy's gravestone. They then repeated this, *ad nauseum*, throughout the week leading up to 1 June.

Did You Know?: 'The WB either misplaced the media roll, or someone took it,' Emma Caulfield told Australian magazine *Big Heat*. 'Media rolls are shown to selected media groups to help them promote *Buffy*. They get a two- or three-month-ahead sneak-peek. We wrapped-up filming of the season finale then Sarah flew out to the Gold Coast for *Scooby-Doo*. She was flown back in [on a] Sunday night to re-shoot the stolen scenes. It's been panic here because we had to change the whole last fifteen minutes because of the stolen footage. Joss is far from impressed.' This revelation has given rise to a popular fan-rumour that the ending of the episode as originally filmed was to have featured Dawn sacrificing herself instead of Buffy.

Did You Spot?: The 'Previously on *Buffy the Vampire Slayer*' reprise includes clips (often as short as a single frame) from all 99 previous episodes. Use your remote control and see how many you can identify.

Joss Whedon's Comments: 'I did warn UPN,' Joss told *Dream-Watch*, ' "Guys, you might see something in the final episode that disturbs you slightly!" ' After the episode's broadcast, Joss told panicking fans on the *Posting Board* that the series *would* return. 'Just want to say again, finally, definitively, that *Buffy* will be back next season, starring Sarah Michelle Gellar, on UPN, Tuesdays at 8 p.m. How will we bring her back?' he rhetorically asked. 'With great difficulty, of course. And pain and confusion. Will it be cheesy? I don't think so. The fact is, we had most of next season planned before we shot this episode. Same writers you know, same actors you love, same crappy little warehouse in Santa Monica we've been shooting in for five years. Different network. But we've never been controlled by the network. The only difference is that Marti [Noxon] will share executive producer credit with me. The story is in charge, the story that keeps on speaking to me, that says there is much more to tell about these characters. An ensemble this brilliant could easily carry the show even without the Slayer. But even though she reached some closure, Buffy's story isn't over. When it is, I'll know. And we'll stop.'

> *BUFFY ANNE SUMMERS*
> *1981–2001*
> *BELOVED SISTER*
> *DEVOTED FRIEND*
> *SHE SAVED THE WORLD*
> *A LOT*

The Outsiders

'The brilliant thing about Joss is he's got all these people
sucked in watching this fantasy, but in the meantime he's
making them think about the kid that they've ostracised
and the kid who's in trouble . . . He explores a lot of things
that are going on with kids today.'

– Kristine Sutherland

For some people memories of school are as Muriel Spark describes them in *The Prime of Miss Jean Brodie*: 'the happiest days of their lives'. For most of us, however, it was a time of intense pressure and loneliness when, cruelly, we were nowhere near mature enough to deal with many of these emotions. That's the central paradox of the teenage years that *Buffy the Vampire Slayer* articulated. Many TV series had talked about how hard growing up can be (from *Happy Days* and *The Wonder Years* to *Press Gang*). Few, however, have been as honest or as painfully accurate as *Buffy*. When Buffy is overwhelmed by the thoughts of her fellow students in **52**, 'Earshot', from the cacophony certain phrases stand out: 'It's got to get better. *Please* tell me it gets better'; 'I *hate* my body'; 'What if I *never* get breasts?'; 'I *hate* her'; 'No one's *ever* gonna love me'.

'I was a pathetic loser in school,' confessed Joss Whedon but, despite his stated intention to make Buffy's conflict with the monsters she fought 'a metaphor about just how frightening and horrible high school is', there are few metaphors in *Buffy*'s treatment of the teenage years themselves. Here, an outsider *is* an outsider. The aspirations of parents and teachers place a burden on young shoulders that needs no subtext to amplify it. Self-doubt, especially in those with identity or image problems, was never far from the surface. (Xander acknowledges his shortcomings in **3**, 'The Witch', saying: 'For I am Xander, King of Cretins. May all lesser cretins bow before me.') The fear of failure and peer-rejection was the topic of many conversations. As Willow tells Xander in **6**, 'The Pack': 'You fail math, you flunk out of school. You end up being the guy at the pizza place that sweeps the floor and says, "Hey, kids, where's the cool parties this weekend?" ' The obsessions of sex and peer-acceptance were always crucial to the way that characters regarded themselves. Cordelia's dream in **3**, 'The Witch', is: 'Me on the cheerleading squad, adored by every varsity male as far as the eye can see. We have to achieve our dreams, or else we wither and die.' In **11**, 'Out of Mind, Out of Sight', Cordelia seems sympathetic towards Marcie, the Invisible Girl saying 'it's awful to feel that lonely'. When Buffy asks how *she* would know, Cordy replies: 'You think I'm never lonesome 'cos I'm so cute and popular? I can be surrounded by people and be completely alone. It's not like any of them really know me. I don't even know if they like me half the time. People just want to be in the popular zone.' Buffy then asks why, if Cordelia feels like this, she works so hard at being popular; Cordelia says simply that it 'beats being alone all by yourself'.

'The anger of the outcast', central to **11**, 'Out of Mind, Out of Sight', was to become a touchstone for the entire series. 'On the exterior it's about demons and vampires and the mythology of the Slayer, but underneath it's strictly about growing up,' Kristine Sutherland told Paul Simpson. Most *Buffy* episodes concern one form of outsider or another. Buffy herself, from the first episode, is a textbook example. A girl in a new town and school, struggling to keep her head above waves that could drown someone with less mental toughness (as, indeed, it does Marcie). Battling the preconceptions of others, whether it's hated authority figures like Snyder, or the expectations of her friends. Others deal with the pressure in different ways. Willow keeps her head down and hopes to avoid Cordelia's sarcasm. Xander becomes the class clown, with a witty comeback for every loser put-down. When Willow asks Giles why Marcie is doing the terrible things she does, he replies: 'The loneliness, the constant exile. She's gone mad.' It's a simplistic answer but, in essence, it describes a heightened version of a form of trauma that many teenagers experience.

In **3**, 'The Witch', Amy was portrayed as a victim of the aspirations of her Nazi-like mother. The issue of parental pressure here (the implication of Amy as a shy little fat girl cruelly beaten into agreeing to Catherine's mad schemes), along with **23**, 'Ted' (a potential stepfather who likes to slap young girls about) and **24**, 'Bad Eggs' (Joyce at the nadir of her *Mommie Dearest* period), reached a violent climax in **45**, 'Gingerbread'. Now the issues was no longer a case of 'I want my kids to be just like me' but rather 'what are my children up to behind my back, and how can I put a stop to it?' **45**, 'Gingerbread's witch-hunt plot concerned attacking the right to freedom of speech, but the belief systems into which Buffy and Willow found their mothers trying to push them are much more frightening. As Buffy tells Joyce when the demon manifests itself: 'Mom, dead people are talking to you. Do the math.' See also, **84**, 'Family' and, subsequently, **141**, 'Empty Places'. The aftermath of Joyce's death in **94**, 'The Body', saw Buffy attempting to take on a parental role that she was manifestly ill-equipped for (**95**, 'Forever'; **97**, 'Tough Love'). The introduction of Dawn, and her metamorphosis from a bratty annoyance to Buffy into the key (in several senses) to her sister's future, helped to change the focus of both the series and the characters. 'She still thinks I'm just her dumb little sister,' Dawn noted in **80**, 'Real Me'. 'Is she in for a surprise.'

Bullying was also a central prop. 'Every school has them,' noted Xander in **6**, 'The Pack'. 'You start a new school, you get your desks, your blackboards and some mean kids.' Whether it was Jack O'Toole pulling a knife on Xander in **47**, 'The Zeppo', or Larry's outrageous sexual innuendo in **27**, 'Phases', the threat of humiliation and pain was never far from the minds of the audience. 'Testosterone is a great equalizer,' noted Giles in **6**, 'The Pack'. 'It turns all men into morons.' In **27**, 'Phases', Buffy tells Willow: 'Welcome to the mystery that is men . . . It goes something like, "They grow body hair, they lose all ability to tell you what they really want".' 'That doesn't seem like a fair trade,' replied Willow, sadly. Ultimately, the theme was examined to breaking point in **38**, 'Beauty and the Beasts', which managed to fudge the tricky subject of male domestic violence, but accurately captured the confusion on both sides when trying to maintain relationships. By the time the gang reach college, bullying has become intellectual rather than physical, something Xander (as an outsider within his own peer group) felt particularly strongly (see **60**, 'Fear Itself'; **61**, 'Beer Bad'; **77**, 'Primeval').

The second year of *Buffy* was the point at which a promising idea suddenly (and, given the formulaic nature of American TV, quite unexpectedly) grew up and got serious. If the initial episodes had been a dip of the toe into a pool of delicious irony, in which teenagers fought vampires between homework and dates, then the second season was a fully clothed dive into the murky waters of the adult world. We had no reason to expect anything so daring, so *challenging* as this. Previously, *Buffy* had been about teenage dreams and desires: Xander's helpless love life, Willow's quest to make Xander notice her. The great taboo 'S' word (sex) was finally spoken (by, of all people, Joyce) in **29**, 'Passion', after the heroine's virginity had been lost in **25**, 'Surprise'.[33] Even Giles was not immune from the great hormonal upheaval going on around him, first winning Jenny Calendar, then mourning her.

Giles was another outsider. The Englishman abroad, lost in a school situation he doesn't understand, working with a girl who speaks a language he doesn't, having to put aside all his preconceptions about what a Watcher is, to deal with the realities of life in Sunnydale. 'But Giles is not a fool,' said Tony Head. 'He's deeply learned. One of the choices I made at the beginning was that [Giles has] prepared for this for some time. There's a lot of theory gone into it, but that [he's] had absolutely no practical experience. So when we first get into the affray, it's a bit of a shock.' In **42**, 'Lover's Walk', when Buffy tells him that when her mother saw her SAT scores 'Her head spun around and exploded', Giles asks, 'I've been on the Hellmouth too long. That was metaphorical, yes?' He *knows* Buffy and is able to spot Faith's lies about her in **49**, 'Consequences'. Of course Giles was an outsider even as a teenager and in **40**, 'Band Candy', we see evidence of his way of dealing with responsibility: 'Let's find the demon and kick the crap out of it!' 'Did anyone ever tell you you're kind of a fuddy-duddy?' Jenny asked him in **20**, 'The Dark Age'. 'Nobody ever seems to tell me anything else,' he replied. In season four, as David Fury noted, Giles became the equivalent of a father who has seen his children leave home. He felt abandoned by them and struggled to create a new identity for himself in a changing world (see **57**, 'The Freshman'; **74**, 'Where The Wild Things Are'), a metaphor that **68**, 'A New Man', took literally. It was almost a relief for him in **66**, 'Hush', when everyone lost their voices and, at last, he had something that connected him with his young friends again.

In Xander we had a paradox. Someone who was (according to **47**, 'The Zeppo') 'not challenged' but who found school such hard going that he surrendered his intellect to the clouds and spent his days dreaming about ... well, sex, basically (hinted it **10**, 'Nightmares'; **26**, 'Innocence' and **47**, 'The Zeppo', and wholly confirmed in **52**, 'Earshot'). But Xander is, as Oz notes in **52**, 'Earshot', 'a very complex man'. 'You are strange,' Ampata notes in **16**, 'Inca Mummy Girl'. 'Girls always tell me that,' confesses

---

[33] Actually, the first use of the word 'sex' in *Buffy* occurs as early as **3**, 'The Witch', albeit in a very different context.

Xander, 'right before they run away.' The only time we see Xander enraged about the abject unfairness of a system to which he was a crushed victim was in **32**, 'Go Fish', when Willow is told by Snyder to up the failing grades of one of the swim team. Xander knows, however, that life is seldom fair (it's a system that, as he freely acknowledged, 'discriminates against the uninformed'). In **17**, 'Reptile Boy', having suffered from a ritual frat party humiliation, his way of dealing with his feelings is mind-numbing violence. Hints of domestic horror (see **78**, 'Restless') give this recurring theme a contextualisation.

Willow's story was different. In **1**, 'Welcome to the Hellmouth', she was simply looking for a friend to call her own. ('Aren't you hanging out with Cordelia?' Buffy asks: 'I can't do both?' 'Not legally,' Willow replies.) Willow never surrendered to the cruelties of life (not even Xander's failure to notice her increasingly desperate advances), but sometimes she longed for change. By **50**, 'Doppelgängland', she was even bemoaning the one quality about herself that she could be proud of. Being 'Reliable Dog Geyser Person'.

There was also Faith, whose way of dealing with the 'outsider-ness' of being a Slayer was radically different from Buffy – as shown in **48**, 'Bad Girls', and her random sexual exploits. 'How many people do you think we've saved by now? Thousands? Because in my book, that puts you and me in the plus column,' she says in **49**, 'Consequences', as the cracks begin to open. Faith turned to the dark side because she was an outsider within the Scooby Gang – none of them, really, wanted her around. Whereas with the mayor, she's cherished in a home rather than alone in a motel room. In **51**, 'Enemies', her sleeping with the enemy is revealed as she tells Buffy: 'I'll be sitting at his right hand. Assuming he has hands after the transformation. I'm not too clear on that part. And all your little lame-ass friends are gonna be Kibbles and Bits.' Ultimately, it could have been so different if only she'd had any love in her life. But, at every step, from her mother's rejection onwards, it was not to be.

In **38**, 'Beauty and the Beasts', Buffy calls Faith's 'all men are beasts' view cynical. 'It's realistic,' Faith replies. 'Every guy, from *Manimal* to Mr "I Love *The English Patient*" has *beast* in him. I don't care how sensitive they act. They're all still just in for the chase.' Redemption was key to Faith's long story, an anguished and world-weary figure; a girl sick of all the horror in her life and of the taint of evil within her. In **71**, 'This Year's Girl' and **72**,

'Who Are You?' (and her subsequent appearances in several *Angel* episodes) we saw Faith reaching, literally, the end of the line, sadistically torturing Wesley for the simple reason that it would make Angel interested enough to kill her. That she, then, chose the path of redemption was almost entirely down to Angel's refusal to play the vengeance game, however much Buffy may have wanted him to.

While in Sunnydale, Angel never really fitted in either. Shaken to his core by Buffy's arrival (in **19**, 'Lie to Me', he tells Willow 'a hundred years just hanging out feeling guilty, I really honed my brooding skills. Then *she* comes along.'), his curse puts him on the outside of his own kind *and* humanity. 'The last time I looked in on you two,' noted Spike in **42**, 'Lover's Walk', 'you were fighting to the death. Now you're back to making googly-eyes at each other again like nothing happened.' When Angel lost his soul in **26**, 'Innocence', note how gleefully happy Angelus was to be back with his own kind – Spike and Drusilla.

For Buffy, the constant struggle was always to balance the different elements within her life. In **40**, 'Band Candy', she challenges Joyce and Giles, saying: 'You're both scheduling me 24 hours a day. Between the two of you, that's 48 hours.' But her rebellion against her destiny was only a tiny part of the complicated double life that she was forced to lead. On occasions (**3**, 'The Witch'; **17**, 'Reptile Boy'; **37**, 'Faith, Hope and Trick'; **111**, 'Gone') she longed for a life free of the burden of her Slayer duties. In **39**, 'Homecoming', she even tried to put it into practice ('This is just like any other popularity contest. I've done this before. The only difference being this time I'm not actually popular.') And with her off-on-off-on again relationship with an older man (old enough, in fact, to be her ancestor) Buffy's confusion reached critical meltdown. Even when she *tried* to find a normal boy (Owen or Scott), Slaying always got in the way.

It's the five episodes that detail the climax and breakdown of the Buffy/Angel relationship (**25**, 'Surprise'; **26**, 'Innocence'; **29**, 'Passion' and **33/34**, 'Becoming') that identify the biggest change to *Buffy*. These were stories in which we saw a young girl being given some heartbreaking lessons in the horrors of the adult world. In the teen-suicide drama **31**, 'I Only Have Eyes for You', Buffy spent the episode believing that the haunting of the school by the restless soul of James was just retribution for what he did to Grace until a more reflective Giles told her: 'To forgive is an action of compassion. It's not done because people deserve it. It's done because they *need* it.' It was only when she realised, in **54**, 'The Prom', that what she was doing had not gone unnoticed by her peers that Buffy's defences finally crumbled. 'It was a hell of a battle,' she noted at the end of **56**, 'Graduation Day Part 2'. She could have been talking about her own struggle to find a purpose in the madness around her.

Denial, thy name truly *is* Sunnydale: how did the average people of Sunnydale look at Buffy and her friends? What did the townsfolk make of Giles, for instance? While he was the school librarian, he at least had an excuse to be hanging around with teenage girls and boys. But he never seemed to have a steady girlfriend, apart from his brief interlude with Jenny Calendar. His home was filled with books on black magic, weapons, shackles and handcuffs. Then, after losing his job, young men and women were regularly seen coming and going from his house at all hours of the night. It was obvious that he must have been selling drugs. And surely the delivery boy noticed that Giles kept a blond man tied up in a chair in his living room.

Look at Buffy herself. How many times was she seen in public with ugly bruises on her face and arms, or cuts on her lip? To anyone who knows her, it must have seemed that she was being regularly abused. And since Buffy never complained to anyone, the natural assumption must be that she tolerated it. The neighbours *must* assume that Joyce, and possibly Giles, are beating Buffy in some sick and twisted sadomasochistic spank-fetish role-play game. It's a wonder the child welfare department never came a-calling. In previous seasons we knew that Buffy was leaving her house every night to hang around the park. Clearly she was a teenage prostitute, often seen in the company of a much older man who one could only guess to be her pimp. As for Xander, he was observed taking a man home to his basement apartment and the man was wearing handcuffs and tied with ropes. What were the Harris' neighbours supposed to believe about him? In fact, what did his family themselves believe? When you look at the Scooby Gang from this perspective, they seemed a right bunch of perverted dysfunctional weirdos.

In **52**, 'Earshot', Buffy finds Jonathan alone on the top of the school clock tower with a gun in his hand. We'd seen him in several episodes before, always the butt of cruel jokes by the likes of Harmony, or intimidated and bullied by others. Buffy tells Jonathan that she's never thought much about him: 'Nobody here really does. Bugs you, doesn't it?' Jonathan asks if she believes he simply wants attention? 'Believe it or not,' Buffy replies, 'I understand about the pain.' Jonathan is incredulous: 'The burden of being beautiful and athletic, that's a crippler!' he says, echoing Buffy's own disbelief at Cordelia in **11**, 'Out of Mind, Out of Sight'. 'I was wrong,' notes Buffy. 'You *are* an idiot. My life happens, on occasion, to suck beyond the telling of it. Sometimes more than I can handle. Not just mine. Every single person down there is ignoring *your* pain because they're dealing with their *own*. The beautiful ones, the popular ones, the guys that pick on you, everyone. If you could hear what they're feeling, the loneliness, the confusion. It looks quiet down there. It's not. It's deafening.'

Analysing the success of *Buffy* requires us to look hard at our own experiences in our teens. Joss Whedon and the other writers, in using the clichés of horror movies – vampires, demons, possession, robots and so on – to represent the terrors of being a teenager, managed to tap into something buried deep within all of us. It was the subtext stuff – parental pressure, bullying, fear of sex, social exclusion. The characters in *Buffy* were characters that we could empathise with, because we were all once like them. Outsiders.

> Cordelia: '*Are we killing something tonight?*'
> Buffy: '*Only my carefree spirit.*'
> – 'Band Candy'

Changing Channels

It was one of the TV stories of the decade, though it had little to do with what was taking place in Sunnydale. Tension erupted early in 2001 when *Buffy*'s production company, Fox, asked the WB network on which *Buffy* – then reaching the end of its fifth season – was broadcast to pay $2 million per episode, effectively doubling the cost of carrying the show. WB executives replied that they would pay $1.6 million, but no more, claiming this would mean losing money on the series. Although only the WB's third-highest-rated series (behind *7th Heaven* and *Charmed*), *Buffy* was easily its biggest revenue generator, with 30-second advertising spots during episodes believed to be worth $100,000 each to the network.

'If we end up somewhere other than the WB, we'll be exactly the same show. Fox have supported us on everything,' Joss Whedon told the press. 'I think the fans will find us.' Still, Whedon was hopeful that *Buffy* would remain on familiar ground. He wasn't the only one. 'I will stay on *Buffy* if, and only if, *Buffy* stays on the WB,' Sarah Michelle Gellar told *E! Online* in an unguarded moment of clarity at the Golden Globes. The remarks enraged Fox executives, considering that Gellar was securely under contract until 2003, regardless of where *Buffy* ran. If the star was announcing serious intentions to quit, the studio's bargaining position in any forthcoming renegotiation could be seriously undermined. What happened next shows how frantic Hollywood players can become when a major deal is on the line. According to the *Los Angeles Times*' Scott Collins, Fox executive Sandy Grushow rang Gellar's representative Debbie Klein – whom he'd known since they were classmates in fifth grade – and reminded Klein of her client's binding contract. Subsequently, a wholesale retraction from the contrite star appeared in the press. 'I'm not going anywhere. I can't stress that enough,' Sarah said, adding that, 'Fox has been very good to me. I intend to stay with *Buffy* no matter what.'

Next, comments attributed to WB chief executive Jamie Kellner made Joss Whedon furious. 'To dismiss his own product angers me. It doesn't breed love,' Joss told *The Daily News*. Kellner was said to have argued vigorously against paying any more money for *Buffy*, telling *Entertainment Weekly* that it wasn't even the network's top-rated series and – perhaps unintentionally – belittling the series' many adult viewers by asserting that it was a show which appealed, almost exclusively, to teens. 'We have tremendous respect for Joss, Sarah and everyone associated with *Buffy*,' said WB spokesman Brad Turrell, manfully trying to defuse the simmering row. 'They have delivered a consistently excellent program for five seasons.' Within weeks of the move, Kellner was no longer at the WB, having become CEO of the Turner Broadcasting System, like the WB, a subsidiary of AOL/Time-Warner.

A late-February 2001 deadline passed and Fox were now free to consider bids from such parties as ABC and UPN. The latter was an interesting, if rather unexpected, player in the deal. Home to the *Star Trek* franchise, WWF Wrestling and not a lot else, UPN made a bid in March. Nick Brendon broke the news in an interview with *zap2it.com*. 'Apparently, money talks,' he noted. Finally, in April, Fox announced that *Buffy* would be relocating from season six. UPN agreed to a two-year, 44-episode deal, reportedly paying $2.3 million per episode (and, it later emerged, broadcasting at a significant loss). UPN CEO Dean Valentine said: 'We are incredibly pleased to have *Buffy*, not just because it's one of the best shows on air and represents a new era in UPN's direction, but because Joss Whedon is one of the finest writers and producers in television.' Advertising revenue played a huge part in the decision, noted Adam Ware, UPN's chief operating officer, crediting *Buffy* and *Roswell* (which UPN also bought after it was dropped by the WB), for attracting The Gap and Maybelline to UPN.

Joss, was asked by *E! Online* if he watched UPN. 'No,' he replied, 'but then, I don't watch the WB either, apart from my own shows. You'll find that people who make TV [seldom] have time to watch it. The only exception for me is *The West Wing*.'

Although the media had considered UPN a long shot, the network was said to be passionate about the series and 'invested in its long-term success'. Needless to say, the WB was *not* impressed. In a very terse statement it suggested that Fox had made 'an inauspicious decision for the television industry by taking one of their programs off a nonaffiliated network and placing it on a network in which they have a vested interest' (Fox and UPN were allegedly discussing a merger at that time).

There was little reason for anyone outside the two networks to much care about *Buffy* moving. The show's many fans had no difficulty finding it when it returned in September. In a way, what was more interesting was a broader issue. How the WB had succeeded with its strategy of becoming a TV network primarily for teenage girls, and how UPN – with their acquisition of *Buffy* and *Roswell* – seemed to be trying to capture the same demographic. With shows like *Buffy*, *Charmed*, *Angel*, *Popular*, *Gilmore Girls* and *Dawson's Creek*, the WB made itself a first stop for every advertiser selling clothes, cosmetics, CDs and cell phones. 'I think, the [right] strategy is doing shows with a lot of strong teen characters,' Jamie Kellner had noted. 'But teen characters that have family units.' The price UPN eventually paid for *Buffy* made no sense to Kellner. That's because it only made sense *at all* as part of a broader deal that effectively guaranteed UPN's continued affiliation with stations in New York, LA and other large markets.

A year after *Buffy* moved, the watershed shifts in the industry that many predicted at the time had failed to happen. Studios still sold shows to networks with which they shared no corporate affiliation. UPN didn't go out of business due to *Buffy*'s price tag, and the WB didn't collapse without the show. What's more, the WB's charges that Fox sold *Buffy* to UPN because News Corp. (Fox's parent company) was planning to take a stake in UPN didn't happen either. UPN remained a wholly owned subsidiary of Viacom. But there *were* ramifications. Thanks to *Buffy* and their other 2001 hit show, *Enterprise*, UPN finally started to shed its old image. The strong performance of both helped the network's overall 2001–02 ratings to jump 15% in total viewers, 13% in adults aged 18–49 and 19% in the important 18–34 age demographic. It topped the WB in all three categories. The WB, despite a strong May sweep that helped re-establish some momentum, had a somewhat disappointing year, though this wasn't due to declines on Tuesdays. The network smartly shifted *Gilmore Girls* into *Buffy*'s old slot and paired it with its own debut hit-of-the-year, *Smallville*.

One of the key reasons UPN execs gave for buying *Buffy* was its ability to help the network create new programming. However, that didn't happen either and, by the middle of *Buffy*'s seventh season, the UPN deal's $2.3 million-per-episode had started to seem exorbitant – particularly as the series' initally impressive rating had begun to decline. And while *Buffy* helped UPN make dramatic gains in ad revenue, the show's per-episode price always remained far higher than the amount of direct coin it pulled in. UPN president Leslie Moonves called the *Buffy* pact 'a smaller version of Fox's first NFL deal. Fox lost a fortune on that, but as a result, became a major-league player.'

For the WB, losing *Buffy*, while painful psychologically, didn't matter much to the network's bottom line. 'They might have had slightly better ratings with *Buffy*, but they still had a decent year,' noted Josef Adalin. But, Fox/News Corp. seemed to be the deal's biggest winners. Not only was *Buffy* a more profitable show than it had been on the WB, but the company felt hardly a pinch of negative reaction from other networks to the move.

*'Wherever I was, I was happy. At peace. I was warm.
I was loved. I was finished. Complete. I don't understand about
dimensions or theology . . . but I think I was in Heaven.'*
– 'After Life'

Season Six (2001–02)

Mutant Enemy Inc/Kuzui Enterprises/Sandollar Television/20th Century Fox
Created by Joss Whedon
Co-Producers: John F Perry, Marc David Alpert (101–115),
James A Contner (113, 118, 121)
Producers: Douglas Petrie (101–114), David Solomon, Gareth Davies,
Marc David Alpert (116–122)
Consulting Producer: David Greenwalt
Supervising Producers: Jane Espenson, Douglas Petrie (115–122),
Co-Executive Producer: David Fury
Executive Producers: Sandy Gallin, Gail Berman, Fran Rubel Kuzui,
Kaz Kuzui, Joss Whedon, Marti Noxon
Regular Cast:
Sarah Michelle Gellar (Buffy Summers), Nicholas Brendon (Xander Harris),
Alyson Hannigan (Willow Rosenberg),
Anthony Stewart Head (Rupert Giles, 101, 104–108, 121–122),
Kristine Sutherland (Joyce Summers, 117),
Elizabeth Anne Allen (Amy Madison, 109–110, 112),
Dean Butler (Hank Summers, 117), James Marsters (Spike),
Danny Strong (Jonathan Levinson, 104–105, 109, 111, 113, 117–122),
Emma Caulfield (Anya Jenkins, 101–116, 118–122),
Andy Umberger (D'Hoffryn, 116), Marc Blucas (Riley Finn, 115),
Amber Benson (Tara Maclay, 101–110, 113–114, 116–120),[34]
Michelle Trachtenberg (Dawn Summers),
Adam Busch (Warren Meers, 104–105, 109, 111, 113, 117–120),
Amelinda Embry (Katrina Silber, 113, 120),
Tom Lenk (Andrew Wells, 104–105, 109, 111, 113, 117–122),
Jeff Kober (Rack, 110, 120–121), Kirsten Nelson (Lorraine Ross, 112, 117),
Kali Rocha (Halfrek, 112, 114, 116, 118), Marion Calvert (Gina, 112–113),
James C Leary (Clem, 105,[35] 114, 116, 119–120),
Steven W Bailey (Cave Demon, 120–122)

---

[34] Uncredited in **120**, 'Villains'.
[35] Credited as 'Loose Skinned Demon' in **105**, 'Life Serial'.

101
Bargaining

US Transmission Date: 2 Oct 2001
UK Transmission Date: 10 Jan 2002

Writer: Marti Noxon
Director: David Grossman
Cast: Franc Ross (Razor), Geoff Meed (Mag), Mike Grief (Klyed),
Paul Greenberg (Shempy Vamp), Bru Muller (Teacher),
Joy DeMichelle Moore (Ms Lefcourt), Robert D Vito (Cute Boy),
Henry Johnson (Parent #1), Kelly Lynn Warren (Parent #2),
Hila Levy (Pretty Girl), Richard Wharton (Homeowner)

Some months have passed since Buffy sacrificed herself to save the world. The Scooby Gang are using the Buffybot to maintain an illusion and the population of Sunnydale – human and demonic – remain unaware of the Slayer's death. Unfortunately, a vampire accidentally discovers the truth and escapes to tell a gang of biker Hellion-demons about Sunnydale's best-kept secret. Meanwhile, as Giles makes preparations to return to England, Willow, Tara, Anya and Xander perform a powerful and dangerous spell at Buffy's gravesite.

A Little Learning is a Dangerous Thing: Dawn's teacher notes that the kids' model version of a utopian futuristic society includes an extraordinary number of pizza parlours, but no schools.

Denial, Thy Names Are Willow, Tara, Anya and Xander: The resurrection ritual that the Scooby Gang intend to use on Buffy's corpse is, according to Tara, against all laws of nature and practically impossible to do. However, Buffy didn't die a natural death; rather, she was killed by mystical energy. This means, Willow argues, that her soul is most likely trapped in a Hell dimension just as Angel once was (see **34**, 'Becoming' Part 2). Willow offers no supporting evidence for this and, as it turns out, is wholly wrong (see **103**, 'After Life').

Denial, Thy Name is Spike: Spike obviously still bears the scars of an indescribable guilt because he failed in his promise to a lady (see **100**, 'The Gift') to protect Dawn which, indirectly, resulted in Buffy's death. He seems to be dealing with it, however. His disdain for authority briefly surfaces while he's talking to Dawn about school. Then he realises that he's supposed to be a role model.

However, he seems to get upset each time he's near to the Buffybot which, he now realises, is no replacement for the real thing.

The Conspiracy Starts at Home Time: Willow has managed to get the Buffybot's head back on (see **100**, 'The Gift') and it is currently impersonating Buffy to a reasonably satisfactory degree. Enough to fool Dawn's teacher, at least. Willow has programmed the robot away from a penchant for knock-knock jokes, though in trying to insert some new puns, its speech patterns have taken on an abstract edge. Tara and Willow have moved into the Summers' home with Dawn and are living in Joyce's old room.

It's a Designer Label!: Tara's red leather coat shares top honours with the Buffybot's leather pants. Also watch out for several T-shirts with number motifs on them, worn by various Scoobies and clearly meant to mess with the heads of viewers who believed there were hidden references to something significant.

References: Conceptually, *From Dusk Till Dawn* and *The Uncanny X-Men* (Willow *is* Jean Grey in the opening scene. See **100**, 'The Gift'; **122**, 'Grave'), *Night of the Living Dead* ('Scenario: we raise Buffy from the grave. She tries to eat our brains'), *Nightmare on Elm Street* (Razor's Freddie Kruger-style finger weapons). Xander alludes to *The Fury* ('that way lies spooky carnival death'). Also, Dadaism (a nihilistic artistic movement of the early 20th century founded on principles of irrationality and irrelevance towards accepted aesthetic criteria), Video Hut and the Discovery Channel. A *Rock the Vote* poster is briefly visible. Anya found the last known Urn of Osiris,[36] the artefact needed to resurrect Buffy, at the online auction site e-Bay, from a Desert Gnome in Cairo. He drove a hard bargain, but Anya got him to throw in a limited edition Backstreet Boys lunch box (she implies this is for Xander). Dawn's class are reading *Walden, or Life in the Woods* by Henry David Thoreau (1817–62). One of the vampires wears a Hanson T-shirt. The movie *Dude, Where's My Car* is on the billboard at the Sun Cinema. Keen-eyed viewers may spot that it's still on later in the season, almost two years after it last played in most US theatres. The movie is, apparently, a particular favourite of Marti Noxon.

---

[36] Osiris was the Egyptian god of the afterlife, brought back from the dead himself by Isis, his wife, following his murder by his brother Sutekh. A character based on Osiris appears in *Stargate SG-1*.

Bitch!: Anya, on the Buffybot: 'I think the concept of *chi* is a little tough for her to grasp. She's not the descendant of a long line of mystical warriors, she's the descendant of a toaster oven.'

Awesome!: Spike casually setting fire to the fat vampire who's throttling Giles. A lonely Dawn lying on the bed next to the robot of her dead sister. The genuinely touching scene of Giles's departure from the airport, and his final words to his young friends: 'Just be careful.' The climax, Buffy's corpse coming to life.

'You May Remember Me From Such Films and TV Series As . . .': Franc Ross was Tobias in *Amityville: Dollshouse*, and appeared in *A Whisper Kills*, *The West Wing*, *3rd Rock from the Sun* and *Sliders*. Bru Muller's movies include *Eating LA* and *Since You've Been Gone*. She also wrote and produced *Maxwell*. Paul Greenberg appeared in *Ghost Mom* and *The Kids in the Hall*. Robert Vito was in *Chicago Hope* and *Grownups*. Mike Grief appeared in *Big Brother in Trouble*, *King's Pawn*, *Liar Liar*, *Malcolm in the Middle* and *Grosse Pointe*. Hila Levy played Samantha in *Lava Lounge*. Richard Wharton's CV includes *Will & Grace*, *Herman USA* and *The Fence*.

Don't Give Up The Day Job: Paint Foreman Lisa Gamel was a scenic artist on *Barb Wire*. Script Supervisor Suzanne McRobert's movies include *Geppetto*. Production Coordinator Lisa Ripley Becker previously worked on *The X-Files*.

Valley-Speak: Xander: 'Great googly-moogly.'

Cigarettes & Alcohol: Xander wanted to get Giles a can of *Old English 800* as a parting gift. But the guy living in a box in front of the store wouldn't buy it for him. There's a lot of beer drunk in the biker bar.

Sex and Drugs and Rock'n'Roll: Tara blows sobri-root into a vampire's face. It's supposed to confuse him but, instead, it makes him peppy. Tara wonders, briefly, if the vampire might be taking prescription medication.

Buffybot says she admires Spike's brain almost as much as his washboard abs.

Logic, Let Me Introduce You to This Window: The Scoobies are trying to keep Buffy's death a secret from the world – one could suggest, therefore, that the gravestone is something of a give-away. Hidden or not, there's always the possibility that somebody who isn't supposed to will be walking through the Sunnydale woods and discover it. Why do only the Buffybot and Anya have stakes during the initial hunt (to be fair, Giles also has an axe, but nobody else seems to be tooled up)? And doesn't Anya's pointy stick seem rather blunt to be of much use? When Willow enters the Magic Box after getting the last ingredient for the spell, Tara says she's late, indicating that the Scoobies were expecting her earlier. But Willow subsequently tells Xander: 'I thought we weren't gonna meet till later.' The Urn of Osiris is something of a contradiction since the ancient Egyptians mummified rather than cremated their dead. They did preserve vital organs in canopic jars although the vessel seen here doesn't look much like one of those (it's neck is far too narrow to get something like a heart into). The sacrifice that accompanies the resurrection ritual appears to be similar to Greco-Roman necromantic rites rather than anything Egyptian. Giles's flight from Sunnydale airport is said to be 'leaving for Los Angeles and continuing to London.' US airports *do* sometimes use this description for flights that will land at another airport to take on more passengers. But the idea of a transatlantic flight originating in Sunnydale with a stopover in LA (just 80 miles away) is ludicrous. Given that in most respects (location, size) Sunnydale is based on the town of Santa Barbara, it's interesting to note that Santa Barbara Airport is a municipal (dealing chiefly with commuter flights to gateway cities such as Los Angeles, San Francisco and Denver) and not an international one. Why, when the Scoobies know that she exhibits frequently bizarre behaviour, is the Buffybot allowed to patrol the streets on her own? Who is with Dawn while all the other Scoobies are patrolling in the opening sequence? Willow wears a brown skirt in the scene where she asks Dawn to return her clogs. However, in the next scene, in the kitchen, she is wearing the same red shirt, but with a pair a jeans. Later, at Xander's apartment, the skirt returns. Anya, Tara and Xander are much closer together in some shots when they're in a circle with Willow than in others and, at one point, Anya and Tara swap positions.

I Just *Love* Your Accent: Spike wonders if Giles's life flashed before his eyes while being choked: 'Cuppa tea. Cuppa tea. Almost got shagged. Cuppa tea ...'

Motors: A whole gang of demon bikers on nasty great Harley Davidsons.

A Haven For the Bruthas: Hellions are road pirates. They raid towns, usually backwaters, but, with the Slayer seemingly gone, they're thinking about making the Hellmouth their new home.

Cruelty To Animals: A fawn cops it in the neck as part of Willow's resurrection ritual.

Quote/Unquote: Xander: 'Who made you the boss of the group?' Anya: 'You did.' Tara: 'You said Willow should be boss.' Anya: 'You said, "Let's vote," and it was unanimous . . .' Tara: 'Then you made her this little plaque that said *Boss of Us*. You put sparkles on it . . .'

Notes: 'We need the world, and the underworld, to believe that Buffy is alive and well.' *Buffy*, as a series and a concept walks a thin line between doomed magnificence and cheeky observational comedy. Put simply, you never get quite what you expect. We know change is in the air, but this episode has one basic agenda: to reassure viewers, along with the population of Sunnydale (human *and* supernatural), that nothing has changed. New network, same show. But, of course, something *has* changed. Buffy's dead for a start. That's where we begin. For a long time, it's where we stay. So we get some lovely comedy sequences with the Buffybot and a bit of Bambi-murdering and snake-regurgitating to appeal to any passing WWF fans. It was to the relief of this author, therefore, that the production managed to do all this (including retelling the backstory for any first-time viewers) without too much repetition, hesitation or deviation. Best season opener since 13, 'When She Was Bad'.

Giles intends to return to England. He's leaving the Magic Box in Anya's capable hands and intends to be a silent partner. He isn't, however, going anywhere near fast enough for an impatient Anya who wants the shop *now*. Hank Summers has seemingly found out about the death of his wife (see 95, 'Forever') and has been in, at least occasional, telephone contact with Dawn (if not Buffy). Xander still hasn't told his friends about his and Anya's engagement (see 100, 'The Gift'; 106, 'All the Way'). Mr Davis and Ms Lefcourt are two of Dawn's teachers. When Anya was a demon (see 43, 'The Wish') she once punished someone by making them check spreadsheets for eternity. Zombies don't eat brains, according to Anya, unless instructed to by their Zombie masters. When Anya is nervous she says money helps to calm her. Willow mentions Dawn's unsuccessful attempts to resurrect her mother in

95, 'Forever'. Dawn notes that she is no longer the Key (see **83**, 'No Place Like Home') or, if she is, she doesn't open anything since the death of Glory. Xander owns a surfboard. (One popular fan myth is that it was actually the one presented to Sarah Michelle Gellar for Outstanding Lifetime Achievement at the *Teen Choice Awards* in August 2001. However, the July recording date for 'Bargaining' would seem to rule this out.) As previously mentioned in **47**, 'The Zeppo', the alignment of stars and/or planets seems to be of vital significance to resurrection rituals (Tara mentions that Mercury is in retrograde).

Soundtrack: 'Permanence' by Static X can be heard in the demon biker bar.

Critique: 'Unlike *Law & Order*, you never know what's going to happen on *Buffy*,' notes Amy Elz. 'Will Buffy be attacked by her city's mayor who's now a giant snake? Will she be forced to kill her boyfriend to protect the world? Will she suddenly burst into song? Who knows! That is what makes it great.'

'Like *The X-Files* before it, *Buffy* deftly blends action and science fiction with astute writing and surprisingly impressive acting into a unique and fulfilling drama,' noted *Variety*'s Laura Fries. 'While other shows have utilised the sci-fi angle as a gimmick to revive characters, Whedon isn't one to compromise a story arc in order to please fans.'

Did You Know?: When Tara gives Giles the rubber finger monster as a parting gift, she wiggles it on her finger while saying, 'Grrr Arrrgh,' like the vampire in the Mutant Enemy logo at the end of each episode.

Ratings: The two-hour *Buffy* season six premiere was a smash hit with viewers, scoring the second highest ratings in the show's history. UPN were doubtless relieved that the massive cost of snatching the Slayer from the WB seemed to have paid off, as 7.7 million viewers tuned in. In typical mediaspeak, UPN announced that the episodes 'earned the network's best Tuesday ratings ever across all key demographics'. A delighted Joss Whedon told reporters that the figures had put 'a little more bounce in our step today, which is a good thing since we're shooting a musical episode'. He added, 'I don't usually look at ratings, [but] I'm pretty damn thrilled.'

Marti Noxon's Comments: Concerning Tara and Willow, Marti told *DreamWatch*: 'My mom is gay, she came out when I was thirteen. For the latter part of my childhood I was raised by two women so, definitely, some of the stuff that I have written about their relationship has been informed by that. I'd say the only thing that really affected the storyline is something my mother told me: that being gay is really just about loving somebody. It's much less about the sex of that person.'

Joss Whedon's Comments: 'It's not a question of topping ourselves,' Joss told *TV Guide*. 'That's why in season four we did the finale as a dream show, because we'd *done* a giant battle the year before, and we knew that we weren't going to top that.' The move to UPN from the WB allowed Joss a little more freedom, at least when it came to the Willow/Tara relationship. 'I think UPN will probably be a simpler process, because [the first kiss] already happened. They basically said if something reads wrong, they'll let us know.'

102
Bargaining, Part 2

US Transmission Date: 2 Oct 2001
UK Transmission Date: 10 Jan 2002

Writer: David Fury
Director: David Grossman
Cast: Franc Ross (Razor), Geoff Meed (Mag), Mike Grief (Klyed)

Buffy's resurrection goes unnoticed as Razor's gang create havoc in Sunnydale. Confused and disoriented, Buffy wanders through the carnage and eventually runs into the Scoobies, who realise that she had to dig her way from her own grave. When the demons arrive for a final fight, Buffy's Slayer sensibilities kick-in and she defeats them. Dawn eventually finds Buffy at Glory's tower where Buffy, seemingly, wants to jump to her death again.

Denial, Thy Name is Willow: While nobody comes out of this story without having been through quite a bit of soul-searching, it's especially tough on Willow. Weakened by the tests that the Osiris spell put her through, Willow thinks she has blown her only chance of bringing Buffy back from, as she believes, Hell. When she and the others find Buffy alive, she is overjoyed if a little too anxious in making nervous excuses for Buffy's terrified, non-vocal response to them. Anya asks, 'What's wrong with her?' Willow's snappy reply, 'Nothing', is just a touch too quick for comfort.

References: There's a huge conceptual and visual debt to Edgar Allen Poe's *The Premature Burial* (specifically Roger Corman's 1962 movie adaptation). Also, *Peter Pan* ('how long have you known your girlfriend was Tinkerbell?'), the North American Air Defense based at Cheyenne Mountain in Colorado, Sam Peckinpah's *The Wild Bunch* (see **2**, 'The Harvest'; **24**, 'Bad Eggs'), electrical retailers Radio Shack and *Little Red Riding Hood* ('the better to cut you down to size, grandma'). Tara paraphrases Bob Dylan's 'If You Gotta Go, Go Now'.

Awesome!: A wild-eyed Buffy awakening in her coffin, realising she has been buried alive and, subsequently, bursting to the surface. Spike and Dawn on the motorbike. Anya, Willow and Tara's furious attack on Razor when he threatens Xander.

Valley-Speak: Xander: 'This is really starting to grate my cheese.'

Naming All the Stars: Xander tries to navigate by following the North Star. Only what he's actually following turns out to be either an aeroplane or a blimp.

Sex and Drugs and Rock'n'Roll: Razor tells the cornered Scooby Gang that his demons intend to enjoy themselves for a few hours. They might even live through it, he notes, except that some of his boys have certain anatomical incompatibilities that tend to tear up little girls. Note that one of Razor's gang appears to be a girl-demon. One shudders to imagine, therefore, what they have planned for Xander.

Logic, Let Me Introduce You to This Window: Spike complains about the lack of serious weaponry in the Summers household. Wasn't the big trunk he's looking in previously full of weapons (and as recently as **100**, 'The Gift', too)? When did the Scoobies get rid of them? And, why? Buffy's hair, post-exhumation, is remarkably clean for someone who has just dug through six feet of impacted dirt. The fact that it has also become darker since her death, however, *is* an accurate *post-mortem* effect. Dawn appears to follow Buffy into the alley from the same direction that Buffy herself came. So Dawn should have also run past, or been very close to, Willow, Tara, Anya and Xander. Dawn deduces that Buffy has returned from her grave on the strength of some very cryptic and irrational things that the, clearly on-it's-last-legs,

Buffybot tells her concerning 'the Other Buffy'. But she's a smart kid so we can mark that one down as a combination of wishful thinking and a lucky guess. How could the Scoobies be so stupid as not to realise that the resurrection spell would have revived Buffy in her coffin? Where did they think it was going to revive her? Given the levels of Willow's and, to an extent Xander's, guilt and desperation to have their friend back, that's perhaps understandable, but Tara, at least, should have realised.

Quote/Unquote: Xander: 'There's something you don't see every day. Unless you're us.'

Razor: 'I better back off or you might pull a rabbit out of a hat.'
Anya, to Willow and Tara: 'Don't do *that*.'

Buffy: 'Is this Hell?'

Notes: 'We can handle a vampire or two, sure, but we've got a cavalcade of demons here.' The second half of the story takes a dismissive look at the new roads that the first episode offered and, in the midst of their construction, resurrects Buffy and throws her headfirst into an abject nightmare. Not the plot about biker demons – that's *tame*, everyday Sunnydale stuff, and she defeats them with barely a noncommittal dismissive grunt. The nightmare here is that life is actually *worse* than death (see **103**, 'After Life'). This, then, is *Buffy* elegantly reaffirming its ultimate agenda. She's back and, despite some cosmetic changes, she's still beautiful.

Xander bemoans his lack of male friends (something he mentioned, specifically relating to Oz's departure, in **93**, 'I Was Made to Love You'). He does, however, get on well with a guy at work called Tito (see **104**, 'Flooded').

Critique: 'Overall *Buffy* has not been affected by the move to the UPN. It's the same smart, clever and thoroughly entertaining series it has always been,' noted *Cinescape*. 'The show is always reinventing itself, offing characters and bringing in new blood . . . If anything, the series is likely to finally break into the mainstream which has so far eluded the cult show when it received critical and fan accolades for the past five years. *Buffy* lives and let's hope for a long time to come.'

However, had the inevitable *Buffy*-backlash begun? Certainly, some mainstream US media reviewers were distinctly lukewarm in their comments: 'I like the hero-quest mythology in her resurrection a lot more than I do Sarah Michelle Gellar's performance as the born-again Buffy,' wrote David Zuarwik in the *Baltimore Sun*.

'Tonight's two-hour premiere doesn't meet the normally high standards for the show, seeming oddly flat, unmoving and mostly unfunny.' 'Not special at all,' added Tim Goodman, while Alan Sepinwall, in the *New Jersey Star Ledger*, felt the episode 'definitely falls into the "overwrought" category [and was] not pleasant to sit through'.

Did You Know?: The Willow Rosenberg–Bambi Murderer sequence in the first episode, was originally much longer and was edited prior to transmission. Needless to say the broadcast version suffered even further cuts in many overseas markets – notably in Britain – along with the snake-regurgitating sequence and Buffy waking up in her coffin in Part 2. 'Some trims were made to the episode but these were kept to a minimum to make sure the scenes flowed and the essence and integrity of the storyline were maintained,' a Sky One spokeswoman told the *Media Guardian*. 'I believe the first episode was darker and sexier than usual for *Buffy*,' she added. The spokeswoman noted that the rest of the series did not include such adult storylines and would, therefore, not require cutting. It was somewhat surprising, therefore, to discover several cuts were also made to the following episode, **103**, 'After Life'. Fans were eventually given a chance to see these episodes uncut in a late-night repeat run on Sky One.

Cast and Crew Comments: In *TV Guide*, Michelle Trachtenberg revealed that Joss Whedon had discussed two possible spin-off avenues with her: 'I've been asked if a spin-off or a continuation [of the show] would be of interest to me and pretty much it is. I love my character. And the people I work with every day would be wonderful to work with for a while longer.' Michelle was a fan of *Buffy* even before she joined the cast, due to her friendship with her former *All My Children* co-star Sarah Michelle Gellar. 'I began watching because of Sarah,' she told *BBC Online*. 'I always tried to think about ways for me to guest star on the show.' She even visited Sarah on the set some months before casting calls were made for the role of Dawn. 'I love finding little references in the script to past episodes because, as a fan, I know what they're talking about.'

'This isn't a show just for teenagers or just adults,' Sarah Michelle Gellar told *The Buzz*, 'it's for everyone.'

Joss Whedon's Comments: 'If Xander said "Dy-no-mite!" every time he killed a vampire, I'd tear my face off after about six episodes,' Joss told *Maxim* when asked why none of the *Buffy* characters had a catchphrase. Joss also touched on the real-life consequences of increased promiscuity on the show. 'Vampires can't get diseases or make babies, so they're covered. We laid that in so Buffy could have sex with Angel without having to include the inevitable condom-shot.' Asked if he would ever watch an adult film à la the *Friends* spoof *Bouffet, the Vampire Layer*, Joss added 'there probably *is* a porno out there with that name, but I don't watch pornography. I just write it!'

103
After Life

US Transmission Date: 9 Oct 2001
UK Transmission Date: 17 Jan 2002

Writer: Jane Espenson
Director: David Solomon
Cast: Lisa Hoyle (Demon)

The repercussions of the resurrection spell have the Scoobies battling with a malevolent spirit created as a consequence of their actions. Buffy, meanwhile, realises that she was happier in the afterlife but cannot bring herself to tell her friends what they have done. She finds the only sympathetic ear available in Spike.

Dreaming (As Blondie Once Said) is Free: In one of the most revealing moments of the series, Spike tells Buffy that he saved her from dying (see **100**, 'The Gift'). Not when it *counted*, of course. But every night in his dreams. 'I'd do something different. Faster or more clever. Dozens of times, lots of different ways.'

A Little Learning is a Dangerous Thing: Anya describes the demon that possesses various members of the Scooby Gang as a hitchhiker, saying that this is a standard way to travel between alternate dimensions. It subsequently transpires that the reason for the manifestation is thaumogenesis, a by-product from the spell cast to resurrect Buffy.

Dawn mentions five species of demons which move transdimensionally: Skaggmore, Trellbane, Skitterers, Large and Small Bone-Eaters.

Mom's Apple Pie: By the end of the episode Buffy has assumed Joyce's former role within the Summers household and has made Dawn's school lunch.

Denial, Thy Name is Buffy: Pointedly, Buffy not only refuses to discuss where she has returned from, but also spends the episode avoiding thanking her friends for their gift of life. Of course, we subsequently learn that she's got a good reason to be so ungrateful.

The Conspiracy Starts at Home Time: Spike is outraged that, having worked with the Scoobies all summer, and saving all of their lives countless times, he was kept out of the loop regarding Buffy's resurrection. He believes the reason for this was that Willow knew there was a chance Buffy would come back wrong and that Willow would be faced with destroying the resulting abomination. 'She knew I wouldn't let her. That's why she shut me out,' Spike says. Although Xander is dismissive, blaming Spike's reaction on his unrequited love for Buffy, he later questions Tara about whether she or Willow knew there were likely to be consequences from the resurrection spell.

Dig Your Own Hole: Spike immediately recognises the injuries that Buffy's hands have suffered as being consistent with someone smashing their way out of a coffin.

It's a Designer Label!: Lots of nice stuff here: Willow's tropical pink nightshirt and fluffy red sleeveless top, Anya's red pyjamas and Tara's tie-dyed shirt.

References: Xander's 'I've done a lot of fleeing through these mean streets' is a probable allusion to Martin Scorsese's *Mean Streets* although that title itself was part of a quotation from Raymond Chandler's *The Simple Art of Murder*. Also, *Spider-Man* ('my senses are honed for danger'), *Batman* ('holy *crap*!'), *Poltergeist*, *Scooby-Doo, Where Are You?* ('makin' with the big-skeedaddle'), allusions to *I Know What You Did Last Summer* and *Super Friends* (see **51**, 'Enemies').

Bitch!: The thaumogenesis demon attacks Willow and Tara in the form of Buffy: 'Your hands smell of death. Filthy little bitches, rattling the bones. Did you cut a throat? Did you pat its head?' (a reference, seemingly, to Willow's slaughter of the fawn in **101**, 'Bargaining' Part 1).

Dawn tells Xander to drive fast. He protests that he can't. Dawn replies that she could drive faster and she can't drive.

Awesome!: Spike's angry confrontation with Xander. Buffy watching as the faces of her friends on photographs become decayed, skeletal corpses. The shocking moment when Anya is taken over by the demon. Dawn's anguish that the others are considering undoing the spell and sending Buffy back.

Surprise!: The agonisingly sad final scene, and the revelation, to Spike and the audience, that, far from being stuck in Hell, Buffy was actually in paradise (or something conceptually similar).

Don't Give Up The Day Job: Production Designer Carey Meyer's CV includes *Mr Write*, *Payback* and *The Doors*. Lisa Hoyle's stunts can be seen in movies such as *Austin Powers: The Spy Who Shagged Me*, *Go*, *Pearl Harbour* and *Charlie's Angels*.

Logic, Let Me Introduce You to This Window: Spike appears to have been waiting in the alley for some considerable time at the end of the episode as it's bright and sunny just a few meters away in both directions. Willow says she contacted Giles in London to tell him about Buffy's resurrection. But Giles only caught the plane *that* afternoon (see **101**, 'Bargaining' Part 1). As it's now, seemingly, the early hours of the next morning, nowhere near enough time would have passed for him to have arrived in England (it's an 11-hour flight from Los Angeles to Heathrow).

What A Shame They Dropped . . .: From the shooting script, Anya: 'Why are you having us skulk around and meet in the backyard like conspiracy squirrels? Sitting on this arm is making my buttocks hurt.'

I Just *Love* Your Accent: Willow tells Tara that when she spoke to Giles on the phone he was glad to hear that Buffy was alive, but also weirded out. She believes that she actually heard him cleaning his glasses.

Motors: Spike is still riding the motorbike he acquired in the last episode.

Quote/Unquote: Spike: 'The thing about magic, there's always consequences.'

Anya: 'Remember that bookstore? They became one of those books-and-coffee places. Now they're just coffee. It's like evolution only without the *getting-better* part.'

Notes: 'Everything here is hard and bright and violent . . . This is Hell.' If there is one certainty in life, besides death and the rent man, it's that Jane Espenson's scripts can cheer up even a professional misanthrope with a stylish humour that renders other great writers anaemic in comparison. 'After Life' is among Espenson's most challenging work and that's no surprise. That there's hardly a joke in it worthy of the name, however, is. This was *Buffy*'s first hesitant step towards establishing where it intended to go this season. A dark and troubled story – at times *achingly* sad (particularly the ending) – about how friendship can sometimes be blind. (There are early hints that Willow is drifting too deeply into the belief that magic is a cure-all.) Forget **94**, 'The Body', forget **95**, 'Forever'; 'After Life' is, easily, the least life-affirming, least celebratory episode of *Buffy* yet. And therein lies its true beauty.

Willow alludes to the passage of time being different in a Hell dimension to reality (see **35**, 'Anne'; **38**, 'Beauty and the Beasts'). Xander mentions Spike's obsession with Buffy (see **92**, 'Crush'; **96**, 'Intervention'; **100**, 'The Gift').

Critique: Richard Matthews in *The Daily Telegraph* describes *Buffy* as: 'Superb. Great writing, great acting and a sense of invention that never patronises its audience, Joss Whedon re-modelled the teen heroine as a kick-ass vampire hunter and resuscitated the horror genre. Actually, to dismiss it as horror is to do an injustice. Taking a leaf out of *Star Trek*'s book, *Buffy* uses its fantastical premise to explore emotional and psychological home truths. If you doubt its prescience, just click to the episode that prefigured the Columbine massacre and you'll see the light.'

Did You Know?: Before meeting fiancé Freddie Prinze Jr, Sarah Michelle Gellar made it a policy not to date actors, according to the *teenhollywood.com* website. She always avoided relationships within showbiz, but was forced to drop her philosophy when she met Prinze. 'With Freddie it's been difficult in the sense that I've never really had a public relationship,' notes Sarah. 'How much do you talk about it? If you say nothing, it makes them thirst for more. But you can't complain, "I have no privacy." When you take on this job, it's something you're aware of.'

You Sexy Thing: She may have once been voted the most gorgeous girl in the world, but don't tell Sarah Michelle Gellar that she's sexy. Sarah would prefer to be famous for being clever. 'Being sexy is being confident,' she told *Infobeat*. 'It's important to know you don't have silicone breasts falling out and a thigh-high skirt. Sometimes you meet people and they think, "Another cute little blonde actress." That's not who I am.'

Cast and Crew Comments: *Starburst* asked James Marsters whether there is a way in which *Buffy* could tackle something like the 11 September tragedy within its drama. 'They certainly tackled the whole Collumbine [sic] Massacre head-on,' he noted. 'Although it must be said that was more about accidental timing than [the writers] wanting to be topical.'

When he appeared on *Richard and Judy* in Britain, James was asked about his relationship with his fans: 'I enjoy meeting them,' he said. 'I think fans of *Buffy* tend to be pretty sophisticated. The writing on the show demands that you are hip to "get it". Irony is heavily used so, in general, the fans are pretty interesting to talk to. Actually, they're freaks and I'm a freak.' So, Richard Madeley asked, did James get asked really detailed questions about what happens in the show? 'No,' replied Marsters, deadpan. 'They usually just grab my bum!'

Jane Espenson's Comments: In several interviews, Jane has noted that she particularly enjoys writing for the character of Anya, whom she regards as something of an alter ego for herself. Emma Caulfield's reaction to that? 'I'm very flattered,' she told *BBC Online*. 'I love Jane, I love her episodes and I have such a good time playing the character. I'm a lucky girl.'

In an online interview, Jane agreed that 'After Life' was a significant departure from her usual style: 'I don't remember how the assigning happened. I normally write comedy. I remember Joss saying, you don't have to do this one. I thought I'd give it a try and I had a wonderful time writing it. It's interesting finding other ways to be entertaining.' One question that Jane always gets asked is to name her favourite episode: 'I always say **40**, "Band Candy",' she told Rob Francis. 'Because it was my first. However, I'm not sure if that's true anymore. I really like **73**, "Superstar".'

Joss Whedon's Comments: Had Joss really pulled back from the day-to-day running of *Buffy* and *Angel* as contemporary fan rumours suggested? 'Not enough to suit my wife,' he told *Cult Times*. 'The honest answer is yes-and-no. I keep to my own schedule now. I don't have to be here every second of the day-to-day shooting . . . but I still have a great love for this show that I can't cure myself of.'

104
Flooded

US Transmission Date: 16 Oct 2001
UK Transmission Date: 24 Jan 2002

Writers: Douglas Petrie, Jane Espenson
Director: Douglas Petrie
Cast: Todd Stashwick (M'Fashnik Demon), Michael Merton (Mr Savitsky),
John Jabaley (Tito), Brian Kolb (Bank Gurad)

Buffy finds herself having to contend with the financial and physical mundanities of running a household, such as burst pipes and home-improvement loans. She seeks the advice of a returned Giles, who also expresses his concern over Willow's action in bringing Buffy back from the grave. To add to Buffy's problems, she has become the object of mischief for a *troika* of bored, nerdish would-be sorcerers.

Dreaming (As Blondie Once Said) is Free: Buffy tells Giles that she hasn't had trouble sleeping since her resurrection. 'Except, you know, for the dreams.'

Authority Sucks!: An officious bank officer refuses to give Buffy a loan even after she saves his life from an enraged M'Fashnik demon.

Pretty Green: Money is definitely becoming an issue, Willow tells Buffy. Joyce had life insurance which should have left Buffy and Dawn covered, but hospital bills sucked up most this. As the Loan Officer confirms, the only collateral Buffy has is her house, which has been losing equity over the years. For some reason, Sunnydale property values have never been competitive (that'll probably be something to do with the mortality rate).

Mom's Apple Pie: Buffy makes a complete mess of preparing a temporary bed for Giles on the couch, apologising that her mother always did stuff like that. Joyce dealt with this sort of thing every day, Giles tells Buffy after the living room is trashed during her fight with the M'Fashnik. Joyce took one crisis at a time, without the aid of superpowers, and got through them all. So, Giles believes, can Buffy.

Denial, Thy Name is Willow: Buffy hasn't displayed a range of human emotions since she returned, Willow notes, which is why

Willow is so pleased when Buffy briefly gets angry over money issues. The subtext of Willow's confusion (and, even, a pointed annoyance) that Buffy isn't more grateful to Willow for bringing her back from the dead (see also Willow's rather petty conversation with Tara in **103**, 'After Life') spills over into her confrontation with Giles. He clearly suspects that Buffy's return from wherever she was (they still know nothing, he perceptively notes) has damaged her in some way. But this is arrogantly dismissed by Willow, who seems more concerned that Giles should be impressed by her magical prowess than with her friend's welfare. As Giles notes, 'you're a very stupid girl'.

The Conspiracy Starts at Home Time: The M'Fashnik comes from a line of mercenary demons, known to perform acts of mayhem and slaughter for the highest bidder. The *troika* have hired it to create chaos while they rob the bank.

Work is a Four-Letter Word: Xander spends four hours trying to piece Buffy's smashed coffee table together after the fight with the demon, before finally giving up.

It's a Designer Label!: Buffy's sexy grey top, Anya's cute summery dress with roses.

References: An allusion to Genesis 7:15 ('we should start gathering up two of every animal'), *Teletubbies* ('Buffy go bye-bye'), Gloria Gaynor's 'I Will Survive' ('and so you're back . . .'). Anya, Dawn and Xander have a petty (though highly amusing) argument about Spider-Man's *modus operendi* ('Action is *his* reward'). Willow alludes to *The Blair Witch Project*.

Geek-Speak: A whiteboard lists the *troika*'s TO DO list. CONTROL THE WEATHER, MINIATURIZE FORT KNOX, CONJURE FAKE ID'S, SHRINK RAY, GIRLS, GIRLS, and THE GORILLA THING (dialogue suggests this means training gorillas to be their slaves). Jonathan also mentions a plan to create workable jet-packs (see **120**, 'Villains') and adds HYPNOTIZE BUFFY at the end (see **105**, 'Life Serial'). Also, *The Wizard of Oz* (Andrew training winged-monkeys to attack the school play, which seems to have been a version of *Romeo and Juliet* judging by Jonathan's comments), *The Simpsons* and the *Austin Powers* movies (the *troika*'s Super Villain laugh being a hilarious cross between Dr Evil and Monty Burns), *Star Trek* (Jonathan and Andrew voting using the Vulcan hand-gesture) and *The Next Generation* ('make it so'), the Beatles' ('for those long, lonely nights after a hard day's slaughter'), *Happy Days* ('Exactamundo') and *Star Wars* ('the force can sometimes have great power on the weak-minded'). Andrew is upset because Warren won't build him a robot replica of *Sleepy Hollow* actress Christina Ricci (however, see **119**, 'Seeing Red', concerning Andrew's sexuality).

With their ill-gotten gains from the bank robbery, Warren, Jonathan and Andrew have kitted-out their lair with, among other things, a periscope from a Russian submarine, a flame-thrower, numerous action figures and a virtual-reality headset. Their decoration ideas seem to have been taken largely from various super-villain pads in *Batman* and *The Avengers*.

Bitch!: Willow is relieved that Buffy is, at last, showing some emotion. In an, unsuccessful, attempt to provoke another angry response from Buffy, Willow alleges that last semester she slept with Riley. 'What the hell are you doing?' asks Buffy. 'Pissing you off,' replies Willow, to which Buffy responds: 'Yes. True. Why?' When Anya suggests that Buffy charge for slaying vampires Buffy replies: 'That's an idea . . . *you* might have.'

Awesome!: The pre-title sequence in the basement with the burst water pipe. Buffy's fight with the demon in the bank. Giles, Xander and Dawn's discussions on the pronunciation of 'M'Fashnik'. The flashback to the *troika*'s first meeting. Giles's confrontation with Willow. The pissed-off look on Buffy's face after drowning the demon in the basement when Spike casually asks if she was aware the place was flooded.

Surprise!: The revelation that the evil masterminds behind the bank robbery are . . . wait for it, Warren, Jonathan and some other guy we've never seen before.

'You May Remember Me From Such Films and TV Series As . . .': Todd Stashwick appeared in *Angel*, *Law & Order*, *Whacked*, *Dark Angel* and *Lucid Day in Hell*. John Jabaley was location manager on *LA Heat*, *Avalanche* and *The Chaos Factor*. Michael Merton appeared in *Felicity* and *General Hospital*. He's also a scriptwriter on animated series such as *X-Men: Evolution* and *Buzz Lightyear of Star Command*.

Don't Give Up The Day Job: Director of Photography Raymond Stella's CV includes such movies as *What Women Want*, *Blade*, *Apollo 13*, *Braveheart*, *Schindler's List*, *Indiana Jones and the Last*

Crusade, *Jurassic Park*, *The Thing*, *Escape from New York* and *Jaws of Satan*. Editor Lisa Lassak previously worked on *Killers* and *Just Add Love*.

Valley-Speak: Warren, after Andrew's little speech about wormholes: 'Dude. Don't be a geek.'
  Jonathan: 'You guys suck.'

Cigarettes & Alcohol: 'You do research now?' Buffy asks Dawn in the Magic Box. 'You want a . . . pack of cigarettes to go with that?'

Logic, Let Me Introduce You to This Window: When Giles wears a short-sleeved shirt, his Eyghon tattoo is missing (previously seen in **20**, 'The Dark Age'; **40**, 'Band Candy' and **70**, 'Goodbye Iowa'). Shouldn't Tara and Willow help Buffy out with the household finances since they live in the house too? Don't they pay rent or contribute to the food bill? Pfft, sponging students. As Buffy says, rather bitterly, when the phone rings: 'Who'd be calling? Everyone I know *lives* here.' Why does Warren just happen to have Buffy's name, address and phone number on a piece of paper in his back pocket to give to the demon on demand? There had been no forewarning prior to the M'Fashnik turning up that the Slayer would, in any way, be involved in their shenanigans. When the M'Fashnik smashes in the door of Buffy's house, Dawn and Giles are standing next to each other some distance away from it, yet Dawn is dramatically thrown to the floor in a flurry of splinters while Giles remains standing.

I Just *Love* Your Accent: In his few days back in England, Giles met with the Watcher's Council. He keeps a flat in Bath, saw a few old friends and almost made a new one. This, he believes, is statistically impossible for a man his age. He describes Buffy's childhood pillows as whimsical.

Giles's Cranial Trauma: 'Now I know I'm back in America,' notes Rupert, 'I've been knocked unconscious.' He's referring to the numerous occasions in the past in which he ends up getting hit on the head with a blunt instrument (too many to list but watch more than a couple of episodes and you'll find one).

Quote/Unquote: Giles: 'The magics you channelled are ferocious and primal . . . You are lucky to be alive, you rank, arrogant amateur.' Willow: 'You're right . . . I'm very powerful. And maybe it's not such a good idea for you to *piss me off*.'

Notes: 'Aside from the moral issues, and the mess, we can get in trouble for murder.' After three episodes of reformatting, at last, the *real Buffy*. 'Flooded', a razor-sharp tale of wishful thinking, drags the series back to the past. There are three elements of plot: Buffy's newly acquired financial worries, the return of Giles and its effect upon the group dynamic and the arrival of the season's first Big Bad, a *troika* of fanboy evildoers. Jonathan, Warren and Andrew are *fabulous*, a cunning mixture of the incompetence of Dr Evil and the sarcastic reference-dropping of *The Simpsons*' Comic Store Guy. Fans, who either didn't recognise a gentle bit of fun being poked in their direction, or who *did* and got the joke, quickly grew to *love* them. Doug and Jane neatly balance all of the elements necessary for a great *Buffy* episode, although the final scene seemed a shade purfunctory.

When Giles left he signed papers placing the Magic Box in Anya's complete control. Her first, hysterical, words to him on his return are: 'We are so glad to see you . . . *You can't have the store back.*' The *troika*'s headquarters are in the basement of Warren's mom's house (last seen, briefly, in **96**, 'Intervention'). Andrew is the younger brother of Tucker Wells, the insane ex-student who released hellhounds on Buffy's prom night (see **54**, 'The Prom'). Jonathan remembers that he was at that event (he presented Buffy with her Class Protector award) and Warren, seemingly, was too (he sneeringly alludes to the fact that he graduated while Andrew, possibly, didn't). 'I had nothing to do with the devildogs. I trained flying monkey-demons to attack the school play,' notes Andrew defensively. The others, actually, thought *that* was quite cool. Jonathan, like Andrew, isn't keen on the idea of killing Buffy, reminding the others that she saved his life several times (specifically, **22**, 'What's My Line?' Part 2; **32**, 'Go Fish'; **52**, 'Earshot' and **73**, 'Superstar'). Plus, she's hot. When Buffy sits on the porch with Spike and asks 'why are you always around when I'm miserable?' it's not only a reference to the climax of **103**, 'After Life', but also to a similar sequence in **85**, 'Fool for Love'.

Original UPN broadcasts of this episode included, during one of the advert breaks, a 20-second trailer for **107**, 'Once More, With Feeling' (at this stage still being publicly called *Buffy: The Musical*) which featured Alyson Hannigan in the recording studio adding her voice to the chorus of '(They Got) The Mustard (Out)'. Several similar behind-the-scenes trailers featured over the next few weeks in the lead-up to the episode's premiere.

The Comic: 'Reunion', a one-shot comic book authored by Jane Espenson, told the story of what happened during Buffy and Angel's off-screen meeting between Los Angeles and Sunnydale after this episode (and *Angel*: 'Carpe Noctem'). Or, at least, what Xander, Anya and Dawn *speculate* may have happened during the rendezvous.

Critique: 'As *Buffy* gets ever darker, the comic relief offered by Emma Caulfield's irrepressible demon-turned-human Anya is more welcome than ever,' noted *TV Guide*. '[She's] blunt, literal, selfish and mercenary. Yet the vibrant Caulfield makes Anya tremendously likeable.' Concerning the *troika*, *scifi_ign.com*'s Susan Kuhn noted: 'I love that Espenson and Petrie give them all little geeky flourishes (the Spockian gesture when voting, the snorty laugh) without plunging into over-the-top nerd stereotype. It's nice to see Jonathan getting some decent airtime post-'Superstar' – as long as these wannabe Lone Gunmen are handled with a light touch, they should provide plenty of giggles this season.'

Did You Know?: Nick Brendon nearly gave up acting before landing the role of Xander, according to the *Sydney Morning Herald*. Nick told Keith Austin that, having lost over 20 jobs before becoming an actor and during his early days in the profession, 'I was destined to act.' Despite this, Brendon gave up his acting career once, after becoming sick of Hollywood. 'I was really stressed out and I wasn't having fun. The day I quit acting, a big weight lifted.' Fortunately, sometimes life deals out second chances, and within three months of changing his mind, Nick landed the part of Xander. He also spoke about the stresses of singing on **107**, 'Once More, With Feeling'. 'I started having nightmares, like showing up at school without pants on.' So, if Nick were to gain a superpower in real life, what would it be? 'The ability to touch a book and know everything in it without spending days reading it,' he told Rob Francis. 'It's a knowledge-thing but, basically, I'm just a lazy bastard!'

Cast and Crew Comments: Amber Benson revealed that you stand a better chance of a candlelit dinner for two with her if you work behind – rather than in front of – the camera. 'I tend to date the behind-the-scenes guys,' Amber told *Stuff* magazine. 'I've gone through an editor, a writer and a camera operator. I work so hard, I don't have much time to date.' Amber also admits she isn't one for Hollywood celebrity parties. 'If I ever go to one, I'm in the corner with a non-alcoholic drink. I don't feel comfortable. You know what the most fun is? When you're the only sober person there. You watch these people acting like total asses.'

A clever, articulate and talented young woman, Amber has already taken the first steps in establishing a career for herself outside acting, writing and directing her own movie, *Chance*, and scripting issues of the *Buffy* comic and the animated Internet adventure *The Ghosts of Albion*.

Jane Espenson's Comments: 'The co-writing experiences this year were very different,' Jane told the online *Succubus Club* in May 2002. 'Doug and I tried something we hadn't tried before, I wrote a whole draft, he did his rewrite on it. Then I rewrote him and he rewrote me. It didn't really work, because both of us would throw out all the other person's stuff and write our own version. It was two views of Mount Fuji. Fury and I did it completely differently. I wrote a half and he wrote a half. That worked especially well for **105**, "Life Serial".'

'I feel there's a lot of Buffy that speaks to events that are traumatic or painful,' Jane told another online interview. 'They pulled **52**, "Earshot", because of Columbine. I was glad they'd delayed it because the episode felt weird in that context. But I was also glad they finally aired it, because I felt like it was exactly the thing that people needed to hear. You may feel all alone in your pain in high school like everyone is observing you, but in fact, nobody's paying any attention to you because everyone's in [their own] pain, and wrapped up in their own world. That was really important to say.'

Joss Whedon's Comments: 'I tend to plot the major story points, sometimes in conversation with the writers, [but] usually by myself. At the beginning of every year I figure out the basic steps and who will write that script and when and where so-and-so dies,' Joss told Rob Francis. Does it worry him that, particularly on the Internet, fans take everything he says so seriously? 'Sometimes I do worry that I will say something like "Sarah will die – we will kill off Buffy," and then fans will say, "I heard a rumour." People, lighten up!'

105
Life Serial

US Transmission Date: 23 October 2001
UK Transmission Date: 31 January 2002

Writers: David Fury, Jane Espenson
Director: Nick Marck
Cast: Paul Gutrecht (Tony), Noel Albert Guglielmi (Vince),
Enrique Almeida (Marco), Jonathan Goldstein (Mike),
Winsome Brown (Woman Customer), Christopher May (Male Customer),
David J Miller (Rat-Faced Demon),
Andrew Cooper Wasser (Slime-Covered Demon), Richard Beatty (Small Demon),
Jennifer Shon (Rahcel), Jabari Hearn (Steve), Derrick McMillon (Ron),
Clint Culp (Bartender), Mark Ginter (Horned Demon),
Alice Dinnean Vernon (Mummy Hand), Marcia Ann Burrs (Professor Bellamy)[37]

As Buffy tries to acclimatise to her new life as a surrogate parent, return to college and attempt numerous part-time jobs to make money, she again comes up against the *troika*. They plan to test the Slayer by casting spells that make her experience time distortions, magically appearing and disappearing demons and a time-loop. The Scooby Gang's less-than-sympathetic response means that Buffy turns to Spike. And alcohol.

Dudes and Babes: Anya suggests to Buffy that, when selling things to people, she should do what Anya does and picture herself naked.

Authority Sucks!: Anya, mean-spiritedly, suggests that the shipping charges that Buffy neglected to include in her, extremely stressful, first sale at the Magic Box will be taken out of her salary. Buffy quits in protest.

Pretty Green: Buffy's financial woes continue, with her losing two jobs on the first day. But the gift of a, seemingly, large cheque from Giles will hold off the creditors for a while.

A Little Learning is a Dangerous Thing: In Sociology, Willow and her classmates are studying *The Social Construction of Reality* with their professor, Mike. All of this goes right over Buffy's head and she considers that maybe she should ease back in with some non-taxing classes, like introduction to pies, or advanced walking. Tara is taking an Art Appreciation class. From the book she gives Buffy to look at, they appear to be concentrating on the Renaissance.

---

[37] Uncredited.

Denial, Thy Name is Buffy: Buffy says that her meeting with Angel (see **104**, 'Flooded') was intense but refuses to elaborate.

Denial, Thy Name is Giles: He believes that the time anomalies Buffy suffers may be stress-related.

Denial, Thy Name is Xander: When the demons attack the construction site, Xander is horrified, telling Buffy: 'Not at my job. That's *your* job!'

The Conspiracy Starts at Home Time: In their quest to become the crime lords of Sunnydale, the *troika* know that they must stay one step ahead of Buffy. That's why they intend to throw her some magical tests, seeing which of them can shake her up the most.

Work is a Four-Letter Word: Xander gets Buffy a labouring job on his building site. Since she isn't in a union Xander has to call in a few favours. Her strength is an advantage in overcoming the obvious sexism of the crew, but she's actually *too good* at it. As they get paid by the hour she's told to slow down. The foreman Tony seems, as Xander notes, pig-ignorant, rude and a little hostile (with pretentions of sexual harassment). Ultimately, Andrew's demon attack finishes Buffy's construction career. Xander himself is in charge of supervising the sheet rock hangers on the site.

Buffy then, reluctantly, tries retail, working for Giles and Anya at the Magic Box. With hilarious consequences.

It's a Designer Label!: Some horrorshows here: Willow's orange shirt and Buffy's sparkly boob-tube being major offenders. The *troika* wear some of the geekiest clothes seen thus far (especially Jonathan's hooped-top). Buffy's shopgirl outfit is quite tasteful.

References: *Groundhog Day* (and numerous TV homages to it). Republican presidential candidate Bob Dole. Tara and Willow watch Nickelodeon's *Spongebob Squarepants*, apparently. Also, *Gidget* (see **3**, 'The Witch') and *Jeopardy*. Marco calls Buffy little Britney, the series' first reference to Ms Spears with whom it has been linked in the tabloids on so many occasions.

Geek-Speak: Warren and Jonathan find Andrew spray-painting a huge (conspicuous) mural of the Death Star on the side of their van. (When Jonathan points out that one of the Thermal exhaust ports is in the wrong place, Andrew proudly says he's using the Empire's revised designs from *Return of the Jedi*.) Andrew hopes that Buffy solves the time-loop faster than Data did on that episode of *TNG* where the Enterprise kept blowing up ('Cause and Effect'). Or, Warren adds, faster than Mulder did in that *X-Files* where the bank kept exploding ('Monday'). 'Scully wants me so bad,' Andrew says, hopefully (but, see **Sex and Drugs and Rock'n'Roll**). The pair also allude to the Dead Parrot sketch from *Monty Python's Flying Circus*. While observing Buffy's first hesitant steps in retail, Warren suggests the *troika* check the other channels for free cable porn. When Andrew suggests they're like Dr No, a pointless argument ensues about who was the best James Bond. Warren admires Sean Connery, but Jonathan prefers Roger Moore. Andrew liked Timothy Dalton. Warren's angry rant about the comedy aspects of *Moonraker* being inexcusable (the pigeon doing a double-take etc.), although representative of some of the louder, and more boring, voices in Bond fandom, is *way* off the mark. It's funny, and nowhere near as bad as *A View to a Kill*.

Awesome!: The entire mummy's hand/*Groundhog Day* third act. As funny as *Buffy* has ever got. Most of the *troika* scenes are also hysterical, with the three bickering over which Bond was best, and dropping sci-fi injokes all over the place.

'You May Remember Me From Such Films and TV Series As . . .': James Leary played Kevin in *Los Beltrán*. Richard Beatty appeared in *Thick as Thieves* and wrote *Blindside*. Clint Culp was in *Every Dog Has its Day*. Jonathan Goldstein appeared in *The Auteur Theory* and *Stranger*. Paul Gutrecht wrote and directed *What We Have*, and appeared in *The Girl Disappearing Trick*, *Dragonfly* and *Ally McBeal*. Jennifer Shon was in *NYPD Blue* and *Boston Public*. Mark Ginther played Lord Zedd in *Mighty Morphin Power Rangers: The Movie*, appeared in *Angel*, *P.U.N.K.S* and *Con Air* and was stuntman on movies such as *Hoffa*, *Joe Versus the Volcano* and *Hologram Man*. David Miller's films include *Exposé* and *Deep Down*. Derrick McMillon appeared in *D Minus*. Christopher May was in *The Sky is Falling* and *The Keeper*. Andrew Wasser's CV includes *Grounded for Life* and *Beverley Hills 90210*. Alice Dinnean Vernon was a voice artist on *Aliens in the Family* and appeared as Sherry Netherland in the long-running *Sesame Street*. Noel Guglielmi was in *The Fast and the Furious* and *24*. Marcia Ann Burrs appeared in *Judging Amy* and *7th Heaven*.

Don't Give Up The Day Job: Nick Marck began as an assistant director on *Carny*, *10*, *Battlestar Galactica*, *The Postman Always*

Rings Twice and *Rehearsal for Murder* before directing *The Wonder Years, The X-Files, Dawson's Creek* and *Malcolm in the Middle*.

Valley-Speak: Andrew: 'Wicked cool!'

Cigarettes & Alcohol: Giles drinks a glass of wine as the Scoobies have dinner at the beginning. Totally cheesed-off with the *Groundhog Day*-style time-loop, Buffy goes to Spike's crypt to cadge his whisky. He then takes her to a seedy demon bar. This is the third time we've seen Buffy drunk (see **17**, 'Reptile Boy' and **61**, 'Beer Bad'). There are numerous cases of Bacardi in the back room where Spike plays poker with the demons.

Sex and Drugs and Rock'n'Roll: *Double entendre* overload. Concerning fried chicken, Willow notes that she is a breast girl, before turning to Tara and whispering: 'But, then, you knew that.' Anya tells Buffy about a Magic Box customer who wanted to purchase a sapphire ding-dong (a phallus, presumably). Jonathan asks the *troika* to hold hands when he's performing a spell. 'With each other?' asks a horrified Andrew. 'You know what homophobia really means about you?' asks Warren. How very insightful (see **119**, 'Seeing Red'). And as for Jonathan telling the others to 'Stop touching my magic bone,' well . . .

Logic, Let Me Introduce You to This Window: While undeniably fun, the fast-forward-freakout section is logically insane. From the perspective of those for whom time is travelling at normal speed – i.e. *everybody but Buffy* – she must seem as though she's standing in some kind of a trance. 'Zoned out' as Tara puts it. Doesn't anyone think to call an ambulance, sit her down, or do something other than just ignore her including, at one point, somebody knocking her to the ground and not even stopping to ask if she's all right. This is especially true of Tara who, twice, simply walks off and leaves Buffy staring into space. During the fight with the three monsters at the construction site, Buffy (or rather, Sarah Michelle Gellar's stunt-double) dangles from a horizontal bar and does some gymnastic-style kicking. One of her kicks clearly misses its intended demon-target but he still falls down as though hit. How did Jonathan and co. get a mini-camera into the eye-socket of a skull that's in the private area of the Magic Box. No one except the Scooby Gang is allowed in there, as we've previously seen demonstrated (notably, **84**, 'Family'). Jonathan suggests that *The Living Daylights* (1986), the fifteenth James Bond film, was written for Roger Moore. Not, strictly speaking, true. Richard Maibaum and Michael Wilson's script was certainly started during post-production on *A View to a Kill* (1985), but it wasn't even completed to first draft stage by the time Moore left. Indeed, while most of the writing was going on, the actor they were trying to get to play Bond was Pierce Brosnan, then starring in *Remington Steele*. Ordinarily this point would be far too anoraky to include but, hell, this *is* the *troika* we're talking about.

Cruelty To Animals: At the bar, Spike gets involved in a card game with various demons, including Clem, for which the stake is kittens. 'They're delicious,' notes the green-skinned demon.

Quote/Unquote: Giles: 'Think of the store as a library, it'll help you to concentrate on service . . .' Buffy: 'Yes. And then I'm going to marry Bob Dole and raise penguins in Guam.'

Notes: 'Someone's doing stuff to me. Messing up my life. Except that it was kind of pre-messed already.' If there was ever any doubt in the minds of fans that they, themselves, were being satirised by the *troika* (see **104**, 'Flooded') then this episode hits them over the head with the realisation. The dramatic components of this are, at best, questionable. The comedy potential, however, isn't wasted. You *will* laugh at much of this episode and, if you don't, then you're probably dead. *Groundhog Day*-style plot devices and merriment aside, 'Life Serial' also contains a clever piece of social comment concerning the drabness of working life after the freedom of the teenage years. Buffy tries, unsuccessfully, to fit her unique lifestyle in with the awful realities of earning a weekly wage. She tackles labyrinthine bureaucracy, sexism (from Xander's boorish construction site colleagues) and the falseness of customer service-with-a-smile. A smashing episode, then, which deals with big issues, but finds time for fabulous comedy and only really disappoints in the rather stale final act. Otherwise, lots to laugh at and lots to think about. The series in microcosm.

Buffy mentions that she left college when Joyce became sick (see **97**, 'Tough Love').

Soundtrack: 'Kidnapper Song' by the Masticators and 'Boom Swagger Boom' by Murder City Devils.

Critique: Marcus Ferrell, at *ZENtertainment.com* was 'glad [to see] more humor this week; too much darkness can get you down. Although the antics of the dorks were illogical, they were humorous, and an inventive way of testing someone's skills. No doubt this will be met with much weeping and gnashing of teeth.'

Did You Know?: How much of the geek-stuff did Adam Busch need to learn? 'I had to do a lot of research [on] *Dungeons and Dragons*,' he told Matt Springer. 'The first scene we shot together – me, Danny and Tom – was when we sat around the table playing *Dungeons and Dragons* . . . none of us knew how to play.'

Comedy is the New Horror: David Fury began his career as a New York stage actor, and a stand-up comedian, as well as working as a voice artist on numerous films (most famously providing several of the voices on *Raiders of the Lost Ark*. He graduated on to writing sitcom scripts. 'Joss was open to comedy writers rather than people who worked in one-hour dramas,' he noted.

Jane Espenson's story is a similar one. Jane grew up in Ames, Iowa, where, by her own admission, she was a '*Star Trek*-obsessed nerd' who watched far too much television. At age thirteen she attempted to write an episode of *M*A*S*H* and received an encouraging rejection letter from the producers. She attended college at UC Berkeley, studying linguistics. While there, Jane submitted a script to *Star Trek: The Next Generation*, which led to her winning a slot on the Walt Disney writers' fellowship. Subsequently, Jane worked for several years on sitcoms like *Dinosaurs* and *Ellen* and, as she told Rob Francis, several others that readers probably won't have heard of. 'Then I decided I wanted to make the switch to drama and ended up on *Buffy*.' 'When I got this job the show was already established,' Jane told an Internet interview. 'I didn't come to it intending to make any sort of social comment. I knew that it was a metaphor and that I would be talking about what it feels like to be a teenager. But I didn't quite understand that it would end up being so much about what it means to be human. It's not just about the experiences of being fifteen any more, if it ever was.'

Since *Buffy*'s finale, Jane has moved to another highly regarded WB show, *Gilmore Girls*. Asked by *Ain't It Cool* about her own viewing habits, Jane noted that 'I [still] watch a lot of TV, but I find that recently it's oddball stuff: *Iron Chef* and *Junkyard Wars* and the History Channel (they have this English thing called *Time Team*). Scripted stuff sometimes feels like homework.'

Cast and Crew Comments: 'You can expect that Dawn will be getting a little more rebellious,' Michelle Trachtenberg told *Sci-Fi*

Wire. 'Obviously, she has shown signs of being a kleptomaniac,' she added. 'I know that storyline will reach a certain pinnacle – that Buffy and Dawn will have to deal with [it].'

On the set, however, the mature 16-year-old was still treated like a kid by her elder castmates. 'They're all very nice, but I'm not in on the dirty jokes,' she told *TV Guide*. 'No one cusses around me, either.'

Jane Espenson's Comments: '[There were] four different storylines, each in a separate act,' Jane told the Succubus Club. 'I wrote the last two, Mummy Hand in the Magic Shop and the Kitten Poker with Spike. That was a fun one, I like writing the comedies.'

Joss Whedon's Comments: Joss always had faith that *Buffy* would find a niche. 'When I say I'm not surprised that the show has gotten to 100 episodes, I sound like an ego with legs,' he told *The Los Angeles Times*. 'But *Buffy* makes sense to me, and I believed it would make sense to other people.'

106
All the Way

US Transmission Date: 30 Oct 2001
UK Transmission Date: 7 Feb 2002

Writer: Steven S DeKnight
Director: David Solomon
Cast: John O'Leary (Mr Kaltenbach), Kavan Reece (Justin),
Amber Tamblyn (Janice), Dave Power (Zack), Charles Duckworth (Glenn),
Dawn Worrell (Christy), Emily Kay (Maria), Adam Gordon (Carl),
Sabrina Spear (Girl), Chad Erikson (Guy), Dominic Rambaran (Paramedic #1),
Anthony Sago (Paramedic #2), Lorin Becker (Witch Woman),
Lily Jackson (Witchypoo), Steven Anthony Lawrence (Chunky Kid)

After Xander and Anya finally announce their engagement to their friends, Dawn lies to Buffy and spends Halloween night up to mischief with her friend Janice and two boys. She develops a crush on one, Justin, and receives her first kiss. There are problems, however, when the boys reveal themselves to be vampires. Meanwhile, after Willow and Tara have a fight about Willow's abuse of magic, Willow casts a spell on Tara to make her forget.

Dudes and Babes: Xander lovingly looks at Anya and Dawn dancing and tells Buffy, 'I'm gonna marry that girl.' Buffy is *horrified*: 'What?! She's fifteen and my sister . . . oh.'

Tara and Willow have their first significant argument over Willow's casual abuse of magic (see **104**, 'Flooded'). Why use magic, Tara asks, when you can do something naturally? But this seems too hard a concept for Willow to grasp. Willow assumes, wrongly, that Tara and Giles have been talking about her behind her back and says some very hurtful things (Tara: 'What do you want me to do, just sit back and keep my mouth shut?' Willow: 'That'd be a good start'). Then, she regrets it. At the episode's end, with Tara still upset at her, Willow does something even more questionable, and uses a spell to make Tara forget they have been fighting (see **107**, 'Once More, With Feeling', and **108**, 'Tabula Rasa', for the repercussions).

Authority Sucks!: After Dawn's first fumbling steps in teenage romance Buffy leaves it to Giles to hand out the necessary chastisement. He is, clearly, not happy with Buffy avoiding her quasi-parental responsibility (see **107**, 'Once More, With Feeling').

A Little Learning is a Dangerous Thing: Dawn tells Justin that witches don't, generally, look like traditional depictions with broomsticks and warts. When Justin asks if she has any witch-friends she blurts out that she's read about them in books.

Denial, Thy Name is Giles: Buffy discovers the reason Giles is always cleaning his glasses is so that he doesn't have to see what the Scooby Gang are doing.

Theft is a Five-Letter Word: Dawn admits to Justin that she has been stealing for some time, explaining her taking Anya's earrings in **96**, 'Intervention', and noting that she hasn't paid for lipstick since forever (see **114**, 'Older, and Far Away'). She steals an amulet that she finds lying in the Magic Box, which can be seen again, briefly, in her stash box in **107**, 'Once More, With Feeling'.

It's a Designer Label!: The Halloween costumes are fun, especially Anya's. Check out, in particular, Tara's lovely peach top and the skin-tight silver pants worn by the Bronze waitresses.

Dodgy Subject Matter: Mr Kaltenbach designed toy robots in the late 1950s and got enormous pleasure from the joy they gave to children. However, there are dark hints of a terrible secret in his past when he talks about 'one little mistake . . . they took it all away'. This is, potentially, the series' first oblique reference to child sexual abuse (although **30**, 'Killed By Death', does so through metaphor).

References: The title is a Sammy Cahn/Jimmy Van Heusen song most famously recorded by Frank Sinatra. The lady customer at the Magic Box is dressed as Witchypoo, a character from Sid and Marty Kofft's classic 1970s serial *HR Pufnstuff*. Zach's 'Pumpkins, very dangerous, you go first,' is an allusion to *Raiders of the Lost Ark*. Xander paraphrases *Henry V* ('once more into the breach', see **100**, 'The Gift'). During the Magic Box sale Xander is dressed (unimpressively) as a pirate. Giles refers to him as Ahab, the captain in *Moby Dick*. Anya wears a Farrah Fawcett Majors costume. Willow and Tara see a couple in the Bronze dancing suggestively and dressed as Luke Skywalker and Princess Leia: 'Do they *know* they're brother and sister?' Willow asks. Mr Kaltenbach hums 'Pop Goes the Weasel'. Also *Fantasia* (specifically the Mickey Mouse 'Sorcerers Apprentice' sequence), *Toy Story* (Zack uses Buzz Lightyear's catchphrase 'To infinity and beyond'), *JFK* ('just one little mistake'), *A Shot in the Dark* ('Summers' residence'), *Crimes and Misdemeanors*, Xander alludes to 'Not Waving, But Drowning' (see **65**, 'Something Blue'), *WWF Smackdown*, *Superman*, escapologist Harry Houdini (1874–1926) and Bobby Boris Pickett and the Crypt-Kickers' 'The Monster Mash'.

Bitch!: Buffy, on Spike: 'He was so much easier to talk to when he wanted me dead.'

Observe the expression on Willow's face when Xander announces his engagement. A mixture of bewilderment and hurt. Ooo, no subtext there, I don't think (see **21**, 'What's My Line?' Part 1; **39**, 'Homecoming'; **116**, 'Hell's Bells'; **122**, 'Grave').

Awesome!: Stick Giles in a silly costume and you're always guaranteed a good laugh. Plus, Anya doing the *Dance of Capitalist Superiority*. There's *always* something to be said for that. Also, Giles's fight with the two girl vampires. Best bit of the episode is Buffy asking all the assembled vampires if anybody came to the woods simply to make-out, and two rather embarrassed people raise their hands.

'You May Remember Me From Such Films and TV Series As . . .': John O'Leary's impressive CV includes *All the President's Men*, *Demon Seed*, *Airplane!*, *The Haunted* and *Guardian Angel*. Kavan Reece appeared in *That 70s Show*. Amber Tamblyn played Katie in *Ring* and was in *Rebellious* and *General Hospital*. Dave Power appeared in *Band of Brothers*, *JAG* and *U-571*. Lorin Becker played Jenny in *Mid-Century*. Emily Kay was Melissa in *Undressed* and appeared in *Grace Under Fire*. Adam Gordon was in *Kissing Miranda* and *The X-Files*. Steven Lawrence played Beans in *Even Stevens* and appeared in *Jay and Silent Bob Strike Back* and *Sabrina, the Teenage Witch*. Anthony Sago was in *Night Man*.

Don't Give Up the Day Job: Chad Erikson was a Camera Intern on *High Fidelity* and a Grip on *Placebo Effect*. Editor Marilyn McMahon Adams previously worked on *Dark Skies*, *Streets of Fire* and *Shattered Vows*.

The Drugs Don't Work: Spike likes to stir burba weed into the blood he drinks. This makes it hot and spicy, apparently.

Valley-Speak: Dawn, on Justin: 'He's OK.' Janice: 'OK? Or, like, "Oh my God, I think I'm gonna pee my pants"?'
   Zack: 'Don't make me go *kung-fu* on you, man!'
   Willow: 'Hard to believe such a hot mama-yama came from humble, geek-infested roots?'

Cigarettes & Alcohol: Plenty of booze at the engagement party and, later, at the Bronze.

Classic *Double Entendre*: Xander intends to teach Anya a new game called *Shiver Me Timbers*. 'I'm not really much for the timber,' notes Tara.

Logic, Let Me Introduce You to This Window: Dawn doesn't react when Justin kisses her – surely it should be obvious that he's a corpse? Buffy tells Xander that she was out of commission for three months. However, in **103**, 'After Life', Buffy asks Spike how long she was gone, and he replies 147 days, which is almost five months. How, even with Slayer-strength, can slamming a car door on somebody's head decapitate them? Is Dawn ready to give herself to Justin and become a vampire just before Giles shows up? And, if she is, what changes her mind between this scene and the one a few minutes later when she and Justin are alone and she admits to liking him, before staking him? Is it because he says she's special because she's the Slayer's sister?

I Just *Love* Your Accent: Spike uses the British slang-phrase 'nick', meaning to steal. When Xander and Anya announce their engagement, Giles notes: 'Where I come from, this sort of thing requires much in the way of libation.' Except we don't normally call a night on the razzle *that*. 'God save the queen,' toasts Xander. The Pistols' version, hopefully.

Quote/Unquote: Buffy (outraged): 'Were you *parking*? With a vamp?' Dawn: 'I didn't know he was dead.' Justin: 'Living dead.' Dawn: 'Shut up.'

Spike: 'It's Halloween, you nit! We take the night off. Those are the rules.' Carl: 'Me and mine don't follow no stinking rules. We're rebels.' Spike: 'No, *I'm* a rebel. You're an *idiot*.'

Notes: 'So what do you think? Lunchables? Or should we go all the way and turn 'em?' *Buffy* Halloween episodes traditionally tend towards the lighter end of the dramatic scale. This year's effort, once some hilarious establishing scenes in the Magic Box are done-and-dusted, goes for a more serious approach. Dawn takes centre-stage in a story about teen-romance. Of course, this being Sunnydale, you know automatically that the apparently nice high school boy she's kissing in the woods isn't all he seems. And the *obviousness* of that subplot's execution (and resolution) is why 'All the Way' is the least-apt title imaginable. That the episode doesn't really work is a shame because DeKnight's script has several sparkling moments and a deal of tasty *double entendre*. Sadly, though, the dramatic weight is carried almost entirely by the continuing story arc of Willow's abuse of magic and of Tara's growing concern. 'All the Way' is an episode that, while it's important in the overall theme of season (growing up), neverthe- less sees the series – for one week at least – running on the spot.

When Anya sends Buffy to the Magic Box basement for supplies, Buffy notes: 'Don't blame me if we have this conversation over and over,' a reference to **105**, 'Life Serial'. Buffy talks to Giles about previous Halloween calamities: costumes that take over people's personalities (**18**, 'Halloween') and Irish fear-demons (**60**, 'Fear Itself'). Dawn wanted to get a tattoo while Buffy was dead, but Willow says they wouldn't let her. The book Willow holds while angrily berating the Halloween witch over the perpetuation of stereotypes is called *Everyday Witchcraft*.

Soundtrack: 'Even If (It Is Love)' by Lift, 'How Do You Make Me Feel?' by Opus 1 Music Library, Colin Monster's 'Body Of Binky', 'Living Life' by Box of Music, Strange Radio's 'Make Me A Star', Nikka Costa's 'Everybody Got Their Something' (which Willow, Xander and Anya are dancing to before Giles turns off the radio), 'Around My Smile' by Hope Sandoval and the Warm Inventions and Fonda's 'The Sun Keeps Shining On Me'. Man of the Year perform 'Just As Nice' at the Bronze.

Critique: 'Vampires, in *Buffy*, mutate horribly when they are about to suck blood (for which read, "have sex"),' noted Zoe Williams in the *Guardian*. 'They are aping the bodily aspects of puberty . . . [and] the vampiric lifestyle in *Buffy* is characterised by alienation, loneliness, guilt and self-loathing. Modern *Buffy* critics, therefore, find strong [elements] of Jean-Paul Sartre in the undead . . . Given its associations with the rite of passage into adulthood, vampire congress has long been taken as a metaphor for sex. It pretty much still is.'

Did You Know?: Oz fans hoping for the return of the popular werewolf guitarist were disappointed to learn that a planned appearance by Seth Green in this episode was scuppered at the last minute. *E! Online* reported that while Seth was initially slated to appear in 'All the Way', he had to pull out due to scheduling conflicts.

Cast and Crew Comments: Spike's craving for nicotine may be second only to his thirst for blood, but in reality James Marsters had given up cigarettes. As he told Kate O'Hare, '[I've been] on the patch.' James now resorts to the same trick as *The X-Files*' Cigarette Smoking Man, William B Davis. 'Horrible herbal cigarettes. We smoke Morley's. We're the only two characters on TV that do.'

Head On: When Tony Head appeared on *The Johnny Vaughan Show* in February 2002, he admitted that when he was in the musical *Chess* in London, he was pestered by a stalker: 'Stupidly, when we first got our flat in Battersea, I put my name in the telephone directory. [The Stalker] was on the phone and basically you'd say "Oh for God's sake, Carol, go away" and you'd put the phone down. Half an hour later you'd pick it up and she'd still be there.'

Joss Whedon's Comments: Asked about his writing process on the *Posting Board*, Joss noted, '[It's] about two things: structure and emotion. I'm incredibly strict about working out a tight structure, every piece fitting, so there are not too many surprises in a first draft. But it all stems from emotion. What do we need to feel? What do [the characters] need to feel? With **78**, "Restless", I had to throw structure out the window. It was a poem. Though I knew what it meant and what the dramatic flow was, I literally had to sit there (or lie there – I got my appendix out during that script) and wait for the next thing. It was very liberating for me.'

107
Once More, With Feeling

US Transmission Date: 7 Nov 2001
UK Transmission Date: 14 Feb 2002

Writer: Joss Whedon
Director: Joss Whedon
Original Songs, Music and Lyrics: Joss Whedon
Songs Produced and Arranged: Jess Tobias, Christophe Beck
Choreographer: Adam Shankman
Cast: Hinton Battle (Sweet), David Fury (Mustard Man),
Marti Noxon (Parking Ticket Woman), Daniel Weaver (Handsome Young Man),
Scot Zeller (Henchman), Zachary Woodlee (Demon/Henchman),
Timothy Anderson (Henchman), Alex Estronel (Henchman),
Matt Sims (College Guy #1), Hunter Cochran (College Guy #2)

For some mysterious reason, everyone in Sunnydale is compelled to reveal their innermost feelings through song and dance. While searching for the demon behind this disturbing phenomena, Buffy finally tells the gang the truth about where she was after she died, leaving Willow, in particular, devastated. Meanwhile, Tara discovers Willow's spell to make her forget their argument, and both Giles and Spike come to decisions concerning their future relationships with Buffy.

Dudes and Babes: When a couple of boys check out Tara as she and Willow are walking through the park, and Willow lovingly draws Tara's attention to it, Tara is amused: 'I'm cured. I want the boys!'

A Little Learning is a Dangerous Thing: Dawn notes that her maths homework seemed much more interesting at school when they were singing about it.

Denial, Thy Name is Everyone: The entire episode concerns those secrets that everyone is trying so hard to keep, and failing miserably: Buffy's knowledge of having been torn from paradise and of, subsequently, finding life tough to deal with; Xander and Anya's fears about their impending marriage and their suitability towards each other; Giles's belief that his presence in Sunnydale, and his attempts to play the father, are stopping Buffy from achieving all that she can and giving her an easy option each time a crisis looms; Spike's depth of feeling for Buffy and annoyance that she can't seem to make up her mind whether she wants to kill him or kiss him; and, Tara and Willow's fractured relationship through the seductive power of magic on Willow. Only Dawn manages to keep *her* secret (rampant kleptomania, see **96**, 'Intervention'; **106**, 'All the Way') intact. For the moment at least (see **114**, 'Older, and Far Away').

The Conspiracy Starts at Home Time: Believing that the charm she, allegedly, found in the Magic Box is her own, Sweet tells Dawn, 'I come from the imagination/And I'm here strictly by your invocation.' He intends to take her to his underworld domain as his queen ('You and me wouldn't be very regal,' Dawn sings, horrified. 'I'm fifteen, so this queen-thing's illegal!'). It subsequently turns out that it was Xander who accidentally summoned Sweet by wishing for a happy ending (see **127**, 'Selfless'). Sweet, though tempted, ultimately let's Xander off with the underworld queen-thing.

It's a Designer Label!: They really pushed the budget out on this one: Buffy's leather jacket and stylish-yet-affordable boots, Tara's gorgeous Medieval-style turquoise top with padded sleeves and gypsy dress, Anya's black butterfly dress and red underwear, Xander's silk dressing gown, Willow's big furry coat and Dawn's light-blue sweater.

References: The title is a quotation from Joan Armatrading's 'Love And Affection' (see **57**, 'The Freshman'). The trio of street-sweepers that Giles, Xander and Anya walk past appear to be performing the dance of the Chimney Sweeps from *Mary Poppins*. Spike alludes to the African hymn 'Kumbaya' and the Rolling Stones *Get Your Ya-Ya's Out*. Buffy paraphrases Shakespeare's *As You Like It* ('Life's a show and we all play our part') and I Timothy 6:12 ('fight the fight'). Spike refers to '76 Trombones' from *The Music Man*. Also, visual reference to the title sequences of the James Bond movies (specifically *The Spy Who Loved Me*), Tim Burton's *Batman* (Sweet's Joker-style suit and attitude) and Michael Powell and Emeric Pressburger's ballet masterpiece *The Red Shoes* (Dawn's dance with Sweet's minions), *Pinnochio* ('some day he'll be a real boy'), *Snow White and the*

Seven Dwarfs ('Whistle while you work'), *The Karate Kid*, The Isley Brothers' 'Twist And Shout', *That's Entertainment*, *The Avengers* ('we're needed'), *The Addams Family* ('show-time!'), *Superman* ('Merciful Zeus!'), award-winning journalist David Brinkley, Peruvian mambo singer Yma Sumac and *The Lord of the Dance*. Sweet claims to have bought the Emperor Nero (AD 37–68) his first fiddle (presumably the one he, allegedly, played while Rome burned). Xander's 'Respect the cruller, and tame the doughnut' is a probable reference to an extremely crude Tom Cruise line in *Magnolia* concerning male and female genitalia. 'Going Through the Motions' paraphrases Duke Ellington's 'It Don't Mean A Thing (If It Ain't Got That Swing)'.

Bitch!: Buffy: 'So, Dawn's in trouble. It must be Tuesday.'

Awesome!: The brilliantly silly opening graveyard/'Going Through the Motions' sequence. Anya's hysterical rock-opera Bunnies rant. The initial discovery that it's not just the Scoobies who have the urge to share their feelings through song ('They got/the mustard/ *OUT!!!*'). Tara's love song for Willow by the lake, and particularly the bit where two girls sitting nearby suddenly get up and start dancing. Xander and Anya's amusing retro-pastiche production number. James Marsters giving it the works in 'Rest In Peace'. The moment of horror on the faces of the Scoobies when Buffy tells them it wasn't Hell they brought her back from, but rather paradise. Spike saving Buffy from a fiery end with some harsh truths about living. The showstopping 'Where Do We Go From Here?'

Surprise!: Buffy and Spike's big kiss at the end.

'You May Remember Me From Such Films and TV Series As . . .': Broadway veteran Hinton Battle played Cat in the US version of *Red Dwarf* and the Tin Man in *The Wiz* and appeared in *Quantum Leap* and *These Old Boards*. Timothy Anderson's movies include *Boys and Girls*. Daniel Weaver played Vanilla Ice in *Austin Powers: International Man of Mystery*. Zachary Woodlee was in *Rock Star* and *Not Another Teen Movie*. Scot Zeller appeared in *America's Sweetheart*, *Charmed* and *Gilmore Girls*.

Do any of you really need to know who David Fury and Marti Noxon are? Fury played the pizza guy in *Chance* and the Goat Slayer in *Angel*: 'Reprise', *while* Noxon sang the 'Cordy' theme song on *Angel*: 'Birthday'. Satisfied?

Don't Give Up the Day Job: Jesse Tobias was guitarist with Red Hot Chilli Peppers, Alanis Morrisette and, latterly, Splendid. Adam Shankman was choreographer on *The Flintstones*, *Boogie Nights*, *Scream 2*, *She's All That*, *Inspector Gadget* and *The Wedding Planner* (which he also directed). The episode also saw the welcome return to *Buffy* of its Emmy-winning former composer Christophe Beck whose effortlessly evocative music also graces *Stealing Harvard*, *Wolf Girl*, *Bring It On*, *Bone Daddy*, *Life During Wartime*, and *Slap Her, She's French*.

Valley-Speak: Handsome Young Man: 'How can I repay ...?' Buffy: 'Whatever.'

Cigarettes & Alcohol: Spike has a bottle of red wine that he intends to share with Buffy but which he, instead, throws against the wall of his crypt when his song gets emotional.

Sex and Drugs and Rock'n'Roll: Tara and Willow get all giggly at the Magic Box and, on a very obvious pretext, return home to go to bed. This is, surprisingly, much to Xander's disgust, describing it as get-a-roominess and then becoming embarrassed when he realises that Dawn is sitting beside him. Dawn, herself, thinks Tara and Willow's attraction is romantic. Xander and Buffy chorus, simultaneously, that it's not. Subtext question: borderline homophobia? Or a wish to get more research done into the causes of the singing and dancing? The author leaves it to the reader to decide.

Anya says she's seen some previous examples of underworld child-bride deals, and they never end well. Except, maybe, once.

Logic, Let Me Introduce You to This Window: When Buffy enters the Magic Box she says 'good morning'. Subsequently, Dawn arrives from school. This, presumably, means the Scoobies were researching all day. Didn't Xander have to go to work and Tara and Willow to college? How did Sweet get in the Bronze when it's closed? Maybe he's a breaking-and-entering demon as well as a signing-and-dancing one? Immediately after Tara leaves Dawn alone at the house, Sweet's puppet-faced minions kidnap Dawn. But how did *they* get into, and out of, the house without Tara seeing them? During the dance number featuring Tara, Anya and Buffy, Emma Caulfield ends up about half-a-step behind in the movements. You can actually see Amber Benson glance off-camera as she notices this and, as she and Emma back out of focus, a grin appears on Amber's face. The entire Xander-summoned-Sweet plot-twist seems illogical. Xander gives absolutely no indication prior to the end that he knows why any of this is happening despite his desperation to end it (surely he would have tried to hint at what he may have inadvertently set in motion to his friends, even if he didn't want to implicate himself?). A funeral is, seemingly, taking place *at night* while Spike does his big production number. Well, this is Sunnydale; I guess nothing should surprise us. Wouldn't it be interesting to know what Jonathan, Warren and Andrew were singing about while all of this is going on? Bet it had *something* to do with *Star Trek*.

I Just *Love* Your Accent: Spike tells Giles not to be a stupid git.

Quote/Unquote: Giles: 'That would explain the huge backing orchestra I couldn't see and the synchronised dancing from the room service chaps.' And: 'I was able to examine the body while the police were taking witness arias.'

Anya, on bunnies: 'They're not just cute like everybody supposes/They got them hoppy legs and twitchy little noses . . .'

Buffy: 'I'm just worried this whole session's going to turn into some training montage from an eighties movie.'

Notes: 'All those secrets you've been concealing/Say you're happy now, once more, *with feeling*/Now I've gotta run, see you all in Hell!' If **66**, 'Hush', was a variant on Marshall McLuhan's mantra that when people stop talking, they *start* to communicate, then 'Once More, With Feeling' takes such theoretical McLuhanism to an entirely new level. But even this description doesn't really do this episode justice. When Joss Whedon first envisioned a musical episode of *Buffy*, some fans were loudly horrified. We needn't have worried. From its *Bewitched*-style title sequences and knowing musical-comedy opening scenes to the closing, big-chorus-kiss-and-curtains, this is 50 minutes of quite extraordinary television that displays more wit and imagination and has more things to say about relationships than most series can manage in their entire run. A story about hidden secrets, unspoken truths, stifled laughter behind half-closed doors and of the lengths to which people can go to avoid hearing what they don't want to hear, 'Once More, With Feeling' may well be the best *Buffy* episode yet. It's certainly the strangest. For the most part Whedon adheres to standard musical clichés while cleverly using his actors to their strengths. Tony Head, Amber Benson and James Marsters – all fine singers – carry-off their well-staged set pieces with considerable aplomb. Sarah Michelle Gellar (a novice, apparently) does a good job with her three songs, while the amusing Emma Caulfied/Nick Brendon duet 'I'll Never Tell' is the episode's comedy highlight. Expect something different and you'll get what you want. Expect to be cringingly embarrassed by tone-deaf actors strutting their non-funky stuff, and you may be very pleasantly surprised.

At the end of 'Something To Sing About', Dawn tells Buffy that the hardest thing in this world is to live in it, repeating what Buffy told her in **100**, 'The Gift'. There are numerous continuity references within the songs: Willow's theory that some kid is dreaming and they are stuck inside his wacky Broadway nightmare is a musical summation of **10**, 'Nightmares'. Tara's song is literal – she *is* still under Willow's amnesia spell (**106**, 'All the Way'). Anya notes that Xander's 'Penis got diseases from the Chumash tribe' (**64**, 'Pangs'). It's do or die, sing the Scoobies. 'Hey, I died twice,' replies Buffy, casually (**12**, 'Prophecy Girl'; **100**, 'The Gift'). Giles is staying at a hotel having, presumably, got tired of sleeping on Buffy's couch. He mentions having brought his guitar with him to Sunnydale (see **74**, 'Where the Wild Things Are'). In addition to bunnies, Anya also seems to have a fear of midgets. Xander has a couple of the lava lamps in his apartment, along with the dartboard from his old basement seen in **65**, 'Something Blue'. The headline of *Sunnydale Press* (see **17**, 'Reptile Boy'; **33**, 'Becoming' Part 1; **48**, 'Bad Girls'; **55**, 'Graduation Day' Part 1; **66**, 'Hush'; **73**, 'Superstar'; **92**, 'Crush') is: MAYHEM CAUSED – MONSTERS CERTAINLY NOT INVOLVED OFFICIALS SAY.

The premiere broadcast of this episode ran approximately eight minutes longer than normal. Subsequent repeats in the US were edited to standard – circa 42-minute – length. Most initial overseas broadcasts, however, were the 50-minute version and that's the one that was released commercially in the UK in 2002. In Marti Noxon's parking ticket song, the last (almost inaudible) line is: 'I'm not wearing underwear.' This is the first episode to feature a different title sequence and theme music, and the first to have an on-screen title. The Mutant Enemy logo monster *sings*, 'Grrr Arrrgh' at the episode's end.

Soundtrack: The original songs featured are: 'Overture/Going Through The Motions', 'I've Got A Theory', '(They Got) The Mustard (Out)', 'Under Your Spell', 'I'll Never Tell', 'The Parking Ticket', 'Rest In Peace', 'Dawn's Lament', 'What You Feel', 'Standing', 'Walk Through The Fire', 'Something To Sing About', 'What You Feel (reprise)' and 'Where Do We Go From Here?'

The soundtrack is available on CD together with selections from Chris Beck's music from **78**, 'Restless'; **66**, 'Hush' and **100**, 'The Gift'.

Critique: Predictably, this high-profile episode gained *Buffy* huge press coverage. Not since **94**, 'The Body' (and, before that, **66**, 'Hush') had we seen such a range of magazines and newspapers lining-up to heap praise on Joss's shoulders. 'Magnificently inspired,' wrote long-time champion Matt Roush in *TV Guide*. 'A wildly ambitious, entertaining and unexpectedly moving experiment in form by the show's gifted creator Joss Whedon ... At moments I could have sworn I'd died and gone to TV heaven.'

'Skepticism among even fans of the show is understandable,' noted Scott Pierce. '[But] this episode is a triumph ... It's funny, shocking and heartfelt. It mocks itself without becoming a parody ... This is the sort of risk-taking TV that the Emmys ought to reward but won't. Whedon was absolutely right when he says, "There are people who never take genre shows seriously. It's a prejudice that I'll never understand. Because anything to do with fantasy turns them off, and anything humorous must not be meaningful." '

'Perhaps Whedon's best trait is that he's one of the most consistent writers in Hollywood, the equal of Aaron Sorkin or David E Kelley without question and one of the few whose work almost never takes a misstep,' wrote Tim Goodman, who added that 'Once More, With Feeling' was not just an episode, 'it's a TV event ... Forget audience-pleasing chestnuts. The impressive aspect is that these myriad song styles all contain original material that moves the narrative along while jump-starting the season. It's hard to overstate how thrilling this episode is instantly recalling the sophistication of Dennis Potter.'

'Not as good as **66**, "Hush" from two years ago, but better than many of this season's downer episodes (TV to slit your wrist by),' noted the *Post Gazette*. 'Whedon's talent as a clever lyricist almost equals his work as a dramatist. The songs advance the show's serialized plot while further defining the characters. He's clearly a musical theater buff, paying homage to the various styles within the genre.'

Time magazine declared the episode one of the ten TV highlights of 2001: 'You could apply the title of this audacious musical episode to the whole season of *Buffy*, which survived an acrimonious move from the WB to return smarter, funnier and dramatically richer than ever. Who'd have thought creator Joss Whedon (who taught himself piano to write the episode's surprisingly tuneful score, as well as the nimble lyrics) studied his Sondheim along with his sarcophagi?'

'A hugely clever premise that immediately excuses the essential absurd conceit of musicals – why is everybody suddenly breaking into song and dance?' added *The Washington Post*. 'A plot mechanism that makes perfect sense in a *Buffy* universe, where demons' spells continually undermine logic and the laws of nature. Whedon created an organic episode that not only referenced events in prior episodes and advanced existing plot points but also foreshadowed major developments.'

The Punk and the Godfather: James Marsters warned *TV Guide* not to expect a Celine Dion power ballad from Spike. 'We were in London on the dance floor, and Joss Whedon actually stopped dancing, going, "I'm in the middle of your song – I'm on fire, I can't get it out," ' relates the actor, who covers Tom Waits and Bruce Springsteen songs in his own one-man stage show. 'Just today he said, "The last stanza needs more balls." He wants it to be really rock'n'roll.'

'The fact that Spike is truly in love can motivate him to great acts of heroism as he tries to become the kind of man that Buffy could love,' James observes. 'Or, if spurned, it could drive him to great acts of villainy. I don't know if Buffy will ever reciprocate Spike's feelings. I really think Spike is kind of beneath her. He's evil – he just happens to be in love with a good person.'

Did You Know?: Sarah Michelle Gellar intended to have someone else sing her songs, which she would merely lip-synch. When she realised how emotional they were, however, she didn't want anyone else singing them. In a television interview with Richard Blackwood, Sarah stated that she *did* mime the songs, but presumably she meant that she mimed while on set, having already recorded the soundtrack. Alyson Hannigan, on the other hand, was so lacking in confidence concerning her voice that she specifically requested to have no song of her own and very few singing lines.

Cast and Crew Comments: 'I'm not a singer and I hated every moment of it,' Sarah Michelle Gellar confirmed. 'It took 19 hours of singing and 17 hours of dancing in between shooting four other episodes.' She wasn't the only one feeling apprehensive. 'Some of [the cast] were terrified,' says Joss. 'But they embraced it amazingly. They had to work after hours, doing singing lessons, dance rehearsals, training.' 'I'm more nervous about singing than dancing,' noted Michelle Trachtenberg. 'But I [took] some lessons and [in the end] it was fun.' By contrast, Anthony Stewart Head couldn't have been happier. But then he *was* in the middle of recording his debut album, *Music for Elevators*, at the time. 'Every season I would ask, are we going to do the musical episode?' he recalled. 'Joss would say he wasn't ready.'

'The episode is not for everybody but I think it's a thing of brilliance,' noted Joss's collaborator Chris Beck. 'I consider it an honor to have been involved.' 'It's the most fun I've ever had,' Joss told the *Posting Board*. A self-confessed fan of Stephen Sondheim, Joss spent all summer writing the episode. '[He] came up with lyrics, melodies, the underlying chords/harmony, as well as general stylistic direction for each of 16 numbers,' continued Beck. 'The songs started out as four-track recordings Joss made himself. I co-arranged and co-produced the songs with Jesse Tobias of Splendid. Joss was very much involved at every stage and often surprised me with the detail and specificity of his ideas, considering his lack of formal training and comparatively light musical experience.'

Marti Noxon's Comments: Marti insists the musical episode did not represent Joss's follow-up gimmick to Buffy's resurrection. 'It's definitely a privilege of our baroque period, but Joss has been wanting to do a musical since we started,' she told the *Seattle Times*. 'The question was more of when would be the right time.'

Joss Whedon's Comments: 'Yes, the musical is going to be longer, maybe by about six minutes. So set your VCR's accordingly, particularly since Tuesday night is the *only time* the show will be broadcast in its entirety,' Joss told the *Posting Board*. 'It will run again but cuts will be made. Has anyone seen the bills posted in LA? I designed (with much help from the masterful Jeph Loeb) a classic old style musical poster and the brilliant Adam Hughes (he does covers for *Wonder Woman* comics) painted it. It's something to see. After all this effort, I sure hope you don't all hate the thundering crap out of the show. That'd be *oops*!'

108
Tabula Rasa

US Transmission Date: 13 Nov 2001
UK Transmission Date: 21 Feb 2002
Writer: Rebecca Rand Kirshner
Director: David Grossman
Cast: Raymond O'Connor (Teeth), Geordie White (Vamp #1),
Stephen Triplett (Vamp #2), David Franco (Vamp #3)

Grief-stricken over her stupidity in resurrecting Buffy, Willow tries a spell to make Buffy forget that she was in paradise. As one might expect, given Willow's recent track record with magic, the spell goes awry and the Scooby Gang all awake with amnesia, forgetting everything about their lives including their relationships with each other, and the existence of vampires.

Babes and Babes (Bring Your Own Subtext): Even with amnesia it's blindly obvious to both Willow and Tara that they are attracted to each other. It's interesting that Willow uses the word selfish to describe herself (in relation to the spell to resurrect Buffy). The last time she said something similar was in **65**, 'Something Blue', an episode which also concerned a spell of hers going disastrously wrong and having serious consequences not only for herself but also for her friends.

A Little Honesty is a Dangerous Thing: In what could be her mantra after saying something remarkably tactless and inappropriate, if completely true, Anya sees Xander's horrified look and notes: 'I'm just saying what everyone's thinking,' (see **109**, 'Smashed').

Denial, Thy Name is Willow: Realising how selfish her actions were in bringing Buffy back (see **101**, 'Bargaining'), Willow suggests using yet more magic, a spell to make Buffy forget, similar to the one used on Tara in **106**, 'All The Way'. Tara, needless to say, is outraged. Having discovered the violation of her own mind (a particularly insensitive thing for Willow to do considering Glory's brain-suck on Tara in **97**, 'Tough Love'), Tara threatens to leave Willow if her abuse of magic continues. But Willow is blinded by her desire to, she believes, help. That may have been how it started, Tara argues, but now Willow is using spells to fix anything she doesn't like, including Tara herself. Tara asks Willow to go a week without magic. But, of course, she can't and after her spell goes disastrously wrong yet again, and her deception is discovered, Tara leaves her.

Real Gone Kid: Having finally admitted to himself in **107**, 'Once More, With Feeling', that his presence is holding Buffy back, Giles tells her that as long as he stays she will always turn to him if there's something that she feels unable to handle. And he'll step in because he can't bear to see her suffer (as in dealing with Dawn in **106**, 'All the Way'). He has taught Buffy all that he can about being a Slayer and, he notes, he mother taught her what she needed to know about life. But she is not going to trust that until she is forced to stand alone. Therefore, Giles is heading back to England and – this time – he plans to stay indefinitely.

Work is a Four-Letter Word: Teeth asks Buffy if she has ever given any thought to freelance work in the area of debt collection.

It's a Designer Label!: Buffy's long white coat and matching poloneck, Willow's purple blouse. On the so-bad-it's-hilarious side, there's Spike's tweed suit, dickie-bow tie, and deer stalker hat, worn as a disguise.

References: How revealing that the name Buffy gives herself when she loses her memory, Joan, is that of a legendary teenage warrior and martyred saint. Messianic complex, anyone? Spike refers to the climax of the previous episode (kissing Buffy) as being like *Gone With the Wind*. The title is Latin for blank tablet. Buffy paraphrases *Macbeth* ('what we did is done'). Also, Allen Funt, the first host of *Candid Camera*, *Shazam!* ('holy moly') and *Mary Poppins*. Unsure of his religious beliefs, Xander chants the traditional Christian prayer 'Now I lay me down to sleep', *Shema Yisrael*[38] and the Buddhist meditation mantra 'Om'. Spike quotes *The Book of Common Prayer*. Giles sword-fighting with the animated skeleton is a nod to Ray Harryhausen's special effects on *Jason and the Argonauts*. Xander suddenly laughs when he gets his memory back of seeing the movie *King Ralph*. Dawn sings the children's song 'The Ants Go Marching One by One', one of many variants on the civil war standard 'When Johnny Comes Marching Home'.

---

[38] The beginning of one of the most important Jewish prayers: *Shema Yisrael, Adoshem Elokainu, Adoshem Echud*, which translates as: 'Hear, O Israel, the Lord is our God, the Lord is One', and appears in Deuteronomy 6:4.

Awesome!: Spike's assumption that, because he and Giles are both English, they're related ('There *is* a ruggedly handsome resemblance,' says Anya). Spike *does* inspire a particular feeling of familiarity and disappointment Giles adds, helpfully. Giles must be his father, Spike decided, and he adds how he must hate Giles and his tarty stepmom (Anya). Also, the Scoobies screaming when they open the door to find two vampires waiting. And, subsequently, Xander fainting. What a girl.

'You May Remember Me From Such Films and TV Series As ...': Raymond O'Connor appeared in *The Rock*, *Girls in Prison*, *Life Stinks* and *Babylon 5*. Stephen Triplett was in *Surveillance*. David Franco played Morgan in *24* and appeared in *Holy Smoke* and *ER*.

Valley-Speak: Dawn: 'Fine, that's your purgative.' Buffy: 'Prerogative.' Dawn: 'Whatever, *Joan*.'

Sex and Drugs and Rock'n'Roll: At one point during the memory lapse, Willow tells Dawn, 'I think I'm kind of gay,' repeating her thoughts about her vampire alter-ego in **50**, 'Doppelgängland'. Revealingly, Xander assumes that, because Willow is wearing a jacket with the name Harris sewn into it, and that this is also his name, maybe he has *a brother* whom Willow is dating. Almost as revealing as Spike's secret wish to be Angel (see **Quote/Unquote**). And Spike and Buffy move on from spell-induced snogging (**107**, 'Once More, With Feeling') to ending this episode doing some trauma-related making-out in the Bronze.

Slash-Fiction Spank-Fantasy Moment: Giles, to Spike: 'You're not too old to put across my knee, you know, sonny.'

Logic, Let Me Introduce You to This Window: Why does Giles come to the conclusion that he was leaving Anya because he had a one-way ticket to England? Maybe Anya had another ticket herself. It's a bit of a leap (to, admittedly, a correct conclusion). When Xander breaks the crystal in the sewers, it's logical that Tara would guess what had happened, but how do Dawn and Xander seemingly know that it was Willow's spell that caused their amnesia? Willow certainly doesn't say anything. Giles's plane ticket on Global Airlines is going from Sunnydale to Los Angeles and then to London Heathrow (see **101**, 'Bargaining' Part 1, for the implausibility of this).

I Just *Love* Your Accent: One of Spike's finest moments as, during the amnesia, he sneers at Giles, noting that Giles has his crust all stiff and upper with a nancy-boy accent. He goes on to observe that 'you Englishmen are always so . . .' The he pauses, reels off a string of expletivies – bloody hell, sodding, blimey, shagging, knickers, bollocks – and realises that he is, himself, English. 'Welcome to the nancy-tribe,' notes Giles, dryly. Believing his name to be Randy, Spike asks why Giles didn't name him Horny or Desperate-for-a-Shag.

Anya says that she never knows what Giles is talking about, listing words like loo, shag and brolly as examples. Giles also uses balderdash and chicanery in everyday conversation.

Motors: Spike suggests that the memory-challanged Scoobies take Giles's car to go to hospital, adding that he is sure Giles has some sort of mid-life crisis transport. Something red, shiny and shaped like a penis. Ironically Giles *did*, indeed, have just such a motor, introduced in **80**, 'Real Me'.

Cruelty To Animals: Spike owes Teeth 40 kittens in gambling debts (see **105**, 'Life Serial'). Even with her amnesia, Anya's terror of rabbits continues and she, incompetently, manages to conjure up dozens of the poor creatures.

Quote/Unquote: Amnesiac Willow, after Buffy has staked a vampire and watched it explode into dust: 'What did you just do?' Amnesiac Buffy: 'I don't know. But it was *cool*.'

Amnesiac Spike: 'I must be a noble vampire. A good guy. On a mission of redemption. I help the hopeless. I'm a vampire with a soul.' Amnesiac Buffy: 'A vampire with a soul? How *lame* is that?'

Notes: 'You did it the way you're doing everything. When things get rough, you don't even consider the options. You just do a spell. It's not what magic is for.' Not without some welcome belly-laughs (the entire second act with the bewildered amnesiac Scoobies in the Magic Box is particularly impressive), there's a bittersweet element to 'Tabula Rasa'. This *is* the end of an era in many ways, the departure of Tony Head being not least among them. The amnesia stuff leads to some genuinely hilarious conceits, though the least said about the downright silly subplot involving Spike, some kittens, and a Shark-headed extortion-demon who looks like a reject from *The Paul Merton Show*, the better. 'Tabula Rasa', to its credit, manages to work as both a characterisation exercise and a piece of action-drama. With its emphasis on the contradictions of the Scooby Gang (just why *aren't* Willow and Xander a couple?), the episode has the chance to play subtle games and allow the audience, for once, to be several steps ahead of the characters. But the odd structure, and somewhat hurried and depressing nature of the final act end the episode on a downbeat note.

The suit that Spike wears for most of the episode is reminiscent of the one he wore in Xander's dream in **78**, 'Restless'. During the same dream sequence, Giles said he thought of Spike as a son, and here Spike comes to that same conclusion. When asked by Buffy what he wants, Teeth replies a house in Bel Air with a generous-sized swimming pool. Don't we all?

Soundtrack: Michelle Branch performs a gorgeous version of 'Goodbye To You' in the Bronze at the episode's climax, intercut with various shots of Tara leaving Willow, Giles leaving on a jet plane, and Buffy and Spike getting interactive with their tongues. Her guitarist and musical director is Jesse Tobias (see **107**, 'Once More, With Feeling').

Critique: 'For five years, *Buffy* has been the least-watched great show on television, the most ridiculed by ignorati who think they're literati. Like its peers (*The West Wing, The Sopranos, ER*), Buffy is better than movies because its writer is the most important guy on the set,' noted Tim Appelo. 'A lack of sameness is why *Buffy* is confined to tiny networks and snubbed by Emmys.'

Did You Know?: Sarah Michelle Gellar doesn't have a high opinion of some of the *Buffy* merchandising currently filling the shelves. '[The Buffy action figure] looks more like Erik Estrada of *CHiPS* than me,' she told *BBC Online*. Besides which, 'The audience of *Buffy* don't quite seem like doll-playing people, if you know what I mean.'

You always know when a TV show has reached the merchandise hall of fame, however, when you can buy a pair of knickers with its name on them. Such an honour was bestowed on *Buffy* during early 2003. The black pants, emblazoned with a Slayer logo, are currently only available in small or medium sizes. Large and extra large versions are, apparently, on the way.

Head On: 'I've always had a wonderful time on the set, because they're all wonderful actors, and the casting is excellent,' Tony told Melissa Perenson. 'I always enjoy scenes I do with Sarah. We have a great deal of respect for each other, and they have a real resonance, which I think shows on screen. When I watch our scenes, you can always feel that there's a real strength there, a bond. And doing scenes with Alyson – fantastic. Nicky, James . . . they're all rare talents.'

Cast and Crew Comments: 'I've behaved like an unappreciative, almost disgruntled brat,' Emma Caulfield told *The Boston Globe*, describing her adversarial approach to the film and TV industry. 'I've peed on this business. So many people would kill to be in the position I'm in. I haven't deserved what I've gotten.' Emma's charmingly frank views are reminiscent of the character she played. The actress had, at one point, quit acting after her stint as Brandon's girlfriend, Susan, in *Beverly Hills, 90210*. When she first guest-starred on *Buffy* in 1998, it was, she noted, merely to make some quick cash and be on a show that she liked. While in Australia in 2002, Emma had what she describes as an epiphany. 'I had this awakening there and I made peace with the fact that this business is not what I'm supposed to do. It's really a stepping stone for other projects,' she said. The owner of two cats, Caulfield wants to 'effect great change for the animals of the world.' On a similar theme, she told Rob Francis, 'For a while I've had the feeling that there's something I'm supposed to be doing but that I've somehow missed my calling. I think it has something to do with animal rights which I'm very passionate about.'

Marti Noxon's Comments: Talking to *BBC Online*, Marti stated that, if the Giles spin-off series *Ripper* is made, there may be crossovers to other parts of the Buffyverse. 'It would primarily be a new cast, but, time and work permits and technicalities permitting, you'd see guests from the *Buffy* world,' she told an online chat. Marti may even grace our shores herself. Asked if she would be working on *Ripper*, she noted: 'I'm actually eligible for dual citizenship. My father was born in Britain so my brother has worked in London and I know I can get a work permit. We get such a strong reaction from British fans, and we feel very gratified.'

109
Smashed

US Transmission Date: 20 Nov 2001
UK Transmission Date: 28 Feb 2002

Writer: Drew Z Greenberg
Director: Turi Meyer
Cast: Patrice Walters (Woman), John Patrick Clerkin (Man),
Jack Jozefson (Rusty), Rick Garcia (Reporter), Kelly Smith (Innocent Girl),
Jordan Belfi (Ryan), Adam Weiner (Simon), Melanie Sirmons (Brie),
Lauren Nissi (Girlfriend)

After breaking up with Tara, Willow successfully transforms Amy Madison back from her rat-like state and the two witches have a night of fun, drawing Willow further into her growing addiction. Spike notices that his chip doesn't affect him when he hits Buffy, leading him to believe that she's no longer human.

Dudes and Babes: Amy believes she's been a rat for a mere matter of weeks and still thinks that the Sunnydale High prom is coming up (see **54**, 'The Prom') and that there's a possibility Larry will take her. Willow, sadly, has to inform her that (a) Larry's gay (see **27**, 'Phases'), (b) Larry's *dead* (see **56**, 'Graduation Day' Part 2) and (c) high school was over nearly three years ago, destroyed by a giant-snake-thing. Amy later confides to Buffy that she's shocked that Willow is dating girls.

When Willow tells Amy that Xander is engaged, Amy wants to know what his fiancée is like. A thousand-year-old capitalist ex-demon with rabbit phobia, notes Willow. 'That's *so* his type,' replies Amy who, herself, had a brief magic-influenced fling with Xander (see **28**, 'Bewitched, Bothered and Bewildered').

Divorce Sucks!: Dawn's reaction to the break-up of Willow and Tara is similar to that of a child caught in the middle of a separation triangle. Of course, she has been through a similar experience before (at least, in the memories the monks created for her – see **83**, 'No Place Like Home') when Joyce and Hank divorced. Tara acts very like a mother towards her, taking her to a movie and for a milkshake but asking Dawn to promise she'll eat something green tonight.

A Little Learning is a Dangerous Thing: Buffy can't remember how the time difference between California and Britain works. For the uninitiated, Britain is eight hours ahead. So, when it's midnight in California, it's 8 a.m. in London.

Xander finds reference to what he believes may be the diamond eating frost-monster that they're looking for in a *Dungeons and Dragons* manual. Maybe that's where Warren and co. got the idea for the robbery in the first place?

Mom's Apple Pie: Buffy invites Amy to stay at the Summers' house until she gets her bearings. Everybody does, she says, rather bitterly (see **103**, 'After Life', and her comments to Giles in **104**, 'Flooded').

Denial, Thy Name is Spike: As soon as he believes that his chip has stopped working, it's significant that Spike immediately tries to murder an innocent woman. For all of his protestations of having been changed by the experience, and by his love for Buffy, he is still, when all is said and done, a cold-blooded killer.

Denial, Thy Name is Buffy: Responsible people are always so concerned with being good all the time that when they finally get a taste of being bad they can't get enough of it, argues Anya concerning Willow. Buffy dismisses the suggestion that Willow can't handle magic. Xander also believes that Willow has had a taste of something powerful and Anya adds that Tara was the only one holding her in check, and now she's gone (see **110**, 'Wrecked').

Honesty, Thy Name is Anya: When Xander and Buffy seem reluctant to comment on Willow's use of magic while checking computer records, Anya is more forthright. Saying that the others are 'la-la-la-ing' around the subject of Tara's leaving and scared to say anything to Willow. Then she stops and asks Xander if this – her lack of tact – is one of those things he was commenting on. One imagines *that's* a conversation they've had more than once (see, **66**, 'Hush', and Anya's comments concerning Giles's orgasm friend and **108**, 'Tabula Rasa').

The Conspiracy Starts at Home Time: Buffy is about to admit her tryst with Spike over the previous two episodes to Willow but is distracted by Amy's return and the moment is lost (see **113**, 'Dead Things').

It's a Designer Label!: Willow's red T-shirt, Andrew's I ♥ Touring T-shirt, Dawn's sparkly top, Buffy's leather skirt and, best of all, Spike's blue shirt, Amy's suede miniskirt and knee-length black leather boots.

References: Buffy calls Spike Jessica Fletcher, the amateur sleuth played by Angela Lansbury in *Murder, She Wrote*. Also, allusions to the Rolling Stones' 'Rocks Off', the bitter divorce of Tom Cruise and Nicole Kidman, *The Exorcist* ('head spinning?'), *Ellen* and *Star Trek: The Next Generation* ('you can play holodeck another time'). Dawn says of the movie that Tara took her to see: 'It was ironic when all those cute inner-city kids taught their coach a valuable lesson,' a probable allusion to the Keanu Reeves vehicle *Hardball*.

Geek-Speak: In the *Buffy*-universe, seemingly, not only do all 703 episodes of the legendary British science-fiction TV series *Doctor Who* still exist,[39] but they are also all available on DVD. In Region 1, at least. The 1980s comedy-SF show *Red Dwarf*, seemingly, isn't. Andrew descends from the ceiling of the museum à la Tom Cruise in *Mission: Impossible*. Or, for that matter, Frohike in the pilot episode of *The Lone Gunmen*. The reference to the Disney Hall of Presidents is a probable allusion to *Bill and Ted's Excellent Adventure*. The *troika* have a glitterball in their lair.

This episode sees the first hints of another layer to the *troika*: Andrew and Jonathan are in it for the chicks, the money and a decent boost of self-esteem. And, mostly, cos they get to play with such wonderful toys. But with Warren, there's clearly a darker motive (see **113**, 'Dead Things').

Bitch!: Spike: 'You're a tease, you know that, Slayer? Get a fellah's motor revving, let the tension marinate a-couple'o-days, then *bam*. Crown yourself the ice queen.' And, to Warren: 'Help me out here, Spock, I don't speak *loser*.'

Awesome!: Warren gets to use the blowtorch because his evil comrades are allergic to methane (Jonathan) and afraid of *hot things* (Andrew). The freeze-ray. The moment of realisation for Spike when he hits Buffy and doesn't suffer from a headache. Dawn guilting Tara into staying. It's really sweet that Dawn knows the buttons to push and, even though she knows that she's being manipulated, Tara stays anyway. Amy and Willow causing mayhem at the Bronze.

Surprise!: Amy, after Willow finally works out how to return her to human form (see **46**, 'Gingerbread'), screaming.

---

[39] In reality over 100 of the 1960s monochrome *Doctor Who* episodes, from the William Hartnell and Patrick Troughton eras, are missing, presumed wiped, from the BBCs shamefully incomplete archives. Occasionally, film prints of an episode turn up in some Third World dictatorship or in the hand of a private collector (the most recent find was in early 2004), but it's unlikely that we'll ever see television masterpieces like 'The Evil of the Daleks', 'Fury From the Deep' or 'The Web of Fear' in their entirety again.

'You May Remember Me From Such Films and TV Series As . . .': Patrice Walters appeared in *LA Confidential* and *The Practice*. Rick Garcia was in *Collateral Damage*, *24*, *The American President*, *The Fall Guy*, *Airwolf* and *The Incredible Hulk*. Jordan Belfi appeared in *Virgil* and *Remote* and was Camera Assistant on *Wild Wild West*. Jack Jozefson's CV includes *Trade Day*, *Vic*, *Parker Lewis Can't Lose*, *Wild at Heart* and *Gas Pump Girls*. Adam Weiner played Alex in *Voyeur.Com*. Kelly Smith was in *Dead on Page Six* and *Naked Horror*.

Don't Give Up the Day Job: Drew Greenberg has also written for the US version of *Queer as Folk* and acted in *The Rules of Etiquette*. Turi Meyer directed *Candyman: Day of the Dead* and *The Lot*.

Valley-Speak: Warren: 'Dude, that is so cool.'
   Jonathan: 'That's really neato, and stuff . . .'

Cigarettes & Alcohol: Amy and Willow go for a night of debauchery and mischief at the Bronze where they appear to be drinking martinis.

Sex and Drugs and Rock'n'Roll: When she kissed him at the end of **108**, 'Tabula Rasa', Buffy tells Spike, she was thinking about Giles. 'I always wondered about you two,' Spike replies angrily. When Spike tells Buffy that he's in love with her, she corrects him. Spike is in love with *pain*, she notes, and a fascinating discussion about sadomasochism ensues. To put this brutally, Buffy's treatment of Spike for a long time has been less than satisfactory even if he is evil. He's, seemingly, a more than acceptable (even trusted) bodyguard for Buffy's sister, good enough to be used as an emotional crutch on more than one occasion, but not to be treated as someone with feelings. 'You're a *thing*,' Buffy tells him bitterly. Emotional trauma aside, it's not hard to see why all the Spike fans (they're mostly women, inevitably) often dislike Buffy so much. She's spent the last two seasons beating the roaring crud out of someone who, effectively, can't fight back. So, having acknowledged the unresolved sexual tension that's been building since the middle of season four (at least), they end the episode wrecking the abandoned house that they find themselves in and then, ahem, *doing it*.

Logic, Let Me Introduce You to This Window: There's no station ID on the news report on KOUS (previously seen in **66**, 'Hush') as there are on all US TV broadcasts. The Boba Fett action figure is described as a limited-edition mint-condition 1979 vintage. *The Empire Strikes Back* wasn't released until May 1980.[40] It would also be worth an awful lot more if it was still in its original packaging. When Warren takes the device to Spike's head, a reflection from Spike's skin can be briefly seen. And what exactly *is* the device and how does it enable Warren to take a look at the chip without involving some surgery? From the results Warren gets, all it seems to do is measure the strength of the signal being emitted, which doesn't rule out several other types of malfunction. How come when Amy returns to human form, her hair is a different colour and a lot longer than it was in **45**, 'Gingerbread'? It's also ironic she says how sorry she is about Joyce's death since the last time Amy saw her, Joyce was part of a crazed mob of Sunnydale parents wanting to burn Amy alive. Where does Amy, who's taller than both Willow and Buffy, and thinner than Tara, get the various clothes that she wears and that all seem to fit her perfectly? In the Bronze, Amy and Willow play telepathic pool and nobody bats an eyelid. OK, it's nothing compared to the shenanigans they get up to later on and, as ever, this *is* Sunnydale we're talking about. But, surely *somebody* would have stopped to check out their impressive display of mind control. The only crowd they seem to draw are two meatheads who want to dance with Amy. The question's been asked before, but it bears repeating: How do vampires have sex? Biologically speaking, it takes a deal of increased blood circulation for a man to get an erection. Plus it must be rather uncomfortable for Buffy (see **25**, 'Surprise'). Does Spike really strike anybody as the sort of person who'd be conversant with *Star Trek* terminology? Maybe it's not just *Passions* that does it for him (see **65**, 'Something Blue'; **90**, 'Checkpoint')? After all, he knew a bit about *The Empire Strikes Back* in **15**, 'School Hard'.

I Just *Love* Your Accent: The diamond that the *troika* stole was on loan from the British Museum. Spike orders Warren to look at his chip. Is that a British slang term asks Warren?

Cruelty To Animals: If rats could dance, they probably wouldn't gnaw so much, notes Amy.

---

[40] Some sources suggest the Fett action figure was, in fact, released in America in late 1979 to catch the Christmas market. Confirmation of this has proved impossible.

Quote/Unquote: Buffy: 'How've you been?' Amy: 'Rat. You?' Buffy: 'Dead.'

Willow, on Amy: 'I keep expecting her to do ratty stuff. You know, licking her hands clean, shredding newspaper, leaving little pellets in the corner.' Buffy: 'Let's definitely not leave her alone in the house too long.'

Notes: 'Nothing wrong with me. Something wrong with *her*.' The funniest debut-script since **40**, 'Band Candy', 'Smashed' is a statement of intent from a writer new to the series. Didn't *Buffy* used to be, like, all funny and stuff? Drew Greenberg seems to be asking. The return of Elizabeth Anne Allen is an obvious highlight as Amy takes Willow to the borders of the Dark Side for a night of witchy debauchery. Then, just when you think the episode can't possibly get any funnier, the *troika* turn up to steal a diamond using a freeze-ray. 'Smashed' has all of this *and* some wonderful observational comedy surrounding Dawn and her relationship with Willow and Tara, though the episode's end – Buffy and Spike getting passionate – is signposted by two previous attempts to do, more-or-less, the same thing (see **107**, 'Once More, With Feeling'; **108**, 'Tabula Rasa'). Nevertheless, this represents the most witty and, musical episode aside, most inventive *Buffy* in some considerable time.

Amy discovers that Principal Snyder was eaten by the mayor (**56**, 'Graduation Day' Part 2). Her father is mentioned (see **3**, 'The Witch'; **110**, 'Wrecked'). She says she wishes there was a way to make him forget about the last three years. Willow says she might be able to help her out there but it would be an idea to sew her name in her clothes first (see **108**, Tabula Rasa'). When Buffy mentions all the weird things that have been going on recently, Xander adds exploding lint to her list, a reference to Buffy's description of the self-destructing surveillance device planted on her in **105**, 'Life Serial'. Buffy always wanted a pony. The headline of the newspaper (presumably *Sunnydale Press*, see **107**, 'Once More, With Feeling') is: MUSEUM GUARD ATTACKED, FROZEN – BODY THAWED, REMAINS UNCONSCIOUS.

Soundtrack: Grunge rockers Virgil perform 'Vermillion Borders', 'Parachute' and 'Here' at the Bronze. When Amy and Willow do their prestadigitation, they are briefly replaced by girl-band Halo Friendlies doing a cracking version of 'Run Away'.

Critique: ' "Why can't I feel," sang Buffy in a recent episode of the series on which teenagers go through hell – literally,' noted *The Boston Globe*. 'She'd already found eternal bliss in Heaven, but after a rude awakening of John Miltonian proportions, she lost paradise when her Scooby pals summoned her back to her so-called earthly life. Talk about teen angst; poor Buffy can't even enjoy the simple joys of resurrection.'

Did You Know?: Many fans would love to see *Buffy* in widescreen. But, except for special occasions like **107**, 'Once More, With Feeling', this was never an option. Joss Whedon preferred it that way: 'I like the idea that *Buffy* stays square,' he told *zap2it.com*. 'Most TVs are still square. Whereas *Angel*, [filmed and broadcast in widescreen] I think of as a dark, melodramatic film, *Buffy* [is] a comforting TV show, even though it's the darkest, bleakest world. I want to keep it that way.'

The Love That Dares Not Speak its Name: So how will the Buffy/Spike relationship be resolved? 'There's going to be quite a bit of punching of noses, believe me,' hinted Marti Noxon. 'It's going to be a wild ride, that's for sure.'

Cast and Crew Comments: Understandably, Sarah Michelle Gellar often got quite defensive about *Buffy*. After all, in many quarters, the series never received anywhere near the respect it deserved. Which was why Gellar had no patience with people who couldn't see past the – admittedly offbeat – title. People whom Gellar described, bluntly as stupid. 'I don't mean to be rude,' she told *Deseret News*, 'but I think it's ignorance. This show is the most wonderful mix of witty writing, phenomenal performances and evolving stories.'

Joss Whedon's Comments: 'The reason we stayed on the air in our first 13 [episodes] was because we had this incredibly strong Internet fanbase,' Joss told the *Chicago Tribune*. 'Thanks to those fans, *Buffy* is the highest profile cult show on television.' Joss promised in the same interview that he would never abandon *Buffy*'s cult roots in a bid for higher viewing figures. 'I'd rather have 100 people who *need* to see my show than 1,000 people who *like* to,' he said. 'I'll take the badge of *cult* and wear it very proudly. It means the show's affecting people on a different level.'

110
Wrecked

US Transmission Date: 27 Nov 2001
UK Transmission Date: 7 Mar 2002

Writer: Marti Noxon
Director: David Solomon
Cast: Fleming Brooks (Mandraz), Mageina Tovah (Jonesing Girl),
Michael Giordani (Jonesing Man), Colin Malone (Creepy Man),
Mark Oxman[41] (Espresso Pump Worker)

Buffy is ashamed of herself after having sex with Spike and determines to keep her liaison a secret from her friends. Meanwhile, keen for bigger thrills, Amy takes Willow to a warlock, Rack, whose powerful brand of spells quickly sees Willow hooked. While looking after Dawn, Willow decides that she needs another fix. To escape a demon summoned by Willow's carelessness, she and Dawn steal a car.

Dreaming (As Blondie Once Said) is Free: Willow's magic-induced hallucination featuring a red-skinned demon hiding in the grass. It ends with that traditional horror movie motif, a woman in dire peril. And with Willow screaming her head off. That'll teach her to mess with the black arts.

A Little Learning is a Dangerous Thing: Xander realises that Willow's closeness to Amy is potentially dangerous. He describes the coupling as Willow making herself a playmate who won't monitor her use of magic as Tara previously did. Seems he's learning a thing or two about honesty from his fiancée. Sadly, he doesn't say any of this to Willow herself.

Mom's Apple Pie: Having noted in **109**, 'Smashed', that Dawn's relationship with Tara is very much mother/daughter, here we've got Willow presented as a classic incompetent father-figure. Always trying to do the right thing and usually making a complete thoughtless hash of it. Where, exactly, that leaves Buffy in the equation is open to question, something neither Buffy nor Dawn themselves seem entirely sure about (see **111**, 'Gone').

Denial, Thy Name is Buffy: Buffy is back living in the land of denial, trying to forget that she ever slept with Spike. After

---

[41] Uncredited.

spending her time wavering between a sort of acceptance of the situation and angry rebuttals of him (see **109**, 'Smashed'), she makes the decision to try to cut him out of her life completely and ends the episode with her bed surrounded by garlic and clutching a cross. Too late, love. As he himself notes, 'I'm in your system now.' Yet still she treats him like pond scum, even after he has tenderly taken care of her injured sister while she's too busy sorting out Willow. Poor deluded woman (see **111**, 'Gone').

The Conspiracy Starts at Home Time: Rack is a warlock/pusher who deals, according to Spike, in dangerous black magic. His home/consulting rooms are downtown and are cloaked in that they seem to exist in a different dimension altogether. They move around periodically to, as Amy suggests, keep Rack out of trouble. Spike notes that you have to be either a witch or a vampire to be able to sense the building's presence. Rack is obviously powerful (he was aware of Amy's life as a rat, see **45**, 'Gingerbread', noting that she was messing with spells that were out of her league and she should leave that sort of thing to professionals).

It's a Designer Label!: For the forthcoming wedding, Anya can't decide whether to put her bridesmaids in cocktail dresses or the traditional burlap with blood larva (see **116**, 'Hell's Bells'). We get another look at Buffy's stylish-yet-affordable boots (see **107**, 'Once More, With Feeling'). Amy's extremely tight black dress, Willow's studded denim jacket, Dawn's blue sweater and a whole episode full of cool leather coats (Buffy, Willow, Spike etc.). Check out, also, Anya's freshly dyed super-blonde hair.

References: Anya believes that home and garden guru Martha Stewart is a witch ('nobody could do that much decoupage without calling on the powers of darkness'). Also, actress Joan Crawford (Dawn's reference seems to be to the notorious biography movie about her as an abusive mother, *Mommie Dearest*).

Bitch!: Notice how downright spiteful and condescending magicked-up-Willow is towards Dawn.

Awesome!: Dawn slapping Willow across the face, and the later scene as Willow, addicted and in pain, literally hits rock bottom, and lies in the dirt at Buffy's feet weeping. 'Get up,' an angry Buffy tells her. Also, the conversation between Buffy and Spike as they search for Rack's place is brilliant characterisation – Spike turning from a sleazy pervert obsessed with a girl who is out of his class into a totally out-of-the-closet romantic within the space of about three lines of dialogue. Best of all, Willow blissfully wallowing in the excesses of her magic-addled state, up on the ceiling and, like, *gone* (see **121**, 'Two to Go').

'You May Remember Me From Such Films and TV Series As . . .': Mageina Tovah was in *YMI*. Michael Giordani appeared in *We Were Soldiers*. Colin Malone's CV includes *Art House*, *G vs E* and *Seinfeld*. Mark Oxman appeared in *The West Wing*, *Felicity* and *Catch Me If You Can*.

The Drugs Don't Work: Rack's price for feeding Willow's increasing addiction is to, as he describes it, take a little tour, which seems to involve him feeding from the powerful vibes that Willow gives off. It appears to be something of a quasi-erotic experience for both, ending with Willow smiling like she's just reached orgasm and Rack whispering that she tastes like strawberries (see **121**, 'Two to Go'). Later, we see Amy spinning around, like a dervish and, clearly, as high as a kite. Rack reclines on a sofa, holding in his hands what looks like a glass ball with a reflection of Amy trapped inside it. Rack looks up and there's Willow, literally on the ceiling, writhing in ecstasy.

Valley-Speak: Dawn: 'A mother of all night-wedgies.'
    Amy: 'It was awesome. This blowhard dude, first she made his mouth disappear?'

Cigarettes & Alcohol: The smelly guy in Rack's waiting room seems ready for a long wait as be puts his cigarettes and lighter on the table. Disgusted, Dawn leaves him to it.

Sex and Drugs and Rock'n'Roll: The opening shot. Rubble. Bits of splintered wood and plaster everywhere. The camera pans across to reveal a bare foot. Suddenly Buffy sits up, naked and holding her skirt to her chest. She looks around frowning, sensing that Spike is awake. Bruised and scratched, he looks up at her. 'When did the building fall down?' asks Buffy, confused. Yeah, I've had mornings like that too.
    Spike implies that he suspected the only thing better than killing a Slayer would be having sex with one and that Buffy, herself, seems to be something of a vampire groupie. Only one vampire ever got me hot, Buffy replies, but he's gone. Spike, on the other hand, is just *convenient*. Spike is, clearly, hurt by this suggestion and asks if Buffy now intends to go back to treating him like dirt

until the next time she has an itch requiring scratching. I'm disgusted with myself, notes Buffy. That is the power that Spike's charms had on her. Last night was the most perverse, degrading experience of her life, she concludes. Spike seems rather pleased with this description.

Anya notes that she doesn't intend asking Xander to perform the groom's traditional rite of self-flagellation at their wedding. Given that the couple have enjoyed spanking (**69**, 'The I in Team') he'd probably have got-off on that.

Logic, Let Me Introduce You to This Window: Buffy wakes up next to Spike and immediately starts dressing. Before she leaves, Spike reveals he has her underwear. Surely she noticed that she didn't have them on while she was getting dressed? Rack must have been around Sunnydale for some time if Amy knows him since she's been a rat for three years. How, therefore, have his and Buffy's (or, more importantly, Willow's) paths never crossed before now? Amy says she'd better be getting home as her dad is expecting her. Since when? In the previous episode she was reluctant to contact Mr Madison and try to answer the inevitable questions about her absence. She may, of course, have telephoned him while she and Willow were out overnight (after they'd finished their amusing escapades at the Bronze). Bet that would have been a good conversation: 'Hi, Dad. No, I didn't run away from home, I've spent three years as a rat . . .' Willow says that the one thing she won't miss about magic is the time she kept stinky yak cheese in her bra. Wouldn't that have been a bit conspicuous in making her smell somewhat? Why, exactly, was Amy stealing sage (and other kitchen herbs) from Buffy's house? To give to Rack in exchange for another dose of his magic? Maybe, but, *sage*? Perhaps he's got some onions and wants to stuff a chicken?

I Just *Love* Your Accent: Spike uses the word bollocks for the fifth time in the series (**76**, 'The Yoko Factor'; **80**, 'Real Me'; **85**, 'Fool for Love'; **108**, 'Tabula Rasa').

Motors: When being chased by the demon, Willow and Dawn leap into a convenient car, which Willow commands to drive off. And crashes.

Quote/Unquote: Dawn: 'It was like a meat party in my mouth. OK, I'm just a kid, and even *I* know that came out wrong.'

Notes: 'She's as bad as I am. Worse. Bet she's at Rack's right now.' It had been some time since we'd seen a decent example of

'*Buffy*-as-metaphor', which was, let's remember, once such an important part of the series' success. Doubly welcome – in an episode short on tension but high on blood-pumping, testosterone-soaked adrenaline – was a thoroughly harrowing and unpleasant study of the horrors of addiction. In the *Buffy* equivalent of *The Man With the Golden Arm*, Alyson Hannigan acts her little cotton socks off. 'Wrecked' is a strange, out-of-focus look at the dark path that Willow travelled down during the previous year and a half. Echoing Faith's flirtation with the Dark Side in season three, Marti Noxon uses a clever mixture of Joyce Summers-style denial and pain to push Willow to the brink. That's all terrific stuff. Where 'Wrecked' is less successful is in its continuation of the Buffy/Spike riff that had, frankly, been mined to excess over the previous three episodes. How many more times did we need variations on the same basic episode end/beginning of Buffy and Spike get-it-on followed by Buffy angrily regretting it? The scenes work because Marsters and Gellar are, you know, *good*. But there's only so much repetition that a series can take before something radical is needed to shake it from its lethargy.

Xander catches Anya reading yet another bridal magazine (*Bride and Joy*). Some of the metaphors in the episode are really subtle (the burnt pancakes Tara was making for Dawn are a subconscious representation of her and Willow's incendiary relationship). Buffy accuses Spike of drawing out the search for Dawn, noting that he's done this sort of thing before (that's a bit unfair, the previous only occasion was in 92, 'Crush'). Dawn suffers from a broken arm in the crash (see 111, 'Gone').

Soundtrack: Laika's sexy 'Black Cat Bone' plays as Willow floats on the ceiling at Rack's place. The episode is also notable for Thomas Wanker's spooky score.

Critique: 'More daring than ever, *Buffy* is glorious and revelatory in its willingness to face up to the messiness and potential danger of sex,' wrote Stephanie Zacharek. 'It may be the greatest postcoital line ever: "When did the house fall down?"'

Did You Know?: This episode is dedicated, onscreen, 'In Loving Memory of JD Peralta', a production assistant on *Buffy* who died in November 2002 while 'Wrecked' was in production.

Cast and Crew Comments: 'People have stopped me in the street,' Tom Lenk told Lisa Kincaid. 'In fact I got stopped in a store by the night manager. [He said] "I have to know, are you on *Buffy*?"'

We had a twenty-minute conversation. Fans always have something great to say.'

Marti Noxon's Comments: Marti revealed to *zap2it.com*, that the much-speculated scene in which Spike and Buffy finally have sex was the short version. It had to be cut after UPN executives complained that the original was too explicit. As much as 15 seconds were removed – an enormous amount in TV terms. Marti also commented on the decision to allow the tension between the characters to come to fruition. 'It's really a love-hate relationship in the strictest definition,' she said. 'It's still probably not the best choice for her [but she] kind of likes dark guys. The relationship is really about choosing someone who, in the long run, some of the safety of it is that you know it can't work.'

111
Gone

US Transmission Date: 8 Jan 2002
UK Transmission Date: 14 Mar 2002

Writer: David Fury
Director: David Fury
Cast: Daniel Hagen (Frank), Susan Ruttan (Doris Kroeger)

The *troika* build another new crime toy, an invisibility ray, and, during their latest abortive stunt, accidentally hit Buffy with it. She takes advantage of her new situation by paying Spike a visit and playing devious games with some deserving cases. Jonathan, Warren and Andrew realise that the invisible objects are rapidly breaking down structurally and they kidnap Willow to force Buffy into the open.

Dudes and Babes: Spike finally stands up to Buffy regarding the whole shag-and-run situation. He feels that she's using him, and he's right.

There's a Ghost in My Crypt: Previously, **31**, 'I Only Have Eyes For You' had confirmed that ghosts exist in the *Buffy*-universe, and Spike is aware of this. Albeit, he seems to believe that spooks are tangible since this one is keen on grabbing his butt.

A Little Learning is a Dangerous Thing: Dawn's grades have fallen sharply in the last year, due in part to her frequent lateness and absences from school. She has a special affection for a fertility statue of the god Kokopelli that originally belonged to her mother. Hopefully she's still naive enough not to know what it's actually for (see **3**, 'The Witch'). Spike watches *Night of the Living Dead* on TV in his crypt.

Mom's Apple Pie: Willow is seemingly a dab-hand at cooking breakfast, making a tasty-looking ham omelette for Dawn, which the latter refuses as she's still mad at Willow for endangering her life by stupidity.

Denial, Thy Name is Xander: When Xander walks in on Invisible-Buffy and Spike having sex in Spike's crypt, the only way he could not know what's happening here would have been if he was nine *and* wasn't aware of Buffy's invisible status. Since Xander doesn't have either excuse one can only assume that he's having a Joyce Summers-style dose of deep denial.

Denial, Thy Name is Buffy: If Buffy is beginning to realise that her 'vacation from me' is a front for a deeper unhappiness, then a useful initial step mustn't end with her 'I don't want to die' conversation with Willow. Taking responsibility for ones own actions instead of crying about and/or avoiding the consequences of them is an important one. Buffy's harassing an annoying social worker insane is understandable enough, though she was simply doing her job trying to ensure Dawn's welfare (which, as Doris points out, is something that Buffy should also be concerned with). Having sex with Spike when she is, quite literally, not herself means that Buffy doesn't have to, psychologically, deal with the consequences.

The Conspiracy Starts at Home Time: The diamond stolen from the museum (see **109**, 'Smashed') is called the Illuminata. There are rumours of it having quasi-mystical quantum properties. The *troika* need it to power their invisibility ray.

It's a Designer Label!: Buffy's tight red pants and puma T-shirt. There are lots of interesting T-shirt motifs on display including Bongo Bongo (Andrew), Los Angeles USA (Jonathan) and Skinny Skulls (Willow).

References: *The Shining* ('all work and no play make Doris a dull girl'), *The X-Files* ('Xander and Anya are . . . Muldering out what happened'), *Goldilocks*, *The Thing* ('for all we know she could be one of us'), *A Christmas Carol* ('I am the ghost of fashion victims past'), the Doors' 'The End' ('kill, kill, kill', see **19**, 'Lie to Me'), black actor Geoffrey Cambridge, Linda Creed and Thom Bell's blue-eyed soul classic 'Betcha By Golly Wow' (the most famous version is by the Stylistics) and *White Heat* ('so long, copper!'). When Buffy walks between parked cars outside the hairdresser's one minivan has bumper stickers reading *God Bless America* and *United We Stand*.

Geek-Speak: When Andrew sees the Invisibility Ray he says that he'd pictured something cooler. 'More ILM, less Ed Wood.' Industrial Light and Magic are a division of George Lucas's production company, and are mainly responsible for creating state-of-the-art special visual effects. Ed Wood was a director who made notoriously cheap and campy movies including the legendary *Plan 9 from Outer Space*. Warren calls Jonathan Frodo, after the vertically challenged hobbit from *The Lord of the Rings*. Also, Superman's nemesis Lex Luthor.

Bitch!: Willow knows that she deserves the wrath of Dawn over the events of **110**, 'Wrecked', but she's uncertain as to why Buffy is getting cold-shouldered too. Because I let it happen, notes Buffy, sadly.
Xander, to Spike: 'Still trying to mack on Buffy? Wake up already. Never gonna happen. Only a complete loser would ever hook up with you. Unless she's a simpleton like Harmony, or a nut-sack like Drusilla.'

Awesome!: Buffy and Spike's fumbling performance in front of Doris, the officious Social Services lady and, subsequently, Buffy's invisible revenge on her. Spike, trying to hold a conversation with Xander while Invisible-Buffy plays sexy games with his ears. Warren's incompetent declaration of the *troika*'s identity to Buffy: 'We're your arch-nemesis . . . ses.' And, the *troika's* dreadfully poor subsequent escape attempt.

'You May Remember Me From Such Films and TV Series As . . .': Susan Ruttan gained a cult following as Roxanne in *LA Law*. She also appeared in *Love Kills*, *The Sure Hand of God*, *Popular* and *Take My Daughter, Please*. Daniel Hagen was in *The Deep End of the Ocean*, *Roswell*, *Friends*, *Mad About You* and *Bonfire of the Vanities*.

Valley-Speak: Jonathan, to Warren: 'You *penis!*'
  Buffy: 'You know kids today and their buggin' street-slang.'

Cigarettes & Alcohol: Spike's cigarette lighter plays an important part in the plot. He has a glass of whisky while having a serious post-coital talk with Invisible-Buffy.

Sex and Drugs and Rock'n'Roll: The *troika* are planning to turn themselves invisible so that they can get into a women-only bikini-wax spa.

Logic, Let Me Introduce You to This Window: When Buffy and Spike are talking in his crypt, Spike tells Buffy to find her clothes if she can and push off. As her clothes are also invisible (and scattered all over the crypt), it's probable that Buffy couldn't find some or all of them, but when Willow restores her visibility Buffy is fully dressed. In Buffy's kitchen there are rays of sunlight and Spike seems to be in their direct influence. Buffy tossed Spike's lighter into the box of magic stuff to be thrown out. Next time we see it, Spike is fishing it out of the pocket of Buffy's jeans.

Motors: Willow hacks into the Department of Motor Vehicles to find out the details of the mysterious black van that has been stalking Buffy since **105**, 'Life Serial'.

Quote/Unquote: Xander: 'Kidding aside, Spike, you really should get a girlfriend.'
  Buffy: 'For the first time since . . . I'm free. Free of rules and reports. Free of this life.' Spike: 'Got another name for that. Dead.'
  Warren: 'You haven't won yet, Slayer.' Buffy: 'No, that part comes after I beat the snot out of you.'

Notes: 'Kind of fits the day I've had. Willow's still a wreck, Dawn's mad at both of us, and the Social Services lady put me through a wringer. Says she's gonna watch me. I'd like to see her try now.' Metaphors. Funny things. Like London buses, you wait for ages for one to turn up, then two come along at once. On the surface, 'Gone' is little more than a remake of **11**, 'Out of Mind, Out of Sight', with the plight of the invisible girl, in this case, being Buffy herself. Normally, when a series starts remaking its own previous episodes, it's in trouble. But 'Gone' is much more than a revisitation of the past. In vanishing, Buffy is given exactly what she wants – a chance not to be herself. She has fun with her new gift at first; she can shag Spike without conscience or regret because, hey get this, *it's not really her* doing it. Spike, in what was becoming a regular part of the show, was required to talk some sense into her. 'Gone' reflects the changing nature of *Buffy* by presenting us with the kind of episode they used to make – funny, thoughtful, and with a metaphor at its heart – but in a much more schizophrenic and dark world that season six inhabited. For those who prefer Chicken Tikka to a Mars Bar.

When Invisible-Buffy is leaving the social services centre she whistles a few bars of 'Going Through The Motions' (see **107**, 'Once More, With Feeling'). Xander asks Buffy if she has been ignored lately, referring to the cause of Marcie's invisibility **11**, 'Out of Mind, Out of Sight'. In discussing the seating arrangements for their wedding, Anya tells Xander that she's invited her former boss, D'Hoffryn (see **50**, 'Doppelgängland'; **65**, 'Something Blue'). Xander's Uncle Rory is mentioned (see **20**, 'The Dark Age'; **47**, 'The Zeppo'; **60**, 'Fear Itself'; **116**, 'Hell's Bells'). Among the magic paraphernalia that Buffy is throwing out to help Willow avoid the temptation are tarot cards, a crystal ball and lots of candles. The hairdresser that Buffy uses is called Continental Hair Design.

Soundtrack: 'I Know' by Trespassers William.

Did You Know?: Adam Busch told *zap2it.com* that the *troika*'s anorakish squabbles were wholly inspired by fights between the *Buffy* writers. '[Joss] said the arguments they have in the writing room they put directly in the script – about who's the best James Bond, that kind of stuff,' he claimed. Despite the evil threesome's internecine wrangling and substantive comic potential, however, Marti Noxon indicated that they were a serious threat. 'They're not simply meant for comic relief, and we throw some surprises out in all of those characters,' she noted.

Joss Whedon's Comments: 'My plans every season extend a year past where I am', Joss told Dana Meltzer. 'But I don't have a giant, overriding plan. It's the journey of life. There are certain points I want to make about female empowerment and the pain of growing up but, beyond that, every episode is an opportunity to explore how I feel about the world. I only learn that day to day.' So what did Joss plan for the upcoming season? He promised more sin and debauchery. 'We have horrible misery and sex in store for everybody,' he noted. 'It's not a bad combination.'

112
Doublemeat Palace

US Transmission Date: 29 Jan 2002
UK Transmission Date: 21 Mar 2002

Writer: Jane Espenson
Director: Nick Marck
Cast: Pat Crawford Brown (Wig Lady), Brent Hinkley (Manny the Manager),
T Ferguson (Gary), Douglas Bennett (Phillip), Andrew Reville (Timothy),
Kevin C Carter (Mr Typical), John F Kearney (Elderly Man),
Sara Lawall (Housewife Type), Victor Z Isaac (Pimply Teen)

Strapped for cash, Buffy gets a job at a fast-food restaurant where
the weird manager and high turnover of employees has her more
than a little suspicious. When co-workers end up in pieces, the
mystery behind the burgers secret ingredient comes into question.

Dudes and Geeks: Xander says he understands Warren being the
supervillainy type (see **93**, 'I Was Made to Love You'), but he
thought Jonathan had learned his lesson from the events of **73**,
'Superstar'. Willow describes their headquarters as the nerd
natural habitat. Buffy found spell books, parchments, charmed
objects and a conjurer's harp at the *troika*'s headquarters.

Authority Sucks!: Manny, the humourless and horribly clothed
manager of the Doublemeat Palace seems to be a sinister corporate
murderer for most of the episode, but ends it having been eaten by
the monster.

A Little Learning is a Dangerous Thing: One of Anya's ex-demon
colleagues, Halfrek, shows up after receiving a garbled message
concerning the wedding (she notes, rather chillingly, that vengeance-demons spend much of their time maiming the wrong
man). She thinks she's been summoned by a scorned woman to
wreak a terrible vengeance upon Xander.

Mom's Apple Pie: Dawn's friend Janice (see **106**, 'All the Way')
has a sister who is a lawyer. Dawn sadly notes that Buffy's never
going to be either a lawyer or a doctor. Buffy's the Slayer, says
Xander, she saves the world. But this means that she's going to
have crappy minimum-wage jobs her entire life to fit in with her
Slayer duties, Dawn adds. Maybe Dawn will get a job with a
massive salary, Xander suggests. Then she can use her money to
support her deadbeat sister.

Denial, Thy Name is Anya: Anya's conversation with Hallie is a fascinating example of peer pressure and in showing how far removed Anya is from the character she presented when first becoming human (see **50**, 'Doppelgängland'). Hallie suggests this is quasi-domestication and that Xander's little habits, like criticising Anya's lack of tact (see **109**, 'Smashed'), should be a source of annoyance to Anya herself. Cleverly, however, she never actually criticises Xander directly, merely questioning each point in his favour that Anya highlights in a seemingly reasonable, but actually really pointed, way.

The Conspiracy Starts at Home Time: The Doublemeat Palace is one of California's biggest fast-food chains. Their speciality, the Doublemeat Medley, made from the harvesting of two special meats includes a closely guarded secret ingredient, which Buffy speculates, due to a few circumstantial bits of evidence, is actually *people*. It isn't; rather it's a vegetable product. The company, nevertheless, are keen that their customers don't discover they're actually eating veggie burgers. Buffy, having been sacked for her outburst in the restaurant, gets her job back by promising to keep the secret a secret.

Work is a Four-Letter Word: When Anya was a vengeance-demon, she caused pain and mayhem. But, she notes, she put in a full day's work and got compensated appropriately. 'Welcome to today's episode of *Go Money Go*,' replies Xander.

It's a Designer Label!: A strange bunch, with Xander's horrible shirt falling into the fashion victim's column (he wears a much more sartorial red one later when meeting Halfrek). Also, Anya's white top and crimson velvet pants, Willow's ill-fitting jumper, Dawn's red jacket and Buffy's cute black star T-shirt.

References: Visually, *Alien*. Conceptually, *Society* and *Eat the Rich*. Also, Jolene Blalock (Willow notes that the *troika* had numerous pictures of 'that Vulcan woman on *Enterprise*'), *Sleepless in Seattle* and its stars Meg Ryan and Tom Hanks, *Friends* ('hey, standing right here'), Disneyland and the Lollapalooza tour. Buffy's 'variety is the spice of bad' is a paraphrase from *The Timepiece* by William Cowper (1731–1800).

Awesome!: Xander's reaction to the *troika*'s taste in Vulcan sex-symbols. The dreadful company training video that Buffy watches – so *Simpsons*esque that the only thing missing is a Troy

McClure narration. Xander's startled expression when Halfrek appears, and then at the sudden transition to girlie-talk when Anya walks in. Buffy clearly having sex with Spike against the wall outside the diner. Willow angrily ending her friendship with Amy in a staggering metaphor for the inherent problems of abuse recovery when you are surrounded by junkie friends. And, of course, the giant penis-shaped monster that squirts liquid at Willow, who screams and runs away. No intended Freudian symbolism there, clearly.

'You May Remember Me From Such Films and TV Series As . . .': Brent Hinkley was in *The Silence of the Lambs*, *The West Wing*, *Bob Roberts*, *Carnival of Souls*, *Falling Down* and *Ed Wood*. Pat Crawford Brown's CV includes *Jack Frost*, *Moonlighting*, *Sister Act*, *The Rocketeer*, *Johnny Skidmarks*, *Reality Bites* and *Coach*. Kirsten Nelson played Lani in *Three Women in Pain* and the young Dolores Landingham in *The West Wing*, and appeared in *The Fugitive*. John Kearney appeared in *Giro City* and *Judgement*. Kevin Carter's movies include *Ripple* and *Stonewashed*. Sara Lawall was in *The Cable Guy*. The director/producer of *Hungry*, Douglas Bennett, was also in *Gone in Sixty Seconds* and *CSI*.

Don't Give Up the Day Job: Puppeteer Pons Maar previously worked on *Phantoms*, *Return to Oz* and *Theodore Rex*. He was also the voice of Roy in *Dinosaurs*.

The Drugs Don't Work: When Gary gives Buffy a soda cup and tells her to fill it she replies that she wasn't aware they'd be drug-testing on the job. Amy says that she understands Willow is working on a whole cold turkey-thing.

Sex and Drugs and Rock'n'Roll: In the alley outside the Double-meat Palace, a tired and depressed Buffy lets Spike have his way with her.

Logic, Let Me Introduce You to This Window: Whose was the finger and how did it get into the grinder? This is never made clear. How does Anya know just after she's arrived at the Magic Box after her reunion with Halfrek that the chemistry Willow is performing concerns the ingredients of the Doublemeat Palace burgers? What, exactly, are the opening hours of the Doublemeat Palace? Gary was said to be coming in early, around 7 a.m. to open up, so we can assume it opens around 7.30 or 8 o'clock (although Buffy is subsequently shown clocking-in for her shift a few minutes after 9, and she's not alone). More problematic is closing time. Most fast-food chains close around midnight. While Willow is working on the contents of the burger, with Xander and Dawn, Buffy goes to the Doublemeat which is now closed. So if it's, say, just after midnight, and it was Sunday the day before (the only explanation as to why both Anya and Xander would be at home in the middle of the day when Halfrek arrives, and why Willow's at home and not at college) then why is Buffy not bothered about Dawn still being up in the early hours of the morning with school the next day? When Willow arrives, even though the interior is in darkness, the exterior is lit-up as though the store is still open, and the drive-thru intercom is still working. Did Buffy tell Spike she was working at the Doublemeat Palace? If so, why? And if not, how does he know? Not illogical *per se*, but certainly a crime against all laws of God and man: what the hell is up with Willow's hair? She looks like she's had an accident with an electrical implement. Why does Buffy, who has always been so keen to keep Dawn away from Slayer business (see **122**, 'Grave'), show her the severed finger?

Cruelty To Animals: The company video, telling the story of how a cow and a chicken come together to form the Doublemeat Medley was, according to Buffy, kind of graphic with the slaughter. Manny notes that curiosity killed the cat. Buffy mutters, 'Theory number five. Cat burgers.'

Quote/Unquote: Spike: 'What's in the Doublemeat nuggets?'
Buffy: 'That's just great. I try to do the simplest thing in the world, get an ordinary job in a well-lit place and, look, I'm back where I started. Blood and death and funky smells.'

Notes: 'We have a lot of turnover here.' If the old saying is true and we are what we eat then *Buffy*, by way of its constantly healthy diet of horror pastiche, wry social comment and cunning observational comedy is in far better shape than most of the competition. Ah, Magic Jane, where would we be without her? A witty parody on some of the more disturbing aspects of the processed food industry and of the awful realities of the minimum wage lifestyle, which many viewers will be able to identify with, 'Doublemeat Palace' has more jokes per square inch than the Edinburgh Comedy Festival. Much of the delightfully queasy subject matter centres on the secret ingredient in the burgers and whether it has anything to do with the high turnover of staff.

Comedically obvious? Certainly. But it's done with such clever, knowing glances that you can't help but be impressed at the sheer nerve of the thing. *Buffy* usually works best when it's making you laugh at the same time as making you think. 'Doublemeat Palace' does both. With fries.

Buffy mentions waitressing in a diner 'that summer in LA', referring to the events between **34**, 'Becoming' Part 2 and **35**, 'Anne'. Xander, too, has been employed in the fast-food industry (at Hot-Dog-On-A-Stick, see **64**, 'Pangs', and as a pizza delivery boy, **67**, 'Doomed'). Amy asks Willow if she can have the rat cage she lived in for three years, citing sentimental reasons, and Willow agrees. In reality, Amy probably wants to sell it and use the money to get another fix from Rack.

Soundtrack: Warren Bennett's 'The Twist' and Austin and Hughes's 'Pow!' and 'Power Play' play during the Doublemeat Palace training video.

Critique: 'It may seem strange to see a gruesome tale about a burger bar run by a parasitic monster as welcome light relief,' wrote John Binns. 'The first two-thirds remind us how good *Buffy* can be at lampooning the horror genre. Inevitably, perhaps, the resolution is more disappointing: other than the slight wry smile raised by the idea that a burger chain's secret might be that it's products are vegetable-based.'

'The episode never sold a real threat,' noted Sharon Goodman on *FanboyPlanet.com*. 'The idea that there was something fishy going on was easily explained by Buffy's boredom. By the time we find out there was evil afoot, we stopped caring. I have to think the writers are saving up the good stuff for February sweeps.'

Did You Know?: The exterior location used for the Doublemeat Palace diner in this and future episodes was a hot dog restaurant called *Hipperty Hopperty Dog* which can be found on Sepulveda Blvd close to Los Angeles airport.

'Doublemeat Palace' is the only *Buffy* episode that ever caused advertisers to pull out of supporting the series. 'They did *not* like us making fun of fast food,' Joss Whedon told *DreamWatch*.

Cast and Crew Comments: Sarah Michelle Gellar revealed her tips for staying healthy. 'I carry a bottle of water with me all the time,' she told the *National Post*. 'I don't really drink anything except water and iced tea.' Vitamins play a part in the Gellar health regime too. 'I really believe [they] can fix almost anything: skin and hair problems, energy problems, colds. I always take my vitamins, usually a multi and a vitamin C.'

When asked by *FHM* if she'd heard about a *Buffy* drinking game where, every time the viewers catch a glimpse of Buffy's bra-strap, they have a drink, Sarah noted: 'In the first season they always made me wear tank tops. I was about 15 pounds heavier and a full cup size bigger and I wasn't going to wear tank tops without a bra, so you *always* saw the straps. I was thinking, "Great, I'm adding to the drunk-rate in America." But for the second season I discovered strapless bars and it ruined the whole game.'

Jane Espenson's Comments: Was the Doublemeat Palace demon's symbolism deliberate, asked the *Succubus Club*, and if so what was it symbolising? 'It was an enormous penis,' Jane replied candidly. 'We didn't know it was going to look like that. It wasn't intentional. Would we have a lesbian cut off a giant penis? That's icky and strange. However, once it had happened, we felt free to comment on it.'

'[All of the writers] had fast-food experiences except me,' Jane noted in the same interview. 'Marti worked at McDonalds and had a lot of insight. My boyfriend worked at some dreadful fast-food places in Ohio. Really awful-sounding places so he had all the information about the buttons and the grill. We almost backed away from having her in fast-food when Joss remembered she had waitressed before. But fast-food is a whole different kind of job than working in a diner. You wouldn't believe the amount of the conversations [we had] about what Buffy should do for a living. It needed to be something awful. Fast-food was about as awful as we could think of.'

Joss Whedon's Comments: Ever since John Ritter appeared in 23, 'Ted', *Buffy* has been lacking in celebrity guest stars. Hasn't anyone famous asked if they could do a cameo? 'I heard a rumor that REM wanted to be on the show,' Joss told *Maxim*, 'but I haven't confirmed that. Famous people aren't going, "I want to be on the show!" Which is OK, because this isn't *Friends*.'

113
Dead Things

US Transmission Date: 05 Feb 2002
UK Transmission Date: 28 Mar 2002

Writer: Steve S DeKnight
Director: James A Contner
Cast: Rock Reiser (Desk Sergeant), Bernard K Addison (Cop #1),
Eric Prescott (Cop #2)

The *troika*'s latest riotous escapade is to turn Warren's ex-girlfriend, Katrina, into their sex-slave. Inevitably, it goes horribly wrong when Warren kills her. They use sorcery to make Buffy believe that *she* killed Katrina – and it seems to work as Buffy's world begins to fall apart.

Freudian Guilt-Trip: Believing, like Buffy, that she has killed an innocent girl in the forest, Spike manages to get Buffy home. There, she suffers a terrifying erotic nightmare full of lesbian overtones, penis and bondage metaphors (the stake, the handcuffs) and guilt with a capital G. For the psychology student this has got, literally, *everything*. Subtext: Buffy is so appalled by her continued involvement in an abusive tryst with a vampire who is unredeemed by a soul, and by her shame that, after two essentially noble boyfriends, she's been reduced to *this*, she is seeking some severe punishment for it. As her mom's dead and a spanking's probably out of the question, what better than a long stretch in prison? It's the best bit of the episode by a mile, but it also highlights everything that's, conceptually, wrong with 'Dead Things'.

Dudes and Babes: Unable to confide in Willow, Buffy tells Tara that Spike can hurt her and asks about the resurrection spell. Does this mean that Buffy came back as a demon? Tara uses numerous texts including *The Brekenkrieg Grimore* to check and, ultimately, tells Buffy that there's nothing wrong with her. She *is* slightly different as, when her essence was funnelled back into her body, it subtly altered Buffy on a molecular level. Probably just enough to confuse the sensors in Spike's chip. Tara compares it to nothing worse than bad sunburn. Buffy then, tearfully, confesses to Tara that there *must* be something wrong with her otherwise why would she let Spike do these things to her (there's that subtext again). Buffy suggests that while Spike stands for everything she hates, the only time she *feels* anything since she returned from paradise is when she's with him. Tara sympathetically asks Buffy if she loves Spike, stressing that, despite his less-than-admirable qualities, he *has* done a lot of good and, in his own way, he very definitely *does* love Buffy. However, Buffy finally realises that she's been using him.

A Little Learning is a Dangerous Thing: Anya notes that human perception is based on a linear chronology. Being exposed to the Rwasundi (the demons that Jonathan seemingly summoned) for more than a few seconds can cause vivid hallucinations and a slightly tingly scalp. However, Buffy has regained enough of her awareness by this point to realise that Warren *must* have had something to do with Katrina's death. And, thus, she herself didn't.

Denial, Thy Name is Buffy: She's got it as bad as her mom ever did. You don't have a soul, she screams at Spike. There is nothing good or clean in him. He's dead inside. Denial transference? This is, in many ways, a pivotal episode for Buffy, character-wise. She finally climbs out of the hole of denial into which she's been sinking since **103**, 'After Life', in the closing moments, weeping on Tara's knee. At least she has now admitted that she's been using Spike, but it's been a long, slow process to get to this point. Buffy is also very bloody-minded about going to the police, and is seemingly oblivious that this will really mess-up Dawn's life (even if Buffy could convince the authorities that killing Katrina was an accident, Dawn would still be put into care immediately). Of course, this isn't the first time that Buffy has believed she's killed someone human (see **23**, 'Ted'). The part of her that isn't a Slayer is still a bewildered 21-year-old girl who knows that she's done something appalling and needs to atone for it to rid herself of the guilt. Nevertheless, Dawn is correct when she says that Buffy's unhappiness since she returned from paradise is partly the reason she's so keen to go to the police. Prison, in many ways, is an ideal place for people who don't want to deal with their more complex issues. Buffy *has* responsibilities – both as a surrogate-mother to Dawn and as the Slayer to the world at large – neither of which she can walk away from no matter how tempting that solution may be. And, really, she *knows* that.

The Psychology Starts at a Dramatically Appropriate Time: The entire season, in some ways, can be viewed as a subtextual essay on both personal and social perceptions, and this episode is the key text in this reading. Both Buffy, post-resurrection, and, especially, Warren have a problem in seeing other people as an entity in and of itself (Buffy's treatment of Spike is frequently appalling; with Warren it's an almost sociopathic disregard for anything other than an abstract concept of life as a kind of hedonistic toyshop; we saw this in **93**, 'I Was Made to Love You', and it's even more evident here). His friends don't seem immune to this either; after Katrina's death note how Jonathan refers to Warren's dead girlfriend as 'her' once and then, looking at the body, notes 'we have to get rid of *it*'. Andrew merely seems intoxicated at the end of the episode that they have, in effect, gotten away with murder (something that will grow fatter and more rancid as the season progresses). Spike, for his part, has the same problem that many serial killers have: an inability to view humans as humans rather than just lumps of meat. Katrina is only real to him in the sense that she's a dead body, the discovery of which will get Buffy in trouble. Spike dumps her in the river and genuinely can't understand why Buffy is willing to give up everything because of this faceless girl's death.

Work is a Four-Letter Word: Buffy's still putting in long hours at the Doublemeat Palace, to the extent that Dawn is becoming even more distanced and intolerant of her.

It's a Designer Label!: Warren's *urban pimp* pickup suit. *Nice threads*. Also, Xander's purple shirt, Buffy's green strapless top, Willow's suede jacket and Tara's lumpy green sweater. Anya is vision in red at the Bronze.

References: The title may be an oblique reference to the movie *Very Bad Things*, which also concerned an elaborate cover-up of a woman's accidental death. Buffy refers to cult movie director David Lynch (*Eraserhead*, *Twin Peaks*, *Wild at Heart*, *Mulholland Drive*) and claims to have some New Kids on the Block posters. Also paraphrases from *The Wacky Races* ('And, she's off'), *The Simpsons* ('Gentlemen, to crime'), *I Dream of Jeannie* ('I love you, Master'), *The X-Files* ('this isn't happening') and allusions to *Soul Train*, *Rosemary's Baby* (Buffy's dream sequence) and the Mills Brothers' 'You Always Hurt The One You Love'.

Geek-Speak: Jonathan steals Andrew's copy of Peter Frampton's *Frampton Comes Alive*. Later, the pair spar with plastic *Star Wars* lightsabers.

Awesome!: While there *is* something inherently amusing about Jonathan and Andrew chanting "BAZOOMBAS!", the fact that this occurs in a scene where they are aiding Warren to procure an intended rape-victim renders this somewhat tacky. Whatever one may think of Spike, his love for Buffy in this episode is demonstrably clear. When he says that he loves her and Buffy replies that he doesn't, Spike's response is particularly impressive: 'You think I haven't tried *not to*?' The final scene, with Buffy tearfully begging Tara *not* to forgive her for having sex with Spike *is* cathartic and *almost* cancels out some of the episode's less savoury aspects.

'You May Remember Me From Such Films and TV Series As . . .': Rock Reiser appeared in *Never Been Kissed*, *Gideon's Crossing*, *Melrose Place* and *Space: Above and Beyond*. Eric Prescott was in *Days of Our Lives*. Bernard Addison's CV includes *Frasier* and *Celebrity*.

Don't Give Up The Day Job: Producer John Perry previously worked on *Midnight Caller* and *Falcon Crest*.

The Drugs Don't Work: Willow has been spell-free for 32 days (presumably that was how long ago the events of **110**, 'Wrecked', took place). She did some involuntary magic in **112**, 'Doublemeat Palace', but it was Amy who cast that spell against Willow's wishes so she's probably not counting that.

Valley-Speak: Andrew: 'Dude, *that* is messed-up.'

Cigarettes & Alcohol: When the Scoobies are planning to go to the Bronze, Xander promises tall glasses of frosty relaxation on him. In the bar, Katrina is drinking red wine. Warren dumps his ear-piece into a cocktail. The *troika* toast the, initial, success of their cerebral dampener with champagne (which Andrew thinks tastes funny). Spike smokes while drinking his blood in the crypt.

Sex and Drugs and Rock'n'Roll: Yet another torrid episode opening full of grunting and nakedness with Spike and Buffy going at it on the floor of his crypt. The way that Buffy makes it hurt in all the wrong places, notes Spike: 'I've never been with such an animal.' Buffy angrily replies that she's not an animal. Spike asks her if she'd like to see his bite marks. Sexually, at least, they *do* seem to have a good time. Nevertheless, Spike remains concerned about what, exactly, is going on between them and asks Buffy if she even likes him. Sometimes, she replies, honestly. Then, holding up a pair of handcuffs, Spike asks Buffy if she trusts him. Never, is the obvious reply.

Warren's latest deranged plan, aided by Jonathan's bone-magic, involves a cerebral dampener that will make any woman the *troika* desire into their slave. Of course, it all goes horribly wrong when Katrina, dressed – inevitably – in a sexy French-maid's outfit straight out of *The Benny Hill Show*, suddenly throws off her conditioning, realises what's going on, gives a dramatic little rape speech, and then gets murdered with a blunt instrument. Jonathan, who otherwise comes out of the episode fairly well (certainly better than Andrew and Warren), nevertheless says he could have used a cerebral dampener in high school. As opposed to, say, a gun (see **52**, 'Earshot')?

Logic, Let Me Introduce You to This Window: At one point Buffy turns her head, revealing her neck. Since she's been bitten on at least three occasions in the series (**12**, 'Prophecy Girl'; **56**, 'Graduation Day' Part 2; **79**, 'Buffy vs Dracula') shouldn't she have scars, as shown in previous episodes (notably the one Parker comments upon in **59**, 'The Harsh Light of Day')? Buffy and Spike have a huge fight beside a police building and yet aren't spotted or arrested for affray. Principal Snyder's line about the police of Sunnydale being deeply stupid (**34**, 'Becoming' Part 2) is something the writers – not unjustifiably – keep on coming back to (see **122**, 'Grave'). What's Katrina doing back in Sunnydale? In **93**, 'I Was Made to Love You', it was revealed that she came from out of town. It's difficult to imagine that, after the horrors she went through in that story, she would have any reason to ever come back. Katrina is wearing mainly black clothes in the bar. Next time we see her, the *troika* have changed her into the French-maid outfit. After her death, the scenes in the woods have both her and Jonathan impersonating her wearing a short blue skirt and a blue sweater – where did *those* come from? The whole deal with the Rwasundi is rather confusing. Who summoned them? Jonathan, seemingly, since he's the one interacting with them, though isn't Andrew normally the *troika* member with responsibility for the demony-type stuff? Additionally, if the Rwasundi cause the time distortion then why isn't Jonathan (who's impersonating Katrina) affected by this along with Buffy and Spike?

I Just *Love* Your Accent: Tired of talking bollocks (see **110**, 'Wrecked'), seemingly, Spike uses another British variant: 'Oh, balls!'

Quote/Unquote: Spike, on Buffy's friends: 'You try to stay with them. But you always end up in the dark places. With me.'

Notes: 'This isn't some fantasy you freaks, it's rape . . . I'm going to make sure they lock you away for this.' There are many laudable things in this episode's story of shallow desire versus mature needs. Unfortunately, a thoroughly sick, venal aberration within the presented characterisation (particularly of the *troika*) and a series of highly unsavoury BDSM-gags in the Buffy/Spike relationship, which seem to be there purely to get up the noses of *The Parents Television Council*, drag a promising script into some murky depths. A *Buffy* episode including rape and bondage allusions? How desperately grown-up. Watching **113**, 'Dead Things', frankly, is like wading through a cesspool in search of a diamond. Like **49**, 'Consequences' (which, on more occasions than is truly healthy, this episode greatly resembles) 'Dead Things' plays with the idea of the Slayer equivalent of collateral damage. Only this time, Buffy, rather than Faith, is the central figure. All of this occurs as she's getting a depressing dose of victim-culture concerning her continuing morbid fascination with Spike. Sadly, elsewhere, the episode plays dangerous, disturbing games with what this season seems to have as the central theme. It's all very well to say 'oh, grow up' to fat immature fanboys who live in the basement with their comic collection and *Star Wars* figures. But when that growing up process turns them into Jeffrey Dahmer, is it really such a good idea to pick at this raw scab? This is, by no means, the first time that a *Buffy* episode has disturbed me. Unlike **66**, 'Hush' or **94**, 'The Body', however, what's disturbing about 'Dead Things' is what it says rather than the way it says it.

Spike remembers that he ate a decorator once. Katrina mentions Warren's wind-up slut who tried to choke her to death (see **93**, 'I Was Made to Love You'). Dawn is staying at Janice's (**106**, 'All the Way') where Janice's mom intends to teach her how to make tortillas. The coroner who reports on Katrina's death is called Willard Batts. Dated 1 February 2002, this states: 'Victim sustained injuries consistent with a fall. Twenty-one-year-old Katrina Silber's death appears to have been caused by an accidental drowning or suicide.'

Soundtrack: 'Boo Wah Boo Wah' by Red & the Red Hots plays at the Bronze when Anya, Xander and Willow are dancing. Also, 'Sleeping Beauty Waltz' by Piotr Tchaikovsky, 'Out Of This World' by Bush (the highly charged scene in which Buffy almost-but-not-quite enters Spike's crypt) and 'Fingersnap' from the Non-Stop Music Library.

Did You Know?: Two British teenagers who tried to push a girl over a cliff and threatened to bite her after watching a *Buffy* episode escaped a custodial sentence in March 2002. Nicola Millar and Kelly Brannigan, from Stevenston, Ayrshire, carried out the attack on their victim and left her on waste ground, an Edinburgh court heard. Both pleaded guilty to charges of assault. The judge took into account that they were first-time offenders, placed both on probation for three years and ordered them to do 240 hours' community service.

Joss Whedon's Comments: Which movies does Joss wish that he'd written? '*The Matrix, Magnolia, Three Kings, Casablanca, South Park, Sense and Sensibility* and *Firestorm* with Howi Long,' Joss told the *Posting Board*.

114
Older, and Far Away

US Transmission Date: 12 Feb 2002
UK Transmission Date: 4 Apr 2002

Writer: Drew Z Greenberg
Director: Michael Gershman
Cast: Ryan Browning (Richard), Laura Roth (Sophie),
Elizabeth Cazenave (Teacher)

Friends new and old gather at Revello Drive for Buffy's 21st birthday party and (for once) it all seems to go off without a hitch. However, feeling neglected by Buffy, Dawn's wish to keep people from leaving her is answered by Anya's former colleague Halfrek, who binds the attendees of the party to the house. When Tara tries a spell to free them, she only makes the situation worse by accidentally releasing a demon.

Dudes and Babes: Tara suggests that Richard, the proposed date that Anya and Xander have set Buffy up with is cute, although she admits she's not a very good judge of cuteness in boys. Clem agrees with her. Spike just scowls at them both.

A Little Learning is a Dangerous Thing: Amusingly, after all of the grief the Scoobies have given Willow, it's Tara's magic that goes disastrously wrong on this occasion.

Mom's Apple Pie: Despite having to run out on Dawn, yet again, in the opening scene Buffy does find the time to tell her sister to finish dinner, do her homework, and don't stay up too late.

Denial, Thy Name is Dawn: Proving, not for the first time, that when the mood takes her she can be a right stroppy, attention-seeking drama queen, Dawn accidentally sets in motion the events of the episode. Not that she doesn't have some legitimate grievances in her life (Glory, Joyce's death, Buffy's death) *and*, to be fair, she's handled herself with a great maturity for much of the time. It must be hard for the lass, especially as even the one member of Buffy's crowd that she really likes and that everyone else can't stand, Spike, has been more interested in shagging her sister than hanging out with her like he used to. But she's been dealing with many of these insecurities through kleptomania, perhaps hoping that when she gets caught she'll finally receive some attention. Even before Halfrek's intervention, her stolen birthday present for Buffy was an incredibly blatant cry for help, literally demanding that Buffy ask questions about its purchase. Hanging out with the people she does, it's reasonable to assume that Dawn should know better than to make a wish to a stranger, but the phrase 'sometimes, I wish . . .' is a part of every teenager's vocabulary. Buffy's sense of just how lonely Dawn has become may, perhaps, help her with her own disassociation complex (see **113**, 'Dead Things'). Still, the theft-thing finally comes home to roost. Anya, the owner of most of the trinkets in Dawn's secret stash, *is* in mood for forgiveness, but at a price: 'We're gonna talk about payment,' she notes. 'There are two words I want you to get used to. Punitive damages!'

The Allergies Start at Party Time: Sophie, Buffy's seemingly school-age friend, is allergic to chocolate, egg yolk and peanuts. And, sometimes, dairy products. And alcohol (because of the barley).

Presents: Buffy's birthday gifts include a battery-operated back massager (probably from Willow), a gorgeous black leather jacket (which Dawn shoplifted) and a weapons chest (which Xander built and Anya offered helpful suggestions about).

It's a Designer Label!: Dawn's red top (which also appears in the next episode). Loads of cool party clothes including Buffy's strapless black top, Willow's gorgeous see-through blouse and Tara's crimson skirt.

References: Witty allusions to *Children of the Corn* ('only thing missing is a cornfield') and *Night of the Living Dead*. The title is a quotation from the novel *Empire of the Sun*. An issue of Neil

Gaiman's *The Sandman* ('24 Hours') about a group of people trapped in a diner is, conceptually, similar to this episode. Also, *Moonlighting* (Buffy and Spike's argument, and especially both repeating 'fine' to each other is *very* Maddy/David), *Stargate SG-1* ('well, *this* can't be good'), *The Simpsons* ('that was sarcasm by the way') and *The Addams Family* ('you rang?').

Awesome!: Xander gets most of the good lines, and Spike most of the pithy ones. Tara suggesting Spike put some ice on his muscle cramp. Sophie noting that she'd sooner stay trapped in the house than do a shift at the Doublemeat. Anya's hilariously claustrophobic panic-attack and Halfrek's dramatic *deus ex-machina*-style arrival before being trapped by her own curse. Also, Clem's closing line: 'Cool party!'

'You May Remember Me From Such Films and TV Series As . . .': Ryan Browning appeared in *Stealing Sinatra*, *Losing Grace* and *Baywatch*. Laura Roth was in *Once and Again* and *Malcolm in the Middle*. Elizabeth Cazenave appeared in *The Mothman Prophecies*.

Don't Give Up The Day Job: Visual Effects creator Randy Goux's talents can also be seen on *X-Men* and *The Lord of the Rings*.

Valley-Speak: Richard: 'You have some weird friends.' Xander: 'News from the file marked *duh*.'

Cigarettes & Alcohol: Spike arrives at the party with a six-pack of beer.

Logic, Let Me Introduce You to This Window: Buffy's birthday has been established as being mid-January (see **25**, 'Surprise'; **36**, 'Helpless'). Yet for the last two seasons the episode that contains her birthday has been broadcast in February. When Buffy pulls Spike away from the group after he jokes about eating Richard you can see Spike's reflection in the hall mirror. When Tara casts the release spell, why is Spike getting ready to rush the door, into broad daylight, without a blanket or any other form of protection from the sun? Also, how can Spike be in Dawn's room where there is sunlight pouring through the open windows without him bursting into flames? Moving someone with a heavy stomach wound up a flight of stairs isn't recommended emergency medical treatment. When Richard is stabbed, it appears that the blade went deep enough to rupture a major organ, yet he lives for several hours while trapped in the house, and the Scoobies don't even bother to put on a bandage (although Tara does dab at the wound with something). How did Dawn get the jacket out of the store with the security tag still attached? Anya claims that only a vengeance-demon can break his or her own spell. She, of all people, should know better. Giles destroying her amulet in an alternate reality broke her spell for Cordelia and trapped Anya in human form (**43**, 'The Wish'). If Willow and Tara have classes in the morning then shouldn't Dawn, also, have to go to school? She certainly doesn't seem like she's getting ready to go.

Cruelty to Animals: When Xander suggests the boys play poker, Clem says it's weird without kittens (see **105**, 'Life Serial').

Quote/Unquote: Spike: 'I had a muscle cramp. Buffy was helping.' Tara: ' . . . In your pants?'

Notes: 'People have a tendency to go away . . . Sometimes I wish I could make them stop.' Buffy's birthday parties always seem to end with some catastrophe for her friends. 'You ever think about *not* celebrating?' asks an exasperated Spike at one point. The pain of her perceived and constant rejection by Buffy and a craving to be the centre of attention for once forces Dawn into her own, private version of **43**, 'The Wish'. Thus, we get a classic bottle-show in the tradition of all good slasher movies (and some bad ones), with ten characters trapped in a house. Drew Greenberg's previous script, **109**, 'Smashed', hinted at a real talent emerging and, while 'Older, and Far Away' isn't a patch on *that* riotous collection of comedy hijinx, it does show a writer developing a unique and interesting new voice in the *Buffy* oeuvre. Well directed and as sharp as a needle when it's going for the joke-shock-joke two-step (let's pretend that a thoroughly slovenly middle section without hardly a laugh in sight never happened) once again *Buffy* proves that even when it's taking shortcuts, it can still produce innovation.

Spike has a black eye from the beating Buffy gave him in **113**, 'Dead Things'. Tara says she thought that cursing unfaithful men was all that vengeance-demons did. Halfrek says this was Anya's *raison d'être* but they all have different specialities. And that they prefer the more ideologically acceptable term justice-demon. Halfrek's main area of work is protecting neglected children and punishing their parents and she originally came to Sunnydale because she heard Dawn's cries for attention (Daddy issues, says Anya, very bitchily). In one of the most clever pieces of continuity the series ever did, when Halfrek sees Spike she calls him William and then, embarrassed, they both try to pretend that they don't know each other (Kali Rocha played the then-human William's unrequited love interest, Cecily, in **85**, 'Fool For Love'). The Magic Box's range of Essence of Slug candles are mentioned again (see **105**, 'Life Serial'). Willow appears to be attending a group of like-minded witches who are trying to give up magic. They're called Spellcasters Anonymous although they're said to be looking for a better name. Richard works with Xander at the construction site. Dawn refers to the events of **50**, 'Doppelgängland', while Xander alludes to his invocation of the musical amulet in **107**, 'Once More, With Feeling'.

Soundtrack: Mint Royale's 'Rock And Roll Bar', 'The Race' by Gwenmars, 'California Calling' by Opus 1, 'Seconds' by Even, 'Down, Down, Down' from the Extreme Music Library, 'Pictures Of Success' by Rilo Kiley and Aberdeen's 'Clouds Like These'.

Did You Know?: James Marsters appeared naked in his first acting job – a Chicago stage production of *The Tempest*. But having to get his kit off regularly on TV necessitates some discipline, as he told *Sci-Fi Wire*. 'Luckily, Sarah and I have built up trust and friendship, so we lean on each other. She taught me that love-scenes are much like fight-scenes. You're going to a level of unreality that's beyond normal acting. We did eight takes. Finally, Sarah said, "Just don't do anything. Do the worst acting in your life. Think about breakfast." We did it again, and that's the take you see.'

Cast and Crew Comments: Michelle Trachtenberg, according to *CT Now* website, had previously set her sights on going to Yale and studying theatre and English. However: 'I realised I wanted to consider other colleges and decide what subjects I really wanted to study,' she says. 'I know what to do before the cameras. Now I want to learn what to do behind them. I'm even thinking of taking a year off after I graduate and maybe making a movie in a place like Italy. That would give me a chance to travel and work at the same time. Education is important to me. So is work. But the most important thing in my life is my family – my mother, my sister, my father and my cat, Casey.'

Joss Whedon's Comments: When *Buffy* actors get questions concerning future developments in interviews, they always seem to answer with horrific threats like: 'I can't tell you, Joss will rip out my tongue and feed it to wolves.' So, does Whedon *actually* say things like that? 'I'm a very gentle man, not unlike Gandhi,' Joss told Tasha Robinson. 'I don't threaten them. There is, sort of hanging over their head, the thing that I could kill them at any moment. But that's just if they annoy me. They know that I'm very secretive about plot twists, because I think it's better for the show. But anybody with a computer can find out what's going to happen, apparently even before I know. So my wish for secrecy is pathetic.'

115
As You Were

US Transmission Date: 26 Feb 2002
UK Transmission Date: 11 Apr 2202

Writer: Douglas Petrie
Director: Douglas Petrie
Cast: Ivana Milcevic (Sam Finn), Ryan Roberts (Todd),
Adam Paul (Skanky Vamp), Marilyn Brett (Lady),
Alice Dinnean Vernon (Baby Demon Puppeteer)

Riley Finn pursues a demon to Sunnydale and seeks Buffy's help in capturing it. He also comes with a surprise ... he's happily married. His wife, fellow military demon hunter Sam, befriends the Scooby Gang. But Buffy's own relationship with Spike comes into question when her ex's perfect romance illustrates to her what she, herself, no longer has.

Dreaming (As Blondie Once Said) is Free: Xander says he's starting to have dreams of gardenia bouquets and is glad his manly co-workers couldn't hear him confess this to Anya.

Dudes and Babes: Sam gives Willow a sweet little pep-talk over Willow's bravery in facing up to her addiction. Riley's team, Sam notes, had two hard-core shamans working for them. Both got addicted and neither survived the ordeal. Sam tells Willow that she's never met anyone with enough strength to quit before now.

A Little Learning is a Dangerous Thing: In a pointed moment, Doublemeat Palace know-all Todd reminds Buffy that she dropped out of college. Todd, himself, is attending night classes working for his MBA so he doesn't have to spend all his life flipping burgers. Later, Buffy receives a rejection letter for her application to re-enrol at UCOD from Surrinda Blackmaster, the assistant to the dean.

Denial, Thy Name is Buffy: Shaken by Riley's return, and the fact that he's managed to get over her by marrying (in effect) a female clone of himself, Buffy goes to Spike, ostensibly for information, but actually so that he can comfort her. Tell me you love me, she demands before they go to bed. After the discovery that Spike *is* responsible for obtaining the demon eggs, Riley offers to kill Spike if Buffy would like. Buffy asks Riley if he deliberately waited until his life was absolutely perfect before returning to find her sleeping with a vampire. Despite Buffy's self-proclaimed incredible patheticness, none of that means anything to Riley because it doesn't touch the real Buffy, he notes. She is still the first woman Riley ever loved. Buffy admits that on the night he left Sunnydale (**88**, 'Into The Woods') she never had the chance to tell you him how sorry she was about what happened between them. She never has to, replies Riley.

After Riley's departure, Buffy returns to Spike and tells him that their relationship is over: She *does* want him, she reveals, sadly. Being with him makes things simpler. But, she admits, she's using him. 'I'm just being weak and selfish. And it's killing me.'

The Conspiracy Starts at Home Time: Riley and Sam are tracking a Suvolte demon, which is rare, lethal and nearly extinct. They've been following it through every jungle from Paraguay. Suvoltes start to kill from the moment they hatch and reach full maturity around three months. Sam believes the demon's eggs are being sold on the black market. There are foreign military powers that would love to have their own Suvolte. You could never train it, but drop it on an urban population and it would cleanse the area. When they approach the demon, Riley tells bystanders that he's from the National Forestry Service and there's a wild bear on the loose.

It's a Designer Label!: Buffy's disgusting yellow duffel-coat. Much better is the ninja-wear state-of-the-art kevlar combat gear that Riley provides.

References: Allusions to Nicolo Machiavelli (1469–1527, Italian political and military theorist), *Thunderbirds* ('m'lady'), Lyndon Johnson (1908–73) and his successor Richard Nixon (1913–94), golfer Arnold Palmer, James Bond, *Goldeneye* ('boys with toys'), the June 1944 Allied invasion of Normandy (as portrayed in movies as diverse as *The Longest Day* and *Saving Private Ryan*), the Broadway showtune 'If I Knew You Were Coming I'd Have

Baked a Cake', most associated with Ethel Merman (1908–84), although the hit version was by Eileen Barton, the Small Faces' 'Tin Soldier' and Neil Armstrong's 1969 moon-landing speech ('that's a first big step'). Riley paraphrases 2Unlimited's 'Get Ready For This'. Xander's description of Riley and Sam as Nick and Nora Fury is a reference to Nick and Nora Charles, the sleuths of Dashiell Hammet's *The Thin Man*, and to Nick Fury, the cigar-chomping Marvel comic hero.

Geek-Speak: When Riley describes the Suvolte's breeding habits, Buffy notes: 'So they're like really mean tribbles?' She then apologises, noting that she's been dealing a lot with the *troika*. Later, she asks Riley if he's got a jet-pack (see **119**, 'Seeing Red').

Bitch: Being hyper-supportive of her best friend, Willow tells Buffy that she's prepared to hate Sam in any way Buffy wants. 'I don't wanna seem petty,' says Buffy who, it turns out, rather likes Sam. That's the beauty, replies Willow. 'Let me carry the hate for both of us!' Willow subsequently gets on really well with Sam too, and they swap e-mail addresses. But, as the helicopter carrying Sam and Riley leaves, after waving them off Willow turns away scowling and tells Buffy, brilliantly: 'What a bitch!'

Awesome!: The vampire refusing the eat Buffy once he realises that she's been eating Doublemeat burgers. Buffy's dim-witted response to Riley's surprise arrival: 'My hat has a cow.'

'You May Remember Me From Such Films and TV Series As . . .': Bosnian-born Ivana Milicevic was Emma in *Vanilla Sky* and Roxana in *Head Over Heals*. She also appeared in *Postmortem*, *The Devil's Child*, *The Nanny*, *Felicity* and *Jerry Maguire*. Marilyn Brett was, memorably, in *American Pie 2*, *Going Nomad* and *Girl, Interrupted*. Adam Paul's movies include *Biohazard* and *The Pentagon Wars*.

Don't Give Up The Day Job: Key Grip George Palmer worked on *Titanic*, *Independence Day*, *Tales from the Crypt* and *Cutting Class*. Chief Lighting Technician Chris Strong's CV includes movies such as *Alien: Resurrection*, *Nixon*, *Se7en* and *Speed*.

Cigarettes & Alcohol: Xander has a beer with his nachos at the Bronze as he and Anya argue about the wedding arrangements.

Logic, Let Me Introduce You to This Window: As with Spike in **112**, 'Doublemeat Palace', how does Riley know that Buffy works at the diner? Riley notices Buffy's new haircut, but he doesn't question further her comment that she died (nor the fact that Joyce is absent – presumably all of this was done off-screen in one big catching-up session. He subsequently knows, for instance, that Xander is getting married). When Buffy stakes the vampire, the stake clearly doesn't go through his heart, but rather the middle of his chest, yet he still explodes. Wasn't Xander supposed to be at Buffy's house watching Dawn while Buffy, Sam and Riley were out? Instead he was at *his* house with Anya hiding from his relatives. More queries about the Doublemeat Palace's opening hours: Buffy was said to be 'working till close', then she did a quick patrol, had sex with Spike, and finally went home and told Dawn, who is going to the Bronze with Willow, to be home by eleven. Wouldn't it already be well past eleven by the time she got home (assuming a late shift is just that, see **112**, 'Doublemeat Palace'). If, as soon as one Suvolte is killed, a dozen take its place, as Riley suggests, then how is the race nearly extinct? Spike is now an international criminal mastermind, seemingly. Despite Buffy and Riley's low opinion of his intelligence ('incompetent' and 'an idiot' respectively), Spike's a sharp enough kiddie to be unlikely to store anything potentially valuable without making sure he knew how to keep it in good condition. And why would he use the street name Doctor? Everybody in the Sunnydale underworld who matters knows exactly who he is. Plus, more importantly, a demon with a very similar name was involved in the worst night of Spike's life (see **100**, 'The Gift'). He might be evil but he's not a masochist. Sunnydale's zip code is 95037, which is actually a code for the town of Morgan Hill at the southern end of the Santa Clara Valley south of San Francisco.

I Just *Love* Your Accent: Spike is the first person to use the phrase it's a fair cop on TV since 1971. He tells Riley that Buffy isn't 'your bint any more' (see **59**, 'The Harsh Light of Day'; **82**, 'Out of My Mind'). Dawn suggests Willow is awfully chipper tonight. Must be Spike's influence rubbing off.

Quote/Unquote: Buffy, to Sam and Riley after their revelation: 'Husband? Wife? Those aren't code names like Big Dog or Falcon?'

Riley: 'I'm taking this place apart until I find that nest.' Spike: 'Over my dead body.' Riley: 'I've seen enough of your dead body for one night, thanks.'

Notes: 'You want me to say that I liked seeing you in bed with that idiot? Or blinding orange is your best colour? Or that burger smell is appealing?' The prodigal returns. Riley Finn, fresh from a glut of demon slaughtering in South America, comes back to Sunnydale. 'As You Were' neatly ties up the loose ends left from Riley's sudden departure (see **88**, 'Into the Woods'). Like why it happened, for instance. In offering up Riley to the sacrificial alter of fandom, Joss Whedon stated that such a Gary Cooper-like character could not function in the *Buffy*-universe. Except, perhaps, as a comic feed which is the role Marc Blucas gets to play here and, credit to the lad, he pulls it off very well. Amid the torrid and sandblasted emotional lives of the Scooby Gang, we also have the most *Buffy*-like episode of this season thus far: a story about tracking a demon nasty in which Xander and Willow keep out of the way and say funny things, Buffy and Riley (plus Mrs Finn) get proactive with the murdering and Spike is actually evil for a change. There are lots of little throwaway comedy gems in Petrie's script (Spike's delight at Riley finding him *in-flagrante* with Buffy is particularly noteworthy). Very much as you were, then, with just a hint of that which is yet to come.

When Willow was little she spent many hours imagining what her eventual wedding to Xander would be like. Anya and Xander are going to the airport to pick up Xander's often mentioned alcoholic uncle, Rory (see **116**, 'Hell's Bells'). Xander says he hates him and, indeed, his whole family. Riley and Sam have been married for four months. Sam asks Buffy if she has a safehouse. Buffy replies she has a house and it's usually safe. Sometimes you can't even leave (see **114**, 'Older, and Far Away'). Riley mentions Willy's Bar (he was last seen there in **86**, 'Shadow', getting some vampire-love from Sandy). Sam went to Central America with the Peace Corps where her whole infirmary was slaughtered by something supernaturally horrid. She subsequently joined the government's latest version of the Initiative (see **63**, 'The Initiative') which she calls the squad and, in her first firefight, met Riley.

Soundtrack: 'Sound of the Revolution' by Lunatic Calm and 'Washes Away' by Trespassers William.

Critique: 'The bleakness of the themes puts the series closer to Philip Roth, even Samuel Beckett, than Anne Rice,' noted Robert Hanks in the *Independent*. 'All this makes it sound pretentious and heavy going. But the other point to make about *Buffy* is that it is deliciously competent. The dialogue [is] unvaryingly slick and witty, up there with the best Hollywood screwball comedies; the storylines [are] brilliantly laid out, and the characters have grown in ways that are recognisable from life, while wholly unfamiliar to television. This is what attracts the intellectuals.'

Did You Know?: An average episode of *Buffy* only requires two days on location away from the Mutant Enemy lot in Santa Monica, which has increased in size dramatically over the last five years. That's a big difference from the early days when the production would be on the road for up to six days per episode. Filming at Torrance High School, which doubled for Sunnydale High in the first three seasons, was an interesting logistical challenge. 'The school were helpful to us and everyone was very nice until the end of season three,' notes producer Gareth Davies. 'We'd told [the local population] that we were going to blow up the school. Unfortunately, we neglected to tell them *when*.' So, when the massive explosion in **56**, 'Graduation Day' Part 2, occurred at 5 a.m. one morning in 1999, many residents were less than impressed. 'We recently went back to the area,' Davies told Rob Francis. 'As soon as we announced it I got a series of irate letters from people over something that happened three years ago.'

Head On: 'When a record company said they were interested in doing an album with me, my first reaction was "Actor in his 40s releases album. Put it on the shelf between William Shatner and David Hasselhoff," ' Tony Head wryly noted. 'But I figured it was safe enough if I made it working with people I respect and love. So, Joss has contributed a song, James is on the album and so are Amber and Alyson.' The fruit of his labours, *Music for Elevators*, was released early in 2002. The record was made in collaboration with noted dance producer George Sarah of THC (who had previously appeared in **61**, 'Beer Bad', and **62** 'Wild at Heart', as part of Veruca's band). A mixture of ambient-trance and folk, the CD included a startling reworking of Lennon and McCartney's 'We Can Work It Out' and the Joss Whedon-written 'Last Time'. James Marsters provides backing vocals on the CD's standout song, 'Owning My Mistakes'.

Joss Whedon's Comments: 'It's going to get worse,' Joss noted, concerning the levels of miserablism in season six. 'We have a lot of humour in store, and a lot of goofy, crazy stuff, but are we bringing on the pain? We *love* pain. But, there's happiness. There's always hope.'

116
Hell's Bells

US Transmission Date: 5 Mar 2002
UK Transmission Date: 18 Apr 2002

Writer: Rebecca Rand Kirshner
Director: David Solomon
Cast: Casey Sander (Tony Harris), Lee Garlington (Jessica Harris),
Steve Gilborn (Uncle Rory), Jan Hoag (Cousin Carol),
George D Wallace (Old Xander), Daniel McFeeley (Warty Demon),
Rebecca Jackson (Tarantula), Mel Fair (Tentacle Demon),
Nick Kokich (Demon Teen), Robert Noble (Night Manager),
Julian Franco (Young Bartender), Susannah L Brown (Caterer Girl),
Joey Hiott (Josh Aged 10), Abigail Mavity (Sara Aged 8),
Chris Emerson (Josh Aged 21), Ashley-Ann Wood (Sara Aged 18),
Megan Kent (Karen)

Xander and Anya's wedding day arrives. While Xander's dysfunctional family go head-to-head with Anya's, mostly non-human,
friends an old man approaches Xander to warn him that his future
life may not turn out to be a bed of roses.

Dreaming (As Blondie Once Said) is Free: The old man claiming to
be Xander from the future shows him an orb in which Xander
receives visions of what his life will, allegedly, be like if he marries
Anya. They will have two children, Josh and Sara (the little girl will
inherit aspects of her mother's genes and grow up with strangely
deformed ears), both of whom will have a strained relationship with
their father. Xander will injure his back fighting demons alongside
Buffy (who is, seemingly, killed in this fight) and will be unable to
work, thus putting financial pressure on Anya. Xander and Anya's
relationship sours after this and, although they stay together,
they're never intimate or happy. Some 30 years after they're
married, Xander will kill Anya during a blazing row, by smashing
her in the face with a frying pan. The only way to stop all of this
from happening, the old man tells Xander, is to abort the wedding.

No Fat Chicks: Xander's cousin Carol is a nervous plump
middle-aged woman – seemingly married on more than one
occasion – with a young daughter, Karen. She asks Xander about
one of Anya's guests, Krevlin, a cheerful (if rather warty) demon.
Carol wonders, if Krevlin could clear up his skin problem does
Xander think he'd be willing to date a woman with a kid? 'I really
can't afford to be very picky!'

Dudes and Babes: Buffy tells Xander that he and Anya give her hope; they're proof that there's light at the end of a long and nasty tunnel (see **89**, 'Triangle').

A Little Learning is a Dangerous Thing: The old man pretending to be future-Xander is, really, Stewart Burns, a philanderer whom Anyanka cursed in Chicago in 1914 by sending him to another (seemingly hellish) dimension.

Denial, Thy Name is Spike: He arrives at the wedding with a skanky Goth-girl. It's an obvious attempt to make Buffy jealous. Is it working, he asks desperately? Yes, Buffy replies, a little. Spike, in one of the episode's best scenes, apologies and tells Buffy that he's pleased to see her happy for a change. Then he takes his date and leaves, having assured Buffy that the Goth chick won't be coming home with him.

The Ceremony Starts at Home Time: The location of the wedding is the Sunnydale Bison's Lodge. Willow notes that the rehearsal dinner last night was like a zoo without the table manners. It's not entirely clear whether she's referring to Anya's demon friends or Xander's family. Concerning the latter, Willow suggests she hasn't seen them so badly behaved since her bar mitzvah (Mr Harris got drunk last night and threw up in Buffy purse). Buffy can't believe that the Harrises bought the cover story about Anya's people being circus folk.

Anya, practising her vows, intends to stick pretty much to the traditional Christian wedding ceremony, promising to cherish and honour her husband. But not to obey, of course, because that's anachronistic and misogynistic 'and who do you think you are, like a sea captain or something?' By later in the episode, she's adding stuff like a pledge to be Xander's friend, confidante and sex poodle, much to Tara's alarm.

In the end, even once he realises that the visions were a lie, Xander still decides not to go ahead with the wedding. He isn't ready and, perhaps understanding that the visions were his own worst-case-scenario perceptions of how the marriage could turn out (possibly based on his own parents' disastrous relationship), Xander tells Anya that he can't go through with it.

It's a Designer Label!: Aside from the horrors of the bridesmaid dresses, look out for Buffy's I Survived T-shirt at the end. A witty summation of the episode and, ultimately, the season.

References: Allusions to actress and cabaret singer Marlene Dietrich (1904–99), *Henry V* ('into the breach with you'), *Stargate SG-1*'s 'Window of Opportunity' (the juggling), the Athenian legend of the Minotaur, *The Godfather* ('I mean no disrespect') and the Beatles' 'Yesterday' ('I'm not the man I used to be'). Elements of the plot may have been inspired by a *Hammer House of Mystery and Suspense* episode called 'A Distant Scream', the *Back to the Future* trilogy and *The Outer Limits*' 'Demon With a Glass Hand'.

Awesome!: The opening, with the dresses. Buffy's increasingly desperate excuses to Anya for the delay, and her entertaining of the wedding guests. And, especially, the moment when it all kicks-off and descends into a brawl.

'You May Remember Me From Such Films and TV Series As . . .': Lee Garlington was Natalie's Mom in *American Pie 2* and Kathy Donovan in *Townies*, and appeared in *Boys and Girls*, *The Babysitter*, *Shame*, *Field of Dreams*, *In the Mood* and *Virtual Obsession*. Steve Gilborn's CV includes *Evolution*, *Nurse Betty*, *The West Wing*, *Ellen*, *The Practice*, *Blossom* and *He Said, She Said*. In a career stretching almost sixty years, George Wallace can be seen in *Bicentennial Man*, *Multiplicity*, *Postcards From the Edge*, *Towering Inferno*, *The Six Million Dollar Man*, *Forbidden Planet*, *Radar Men From Mars*, *Kojak*, *Bonanza* and *Rawhide*. Casey Sander was Rock in *Home Improvement* and appeared in *Dynasty*, *Knight Rider*, *Body Double*, *Grace Under Fire*, *Crosscut*, *Predator 2* and *Dragnet*. Jan Hoag played Bambi in *The Parlor* and was in *Murphy Brown*, *Silk Stalking*, *The Last Dance*, *976-WISH*, *Armed & Innocent* and *Murder, She Wrote*. Daniel McFeeley appeared in *Hunter's Blood*. Robert Noble was in *Robin Hood: Men in Tights*, *Bill & Ted's Bogus Journey*, *Stir*, *Green Acres*, *Mail Order Bride*, *The West Wing* and *Love, Cheat & Steal*. Nick Kokvich played Kevin in *The United States of Leland*. Ashley Ann Wood appeared in *From Earth to the Moon* and *Beyond Reality*. Andy Umberger and can be seen in *Dragonfly*, *The West Wing*, *The X-Files* and *Tempting Fate*. Abigail Mavity was in *100 Mile Rule* and *Strong Medicine*. Chris Emerson appeared in *What Women Want* and *Boston Public*. Joey Hiott was in *That 70s Show* and *Family Law*.

Don't Give Up the Day Job: Musical editor Tim Isle also worked on *Bring It On*, *Whatever It Takes* and *Watching Ellie*. Rebecca Jackson was a scenic painter on *Just a Little Harmless Sex*.

Valley-Speak: Buffy: 'Did you see the guy with the tentacles? What's he supposed to be? Inky the Squid Boy?'

Dawn: 'Spike's here and he brought a total skank. A manic-panicked freak who he's like totally macking with right in the middle of the room.'

Not Exactly a Haven From the Harris Family: Nick Brendon's perceptive 1999 comments to *Entertainment Weekly* about Xander's family background (see **11**, 'Out of Mind, Out of Sight') seem remarkably apt when we finally meet the dysfunctional, proudly Episcopalian, Harrises. Mr Harris senior is a sarcastic, short-tempered, foul-mouthed, *nasty* drunk. His wife, Jessica, is a bag of nerves, insecure over her weight and constantly self-deprecating and belittling herself. Xander's list of jobs for Buffy at the wedding is:

1. Don't let Mr Harris near the bar.
2. Don't let Mrs Harris near the bar.

The oft-mentioned Uncle Rory finally shows up. Most of what Xander had previously alleged about him is confirmed. He likes booze (he's trying to make himself an Irish coffee for breakfast), is an ex-taxidermist and also a lecherous old raver whose target group seems to be girls half his age. He also claims to have invented Velcro and isn't half as funny a practical joker as he thinks he is.

Cigarettes & Alcohol: During Xander's first vision he's got a beer in his hand. In his second, he's drunk on red wine. Tony Harris drinks copious amounts of Jack Daniels during the wedding.

Sex and Drugs and Rock'n'Roll: As Buffy leads a violently drunk Mr Harris away from a confrontation, he looks at her ass and comments: 'Nice chassis, what's under the hood?' After some further lewd suggestions, Buffy threatens him and he goes very quiet.

Logic, Let Me Introduce You to This Window: It appears to be a reasonably bright day outside throughout most of the episode, although it's raining. How, therefore, does Spike get into (and out of) the wedding? Burns says he was a victim of one of Anyanka's curses. In **43**, 'The Wish', when Giles destroyed Anyanka's amulet, he specifically said that this would return her to human form and reverse *all* of the wishes that she had granted.

What a Shame They Cut . . .: A scene from the draft script in which we learn that Giles couldn't attend the wedding because he's fighting daemons (Willow is specific about the spelling) in England. Instead he paid for all of the wedding flowers. Also, in the same scene, Dawn describes her dress as 'the colour of snot'.

Cruelty to Animals: D'Hoffyrn shows up with Halfrek bearing the greetings of Hyman, the god of matrimony. He gives Dawn his gift and tells her to be careful with it. Is it fragile? asks Dawn, taking the box. 'Squirmy,' he replies as tentacles burst out of the box and Dawn looks terrified. Later, Dawn tells a startled Xander that one of Anya's presents got loose.

Quote/Unquote: Old Man: 'You'll hurt her less today than you will later. Believe me. Sometimes, two people, all they bring each other is pain.'

Notes: 'I, Anya, want to marry you, Xander. Because I love you and I always will.' I actually *hate* weddings. Most of those I've attended resemble that funeral in *Steptoe and Son*. Bitter, incestuous and always ending in a huge fight. I'm not sure if Rebecca Kirshner has ever seen any Galton and Simpson, but she's clearly been to a few such horrorshows. 'Hell's Bells', is one of the least amusing and most emotionally draining *Buffy* episodes ever. This is *really* tough going. The plot lurches from one extreme of miserablism to the next – like sitting through 24 hours nonstop of the Jesus and Mary Chain, the Smiths and Radiohead. You'll get to the end and wonder how you made it out alive. At heart, there's a really nihilist core to 'Hell's Bells' which, despite strong material (much of which is eloquently played by the regulars and the excellent guest cast), renders the episode somewhat arch compared to more emotionally involving pieces. Future-imperfect riddles, racism allegories and lots of fear battle for prominence. But in the last few moments we get a scene that is among the most touching, lyrical and saddest of all *Buffy* climaxes.

Willow tells Xander that it's a good thing she realised that she was gay because 'here we are in formalwear', a reference to Willow and Xander's romantic fluke in **39**, 'Homecoming'. After Xander decides not to go through with the wedding, D'Hoffryn suggests to Anya that she has become domesticated and needs to have her demon powers back (see **118**, 'Entropy').

Critique: 'Some fans have felt that the momentum of the sixth season was lost in the mid-season repetition of controversial issues and themes,' noted John Mosby. 'Others felt that this was a clear sign that the show was reflecting the confused journey of teenagers into the adult world where their safety nets are gone, the mistakes greater and the consequences higher.'

Did You Know: It was revealed at the Academy of Television Arts and Sciences *Buffy* event in June 2002 that the *Buffy* cast has frequent get-togethers at Joss's house. The first time they did this (prior to filming the untransmitted pilot episode in 1996), the actors were very nervous and ill at ease so, according to Joss, they all drank a bit to get comfortable. At this point Nick Brendon pointed towards the very pregnant Marti Noxon and said, 'And look what happened!' What *did* happen at a later get-together, Joss noted, was that everyone wound up around a piano, singing. Surprised at how well his actors could sing, Joss noted that it was at this point he realised he had a group who could pull off a musical episode. Alyson Hannigan confirmed that when Joss first wrote the musical, he and his wife Kai sang all of the songs on to tape for the actors to learn. Alyson said this was rather intimidating as Kai has a fabulous voice. (The Whedons' demo of 'Something To Sing About', included on the *Once More, With Feeling* soundtrack CD, confirms this.) Michelle Tractenberg told Joss that while she wasn't too comfortable with her voice, she loved to dance and had studied ballet and tap. So she asked for a production number, which he duly obliged, choreographing the sequence himself. Joss said he wrote each song for the actor and their strengths. He wrote a rock number for James, because 'it had to be', and a ballad for Amber because she's a wonderful ballad singer. The 30s pastiche number for Anya and Xander was based, in part, on the art-deco style of their apartment set. When asked whose musical talent had surprised him the most, Joss responded Emma Calufield's: 'We'd never heard her sing before. She was amazing.'

Joss Whedon's Comments: How does Joss Whedon cope with having two shows on air at the same time? 'One trick is to be behind in everything all the time, which I am,' he told *TV Guide*. 'The other thing is that I have such great crews working on *Buffy* and *Angel* [that] I know they can get a lot done without my supervision. A lot of the machine can run without me now.' Variety helps to spice things up too. 'Every now and then I work on *Angel*, or some other thing. You get juiced up and you actually get more creative.'

117
Normal Again

US Transmission Date: 12 Mar 2002
UK Transmission Date: 25 Apr 2002

Writer: Diego Gutiérrez
Director: Rick Rosenthal
Cast: Michael Warren (Doctor), Sarah Scivier (Nurse),
Rodney Charles (Orderly), April Dion (Kissing Girl)

As an apparent result of the *troika*'s latest attempts to mess with
Buffy's mind, she suffers horrifying hallucinations, imagining
herself a mental patient in a Los Angeles hospital watched over by
distraught parents and puzzled doctors. Sunnydale has been a
figment of her psychotic imagination. But now, seemingly, the
walls are crumbling, the villains have become more mundane, the
friends she has depended upon are less reliable. It's not *fun* any
more.

Dreaming (As Blondie Once Said) is Free: Either in reality or in a
demon-induced hallucination (it's seemingly up to the viewer to
choose which since the episode ends without definitive resolution)
Buffy has been an inmate at the hospital for six years, the victim
of an undifferentiated type of schizophrenia. Buffy's delusions are
multi-layered, the doctor tells Joyce and Hank. She believes that
she is some kind of superhero – the Slayer. But this is only one
level. She has also created an intricate latticework to support her
primary delusion. In her mind, she's the central figure in a
fantastic world surrounded with friends, some with their own
superpowers. Together they face grand overblown conflicts against
an assortment of monsters, both imaginary and rooted in myth.
Every time the doctors think they're getting through to her, yet
more fanciful enemies and allies magically appear. Like Dawn – a
literal key – that Buffy inserted into her delusion, actually
rewriting the entire history of it to accommodate her need for a
familial bond. But this pressing of the cosmic reset button, of
course, created inconsistencies. Buffy starts to ask *obvious* questions. Why, exactly, *does* she sleep with a vampire that she hates?
And what's with Dawn – a ball of energy created by monks to
fight a god?

The doctor convinces Buffy that the only way for her to get out
of her delusion is to kill the things that are keeping her in it: Dawn

and her friends. Buffy tries, and is tempted by the offer of being an only child again, having her mother (and father) back in her life, and not having the responsibilities of being the Slayer. But, ultimately, she decides that Sunnydale is, for better or worse, *her* reality.

Dudes and Babes: Willow nervously practises asking Tara if she'd like to meet for coffee, food, kisses and gay-love, but just as she's about to ask for real, she spots Tara in the university corridor kissing another girl (see **118**, 'Entropy'). Xander says that Anya's suitcase is gone and that there's a closed sign on the Magic Box. She left a couple days ago, Willow confirms. Xander still loves Anya (see **118**, 'Entropy'). He knows that he's a better person with her in his life, but things got too complicated with the wedding (see **116**, 'Hell's Bells').

Mom's Apple Pie: Buffy angrily tells Dawn that she must try harder with her grades, and to stop the stealing-thing (see **114**, 'Older, and Far Away').

Denial, Thy Name is Buffy: Buffy tells Dawn that in her hallucination their parents were together, like they used to be before Sunnydale. She wonders why it is that Dawn is taller than her despite Buffy being older. Drifting back and forth between realities, Joyce asks Buffy to say out loud that she doesn't have a sister. Back in Sunnydale, hearing this, Dawn is upset. 'It's your *ideal* reality. And I'm not even a part of it.'

Buffy tells Willow that she was detached even before the demon injured her and induced the hallucinations. She confesses that when she saw her first vampires (presumably 1996, see **33**, 'Becoming' Part 1) she told her parents and they freaked out. They thought there was something seriously wrong with Buffy and sent her to a clinic. She was only there for a couple of weeks and, eventually, her parents simply forgot about the incident.

'I hope you don't think this antidote's gonna rid you of that nasty martyrdom,' Spike tells her, suggesting that Buffy is addicted to the misery. He alleges this is why she won't tell her friends about Spike. She might be happy if she did. They would either understand and try to help her, or ostracise her. Either way she'd be better off than she is now.

Denial, Thy Name is Spike: Spike hadn't heard about the wedding debacle. He notes that some people can't see a good thing when they've got it, which seems to be as much about Buffy breaking up with him as a reference to Xander and Anya. Having agreed to help Xander track the demon with the unpronounceable name to obtain the antidote for Buffy, Spike says that if everything in their lives really is a product of Buffy's twisted brain it might explain a few things. Like the chip in his head making him soft and turning him into her sex-slave.

Denial, Thy Name is Xander: He clearly *hears* the sex-slave line (he alludes to it later when talking to Buffy). But he convinces himself that it's part of Spike's obsession with Buffy, and not real – despite the evidence of his own eyes in **111**, 'Gone'.

It's a Designer Label!: We see Buffy's first two woolly hats of the season. Also, Willow's red blouse and Buffy's suede jacket.

References: Allusions to *Taxi Driver* and *Blue Velvet* ('you lookin' for me?'), *Julius Caesar* ('friends, Romans . . .'), *Supergirl* and *One Flew Over the Cuckoo's Nest*. The music is highly reminiscent of Bernard Herrmann's celebrated score for *Psycho*.

Geek-Speak: Warren recently took Andrew to see *Ocean's Eleven*. Jonathan mentions Jack Torrence, the hero of Stephen King's *The Shining* (as played by Jack Nicholson in Stanley Kubrick's film adaptation) and the DC superhero comic *Legion of Doom*. Warren says that Andrew's demon has the Slayer 'tripping like a Ken Russell film festival'. Also, *The Hitch-Hiker's Guide to the Galaxy* ('don't panic').

Bitch!: Warren, to Jonathan: 'Midgetor, get back to the monitors.' Xander: 'Just run along.' Spike: 'I guess you know all about that, don't you? The king of the big exit.'

West Hollywood: Xander calls Spike a pathetic pouf.

Awesome!: Jonathan's increasing paranoia that Warren and Andrew are plotting against him (completely correctly as it turns out). Spike and Xander's testosterone-fest in the graveyard. Buffy making her decision and saying goodbye to her mother for the last time.

'You May Remember Me From Such Films and TV Series As . . .': Michael Warren was Bobby Hill in *Hill Street Blues* and appeared in *Cleopatra Jones*, *SWAT*, *A Passion to Kill* and *Buffalo Soldier*.

Don't Give Up the Day Job: Rick Rosenthal directed *Halloween: Resurrection*, *Roar*, *Witchblade*, *Nasty Boys* and *American*

Dreamer and, as an actor, worked on *Better Off Dead*, *Video Vixens* and *Johnny Dangerous*. Joss Whedon's former assistant Diego Gutiérrez has also written for *Dawson's Creek*.

The Drugs Don't Work: Lorraine, Buffy's supervisor (see **112**, 'Doublemeat Palace'), suggests that if she didn't know better she'd swear Buffy was on drugs.

Logic, Let Me Introduce You to This Window: Spike seemingly leaves the house in the middle of the day. It seems strange that Buffy in the alternate reality has perfectly cut and streaked hair, even though she has been in an asylum for six years. If Joyce were alive in an alternate reality, why would Buffy kill her off in her fantasy world? That's *very* Freudian. Perhaps Spike's right and she does enjoy misery and pain. Despite all the research she does on the demon, Willow never tells Buffy exactly what the demon's poison is supposed to do. A doctor expecting a delusional schizophrenic patient to will herself back into reality isn't standard medical practice or anything even remotely like it. Although that inaccurate view of schizophrenia might be further evidence that the sanatorium is the fantasy since Buffy isn't a psychiatry expert. Alternatively, the explanation that the entire series has been the fevered imaginings of a teenage girl might help to explain a few things – like Angel's dreadful Irish accent (presumably, Buffy's never heard a real one to base it on).

Quote/Unquote: Xander: 'You think this isn't real just because of all the vampires and demons and ex-vengeance-demons and the sister that used to be a big ball of universe-destroying energy?'

Joyce: 'I know the world feels like a hard place sometimes, but you've got people who love you.'

Notes: 'All the people you created in Sunnydale. They're not as comforting as they were . . . You used to create grand villains. Now what is it? Ordinary people you went to high school with. Not gods or monsters. Just three pathetic little men.' An unexpected lurch into existentialism, 'Normal Again' plays an interesting game with the audience, casting a weary eye on recent critical analysis. A risky move. This isn't just knocking down the fourth wall and winking (the series did *that* in **47**, 'The Zeppo', three years ago); rather it appears to be full-blown artistic comment. 'Normal Again' is clever and radical and imaginative; can't say that often enough. With a Byzantine complexity, its defiance of traditional dramatic signposts is to be applauded. The episode is really funny in places and also *very* scary – in the way that padded cells are. A primal fear for many people is that madness is simply one bad day away. For all these reasons, and more, Diego Gutiérrez's debut should have been the season's crowning jewel. Sadly, 'Normal Again' is also, whether consciously or by coincidence, a conceptual parallelogram to the *Star Trek: Deep Space Nine* episode 'Far Beyond the Stars'. And this unoriginality renders the episode's climax a crushing disappointment. How tragic that, seemingly, we've all spent our lives watching too much telly.

According to Jonathan it has been some weeks since the events of **113**, 'Dead Things'. When Buffy looks at the photograph of herself as a little girl, it's Alexandra Lee, who portrayed young Buffy in **99**, 'The Weight Of The World'. In one asylum scene, the doctor tells Buffy that she had a momentary awakening during the summer and it was her friends who pulled her back into the delusion, a reference to Buffy's death and resurrection (see **100**, 'The Gift'; **101**, 'Bargaining' Part 1). Dawn's friend Janice is mentioned again (see **106**, 'All the Way'). The musical wind instrument Andrew uses to summon the demon is a didgeridoo (a deep-toned native Australian instrument also, briefly, seen in **105**, 'Life Serial').

Critique: 'The cleverness here lies in how a potentially disastrous dislocation is dovetailed into Buffy's emotional state,' noted the doyen of British *Buffy* critics, Mark Wyman. 'Weak points are sparse. Mostly, it's another sterling example of advancing core character arcs within the most outlandish of stories.'

Did You Know?: 'We get along really well,' Tom Lenk told Matt Springer about the *troika*'s off-screen activities. 'We watch Eddie Izzard videos in Adam's trailer. We're friends outside of work, too. I think our senses of humor all click. The three of us have our own geeky interests, but they're different from the sci-fi stuff. We're theater geeks. I have to admit that I do have a couple *Star Wars* T-shirts from when I was in high school. And I have an autographed picture of Carrie Fisher.'

Cast and Crew Comments: In *Steppin' Out*, Amber Benson talked about a glamour shoot she was about to undertake and noted that, 'I'm a big prude and I don't want to wear anything revealing, but you need to do it [to get ahead in Hollywood] and that's sad. And what's sicker is that Hollywood encourages it. "Oh, she was on the cover of *Maxim*! So if she's in my movie, people will come see it!" '

Despite her reservations, however, Amber concedes, 'If they want me to do something I'm not comfortable with, then I'm going to say, "Screw you." I'm not a size 0. I'm a 6 or even an 8 on a bad day. You don't want to see me in a thong.'

118
Entropy

US Transmission Date: 30 Apr 2002
UK Transmission Date: 2 May 2002

Writer: Drew Z Greenberg
Director: James A Contner
Cast: Edie Caggiano (Mother)

Having become a vengeance-demon again, Anya attempts to curse Xander for all the pain that he caused her. Unable to do this herself, she attempts to enlist the help of some old friends. But it doesn't work out as expected. The Scooby Gang discover that the *troika* have been watching their every move with hidden cameras. And what's currently being captured on video proves to be devastating for everyone.

Dudes and Babes: Tara confirms that the girl Willow saw her kissing in **117**, 'Normal Again', was just a friend. During their conversation with Anya, Tara says that neither she nor Willow hate men. 'We're more centred around the girl-on-girl action,' adds Willow helpfully.

The first sign of Andrew's emerging confused sexuality occurs when the *troika* tune into Spike and Anya copulating. Spike is *so* cool, notes an awestruck Andrew, before hurriedly adding that Anya's hot too.

A Little Learning is a Dangerous Thing: Spike lies, cheats, steal and manipulates, Buffy notes, but she agrees with him that he doesn't hurt Buffy. He tells her that his feelings for her are real and Buffy acknowledges this. But, she says, they aren't feelings that *she* shares and that he must move on for both their sakes. However, it's noticeable that, after he has sex with Anya, Buffy looks at him sourly and says that his moving on didn't take very long.

Mom's Apple Pie: Trying desperately to make up from her attempts to murder Dawn in the last episode, Buffy suggests all sorts of stuff they can do together (hiring a movie, having pizza). Not, she stresses, that this is guilt; she just wants to spend some time with her sister. But then, she realises: 'I'm cramping your teenage style. I'm the embarrassing mom who tries too hard. When did this happen?' Dawn suggests that, rather than Buffy hanging out with Dawn, they could patrol together. Buffy is less than impressed with this idea, saying that she works very hard to keep Dawn away from that side of her life. However, as Dawn rightly points out, this would be a perfectly reasonable argument if Buffy were protecting the world from tax audits. But, with her sister being the Slayer, dangerous things that want to kill Dawn seem to find her.

Denial, Thy Name is Buffy: When Spike again threatens to reveal his relationship with Buffy to the Scooby Gang if she doesn't, Buffy notes that she tried to kill her friends last week (see **117**, 'Normal Again') and they still don't hate her. So, she believes, they'd also be able to deal with the fact she's been sleeping with Spike. She's very wrong, however, as Xander proves at the climax.

Denial, Thy Names Are Anya and Xander: Xander is horrified that Anya would go out and bang the first body she could find, dead or alive. Anya suggests that he is in no position to be judging her. The mature solution for Xander, she says, is to spend his life telling stupid, pointless jokes so that no one will notice that he is a scared, insecure little boy. Xander's reaction to finding out Buffy and Spike were intimate is angry denial: 'I don't wanna know *any* of this.'

The Confessions Start at Home Time: Dawn has returned all of the stolen goods that she still had to various stores. Seemingly, she's been banned from entering these stores. She tells Buffy that she can't go into one because she shoplifted three pairs of earrings, a coin purse and a toothbrush. The latter item amuses Buffy: 'As rebellious teenagers go, you're kinda square.' Dawn offers to work off her debt to Anya at the newly reopened Magic Box.

It's a Designer Label!: Lots of red clothes dominate this episode, which may be an unconscious comment on the state of mind of the characters. Willow's deep red Chippewa Guy, New York sweatshirt, Anya's tight scarlet top, matching skirt and leather boots. Also, Spike's tasty black shirt, Andrew's hilariously mommy's-boy jumper and Buffy's flower-embroidered jeans.

References: 'Things fall apart,' says Tara, quoting *The Second Coming* by Irish existentialist poet WB Yeats (1865–1939). Xander tells Anya 'you had to do it cos he was *there*. Like Mount Everest,' paraphrasing a quote attributed to George Leigh Mallory (1886–1924) before his fatal expedition to the Himalayas. Also, International House of Pancakes, the Who's 'Pinball Wizard' ('he'd have to be deaf, dumb and blind not to'), *Friends* ('how *you* doin'?'), *Diamonds Are Forever* (the mini-bike chase sequence) and a possible allusion to the Smiths' 'I Don't Owe You Anything'.

Geek-Speak: *Star Wars* (Warren calls Jonathan 'Padawan', a term for a trainee Jedi) and *Indiana Jones and the Temple of Doom* (Short Round). Andrew says Jonathan has the same look on his face as he did that time Andrew highlighted in his *Babylon 5* novels.

Bitch!: When Tara and Willow ask Anya if there's anything they can do to help she notes that there is. They are both lesbians, so the hating-of-men will come in handy. She'd like to talk about Xander . . .

Spike says that he can't stand any of the Scoobies except Anya, because she speaks her mind: 'I have nothing but respect for a woman who's forthright. Drusilla was always straightforward. Didn't have a single buggering clue about what was going on, but she was straight about it.'

Halfrek tells Anya about a man she recently cursed who hadn't paid any child support in 11 years. So now, every time he picks up a piece of paper that isn't a cheque for the child, he gets a paper cut.

Awesome!: Anya incompetently trying to get Tara, Willow, Dawn and Buffy to wish all manner of horrors on Xander only to find that, ultimately, that isn't what she really wants. Also, Anya needlessly complicating her options. Spike's an ideal candidate, but he's not a woman, so all she had to do is get someone to wish Spike *were* a woman, and then . . . As Hallie notes, Anya still has a 'female power, Take Back the Night-thing' about vengeance, which Hallie considers sweet. But, she also states, men have an occasional need of vengeance too. Willow averting Dawn's eyes from her computer screen as she focuses on Spike and Anya having sex. Spike's denial that he has a sexy dance. And the moment when Spike says: 'You know, I wish . . .' and Anya, quietly, replies: 'Don't.'

'You May Remember Me From Such Films As . . .': Edie Caggiano played Tina in *The Brothers Grim*.

Cigarettes & Alcohol: Xander's drinking and feeling sorry for himself as the episode opens. Later, Anya and Spike get drunk on Giles's Jack Daniels at the Magic Box.

Sex and Drugs and Rock'n'Roll: Hurt by their rejections (by Xander and Buffy respectively), Anya and Spike get bladdered at the Magic Box and talk about their former lovers. About how uptight and repressed they both are. It's no wonder they couldn't deal with the likes of us, Spike notes. 'We should have been dead hundreds of years ago.' Then the pair seek mutual solace in some meaningless sex.

Logic, Let Me Introduce You to This Window: What, exactly, *is* the disc that the vampires have that the *troika* are so desperate to acquire? It's given huge focus early in the episode, then never mentioned again. Also, the disc that Warren recovers in the opening scene is a completely different colour to the one Jonathan is working on later. Dawn tells Anya that, since the events of **114**, 'Older, and Far Away', she never uses the word wish, spelling it out to be on the safe side. Yet, she uses it in the very next sentence.

I Just *Love* Your Accent: Spike calls Xander a ponce and a wanker.

Cruelty To Animals: Dawn, jokingly, claims she stole goldfish by hiding them in her pockets. She dislikes pet shops as they keep animals in cages and people poke them.

Quote/Unquote: Anya: 'I wish your intestines were tied in knots and ripped apart inside your lousy gut.' Xander: 'They are.' Anya: 'Really? Does it hurt?'

Tara: 'Trust has to build again . . . You have to learn if you're even the same people you were . . . It's a long and important process. Can we just skip it? Can you be kissing me now?'

Notes: 'You could try getting someone to make the wish for you.' An inevitable universal constant, entropy is the thermodynamic quantity that measures disorder and, as a concept, can be seen as a metaphor for a long-running TV series reaching the point where it all comes to pieces. Except in the case of 'Entropy', the episode of *Buffy*, which is a taut and beautiful thing. Never cynical in its targets or execution, 'Entropy' understands that love is a double-edged sword, and that pain is an equal part of the game to all the good stuff. Anybody who has been involved in a relationship that has stalled, or died, will find themselves nodding their heads in quiet sympathy at this episode's depiction of the bewilderment of rejection and the remorse that follows. A bittersweet essay on an inexplicable part of human frailty, 'Entropy' is a clear light shined on an awful part of everyone's life.

This isn't the first time that Spike and Anya have comforted each other due to their mutual frustrations. In **74**, 'Where the Wild Things Are', Anya took Spike as her date to the college party to make Xander jealous. Anya says she hasn't been scorned by a man in a thousand years (the last would have been Olaf, see **89**, 'Triangle'; **127**, 'Selfless'). Willow tells Tara about some of the events of **112**, 'Doublemeat Palace' (asked what the monster in the wig lady's head looked like, she notes: 'Let's put it this way, if I wasn't gay before . . .'); **111**, 'Gone' and **115**, 'As You Were'. Tara is living in the dorms at UC Sunnydale. When Anya suggests that men have been riding roughshod over Buffy for years, Buffy says there have only been four of them. Then, realising that she's including Spike, she quickly amends it to three (Angel, Parker and Riley).

Soundtrack: 'Sao Paulo Rain' by Tom McRae accompanies Xander's moody introspection. The beautiful 'That Kind Of Love' by Alison Krauss is heard at the end of the episode.

Did You Know?: Does Danny Strong get any of the nerd references that the *troika* deal in? 'When they called me "Frodo", a Jane Espenson moment, I asked, "Jane, is this supposed to be Fredo from *The Godfather*?" She's like, "No! *Lord of the Rings*! It's a short reference!"'

Cast and Crew Comments: It may be like filming a mini-movie each week, but for Sarah Michelle Gellar, TV beats the big screen. 'Films don't afford me the opportunities that *Buffy* does,' she told *Cult Times*. 'Until I'm a little older, I'll never get the opportunities in feature films [that] I can do every week on the show.'

Joss Whedon's Comments: While Joss himself established the overall look of Sunnydale, he is quick to credit production designer Carey Meyer and set decorator David Koneff. 'These guys are extremely talented,' he told Bob Blakey. 'They created this world. They've been to all the warehouses. They'll find furniture you couldn't conceive of. Sometimes I have to pull them back because they want to have too much fun.'

119
Seeing Red

US Transmission Date: 7 May 2002
UK Transmission Date: 9 May 2002

Writer: Steven S DeKnight
Director: Michael Gershman
Cast: Amy Hathaway (Blonde Woman), Nichole Hiltz (Beautiful Woman),
Garrett Brawith (Frank), Tim Hager (Administrator), Stefan Marks (Guard #1),
Christopher James (Guard #2), Kate Orsini (Girl at Bronze)

The *troika* initiate their plan to steal a pair of mystical orbs that render the possessor of them invulnerable. A battle between Buffy and Warren goes badly for the Slayer until Jonathan reveals the secret to Warren's power. Buffy defeats Warren but he escapes to take a quite terrible revenge on the Slayer and her friends.

No Fat Chicks: The blonde in the bar is seeking vengeance upon her boyfriend, Carl, who, apparently, slept with her 'fat ugly sister'. Does he like them fleshy? Anya asks. She bets that the woman just wishes Carl would bloat up a couple of thousand pounds and pop like a meat zeppelin.

Dudes and Babes: Willow guesses that Buffy and Spike have been involved and Tara confirms this. Willow asks how Buffy could hide something like that from her best friend. Tara believes that Buffy was afraid of the look Willow would have upon discovering this. Which is, she suggests, very similar to the look Willow is wearing now.

Andrew's repressed love for Warren finally bubbles to the surface, first through innuendo ('I can't wait to get my hands on his orbs') then, when Andrew and Jonathan are arrested, Andrew finally realising that Warren has been using him all along. 'He promised we'd be together. He never really loved . . . hanging out.'

Abuse Sucks!: Warren confronts Frank who, along with his jock-buddies, used to make Warren's life a misery in gym class, and takes his revenge in a suitably violent way.

A Little Learning is a Dangerous Thing: Spike is no longer part of the team, Buffy tells Dawn. Later, Dawn asks Spike if he loves Buffy and he is unable to answer. That, in itself, tells Dawn everything she needs to know. Forcing his way into Buffy's bathroom, Spike apologises for hurting her. He tells Buffy that he's tried everything to rid himself of these feelings and that he wishes she had let Xander kill him. Then he tries to force himself on her. Suitably horrified at what he's done, Spike realises that he's lost every chance he ever had of getting Buffy to take his feelings seriously. After a chance remark by Clem gives him an idea, he leaves Sunnydale on a motorbike, vowing to return a changed vampire.

Denial, Thy Name Isn't Xander: The lone sane voice left in Sunnydale, Xander tells Buffy that he understands why Anya slept with Spike (see **118**, 'Entropy'), but not why Buffy herself did. Buffy suggests that Xander has no idea how hard it has been for her since she was resurrected. 'You could have *told* me,' suggests Xander, with the unspoken implication that, once upon a time, Buffy *would* have. Buffy alleges that Xander's decision-making skills haven't exactly been world class recently. I've made mistakes, Xander admits. But, the last time he checked, slaughtering half of Europe wasn't one of them.

The Conspiracy Starts at Home Time: Xander enters into the soul-vs-chip debate concerning Spike (see **92**, 'Crush').

It's a Designer Label!: Willow's nightshirt. Buffy's cool leather jacket. Dawn's fluffy ice-blue sweater. Warren's Ace of Spades T-shirt. Spike's excellent black sweatshirt.

References: *The Fall and Rise of Reginald Perrin* ('great', 'super'), *High Society*, Frank Sinatra's 'Love and Marriage', *Psycho* (the shower scene), *Thunderball* (the jet-pack), Sherlock Holmes, *The Wizard of Oz* (allusions to flying monkeys), *HR Pufnstuff* (see **106**, 'All the Way'), illusionists Siegfried and Roy (see **55**, 'Graduation Day' Part 1), Mahatma Gandhi (see **35**, 'Anne'), Bob Dylan's 'Blowin' in the Wind', Charles Atlas, *Bring It On*, *Mighty Mouse*, *Knight Rider*, Jiminy Cricket, *The Burns and Allen Show* ('say goodnight, bitch'), Elton John's 'Rocket Man' and *Empire of the Ants*.

Geek-Speak: The *troika*'s buzzsaw-trap for Buffy is outrageously ripped-off from *Indiana Jones and the Last Crusade*. They have a (semi-naked) Xena action figure in their lair. Also, *Star Trek: The Next Generation* (Andrew tells Jonathan that Warren is 'Picard. You're Deanna Troi. Get use to the feeling, Betazoid'). Among the items Buffy recovers from the *troika*'s lair are some love poems written in Klingon.

Bitch!: Blonde Woman: 'He said he loved me.' Anya: 'Gee, then I guess he must have meant it, cos guys never say anything they don't really mean.'

Awesome!: The opening post-sexual-indulgence shot of Willow and Tara. Buffy's less-than-impressed reaction to Warren's jet-pack ('oh, come *on*!'). Dawn's joyous little giggle as she realises Tara and Willow are back together. Anya getting distracted from her vengeance work by her own problems. Dawn confronting Spike. Jonathan giving Buffy the information with which to beat Warren. Xander and Buffy's touching reconciliation.

Surprise!: Tara's death (unless you'd been reading certain Internet spoiler pages).

'You May Remember Me From Such Films and TV Series As . . .': Amy Hathaway played Shelby in *My Two Dads* and Tanya in *Joyride*, and appeared in *In God's Hands*, *Last Exit to Earth* and *The Wonder Years*. Nicole Hiltz was in *Angelic Tuesday*, *Scorched* and *Shallow Hal*. Garrett Brawith appeared in *Black Hole* and *The Invisible Man*. Christopher James was in *Thursday the 12th*. Stefan Marks appeared in *The Sky is Falling*.

Don't Give Up the Day Job: Lead Person Keith Cuba wrote *The Dark Ride* and also worked on *Tremors 2: Aftershock* and *Dangerous Indiscretion*.

Valley-Speak: Dawn: 'I'm totally not here.'
   Andrew: 'Dude, unholy hairgel.'

Cigarettes & Alcohol: Spike drinks vodka and blood in his crypt when Dawn comes to see him. Xander's got several bottles and cans of beer on the go when Buffy calls. He thinks there might be another one in the fridge. Andrew drinks something with lots of fruit in it at the Bronze while Anya shares a martini with the blonde girl.

The Magic Bullet: When Warren fires shots from his gun, they all appear to go reasonably horizontally. If Tara and Willow are on the first floor, the shot that kills Tara would, therefore, have had to be at quite a steep angle for the bullet to have struck her. When Tara is shot, she's facing away from the window. After she sees the blood on Willow's shirt, and falls, there is clearly an exit wound. Wouldn't the bullet, therefore, have hit Willow who was standing directly in front of her?

Logic, Let Me Introduce You to This Window: When Warren is trying to overturn the armoured car the sun has not fully set. But when the camera cuts back to Jonathan and Andrew, it's completely dark. Other shots in this sequence fluctuate between twilight and nighttime. Also, two men carrying brushes appear in the background in several shots when Buffy is fighting Warren but in others they're nowhere to be seen. When Warren activates his jet-pack, two long poles sticking out the back are clearly visible. How did Warren and Andrew hide their jet-packs from Jonathan? Wouldn't he notice something bulkier than usual under their jackets? They're not exactly unobtrusive. How did Warren's jet-pack survive the vicious pummelling that Buffy gave him without something malfunctioning, or short-circuiting? Both Xander and Willow barge into Buffy's bathroom unannounced. We know it's an open house at Revello Drive, but that's *ridiculous*. In the bathroom, the reflection of Spike's foot can be seen in the mirror. There's now a Verizon payphone outside the Magic Box which has never been seen previously.

I Just *Love* Your Accent: Spike refers to the *troika* as wankers.

Quote/Unquote: Spike: 'Great love is wild and passionate and dangerous. It burns and consumes.' Buffy: 'Until there's nothing left. That kind of love doesn't last.'
    Warren: 'You know who I am?' Buffy: 'You're a murderer.' Warren: 'That too. But more to the point, I'm the guy that beat you.'

Notes: 'Tara? Come on, baby. Get up.' At the risk of sounding like a broken record, definitive evidence that someone who was bullied and emotionally crippled in childhood will, as a direct consequence of this, turn into a megalomaniac rapist is rather compelling by its absence. And that's just Spike; wait till you see what it's supposed to have done to Warren . . . 'Seeing Red' is the (literal) living end of an awkward, and at times unbearably close-to-home, plotline that weaved its way throughout this season. In tying several seemingly frayed loose ends, DeKnight did a remarkably mature job of changing the series focus. But there is something darkly unsatisfying about the 'little men, and you *know* you are' riff that marbles much of this episode. 'Seeing Red' is clever, funny and dangerous. And, in its shocking final scene, as emotionally spot-on as *Buffy* has ever been. It's just not very likeable, that's all.

Dawn is sleeping at Janice's yet again (see **105**, 'All the Way'). Xander suggests he's part-fish (see **32**, 'Go Fish'). Clem tells Spike that Buffy is a sweet girl, but she has issues. Clem has a cousin who once got resurrected by a kooky shaman.

Part of this episode was filmed at Six Flags Magic Mountain theme park in Valencia, 35 miles north of Los Angeles. Shooting took place on Thursday 28 February and Friday 1 March, beginning in the late afternoon on both days, with the second day of filming stretching into the early hours of Saturday morning. The Cyclone Bay section of the park featured as the backdrop. For the first, and only, time Amber Benson's name was included on the series' opening titles. The portrait photo of Dawn seen in this episode is one of the official publicity shots from season five.

Soundtrack: 'The Leaves' by Daryl Ann, 'Stranded' by Alien Ant Farm and 'Displaced' by Azure Ray.

Critique: 'Reacting to this accomplished, hugely symbolic drama based on Warren's lone gunman actions, or the horrific bathroom scene, would misrepresent the episode,' wrote Mark Wyman in *TV Zone*. 'There are pure comedy moments, introspection, action, horror. Uneasy viewing, but unforgettable.'

Did You Know?: According to a report in the *Sun* in early 2002, audiences for the *Scooby-Doo* movie were likely to see both more and less of Sarah Michelle Gellar than they might have expected. A scene in the movie, it stated, involved Daphne baring her bottom. However, fans would be disappointed to learn that a body double was used for the scene as Sarah was said to be 'embarrassed by her bum'. When the movie premiered, of course, it contained no such scene or anything even remotely like it.

Jane Espenson's Comments: 'I love Spike,' Jane notes. 'I was worried about the attempted rape because that's not something you play around with. It's hard to come back from. I think we have to be very careful that we are not saying anything about humans. When we say that Spike looked into his soul, at that moment, and saw the demon in him, that's what made him want to go get a soul.'

Marti Noxon's Comments: What does Marti think about the fans who still want Buffy and Angel back together? 'They call themselves shippers,' she told an online interview. 'These are the people who still have their high school sweetheart's picture in a frame on the wall. They can't seem to let go. I think Buffy and Angel's relationship was idealised. It was like a fairy tale, in the way young girls dream about – to have this perfect, unattainable man. But you have to throw curve balls. We gave Buffy and Angel a barrier they couldn't surmount. This locks it into a romantic ideal, because they never fought over who has to do the laundry. They were stuck in the first beautifully passionate stage of love, and that's where it will be forever.' Conversely, some fans want Buffy and *Spike* together. Does that surprise her? 'Sometimes, things don't go the way we intend. It seemed very obvious to us that the Buffy–Spike relationship couldn't work in the long run, so now we need to reiterate why. We need to show people the difference between loving someone who is good to be around and loving someone who is good.'

Joss Whedon's Comments: Within hours of this episode's first broadcast, Joss appeared on the *Posting Board* to tell fans: 'I killed Tara ... because stories, as I have often said, are not about what we *want*. I knew some people would be angry with me for destroying the only gay couple on the show, but the idea that I *couldn't* kill Tara because she was gay is as offensive to me as the idea that I *did* kill her because she *was* gay. Willow's story was not about being gay. It was about weakness, addiction, loss ... the way life hits you in the gut right when you think you're back on your feet.'

120
Villains

US Transmission Date: 14 May 2002
UK Transmission Date: 16 May 2002

Writer: Marti Noxon
Director: David Solomon
Cast: Tim Hodgin (Coroner), Michael Mattheys (Paramedic),
Julie Hermelin (Clerk), Alan Henry Brown (Demon Bartender),
Mueen J Ahmed (Doctor), Jane Cho (Nurse #1), Meredith Gross (Nurse #2),
David Adefeso (Paramedic #2), Jeffrey Nicholas Brown (Vampire),
Nelson Frederick (Villager)

While the paramedics work on Buffy, Willow desperately tries a spell to return Tara to life. She is unsuccessful and goes to the Magic Box, drawing dark power from books she finds there. After saving Buffy's life by removing the bullet from her shoulder, Willow heads off to find Warren. When he discovers that Buffy is not dead, Warren seeks Rack's help against the Slayer, but he is informed that Willow's wrath is a more immediate concern. Willow finds Warren and unleashes her full awesome vengeance upon him, torturing him with the ghost of Katrina and eventually ripping the skin from his body. 'One down . . .'

Dudes and Babes: Spike now appears to be in Africa, striding through the native village like he owns the place. He enters a forbidden cave where he seeks a demon that knows about the Slayer. The demon asks if Spike wishes to return to his former self. Look what she has reduced you to, it tells Spike. 'You were a legendary dark warrior and you let yourself be castrated.' Spike is told that he will be unable to endure the trials required to grant his request. Do your worst, Spike snarls. 'But when I win, I want what I came here for. Bitch is gonna see a change.'

A Little Learning is a Dangerous Thing: Xander and Buffy finally learn that Anya has regained her vengeance-demon powers.

Mom's Apple Pie: Despite Xander's protestations, Buffy is prepared to let Dawn stay with Spike while the Scoobies search for Willow. But when they get to Spike's crypt they find him gone and Clem crypt-sitting while his friend is out of town.

Denial, Thy Name is Willow: In one of the best scenes of the season, Buffy, Xander and Dawn discuss the rights and wrongs of what Willow wishes to do. Xander suggests Warren is as bad as any vampire that Buffy has destroyed. However, Buffy argues, being the Slayer does not give her, or anyone, a licence to kill. More importantly, Warren is human and the human world has it's own rules for dealing with people like him. Xander suggests that those rules don't seem to work very well. Buffy argues that sometimes they do, but that it's impossible to control the universe. If they could, they would be able to bring Tara back, she notes. And Joyce too, Dawn adds, sadly. There are limits to what can be done, Buffy concludes, and it's right that there should be. Willow, seemingly, doesn't want to believe this.

The Psychology Starts at Home Time: The vision of Katrina asks Warren how he could say he loved her and then kill her. Because you *deserved* it, Warren replies angrily. Because Warren *liked* it, Willow suggests. She suggests that Warren never felt like he had power with women until he killed Katrina. Now he enjoys it, hence his attack on Buffy.

It's a Designer Label!: Highlight of the episode, Anya's hilarious spotty pants.

References: Country Time Lemonade, *Puppet Master* (a series by Full Moon about puppets that come to life), *The Wedding Planner*, *Dragnet*, gritty prison drama *Oz* and *The Andy Griffiths Show* (see 37, 'Faith, Hope and Trick'). Also, allusions to French philosopher, physician and (alleged) seer Michal Nostradamus (1503–66), Goth-punk band the Damned, a paraphrase of Psalms 8:2 ('out of the mouths of babes'), *Licence to Kill* and *Monty Python's Flying Circus* ('you take the comfy chair'). Willow giving Warren a vision of the dead Katrina owes a debt to Dostoyevski's *Crime and Punishment*.

Geek-Speak: Andrew is a fan of Matthew Broderick (*War Games*, *Inspector Gadget*, *Glory*, *Election*), in particular his teen-comedy *Ferris Bueller's Day Off*. He's less enthusiastic about Broderick's more recent work ('Broadway-Matthew, I find him cold'). Andrew wonders if the police will let his aunt bring him his Discman in jail.

Bitch!: Rack: 'You're new.' Warren: 'I come bearing dead presidents. Think we can skip the small talk?'

'You're *My* Little Puppy Now': Jonathan nervously notes that a guy in the next cell has been looking at him and, he believes, wants to make Jonathan his butt monkey. Don't flatter yourself, says Andrew, who heard the man talking to the guard. All he's in for is a parking offence. Jonathan, nevertheless, has heard that prison changes a man, and that sex-starved inmates prefer 'the small ones, with little hands like their girlfriends . . .'

Awesome!: Jonathan sarcastically describing Warren as a nice murderer. Dawn finding Tara's body. And, subsequently, Buffy discovering Dawn sitting in the dark with the body because Dawn didn't want Tara to be alone. Willow draining the knowledge from the books, sending her eyes and hair black. Anya making the decision to ignore her demon responsibilities and help Buffy and Xander.

'You May Remember Me From Such Films and TV Series As . . .': Steve Bailey played Cyrus in *Phantasmagoria* and appeared in *Nash Bridges*.

Valley-Speak: Jonathan: 'Oh yeah, that was *rad*.'

Cigarettes & Alcohol: Warren goes into the demon bar and orders a whisky, straight up, and a round for everyone in the house to celebrate killing the Slayer.

Logic, Let Me Introduce You to This Window: The blood splatters on Willow's neck and blouse and Xander's shirt are different in several shots. Why do the medical staff leave the operating theatre when Willow orders them to without so much as an objection when their patient appears to be flatlining? There's no channel ID on the programme on crocodiles that the vampire in the bar is watching. Willow finds the time to change her clothes after absorbing the black books before setting out to save Buffy and bring down her wrath on Warren. Xander changes his bloodstained shirt while at Buffy's after the discovery of Tara's body. So, where did he get these new clothes from? In the woods, Warren is running with nothing in his hands. Then, suddenly, he has an axe. As Willow chases him, creating a psychic path, the cables pulling the trees away from her are visible. It took Warren months to build his first robot (see **93**, 'I Was Made to Love You') and a few weeks to build the second (see **96**, 'Invention'), yet he builds this replica of himself in less than a day. Willow summons Osiris through willpower. In **101**, 'Bargaining' Part 1, she had to use a magical urn. Why doesn't she attempt to get one of the Gora demon eggs for a resurrection spell, as Dawn did in **95**, 'Forever'? The process of entry into the body that a bullet takes, which Willow demonstrates while torturing Warren, is the reverse of what happened to Tara. She was shot in the back and the bullet exited from the front. Buffy's gun-wound looks lower in the hospital than where she was initially shot (see **119**, 'Seeing Red'). How did Spike get all the way to a specific location in Africa in the timespan shown, and do so while avoiding direct sunlight? The bullet that killed Tara, and that we see Willow extract and later put in Warren's chest, seems oddly intact. Dare one suggest, again, *magic* (**119**, 'Seeing Red')? The emergency-room scene with Buffy makes no sense. The doctors are working on her left ventricle but haven't removed her shirt. There's no oxygen mask or sterile covering and she's, seemingly, not hooked up to any medical sensors (although an assistant seems to be reading off a machine giving her heart rate).

Quote/Unquote: Xander: 'I've had blood on my hands all day. Blood from people I love.'

Willow: 'One tiny piece of metal destroys everything. It ripped her insides out. It took her light away from me.'

Notes: 'The magic's too strong. There's no coming back from it.' What is it about *Buffy* and rad-fem revenge agendas? Is there something contractual that says this subject has to be tackled, angrily, once per season or it's a betrayal of the Sisterhood? We've both been there and, like, done that (**38**, 'Beauty and the Beasts'). That this episode is *much* better than previous forays into this field is significant, however. 'Villains' is confused, confusing, touching and truly dreadful (in every sense of the word). Often all at the same time. As with some of the best episodes of this season (and *all* of the worst), it is unbearably intense and, at times, almost unwatchable. There's a viciousness to the points it has to make that matches the bovver-boot nature of the visual presentation. It's a little like watching somebody getting their head kicked in – is it horribly fascinating or fascinatingly horrible? The aftermath of Tara's death sends Willow on a mystical bender; a grief-stricken lust for vengeance. Despite this, Buffy, Anya and Xander still try to stop her. Because she's their friend and what she's doing is *wrong*. And in that one line is the reason – the only reason – why 'Villains' works at all. Essentially, it's about trying to do the right thing, even if it's not the easy thing. Ultimately, 'Villains' is a little like biting into a Cadbury's Creme Egg and finding no yummy bit in the middle. Hollow, but not entirely unpleasurable. There are lots of things that are wrong with this episode, occasionally trite and ham-fisted dialogue not least among them. And much that's shocking (again, in all senses of the word). But, there's also hope for redemption, which is, let's remember, this series' *raison d'être*.

Willow's 'bored now' was the catch phrase of her vampire alter ego in **43**, 'The Wish', and **50**, 'Doppelgängland'. The destination of the bus the Warrenbot boards is San Diego. The scenes of Xander, Buffy and Willow and the Warrenbot are rumoured to have been filmed in Joshua Tree National Park east of Los Angeles.

Soundtrack: Aptly, the Misfits' 'Die, Die My Darling' plays in the scene where Warren's in the demon bar.

Critique: While many lesbian critics saw dark and offensive overtones in Tara's death (see **122**, 'Grave'), Jennifer Greenman was more charitable: 'Despite my feelings of anger, betrayal and sadness, I am grateful for almost three years of an honest, beautiful lesbian relationship,' she wrote. 'I respect Whedon for staying true to his own vision even if I don't agree with it . . . Part of me is sad that I can't see this story the way Whedon must have intended it, where all the characters really are treated the same in death and in life.' Contrasting this was a piece by Emily Almond on *scifidimensions.com* entitled 'Lesbians, Where Art Thou?': 'If they're not dead, they're evil. Why are lesbians denied a sane reflection of themselves in today's media?' noted Almond, and concluded: 'I want a full and unconditional promise of compensatory damages for havoc wreaked. I don't want to have invested what I have in this story . . . It's back to the beginning: Bad lesbians. Bad girls.'

This was also the position taken by Hillary Clay, who wrote that: 'The fact is that Willow and Tara are the only couple even trying to portray a healthy and loving relationship between two people of the same sex. You can't claim equal treatment when you are talking about the only example of its kind. Anything that happens to Willow and Tara is necessarily excluded from equal treatment because they are the only lesbian couple on television. The only equal treatment that Willow and Tara received was [that of] all of the other lesbians in Hollywood. Dead. Evil.'

Did You Know?: Despite failed attempts to feature Britney Spears in *Buffy's* fifth season, several sources continued to report that the Princess of Pop was set for a major role. *Sky News* went so far as to claim that Britney planning to take the part of the major villain in season seven. A *Buffy* insider was quoted as having claimed: 'This will be an amazing sight. Millions will tune-in to see them fighting in their trademark figure-hugging outfits.' Yes, that sounds like *just* the kind of thing someone on the *Buffy* staff *would* say.

We Read Dickens When I Went to School: According to a freelance journalist studying the Slayer for her MA in English Literature at Sussex University, Buffy was much more than just a superhero. Jac Bayles wrote a 17,000-word dissertation – *Drop Dead Monstrous* – which dealt with how the women in the series were more dangerous than the vampires that they hunted. Bayles says that the programme empowered women and girls with its depiction of strong female role models. 'Quite a few academics are now writing about *Buffy*,' she continued. 'Lots of people see the monsters as allegorical for the teenage condition.'

Another academic to recognise the artistic value of *Buffy* is Rhonda Wilcox, an English professor at Georgia's Gordon

College. 'The title invites simplification,' she told the *Globe and Mail*. 'But *Buffy* is the opposite of simple. It recognizes the complexity of art and life. It has a wonderful balance of mythic power and postmodern self-consciousness. It *is* art. Like Shakespeare. Like Dickens. *Buffy* is an example of a *Bildungsroman* (a German term for a novel of growth).'

Cast and Crew Comments: 'This season starts out really dark and heavy,' costume designer Cynthia Bergstrom told style website *katrillion.com*. 'Buffy's wardrobe is rather reflective of that. It's jeans and T-shirts, but as each episode progresses she does change somewhat.' Hello Kitty couture is big on *Buffy* too. 'I saw the Hello Kitty rhinestone T-shirt at Fred Segal, and they were so popular I was only able to get two for Michelle Trachtenberg,' Bergstrom revealed.

Marti Noxon's Comments: Having been quoted as saying that she thought it important that parents knew they could turn *Buffy* off because of the occasionally excessive violence, Marti told Andy Mangels: 'I feel parents should watch with their kids, and they should be aware that not every episode is appropriate for young children. We write to an adult sensibility with a lot of stuff that kids enjoy, but I worry about the violence and, moreso, the sexual content. Sometimes the shows get pretty sophisticated sexually, and we do a lot of equating sex and violence.'

Joss Whedon's Comments: Continuing an annual tradition, Joss announced his plans for season seven even before season six was even completed. 'I always like to get on the Net and reveal everything that's going to happen next year,' Joss told the *Posting Board*. 'That way, you don't spend all summer stressing.' Spoiler fans needn't have worried, however. These alleged teasers were from a man who once promised Zeppelin battles over Neptune and an all-naked, all-gay episode. 'Buffy will become a "vampire slayer"' noted Joss in May 2002. 'I can't really explain what that means yet, cause Doug [Petrie] hasn't explained it to me. But it seems to point towards adventure. Format change: from now on, the first half hour will be about Buffy figuring what the monster is, and the second half hour will be about Sam Waterston [*Law & Order*] prosecuting the monster. We're easing back on the goats. There've been complaints.' Also, 'because of the coincidental movie name, we will no longer refer to the kids as the Scooby

Gang. They will now be known as the "*Scooby Doo*, The Film, Coming This Christmas To Your Local DVD Store" gang.'

Tales of the Slayer: With many of the *Buffy* writers contributing scripts to Dark Horse's hugely impressive monthly *Buffy* comic series (and numerous spin-offs), early 2002 saw the release of the graphic novel anthology *Tales of the Slayer*. This featured seven stories of Slayers of the past and a coda featuring Joss Whedon's futuristic Slayer, Melaka Fray. Written by Whedon, Jane Espenson, David Fury, Rebecca Kirshner, Doug Petrie and Amber Benson, the beautifully illustrated book became a must-have for all *Buffy* fans.

'I chose my period impulsively,' Jane Espenson told the Dark Horse website. 'I like Jane Austen, so when Joss said that everyone who was contributing had to pick a time period, I said, "I want Jane Austen." I realised later that it's not a very comic-book era. It's not about action; it's about words.' The other writers, particularly Joss and Doug Petrie, started writing comics because they grew up as comics fans and loved the medium. Is the same true for Jane? 'Not at all,' she added. 'It started out just being another challenge, but Joss and Doug introduced me to the world of comic books, and I get it now. It's an amazing medium.'

121
Two To Go

US Transmission Date: 21 May 2002
UK Transmission Date: 23 May 2002

Writer: Douglas Petrie
Director: Bill Norton
Cast: Jeff McCredie (Officer), Damian Mooney (Patrol Cop),
Michael Younger (Truck Driver)

Willow goes after Jonathan and Andrew, forcing Buffy into the unlikely role of protector to criminals. Buffy, with Anya's help, frees Jonathan and Andrew from jail and then they all return to the Magic Box to try to find a protection spell to slow Willow down. Meanwhile, Spike undergoes the torrid challenge of an African demon to become what he once was.

Dudes and Babes: Anya tells Xander that, despite what he may think, she *does* care about whether he lives or dies. She's just not sure which. When Xander speculates that things could get ugly with Willow, Anya wonders if he'll chose that moment to propose again (see **100**, 'The Gift'). Xander says that he needs to know if Anya intends to use Willow as an excuse for revenge. Anya replies that, while nothing would give her greater satisfaction than reaping vengeance upon him, she cannot. She notes that Xander should be happy: she can't hurt him, so she'll just have to settle for hating him instead. Xander notes that Anya already *has* hurt him – she did that when she had sex with Spike (**118**, 'Entropy'). That wasn't vengeance, notes Anya, it was solace.

Denial, Thy Name is Willow: Her death-count is now two, Warren and Rack. But Buffy and Xander are still trying to stop Willow before she kills someone anybody actually cares about. However, her callous and downright nasty treatment of Dawn goes far beyond what one would expect from someone suffering from grief-stricken loss. How much of this is Willow and how much is the magic that's now controlling her is a very interesting question, of course. Willow disassociates herself, by talking in the third person (and in very unflattering terms) but, ultimately, she is self-aware enough to use 'me' on at least a couple of occasions. 'Let me tell you something about Willow,' she notes at her most depersonalised. 'She's a *loser*.' Everyone picked on Willow in junior high and high school. Now, she tells Buffy, 'Willow's a junkie.' The only thing Willow was ever good for, she continues, were those moments when Tara would make Willow feel that she was wonderful. Buffy suggests that Willow has always had an addictive personality. This does rather make one wonder why Buffy didn't say something sooner. Like two years ago when Willow first started dabbling casually with the dark mojo.

References: Spike gleefully quotes from Nirvana's 'Smells Like Teen Spirit' ('Here we are now. Entertain us'). The truck-chasing-a-car sequence may be a tribute to Steven Spielberg's *Duel*. Also, Elizabeth Barrett Browning's *Sonnets from the Portuguese* (see **3**, 'The Witch'), REM's *Out of Time*, *Gladiator*, *Sabrina, the Teenage Witch*, *Wayne's World* ('we'll be worthy'), Jesus Jones's 'Right Here, Right Now' and *Shindig*. Willow says 'if at first you don't succeed,' a quotation apocryphally attributed to Scottish king Robert the Bruce (1274–1329). Possible allusions include: *A Clockwork Orange*, *Christina F*, Neil Young's 'The Needle, And The Damage Done' and Julian Cope's 1992 poem *Hanging Out with Emma-Jane When Emma-Jane's a Junkie*.

Geek-Speak: Andrew says that they have mere seconds before *Darth Rosenberg* grinds them all into Jawa-burgers and not one of the Scoobies has the Midichlorians to stop her. Midichlorians are micro-organisms that exist in all living things (*Star Wars Episode 1: The Phantom Menace*). Jedis have many midichlorians, hence their psychic and supernatural abilities. Darth is the title given to a Sith Warrior (e.g. Darth Vader, Darth Maul); Jawas are the scavenger people who live on Tattooine. Also, *The X-Files* ('you're checking for implants?') and allusions to *The Uncanny X-Men* character Dark Phoenix (Jean Grey, formerly Marvel Girl, whose powers included telepathy and telekinesis. Psychically seduced by the Hellfire Club, she was transformed into a power-hungry goddess and, ultimately, killed). Andrew says Lex Luthor had a false epidermis escape-kit in the *Superman versus the Amazing Spider-Man Treasury Edition*.

Bitch!: Anya notes that a witch at Willow's level can only 'go airborne. It's a thing. Very flashy, impresses the locals,' but it takes longer than teleportation which Anya, herself, has the power to achieve.

Awesome!: Jonathan and Andrew's big girlie cat-fight. Anya failing to convince an officious police officer to let the boys out of their cell. Clem and Dawn's scene: here's somebody else who, like Spike, doesn't treat Dawn as a little girl. What a shame all of her best adult friends are demons. Spike's resigned reaction when the hands of the huge thug he has to fight burst into flames.

Surprise!: Giles's arrival at the climax.

'You May Remember Me From Such Films As . . .': Michael Younger appeared in *Crazy in Alabama*.

The Drugs Don't Work: Guess the rehab didn't take, Rack asks Willow.

Don't Give Up the Day Job: Bill Norton's previous work includes *Daughters*, *False Arrest*, *More American Graffiti* (which he also wrote), *Bad to the Bone*, *Freaky Links*, *Angel*, *Roswell* and the memorable TV movie *Gargoyles*.

Valley-Speak: Andrew: 'This is major uncool.'

Logic, Let Me Introduce You to This Window: In 110, 'Wrecked', it was established that only a witch or a demon could find Rack's house (specifically, Buffy couldn't find it without Spike's help). But

Buffy manages to locate it here without any demonic assistance. Willow pins Anya against the wall. Why does Anya scream? Couldn't she merely have teleported away as she demonstrated earlier in the episode? Or thrown Willow aside with her vengeance-demon powers (as Halfrek demonstrated in **114**, 'Older, and Far Away')? Even if Anya couldn't, she's immortal now, so no matter how hard Willow strangles her, or projects magic at her, she's not going to die. If Anya *could* scream for help then she wasn't being strangled *that* hard. What happened to Clem? He was in the waiting room of Rack's house but wasn't teleported to the Magic Box with Buffy, Dawn and Willow. Jonathan says he's known Willow almost as long as Xander and Buffy. In actual fact, given that he talks about Willow packing her own school lunches (the implication is that he's talking about junior high or before), he's known her considerably longer than Buffy, who only met Willow for the first time six years ago. Both Alyson Hannigan and Sarah Michelle Gellar's stunt-doubles' faces are clearly visible during the Buffy/Willow fight. A general error in several episodes, but it's noticeable here: Willow is often referred to as 'a Wicca' when the dialogue is, clearly, talking about her magical prowess, rather than of her as a practitioner of a group of pagan traditions of which witchcraft is only a small part. Not all Wiccas are witches and vice versa. It's ironic that a series that once so successfully lampooned trendy and inaccurate uses of Wiccan terms by so-called Wanna-Blessed-Bes (see **66**, 'Hush') should be guilty of such a crass error themselves.

Motors: Willow destroys Xander's car to delay Buffy getting to the jail and stopping her killing Jonathan and Andrew. So, Xander does what any law-abiding citizen would, and steals a police car. Which leads to the mother of all car chases.

Quote/Unquote: Xander, to Andrew: 'You haven't had even a tiny bit of sex, have you?' Anya: 'The annoying virgin has a point.'
   Willow: 'There's no one in the world with the power to stop me now.' Giles: 'I'd like to test that theory.'

Notes: 'The only time you were ever at peace in your whole life is when you were dead.' Best episode of the season, by miles, 'Two to Go' forgoes much of the legacy that has occasionally stifled creative development in this most uneven of years to deliver, instead, a precise and lyrical essay on human frailty. Buffy and Xander, bound by a friendship that they're determined not to see broken, embark on a mission to save a friend from her herself. And fail miserably. Anya rediscovers the spark of humanity at her core, tells Xander how much he hurt her and then puts her life at risk for him and Buffy because *it's the right thing to do*. Jonathan's sudden lack of moral ambiguity is beautifully fashioned and totally in character. And Willow? Willow's *gone*, baby! Willow's talking about herself in the third person. A disfigured, insane remnant of girl we once knew, who makes Dennis Hopper in *Apocalypse Now* seem *normal*. A sneering Johnny Rotten-style ball of piss and anger, telling the home truths that Buffy doesn't want to hear. A critical nexus of the previous year, and a pointer, just, to the future. A dark, malevolent future devoid of many of the things that made *Buffy* great, maybe. But, in its own way, every bit as good as what's gone before. Some people tried to tell you that this series was running out of ideas. Show them, please, this episode.

Willow mentions that Dawn used to be mystic energy (see **83**, 'No Place Like Home'). Andrew says that he likes following orders. The usual 'Previously on *Buffy the Vampire Slayer*' opening is replaced for this episode by a Nick Brendon voice-over stating 'this is what happened this year'.

Critique: 'Whether standing atop an 18-wheeler truck, or taunting Dawn and Buffy with her angsty yet calm diatribes, Hannigan's Dark Willow remains awesomely powerful,' noted *TV Zone*. *Impact*'s John Mosby added: 'It may have seemed that the "Three Wankers of the Apocalypse" were a small-time concern, but they too factored into the high drama. And, of course, there's *that* entrance from Giles. Superb!' The *Australian*'s Kate MacKenzie considered that: 'While this episode doesn't save the season from being the show's worst so far, it's still a breath of fresh air in a world full of formulaic reality shows and courtroom dramas.'

You Sexy Things: *FHM*'s annual *World's 100 Sexiest Women* poll – published in May 2002 – saw the girls of *Buffy* and *Angel* once again dominating. After being narrowly defeated by Alyson Hannigan last year, the 1999 winner Sarah Michelle Gellar led the *Buffy* charge at number 11. Alyson slipped back from 10th place in 2001 to 21st, but did come third in a separate poll of the magazine's lesbian readers. Emma Caulfield was a new entry at 86, with Eliza Dushku taking 58th position. *Angel* fans also had cause to celebrate with Charisma Carpenter's impressive rise from 29 to 13.

Did You Know?: Anyone jittery about American competence in the vanguard of the war against terror was probably relieved to learn about Anthony Cordesman, a professor at the *Center for Strategic and International Studies*, an influential Washington thinktank which helps to formulate US defence policy. He wrote a treatise entitled *Biological Warfare and the Buffy Paradigm*. 'The US must plan its homeland defense policies for a future in which there is no way to predict the weapon that will be used, or the method chosen to deliver [it],' wrote the professor. 'I would like you to think about the biological threat in terms of *Buffy the Vampire Slayer*; that you think about the world of biological weapons in terms of the "Buffy Paradigm"; and that you think about many of the problems in the proposed solutions as part of the "Buffy Syndrome".' For any three-star generals bemused by this analogy, Anthony went on to explain that *Buffy* is a TV series 'about a teenage vampire slayer who lives in a world of unpredictable threats where each series of crises only becomes predictable when it is over'. Aren't you just beyond glad that you live in a world where Buffy helps the president decide who to bomb next?

Cast and Crew Comments: Nick Brendon described how he transformed Xander from a skinny high school wimp into something of a beefcake. 'I hired a trainer and started working out,' he told *YM*. 'At first Joss really didn't want me to, because it wasn't part of the character, [but] we talked it over and decided I was out of high school and going into the workforce.' Nick also revealed a romantic side when asked what he would like to see more of on *Buffy*. 'Less blood, more love. You *can* quote me on that.'

Head On: Tony Head admitted that despite his reduced role in season six, he wanted to be around more for *Buffy*'s seventh year. 'I'm keeping my card as open as I can so when Joss calls for me, I'm ready,' Tony told *Entertainment Weekly*. 'Obviously there are limitations to that, and things are happening here in the UK. But we have some plans for next season, and we'll see where they lead.' If *Buffy* ended, however, Tony believed that this might not be such a bad thing. 'Personally, I think it would be good if the show finishes on a high. If you pursue something until it's beaten to a pulp, there is no possibility, no future, because everyone's tired of it. I think Joss is on the same wavelength. I would hope the network would allow him to do what he feels is right.' Tony had been very busy since returning to Britain. After the success of his comedy drama series *Manchild*, filming of a second season commenced. '*Ripper* is still on, the BBC wants to do it,' he noted. 'Fox is still interested, so it's ultimately about when Joss has the time. I'm doing another season of *Manchild* until mid-October, so I won't be available at least until then.' Although he missed the *Buffy* cast and crew, returning to Britain meant plenty of action – not least in the bedroom. 'I did a love scene in *Spooks*. I seem to be doing a lot of them for the first time in my life. Very odd. Even in my Taster's Choice [Gold Blend] commercials, we never got our kit off.'

Joss Whedon's Comments: Some *Buffy* and *Angel* fans seem to have been more openly critical than ever during this season. 'It affects me,' Joss told *E! Online*. 'At the same time, I need to give them what they need, not what they want. They need to have their hearts broken. They need to see change. They hated Oz, then they hated that he left. These things are inevitable. If people are freaking out, I'm good.'

122
Grave

US Transmission Date: 21 May 2002
UK Transmission Date: 30 May 2002

Writer: David Fury
Director: James A Contner
Cast: Brett Wagner (Trucker)

Giles's return to Sunnydale may be the last hope of stopping Willow before she destroys the world in her thirst for vengeance. But has he come back too late?

Playing the Homophobia Card: The amount of Internet bandwidth used to discuss the possible subtexts surrounding Tara's death (**119**, 'Seeing Red') and Willow's subsequent actions could have filled Wembley Stadium. In a sense, the outrage that many fans (of all sexualities) felt over the death of a well-loved character was understandable. But that's no different to the emotional response that, for instance, **94**, 'The Body', achieved. This time, the fact that the character in question was gay made the situation more problematic. First, and rightly, a bit of praise: for the previous 18 months *Buffy* had been near enough the only mainstream US drama series to feature two regular characters engaged in a loving same-sex relationship. That simple fact should *never* be forgotten.

Willow and Tara, whether by accident or design, had become positive role models for gay teenagers everywhere. They had shown that you don't have to hide your sexuality or to be an outsider. That ridicule and homophobia are products of ignorance and that *any* kind of love is, actually, all right. The sudden death of one of those characters, while dramatically interesting, obviously raised the question of *agenda* and whether the reason behind this was not, at least in part, a decision that a mistake had been made. In a strongly worded piece on the website *xtremegames.com*, fan Robert Black wrote an essay entitled 'It's not homophobia but that doesn't make it right' in which he argued that the killing of Tara showed a callous disregard for fans, and for the wider gay community. 'To a marginalized segment of the population,' Black noted, 'where there is a constant feeling that one's very existence is being denied, onscreen reflection can be priceless.' Very true. A counter-argument, of course, is that such attacks can be viewed as, at best, misguided and, at worst, as offensively myopic as those postings two years previously on message boards and newsgroups which stated that *Buffy* had just lost a viewer because they had 'turned Willow queer'.

The *positive* presentation of lesbianism over three seasons on *Buffy cannot* be overstated and can only have done gay tolerance good in a wider context. Although generally praised for its sensitive handling of the gay issue, *Buffy* had, previously, come in for some mild (even amused) criticism from the gay community over the way that Willow's sexuality was referenced in both **89**, 'Triangle' (when Anya suggests that Willow is attracted to Xander, Willow replies 'Hello, *gay now*'), and **96**, 'Intervention' (the Buffybot's information on Willow: GAY 1999–PRESENT). Character-wise, Willow certainly *seems* to be bisexual given that she had such an intimate and loving relationship with Oz prior to meeting Tara. It's therefore difficult to believe she is completely unattracted to all men. One theory put forward as to why Willow should describe herself as gay rather than bisexual is that the American public generally associate bisexual women with porn videos, jokes on *Friends* and *The Jerry Springer Show*.[42] They're less comfortable

---

[42] In an interview with *E! Online*, Joss noted: 'Marti and I debated about whether or not Willow was bisexual, experimenting, going back and forth. We thought, after Tara, it really would be disingenuous of us to have her be anything less than gay. So we decided that's pretty much final – that's who she is. To backtrack on that would make it appear as if Tara's death was something other than it was.'

with the term than we are in Britain. Nevertheless, *Buffy* has featured, let's remember, two popular same-sex characters in a wholly positive relationship for nearly 50 episodes. Regardless of how it ended, one cannot wipe away those memories entirely.

But even after Tara's death, the arguments surrounding Willow didn't end. They run something like this: *Buffy* has always had a subtext that *sex is evil* – going as far back as Buffy's relationship with Angel. It's one of the cornerstone metaphors of the show. Of all the Scoobies, Willow is one of only two who ever had a partner killed. It's a bit of a stretch, but as fan-writer Susannah Tiller theorised, this *could* be seen – if one were looking for underlying themes – as a metaphor that lesbian sex is somehow worse than heterosexual promiscuity. Compare, for example, Tara's case with Buffy and Riley's break-up. Riley is 'rewarded' with a happy marriage. Tara gets the bullet. Another of *Buffy*'s few openly gay characters, Larry, also died (see **56**, 'Graduation Day' Part 2). Heterosexual characters, even if they're initially unlikeable, wickedly promiscuous or downright evil (Wesley, Harmony and Faith respectively) all, ultimately, get a decent shot at redemption, Tiller notes. Gay characters in *Buffy*, generally, don't. Tara was killed immediately after she and Willow had sex, making the lesbian-sex-is-evil metaphor even more pointed. So ingrained is this negative portrayal that it has been well documented by film historians as the 'dead/evil lesbian cliché' (most notably in the book *The Celluloid Closet* by Vito Russo). David Fury even admitted during an Internet interview in May 2002 that he believed this juxtaposition within *Buffy* was a mistake: 'In retrospect, I can see the cliché. That was not our intent. We wanted to show them together and happy. It created the impression in a lot of people's minds that [Tara's] death was linked to them having sex.' To some fans, Tara's death also seemed gratuitous. If compared to, for example, Angel's death in **34**, 'Becoming' Part 2, which – as Tiller notes – served a specific dramatic purpose. Angel's was a *noble* death, whereas Tara's felt like an afterthought, and does little but to act as a clumsy plot device for Willow's actions in subsequent episodes.

It's also interesting to compare Willow's behaviour to Giles's reaction to Jenny's death in **29**, 'Passion'. While both are grief-stricken emotional responses, Giles's actions are much more instantaneous. By comparison, Willow's slow and calculated descent into vengeance-driven madness has the awkward potential to be viewed as yet another cliché: a lesbian who loses her partner becoming homicidal to the point of irrationality (or, actually, irrational to the point of genocide). From a psychological point of view, Willow's torture and murder of Warren (**120**, 'Villains') is where the entire plot threatens to fall into the murky world of Freudian stereotypes (perpetuated by popular culture) in which lesbians are frequently depicted as being inherently irrational, unstable man-haters. For some gay fans, perhaps the ultimate slap in the face was that, having decided to destroy the world, Willow is stopped from her apocalyptic designs when her best friend (a man, of course) tells her that he loves her. The Freudian stereotype is therefore complete: a lesbian just needs the love of a good man to make her 'normal' again.

Some of these charges do have a degree of truth in them, although Marti Noxon used an interview with the gay publication *The Advocate* to present the production's proudly pro-gay credentials: 'We never meant for Willow to become a gay icon. Every character on *Buffy* is going to struggle with their dark side; that's the nature of our show. There are people who are unhappy Willow and Tara are not the poster-couple for gay relationships. But to my mind, that's not a fair representation of gay people.' However, Tara's death, Noxon added, was 'the first time we've gotten a public outcry where I can't even read some of the letters, they hurt so much'.

Joss Whedon defended the storyline and remained somewhat mystified by hostile reactions to it. Talking to *E! Online* he said: 'I wanted people to be upset – it's my *job* [to do that]. What was surprising was that there was a lot of hate toward us. It was an episode that was clearly about male violence and dominance, and suddenly I'm a gay basher. It's one thing when you piss off people you want wiped off the planet. It's different when it's people you care about like your audience. But it's frustrating when *they* treat you in the same knee-jerk manner.' It was certainly *very* strange at the time to read articles such as one by author Rodger Streitmatter on *GayToday.com*, in which Streitmatter stated: 'I was very pleased that I could finally recommend *Buffy* as a television program that provided a picture of young gay life that was both realistic and positive. I no longer can.' This, despite the fact that *Buffy* continued to include one proudly and openly gay character. That was, and indeed remains, one more than most TV series can ever manage. Much of the anger directed towards Whedon seemed to be not, specifically, because he had killed Tara, but because Willow and Tara were the only positive lesbian role models on television. Ultimately that was, surely, not Joss's fault but, rather, everyone else's.

A Little Learning is a Dangerous Thing: Giles confirms what the audience already suspected from **90**, 'Checkpoint': that the Watcher's Council hasn't a bloody clue about much of anything. There is, however, a powerful coven in Devon that sensed the rise of a dangerous magic in Sunnydale (see **123**, 'Lessons'). A dark force, fuelled by grief. A seer in the coven told Giles about Tara and they imbued him with their powers and sent him to bring Willow down. Anya asks if Giles knew that Willow was going to take his powers to boost her own and that they were tainted. Giles says that he certainly knew there was such a possibility. The gift he was given by the coven was the true essence of magic, which comes, in all its purity, from the Earth itself. Willow's magic, on the other hand, came from a place of rage and vengeance. That which she took from Giles tapped into the spark of humanity that remained within her. It allowed her to *feel* again, thus giving Xander the opportunity to reach her through love.

Denial, Thy Name is Xander: There are further references to the feelings of inadequacy that Xander had mentioned in the previous episode. He was unable to stop the shooting of Buffy and Tara or to reason with Willow. Here, he sarcastically suggests to Dawn that some people always know what to do in a crisis, indicating he isn't one of them. Later, he bemoans his inability to run away despite this being something that he's had lots of practice at.

Yet, ultimately, this is his finest hour, revealing a man who loses himself so easily in pity and yet is able go to the (literal) ends of the earth to save a friend – and humanity along with it. A man who spends his life telling inane jokes and blurting out confidential information at inappropriate times (you can usually trust Xander with your life, but would you want to trust him with your secrets?) and yet will face down ultimate darkness.

Denial, Thy Name is Willow: Willow tells Giles that he's a hypocrite, suggesting that he waltzed back to Sunnydale with borrowed magics so that he could chastise her. She says that she used to believe Giles had all the answers. Now, she suggests, Giles is really a fraud, jealous of her and unable to bear the knowledge that she is more powerful than he. Having subsequently been given insight into the suffering of the world, Willow decides to summon the demon Proserpexa at a Satanic temple on Kingman's Bluff.

She intends to drain the planet's life force, funnel its energy through Proserpexa's effigy and burn the Earth to a cinder.

Denial, Thy Name is Buffy: Dawn asks why Buffy didn't tell her about Spike attempting to rape her. Dawn didn't need to know, Buffy replies, and notes that she was trying to protect her sister. 'You *can't*,' Dawn explodes. People Dawn loves keep dying; even Buffy can't protect her from *that*. After their battle with the Earth Monsters, Dawn asks if Buffy is crying because the world *didn't* end. Buffy apologises to her sister and tells her that, from now on, everything is going to be better. Buffy wants to see her friends happy again and she wants to see Dawn grow up into 'the woman you're going to become. Because she's gonna be beautiful. And powerful. I don't want to protect you from the world – I want to show it to you.'

The Hilarity Starts at Home Time: When Giles asks what's been going on in Sunnydale since he left, Buffy tells him that Willow has been messing with dark forces, Dawn's a kleptomaniac, Xander left Anya at the altar, Anya became a demon again and Buffy's been sleeping with Spike. Giles does the only thing he can – burst out laughing. Buffy stares in disbelief, until his infectious amusement at the absurdity of what she's just said hits her and she joins in. Between fits of giggles she tells Giles about the events of **117**, 'Normal Again', seemingly the most ludicrous of all that has happened.

References: *The Wizard of Oz* ('fly my pretty'), obliquely *Bill and Ted's Bogus Journey*, *Trading Places* ('it's a miracle!'), *The Mummy* (the insects attacking Spike), Van Morrison's 'Brown-Eyed Girl', *Alice Doesn't Live Here Anymore*, *Friends* (Xander uses Phoebe's occasional catchphrase 'whatcha doin'?'), *Sleepy Hollow* and *Dead Men Walking*. Xander tells Willow: 'I was gonna walk you off a cliff and hand you an anvil, but that seemed too cartoony,' referring to a visual gag often used by Roadrunner on Wile E Coyote. Anya quotes Speedy Gonzalez (*'Holy frijole!'*).

Bitch!: Willow asks Giles if he remember the spat they had when Giles was under the delusion that he was still relevant (see **105**, 'Life Serial').

Xander, on Spike: 'Is this blind spot a genetic trait with you Summers women? The only useful thing that animal ever did was finally leave town.'

Awesome!: Buffy and Anya hugging the returned Giles. Giles asking Buffy how a recovered Willow will be able to live with herself and Willow herself replying: 'Willow doesn't live here any more.' Dawn turning into a fighting machine almost as impressive as her sister as she and Buffy battle the Earth Monsters. 'You think I never *watched* you?' Dawn asks as Buffy looks at her sister proudly, if somewhat incredulously. Jonathan and Andrew escaping with a very scary-looking trucker. The completely unexpected finale, a demon hand reaching out to Spike's chest and telling him, 'Your soul is returned to you.'

'You May Remember Me From Such Films and TV Series As . . .': Brett Wagner appeared in *Finding Kelly*, *Sliders* and *Dark Skies*.

Valley-Speak: Willow: 'Uh-oh. Daddy's home. I'm in wicked trouble now.'

Logic, Let Me Introduce You to This Window: When Xander and Willow hug, in one angle Xander's left knee is drawn up but in another it's on the ground. During the scene where Willow is chasing the stolen car in the truck, parked police cars can be seen in the background, even though by this time they had all, apparently, been driven away from the station. It's easy to forget that the events of the last four episodes have taken place over such a short time scale. The final scene of **119**, 'Seeing Red', to the end of this episode covers approximately 24 hours. It therefore seems unbelievable that Giles and Buffy would be laughing hysterically about the more ridiculous aspects of the season with Tara's body not even cold. Willow being given an insight into the suffering of all humanity is similar to the experience that Cordelia underwent in *Angel*: 'To Shanshu in LA', the main difference being that Cordy emerged with her sanity intact, wanting to help everyone. Willow, conversely, wants to end the world to make her own suffering stop. Lightweight. The previous demonically perpetuated Sunnydale earthquake, mentioned in **2**, 'The Harvest', took place in 1937, not 1932 as stated here. Of course, this could refer to separate events, but even on a fault as active as the San Andreas, two major earthquakes within five years is highly unlikely. Giles refers to Devonshire, as opposed to Devon, by which the county has been much more widely known in Britain for many years. This could, of course, be an example of Giles being Giles, but it's still factually inaccurate. And Tony Head should have spotted this as he lives just a few miles away in Bath. A Wiccan performing what is described as 'a Satanic ritual' is a complete contradiction in terms. Wiccans are pagans who do not believe in *any* Judaeo-Christian icons.

I Just *Love* Your Accent: Spike describes the tests set for him as a bloody doddle and a piece of piss. Willow calls Giles Jeeves (see **43**, 'The Wish').

Quote/Unquote: Buffy: 'You were right about everything. It is time I was an adult.' Giles: 'Sometimes the most adult thing you can do is ask for help when you need it.'

Xander: 'You've come pretty far. Ending the world, not a terrific notion but the thing is, I love you. I loved crayon-breaky-Willow and I love scary-veiny-Willow ... You wanna kill the world, you start with me. I've earned that.'

Notes: 'Is this the master plan? You're gonna stop me by telling me you love me?' So, we reach the end of a very strange road. And a new theme emerges to compete with 'oh, grow up' as the core-value of this disjointed, sometimes unsatisfying, occasionally hollow, but always fascinating year. Love redeems, *Buffy*'s final mission statement (indeed, see **144**, 'Chosen' for proof of that). The circular nature of the season, as with previous years, meant that we ended up, conceptually, exactly where we began; Buffy deep in the earth, surrounded by the dead, Willow knee-deep in dark magic through grief; Xander valiantly trying to keep his friends together in the face of terrible events; Spike searching for meaning in a world that no longer allows him to be what he is; Dawn trying to come to terms with what her sister was, and is. And what Dawn herself will ultimately become. Buffy tells Giles about the events of the season and they laugh hysterically. Sometimes, that's the only answer to such darkness. 'Grave' *is* dark but its overall message, that nothing is ever so bad that it can't be put right through love, is a wonderfully brave statement for a TV series to make in this day and age. In lesser hands, this could have been awful – mawkish and risible. In these hands, however, it's staggeringly appropriate. *Buffy* went through a lot during season six and, at times, it was hard going. Fractious, awkward, challenging telly. But, never less than extraordinary. The final four episodes pull the strands together and make it into a cohesive whole. What will we say in years to come when the next generation asks, 'Daddy, what do you do in *Buffy* season six?' *I'll* say, 'It depressed the hell out of me, son, but it was worth it in the end.'

On her first day in Kindergarten, Willow cried because she broke the yellow crayon and was too afraid to tell anyone. Proserpexa is important in the hierarchy of she-demons. Her followers intended to use her effigy to destroy the world. They all died when the temple was swallowed in the earthquake of 1932.

Soundtrack: Series favourite Sarah McLachlan's version of 'The Prayer of St Francis' closes the season. The two McLachlan songs used in *Buffy*, interestingly, both include direct or indirect allusions to devotional prayers ('Full of Grace' to the *Hail Mary*. See **34**, 'Becoming' Part 2).

Critique: 'The finale belonged, unequivocally, to Willow,' noted Stephanie Zacharek on *salon.com*. 'It didn't have the queasy-making resonance of Whedon's finale last year. But this year, nevertheless, threw the show and its characters into yet another light; it has changed the shape of their shadows, showing us things in them – resources of unusual bravery and cruelty – that we couldn't previously have imagined.'

'Wasn't it cool to watch Willow get evil with her black hair and veiny face?' asked Sonia Mansfield. 'Finally Xander gets his day in the sun and saves the world. You can't ask for a better season-ender than that.'

Giving the episode a generally positive review, Robert Bianco felt that 'even when *Buffy* fails . . . it fails in interesting ways. Most long-running series stumble because the writers . . . exhaust their energy and interest. It's clear *Buffy* suffered from Whedon's reduced involvement – and from the absence of Anthony Stewart Head. But essentially, *Buffy* faltered because it charted a seemingly viable artistic course that simply didn't work. What the show was seeking was a metaphorical expression of real-world problems. Unfortunately, it's hard to sustain 22 weeks of character ennui without inducing the same in an audience.'

'The ending with Xander's defeat of bad Willow and Buffy's subsequent protestations that she now wants to live, to see her friends happy, seemed a bit contrived,' noted Thomas Hibbs. 'Indeed, the dialogue at times reduced the difference between good and evil to a sappy distinction between those who feel and those who don't. But, in a show that has always stressed the dire consequences of decisions and actions, we can be sure that earth will remain closer to Hell than to Heaven.'

Did You Know?: The mausoleum that Xander attempts to enter is named Alpert, after producer Marc David Alpert.

Cast and Crew Comments: Sarah Michelle Gellar was keen that *Buffy* should go out on top. 'This was a little bit of a frightening year. A lot of shows that were very strong went out not with a bang but with a whimper,' she told reporters at a UPN end-of-season press event. 'It is very important to us that eventually when it is time to go, that we go out strong,' added Sarah. 'We don't want to be a show that got cancelled that people say, "Oh that should've been off three years ago." ' Asked when she thought the show would end, Gellar added: 'I don't have an answer to that. I always say that if you would've told me in the beginning this show would have been on seven years, I would have laughed at you. You always want to challenge yourself. You want to constantly keep it fresh. If it's not fresh, exciting and something you passionately want to do, then the audience is going to know.'

*'I'm standing on the mouth of Hell. It's gonna swallow
me whole. It'll choke on me . . . They're not ready.
They think we're gonna wait for the end? They want
an apocalypse? We'll give 'em one . . .'*

– 'Bring on the Night'

Season Seven (2002–03)

Mutant Enemy Inc/Kuzui Enterprises/Sandollar Television/20th Century Fox
Created by Joss Whedon
Co-Producers: John F Perry, James A Contner (125, 134, 141)
Producers: Gareth Davies, Marc David Alpert
Supervising Producer: Douglas Petrie
Co-Executive Producers: David Solomon, Jane Espenson, David Fury
Executive Producers: Sandy Gallin, Gail Berman, Fran Rubel Kuzui,
Kaz Kuzui, Marti Noxon, Joss Whedon
Regular Cast:
Sarah Michelle Gellar (Buffy Summers),
Nicholas Brendon (Xander Harris, 123–128, 130–144),
Alyson Hannigan (Willow Rosenberg),
Anthony Stewart Head (Rupert Giles, 123–124, 130, 132–133, 135–136, 139–144),
Charisma Carpenter (Cordelia Chase, 128),[43] David Boreanaz (Angel, 143–144),
Mark Metcalf (The Master, 123),
Kristine Sutherland (Joyce Summers, 128,[44] 129, 132),
Elizabeth Anne Allen (Amy Madison, 135), James Marsters (Spike),
Juliet Landau (Drusilla, 123, 132, 139), Danny Strong (Jonathan Levinson,
129, 131, 136, 138), Eliza Dushku (Faith, 140–144),
Harry Groener (Mayor Richard Wilkins III, 123, 142),
Emma Caulfield (Anya Jenkins, 123–126, 128, 130–139, 141–144),
Harris Yulin (Quentin Travers, 131), Andy Umberger (D'Hoffryn, 127),
George Hertzberg (Adam, 123), Sharon Ferguson (Primitive, 137),
Michelle Trachtenberg (Dawn Summers), Clare Kramer (Glory, 123),
Abraham Benrubi (Olaf the Troll, 127), Cynthia LaMontagne (Lydia, 131),
Oliver Muirhead (Philip, 131), Kris Iyer (Nigel, 131),
Adam Busch (Warren Meers, 123, 129, 131, 135, 138),
Tom Lenk (Andrew Wells, 129, 131–144), Kali Rocha (Halfrek, 123, 127),

---

[43] Uncredited in **128**, 'Him', appears only in a flashback sequence from **28**, 'Bewitched, Bothered and Bewildered'.

[44] Uncredited in **128**, 'Him', appears only in a flashback sequence from **28**, 'Bewitched, Bothered and Bewildered'.

James C Leary (Clem, 134, 141),
DB Woodside (Principal Robin Wood, 123–124, 126, 128, 131–132, 136–142, 144),
Azura Skye (Cassie Newton, 126, 129),
Sarah Hagan (Amanda, 126, 134, 136–138, 140–144),
Stacey Scowley (Young Woman, 129–130),
Camden Toy (Über-Vamp, 131–133, 137), Iyari Limon (Kennedy, 132–144),
Clara Bryant (Molly, 132–134, 137–138, 140),
Indigo (Rona, 133–134, 137–141, 144), Felicia Day (Vi, 133–134, 137, 142–144),
Lalaine (Chloe, 133, 136), Kristy Wu (Chao-Ahn, 136–137, 140–141, 144),[45]
KD Aubert (Nikki Wood, 136, 138), Nathon Fillion (Caleb, 140–144),
Mary Wilcher (Shannon, 140–141, 144), Dania Ramirez (Caridad, 140, 142–143),
Lisa Ann Cabasa (Injured Girl, 142–144)

123
Lessons

US Transmission Date: 24 Sep 2002
UK Transmission Date: 16 Jan 2003

Writer: Joss Whedon
Director: David Solomon
Cast: Alex Breckenridge (Kit Holburn), David Zepeda (Carlos Trejo),
Jeremy Howard (Dead Nerd), Ken Strunk (Dead Janitor),
Rachael Bella (Dead Girl), Ed F Martin (Teacher), Simon Chernin (Student),
Jeff Denton (Vampire), Ciaran Hope (Cafe Singer),[46] Mark Weathers (Student)[47]

A young woman is pursued through the streets of Istanbul by sinister robed figures and put to death. Meanwhile, in Sunnydale, California, Dawn Summers attends her first day at the newly reopened Sunnydale High School, accompanied by her, frankly nervous, sister.

Dudes and Babes: Dawn tells her new classmates that she loves to dance (see **107**, 'Once More, With Feeling') and cracks a moderately amusing joke about Britney Spears. Then Buffy arrives and causes a big commotion. 'I also have a sister,' notes Dawn, sadly. She is allergic to bees.

When the zombie boy says that he'd like to go out with Dawn, Buffy replies that he's picked the wrong sister – *she* is the one who dates dead people. And, she adds, no offence, but both of those (Angel and Spike) were hotties. The zombie girl notes, angrily, that

---

[45] Uncredited.
[46] Uncredited.
[47] Uncredited.

while Buffy was making out with her dead boyfriend she was being ripped to death by a werewolf. This probably isn't a reference to the events of **27**, 'Phases', as Angel was Angelus during that period. Since Oz never seemed to hurt anyone (at least anyone *innocent*) during his time in Sunnydale, it's probable, therefore, that the girl was killed by either Veruca (see **62**, 'Wild At Heart') or another werewolf entirely.

Dawn makes two new friends on her first day at school. Shy psychic Goth-girl Kit Holburn, and neurotic outsider Carlos Trejo. Potentially her Willow and Xander. Sadly, neither are ever seen again.

Authority Sucks!: The new school principal, Robin Wood, heedless of the fact that his two immediate predecessors were *eaten* (see **6**, 'The Pack'; **56**, 'Graduation Day' Part 2), seems like a genuinely decent man, offering Buffy a low-paid part-time counselling job with the school's Outreach programme, aimed at helping troubled teenagers. One ominous snippet of information: his office lies directly over the Hellmouth. He's obviously, therefore, hiding *some* dark secret (see **136**, 'First Date'; **139**, 'Lies My Parents Told Me').

A Little Learning is a Dangerous Thing: Buffy tells Dawn about all the horrors that await her in high school, mentioning Hyena People (see **6**, 'The Pack'), lizardy-type athletes (**32**, 'Go Fish') and those who are invisible (**11**, 'Out of Mind, Out of Sight'). When Buffy tells Xander that she has probably wrecked Dawn's social life, this alludes to a conversation between Buffy and Giles in **2**, 'The Harvest'.

Spike, in his confused state, tells Buffy that he was never a quick study. He then talks about William's schooldays and an occasion when he was, seemingly, caned for dropping his writing slate into a river. Spike appeared to have been mutilating himself in an attempt to cut out the soul that he acquired in **122**, 'Grave'.

Willow is currently staying in England with the coven that helped Giles in **121**, 'Two To Go'. They are, she notes, the most amazing women she's ever met and are led by a Ms Harkness. They have taught Willow much in the way of natural lore to cure her magic addiction (see **110**, 'Wrecked'; **122**, 'Grave') including elements of Gaia, root systems and molecular connections. But Willow, in a self-flagellatory mood, remains terrified of returning to Sunnydale and facing the friends whom she so recently tried to kill. Giles asks if she wants to be punished. 'I want to be Willow,' she replies, sadly.

Mom's Apple Pie: Buffy is twice mistaken for Dawn's mother (firstly by Wood, then by Carlos). Much to her *chagrin*. Though a quick check in the mirror confirms what she believed all along – that she hasn't got mom-hair.

The Conspiracy Starts at Home Time: Something is rising, Halfrek tells Anya. Something older than the Old Ones (see **2**, 'The Harvest').

The shapechanging evil in the basement appears to Spike as Warren Meers, Glory, Adam, Mayor Wilkins, Drusilla, the Master and, finally, Buffy.

Work is a Four-Letter Word: Buffy quits the Doublemeat Palace to work as a guidance counsellor. 'Sarah was very upset about not getting to wear the [Doublemeat] hat any more,' Joss Whedon told *TV Zone*.

It's a Designer Label!: Xander looks extremely sharp in his suit – he's heading the construction team at Sunnydale High campus. Also, Dawn's stylish-yet-affordable boots and Buffy's gorgeous white top.

References: Giles's conversation with Willow contains dialogue echoes of *The Empire Strikes Back*, JK Rowling's Harry Potter novels, *Picnic At Hanging Rock* and *All the President's Men*. 'If at first you don't succeed' is a quotation apocryphally attributed to the Scottish monarch Robert the Bruce (1274–1329). Also, REM's 'Shiny Happy People', *The Fantastic Four*, *The Twilight Zone*, *Alice in Wonderland*, the Food Channel, James Bond, the nursery rhyme 'What Are Little Girls Made Of?' and an allusion to Genesis 1:1 ('The beginning ... the word'). Visual references include *Poltergeist*, *The West Wing*, *Almost Famous*, *Repulsion* and *Night of the Living Dead*.

Bitch!: Anya was the most hard-core vengeance-demon under D'Hoffryn's charge (see **43**, 'The Wish'; **50**, 'Doppelgängland'; **65**, 'Something Blue'). Halfrek notes that she has always been competitive with Anya and alludes to a particular incident during the Crimean War. (Compare this, however, with the flashback scenes witnessed in **127**, 'Selfless'.) However, since Anya's return to the fold (see **116**, 'Hell's Bells'; **118**, 'Entropy'), her heart no longer seems to be in her work. There have been no deaths or eviscerations and, Halfrek notes, Anya is seldom goading women into anything inventive and not delivering even when she does. For example, a waitress recently wished her cheating husband were a frog. Anya made him French.

Awesome!: Giles and Willow's conversation about an interconnected world. The scenes between Buffy and Wood are a nice juxtaposition of comedy and occasional dramatic insight. Plus, Spike's incredible appearance in the basement.

'You May Remember Me From Such Films and TV Series As . . .': Alex Breckenridge played Charity in *Vampire Clan* and appeared in *Big Fat Liar* and *Charmed*. David Zepeda's CV includes *Grounded For Life*. DB Woodside played Aaron Mosely in *Murder One* and Wayne Palmer in *24* and also appeared in *Romeo Must Die*. Rachael Bella played Rebecca Kotlen in *The Ring* and was also in *The Blood Oranges* and *A Little Princess*. Simon Chernin appeared in *My Brother Jake*. Jeff Denton was in *Mafia Movie Madness*. Jeremy Howard's CV includes *Catch Me If You Can*, *Galaxy Quest* and *Men in Black II*. Ed Martin was in *Chicago Hope*. Ken Strunk's movies include *Hoosiers*.

Don't Give Up the Day Job: Ciaran Hope worked as a music editor on *Killer Bud* and *Fear of Flying*. Mark Weathers was on the swing team on *Die, Momma, Die*.

Logic, Let Me Introduce You to This Window: The coven that Giles worked with in **121**, 'Two To Go', was in Devon. Now, apparently, they're based in Westbury, Wiltshire. A cellphone that works underground? Dawn seems astonished, as she rightly should. The people in the basement are manifest spirits controlled by a talisman, raised to seek vengeance. Does that mean they can answer cellphones? Why did the school authorities fill the basement of the new Sunnydale High with various junk from the old one? Who planted the talisman? How did Spike get back from Africa in his somewhat insane state? Doesn't anyone in her class miss Dawn after she goes to the bathroom? Appearing as Adam, the (as yet nameless) shapechanging evil calls Spike Number 17 instead of Hostile 17. Additionally, as far as we know (certainly from the evidence of **42**, 'Lover's Walk') Spike and Mayor Wilkins, whom the shapechanger also appears as, have never previously met. A whopping great hole in a new building's floor isn't 'contracty goodness', as Xander suggests. It's more likely to mean a lawsuit for shoddy workmanship and a penalty clause for the construction company. For the second time in the series' history viewers are given a glimpse of Sarah Michelle Gellar's legendary tattoo on her back (see **122**, 'Grave'). This occurs just before Buffy, Xander and Dawn head off to school.

The zombie girl claims that the school was built on their graves. However, the new school was constructed on the same spot as the old one, not a cemetery. During the final scene, Drusilla clearly touches Spike's hair, despite it being subsequently established that the First Evil is non-corporeal. When Buffy arrives in the basement she's wearing high heels. Subsequently, when fighting the zombies, these have changed to brown trainers.

General point, not specific to this episode: if one vampire is capable of redemption (see **122**, 'Grave') and a spell for re-ensouling vampires exists (**34**, 'Becoming' Part 2), shouldn't Buffy be trying to re-ensoul and redeem vampires rather than merely slaying them? It's a longer process, perhaps, but it's surely a more humane one. Or, does this only apply to vampires that Buffy fancies?

I Just *Love* Your Accent: There are a couple of scenes involving Willow and Giles in the rural English splendour of a wet and miserable June afternoon in Wiltshire. Willow refers to bangers and mash (a bland sausage and mashed potato dinner, for American readers) before adding that she isn't sure what that is.

Motors: Xander has a new silver Merc (3PCE 187), his previous car having been destroyed by Willow in **121**, 'Two To Go'.

Cruelty To Animals: Buffy makes up a totally ridiculous story to excuse herself from Principal Wood. 'Good luck with that . . . dog tragedy,' he notes.

Quote/Unquote: Buffy: 'It doesn't matter how well prepped you are or how well armed. You're a little girl.' Dawn: 'Woman.' Buffy: 'Little woman.' Dawn: 'I'm taller than you.'

Willow: 'When you brought me here, I thought it was to . . . lock me in some mystical dungeon for all eternity . . . Instead, you go all Dumbledore on me.'

Willow: 'Is there anything you don't know everything about?' Giles: 'Synchronised swimming. Complete mystery to me.'

Wood: 'It's not even noon and I've already bullied my first family member into helping out. I'm gonna be the best principal ever!'

Notes: 'It's about power. Who's got it, who knows how to use it.' Where better to reach the beginning of the end than back where it all started? Unlike many of its contemporary series, the episodes that open a season of *Buffy* seldom conform to accepted dramatic criteria. In short, they don't, normally, seem bothered about setting up the mechanics of what is to follow. Additionally, and these two facts may or may not be related, they don't always satisfy the viewer either. Which is odd since these season-openers are usually written by Joss Whedon. 'Lessons' does *both* of the above, which is disquieting in a way. It's a fine episode, full of pithy one-liners, impressive set-pieces, conceptual depth and terrific performances. Plus the central concept of what's coming in season seven is all over it like a rash. It's therefore not like a *Buffy* season-opener at all. If 'Lessons' is like anything from the series' past, then it's probably 1, 'Welcome to the Hellmouth', which suggests a conscious decision by the production team to return *Buffy* to its conceptual roots. Structurally, having to tell so many fragments of an incomplete story, 'Lessons' is quite messy. The *non sequitur* pre-title sequence, and the coda – which includes fan-pleasing, but rather pointless, cameos for several favourite villains from years past – suggests a complex story arc in the making. But, taken strictly on its own merits, 'Lessons' delivers its message and reminds us that *Buffy*'s strengths have always been in its ability to surprise.

The first vampire that Buffy fought with a stake survived when she missed his heart (see the *Buffy the Vampire Slayer* movie; **2**, 'The Harvest'; **33**, 'Becoming' Part 1). Vampires tend not to be aware of their preternatural strength when first sired (see Angel's comment in **14**, 'Some Assembly Required'). However, as Dawn notes, they all seem to acquire a familiarity with martial-arts skills surprisingly quickly. Among Giles's talents is an ability to ride horses. Wood says that the School Board recommended that he familiarise himself with Buffy's file. Of course, as we subsequently discover, he has a much deeper motive for knowing as much as possible about her (see **136**, 'First Date').

Soundtrack: 'So High' by Strange Radio. Ciaran Hope performs a song that appears to be called 'In My Eyes' in the Espresso Pump.

Critique: 'Tonight's opener goes back-to-basics in Buffy's old high school,' noted the *Calgary Sun*. 'Funny, fast and spooky, it's worth staking out.' 'It seems *Buffy* is out of its funk and hopefully the rest of the season continues on this promising track,' added online reviewer Richard Williams. In an article describing several reasons why *Buffy* would, probably, again be ignored by the

Emmy nomination committee, *Entertainment Weekly*'s Ken Tucker described the series as an 'extravagantly dramatic show that explores adolescent and post-adolescent traumas better than any series since *My So-Called Life*.' Yet, Tucker continued, *Buffy* is also 'not quite "grown-up" enough to draw in adult Emmy voters.'

'Not all the signs are positive,' argued the *Baltimore Sun*. 'The rehabilitation of Willow, whose destructive rage caught everyone off-guard last year, appears to [take] place in a British pasture way-too-immersed in New Age philosophy.'

Did You Know?: The opening Istanbul sequence was filmed at Universal Studios.

Filming for the scenes – in this and the following episode – featuring Giles and Willow took place at Tony Head's home in the village of Timsbury, near Keynsham. Tony told the *Bristol Evening Post* that, 'Joss suggested we use my place and I thought it might be fun. My only regret is the weather.' During the shooting several of the crew stayed at Tony's house, which enabled his daughters, Daisy and Emily, to see some of their American friends. Afterwards, Joss Whedon is reported to have motored up to London and spent three hours buying comics in *Forbidden Planet*. Now *there's* a man who's got his priorities in life sorted.

Throughout this episode's original US broadcast, trailers were aired for the following programme, the premier of *Haunted* featuring an appearance by the band the Goo Goo Dolls. These trailers featured James Marsters.

Cast and Crew Comments: 'We worked out a deal,' Tony Head told the *New York Daily News*. '[I'll be in] a minimum of ten episodes. Thank God I work for somebody who isn't remotely Hollywood. Usually, they say, "You do what we want, or you're not coming back at all".'

Joss Whedon's Comments: A return to a lighter, funnier *Buffy* was promised for season seven, following a year which many fans saw as being too grim for too long. While Joss Whedon was looking forward to taking the show back to its wittier roots, he also, clearly, believed that *Buffy* had accomplished what it set out to do during season six – making the heroine face the inner demons that accompany maturity. 'Every year has its criticism,' Joss told *USA Today*. 'I do think we hit a few of the same notes too many times. But I'm proud of many of the things we did.'

Speaking at an Academy of Television Arts and Sciences symposium in June 2002, Joss noted that when he first saw Tony Head's scene at the climax of **121**, 'Two To Go', he instantly realised how much season six had missed Giles's presence. 'I'm going to England to shoot some second-unit with Tony and Alyson,' Joss told *Sci-Fi Wire*. 'Our first production values ever. Usually it's "We're in Venice. Hand me that goblet' " (a reference to the opening scene of **8**, 'I Robot . . . You Jane'). Asked about his general approach to the coming year, Whedon added, 'it's something I've been gearing towards since the beginning. The climax will be the biggest thing we've ever done. I am looking for closure next year because we're making a more positive statement. This year was just about surviving.'

'Season six was fantastic, but it had a darker tone,' Joss told another online interview. 'Some of the episodes depressed the hell out of me. We're going back to our original mission statement, to the positive view of female empowerment. This year was about adult life and relationships – and making bad decisions. Next year will still be scary, different and strange. People will stop abandoning Dawn. Willow won't be a junkie any more. Buffy won't be dead. The theme . . . [will] be *Buffy Year One*.'

'We're going to be back to Sunnydale High,' Whedon told Patrick Lee of *SciFi.com*. 'We're going to be spending time with Dawn, and facing a lot worse peril than ever because some idiot built that school again.'

124
Beneath You

US Transmission Date: 1 Oct 2002
UK Transmission Date: 23 Jan 2003

Writer: Douglas Petrie
Director: Nick Marck
Cast: Kaarina Aufranc (Nancy), Tess Hall (Punk Girl),
Benita Krista Nall (Young Woman), Jack Sundmacher (Ronnie)

A giant worm-like Sluggoth demon causes mayhem in Sunnydale, a result of Anya's latest piece of deranged wish-granting. Xander and Buffy try to help the demon's intended victim, Nancy. Meanwhile, Spike tells Buffy about his re-ensoulment.

Dreaming (As Blondie Once Said) is Free: The episode begins with Buffy dreaming about a pink-haired Goth-girl being murdered by robed men in Frankfurt. Buffy realises, almost instantly, that this has actually happened in reality and that there are other girls in the same position who are also going to die.

Dudes and Babes: Xander mentions that he has seen Anya at the Bronze a few times and speculates she was probably looking for scorned women (as, indeed, this episode confirms). Buffy refers to Dawn's smoochathon with a vampire last Halloween (see **106**, 'All The Way'). The Sluggoth is, in reality, Ronnie, the abusive ex-boyfriend of Nancy, turned into his present state by Anya.

Authority Spanks!: Wood, semi-seriously, suggests there are only three things that teenagers understand: the boot, the bat, and the bastinado. He's a bit disturbed that Buffy actually knows what the latter is (a Turkish torture implement used to beat the soles of the feet).

A Little Learning is a Dangerous Thing: Wood suggests that Buffy may become popular with the students as she is the youngest, and least stuffy, member of the Sunnydale High faculty.

Mom's Apple Pie: Dawn, concerned that she and Buffy will be at school together, informs her sister that she should, under no circumstances, talk to Dawn. Or hang out with any of her friends.

Work is a Four-Letter Word: Buffy is delighted when Wood confirms that, in her new job, she can give students detention.

It's a Designer Label!: Highlights include Buffy's black top and Spike's tight blue shirt.

References: The opening sequence contains visual allusions to *Alias* and *Run Lola Run*. Also, *A Fish Called Wanda* and *Tremors*. There are dialogue references to the Crusades, *Star Trek: First Contact* and *Batman*. Spike, quasi-Christ-like, burning himself on a crucifix reinforces one of *Buffy*'s core concepts: the idea of redemption through suffering.

Bitch!: Spike says that he cannot apologise to Buffy for his attempt to rape her (see **119**, 'Seeing Red') but can assure her that he has changed. Buffy agrees, but says that she doesn't know *what* he's changed into. She questions his motives and suggests that there is something he isn't telling her. Spike agrees but, since they're no longer friends, he doesn't want to discuss the subject.

Awesome!: The sweet scene in which Nancy hits on Xander, which turns into an effects overload as the worm-creature stages an attack. The Spike/Anya fight. The final church scenes, as Spike admits to Buffy what happened to him in Africa.

'You May Remember Me From Such Films and TV Series As . . .': Kaarina Aufranc appeared in *The West Wing* and *CSI*. Tess Hall's movies include *The Ring*. Benita Krista Nall was in *JAG* and *Minority Report*.

Don't Give Up the Day Job: Musical Supervisor Robert Duncan's CV includes *Starhunter*, *Blue Murder* and *Tru Calling*.

Valley-Speak: Anya; 'Oh . . . penis!' And: 'Bite me, Harris.'

Sex and Drugs and Rock'n'Roll: Xander speculates on the problems likely to be faced by the troubled teens Buffy is to counsel. These include drugs and unwanted pregnancy.

'West Hollywood': In the episode's best scene, as Nancy is introduced to the people who are going to help her, she gleams that their various interrelationships have a somewhat complex history. So, let's get this straight: Buffy once went with Spike; Spike once went with Anya; Anya once went with Xander? 'Is there anyone here who *hasn't* slept together?' she asks. Xander and Spike look at each other awkwardly. Fantastic.

Logic, Let Me Introduce You to This Window: Why does the German girl speak to Buffy in English? Buffy, apparently, sleeps with her window open. Isn't that a fantastically dangerous thing to do in Sunnydale? Given that this episode takes place, at most, a week after the events of **123**, 'Lessons', Spike's self-inflicted wounds seen in the previous episode have almost totally healed. Given that there's a taxi waiting to take Willow to the airport, the next episode, in which she returns to Sunnydale, must begin at most one day after this. Yet in **125**, 'Same Time, Same Place', Anya comments that these events took place 'last week'. Spike's reflection can be seen on a filing cabinet.

Cruelty to Animals: Anya is told that the man she turned into a Sluggoth has eaten a small dog. 'Awww, puppy,' she says, almost reduced to tears. Spike shares his basement with a rat.

Quote/Unquote: Xander: 'Those kids are damn lucky having a Slayer and a friend on campus, I hope they appreciate it. I know I did.'

Dawn, to Spike: 'I can't take you in a fight, even with the chip in your head, but you *do* sleep. If you hurt my sister . . . you're gonna wake up on fire.'

Buffy: 'Have you completely lost your mind?' Spike: 'Well, yes. Where have you been all night?'

Spike's description of his soul: 'I wanted to give you what you deserved. And I got it. They put the spark in me. Now all it does is *burn*.'

Notes: 'From beneath you, it devours.' A truly fine episode from the always-reliable Doug Petrie that gets to the heart of Spike's return, with soul intact, to Sunnydale. It also gives both Xander and Anya a sizeable chunk of the action, and adds a welcome outsiders' view of the alleged freaks who make up the Scooby Gang – something that we haven't, consciously, had an example of since they all left high school. 'Beneath You' advances the season's ongoing plot arc only by inches and there is another *non-sequitur* pre-title sequence. On the other hand, the return of Spike's soul, and the ramifications of this, see James Marsters putting in a beautifully schizoid performance. There are many other great moments in 'Beneath You', the deliberate triple entendre of the episode's title not least among them.

Buffy mentions Principal Flutie's grizzly fate (see **6**, 'The Pack') and, also, the horrors of working at the Doublemeat Palace (see **112**, 'Doublemeat Palace'). Xander spends the episode bemoaning his inability to get a date since his break up with Anya (see **116**, 'Hell's Bells'). He even tells Dawn that this makes him miss high school as, in those days, at least he didn't have that problem. It's Anya who first realises that Spike has acquired a soul (her demon powers, apparently, gives her an ability to sense its presence). Spike says that Angel should have warned him how hard regaining one's soul can be. (Ironically, a similar scene in *Angel*: 'Just Rewards', sees Angel raging wildly about how easily Spike coped with the ordeal compared to the century of horrors that Angel, himself, suffered.) Robin Wood is a vegetarian. The episode's title is, in part, an allusion to Buffy's opinion of Spike in **85**, 'Fool For Love'.

Soundtrack: 'David' by Gus Gus, 'It Came From Japan' by the Von Bondies and 'Stop Thinking About It' by Joey Ramone. The opening scene is accompanied by a Kraftwerk-style techno recording, composed by Robert Duncan. This includes the repeated lyrics '*Von der tiefe verschlingt es*', which is German for 'from beneath you, it devours'.

Did You Know?: 'We're [the same] in the sense of living the difference between being a young adult and being a child at the same time,' Sarah Michelle Gellar noted concerning her alter ego when she appeared on *The View* in July 2002. 'Buffy is basically a single mom with a full-time job. So I think there are comparisons.'

Nightmares in Wax: During October 2002, Sarah Michelle Gellar joined Queen Victoria, the Duke of Wellington and the Beatles (along with various murderers and assassins) as a fixture in London's Madame Tussaud's. This was as part of a Halloween exhibit called *Dracula's Escape from the Chamber of Horrors*. Visitors were given a stake and cloves of garlic in order to help Buffy find Dracula among several actors dressed as the vampire. Buffy's arrival in the museum was, however, somewhat over-shadowed by a counter-attraction, a Kylie Minogue figure, the famous bottom of which got *much* more press attention.

Critique: In *The Financial Times*, Ian Shuttleworth argued that Buffy and her friends combating evil from a high school library could be read as a Marxist parable on the alienation of intellectual labour. Like many commentators on the phenomena, however, Shuttleworth felt that he needed to justify all this chin-stroking over a TV series. 'On the one hand, its zesty wordplay stands comparison with the finest Howard Hawks screwball comedies; on the other, it dealt with ordinary life crises in a way at once thoughtful and feeling.'

Cast and Crew Comments: James Marsters told *Sci-Fi Wire* that he didn't know whether Spike would turn out to be good or evil after his acquisition of a soul. 'I could be unleashed as the big villain, or I could be goody two-shoes,' he said. But Spike's attempted rape of Buffy in **119**, 'Seeing Red', *would* cause a rift between him and Dawn. 'It won't be easy,' Michelle Trachtenberg noted. 'I think he's the one that Dawn connected to the most, because he never treated her like a child. She'll handle the situation in an adult way.'

'I'm blessed with the good writing. They give me great dialogue,' Emma Caulfield told *SciFi.com*. 'Anya comes pretty easy to me. She's sort of a flashy character; she gets to say the funny lines. And she gets to be ridiculous.'

One of the main focuses of interest in the genre press during this period was whether Amber Benson would be returning, in a guest role, to the series that she graced for three years. 'I don't know, and even if I did, I couldn't tell you,' Amber told *Birmingham News*. 'On *Buffy*, one minute you're dead, the next you're giving birth to some horrible creature!'

Joss Whedon's Comments: Some producers make deliberately serious shows. Joss Whedon has never wanted to be one of them. 'I'm not an adult,' he told the *New York Times*, 'I don't want to create shows with lawyers. I want to invade people's dreams.' Whedon has noted that he isn't averse to telling a good story in the name of fantasy fiction, however. Comparing *Buffy* to one of his favourite shows, *Law & Order*, Joss noted that 'We're paying homage to the same thing: storytelling. I want to create a fiction that affects people's lives.' Although a self-confessed atheist, Whedon has a kind of faith – in narrative passion that creates lasting loyalties. 'Every time people say, "You've transcended the genre," I [say] "I believe in genre".'

125
Same Time, Same Place

US Transmission Date: 8 Oct 2002
UK Transmission Date: 30 Jan 2003

Writer: Jane Espenson
Director: James A Contner
Cast: Camden Toy (Gnarl), Anthony S Johnson (Father),
Matt Koruba (Teen Boy), Nicholette Dixon (Sister), Marshe Daniel (Brother)

Willow returns to Sunnydale. For some inexplicable reason her friends are unable to see her and she cannot see them. To complicate matters, a corpse is discovered with its skin flayed from its body. Could Willow have possibly turned evil again?

Dudes and Babes: Anya notes that vengeance is not as fulfilling as it used to be. Willow is surprised by this admission, having always believed that Anya enjoyed inflicting pain on others. Anya replies that it sounds cool in theory but, in reality, it actually isn't. Willow empathises, remembering from her own experiences that power can corrupt. This observation, notes Anya, was somewhat over-dramatically stated but, fundamentally, correct.

At the episode's climax, Willow realises that she, herself, was subconsciously responsible for her invisibility to Buffy, Xander and Dawn. She tells Buffy that she was afraid they would not accept her back. Buffy confesses that she briefly believed Willow might have been responsible for the murder. She adds that Xander, bless him, never did.

Authority Sucks!: Vengeance-demons' ability to teleport isn't a right, it's a privilege. Since Anya withdrew her vengeance spell on Ronnie (see **124**, 'Beneath You') she is being punished and can only teleport for official business. Sadly, she bemoans, she has to file a flight plan.

A Little Learning is a Dangerous Thing: Xander has told both Buffy and Dawn the story of how he prevented Willow from ending the world by reminding her of the time when she broke the yellow crayon in kindergarten (see **122**, 'Grave').

Denial, Thy Name is Everyone: In a moment of clarity, Dawn asks if anyone around her is ever going to ask their friends for help when they need it. Instead, everyone seems content to keep secrets and suffers alone, in silence. Then, she continues, their friends are expected to be sympathetic when, for instance, they rip the skin off people (**120**, 'Villains') or drag their sisters into the basement (**117**, 'Normal Again'). Buffy admits that Dawn has a point.

Work is a Four-Letter Word: The Magic Box remains closed after Willow decimated it (see **121**, 'Two To Go'; **122**, 'Grave'). Anya notes that Buffy's new job involves her helping 'junior deviants'.

It's a Designer Label!: A mixed bunch: Dawn's minxy top, Willow's cool leather jacket and pinstriped flares, Anya's incredibly tight jeans and Buffy's light blue skirt share top-billing.

References: Gnarl is the creepiest nasty to hit Sunnydale since the Gentlemen and shares a conceptual origin in various nursery rhymes. In several interviews, Jane Espenson has noted that Gnarl was, in part, based on the character of Gollum from *The Lord Of The Rings*. The demon's voice is a dead-ringer for the leader of the Blue Meanies in *Yellow Submarine*. The episode includes dialogue allusions to Harry Nilson's 'Everybody's Talkin'' and Arthur Conan Doyle's Sherlock Holmes novels. Buffy's destruction of Gnarl by stabbing him to keep him immobile, then putting out his eyes, refers to both *The Godfather* and *King Lear*.

Bitch!: Anya is surprised to see Willow, having been told that she was with Giles learning 'how not to kill people'. When Willow says that she is sorry for her previous actions, Anya notes that vengeance-demons tend not to accept apologies. They prefer statements like 'Oh God, please stop hitting me with my own rib-bones.'

Awesome!: The Anya/Willow scenes; in fact, pretty much *everything* that Anya says is touched by comedy greatness. Dawn's paralysis-induced helplessness and Buffy, Xander and Anya's amusingly inane and helpless reaction to it. *You* try saying the word 'vomit' without moving your lips and see how far you get. The really touching final scenes – friendships renewed, and strengthened, through adversity.

'You May Remember Me From Such Films and TV Series As . . .': Anthony Johnson's CV includes *Ninja Academy* and *Married . . . With Children*. Matt Koruba was in *Wanted*.

Don't Give Up the Day Job: Musical Supervisor Douglas Romayne also worked on *In Between Days*, *Wolf Girl*, *The Skulls II* and *Interstate 60*. Editor Louise Innes's CV includes *Foxfire*, *The X-Files*, *Dead Poets Society* and *Dead Calm*.

The Drugs Don't Work: Gnarl is a parasite-demon that secretes a substance through the fingernails that is used to paralyse its victims. It then removes and eats the victim's skin while they are still alive. (Dawn notes the process can take hours.) Gnarl is also immune to magic.

Valley-Speak: Xander, on Giles: 'Is he throwing a tasteful British wiggins?' Buffy: 'With extra wig.'

Sex and Drugs and Rock'n'Roll: Anya feels that the locator spell she and Willow perform gets a little sexy when they begin to bare their souls. She seems keen to continue. Willow, on the other hand, makes an excuse and leaves.

Logic, Let Me Introduce You to This Window: On which airline was Willow flying from London to Sunnydale, via Chicago? (See **101**, 'Bargaining' Part 1; **108**, 'Tabula Rasa'.) At the airport, Willow is arriving on an international flight, yet she reaches the point where she expects to meet Buffy, Xander and Dawn carrying only hand luggage. Not possible. Upon entering the US, baggage pickup takes place *before* clearing immigration. Willow had both a suitcase and a large holdall when she left with Giles in the taxi (**124**, 'Beneath You'). Later, she's carrying the case when arriving at Revello Drive. (She appears to leave the case at the back door when entering the house and, subsequently, it's never seen again.) Anya's vengeance takes her all over the world. Yesterday, for example, she was in Brazil where, she notes, they love soccer. Indeed they do, except they call it *football*, just like everyone else in the world except Americans.

Does Xander give his crew a day off every time there's a murder in Sunnydale (see, for instance, **107**, 'Once More, With Feeling')? If so, it's a wonder anything ever gets built. From whom did Spike learn about Willow's murder of Warren? As far as we know his only conversations with anyone since his return from Africa have been those actually seen in the last two episodes and it's certainly not the kind of subject one would expect Buffy or Xander to casually disclose.[48] Both Buffy and Dawn's blouses were torn by Gnarl. However, later in the episode they're undamaged. When Dawn is supposedly paralysed, while she's lying down on the couch with Xander at her side, her head keeps changing positions.

Quote/Unquote: Willow: 'When did *you* get all insightful?' Anya: 'I'm surprisingly sensitive.' Willow: 'Will you help me?' Anya: 'Is it difficult or time consuming?'

Spike, on Xander: '*I'm* insane. What's *his* excuse?'

Anya: 'Wouldn't it be tragic if you were being kind of silly with your comically paralysed sister while Willow was dying?'

Anya, on Gnarl: 'Buffy killed him. It was gross.'

Notes: 'Button, button, who's got the button? My money's on the witch.' Two of the main reasons why *Buffy* has been, for seven years, the most consistent TV show in the world are highlighted in this episode: Jane Espenson and Alyson Hannigan. The former remains, on her day, easily the best writer on the show. The latter, well, Willow just *rocks*. 'Same Time, Same Place' concerns, on one level, Willow's return to Sunnydale from her enforced meditations in England. There's also some stuff about a flesh-eating parasite-demon. That's the surface. Amid a plot that includes literal presentations of the fear of rejection by those on whom we depend,

---

[48] One excellent fan-theory: One of the cave paintings seen when Spike's soul is returned (**122**, 'Grave') appears to depict a skinless man tied between two poles. D'Hoffryn certainly knew of Willow's actions (see **127**, 'Selfless') and noted that one of his colleagues, called Lloyd, has an illustration of these events on his wall. Could the demon in the cave, therefore, have been a vengeance-demon? If so, it's no wonder that Spike suffered as much as he did.

there are many moments in which Willow questions whether her friends will ever be able to accept her again after the terrible things she did. Redemption is only something worth seeking, the argument seems to be, if you think that you're going to actually achieve it. Cos, if you're not, what's the point? All of this, in dramatic terms at least, sounds like hard work, particularly taking into account Anya's sudden admission to Willow that wish-granting just isn't fun any more. Not many laughs here, right? Wrong! In short, this episode sees *Buffy* doing the simple things again and, by this restatement of its addictive core values, rediscovering an ability to laugh both at itself and at the wider world. When Xander tells Buffy and Dawn the story behind why his WELCOME HOME sign to Willow is written in yellow crayon you want to do something big and dramatic in celebration. Talent wins out, again, as it usually does.

From this episode onwards it appears that Willow is sleeping in Buffy's old bedroom while Buffy has moved into her mother's room. This is, probably, because Willow would not wish to sleep in the room where Tara died. Anya notes that Willow killed two people – Warren (see **120**, 'Villains') and Rack (see **121**, 'Two To Go'). Anya is now back in her own apartment. Dawn has become adept at computer research on demons, discussing those that flay their victims and others who collect eyeballs or viscera. Using Willow's AppleMac laptop, Dawn accesses the *Demon, Demons, Demons* website, as frequently used by Cordelia, Fred and Wesley for information in various episodes of *Angel*. Buffy's work telephone number is 555 0101. Xander's office is 555 0148 and Dawn's cellphone is 555 0193. Xander refers to Willy's bar (see **21**, 'What's My Line' Part 1). Clem is mentioned (see **105**, 'Life Serial'). When Spike asks Buffy what word rhymes with glowing, this alluded to **85**, 'Fool For Love', in which William asked a similar poetry-related question of a waiter while composing a love sonnet for Cecily. And also to Spike's sarcastic conversation with Angelus about the lack of poetry in ripping Buffy's lungs out in **28**, 'Bewitched, Bothered and Bewildered'.

Critique: The *Independent* wrote that *Buffy*'s dialogue is always 'sharp, bantering, allusive, drenched in all the quick, knowing irony that Americans, allegedly, don't do'.

Did You Know?: 'I think the method is conducive for film and television because the method [involves] suspending your disbelief like you're asking the audience to,' James Marsters noted during a 2002 convention panel. 'You build an imaginary world and then release yourself into it. Sean Penn calls it "the Cage". Meryl Streep calls it "the Box". I call it "the Sandlot". As sick as it sounds, in my head there is a little Sunnydale, and a Buffy and a Spike. And Spike *loves* Buffy.' In more recent interviews, however, Marsters has noted that using method acting for TV is not a good idea as the actor has to sustain a character for too long. If, as in Spike's case, the character is being tortured or abused, this can really mess with the actor's head. Nevertheless, his *Buffy* colleagues apparently find James's working methods rather amusing. 'Sarah is always making fun of me,' James told the DragonCon audience in 2003. ' "Oh, I'm a tree." '

Cast and Crew Comments: Alyson Hannigan believed that Willow's greatest challenge in the coming year would be 'winning the fans' love back. They probably hate me now,' she told a convention audience prior to season seven. 'I hope they forgive my evilness in the last few episodes.' Hannigan added that Willow's addiction to magic would remain an issue. 'Once you go that far, you deal with it for the rest of your life. She's got to have time to recover.'

Jane Espenson's Comments: Concerning 'Same Time, Same Place', Jane told Joe Nazzaro that, 'It's got a lot of funny in it, but there's also a tone throughout. It's got [some] melancholy.' She also revealed that the episode has been written quickly due to her working simultaneously on her script for the *Firefly* episode 'Shindig'.

Marti Noxon's Comments: Marti outlined her plans to juggle season seven, motherhood and office gossip, revealing that her biggest challenge was probably 'keeping Joss from exploding'. As she told *Sci-Fi.com*, 'We're going to have to really get economical.' Part of the writing staff's daily routing was also changed – even though many of *Buffy*'s most innovative ideas have stemmed directly from it. 'We're going to have to stop talking about the movies we saw and what we did over the weekend for three hours every day,' noted Noxon. '[And] stop making dumb jokes about 70s TV shows [even though] that's part of the creative process.'

126
Help

US Transmission Date: 15 Oct 2002
UK Transmission Date: 6 Feb 2003

Writer: Rebecca Rand Kirshner
Director: Rick Rosenthal
Cast: Zachery Bryan (Peter), Glenn Morshower (Mr Newton),
Rick Gonzalez (Tomas), Kevin Christy (Josh), Beth Skipp (Student),
Anthony Harrell (Janitor), Jarrett Lennon (Student with Coins),
J Barton (Mike Helgenburg), Daniel Dehring (Red Robed #1),
AJ Wedding (Red Robed #2), Marcie Lynn Ross (Dead Woman),
Troy Brenna (Avilas Demon)

During Buffy's first day at her counselling job she meets Cassie Newton who has been sent because of her failure to do her homework. Cassie tells Buffy that this is pointless since she is going to die next Friday. Buffy determines to make sure this does not happen.

No Fat Chicks: A girl wearing a wide-load pair of cream jeans walks through shot as the camera pans towards Buffy's office.

Dudes and Babes: As he prepares to kill her, Peter tells Cassie it's nothing personal. She does, however, have a death-chick-suicidal-vibe going for her and that she's unlikely to be missed.

Authority Helps: Buffy's first counselling case is Amanda (see **134**, 'Potential') who says that she's been sent because a boy was teasing her. Buffy notes that the bully is probably insecure. Later she says that Amanda shouldn't sit back and take it. Amanda is pleased and happily notes that she didn't – she beat the crap out of her tormentor. That's the *other* reason she was sent to the counsellor. Amanda asks if Buffy thinks she should pound on the boy some more.

 Another of Buffy's cases is Tomas. He confesses that he's scared his brother, who has joined the Marines, will be killed in action. Buffy says that it's OK to be worried about someone you love and suggests that Tomas talk to his brother about his feelings.

The Conspiracy Starts at Home Time: Buffy asks Spike if there's something evil in the school basement. Spike confirms that there is. But, in his confusion, he appears to be talking about himself. It's interesting that, like Angel, Spike seems to draw a distinct line between himself and his persona pre-soul, describing William, as opposed to Spike, as a very bad man.

It's a Designer Label!: Highlights include Buffy's succession of cool tops and Willow's gorgeous black velvet blouse and red gypsy skirt.

References: Xander mentions the popular advertising slogans 'I like Ike' and 'Milk: It does a body good.' Cassie wears a T-shirt celebrating the Detroit thrash-rock duo the White Stripes. She's reading Kurt Vonnegut's classic novel *Slaughterhouse Five*. Also, *Bewitched*, the Google Internet search engine, New York's Rockerfeller Center, locker stickers for the bands Devil Doll and Flammable and the movie *Thank God It's Friday*. Buffy alludes to 1970s diabolist rockers Blue Öyster Cult, most famous for '(Don't Fear) The Reaper'.

Awesome!: The opening funeral home sequence and, particularly, Dawn's complaint about always having to go in the kid's coffin despite being taller than Buffy. Willow is, yet again, having a crisis of confidence over whether she can control her magic. Xander draws a parallel between Willow's magic and using a hammer. The user, he notes, has either power or control, but seldom both. This is followed by the touching scene of Willow visiting Tara's grave. Also, the final sequence, after Cassie has died from a congenital heart defect, with Buffy, Xander, Willow and Dawn discussing fate, freewill and other Big Concept ideas.

'You May Remember Me From Such Films and TV Series As . . .': Glenn Morshower is one of only two men who work in the administrations of both Presidents Bartlet and Palmer, playing Defence Analyst Mike Chysler in *The West Wing* and Secret Service Agent Aaron Pierce in *24*. He's also appeared in *Black Hawk Down*, *CSI*, *The Core*, *Godzilla*, *Air Force One*, *Under Siege* and *JAG*. Azura Skye's CV includes *Red Dragon*, *Confessions of an Ugly Sister*, *28 Days* and *Zoe, Duncan, Jack & Jane*. Zachery Bryan appeared in *Longshot* and *Home Improvement*. J Barton was in *Boston Public*.

Kevin Christy appeared in *Sin*, *Seven Days* and *Dude, Where's My Car?* Rick Gonzalez was in *Laurel Canyon*, *The Rookie* and *Boston Public*. Daniel Dehring appeared in *Hollywood Fame*. Sarah Hagan played Millie Kentner in *Freaks and Geeks* and Sarah in *Orange County*. Anthony Harrell was Eric in *Saved By The Bell: The New Class*. Jarrett Lennon's CV includes *She's All*

That, *ER*, *Highway To Hell* and *Cheers*. Beth Skipp appeared in *Alternate Realities* and *Monk*.

Don't Give Up the Day Job: Troy Brenna is a stuntman who has worked on *Hulk*, *X-Men* and *3000 Miles to Graceland*. AJ Wedding was the writer/director of *OB-1*. Production Designer Thomas Fichter's CV includes *The OC*, *3 Strikes*, *Melrose Place* and *Scream 3*.

Logic, Let Me Introduce You to This Window: Dawn says that Buffy borrows her clothes without asking. Surely they'll be different sizes? Why would a coffin have a child-lock on the inside? OK, this *is* Sunnydale we're talking about. How could Xander, Buffy and Dawn breath for over 30 minutes while inside closed caskets? Where did Willow get the picture of Cassie and Mike from? When Buffy talks to Wood after first meeting Cassie, her top's neckline changes. Some of the episode's time scale is defective, particularly during a montage series of scenes supposedly taking place on a Friday – some of which occur in daylight while preceding scenes were set after dark. When Cassie falls, her head is upright, looking up at the ceiling. In the next shot she's looking towards Buffy. Then, she's facing the ceiling again. Michelle Trachtenberg's hairstyle changes at least twice between scenes that are set on the same day.

Quote/Unquote: Xander: 'Poems. Always a sign of pretentious inner turmoil.'

Buffy, to Mike: 'You're asking my sister to the dance? And she's your *second* choice?'

Peter: 'Help me, please, I'm bleeding.' Buffy: 'Sorry, my office hours are ten to four.'

Notes: 'Next Friday I'm gonna die.' The episode that generated its own website. Well, there are worse things to be remembered for than as an example of pop-culture eating itself. Strictly in terms of dramatic ambitions, 'Help' is not really deserving of the shoeing that I'm about to give it. But, as we all know from bitter experience, ambition and realisation are two different beasts. 'Help' is, on one level, a very touching, and beautifully played, story about the whims and caprices of fate. The episode has, at its heart, a sense of righteous pain that, sometimes, we simply cannot help, change or militate against what the world has planned for us and others. So far, so good. In the midst of all this, though, is a *deeply* unsatisfying episode of *Buffy*. For some reason the good things in 'Help' never quite overcome some major problems associated with it. Perhaps the biggest is in the central guest performance. Azura Skye manages to make the audience care about Cassie and her predicament extremely well. She's very sympathetic and her dialogue has a quaint, rather poignant quality to it. Sadly, what fate ultimately has in store for Cassie is also, in dramatic terms at least, a massive let down. And all the hidden websites in the world aren't gonna change the basic fact that 'Help' is hollow. Because of this, an episode that had the potential to say some important things about teenage trauma sees its message getting lost amid a periphery of fractured subplots and godawfully pretentious poetry. Primarily, this episode is the first character-building exercise for Buffy herself this season, meaning that Sarah Michelle Gellar gets a chance to remind us what a fabulous actress she is. Deft at handling light comedy and Bondian-style pithy quips, she's equally adept at facing off against a suspected abusive parent. Buffy, as Willow notes, is the kind of friend that we all wish we'd had when we were going through the emotional horrors of school. But she learns a valuable lesson before this episode is over, and the audience learn it with her. That, sometimes, all the good intentions in the world are, simply, not enough – even if you've got your own website.

This is the third occasion that Buffy has used the term 'Buffy the Vampire Slayer' (see **12**, 'Prophecy Girl' and **35**, 'Anne'). When Buffy tells Principal Wood that she doesn't usually get a heads up before someone dies, she adds 'not since . . .' then pauses: this is a possible allusion to **12**, 'Prophecy Girl'; **52**, 'Earshot' or **96**, 'Intervention'. Willow once wrote love poems about Xander and posted them online. (Even more embarrassingly, she also wrote fan-fiction based on the 1990s TV series *Dougie Howser MD*.) Dawn was in the same ceramics class as Cassie. Tara's gravestone reads: TARA MACLAY (16 OCTOBER 1980–7 MAY 2002). The cemetery where Tara is buried is close to a lake (quite possibly the same one that she and Willow visited in **107**, 'Once More, With Feeling'). Principal Wood grew up in Beverly Hills (however, see **139**, 'Lies My Parents Told Me') and was once suspended from high school when he attacked someone who bullied him. Mr Miller (see **31**, 'I Only Have Eyes For You') is mentioned. The other occasion in which the series has portrayed students engaged in demonic worship on campus was in **17**, 'Reptile Boy'. It's worth noting that both episodes feature a demon offering power and wealth in exchange for young girls being sacrificed to it. Willow placing the stones on Tara's grave is a common Jewish practice. The stones are used to honour the deceased and to show that the grave has been visited.

That Website Story in Full: While trying to help Cassie, Buffy and Willow stumble across her website, *www.cassienewton.com*. Some viewers who saw Buffy typing in this address rushed to their computers and gave it a try. They were rewarded, if that's the right word, by accessing the same site, full of Cassie's miserablist death-obsessed poems and artwork supplied by author Rebecca Rand Kirshner. 'One of the most frightening things,' Kirshner told *zap2it.com*, 'is tapping back into my high-school journals [and] all those apoplectic teenage memories. I didn't crib any of my own poetry, but I did crib my own mentality.' Joss Whedon had suggested making the site real during the creation of 'Help'. Chris Buchanan, Mutant Enemy's president, helped to design the domain. 'We had 70,000 hits in two days,' he noted. 'We set it up on Geocities, a free server, but we had so many hits that I'm now having to pay.' 'I'd like to leave it up to see what the next mutation is,' Kirshner added.

Critique: 'I've always been supportive when *Buffy*'s creators take risks, but I'm not convinced that an action show can sustain this level of ambiguity,' wrote Rachel Lovinger. 'Isn't *Buffy* all about demonizing life's problems so we can watch the heroine slay them?'

Did You Know?: 'The audience can relate to what *Buffy* wears because she's one of them. She's not sixteen any more, but she is living the life of a young person,' costume designer Terry Dresbach told Maxine Shen. 'We shop at the stores everyone else does – every mall in America has a Rampage in it. What you see on *Buffy*, you can go out and buy.'

Cast and Crew Comments: 'I think Joss created a character that felt unique in Buffy,' Emma Caulfield told Jennifer Dudley. 'Before Buffy, you had superheroes like Wonder Woman. That wasn't relatable. Buffy's still a girl, with a lot of weaknesses and emotions.'

In an interview with *Abercrombie and Fitch*'s website, Emma was asked if she had ever encountered any dangerously obsessed *Buffy* fans. Emma replied that, at a convention in London, she was approached in the hotel bar by a woman who offered to buy her a drink. Politely, Emma declined, noting that she was just about to leave, only to be told by the outraged fan, 'These conventions might be your only source of income one day.'

'People have this idea I'm some crazy right-wing fascist,' Emma confessed to *Premiere*. 'I'm *so* not. It stems from the fact that I said I'd help Elizabeth Dole [get elected]. But I would never admit to being a Republican in this town. I want to work.'

Joss Whedon's Comments: 'I suspect this may be *Buffy*'s last season,' Joss told *TV Guide Online*. 'Nothing's official, but it's starting to feel possible. The way people are talking, there's a finality to it.' Compared to the previous year, *Buffy*'s ratings had dropped an alarming 16%. In fact, during this particular week more viewers watched *Angel* than *Buffy*. 'It had a really good seven-year run and it's time to call it quits,' noted *Mediaweek* columnist Marc Berman. 'Leave with some dignity.' For his part, Joss insisted that his gut instinct is not numbers-driven. 'I never check Buffy's ratings,' he noted. 'It doesn't affect me.'

127
Selfless

US Transmission Date: 22 Oct 2002
UK Transmission Date: 13 Feb 2003

Writer: Drew Goddard
Director: David Solomon
Cast: Joyce Guy (Professor), Jennifer Shon (Rachel),
Taylor Sutherland (Villager #1), Marybeth Scherr (Villager #2),
Alessandro Mastrobuono (Villager #3), Daniel Spanton (Viking #1),
John Timmons (Viking #2), David Fury (Mustard Guy),[49]
Marti Noxon (Parking Ticket Lady)[50]

Anya grants a wish to a scorned college girl, which has devastating consequences. Horrified by the carnage that she has, inadvertently, caused, a shocked Anya suffers from a severe dose of the flashbacks. Meanwhile, Buffy is faced with an awful decision.

'Funny Historical Sidebar': 'Selfless' details Anya's transformation from a Nordic housewife in the dark ages into the powerful vengeance-demon that we knew pre-**50**, 'Doppelgängland'. As a human, Anya (then called Aud), was a rabbit-loving girl from

---

[49] Uncredited.
[50] Uncredited.

Sjornjost in rural Sweden in the late 9th century. Unlike her capitalist leanings of 1,100 years later, Aud preferred exchanging things for goodwill and the sense of accomplishment that stemmed from selflessly giving to others. Her husband, Olaf (see **89**, 'Triangle'), believed that Aud's logic was happenstance, like that of a troll. It was, he noted, little wonder that the local bar matrons made jokes about her. Aud always spoke her mind, asked irksome questions and confused people with her literal interpretations. So, some things *never* change, it seems. When Olaf cheated on her, Aud used a Woodlow Transmogrific Spell, Thornton's Hope, on him. One ingredient, Eelsbane, turned him into a troll. This brought her to the attention of D'Hoffryn, the Lord of Arashmaharr, 'he that turns the air to blood', the patron of Vengeance-Demons, who rechristened her Anyanka.

Subsequently, Anya and her friend Halfrek caused chaos throughout the centuries – witness the sequence set in St Petersburg at the time of the 1905 October Revolution. (Halfrek indicates that Anya, herself, was more than a little responsible for these events. The workers will, inevitably, overthrow absolutism and lead the proletariat to a victorious Communist revolution, resulting in socio-economic paradise on Earth, noted Anya, absent-mindedly.)

A Little Learning is a Dangerous Thing: Willow is about to return to UC Sunnydale. Her psychology professor noticed a drop in Willow's grades at midterms last year and was somewhat concerned. But then, happily, Willow aced all of her final exams. Just like magic.

It's a Designer Label!: Highlights include Dawn's tight red top, Buffy's leather jacket and Willow's grey miniskirt and lurid red tights.

References: Buffy alludes to *Judge Dredd*, telling Xander, 'I *am* the law' (Faith expressed similar sentiments in **49**, 'Consequences'). D'Hoffryn observes the carnage that Anya caused and notes that it's like someone slaughtered an Abercrombie and Fitch catalogue. Also, an allusion to Elvis Costello's 'Alison'. There's a statuette of Marilyn Monroe (1926–62) in the Frathouse. The Swedish sequences seem to be influenced by the films of Ingmar Bergman. When Aud speaks, she sounds uncannily like the Swedish Chef from *The Muppet Show*.

What A Shame They Dropped . . .: A scripted sequence in which Halfrek tells Anya that she once gave a chimney sweep's parents tuberculosis.

Bitch!: Dawn gives Willow some sage advice concerning fitting in with a peer group (which, apparently, consists of nodding and smiling a lot).

Awesome!: Spike confessing his innermost thoughts to Buffy. And the disappointment that the audience collectively feels when it's revealed that Spike has, actually, been talking to the shapechanging evil entity. Also, the touching final scenes between a heartbroken Anya and a supportive Xander.

Surprise!: When Anya tells D'Hoffryn that she wants to undo the chaos she has caused, D'Hoffryn notes this is difficult, but not impossible. Anya is a big girl, he adds, she knows the rules. The proverbial scales must balance. In order to restore the lives of the (dozen or so) victims, a sacrifice is required: the life, and soul, of a vengeance-demon. Anya realises this and is prepared to give up her life. Instead, D'Hoffryn summons Halfrek and destroys her instead. Did Anya think it would be *that* easy, D'Hoffryn says, asking if Anya has learned nothing from her millennia working for him. 'Never go for the kill when you can go for the pain' (see **128**, 'Him').

'You May Remember Me From Such Films and TV Series As . . .': Joyce Guy's CV includes *Sunset Beach*, *Chicago Hope*, *Shocker* and *Felicity*. Taylor Sutherland's movies include *Gangland*. Alessandro Mastrobunono appeared in *The Gin Game*. John Timmons was in *Hard As Nails* and *The Pandora Directive*.

Valley-Speak: Xander: 'Did everybody have their crazy-flakes today?'

Cigarettes and Alcohol: Olaf indulges in much mead-quaffing.

Sex and Drugs and Rock'n'Roll: Anya lies to Willow that she has a new student boyfriend. They enjoy having, Anya continues, lots and lots of sex.

Logic, Let Me Introduce You to This Window: In **89**, 'Triangle', Olaf constantly referred to Anya as Anyanka. Here, however, we discover that when she was his wife (not his girlfriend, as stated in 'Triangle') she was called Aud. She was still going by that name when she turned Olaf into a troll. Of course, there's nothing to suggest that they didn't meet again subsequently and that he learned her demon name then. Why do Aud and D'Hoffryn converse in Sweden in 880 in English? With American accents? Willow, seemingly, kept the talisman that D'Hoffryn gave her in **65**, 'Something Blue'. Why? One of the flashbacks takes place the night before **107**, 'Once More, With Feeling'. But Anya's hairstyle is totally different to that episode. 'Bar' wasn't a term typically used for a 9th-century drinking venue. Tavern would have been more appropriate. During Anya's song, she sits on Xander's chair and there is a revolving shot from above. A circle on the floor can be seen, presumably marking the point at which the contraption that's spinning the chair begins. Anya's song alleges that she is 'good with math'. She must, therefore, have improved since **50**, 'Doppelgängland', when she was flunking the subject at Sunnydale High. Spike's hair is more bleached in this episode than the last. Yet he seems not to have left the basement in the meantime. The bleeding on Anya's lip disappears and reappears between shots.

I Just *Love* Your Accent: Spike uses the term 'sack of hammers' to describe Drusilla's mental instability. It sounds like a plausible cockney expression; however, neither *Cassell's Rhyming Slang* or *The Oxford Dictionary of Slang* feature the phrase.

Quote/Unquote: Olaf tries to persuade Aud that he has no interest in Rannveig: 'Her hips are large and load bearing. Like a Baltic woman . . . Your hips are small. Like a Baltic woman from a slightly more arid region.'

Viking 1: 'The troll is doing an Olaf impersonation.' Viking 2: 'Hit him with fruits and various meats.'

Anya: 'Vengeance?' D'Hoffryn: 'Only to those that deserve it.' Anya: 'They *all* deserve it.' D'Hoffryn: 'That's where I was going with that, yeah.'

Xander, to Buffy: 'This isn't new ground for us. When our friends go crazy and start killing people, we help them.' Willow: 'Sitting right here . . .!'

D'Hoffryn: 'Isn't that just like a Slayer? Solving all her problems by sticking things with sharp objects?'

Notes: 'Vengeance is what I am.' The funniest, most touching and intelligent *Buffy* episode since **107**, 'Once More, With Feeling' (to which it is an, indirect, sequel), 'Selfless' is Anya's *Year One* story in much the same way that **85**, 'Fool for Love', detailed Spike's tragic origins. Interestingly, the numerous flashback sequences are all, in one way or another, quasi-comic variations on the dark and serious situations that are emerging in contemporary Sunnydale. The comedy, the pathos and the horror all work *with* each other; the pacing is brilliant and there are charming scenes for most of the regulars. Nick Brendon, in particular, proves once again just how vital Xander is to a good *Buffy* episode. Xander's unreciprocated, unrequited love for Anya is still strong enough for him to defy a determined Slayer. Then there's Emma Caulfield: beautiful, funny and dangerous in equal measure. 'Selfless' is, simply, *Buffy* at its very best.

Buffy finally discovers that Xander lied to her in **34**, 'Becoming' Part 2, when Xander gave Buffy what he alleged was Willow's message to kick Angelus's ass. As Willow loudly protests here, she never said any such thing. Anya repeats her full 'lame-ass' name (Anya Christina Emmanuella Jenkins), previously mentioned in **90**, 'Checkpoint'. A fantastic bit of continuity: note that, while the sleeping Xander is muttering about wanting a happy ending, he's holding the amulet that, presumably at this exact moment, summons Sweet for the musical episode. Spike says that Drusilla used to see things. She was always staring into the sky, watching cherubs burn or the heavens bleed. The spider creature that Anya summoned to rip out the hearts of the cruel students was a Grimslaw Demon. D'Hoffryn was impressed with Willow's flaying of Warren (see **120**, 'Villains') calling it water-cooler vengeance.

Soundtrack: Joss Whedon's 'Mrs' sung, beautifully, by Emma Caulfield (note that the lyrics allude to 'I'll Never Tell', the song that Anya and Xander performed in **107**, 'Once More, With Feeling'). Listen out, too, for a half-heard operatic prequel to '(They Got) The Mustard (Out)' sung by David Fury and Marti Noxon. Also, Haydn's 'String Quartet No. 2 in F Major'.

Critique: 'Selfless' is a reminder of the powerful recipe of hilarious dialogue, cringe-inducing monsters and gut-wrenching human drama that first turned a valley-girl joke of a movie into an acclaimed TV series, noted *Entertainment Weekly*'s Rachel Lovinger. 'With an eye-poppingly entertaining back-story and all the pathos that can be wrung from the collision of love, betrayal, and responsibility, it's near-perfect.'

The episode, as Mark Wyman wrote in *TV Zone*, has a list of ingredients that almost defies critical reflection. Calling 'Selfless' an extraordinary episode, Wyman continued, 'it's a truism that first-time writers are prone to throwing in too many unwieldy motifs. But the prickly results here are finessed into a powerful, at times breathtaking, whole.'

Did You Know?: The boxing skills that 25-year-old Renee Farster learned in the military came in handy during rehearsals for the Boston theatre group Queer Soup's production *Buffy the Vampire Slayer's High School Reunion*. The company chose an adaptation of *Buffy* as their first production for a variety of reasons, not the least of which was because most members were fans. But they also believed that *Buffy* addressed real issues. Among other things, the show had portrayed gay relationships with honesty and integrity, Farster noted. Lesbian characters like Willow and Tara are open about their relationship – and avoid gay stereotypes often seen on network television.

Cast and Crew Comments: 'Joss realizes that *Buffy* is bigger than one person,' Emma Caulfield told *Fangoria* magazine. 'There's a talented group of performers that can continue carrying the show if anyone leaves.' However, that would not include Emma herself, who announced that her contract was up at the end of the season and that she felt it was time to go. 'I want to do other things with my career. How'd you like to do the same thing every day for five years?'

Joss Whedon's Comments: How important was the medium of the Internet in spreading the word about *Buffy*, Whedon was asked during an online AOL question and answer session: 'I think it's been essential,' he noted. 'The way *Buffy* and the Internet have interacted has been unprecedented. I knew I had fans before I got a chance to see and understand what ratings were. The community that started out at the beginning has grown and grown. It's a mob scene now!'

128
Him

US Transmission Date: 5 Nov 2002
UK Transmission Date: 20 Feb 2003

Writer: Drew Z Greenberg
Director: Michael Gershman
Cast: Thad Luckinbill (RJ Brooks), Brandon Keener (Lance Brooks),
Yan England (O'Donnell), Angela Sarafyan (Lori), David Ghilardi (Teacher),
Riki Lindhome (Cheryl)

Dawn's crush on her school's star quarterback, RJ Brooks, surprises Buffy until she also falls head over heels for the boy's charms. And she isn't the only one. With their female friends all desperately trying to win RJ's affections, Spike and Xander team up to discover why the teen has such an infatuating effect on women.

No Fat Chicks: Cheryl, the girl with a broken leg, must be the world's largest ever cheerleader. Also, when Dawn runs, crying, out of the school, a portly girl wearing a tight grey T-shirt can be seen walking behind her.

Dudes and Babes: We've already been introduced to Dawn's potential Willow and Xander (see **123**, 'Lessons'). Here, we meet her Cordelia – the bitchy, full-of-herself cheerleader Lori.

Xander greatly admires the hot slutty-girl hussy who is provocatively dancing with RJ at the Bronze. Then he discovers that it's Dawn and becomes extremely agitated because (a) he's baby-sat her more often than he cares to remember and (b) Buffy is standing next to him. Even more alarming is that Willow, seemingly, was also turned on by Dawn.

Buffy notes that Anya is probably seducing RJ while the rest of the gang search for Dawn. Anya, she notes, was recently evil so she certainly wouldn't put seduction past her. Willow adds that she, too, was recently evil and grumbles about why she should miss out on all the fun.

Authority Sucks!: Having just experienced a hard time with Principal Wood, RJ is somewhat distressed when Buffy also interrogates him. Once he slips his jacket on, however, her stern, school-ma'am attitude changes to something closer to a rampant sex-bunny.

A Little Learning is a Dangerous Thing: RJ's brother, Lance, was a football jock a couple years older than Xander and Buffy. He used to stick chewing gum in Xander's hair. Since graduating (and giving his letterman jacket to RJ), Lance has put on weight and now works as a pizza deliveryman. Lance notes that, before he gave RJ his jacket, RJ was something of a geek who was into comic books and poetry. Lance adds that *he* got the jacket from his father who met their mother (a former Miss Arkansas) while wearing it. Nobody knows where Mr Brooks senior got it from.

Dawn tries hard to understand the complications of the Scooby Gang's relationships. Discussing Spike's recent acquisition of a soul with Buffy, she notes that Xander also had a soul when he left Anya at the altar (**116**, 'Hell's Bells').

'West Hollywood': Spike is, once again, sharing Xander's apartment (see **66**, 'Hush'). He is going to live in a small room that *looks* like a closet, but, actually, isn't.

Denial, Thy Names Are Buffy, Dawn, Anya and (Particularly) Willow: In the episode's best scene, the four girls – all radically affected by RJ's love-spell – argue over which of them loves him the most. Willow makes the persuasive argument that since she's prepared to look past that whole orientation thing she, clearly, loves him more than the others. Anya suggests that she would kill for RJ, which promptly gives Buffy the idea of murdering Principal Wood. Anya notes this is hard to top, but Willow is still determined and considers using magic. Anya asks if Willow intends to turn RJ into a girl, and then regrets giving her *that* notion. Dawn, meanwhile, realising that she has no chance against such strong opposition, decides to commit suicide, arguing that RJ will know someone loved him so much she was prepared to die for him. Once the effects of the spell have worn off, Dawn is mortified that she was so stupid over a guy, despite Buffy telling her that it wasn't her fault. Get ready to feel even stupider when there's no magic involved, Buffy notes, sadly.

The Conspiracy Starts at Home Time: Xander and Spike's cunning plan to stop RJ's love-spell is to mug him in the street, steal his jacket and then burn it. Which they do quite successfully. Excellent plan, gentlemen. (Before destroying the jacket, Xander, apparently, tried it on. But it didn't fit.)

It's a Designer Label!: Loads of good stuff: Spike's tasteful black shirt and whup-ass boots; Buffy's pink jacket, vampy sunglasses and short pleated Catholic schoolgirl-style skirt; Dawn's multi-coloured top and the incredibly tight jeans and shirt that she wears to the Bronze. Also, Anya's black waistcoat and white T-shirt.

References: Visual homages to *The Graduate*, *Mission: Impossible*, *24*, *The Brady Bunch* and, possibly, *Friends*. Dawn alludes to the *Monty Python's Flying Circus* Spanish Inquisition sketch. Wood makes an oblique reference to Allen Ginsberg's 'Howl'. Also, the LA Lakers' cheerleaders the Laker Girls, Mr Wizard, the Animals' 'It's My Life', *The Sweet Smell of Success*, Chaka Khan's 'I Feel For You' and *Apocalypse Now*. Posters for Amnesty International and the band Say ZuZu are seen. Buffy drinks a can of Mountain Dew.

Bitch!: Lori and Dawn fight in the alley, causing Buffy to berate her sister: 'First with the lap-dance, now with the cat fight. Wanna get drunk and barf next?'

Awesome!: Dawn falling over. Twice (always a comedy highlight, see also **125**, 'Same Time, Same Place'). Xander discovering Buffy and RJ, ahem, doing it. Anya's cunning plan to win RJ (rob a bank!). Buffy's silent attempts to kill Principal Wood, thwarted by Spike.

'You May Remember Me From Such Films and TV Series As . . .': Thad Luckinbill's CV includes *The Young and the Restless*, *Boys to Men*, *Undressed* and *8 Simple Rules . . . for Dating My Teenage Daughter*. David Ghilardi's movies include *Spaceman*. Yan England was in *I Witness* and *Haute Surveillance*. Brandon Keener appeared in *Full Frontal*, *Traffic* and *The Limey*.

Don't Give Up The Day Job: Editor Joshua Charson's movies include *Between the Lions* and *Four Corners*. Assistant Director Christine Tope also worked on *Dude, Where's My Car? Ugly Naked People* and *She's All That*. Set Decorator Susan Eschelbach's CV includes *The House on Carroll Street*, *The Nanny* and *Tucker*. Studio Teacher Cheryl Diamond also worked on the sets of *Go Fish* and *Grounded For Life*.

Valley-Speak: Xander: 'Don't teens in a snit like pizza?'

Cigarettes and Alcohol: Xander, Spike and Lance share a beer.

Sex and Drugs and Rock'n'Roll: 'Him' includes more references to sex than just about any other *Buffy* episode. Buffy notes that she's just like RJ, only with *much* more sexual experience.

Logic, Let Me Introduce You to This Window: Buffy intends to use the rocket launcher which Xander acquired for her to destroy the Judge (**26**, 'Innocence'). Where the hell's *that* been for the last four years and why didn't she use it during any of her other life-or-death battles during this period? Spike's reflection is visible both in a picture frame and a store window. How did Spike get to Xander's apartment on a sunny afternoon without being destroyed? When Dawn talks to Principal Wood, her book-bag is on her chair and she leaves without it. However, subsequently, she walks down the hall with it over her shoulder. Buffy tells Dawn that no guy is worth dying for. Except, seemingly, Angel (see **55**, 'Graduation Day' Part 1). And, possibly, Riley (see **77**, 'Primeval'). The sequence in which Buffy saves Dawn from suicide goes on far too long and is logically flawed in several aspects (notably the positions of the relative trains and the tracks that they're on). Why is a Top 40 band like the Breeders playing a small town venue like the Bronze?

I Just *Love* Your Accent: Xander asks if Spike requires some kind of English-to-constant-pain-in-the-ass translation. Spike uses the common English words 'bollocks' and 'mollycoddling'.

Quote/Unquote: Buffy, to Dawn: 'You have plans for later, or you just gonna go down to the docks and wait for the fleet to come in . . .? Anna Nicole Smith thinks you look tacky!'

Buffy, on Willow's sudden infatuation with RJ: 'You're a gay woman. And he *isn't*!' Willow: 'This isn't about his physical presence . . .' Anya: 'But his physical presence has a penis.'

Xander: 'RJ's a guy.' Willow: 'That's why I'm doing my spell. Cos, you know, he doesn't *have* to be.'

Dawn, to Buffy: 'You're older and hotter. You have sex that's rough, and kill people.'

Anya: 'It was a spell. We aren't responsible for anything we did. Morally, or, you know, legally.'

Notes: 'Maybe I don't want advice from the dysfunction queen. You have no idea what real love is.' Dawn, amusingly, turns into a doe-eyed teenager in love. And so do Buffy, Willow and Anya. OK, that had potential even for a professional misanthrope. Drew Greenberg was the emergent star of the, by general consensus, comedy-free-zone of *Buffy*'s sixth season. Though it has a few stomach-churningly embarrassing moments of Dawn, smitten by her first crush, and takes a while to tell its story, 'Him' wears its source material like a badge of authenticity. It also provides a further example of *Buffy* going for the funny bone instead of the throat. What appears, on paper, to be a basic remake of **28**, 'Bewitched, Bothered and Bewildered', is given a successful push in an alternative direction by some unusual character pairings. And a couple of set-pieces that transcend what could have been very obvious execution to become true gems. One, in particular, involving Spike, Buffy and Principal Wood is as good a visual joke as *Buffy* has ever attempted. Not the most original *Buffy* episode, then, that's probably fair to say. But originality can sometimes lead one into troubled waters of obscurity and naval gazing. You know what they always say: if it ain't broke, don't fix it.

'Him' includes both dialogue allusions to, and a flashback from, **28**, 'Bewitched, Bothered and Bewildered', during which Xander also discovered the hilarious (and dangerous) consequences of a love-spell gone wrong. During that episode Xander seemed to regard the experience as something he never wished to repeat. Yet here, when reminded of it, he smiles and says 'good times'. Selective memory, seemingly. He also alludes to his dysfunctional, argumentative family (see **44**, 'Amends'; **116**, 'Hells' Bells'). Xander's apartment is No. 22. Anya's is No. 24 (though, presumably, not in the same building). D'Hoffryn has, after all, sent a demon to kill Anya following the events of **127**, 'Selfless' (which is said to have taken place a week ago). Fortunately, Buffy saves Anya's life. Dawn uses Buffy's cheerleader uniform last seen in **3**, 'The Witch'. Buffy mentions Principal Snyder. Dawn's English teacher is called Mr Gurin. Coach Wheeler is in charge of the football team.

Soundtrack: Kim and Kelley Deal were contacted after Joss Whedon heard their version of *The Buffy Theme*, which had become a mainstay of the Breeders live set. The popular band perform 'Little Fury' and 'Son Of Three' in the Bronze. 'We flew straight from Mexico City. From LAX, we went straight to the set. We hadn't slept at all, but we were so thrilled we didn't care,' Kelley Deal told Angelique Campbell. The band spent the day performing and sleeping between takes. But they did get the chance to check out the *Buffy* set. 'We saw the Bronze of course, the school and Buffy's office, ' added Deal.

The episode makes extensive use of Max Steiner's classic 'Theme from *A Summer Place*' (previously mentioned in **18**, 'Halloween'), plus 'Warning Sign' by Coldplay, 'New Slang' by the Shins, 'Handsome Drink' by Aberdeen, Silvera Tamara's 'Let You Know' and 'School Blood' by King Black Acid.

Critique: 'I loathe defending *Buffy* to other fans,' wrote author Justine Larbalestier. 'I feel like I'm defending a close relative. While defending the show I will say anything, no matter how illogical. I frequently contradict myself. I don't care.'

Did You Know?: Sarah Michelle Gellar light-heartedly revealed to *Teen Hollywood* that, 'I want to see more women action stars. I don't see why James Bond has to be a man all the time. When Pierce Brosnan retires I'm going to be the next Bond.'

Cast and Crew Comments: '*Buffy*'s certainly presented many challenges to myself. That's why I've been happy to be around as long as I have,' Michelle Trachtenberg told the *Queensland Courier-Mail*.

The End . . .?: Addressing reports that this was to be the final season of *Buffy*, Sarah Michelle Gellar told *Access Hollywood* that this was not necessarily so. 'I read that this morning in the paper,' Gellar noted. 'There have been absolutely no decisions.' Two days later, on 1 November, *SciFi Wire* quoted Joss Whedon as saying that, 'The chances for an eighth season are good. Whether or not they will include Sarah, I don't know, but I suspect there may be some kind of incarnation of the show, even if she decides to pull out.'

Joss Whedon's Comments: 'I love whatever show I'm working on,' Joss told the *Houston Chronicle*. '*Buffy* was my first child and made an inroad into popular culture that I'll probably never equal.' However, he added that *Angel* has 'lots of my best friends on it, is the most fun for me to shoot. And *Firefly* is the most adult work I've ever done and has an unbelievable cast and incredible crew.'

129
Conversations With Dead People

US Transmission Date: 12 Nov 2002
UK Transmission Date: 27 Feb 2003

Writers: Jane Espenson, Drew Goddard, Marti Nixon (uncredited),
Joss Whedon (uncredited)[51]
Director: Nick Marck
Cast: Jonathan M Woodward (Holden Webster)

While patrolling, Buffy meets a former classmate, Holden, who is now a vampire. Holden gets Buffy to reveal her insecurities.

---

[51] Interviewed by the online Succubus Club, Drew Goddard noted that Marti Noxon had written the Willow/Cassie scenes, Joss Whedon had contributed the bulk of the Buffy/Holden story, Goddard himself wrote the Andrew/Jonathan/Warren sequences and Jane Espenson was responsible for the Dawn/Joyce scenes.

Meanwhile, Dawn faces a night of horror as an invisible force trashes the Summers home and the ghost of Cassie Newton visits Willow, saying that she has been sent by Tara.

Dudes and Babes: Holden Webster went to school with Buffy (they had a European History class together). After school, he went to college in Dartmouth (where he got heavily into tai kwon do) and majored in Psychology. He has taken a year off to do an internship at the Sunnydale Mental Hospital.

Cassie tells Willow that Tara says she must be strong, like an amazon (see **94**, 'The Body').

A Little Learning is a Dangerous Thing: Andrew and Jonathan have been living in Mexico since escaping from Sunnydale (**122**, 'Grave'). When Jonathan begins to talk fondly about Sunnydale High, Andrew is incredulous, noting that he has spent the last few years trying to forget about his painful high school experiences. Time changes perception, Jonathan notes. Eventually, all the cruelty, pain and humiliation washes away. Jonathan says that he misses the people he went to school with – his friends, his enemies, even the people who never even knew that he existed. All of those, however, don't share Jonathan's feelings about Jonathan himself, Andrew suggests.

Mom's Apple Pie: As both Buffy and Willow are out, Buffy leaves Dawn 20 dollars to buy some food. But not pizza – which, inevitably, Dawn *does* order.

Joyce appears to Dawn and tells her that bad things are coming. And that when the time comes, Buffy will not be there for Dawn (see **143**, 'End of Days').

Denial, Thy Name is Buffy: Holden may be an evil bloodsucking fiend, but a lot of the points that he makes about Buffy's inability to connect with people and her various complexes (superiority in relation to her slaying, inferiority relating to pretty much everything else) are both perceptive and accurate. However, at least Buffy is beginning to come out of her denial phase with regard to her relationship with Spike towards whom, she notes, she acted like a monster. Buffy says that she's afraid of falling back into the way that she was last year. She believed that she was nothing, having so much power that she didn't ask for or, for that matter, deserve. During the period when she was secretly having sex with Spike, she reveals, she was guilty over this and felt that she deserved to be punished (see **113**, 'Dead Things'). Spike really loved her, she adds, in his own sick and soulless way. But she didn't want to be loved (or, at least, wasn't capable, at that time, of reciprocating). When she says that she has to fight the coming evil, Holden asks if she must do so alone. I have friends, Buffy notes; they fight with her. Sometimes they fight in spite of her, but they continue to fight because they're decent people. Buffy, on the other hand, fights purely because she was *chosen* to do so (see **144**, 'Chosen').

The Conspiracy Starts at Home Time: The shapechanging evil entity appears to Andrew as Warren and forces Andrew to stab and kill Jonathan over the mysterious Seal of Danzalthar on the Hellmouth. There's a first reference to the *troika* becoming gods (see **138**, 'Storyteller') once Warren's masterplan comes to fruition.

The shapechanging evil impersonating Cassie tells Willow that the last year is going to seem like nothing after what the entity has in mind for Willow and her friends. The entity is not, it adds, a fan of easy death. However, the entity is done with the whole good and evil balancing the scales thing and has a big finish planned for humanity.

It's a Designer Label!: Willow's sleeveless black top.

References: In a possible homage to *The X-Files*, the episode begins with a caption giving the date and time (12 November 2002, 8.01 p.m.). Dawn rings Kit (see **123**, 'Lessons') to discuss a horror movie that she's watching. There are visual references to *The Shining* (the blood-writing on the wall), *The Craft* and *The Exorcist*. Also, Tom Hanks, Czech Premiere Vaclav Havel, *True Confessions*, the musical *Pippen*, *The Evil Dead*, an allusion to *Julius Caesar*, MTV's *Celebrity Deathmatch*, French Empress Joséphine Bonaparte (1763–1814), the character of Pinhead from the *Hellraiser* movies, *Raiders of the Lost Ark* and *The Lord of the Rings*.

Geek-Speak: When Andrew complains that he couldn't understand Spanish (or Mexicoan, as he calls it), Jonathan notes that Andrew once learned the entire *Klingon Dictionary* in two and a half weeks. That was different, Andrew adds. It had much clearer transitive and intransitive rules. Andrew alludes to the *Back To The Future* movies ('think McFly!') and *Star Wars*. Warren called Jonathan Short Round (from *Indiana Jones and the Temple of Doom*).

Bitch!: Buffy angrily tells Holden she hates the way that, to vampires, sex, death, pain and love all equate to the same thing.

'West Hollywood': Holden tells Buffy that he was sired by Spike.

Awesome!: Dawn's poptastic 'anchovies' poem. Buffy's description of her conversation with Holden as 'insane troll logic' (see also **89**, 'Triangle'; **127**, 'Selfless'). Andrew falling from the roof. Dawn attempting to cast out the entity that is, she believes, torturing her mother's spirit.

'You May Remember Me From Such Films and TV Series As . . .': Jonathan Woodward appeared in *Pipe Dream* and *Still Life*. Subsequently, he was cast as Knox in *Angel*. Stacey Scowley's CV includes *Hell Asylum* and *Alias*.

The Drugs Don't Work: Jason Wheeler, an extrovert contemporary of Holden and Buffy, has been in a mental institution since graduation (see **56**, 'Graduation Day' Part 2).
   According to Willow, Giles believes that her quitting the use of magic, cold turkey, could be even more dangerous than her occasionally using it.

Valley-Speak: Jonathan: 'Dude, I'm right here.'

Cigarettes and Alcohol: Spike sits alone in the Bronze drinking Jack Daniels. A girl enters and places her cigarettes next to him on the bar as a 'come and get it, big boy'-style introduction. He subsequently accompanies her home and kills her.

Sex and Drugs and Lexicography: When Holden refers to nemeses Buffy asks if *that's* how the word is pronounced. (See **111**, 'Gone', and Warren's assertion that he, Andrew and Jonathan were Buffy's 'arch-nemsis-es.')

Logic, Let Me Introduce You to This Window: Cassie refers to **107**, 'Once More, With Feeling', saying that Tara and Willow sang to each other at the bridge. However, it was Tara who sang to Willow. In some of the graveyard scenes someone can be seen moving in the background behind Holden. When Jonathan and Andrew are using their walkie-talkies, a flashlight shines on Jonathan's face. But Andrew isn't pointing his torch toward Jonathan. When Dawn unplugs the television set, she's holding the plug in a different position between frontal close-ups and rear shots. Since when did Sunnydale have its own mental hospital? During season five, all of those affected by Glory's brainsucking were housed in the regular hospital (the same one Joyce attended for her operation). Is Holden the First or a genuine victim of Spike? This is never clarified, although the fact that he's corporeal suggests the latter. However, if the First cannot touch anything, how does Cassie sit on a chair and lean on the table while talking to Willow?

Quote/Unquote: Andrew's translation of 'From beneath you, it devours': 'It eats you. Starting with your bottom.'

Andrew: 'We alert the Slayer, we help her destroy it, we save Sunnydale. Then we join her gang. And, possibly, hang out at her house.'

Holden: 'Oh my god. Well, not *my* god, 'cause I defy Him and all his works. Does He exist, by the way? Is there word on that?' Buffy: 'Nothing solid.'

Cassie, to Willow: 'I can see it now, candlelight, the Indigo Girls playing. A picture of your dead girlfriend on your bloody lap.'

Notes: 'Everyone's got issues.' One of the most interestingly structured episodes of a TV show in years, 'Conversations With Dead People' sees *Buffy* wandering into areas of psychology, pain and rejection. This is deep, complex and challenging territory. Dawn's miserable existence since she became a human is given a literal, bewilderingly supernatural context that tugs at the heart-strings; Willow's inner moppet gets a trousers-down whupping and Buffy has to endure a chilling taste of her own pop-psych medicine from an unlikely source. If 'Conversations', conceptually, has a soulmate within this series' past then it may be **94**, 'The Body', the only other *Buffy* set-piece to approach some of the more self-analytical corners of the often too-bright Sunnydale Hellmouth experience. In 45 minutes we get at least four of the biggest '*did you see that?*' moments in *Buffy*'s history. Sadly, this is only part of the story and there are key elements that misdirect 'Conversation With Dead People' from where it should have taken the audience. There are holes in the plot where the rain leaked in, particularly during the scenes involving Willow and Cassie – whose second appearance this season is equally as compelling as her first, if also as frustratingly incomplete. Spike's story, too, has visual impact but little in the way of conceptual depth, although in this particular case, there's a more ready explanation for people missing the point. It's also difficult to detect any of Espenson or Goddard's traditional strengths in a story about loss, deceit and betrayal. Hard subjects, but not entirely unrewarding ones.

'Conversations With Dead People' tries hard and for that, if nothing else, we should be grateful.

In school, Buffy was considered very mysterious by most of the boys. There were rumours that she was dating a really old guy (which, of course, she was). Holden tells Buffy that her ex-boyfriend Scott Hope (see **37**, 'Faith, Hope and Trick'; **38**, 'Beauty and the Beasts'; **39**, 'Homecoming') came out of the closet last year. (This is a possible oblique reference to Fab Filippo, the actor who played Scott, now appearing as a gay character in Showtime's *Queer as Folk*.) When asked whose fault her parents divorce was (see **33**, 'Becoming' Part 1), Buffy notes that it was her father's, who cheated on Joyce. There are dialogue allusions during the Dawn/Joyce sequences to **94**, 'The Body', and also both visual and musical references to **87**, 'Listening to Fear'. Andrew suffers from shin splints. Jonathan remembers that his high school locker combination was 36-19-27. Both Andrew and Jonathan have been suffering from prophetic dreams concerning the coming apocalypse (see **138**, 'Storyteller').

Soundtrack: Angie Heart, of series favourites Splendid, sings the episode's key song, 'Blue' (co-written by Heart and Joss Whedon). Also, 'Never Never Is Forever' by Scout and 'Nicolito' by Los Cubaztecas.

Critique: 'This startling episode shifts seamlessly from horror to humor while shifting the season's main story-arc into gear,' noted Robert Bianco. 'Fans will love it, but so will anyone who loves good writing and inventive storytelling.' Though *Buffy* has always been versatile, continued Bianco, its ability to find new dramatic forms to express its fantasy metaphor is still remarkable, as is its ability to surprise. 'No series is better at providing a last-second shock.'

Missing in Action: One hardly needs to be a genius to realise that Cassie Newton's part in this episode was originally written with Tara in mind. However, as the episode went into production, Joss Whedon announced that Mutant Enemy had been unable to reach an agreement with Amber Benson. The actress was interviewed around this time on the *E! Online* website, and stated that she felt 'protective' towards the character of Tara. Some fans immediately jumped to the conclusion that Benson had rejected the offer because of this. 'I miss *Buffy*. It was an amazing group of people and a lot of fun,' Benson noted. 'I knew what was going to happen to Tara long before anybody else did. I feel there was a good reason why [Joss] did it. He wanted to take Willow to another level, and the only way to do that was to absolutely decimate her relationship with Tara.' Although Tara's death had hurt a lot of people, Benson added that 'you can't thwart what is already set in motion'.

Did You Know?: Danny Strong's run as a living character on *Buffy* (stretching back to the untransmitted pilot episode) came to a sudden end when Andrew stabbed Jonathan in this episode. Like most deaths on the show, it was kept a secret, even from Strong. 'I was in a cab in London. Tom [Lenk], Adam [Busch] and I were reading the scripts together,' Strong told Jennifer Dudley. 'I skipped over that part and said, "This is open-ended, we get to come back." Tom said, "It didn't go so well for you." I read it back and took the news very professionally.'

Fan rumours persist that Eric Balfour, who played Xander's friend Jesse in 1, 'Welcome to the Hellmouth' and 2, 'The Harvest', was offered the chance to return in a confrontation with Xander as a substitute scene for the proposed Willow/Tara scene. However, Balfour's schedule made this impossible.

Cast and Crew Comments: Although Kristine Sutherland admitted that she was as upset as many viewers when her character died in 94, 'The Body', she had no complaints about her alter ego's afterlife. 'There are a few frightening images of Joyce after she went to the other side,' she told *TV Guide*, 'but it was much better than being in the morgue.'

Jane Espenson's Comments: 'The episode dealt, in part, with Buffy's ambivalent feelings about her calling,' Jane noted in an article on the writing process which appeared on the *Firefly* website. 'She explored [these] feelings during a mock therapy session with a vampire she was destined to kill. Notice that the episode ideas *begin* with what she's going through and never with what would be a cool Slaying challenge?' Although many fans have speculated on whether the Joyce who appeared to Dawn was the First or *really* Joyce's ghost, Espenson has revealed in several interviews that it was always the production's intention for it to be the First cruelly manipulating Dawn.

In an interview with *TV Zone*, Jane noted that the writing of the episode was split by story rather than by act. 'I only wrote the Dawn material; I wasn't given the Andrew/Jonathan [scenes]. I had my heart set on writing the nerds. I couldn't believe it when that was given to Drew Goddard. I was concerned because I wasn't sure if I could write horror. I'm pleased that people liked [the outcome].'

Joss Whedon's Comments: 'I'm very fond of "Conversations With Dead People",' Joss told *USA Today* when asked about his favourite *Buffy* episodes. 'I thought structurally and tonally it was interesting and had a lot to say. And I got to write another song.' Other episodes in Joss's list included **26**, 'Innocence'; **107**, 'Once More, With Feeling' and **66**, 'Hush'.

130
Sleeper

US Transmission Date: 19 Nov 2002
UK Transmission Date: 6 Mar 2003

Writers: David Fury, Jane Espenson
Director: Alan J Levi
Cast: Robinne Lee (Charlotte), Rob Nagle (Robson), Lisa Jay (Linda), Kevin Daniels (Bouncer), Linda Christopher (Nora), Aimee Mann (Herself),[52] Hans Hernke (Student)[53]

Holden's allegation that he was sired by Spike forces Buffy and the Scoobies to keep a close eye on the vampire. Subsequently, Spike seduces and kills a girl while, seemingly, under the influence of the shapechanging entity. Meanwhile, in England, Giles has problems of his own.

No Fat Chicks: Having been caught rummaging through Spike's gear, Anya thinks fast and says that she wants to have sex with him, adding, helpfully: 'Let's get it on, you big bad boy!' When Spike spots that she's also carrying a stake, she observes this is her idea of kinky sex. When their fumbling attempts at interaction prove unsuccessful, Anya notes this is probably because Spike thinks she's fat.

A Little Guilt is a Dangerous Thing: Spike tells Buffy that he can barely live with the haunting memories of the atrocities he committed when he was William the Bloody. However, he

---

[52] Uncredited.
[53] Uncredited.

continues, as bizarre a notion as Soulful Spike the killer is, this is nothing compared to the idea that any woman other than Buffy could mean anything to him. His chip, he adds, is something that the Initiative did to him; he couldn't do anything about it. His soul, on the other hand, he got on his own. For Buffy.

Denial, Thy Name is Sunnydale: Everyone in the Bronze sees a vampire turning to dust, pauses for a moment, then continues acting as normal. As with many previous examples, we'll have to put this down to collective 'Joyce Summers syndrome'. Having said that, Aimee Mann telling her band that she hates playing vampire towns suggests that Sunnydale's infamy has spread somewhat further afield than we'd previously been led to believe.

The Conspiracy Starts at Home Time: The shapechanging evil entity appears to Spike in this episode, variously, as Buffy, Spike himself and the old man playing harmonica. There is, the entity tells Spike, an order to its plans. Others must die before Buffy.

Work is a Four-Letter Word: Xander has a client meeting at work.

It's a Designer Label!: Some cracking stuff: Spike's leather jacket, Buffy's black sweater, Dawn's scarlet blouse and Anya's cheeky light-blue top.

References: Spike has, seemingly, told Buffy that Billy Idol stole his entire image from Spike. He alludes to Cat Stevens' 'The First Cut Is The Deepest' and *Very Bad Things*. Xander namechecks *CSI: Crime Scene Investigation*. Buffy quotes from *Dragnet*. The rising of the vampires features the visual influence of *The Plague of the Zombies* and *Night of the Living Dead*. Xander has a Halloween skull-mask on his apartment wall.

Awesome!: Anya's hilariously incompetent attempts to seduce Spike. The shapechanging evil entity appearing to Spike, as Buffy, and encouraging him to bite the girl that he's with.

Surprise!: The episode's stunning climax: Giles, apparently, about to be beheaded.

'You May Remember Me From Such Films and TV Series As . . .': Robinne Lee played Bethany in *Deliver Us From Eva*. Rob Nagle appeared in *American Wedding* and *Dawson's Creek*. Kevin Daniels was in *Daria*. Lisa Jay's movies include *Death Factory*.

Don't Give Up The Day Job: Hans Hernke was Hank Stone's stand-in on *Dunsmore*. A singer with 80s chart band 'Til Tuesday, Aimee Mann's work is probably best known via her soundtrack for *Magnolia* (particularly the hit single 'Save Me'). Shortly before her appearance on *Buffy* she had a similar guest-slot on *The West Wing*. Alan J Levi's CV includes *Daytona Beach*, *Columbo*, *Quantum Leap*, *Miami Vice*, *Gemini Man*, *McCloud*, *The Incredible Hulk* and *Go West, Young Girl*.

Valley-Speak: Xander: 'Sweet mamalooshin.'

Cigarettes and Alcohol: Spike has a hip-flask. Xander drinks a Budweiser while watching TV.

Sex and Drugs and Rock'n'Roll: Asking the Bronze's bouncer if he's seen Spike, Buffy describes Spike as having bleached-blond hair, a leather jacket and a British accent. He is, she notes, somewhat sallow, albeit in a *hot* way.

Logic, Let Me Introduce You to This Window: Buffy is at Xander's apartment at 4 a.m. looking for Spike. Willow arrives home subsequent to this. But her conversation with the shapechanging evil entity in the previous episode took place in the UC Sunnydale library which, presumably, isn't open all night? Spike admits to killing several girls. The Bronze's bouncer notes that Spike left the club with different girls each night. Then Willow discovers, via the Internet, that there have been several disappearances, mostly female. Yet the basement vampires are mostly male. As, indeed, was Holden (see **127**, 'Conversations With Dead People'). We can imagine how Spike is able to pick up girls so easily, but how did he persuade several men to accompany him into a dark alley? Did he pretend to be gay, or offer them outside for a fight, or what? Why do all the vampires rise at exactly the same time? They were sired over a period of some days. When Spike punches Xander, he doesn't seem to feel much pain. Buffy tells Willow that Holden alleged Spike sired him two days ago. Later, however, she suggests to Spike that the siring took place last week. When Willow explains to Buffy about the horrible events of the previous night that she and Dawn, individually, suffered, Buffy changes position between shots. As with the Breeders, why is a best selling artiste like Aimee Mann playing the Bronze? Especially given her low opinion of vampire towns. When did Buffy give Spike her cellphone number?

I Just *Love* Your Accent: 'Sleeper' includes obvious stock footage of London (verily, yonder, is this a red telephone box I see before me?), but we'll forgive the production this indiscretion since it's mercifully brief. Also, note the outrageously ancient telephone on Robson's wall.

Motors: The London scenes feature two black taxis and a red Nissan Micra (W291 LHU). If this is *your* car, write to the production office and claim your royalties instantly.

Quote/Unquote: Anya: 'If I get vamped, I'm gonna bite your ass.' Xander: 'Wouldn't be the first time.'

Anya, when she fails to seduce Spike: 'Soulless-Spike would've had me upside down and halfway to Happyland by now.'

Charlotte, to Spike: 'Is that all I was to you? A one-bite stand?' Spike: 'I can't cry this soul out of me.'

Notes: 'This Big Evil that keeps promising to devour us? I think it started chomping.' If the previous two episodes showed different strengths of the series – even in their most wilfully obscure moments – then 'Sleeper' falls into yet another category. It's as different a story from its predecessors as they were to each other. An episode whose story is largely based on a central metaphor that trust is something one earns rather than an automatic right, 'Sleeper' features a couple of magical, jaw-hitting-the-floor moments. In fact, if truth be told, 'Sleeper's main fault is also what ultimately cursed 127, 'Conversations With Dead People' to damning with faint praise; that they're both, obviously, parts of a much larger story. As such, and taken as a stand-alone piece, 'Sleeper' doesn't make an awful lot of sense, except on a visceral level, on first viewing. Or on second viewing for that matter. With hindsight, once the season's greater ambitions became clearer, many viewers revisited this episode and lavished much deserved praise upon it.

This episode begins moments after the previous one ended. In England, Giles discovers that a fellow Watcher, Robson, has been attacked by a robed figure, and the young girl in his care was murdered. The house in which Spike has buried his recent victims is at 634 Hoffman Terrace.

Soundtrack: Aimee Mann performs 'Pavlov's Bell' and 'This Is How It Goes' in the Bronze. Also, Joe Faraci's 'Medusa', 'Red' by Sandra Collins, 'Street Harmonica Player' by Tommy Morgan,

'She Was No Good For Me' by David Grahame and the traditional English folk-ballad 'Early One Morning' (also known as 'The Maiden's Song').

Critique: 'The best show on television deals, improbably, with a high school guidance counselor who secretly vanquishes evil menaces in her spare time,' noted the *Ain't It Cool* website reviewer Hercules. 'Half the episodes aired since September manifested world-class filmed entertainment by any reasonable standard, and allowed the series to reassert itself as the funniest and best-written on television.'

Did You Know?: The episode's original script featured a different song used to trigger Spike into his killing spree – 'I'll Be Seeing You' rather than 'Early One Morning'.

Cast and Crew Comment: 'Spike has been used in different ways,' James Marsters told the *Washington Post*. 'As disposable villain, hapless wreck for comedic purposes, wacky neighbor by design, and then love interest.' James also noted that he was thankful that the show's writers had, as a consequence, been forced to explore the character so that Spike would 'fit into these different roles.'

Marti Noxon's Comments: 'This season feels really strong. We feel like we're hitting all cylinders,' Noxon told *Entertainment Weekly*. 'I have mixed feelings about going on. I want to do work I feel proud of before the idea of killing vampires is like sticking a hot poker in my eye.'

Joss Whedon's Comments: Joss is not interested in becoming another TV factory, such as those associated with writer/producers like Steven Bochco or David Kelley. 'It's time I made some movies,' he told Mike McDaniel. 'I don't want to turn out series for the sake of it. I have lots of ideas and some of them are TV series. But this year, [producing] three is unlike anything I've ever experienced. I never want to do it again because it would kill me. I won't turn out two good series and one contractual obligation.'

131
Never Leave Me

US Transmission Date: 26 Nov 2002
UK Transmission Date: 13 Mar 2003

Writer: Drew Goddard
Director: David Solomon
Cast: Donald Bishop (Butcher), Bobby Brewer (Hoffman),
Roberto Santos (Grimes)

Spike is held as a captive while the Scooby Gang ponder their options in the aftermath of his killing spree. Willow finds Andrew buying blood and he becomes another prisoner of Buffy and her friends.

Dudes and Babes: Spike tells Buffy about the pain he went through to acquire his soul (see **122**, 'Grave'). However, despite this, he notes that this is all relative because he has redefined the concepts of suffering since he fell for Buffy. Having a soul, he adds, is about self-loathing. He now understands why Buffy used him sexually (see **113**, 'Dead Things'). It was because she hated herself. William the Bloody has insight into the concept of violence, Buffy notes sarcastically, but Spike says that as bad and wretched as he was, he never truly loathed himself before acquiring a soul.

Spike believes that Buffy does not know the real him, the killer that he was before he came to Sunnydale. He asks if Buffy knows how much blood a vampire can drink from a girl before she will die? He knew *exactly* how much damage to inflict so that they could still cry. Because, he notes, it wasn't worth it if they couldn't cry.

Authority Sucks!: Two recidivist troublemakers are summoned to Principal Wood's office. He threatens them with placing their latest graffiti-painting incident on their permanent record. He then admits that, actually, he's bluffing. The whole permanent record thing is a myth. Colleges never ask for anything beyond a student's SAT scores and it's not as if an employer is ever going to check how many days someone was absent in high school.

A Little Dying is a Dangerous Thing: The First appears as Jonathan to Andrew who says that he hopes he didn't hurt his friend when he killed him (see **129**, 'Conversations With Dead People'). It actually wasn't that bad, Jonathan suggests, noting a sharp pain, a burning sensation, then general queasiness. It was, he adds, a little like when he used to get ulcers in high school, only at the end he became one with Light and Hope.

The Conspiracy Starts at Home Time: Due to the fact that Jonathan is anaemic, his murder did not produce enough blood spilled on to the Seal of Danzalthar to open it.

The shapechanging evil entity, revealed in this episode to be the First Evil, appears as Warren and Jonathan to Andrew and Spike and Buffy to Spike. The First, and it's minions, the Bringers (or Harbingers) were previously seen in **44**, 'Amends', during which the First attempted to persuade Angel to commit suicide.

Work is a Four-Letter Word: Following the events of **129**, 'Conversations With Dead People', Xander is, once again, performing much needed DIY on Buffy's home. He puts in new windows while simultaneously giving Willow a lecture on proper tool maintenance. Since this isn't Willow's area of expertise, she takes any excuse she can find to get out of the house.

It's a Designer Label!: Highlights include Willow's crimson velvet top and Anya's sweatshirt.

References: Xander gives the girls a precise essay on brainwashing techniques and how a song can be used to trigger a sleeper agent into performing their nefarious tasks. Willow asks if this knowledge comes from Xander's soldier-memory (see **18**, 'Halloween'). Xander, however, says that it's actually taken from every espionage movie he's ever seen. Also, the Sears catalogues, *Indiana Jones and the Last Crusade* ('junior!'), the Who's 'The Real Me', *Iron Fist* and Roy Rogers's horse Trigger. Travers quotes Winston Churchill ('We are still masters of our fate') and Proverbs, 24:6. ('For by wise counsel, you shall make your war'). The fight sequence includes stunts inspired by the movies of Jackie Chan (Buffy using Andrew as a battering-ram).

Geek-Speak: Warren alludes to the climax of *Star Wars* and suggests his non-corporeality makes him like Obi-Wan Kinobe (in *The Empire Strikes Back*). Or Patrick Swayze (in *Ghost*) adds Andrew. When about to kill the piglet, Andrew observes that *Babe 2: Pig in The City* was a really underrated movie. Warren suggests that Andrew imagine himself as Conan The Destroyer. In the butcher's shop, Andrew alludes to *Monty Python's Flying Circus* ('a halibut').

Bitch!: While trying to scare Andrew with tales of Anya's vengeance curses, Xander talks about a man who once broke her heart. She had her revenge by replacing *his* heart with darkness. Then she made him live his life this way, as a hollow shell. It's obvious that he's alluding to himself. Then, getting back into character, he adds that she tore out the man's intestines, rubbed them in his face and took pictures of it.

Awesome!: Andrew's completely incompetent attempts to convince Willow that he has access to powerful magics. And, subsequently, Willow convincing Andrew that she's still Evil-Willow ('I am Death!'). Xander and Anya's interrogation of Andrew, and Anya's glee when her bullying makes Andrew cry. Buffy and Spike's lengthy discussions on redemption. The huge fight sequence between the Scoobies and the Bringers (which turns out to be a diversion to capture Spike). The climactic appearance of the Über-Vamp.

Surprise!: The revelation regarding Robin Wood, when he discovers Jonathan's body in the school basement and buries the evidence. And, the explosive ending.

'You May Remember Me From Such Films and TV Series As . . .': Donald Bishop's CV includes *Bye Bye Love*, *The China Syndrome* and *The Rockford Files*. Bobby Brewer was in *Magnolia*.

Don't Give Up The Day Job: DG trainee Mindee Clem's CV includes *CSI* and *Gilmore Girls*. Script Coordinator Tamara Becher also worked on *Wonderfalls*.

Sex and Drugs and Rock'n'Roll: Andrew mentions the time that he watched Anya and Spike have sex (see **118**, 'Entropy'). Spike asks Buffy if she has never wondered why she, seemingly, cannot kill Spike despite all that he's done to her and her friends. It's not love, they both know that. Buffy suggests it's because he has fought with her but Spike knows this can't be rationalised into some noble act. The truth is that Buffy likes bad men. He doesn't mean troubled or brooding men, he's referring to men who physically (and emotionally) hurt her. She needs the pain they cause her and the hate she gets from this. It gives her the strength to be the Slayer. But, Spike concludes, it's also killing her.

Logic, Let Me Introduce You to This Window: *Babe 2: Pig in the City* is not an underrated movie in any way, shape or form. When Willow talks to Andrew in the alley, her hair is sometimes tucked behind her ears. On other occasions, it isn't. Several of the Scooby Gang are hit, forcefully, with the Bringers' weapons. Yet, they apparently suffer no ill-effects from this as they're immediately back on their feet in just about every case. Spike bursts through a wall to attack Andrew, leaving a hole big enough to pull Andrew through. Subsequently, when Anya and Xander burst into the room, they use the door. Wouldn't it have been simpler to have gone through the hole that Spike created? The First – as Warren

– tells Andrew that it cannot take corporeal form. Andrew tests this by putting his hand through Warren. Yet, in **44**, 'Amends', the First, then in the form of Jenny Calendar, could, and did, interact with Angel. And, in several of the earlier episodes of this season, the First was seen to touch inanimate objects. Or, in one case, Spike. In **123**, 'Lessons', Spike showed Buffy his scarred chest. There's no evidence of such wounds in this episode. We know vampires are supposed to heal quickly, but Spike has a scar on his eyebrow, apparently given to him by the Chinese Slayer in 1900 (see **85**, 'Fool For Love') so clearly not all wounds heal completely. Spike's reflection is visible in a mirror. Travers implies that since Giles left Sunnydale, he hasn't been part of the Watcher's Council and they have no idea of his whereabouts. Yet he was in an all-day meeting involving the Council when Willow tried to ring him during **125**, 'Same Time, Same Place'. Where did Andrew acquire the piglet from?

I Just *Love* Your Accent: Buffy tells Travers that he doesn't have to get 'all British and dodgy', whatever that means.

Cruelty to Animals: Buffy notes that Spike has been feasting on humans for weeks and that he is in withdrawal. They need to get him some blood. Willow offers to kill Anya, but Buffy thinks they should probably ween him off humans. He will, therefore, have to make do with animal blood.

Andrew obtains a piglet to sacrifice and open the seal. However, it proves more difficult than it looks.

Quote/Unquote: Dawn gives Wood her sister's excuse for being off work: 'Her exact words were, "I've got stuff coming out both ends".' Wood: 'Thank you. That's very helpful.'

Warren: 'That was the worst attempted pig-slaughtering I've ever seen.'

Buffy, on Spike: 'He was talking to someone up there . . . And then he started singing.' Anya: 'Maybe it's another musical. A much *crappier* musical.'

Buffy: 'You faced the monster inside you and you fought back. You risked everything to be a better man . . . I believe in you, Spike.'

Notes: 'Spike and I were talking, and he was fine . . . when I came back it was like he was a completely different person.' The series' most formidable presentation of *Evil Since the Dawn of Time*, the First, is back. And this time, it's *totally* after kicking Buffy's ass. A necessary change of pace from its immediate predecessors,

'Never Leave Me' is a bit like a beautifully constructed sandwich filling; a meaty chunk of unadulterated plot which provides some answers while simultaneously setting up the potential avenues down which the next half-dozen shows would travel. There's some fabulous comedy – Xander and Anya get to play out a hilariously absurd version of the Good Cop/Bad Cop dramatic cliché that's worth the entry money on its own. And Dawn is the voice for yet more scatological humour – something of a recurring theme this season. There are, also, a bunch of tender and bittersweet moments between Buffy and Spike. All of this in a bottle-show that seldom strays too far from the Summers' residence. Yet the episode ends a continent away for the second wholly surprising and unsignposted death of a semi-recurring character in three episodes. 'Never Leave Me' sees the *Buffy* production team giving the viewers a parade of little conundrums to solve, with an obvious answer never far from reach. But, always underlying this, is a deeper and more complex plot struggling for freedom. Tied with ominous, brutal action sequences, some disquieting imagery and an unexpected lurch into existentialist melodrama – for no reason other than that the writers probably thought it was funny – the charming veneer of the season's early episodes begins to fade. A much harder, darker and disturbing Sunnydale emerges, scrambling through the dirt at the episode's climax. This, then, is *Buffy* at its most schizophrenic, and its most rivetingly brilliant. This series is never better than when it's taking risks. 'Never Leave Me' walks a tightrope and does a triple back-flip, with pike, before emerging with its dignity intact.

This episode takes place directly following the previous one (note that everyone is wearing the same clothes). 'Never Leave Me' marks the destruction of the Watcher's Council in the *Buffy*-universe (at least, until *Angel*: 'Lineage' a year later). They had headquarters in Munich, Switzerland, Rome and Melbourne, as well as London. All are, seemingly, destroyed. A copy of *The Sunnydale News* can be seen outside Wood's office. Tucker, Andrew's brother (see **54**, 'The Prom'), is mentioned.

Critique: Spike, as many – mainly female – fans have noted, is *Buffy*'s Byronic character: To some he does, indeed, walk in beauty like the night with his chiselled good looks and Sid Vicious sneer. As 12-year-old fan Caroline Adley succinctly puts it, 'He's *hot.*' 'The reasons to love Spike are many,' noted *New York Magazine*'s Mim Udovitch. 'The mass-cultural landscape is not exactly crowded with figures who, like Spike, drink blood and exude danger and romance and wear dark nail polish and smoke.'

Did You Know?: When Wesleyan film student Joss Whedon submitted his final term project, a 1987 post-apocalyptic western on Super 8mm, the results were disappointing. 'It was pretentious,' Whedon told William Weir. However, his film's hero, the Woman With No Name, proved to be his first in a long line of female heroes. In the last decade, the university's prominence in Hollywood has grown so much that insiders have dubbed its network of alumni the *Wesleyan Mafia*. Those who have passed through the university's film programme have included *Pearl Harbor* director Michael Bay, *The Good Girl*'s Miguel Arteta and Paul Weitz, one of the creators of *American Pie*.

Head On: 'It's not winding down, it's coming to an end,' Tony Head told *SciFi Wire* concerning the likelihood that the seventh season would be *Buffy*'s last. 'Joss has brought it back full-circle. In terms of telling Buffy's story – how she learned to deal with her gifts and how it's affected her life and the lives of all around her – it's reached the end.'

Head was back in LA to shoot several episodes. 'We're in debate [as to how many].' He also noted that his first big scene back had, perhaps inevitably, been a lengthy exposition piece. 'Give the English guy the big words.'

Cast and Crew Comments: 'I love working with Sarah,' DB Woodside told *E! Online*. 'She's absolutely crazy. Her sense of humour is amazing. She's like Minnie Mouse on speed.'

Joss Whedon's Comments: '*Buffy* is made by a bunch of writers who think very hard about what they are doing in terms of psychology and methodology,' Whedon told an AOL online chat. 'We take the show very seriously. We are, perhaps, the most pompous geeks of all. When somebody says there is a philosophy behind *Buffy*, that's the truth. When they say there's symbolism and meaning in what we're doing, that's also true. On any show, [there are] sociological patterns we aren't in control of.'

Intellectualisation: Some fans will tell you that *Buffy* was just an ordinary TV series until the academics discovered it. Actually, that's not, quite, true. From very early in the series' life, it acquired – in addition to the reasonably normal rabidly obsessive TV fandom – a foothold among the more cerebral end of critical analysis. Sometimes this amounted to little more than college-going *Buffy* fans writing vast articles that used ten words where three would normally do. (This author is, *by no means*, immune to such verbosity himself.) Nevertheless, while many television shows have acquired an intelligentsia following (*Star Trek*, *Doctor Who* and *The X-Files* are the three outstanding examples), few have been as invasive into the heart of highbrow critique as *Buffy*. Or as widely referenced.

Three particular published academic works neatly illustrate this trend: *Reading the Vampire Slayer: An Unofficial Critical Companion to Buffy and Angel* (2001, edited by Roz Kaveney),[54] *Fighting the Forces: What's at Stake in Buffy the Vampire Slayer* (2002, edited by Rhonda V Wilcox and David Lavery)[55] and *Slayer Slang: A Buffy the Vampire Slayer Lexicon* (2003, by Michael Adams).[56] Kaveney places *Buffy* academia in the context, not of other series that have acquired an intellectual edge to their cult-status, but of far older phenomena like Sherlock Holmesiana. 'Some areas of fiction,' she notes, 'are good at generating mythopoeia; this is one of the things that TV, at its best, does.' Sociologists and philosophers regularly generate *Buffy*-related essays, many of which are reprinted in a frequently fascinating Internet quarterly called *Slayage: The Online International Journal of Buffy Studies* and also in regular academic conferences.

For example, Sheryl Vint, professor of English at the University of Alberta, has written in-depth on whether Buffy is, primarily, a figure of empowerment for young women or a lust object for men.

---

[54] Among the essays in *Reading the Vampire Slayer* are Boyd Tonkin's 'Entropy as Demon: *Buffy* in Southern California', Karen Sayer's 'It Wasn't Our World Anymore. They Made It Theirs: Reading Space and Place' and Esther Saxey's 'Staking a Claim: The Series and Its Slash Fan-Fiction'.

[55] *Fighting the Forces* includes articles such as Wilcox's own 'Who Died and Made Her Boss?: Patterns of Mortality in *Buffy*', Patricia Pender's 'I'm Buffy, and You're . . . History: The Postmodern Politics of *Buffy*' and Justine Larbalestier's '*Buffy*'s Mary-Sue is Jonathan: *Buffy* Acknowledges the fans'.

[56] Never one averse to free publicity (and, at the risk of implying that the *Buffy* publishing industry is the subgenre that celebrates itself) this author was delighted to discover that *he*, and an earlier edition of *Slayer*, are referenced in *Slayer Slang* on more than a dozen occasions. Seemingly, at least in *Buffy* circles, I'm the originator of the word 'vampiry' (*adj*: 'exhibiting features of a vampire', *Slayer* 2000 edition, page 26). I'm not sure that I was, actually, but I'll certainly accept the compliment. As someone who has spent years trying to get *The Simpsons*' word 'cromulent' into the *OED*, 'invented a word' is a fabulous line to stick on your CV!

Vint notes that young women often reject 'a feminist identity because they associate [this] with the negative stereotype of a man-hater . . .' It is imperative, Vint continues, that feminism finds a way to connect with young women's cultural lives, and *Buffy* helped greatly in this regard. However, Vint was also worried that 'secondary texts' were in danger of subverting this image: 'In magazines targeted at men, the desire to show Sarah [Michelle Gellar] as an object for sexual consumption becomes the dominant meaning of the text . . .' Other critics tend to argue that *Buffy*'s central female-empowerment theme is strengthened rather than diminished by the sexuality of her character: 'Post-feminist icons such as Buffy, the Powerpuff Girls and Lara Croft show women that they can be tough, use deadly force, and still look good in a skirt,' noted a (presumably female) Rutgers University *Daily Targum* writer in an article entitled *The Grrl Power Generation*. For *Buffy*'s writers, this is obviously a double-edged sword. 'I think that when the paradigm is flipped, and women take the strong centre roles, in any good drama you need your fall guys. In our show, they become *literal* fall guys,' Marti Noxon subsequently told Allie Gottlieb. Nevertheless, as a contrast to post-feminist commentators who deconstruct the show from an antifeminist perspective, Gottlieb was happy to note in that 'the male [*Buffy*] characters take on what are, typically, considered feminine traits – loving, nurturing, pining, irrationality, being physically weak but having strong emotions. Yet they are still attractive.' In a superb think-piece on the series in the *Los Angeles Times*, Lisa Rosen has noted that 'Buffy was the first young woman on television who was both empowered *and* realistically portrayed. She never patronized her audience.'

The English section of *Buffy*'s intelligentsia following even had their own public forum when the University of East Anglia held a two-day *Buffy* conference during October 2002. According to the UAE website, the event sought to 'address the diversity of ways in which the series has permeated popular and academic discourse and cultural contexts alike'.[57] 'I must confess to having seen a few

---

[57] Papers presented at the event included: 'Unaired Pilot or Bad Quarto: Textual Problems in *Buffy* and Shakespeare in an Internet Age', 'Playing with *Dracula*: Joss Whedon's Creative Adaptation of the Vampire Genre', 'Blood sausage, bangers, and mash: British English and Britishness in *BtVS*', 'Teen-Witch in *BtVS* and Its Impact Upon Teen Girl Identity in Contemporary Britain' and ' "You hold your gun like a sissy girl": Firearms and Anxious Masculinity in *BtVS*'.

Buffy programmes because my youngest son is a fan,' noted Janet Garton, the outgoing Dean of the School of Language, Linguistics and Translation Studies. 'But now there will be more intellectual justification for watching.' Of course, the question *must* be asked, does one *need* an intellectual justification for watching popular entertainment or is such a conceit an example of gross pretentiousness? It's notable that many commentators on the *Buffy* phenomena (in all medias) tend to begin their essays with exactly this sort of disclaimer (the **Critique** sections in this book are, literally, *full* of such comments). Once again, this author has, once or twice, been guilty of the same thing himself. And also of inverse snobbery when, writing in *TV Zone*, I bemoaned the publication of further examples of 'tiresome "No, *really*, forget the title, it's a good show" articles from some trendy journalist in the *Guardian* or the *Washington Post*. Excuse the quasi-comedic bitterness, it's just *I* liked this show before it was fashionable to.' I apologise to trendy journalists *everywhere*. You have as much right to like *Buffy* as me, or anyone else for that matter.

Then, there's the theological aspect of the series which, possibly even more than feminism and sexuality, is one of the main focuses of critical analysis concerning *Buffy*. Jana Riess, the religion editor for *Publishers Weekly*, has written a self-help book called *What Would Buffy Do? A Vampire Slayer as Spiritual Guide*. 'Whedon may call himself an atheist,' she says (which, indeed, he does – quite vociferously), 'but *Buffy* deals with profoundly religious themes. It serves as a strong moral example most of the time.' So *Buffy* is, seemingly, both pro-feminist *and* pro-faith, something that actually – and often despite itself – is difficult to argue against. But is the show also pro-war? Anthony Cordesman, chairman of the Center for Strategic and International Studies, published a treatise called *Biological Warfare and the Buffy Paradigm*. He told *The Washington Post*: 'I was trying to explain modern warfare to people who seem incapable of understanding the subject. It's a fairly esoteric topic. I thought if I related it to something in pop-culture, it would be more easily understood.' This metaphor was taken to a grotesque extreme by Jonah Goldberg in an article entitled 'Buffy the UN Slayer' published in the *Washington Times* in which the writer drew parallels between Buffy's triumphant coup against the Watcher's Council in **90**, 'Checkpoint', and President Bush's speech to the United Nations seeking help for America's fight against the alleged threat of Baghdad. 'The UN really can't back up its rhetoric or defend its honor, it needs a

Slayer for that,' wrote Goldberg, doubtless to the horror of the millions of pacifist liberals who both write for and watch *Buffy*.

So, is all this intellectualisation of an admittedly pretty good television series desirable or not? The University of South Australia's communications lecturer, Geraldine Bloustien, held a one-day academic symposium on the series in 2003. Bloustien noted that *Buffy*'s production values, rich text, pop-culture references and use of metaphors would continue to interest scholars for years. 'In spite of it being about vampires and monsters, it's actually recognised that these are metaphors for other issues,' she noted. 'It's much more about how to get on in life, how to cope with high school, university, jobs, relationships.' That's all very true. But *Buffy* is also, let's remember, a show about vampires and monsters *as well*. That's the intrinsic beauty of *Buffy*, that it works on at least three levels: as substance, metaphor *and* subtext.

Joss Whedon, it appears, finds this intellectualisation process interesting, although one senses that perhaps he may be slightly suspicious about the agenda of some of those who write so deeply about his creation. In the *New York Times*, he elaborated: 'I think it's great the academic community has taken an interest. It's always important for academics to study popular culture, even if the thing they are studying is [inherently] idiotic. If it's successful, or has made a dent in culture, then it's worthy of study to find out why.'

132
Bring on the Night

US Transmission Date: 17 Dec 2002
UK Transmission Date: 20 Mar 2003

Writers: Marti Noxon, Douglas Petrie
Director: David Grossman
Cast: Courtnee Draper (Annabelle), Chris Wiley (Roger)

Giles returns to Sunnydale with three potential Slayers in tow. He believes that the First's plan is to kill off the future Slayer-line before opening the Hellmouth and unleashing the forces beneath. Buffy faces an ancient vampire whom Giles recognises as the Turok-Han.

Dreaming (As Blondie Once Said) is Free: Tired, during a mammoth research session, Buffy falls asleep and dreams that her mother comes to her, offering advice that Buffy should get some rest. Buffy assumes that this is another First-induced manipulation, but she's very definitely sleeping when Xander wakes her so, who knows?

A Little Learning is a Dangerous Thing: Willow notes that she hasn't been able to find any documentation on the First. That's because the entity predates written history, suggests Giles. The only records of its existence were in the Council of Watchers' library. And that is a large pile of ash and rubble now.

Denial, Thy Name is Joyce: When Joyce appears in Buffy's daydreams for the second time in the episode, it's almost certainly the First pretending to be her. However, the assertion that the last thing Buffy probably needs is one of helpful Mom's guilt-trips certainly *sounds* like Joyce at her finest. The subsequent observations that Buffy's friends put too much pressure on her, that there are some things Buffy cannot control and that evil is a natural part of everyone, all suggest that this is the First speaking and not either a ghost or a figment of Buffy's imagination.

The Conspiracy Starts at Home Time: The episode's script, which quickly leaked on to the Internet, included a comment to the effect that it was very important that Giles should not touch, or be touched by, anything. This led to all sorts of fan-theories that Giles wasn't really Giles but was, rather, a manifestation of the First. Giles notes that potential Slayers all over the world are being killed (such as those in Istanbul in **123**, 'Lessons', and Frankfurt in **124**, 'Beneath You') along with their Watchers (like Robson in **130**, 'Sleeper'). There were many potentials but now only a handful remain and they're all on their way to Sunnydale. The First's plan, it seems, is to erase all the Slayers-in-waiting, then Faith, then Buffy. With them eliminated, Giles adds, the Hellmouth would no longer have a guardian.

The records that Giles stole from the Council state that the First can change form, but only appear in the guise of the dead. (Note that everyone whom the First is seen to manifest itself as throughout the season is, or has been at some point, dead. This includes Buffy: see **12**, 'Prophecy Girl'; **100**, 'The Gift'.)

The First appears as Spike and Drusilla. It also, briefly, inhabits Willow when she tries a locator spell to find it.

Work is a Four-Letter Word: Xander feels that he's doomed to replace Buffy's windows for eternity after the Bringers attack in

131, 'Never Leave Me'. He mentions being stuck in a time-loop, à la Buffy's experiences in **105**, 'Life Serial'.

'West Hollywood': Kennedy persuades Willow that she'd make a much better roommate than Molly (who chatters incessantly) or Annabelle (who snores). Then, flirtatiously, Kennedy says that Willow better not hog the covers.

It's a Designer Label!: Bonus points for Giles's brown jacket, Willow's navy-blue top and Molly's 'Kill Germs in 60 Seconds' T-shirt.

References: The title is a song by Sting. 'Bring on the Night's script describes Molly's appearance as 'very *Ghost World*. Pigtails and a miniskirt.' Xander alludes to the climax of *Signs* and the film's director, M Night Shyamalan. Also, the Cliff Notes series, *Sleeping Beauty*, the First Bank of Delaware, *Jackass*, I Timothy 6 ('the root of all evil') and *Star Trek: The Next Generation*. There are conceptual allusions to *Die Another Day* and *Dracula Has Risen From The Grave*. When Wood finds Buffy using an Internet search engine to research the First, she changes her keyphrase, 'Manifestations of Evil', to add 'in the Movies'. Buffy says that she's a fan of *The Exorcist* and *The Blair Witch Project*. As opposed to, say, Rob Schneider's oeuvre? asks Wood. That, Buffy notes, is a different kind of evil. Wood doesn't enjoy scary movies. Even the hokey ones sometimes go to a place that, he believes, the young should avoid. Asked what sort of movies he likes, Wood replies mysteries.

Geek-Speak: Xander's re-emerging geek credentials: Spider-Man one can live with, but an encyclopaedic knowledge of *Wonder Woman*? When Andrew is told about the First, he notes the entity's name isn't very ominous sounding. An evil name, he continues, should be like *Superman*'s Lex Luthor or Harry Potter's Voldemort. Andrew subsequently compares himself with the comic supervillains Dr Doom, Apokalypse and the Riddler. But now, he says, he has returned from the Dark Side, like Darth Vadar in the last five minutes of *Return of the Jedi*.

Awesome!: Anya and Dawn's flagrant abuse of the Geneva Convention towards their prisoner, Andrew. Buffy finding the Bringers cave entrance. Plus the Über-Vamp giving Buffy a damn good chinning. Twice. Buffy's mighty closing speech.

What A Shame They Dropped . . .: A filmed sequence in either this episode or the next (sources vary) was allegedly removed for timing reasons. This had Willow and Kennedy talking about Miss Kitty Fantastico and a painting that Tara had done.

'You May Remember Me From Such Films and TV Series As . . .': Clara Bryant appeared in *Due East* and *Star Trek: Deep Space Nine*. Iyari Limon played Zoe Gold in *Double Teamed* and appeared in *King Cobra*. Courtnee Draper's movies include *The Yard Sale* and *Kidnap Madonna's Baby*.

Valley-Speak: Spike: 'Get bent.'
Andrew: 'This is gonna get hairy. I'm talking weird with a beard.'

Cigarettes and Alcohol: Dawn mentions Red Bull.

Sex and Drugs and Rock'n'Roll: When Buffy says that the First is the original evil, older than time itself, Anya is incredulous. She notes that she often heard similar lines to this during her demon days. Creatures claiming to be so rotten they don't even have a name for it. Then, they normally asked if this made Anya horny.

Logic, Let Me Introduce You to This Window: This episode seems to take place immediately after the previous one; note everyone is wearing the same clothes as at the end of **131**, 'Never Leave Me'. It's also, apparently, late December, just before Christmas. **129**, 'Conversations With Dead People', began on 12 November and concluded in the early hours of the next morning; **130**, 'Sleeper', followed directly from that, covering approximately two days; **131**, 'Never Leave Me', followed directly from *that* with a similar time scale. The events of this episode, therefore, should be dated no later than 18 or 19 November. There are further timing issues: it's daylight outside when Andrew tells Buffy about the seal. However, when they subsequently go to the school, it appears to be nighttime. Furthermore, Wood is wearing the same clothes as he was the previous evening when he buried Jonathan (and is still carrying the shovel he used). He expects to see Buffy at work tomorrow. Later, when Giles arrives with the potentials, it's daytime again, but a whole day and night's worth of adventures occur before Buffy does attend school again the next day.

Once again, Dawn's hairstyle changes style between scenes. It's straight at the beginning, has a layer of curls when the Scoobies go to the school, then it's straight again. Buffy is surprised that the Turok-Han can't be killed with a stake. But this isn't the first time that she's faced a vampire immune to staking (Kakistos in **37**,

'Faith, Hope, and Trick', for example). When Buffy finds Annabelle's body, she's lying flat on her back. During the subsequent fight between Buffy and the Über-Vamp, the body is seen again. Now, Annabelle rests on her right shoulder. What's the point of the Turok-Han holding Spike's head underwater? He doesn't breathe; therefore, he can't drown.

I Just *Love* Your Accent: A smallish complaint: how many girls born in England during the 1980s do readers know with the Christian name Molly? Not 1870s serving wenches with a nice line in Teutonic Mummerset, but girls born when the most popular female names in this country included Tiffany, Kylie and Natasha. Furthermore, how many of them have an accent one degree shy of Dick Van Dyke in *Mary Poppins*? She also uses several very out-of-date slang British terms (like 'brill', for example). Kennedy apologises to Buffy for the British invasion when both Molly and Annabelle suffer from jet lag.

Quote/Unquote: Dawn: 'There's blood on this. Looks like the First made another sacrifice. Or a music video.'
  Giles: 'Sorry to barge in. I'm afraid we have a slight apocalypse.'
  Xander, to Andrew: 'Of course you've got a bad feeling, dude. You're tied to a chair.'

Notes: 'From now on we won't just face our worst fears, we'll seek them out, find them and cut out their hearts, one by one, until the First shows itself . . . Any questions?' The inclusion of one horribly clichéd and dated example of Englishness (in a series that's usually so careful in this area) is the sole negative point in 'Bring on the Night'. This is a truly great *Buffy* episode by *any* standards. But especially in the context of this season's developing story-arc, the newly declared and very literal 'war on terror' that Buffy talks about at the climax. The First's plans for Spike, involving both physical and psychological torture, might be difficult for some viewers to stomach, but these sequences are carried off with such bravado, and even a kind of dignity, that one can't help but be impressed. Elsewhere, in tiny snapshots, like Anya and Dawn's sneaky cruelty to Andrew, and the return of a cold, aloof Giles, *Buffy*'s core values are given a twist of lemon. The sharp, bitter aftertaste that often follows something sweet and eloquent. Then, in the midst of this, we have a ten-minute fight sequence, as harsh and unrelenting as anything that the series has ever attempted. Yet the message that emerges from the bruised lips and bloodied knuckles is that whatever gets you through the night is all right. Epilogued by what may become the *Buffy* equivalent of the St Crispen's Day speech, total war has come to Sunnydale.

Buffy has a photo of Dawn in her office. One of the books that Buffy reads for research is *The Watcher's Codex*. Willow uses the *Demons, Demons, Demons* website in her fruitless search for information on the First (see **125**, 'Same Time, Same Place'). The Turok-Han are, Giles says, similar to what Neanderthals were to human beings; ancient, primordial, ferociously strong killing machines. They are the vampires that other vampires fear. Until seeing one, Giles always believed that they were a myth. Spike says he never figured Drusilla for an existentialist and adds that she hated Paris (see **22**, 'What's My Line?' Part 2).

Critique: '*Buffy* possesses a clear moral center,' wrote Simon Groebner. 'Although the series has come under fire by religious groups for its subject matter, its protagonists have a sense of right and wrong, and characters who commit evil eventually suffer for it.'

Did You Know?: 'I'm the luckiest guy in the world,' Alexis Denisof noted, concerning his engagement to Alyson Hannigan in late 2002. 'We were driving to my family in Seattle during the Christmas break. I had the ring. I thought of a hundred different romantic, complicated plans of asking her,' he told *SciFi Wire*. 'We drove all night from LA to north of San Francisco, so we could spend the following day in Napa Valley. We were having the most perfect day. We stopped at a winery, got some food to make a picnic, then we drove up to a mountain lake. It was there that I asked her. She said yes.'

When she appeared on Conan O'Brien's chatshow *Late Night* shortly after this episode was broadcast, Alyson had what was described, by O'Brien, as an 'awkward celebrity moment' with Luke Perry who was also on the show. On a happier note, around the same time, Alyson also appeared on *The Caroline Rhea Show* and revealed that she seldom has problems learning dialogue for *Buffy*, except for when she is given spells to cast.

The Kennedy Assassination: The introduction of a new love interest for Willow, in the form of the self-confident Kennedy, was not a popular move with some *Buffy* fans. (The most vocal of these appeared to be those fans that had invested a lot of emotional involvement in the presentation of Tara and Willow's relationship.) This line of thinking is possibly best summed up by *TV*

Zone's Kate Brown who wrote that, 'Kennedy never felt like anything other than Mutant Enemy's answer to accusations of homophobia.' Brown also noted that the introduction of another girlfriend for Willow both missed the point of Tara's death (she died to serve a particular plotline, *not* because of her sexuality) and demeaned Tara's memory by 'having Willow move on far too quickly'. Additionally, the more dom/sub aspects of Kennedy's sexual pursuit of Willow during certain episodes (for example, **133**, 'Showtime' and **135**, 'The Killer in Me') was a radical juxtaposition to the lengthy and tender build-up to Willow and Tara's first kiss (see **94**, 'The Body'). The website *filmforce.ign.com*, when interviewing Joss in July 2003, voiced the concerns of a section of *Buffy* fandom when they noted that Kennedy's relationship with Willow seemed to be an almost predatory stalking. 'I wanted an anti-Tara,' Whedon noted in justification. 'Tara was very reticent, Willow caused [her] to blossom. What I wanted was somebody who was further on in dealing with her sexuality than Willow. Somebody who was totally confident. I wanted to explore the concept of Willow moving on.'

Cast and Crew Comments: 'David Grossman is one of my favourite directors,' James Marsters told a convention audience in 2002. 'He's fabulous. He'll kick you in the butt if you're not doing something. He has absolutely no fear of, or respect for, the regulars. That's exactly what you need to be as a director.'

Marti Noxon's Comments: Throughout *Buffy*'s run, Sarah Michelle Gellar came to play an increasing influence upon her character's style. She would often go shopping on her own, or bring in clothes from her own wardrobe. 'She had a tremendous say,' Marti Noxon told Farrah Weinstein. 'There was a period where she was dating Spike. She came to me and said she wanted to start wearing darker, punk-influenced clothes. So, for a while, she was wearing black chokers just on the hint of S&M.'

Joss Whedon's Comments: 'I knew young audiences would like anything that took teenagers seriously and wasn't written by really old people trying to teach teenagers what they think,' Joss told John Beifuss. 'Certain things that the show does are very necessary, really important and empowering.'

This was a good period for Joss, despite the cancellation by Fox of his sci-fi western series *Firefly* a few weeks earlier. On 18 December, Joss's wife Kai gave birth to the couple's son, Donavan.

133
Showtime

US Transmission Date: 14 Jan 2003
UK Transmission Date: 27 Mar 2003

Writer: David Fury
Director: Michael Grossman
Cast: Amanda Fuller (Eve)

More potentials arrive in Sunnydale. One of them, a girl called Eve, creates tensions within the group by claiming that Buffy is not strong enough to protect them against the threat of ultimate evil. Buffy and Xander subsequently discover Eve's body in a motel, meaning that the First has been among them for two days, sowing discord.

Dreaming (As Blondie Once Said) is Free: Spike hallucinates a scenario in which he escapes from his shackles, kills a couple of Bringers and then, as he reaches the cave entrance, meets Buffy. He's rudely brought back to reality by the First.

Dudes and Babes: Four further potential Slayers have arrived to join Kennedy and Molly. They are called Chloe, Vi, Rona and Eve. (The latter doesn't survive the episode.)

Sex and Drugs and Rock'n'Roll: Saucy Kennedy continues with her teasing of Willow concerning the pair sharing a bed. (Will, the poor lamb, cowers rather appalled in her sleeping bag on the floor during the innuendo.) Later, there's a pointed exchange with Kennedy saying that she would love a glimpse of Evil-Willow (see **135**, 'The Killer in Me'). While all of this Sapphic malarkey is going on, Giles and Anya hope that a pan-dimensional entity, Beljoxa's Eye, can offer a solution to the First's threat. Unfortunately, a demon is needed to open the portal to it so Anya tries some sexual bribery with a former acquaintance named Torg. 'Wouldn't touch *you* for all the kittens in Korea,' he notes, disgusted at her, now human, physiology. Anya is *appalled* at this. 'What am I, a leper in this town? I can't even give it away.' Torg, who has six spleens, two stomachs and no heart, once dated Anya after they were accidentally invited to the same massacre. It's implied that they shared a night of passion afterwards.

The Conspiracy Starts at Home Time: Beljoxa's Eye notes that the First Evil has existed since before the universe was born and will continue long after its demise. If the First has been around for all that time, asks Giles pertinently, why hasn't it attempted something similar before now? The opportunity has only recently presented itself, answers the Eye. The mystical forces surrounding the Slayer line have been irrevocably altered and become vulnerable. And it was the Slayer, herself, who seemingly caused this to happen, giving the First it's opportunity. (This is, possibly, a reference to their being, for only the second time in history, two Slayers active at the same time. Later, however, Anya seems to imply that this is directly related to Buffy's death in **100**, 'The Gift'. Maddeningly, this aspect of the backstory is never fully clarified.)

The First appears as Buffy and Eve in this episode.

Work is a Four-Letter Word: The construction site where the Scoobies hide is, Xander notes, the new Sunnydale Public Library. It is due to open in May 2003. That is, if he ever gets back to work on it (however, see **144**, 'Chosen').

It's a Designer Label!: Watch out for Buffy's way-cool leather jacket, Anya's red coat and Dawn's ginger sweater.

References: 'Here endeth the lesson' is a quote from *The Untouchables* (previously used by both the Master in **12**, 'Prophecy Girl', and Spike in **85**, 'Fool For Love'). There are allusions to *The Land That Times Forgot*, *The Spy Who Came In From the Cold*, *The Thing* ('it could be any one of us'), Frankie Goes to Hollywood's 'Welcome To The Pleasuredome', *WWF Smackdown* and *Mad Max Beyond Thunderdome*.

Geek-Speek: Andrew's description of how bored he is involves a simile to *Star Wars Episode One: The Phantom Menace*. Harsh, but fair. Buffy asks Andrew if he ever saw the movie *Misery*. He replies that he did, six times. But he believes Stephen King's novel is much scarier. Then he realises that Buffy is threatening him with something similar to what Kathy Bates did to James Caan in the movie and quickly shuts up. After Buffy's inspiring speech to the potentials about sticking together, Andrew adds that the Justice League put aside their differences to stop the Imperium and his shapeshifting alien horde. Also, references to *Star Trek* ('deflector shields up'), James Bond producers Albert and Barbara Broccoli, the movie *Licence To Kill* and its star Timothy Dalton (Andrew's admiration for whom had previously been mentioned in **105**, 'Life Serial') and 'Six Degrees of Kevin Bacon'.[58]

Bitch!: Giles finally persuades Torg to open Beljoxa's Eye with a promise that Buffy won't kill all his clientele and burn his establishment to the ground.

Awesome!: Buffy's brilliant coup, with Willow and Xander's telepathic aid, to inspire the potentials. In the episode's best scene Andrew and Dawn discuss why the Slayer is always a girl (and not, for instance, a *Silent Warrior*-style boy-ninja – hopefully with kung-fu moves somewhat more impressive than Andrew's). Dawn alleging that Buffy told her if Andrew spoke too much, Dawn had permission to kill him. Also, Buffy's knife throw that kills the Bringer in the pre-title sequence.

'You May Remember Me From Such Films and TV Series As . . .': Felicia Day appeared in *They Shoot Divas Don't They?* Amanda Fuller's CV includes *That 70s Show* and *Til There Was You*. Indigo (real name Alyssa Ashley Nichols) played Cheyenne Webb in *Boston Public*. Lalaine Vergara-Paras was Miranda in *Lizzie McGuire* and also appeared in *You Wish!*

'West Hollywood': There are some further, slyly homoerotic, allusions concerning Andrew and Xander ('Watch it. That's my joystick hand', 'Not touching that one').

Logic, Let Me Introduce You to This Window: After Buffy stabs the Turok-Han in the eye with an arrow, in the next shot the arrow is still, visibly, in her hand. There's no morphing sound effect when the First, as Eve, becomes Buffy. It then appears to touch Spike's face, despite being non-corporeal. The Turok-Han cannot be killed with a stake (see **132**, 'Bring on the Night'). So why did Molly bring a stake with her? Stupid girl. From where did Molly and Kennedy get the fresh clothes that they wear in this episode? When they arrived with Giles, neither appeared to be carrying any luggage. Molly's accent changes from bad cockney to bad West Country at one point. Seemingly, the First was in 1630 Revello Drive for at least two days, posing as Eve. Yet during that time it managed to avoid touching anything or anyone (note, for instance,

---

[58] Also known as 'Six Degrees of Separation', a much-played party game for movie-nerds everywhere.

that the first time we see Eve she's sitting on the floor between Chloe and Vi and is within centimetres of both). After Buffy and Xander find Eve's body and return home, Buffy enters her house by herself. Where did Xander go? Buffy then goes downstairs with Dawn, Willow and Andrew to confront the First. Xander suddenly reappears on the stairs behind her. When the Turok-Han enters the house Buffy isn't wearing a jacket. She and the others run outside and begin fighting the Bringers and suddenly Buffy *is* wearing one. Vi's Watcher once showed her a blurry photo of a vampire. As previously noted, vampire's should not photograph *at all*. How can Buffy use a piece of barbed wire to garrotte the Über-Vamp without cutting her own hands to ribbons?

I Just *Love* Your Accent: Anya tells Rona that peckish is English for hungry.

Quote/Unquote: Buffy: 'Next time you're attacked . . .' Rona: 'You saying I'm gonna get attacked again?' Buffy: 'Welcome to the Hellmouth!'

Anya refers to the demon community. Xander: 'They're a *community* now? What next, a ladies' auxiliary?'

Notes: 'The time has come for all good children to say goodnight.' 'Showtime' opens with a quintessential *Buffy* set-piece, full of action and wit. The episode, thereafter, is something of a curate's egg, parts of which are as good as anything we've seen this season but which, overall, doesn't quite live up to its potential. The, long overdue, exploration of the Slayer-myth is well handled. There's a clever discussion about whether the younger or older apprentices are likely to be the next chosen and about the vastly differing levels of training that each of them possesses. The centrepiece battle with the Über-Vamp, and the subsequent freeing of Spike from his underground torture chamber, however, are somewhat disappointing. All it takes to defeat the Über-Vamp, seemingly, is a bit of barbed-wire-related decapitation.

Willow tells Kennedy that Giles has the Coven (see **121**, 'Two To Go'; **123**, 'Lessons') searching for other potential Slayers. One of the group, Althenea, speaks to Willow on the phone. Kennedy has a half-siser. She seems to be from a rich family background, noting that the house she grew up in had at least two wings. They also had a summer house in the Hamptons. She has been proficient with a crossbow since she was eight. Beljoxa is an oracle-like creature that exists inside a dark dimension. Or, according to

Anya, an eternal vortex. Andrew has an inner-ear infection that makes him nervous of heights.

Some of the location filming for this episode, which had originally taken place on 26 November, had to be remounted on 14 December during the filming of **134**, 'Potential'.

Critique: In the UK magazine *Word*, acclaimed rock critic Charles Shaar Murray noted that genre TV has no right to be *this* good. '*Buffy* and *Angel* have taken long-running episodic fantasy television to its highest artistic peak while avoiding the Scylla of triviality and the Charybdis of pomposity.'

During their final issue of 2002, the *Toronto Star* jointly recognised *Buffy* and *Friends* with an award for 'The Best Comeback After a Slump'.

Did You Know?: 'I don't smoke at all. I've got the patch on now,' James Marsters told a convention audience in 2002. 'I smoke herbal cigarettes. My biggest problem with this is they don't show up on film as well as tobacco smoke [which is] heavy and beautiful.' Marsters also noted that he first became interested in acting when he was in the Fourth Grade. 'I got bitten really early. There's a beautiful film called *Illumanata*. One of first nights I went over to Joss's house, he showed me that movie. It gives you insight into his kind of whole mind-frame about his little company of *Buffy* which is a bunch of theatre nerds who are weird, kinky, strange and outcasts. We're all freaks. None of us were popular in high school.'

Marti Noxon's Comments: 'It is such a melding of different genres and it hits on different levels. There are other shows that are beautifully written and have loyal followings, but I think that one of the great things about watching *Buffy* is that we continue to get the opportunity to subvert people's expectations,' Marti told *SciFi.com*. 'It's such a rich universe that Joss created, that people get really addicted to it. As much as that would sound weird to someone who has never seen the show and only watched *The West Wing*.'

Joss Whedon's Comments: 'I love the function that horror performs, the metaphors. I don't like gore [or] misogyny, I don't like many of the things you find in bad horror movies,' Joss revealed in an interview with *Go Memphis*. 'In the early days, people would send me severed doll's heads. I'm not one of those kinds of aficionados.'

134
Potential

US Transmission Date: 21 Jan 2003
UK Transmission Date: 3 Apr 2003

Writer: Rebecca Rand Kirshner
Director: James A Contner
Cast: Derek Anthony (Imposing Demon)

While Buffy and Spike commence the training of the potential Slayers, Willow attempts a locator spell and discovers another potential is resident in Sunnydale. Remarkably, it seems that Dawn Summers has been chosen as one of her sister's possible successors.

Dudes and Babes: The apprentices just *love* hanging out with Spike. What teenage proto-killing machine, in all honestly, wouldn't? They also, judging from telephone comments that Buffy makes to Xander, seem more than a little interested in the Xan-Man too; some of them walked in on him while he was taking a shower. Giles, meanwhile, has been in Shanghai, to find another potential, Chao-Ahn (see **135**, 'The Killer in Me').

Andrew considers the calling of the Slayer as a superb metaphor for womanhood. A flowering that happens when a girl realises that she is part of a fertile heritage stretching back to Eve. (Yet another Judaeo-Christian allusion in the, supposedly, humanist *Buffy*-universe. See also **2**, 'The Harvest'; **15**, 'School Hard'; **103**, 'After Life'; **129**, 'Conversations With Dead People' etc.)

Amanda (**126**, 'Help') sees Buffy in her counselling role again and suggests that people think she's weird. It is subsequently revealed that she, and not Dawn, is a potential Slayer. Encouraged by Dawn, Amanda unleashes her fiery wrath in a battle with three Bringers and a vampire.

This author remains, frankly, annoyed that Molly isn't *dead* yet. Although, even he isn't immune to the charm of her fishnet tights and miniskirt.

A Little Learning is a Dangerous Thing: Dawn's school lab-partner, Margo, is – allegedly – a freak who once fainted during a dissection.

Denial, Thy Name is Dawn: Dawn is overwhelmed by the revelation that she may be a potential Slayer. Both Xander and

Willow see the positive side of this avenue, although Anya, perhaps inevitably, notes some of the negatives (a shortened lifespan for one).

The Conspiracy Starts at Home Time: Since the destruction of the Über-Vamp in the last episode, the First's manic activities appear to have been scaled down. However, Buffy and her friends realise that the First has not simply abandoned its apocalyptic plans. They determine, therefore, to use this opportunity to schedule training for the potential Slayers.

Amanda tells Dawn about some of the rumours circulating town concerning Buffy. Some people believe that Buffy is a kind of high-functioning schizophrenic. Others, however, clearly know she has abilities of some description and that she can help with problems of the more unusual kind. (This ties in with information gleamed from **54**, 'The Prom' and **93**, 'I Was Made To Love You', which indicate that many of Sunnydale's inhabitants, particularly those of Buffy's own age group, know that she's different from other girls.)

It's a Designer Label!: Impressive items include Kennedy's pink vest, Molly's 'Bonjour Paris!' T-shirt and Willow's cute black and silver top.

References: These include *Top Gun*, singer Chaka Khan, *The Guinness Book of Records*, Orville Redenbacher popcorn, *Batman* ('holy crap!'), *Star Wars*, the Masons and their secret handshake, the History Channel, *Anywhere But Here*, *Alien*, *The Thing* and the Pope. Buffy gets Clem to scare the potentials with a sight-gag straight out of *Beetlejuice*.

Geek-Speek: Andrew insists to Buffy that he's reformed, like Vagita from *Dragon Ball Z*. He used to be a pure Sayan, he continues, but now he fights on the side of Goku.

Awesome!: Vi's little squeal as, she believes, Spike is about to bite her. Anya's tactlessness when Dawn's apparent destiny is revealed. The juxtaposition between the potentials first fight with a vampire and Dawn and Amanda facing another one in the school.

'You May Remember Me From Such Films and TV Series As . . .': Derek Anthony appeared in *The District*.

The Drugs Don't Work: Amanda doesn't know if Buffy and her friends are into drugs. However, she suspects the worst when she's hit by a strange orange cloud and becomes, as she notes, dizzy and discombobulated.

Valley-Speak: Xander: 'No problemo.'

Not Exactly A Haven For The Sisters: During the pre-title sequence, Spike launches a surprise attack on Vi and Rona and tells the watching potentials that these two are now dead. When he asks why, Rona suggests that, traditionally, the black chick always gets it first.

Cigarettes and Alcohol: Buffy takes the potentials to a demon bar; it is, Vi notes, like a gay bar – only with demons. Drinks available include yak's urine shots and pig's blood spritzers. Spike says that, at the price they charge, punters should get human blood straight from the body.

Sex and Drugs and Rock'n'Roll: There are some nice metaphors, in Buffy's conversation with Amanda, surrounding the emotional (and, occasionally literal) sadomasochism inherent in many relationships. This occurs as Buffy and Spike are getting to the holding-hands stage in whatever it is that they share between each other these days. Some *Buffy* fans regarded this as sickening in a man who, under a year ago, was attempting to rape the object of his hand-holding (see **119**, 'Seeing Red'). Others, alternatively, see it as an example of the redemption that Spike's character has undergone and which Buffy talked about so eloquently in **131**, 'Never Leave Me'.

Logic, Let Me Introduce You to This Window: Amanda was outside the door when the spell was cast. Yet later that evening, Dawn and Amanda run into each other. Assuming that Dawn is walking away from her house, why would Amanda be going *back* to the Summers residence when she subsequently notes that she ran away from the orange glowing stuff? When Buffy dies, no new Slayer will be called (the line of succession now goes through Faith; that's been clearly established elsewhere). So why do both Buffy and Dawn say that a new Slayer will be called when she dies? Where is Chloe? Xander isn't exactly hurrying when arriving at the school on a rescue mission. How did he and, indeed, Buffy and Spike know that this was where Dawn would be? Amanda's forehead cut disappears in some shots.

Xander's Special Moment: As Dawn sits, somewhat disappointed that she isn't after all to be potential Slayer, Xander notes that most of their group are special. But not one of them, not even Buffy, knows how much harder it is for him and for Dawn. For seven years he's watched his friends become powerful – a witch, a demon etc. Even Oz had his wolf-powers come a full moon. Xander is, ultimately, the guy who fixes the windows afterwards. Dawn points out that he did have some army training (see **18**, 'Halloween'). The others will never know how tough it is to be the one who *isn't* chosen, Xander continues. To live so near the spotlight and yet never step into it. Maybe this is Xander's power, suggests Dawn. Seeing and knowing (see **140**, 'Dirty Girls').

Cruelty To Animals: Andrew mentions how hard it is to kill a pig (see **131**, 'Never Leave Me').

Quote/Unquote: Anya, on Dawn becoming a potential: 'One moment you're this klutzy teenager with false memories and a history of kleptomania. Then, suddenly, you're a hero. With a much abbreviated lifespan!'

Rona: 'We're a bunch of fifteen-year-olds in a demon bar. How much blending did you think we were gonna do?'

Xander, to Dawn: 'I see more than anybody realises, cos nobody's watching me . . . You're not special. You're *extraordinary*.'

Notes: 'Death is what a Slayer breathes. What a Slayer dreams about when she sleeps. Death is what a Slayer lives.' A two-fronted assault on the concept of sleeping and awakening potential, Rebecca Kirshner's story contrasts one day in the rapidly changing lives of the four apprentice Slayers, and the equally brutal *cruciamentum* that Dawn goes through. The awakening of Slayer powers is, beautifully, described as a metaphor for emergent womanhood. Ultimately, in an episode full of false clues and double-bluffs, it's left to Xander, as so often in the past the true human heart of *Buffy*, to show Dawn where her *true* potential lies. All of this, plus a return for fan-favourite Clem, some clever observations on empowerment, and an acknowledgement of just how far Buffy, herself, has come on her journey to what is, in effect, motherhood. A rich, dark and complex episode that easily maintains the quality of this extraordinary year.

Buffy has a poster of a rainbow in her office. She considered Spike's crypt (which she saw quite a bit of in season six) to be 'comfy'. Andrew asks if Buffy intends to get the microwave fixed, a reference to **129**, 'Conversations With Dead People', in which

Dawn smashed it. (They appear to have bought a new one by **136**, 'First Date'.) Willow mentions that Dawn has the same blood as Buffy (see **91**, 'Blood Ties'). Amanda is in the school swing choir who have a rivalry with the marching band (see **9**, 'The Puppet Show'; **38**, 'Beauty and the Beasts'). Andrew seems very fond of the potentials (especially considering that he's gay). The dating of this episode is less clear than those previously: some time has obviously passed since **133**, 'Showtime' – note that all of Buffy and Spike's visible injuries have cleared up (although Spike still has some pain in his ribs). Also, Xander refers to 2003, indicating that both Christmas and New Year have passed and we're into January.

Soundtrack: 'I Love You' by Citizen Bird is heard in the demon bar.

Critique: What was missing during season six was not so much a sense of humour, noted Robert Bianco, as much as a sense of purpose. 'No such problem this season, as Buffy once again fights to save the world. Along with its spin-off, *Angel*, which is also having an exceptional season, *Buffy* remains TV's best developed and most entertaining fantasy.'

Mark Wyman considered that 'Potential's final scene was 'quietly powerful compensation' for the discovery that Dawn was not to be a potential Slayer. Calling this sequence 'an inspiring coda', Wyman described the episode, overall, as 'a confidence booster'.

Did You Know?: Initially conceived as a combination of Sid Vicious, Billy Idol and *The Lost Boys*-era Kiefer Sutherland, Spike was never intended to be a long-term character. 'I was told bluntly: "Dude, you're cannon fodder",' James Marsters told Richard Harrington. 'I did ten episodes and the story-arc was completed. They brought me back for an episode in season three and I thought, maybe I'll get one next year too.' It was, apparently, when Joss Whedon saw Spike portrayed as pitiful and human in **42**, 'Lover's Walk', that he realised the character could become sustainable.

Busty the Vampire Slayer: Sarah Michelle Gellar was, according to the *Sun*, 'gobsmacked' (what a marvellously Californian word that is) by a conversation she had with a total stranger at her LA gym. 'This girl was topless in the changing room and, out of the blue, asked me "What do you think of these? I've just had my boobs done." I hate fake breasts,' Sarah added, noting that 'if a tidal wave hits LA, just grab a fake boob for safety'.

Joss Whedon's Comments: Whatever small part of Joss is within the character of Buffy herself, Whedon has always argued that his true alter ego on the show is Xander. 'We pretty much made the statement when Dawn said, "That's your power, seeing everything",' Joss told *zap2it.com*. 'Basically that's me saying, "You're the writer, not the star." You couldn't have made him more mine [with] the writers' proxy than that.'

In an online interview with *SciFi Wire*, Joss noted that *Buffy* had, conceptually, exceeded all his expectations: 'It's been very close to what I envisioned, except that it grew up a lot more,' Whedon noted. 'When I started the show, I didn't know its full potential. I just had the basic notion of "It's tough to make it in high school, and it'll be funny, evolving, scary and hit on things that people can relate to".'

135
The Killer In Me

US Transmission Date: 28 Jan 2003
UK Transmission Date: 10 Apr 2003

Writer: Drew Z Greenberg
Director: David Solomon
Cast: Megalyn Echikunwoke (Wiccan Group Leader),
Rif Hutton (Initiative Commander), Terence Bernie Hines (Shop Keeper),
Anna Maria Maccarrone (Waitress)

After sharing a kiss with Kennedy, Willow is magically transformed into Warren and must confront both the loss of Tara and the rage within her that turned her into a murderer. Meanwhile, Spike's chip begins to malfunction and Buffy must ask the Initiative for help. Giles takes the potential Slayers on a journey of self-discovery just as the rest of the Scoobies begin to suspect that their mentor may be a manifestation of the First.

Dudes and Babes: Willow's mother (see **46**, 'Gingerbread') is said to be proud of her daughter's gayness, considering it a form of political statement which is an interesting parallel to some of the accusations from less enlightened fans concerning the production team's own nervousness about tackling the subject. Nevertheless, Willow notes that her mother barely even knew Tara.

As the Scoobies discuss the forthcoming trip, Molly and Rona are said to be in the car fighting over who gets to drive the first leg. Anya subsequently notes that Rona won and locked Molly in the trunk.

A Little Learning is a Dangerous Thing: Giles is taking the potentials into the desert to perform the vision-quest. The girls need this trip to understand the source of their power and how to use it. Giles is alarmed to discover that someone has, apparently, told the potentials that the vision-quest consists of Giles doing the hokey-pokey until a spooky-rasta-máma-Slayer appears and talks to them in riddles (see **96**, 'Intervention').

Denial, Thy Name is Willow: Amy cast a penance malediction on Willow some time after the events of **122**, 'Grave'. This simply waited for Willow to find an excuse to punish herself, the spell taking Willow's thoughts and making them manifest. Thus, when Willow and Kennedy kissed, the repressed guilt and rage inside Willow over what she did to Warren (**120**, 'Villains') and her belief that, by kissing another woman, she is effectively accepting Tara's death turn her, quite literally, into the man that she killed.

The Conspiracy Starts at Home Time: Spike's brain chip begins to malfunction.

It's a Designer Label!: Highlights include Giles's sheepskin coat, Amy's cleavage-revealing black dress, Willow's red shirt, Dawn's black blouse and Buffy's denim jacket.

References: Kennedy notes that she first discovered her true sexual orientation when she saw Vivienne Leigh's performance as Scarlett O'Hara in *Gone With the Wind* as a five-year-old. She says that Willow always turns off the *Moulin Rouge* DVD at chapter 32 so that the movie has a happy ending. Also, allusions to *Ghostbusters* ('who you gonna call?'), *Pulp Fiction*, *A Shot in the Dark*, *Death Line*, *Hex* and *Sleeping Beauty*.

Geek-Speek: Andrew collects the classic Alan Moore comic *The League of Extraordinary Gentlemen* (as, seemingly, does Xander).

Bitch!: Vi leaves her notebook next to the TV. Giles asks Dawn if she would take it out to the car. And, perhaps, whack Vi over the head with it as a reminder not to leave it lying about. Dawn seems quite prepared for that eventuality.

Awesome!: The half of the conversation that we hear when Buffy tries to telephone Riley and the Initiative. And the scene when the Initiative actually turn up ('Government conspiracy! I knew it!'). The moment when Willow, inhabiting Warren's body, establishes to her friends that she is, in fact, herself. She notes that there are non-yellow-crayon stories from kindergarten (see **122**, 'Grave') in which Xander doesn't come out in nearly such a good light (particularly an incident involving Aquaman underwear).

'You May Remember Me From Such Films and TV Series As . . .': Megalyn Echikunwoke played Shannon in *BS** and Nicole Palmer in *24*. She also appeared in *Funny Valentines*. Rif Hutton's CV includes *JAG*, *The Thirteenth Floor*, *Doogie Howser MD* and *LA Law*. Terence Bernie Hines's movies include *Identity*.

The Drugs Don't Work: Since she was last seen (in **112**, 'Doublemeat Palace'), Amy has joined the UC Sunnydale Wiccan group (**66**, 'Hush') because, she says, she wants to control her previously reckless use of magic. Much of the episode works as a pointed metaphor concerning the horrors of addiction (see also **109**, 'Smashed'; **110**, 'Wrecked'). Amy's conversation with Kennedy is particularly interesting. In it, she speaks of her anger that, despite Willow surrendering far more to the dark side than Amy herself ever did, Willow was still accepted and helped by her friends while Amy was faced with a more difficult and painful rehabilitation alone.

Valley-Speak: Andrew: 'Are things always that wackadoo around here?' Anya: 'Ha! Newbie.'

Lesbian Sex and Drugs and Rock'n'Roll: Having truanted from the field trip, Kennedy takes Willow to the Bronze where they discuss their sexuality. Willow notes that she has been gay for three years and that she only ever loved one woman. Kennedy says that they like the same things: Italian food, skate punk, Robert Parker mysteries and fighting evil. Willow points out that she, actually, only enjoys the last of those. And even then, she prefers a nice foot massage. Then they kiss and hijinx ensue. Kennedy considers that Willow is sexy when she pouts, and that her freckles are 'lickable'. Buffy is, seemingly, aware that Willow is attracted to Kennedy long before Willow is herself. Willow is ultimately saved from the spell by a second kiss.

Cigarettes and Alcohol: At the Bronze, Willow and Kennedy drink orange-coloured cocktails with little umbrellas in them.

Logic, Let Me Introduce You to This Window: The underground Initiative complex was supposedly filled with concrete (**77**, 'Primeval'). Andrew puts his hand on Warren, but from a different angle; the next shot shows him reaching out to do so. The length of Amy's crystal necklace changes from scene to scene. When Amy transports Kennedy to the garden, Kennedy arrives in broad daylight. This means that several hours must have passed during transit. Giles hasn't renewed his Californian driver's licence but, so long as he still has a valid British one, that shouldn't prevent him from driving in the US. How was Willow able to buy a gun without encountering the mandatory 72 hours waiting period? That's compulsory in all states of the US. (Is it because Warren was an existing customer and had, therefore, passed all of the various checks?) Robson seemingly survived the events of **130**, 'Sleeper'. However, he's waited a long time to try to contact Buffy and her friends to warn them of the potential danger in their midst (see **132**, 'Bring on the Night', concerning the various dating problems in these episodes). Sarah Michelle Gellar clearly had a cold during the filming of this episode (this is particularly noticeable in the opening scene). What is the source of the red light that features prominently inside the, supposedly, long-abandoned Initiative complex?

Quote/Unquote: Buffy: 'We'll get the gang on it, hit serious research mode.' Spike: 'Try "behavioural modification software through the ages".'

Kennedy: 'You turned into a guy. If you take a step back, seriously, there's a certain element of humour here.' Willow: 'I killed him. It's hard to see the chuckles.'

Xander: 'You're not coming.' Andrew: 'Why? Cos I used to be evil?' Xander: 'Actually, no, cos you're annoying.'

Giles: 'You thought I was evil because I took a group of young girls on a camping trip and *didn't* touch them?'

Notes: 'Remember when things used to be nice and boring?' Starting with one of the longest ever '*Previously on Buffy*' recap-segments, covering almost seven years' worth of plots, 'The Killer in Me' sees the necessary tying up of some long-term loose ends. A *Buffy* version of *The Empire Strikes Back*, if you like, only, hopefully, without the disappointment of *Return of the Jedi* to come. We're treated to welcome return visits from fan-favourite Amy Madison, a sampling of the Wanna-Blessed-Be's from **66**, 'Hush', the Initiative and a restaging of the final moments of **119**,

'Seeing Red', in all its disturbing glory. Giles takes most of the potential Slayers to the desert to do the 'hokey-pokey' thing from **96**, 'Intervention', leaving the Scoobies with some free time. So far, so good. But, Spike's malfunctioning chip, Amy's hard-core desire for revenge and Willow's Third-World-country-sized guilt complex over previous misdeeds cause awkward complications. There's one truly great sequence in which Xander, Anya, Dawn and Andrew try to find out if Giles is non-corporeal evil, or otherwise. Elsewhere, the story somewhat meanders around the important stuff. Willow's growing relationship with the pouty, empathic proto-Slayer, Kennedy, is starting to bear fruit, although it's used as a redemptive key in a story about the extremes of emotion that some fans loudly (and vocally) hated. So, nothing new there. Willow, ultimately, finds a sort of redemption. That she achieves this through love and by, conceptually, experiencing Warren's grief over his killing of Tara should be a final, and welcome, nail in the coffin of those homophobia charges (see **120**, 'Villains'; **122**, 'Grave'). If only for that reason, 'The Killer in Me' deserves much praise. That, and Giles touching and being touched of course.

Spike is currently sleeping on a camp bed in Buffy's basement. Giles mentions several things which are unlikely to go wrong in his absence: Buffy getting shot (**119**, 'Seeing Red'), her throwing everyone in the basement and trying to kill them (**117**, 'Normal Again') and Willow turning evil (**120**, 'Villains'). Buffy is given the option by the Initiative of either repairing Spike's malfunctioning chip or having it removed. She chooses the latter (see **136**, 'First Date'). The Initiative officer to whom Buffy speaks notes that Riley referred to Hostile 17 as 'ass-face' (see **115**, 'As You Were'). There is, Buffy notes, nothing good on TV tonight. Willow alludes to the events of **108**, 'Tabula Rasa'. Presumably, at some point during this episode, Dawn received a, very brief, telephone call from Angelus (see *Angel*: 'Salvage'). Kennedy has a brother who is a vegan. The campus Wiccans still have bake sales on the second Tuesday each month.

Soundtrack: In the Bronze, Aberdeen perform 'Sink Or Float' and 'Cities And Buses'.

Critique: 'After so many weeks of keeping us waiting over the fate of Giles, it's surprising and refreshing to see the conclusion of the storyline played for comic relief,' noted John Binns.

'The writers have led us exactly where they wanted to with the

Giles storyline, and he's given one of his best ever lines,' noted Paul Spragg. 'Few things are scarier in *Buffy* than someone with a gun.'

Did You Know?: 'When I'm here, I do touristy things,' Alyson Hannigan told *The Times* on a trip to London. 'I shop at Marks & Spencer – I love the custard pies – and often hire a car to drive out of the city.' On a previous trip, Alyson went to Ireland to search out the Hannigan family history. 'I drove down the M4, into Wales, took a ferry over and ended up in Cork,' she noted. 'I thought I was a lot more Irish than I really am. I'm a weak drinker – one glass of wine or Guinness and I am fuzzed.'

Joss Whedon's Comments: Concerning Joss's frustration with those who mistake his creations for guilty pleasures, he told the *Must-See Metaphysics* website that 'I hate it when people talk about *Buffy* as being campy. I *hate* camp. I don't enjoy dumb TV. I believe Aaron Spelling has single-handedly lowered SAT scores.' Nevertheless, Whedon uses the medium forcefully. 'It's better to be a spy in the house of love,' he says. 'If I produced *Buffy the Lesbian Separatist*, a series of lectures on PBS [about] why there should be feminism, no one would be coming to the party. The idea of changing culture is important to me [but] it can only be done in a popular medium.'

136
First Date

US Transmission Date: 11 Feb 2003
UK Transmission Date: 17 Apr 2003

Writer: Jane Espenson
Director: David Grossman
Cast: Ashanti (Lissa)

Buffy goes on a date with Robin Wood in an attempt to discover if he has any hidden secrets. After they are attacked by vampires he reveals that he is the son of a former Slayer. Xander, too, finds himself a date. However, the gorgeous Lissa's interest in *him* is much more pragmatically demonic. Meanwhile, the First contacts Andrew in another attempt to destroy the potentials.

Dudes and Babes: With Robin Wood's office being situated directly over the Hellmouth (see **123**, 'Lessons'), Buffy considers that the principal may be what she describes as a bidet of evil. But she's prepared to take the risk; like many unattached people in their mid twenties who have been burned before, she's desperate for a lasting relationship. Once the date begins, however, Buffy discovers a *huge* revelation about Wood's past and motivations.

A Little Learning is a Dangerous Thing: Willow and the girls are unable to find any computer records of Robin Wood prior to his recent move to Sunnydale. As it turns out, there is a reason for this: Wood's mother was Nikki, the Slayer killed by Spike in New York in 1977 (see **85**, 'Fool For Love'; **139**, 'Lies My Parents Told Me'). She died when Robin was four and he was raised by Nikki's Watcher (see **126**, 'Help'; **139**, 'Lies My Parents Told Me'). Robin went through a rebellious vengeance phase in his twenties, slaying as many vampires as he could on the assumption that, eventually, he'd find the one who killed his mother. Wood admits that, although he enjoys his day job, he manoeuvred himself into his position at Sunnydale High specifically to be near to the Hellmouth, just as he manoeuvred Buffy into *her* job (much to Buffy's disappointment – she thought that she'd been hired for her counselling skills). Wood, like many on the periphery of the demon underworld, knows that something big and nasty is coming soon. A Slayer's children do not, seemingly, inherit their mother's supernatural powers (although Robin is said to be the only known offspring of a Slayer, so maybe he's the exception rather than the rule).

At the episode's climax, the First appears to Wood in the guise of his mother. Wood knows that he's being manipulated but is nevertheless grateful to be given the knowledge that he has sought all of his adult life: the identity of Nikki's killer.

Work is a Four-Letter Word: Lissa asks Xander if he can recommend a strong type of rope. Xander notes that this depends on the purpose for which she needs it: something functional or recreational. By which, he quickly adds, he means boating or mountain climbing. As opposed to tying up someone for bondage-type shenanigans. At this point, they arrange to meet for coffee.

Denial, Thy Name is Xander: In his conversation with Buffy and Willow, Xander speculates that if Lissa is interested in him then, chances are, she's a demon. But, as ever, he's hopeful that she may be an ordinary woman. Lissa, inevitably, turns out to be the former: a yellow-eyed demon who wants to open the Seal and raise a Turok-Han of her own for the coming war. Poor Xander. Maybe he's right; perhaps there *is* something about him that genuinely makes him a magnet for demons (see **65**, 'Something Blue'). It's noticeable that just about every girlfriend he's ever had has ended up trying to kill him. Except for Cordelia, of course. But even then, if we take the world that Anya created from Cordy's wish in **43**, 'The Wish', as a literal presentation of her deep-rooted fantasies, she too had the same idea (Xander, of course, is a vampire in that episode). After the horrors of **4**, 'Teacher's Pet'; **28**, 'Bewitched, Bothered and Bewildered'; **49**, 'Consequences' and **116**, 'Hell's Bells', it's hardly surprising what comes next.

'West Hollywood': Returning home, Xander begs Willow to make him gay in a bizarre rant that is sure to have numerous slash-fiction authors planning an *Enterprise* crossover on a website near you very soon.

The Conspiracy Starts at Home Time: When the First asks Andrew to kill the potential slayers, Andrew demands to know the purpose of this. The First, in the form of Jonathan, explains that they are the future of the Slayer line. When they're gone, the line will end. So, why not have Spike do the dirty deed? Andrew asks. The First notes that it's not yet time for Spike to re-enter the game. Andrew then asks whether the First has any inherent weaknesses that he should be aware of and if the entity is composed of the evil impulses of all humanity. The First realises that Andrew is no longer under its control and is wired up to gain information.

It's a Designer Label!: Anya tries to get rid of a red stain on Buffy's shirt. She says that it's either blood or pizza. This appears to be the pizza stain that Dawn got on the same shirt in **129**, 'Conversations With Dead People'. Also, Anya's pink top with poodles on it, Lisa's slinky black dress, Kennedy's extremely tight blouse and Buffy's chunky sweater. However, what on earth is Buffy wearing on her date? It's a mad combination of a stylish black top and shabby jeans. Not so much ambiguous as sloppy. If Xander succeeds in getting Willow to turn him gay then, as he notes himself, he'll need a whole new stylish wardrobe.

References: Allusions to *Joe Millionaire*, the Industrial Revolution, the *Friends* episode 'The One With Monica's Thunder', *JFK*,

Picket Fences, Matthew 6:23 ('get thee behind me'), *From Beyond the Grave*, the Google search engine, A Taste of Honey's 'Boogie, Oogie, Oogie', Kryptonite and *Quantum Leap* and *Enterprise* star Scott Bakula.

Bitch!: Spike: 'You tried to record the ultimate evil? Why? In a complex effort to royally piss it off?'

Awesome!: Chao-Ahn's subtitles and Giles's unhelpful flashcards (see **66**, 'Hush'). One of the finest ever scenes involves Buffy and Xander telling Willow about their respective dates and speculating on whether there's likely to be evil activity involved; about five minutes of sparkling dialogue, witty allusions and beautiful characterisation, an example of Espenson at her finest. Also, Andrew's description of the contents of Buffy's underwear drawer. Does she really wear thongs?

'You May Remember Me From Such Films As . . .': KD Aubert's movies include *The Scorpion King* and *DysEnchanted*. Kirsty Wu played Jenny in *What's Cooking?*

Don't Give Up The Day Job: Soul diva Ashanti Douglas is best known for hits such as 'Foolish', 'Always On Time' and 'What's Luv?'

Valley-Speak: Buffy: 'My bad.'

Not Exactly A Haven For The Watchers: Giles notes that he hates the Sunnydale Mall (see **26**, 'Innocence'). The clerks are rude and everything in the food court is sticky.

Sex and Drugs and Rock'n'Roll: Giles believes that it doesn't matter if Buffy and Spike are intimate with each other as there is now a connection between them. They rely upon each other and this, Giles notes, it what affects Buffy's judgement in all matters related to Spike. They then have a lengthy discussion on the old soul-versus-chip debate (see **92**, 'Crush', and most of the episodes in season six). Note, also, that when Buffy tells Spike about her forthcoming date and Spike says that he is genuinely fine with this information, Buffy looks rather disappointed.

Buffy alleges that Willow and Kennedy hold hands with each other under the dinner table and think that nobody else notices. Willow suggests that Buffy could be considered a frisky vixen by any potential boyfriend.

Logic, Let Me Introduce You to This Window: After overpowering Giles in the graveyard, Spike notes that Anya told him Giles was the First. However, Anya, Xander and the others didn't even consider that Giles might be evil until after Spike and Buffy had left for the Initiative (see **135**, 'The Killer in Me'). They subsequently disproved this theory long before they would have encountered Spike and Buffy again. Even if Spike *had* been told this, how did he expect to tackle a non-corporeal opponent? (Giles even asks this question. Spike doesn't have an answer.) Willow tries to call Buffy, gets no answer, so Spike leaves immediately to find her. Later, when Buffy asks Spike how he knows where Xander is being held, he replies that Willow used a locator spell. When? In **132**, 'Bring on the Night', the Turok-Han didn't come out of the Hellmouth until the seal was fully opened. Why didn't the Turok-Han's arm turn to dust when the seal amputated it? If that particular dark alley is so infested with the vampires, how does anyone get into the restaurant without getting killed? It should have gone out of business long before now, surely, even if it is the best in town. When Buffy and Wood enter the alley, the first vampire who comes around the corner is not among the five that they subsequently kill. How could Xander text-message Willow while being suspended by Lissa? Doesn't Wood notice Spike's lack of a reflection in his car's rear-view mirror? Xander is bound to the wheel by both his hands and feet. But Wood only cuts the ropes on his hands to free him. Wood then tells Buffy that he believes her friend will be OK. This suggests that he's never previously met Xander. Which is highly unlikely as Xander is in charge of construction at Wood's school.

I Just *Love* Your Accent: Giles calls Spike a berk (see **52**, 'Earshot').

Quote/Unquote: Willow: 'How about yours, Xander? Is she evil?' Xander: 'She's interested in me, so there's a good chance. But I'm hoping for the best.'

Andrew: 'What do you want from me, Jonathan-slash-the-First?!' And: 'I'm frightened and my chest hurts where the tape was.'

Anya, to Buffy: 'Fine, leave me to stew in my impotent rage . . . I'm also gonna pee, so you should probably go.'

Notes: 'It can't just keep happening that demon women are attracted to me.' Trust Jane Espenson to do an episode about the awkwardness of blind dating that comes three years after the Scooby Gang all ceased to be teenagers and left high school behind them. And, to make it funny, but also thickly layered with a mature intensity. 'First Date' is *Buffy* doing that old metaphor-thing again, sunk deep into the overall season-arc, but with enough stand-alone set-piece moments to attract those who find themselves outside the chalk-circle of rabid fandom. Elsewhere, Anya's jealousy over Xander is great and there are a few amusing moments with the new Chinese potential Slayer. These positive points are somewhat derailed by Giles trying to inject common sense into the comedy in a scene that is, frankly, badly overwritten. But Buffy's argument with Giles over her decision to remove Spike's chip in the previous episode is central to both the episode and the season's main themes. Spike can be a good man, Buffy argues, but only if he's given the chance to be. That's Jane Espenson's central philosophy for *Buffy*, made flesh.

Buffy mentions the skanky punk girl whom Spike took to Xander and Anya's wedding in **116**, 'Hell's Bells'. Giles says that he was able to survive the Bringers' attack on him (**130**, 'Sleeper') because he heard the man's shoes squeak. He speaks little Mandarin and almost no Cantonese. Like many Asians, Chao-Ahn is lactose-intolerant. The First Evil cannot be recorded on audiotape. In the opening scene, a grave with the inscription Snyder is briefly glimpsed. Presumably this contains whatever was left of the former principal who was eaten by Mayor Wilkins in **56**, 'Graduation Day' Part 2. Jonathan remembers Andrew crashing his jet-pack (**119**, 'Seeing Red'). When the First tells Andrew that Buffy will never allow him to join her gang because he's a murderer, Andrew notes that, actually, several of the Scoobies are: specifically Anya, Willow and Spike. Wood keeps a lethal collection of sharp weaponry behind a white board in his office.

Soundtrack: 'Ammunition' by Trembling Blue Stars and 'Still Life' by Patty Medina.

Critique: 'Despite being perpetually snubbed at the Emmy Awards, *Buffy* has become a critics' darling and inspired a fervent fan base among teenage girls and academics alike,' wrote online reviewer Emily Nassbaum. 'The show's influence can be felt everywhere on television these days, from tawdry knockoffs like *Charmed* to more impressive copycats like *Alias*.'[59]

Did You Know?: Fan Brianna Jacobson has flown 16,800 miles to and from Indianapolis to quench her addiction for *Buffy*. 'Conventions give me strength, mentally and emotionally,' Jacobson told the *Indiana Daily Student*. 'Plus it's an honor to meet all of the actors. They are so beautiful and interesting. I feel special and important when I meet that person.' This view was shared by another fan, Steve Cribb, who, according to *This is Lincolnshire*, was clearing out his collection of British comics to make room for his new obsession for *Buffy*. 'I've got posters of characters from the series all over my bedroom walls, some of the magazines and even a few autographs,' he noted. '*The Beano* was a good friend to me but I've moved on.'

Head On: 'The only reason I've been able to do [*Buffy*] is because of Sarah. She's been so tolerant. She was, basically, a single parent for six years but she was willing to do whatever it took,' Tony told the *Bristol Evening Post* concerning his partner, Sarah Fisher. Success in *Buffy* has meant that Tony spent over five years commuting between his West Country home and LA. He often spent as much as nine months a year away from his family. 'Every time I had six days off, I'd jump on a plane. We put the girls in American schools a couple of times, but I wouldn't want to raise children in the US. I think the upheaval would unbalance the family more than my being away.'

Cast and Crew Comments: 'It's really chaotic because there are all the Slayers coming in,' Alyson Hannigan told Kate O'Hare of

---

[59] Possibly the most obvious example of *Buffy*'s influence on US television, *Charmed* – produced by the Aaron Spelling organisation – joined *Buffy* on the WB in September 1998. Usually regarded by more myopic commentators as mere eye-candy, while *Charmed* undeniably lacks the quick-fire humour of *Buffy*, it *does* possess its own quietly confident and acid-tongued wit. It's true that *Charmed*'s attempts to straddle two vastly different genres has led to gross miscalculations of taste and, at its worst, *Charmed is* cosy and undemanding fluff. *Buffy-lite*, basically. However, *Charmed*'s coy aloofness in form and its frequent nods towards dysfunctional family values are often its salvation. Sometimes the series' pat characterisations and *deus ex machina* plots renders it gauche beside, for example, *Stargate SG-1*'s urbane recontextualisations of classic myths and positively anaemic compared to the sophisticated metaphors of *Buffy*. Nevertheless, it's a source of some annoyance to many fans that *Charmed* has always had higher ratings than *Buffy*, a fact that says much about the average television viewer's priorities.

zap2it.com. 'The other day, we had a six-page scene with twelve principals. It's insane. I'm sure that it's going to go off at the end of the year. Everybody's sort of expecting it to be the end. Knowing Joss, he'll just make it amazing . . . with the possibility that it could continue.'

Joss Whedon's Comments: During an online interview, Joss was asked what was the most difficult episode of *Buffy* to write or direct. His reply was **100**, 'The Gift', 'because it was right in the middle of the Fox/WB wars. My spirit left the building while I still had a week of filming to go.' That said, Whedon noted, they've all been hard to a greater or lesser degree. 'I've spent two weeks trying to rewrite half a page of somebody else's show and [on the other hand] written an episode of my own in three days. [Some] were challenges, like **66**, "Hush", and **94**, "The Body", and the musical. But I can't describe those as hard, because they were so much fun.'

137
Get It Done

US Transmission Date: 18 Feb 2003
UK Transmission Date: 24 Apr 2003

Writer: Douglas Petrie
Director: Douglas Petrie
Cast: Geoffrey Kasule (Shadow Man #1), Karara Muhoro (Shadow Man #2),
Daniel Wilson (Shadow Man #3)

Principal Wood gives Buffy a bag full of items that belonged to his mother. These include weapons, a book and a sealed box. Opening this, Buffy and her friends discover a portal to the distant past. There, Buffy meets the originators of the Slayer line: three Shadow Men who offer her power to fight the First Evil. But at a huge personal price.

Dreaming (As Blondie Once Said) is Free: The first Slayer comes to Buffy again in her dreams. Elements of the Slayer origin myth described in this episode tie in with the imagery previously seen in Buffy's dream in **78**, 'Restless'. In that, Buffy saw the first Slayer chained to the ceiling. Here, the Shadow Men chain her to the ground while they invoke a demon's spirit to enter her. The bag that Robin gives to Buffy is the same one that she pulled mud from to cover her face in 'Restless'. Also, when Buffy told Adam, 'We are not demons', he queried this suggestion. He was, seemingly, referring to the Slayer's power that, as this episode makes clear, was created via the essence of a demon.

No Fat Chicks: Well, not once Chloe has hanged herself, anyway . . .

Dudes and Babes: Buffy discovers the origins of the first Slayer and how this was achieved: by giving a primitive human girl the spirit of a demon. Buffy also learns that the girl did not volunteer for this responsibility but that it was forced upon her by the Shadow Men. This contradicts Buffy's previously stated belief that she herself does not have a dark side. This episode implies that such a juxtaposition somewhat goes with the Slayer territory. The meeting with the Shadow Men is important to Buffy in two specific ways. First, because she chooses not to accept their offer of more power to fight the First Evil, as this would require her to subjugate herself to a demon placed within her. And, second, Buffy begins to question the previously accepted idea of the One Slayer. This puts her on the road to the decision that she would subsequently make in **144**, 'Chosen', which effectively ends the male-dominated concept of what a Slayer was/is/will be. Thus, Buffy is able to deliver true empowerment to the sisterhood by her own actions.

A Little Learning is a Dangerous Thing: Magics work within the laws of physics, notes Willow. However, Anya adds that they only do so with the aid of a catalyst. If Willow is talking about transferring energies, she will need some kind of conduit. Among those mentioned are a Kraken's tooth, the skin of a Draconus and ground-up Baltic stones.

The language that the Shadow Men speak is Swahili, an East African dialect. The Summers household has translation dictionaries in Greek, French, Spanish and Norwegian.

The Conspiracy Starts at Home Time: Buffy is told by the Shadow Men that she is the Hellmouth's last guardian (technically, that's true – see **144**, 'Chosen').

The First appears as Chloe (she, apparently, convinced the girl to kill herself. That's the second time the entity has tried this stunt, but the first time that it's been successful. See **44**, 'Amends').

It's a Designer Label!: Buffy tells Principal Wood that he's a snappy dresser. Damn straight. Spike mentions to Wood that he acquired his leather coat in New York (see **85**, 'Fool For Love').

References: There's a John Barleycorn ornament outside Buffy's home that will be a familiar icon to anyone who's seen *The Wicker Man*. Willow alludes to *Bring It On*. Also, *Winnie the Pooh* and the character of Tigger, *The Muppet Show*, *Pulp Fiction*, 'Kumbaya' (see **107**, 'Once More, With Feeling'), *The Changes*, Joy Division's 'Shadow Play' and the movies of Bruce Lee (Wood's use of throwing stars). The final shot is a visual tribute to *The Lord of the Rings*.

Bitch!: During Buffy's bitter rant after Chloe's death, Xander asks her to remember that they are all Buffy's friends. Anya, surprisingly, says that she isn't. (She was happy enough to have Buffy as a bridesmaid a little under a year ago – see **116**, 'Hell's Bells'.) In which case, why are you here, asks Buffy? Besides requiring the occasional rescue, what does Anya actually contribute to the group? Anya notes that she provides much needed sarcasm. Xander is annoyed. He thought that was *his* job.

Awesome!: Andrew's oven-mitts and 'Big Board' (see **138**, 'Storyteller'). Willow's panicky babbling when she first meets Principal Wood. The two testosterone-charged confrontations between Wood and Spike. The book changing from Sumarian to English before Dawn's very eyes. And that amazing final shot.

'You May Remember Me From Such Films As . . .': Daniel Wilson appeared in *Almost Famous* and *Bloodfist*. Kahara Muhoro's movies include *Phone Booth*.

Not Exactly A Haven For Anyone: Wood tells Buffy about the increased tension at school: fighting in the cafeteria, vandalism and three students having gone missing. This is, seemingly, due to the malign influence of the Hellmouth and will be much worse by **138**, 'Storyteller'.

Sex and Drugs and Rock'n'Roll: Spike and Anya go out on what is, very definitely, a non-date for the sole purpose of getting drunk. At which, they both stress, there will be no sex either under, or on top of, tables (see **118**, 'Entropy').

Logic, Let Me Introduce You to This Window: Spike left his leather coat on Buffy's stairway banister before he attempted to rape her in **119**, 'Seeing Red'. When he subsequently left town on his motorcycle he was wearing a cloth jacket. The coat hasn't been seen since, so when did Spike go back to the Summers' house to retrieve it and then store it away in the school basement? When Buffy and Dawn discovered Chloe hanging in her room, the door behind them was open. In the next shot, it's closed. It seems rather unlikely that Dawn would be able to decipher the ancient text. When did she have the opportunity to learn an entire dead language? Why, other than brazen self-aggrandisement, has Kennedy suddenly assumed command of the other potentials? Who, exactly, made her Queen of the World? Also, when Buffy tells Dawn to get the potential Slayers upstairs while the Scoobies examine the contents of the bag, how come Kennedy is allowed to remain with them? It's because she's Willow's girlfriend, isn't it? How does Chao-Ahn know what Kennedy is saying during the training session? Anya says that she's a bright girl who had a good education. Is she talking about her 9th-century Nordic schooling, which would have been virtually non-existent, or her few months in 1999 at Sunnydale High when she was flunking math (see **50**, 'Doppelgängland')?

Quote/Unquote: Spike: 'You're like a dog with a bone.' Anya: 'So what?' Spike: 'It's *my* bone! Just drop it.'

Dawn: 'Did you know the ancient Sumerians didn't speak English?' Buffy: 'They're worse than the French.'

Xander: 'Every time instructions get cryptic, someone gets hurt. Usually me.'

Notes: 'The Hellmouth is starting its semi-annual percolation. It usually blows around May.' A brick in an imposing wall of aggressive plot, 'Get It Done' is a necessary, if somewhat unwelcome, arc-heavy deviation from the fun and games that surround it. The potential Slayer ranks have swollen into what is not far short of an army, but Buffy knows that even this isn't going to be anywhere near enough for the coming war. The shocking, lonely death of one of Buffy's young followers focuses the Slayer on the need to seek help via a supernatural route. A story about what it truly is to be a Slayer, 'Get It Done' sees Buffy learning that she is the Hellmouth's last guardian. Her speeches to her young charges may be starting to get broken record-like (something that the next episode openly acknowledges), but at least the story is moving forward. Elsewhere, the strain of Buffy's single-minded determination to find answers is beginning to take its toll on relationships within the group. Consequences do, indeed, arrive as the story takes time to restate and reintroduce several key elements from the series' own iconography. Filled with excellent in-jokes and well-drawn characterisation, here's another little piece of the puzzle, built on rocks, not sand.

Buffy has seemingly told Robin Wood that Spike is a vampire, albeit one with a soul. Much to Spike's obvious chagrin. Wood guesses that Spike was sired in the mid-to-late 19th century (see **85**, 'Fool for Love'). When Spike says he is more-or-less unique, he's seemingly referring to Angel also having a soul. Willow considers that Wood is much cooler than Mr Snyder. D'Hoffryn is *still* sending demons on missions to kill Anya (see **128**, 'Him'). Dawn reminds Buffy that their grandmother's closet smelled weird. There are dialogue allusions to the titles of several previous Buffy episodes (for example **9**, 'The Puppet Show' and **14**, 'Some Assembly Required').

The desert dream sequences were filmed in the Joshua Tree National Park, east of LA.

Cuts: The BBC's transmission of this episode, in December 2003, cut the sequences relating to the discovery of Chloe's body. Thus, viewers were treated to the baffling sight of Buffy burying someone and having absolutely no idea who for some time afterwards. On Sky One that sequence was left intact, although they *did* remove the masturbation line from **138**, 'Storyteller'.

Soundtrack: The song played in the UPN promo for this episode was 'Just A Little Girl' by Amy Studt. For subsequent trailers through to the end of the season, much use was made of Michelle Branch's excellent 'Goodbye To You' (see **108**, 'Tabula Rasa').

Critique: According to Martin O'Malley and John Pungente, in their book *More than Meets the Eye: Watching Television Watching Us*, *Buffy* comes closer to depicting the reality of teenage life than anything else on television. 'Don't be fooled by the weekly dose of vampires and monsters. The obvious joke has always been that vampirism and lycanthropy are metaphors for really raging hormones.' The essay also notes that, while other shows deal with teenage reality – issues like sex, peer pressure, school, family problems, body image, insecurity and self-esteem – *Buffy* adapts an existing literary and film genre for television. 'The vampire myth and the sexuality it evokes speak powerfully to today's teenagers.'

Did You Know?: Long before he dyed his hair, James Marsters was grooming his bad-boy image. First, as a rejected student from the famed acting school at Juilliard, then as a Chicago-based theatre actor. But he also had ambitions within a different field. With *Buffy*'s end in sight, James was planning to spend the summer of 2003 touring around Europe with his punk band Ghost of the Robot. How did that come about? 'Frankly, the initial interest is through *Buffy*,' James told the *Chicago Tribune*. 'We don't have a problem with that. We all have to eat. OK, so mine are paid for thanks to the show, but everyone else in the band has to eat.'

The End (Slight Return): In an exclusive, front-page *Buffy Quits* interview with *Entertainment Weekly* in March 2003, Sarah Michelle Gellar noted that, 'At the beginning of this season, Joss and I had a conversation outside my trailer. We both [acknowledged] that this was the end, that we should make that decision and say it publicly.' Among the reasons given by Gellar for her decision to quit the series was so that she could concentrate on her marriage to Freddie Prinze Jr. This news, reportedly, came as a shock to many working on the show. 'It wasn't that big of a surprise, but finding out from a magazine article, that *sucked*,' was, according to the Internet Movie Database, Alyson Hannigan's quoted opinion. 'I'm really upset that's the way the cast and crew found out they would be unemployed.' Alyson was reported to have added that neither she nor anyone else connected to the show had subsequently received an apology from Gellar.

Marti Noxon's Comments: 'The whole idea of being a superhero is the idea that you are unlike other people, and people are drawn to that, but at the same time, it makes you "the other". Someone that may have trouble relating,' Marti told CBC Radio's Mary O'Connell. 'It's inherently a lonely thing. I think it's Joss's life story. He's exceptionally brilliant and has abilities other people don't. He lives in a world where his brain functions faster than most people's. Not that he can leap tall buildings, but the more I look at Buffy's struggle, I see it as a study of being exceptional.'

Joss Whedon's Comments: In *SFX* magazine, Joss Whedon revealed that his favourite British TV show remains *Monty Python's Flying Circus* and that his favourite British swearword begins with a C and ends with a T. ('It's horrible when Americans say it, but oddly endearing with a British accent.') Expressing a love for *Once Upon a Time in the West*, *The Matrix*, Richard Slotkin's *Abe*, *The Simpsons* and Sean Connery's James Bond, Joss noted that he had always preferred the Beatles to the Rolling Stones and that his hero is Vincent Van Gogh ('he produced epic shit with zero approbation'). Neil Young's *Decade* was described as the record that had most changed Joss's life, while he considered Alexis Denisof to be the most underrated person on television. If Joss could live anywhere in the world, other than LA, he would choose London, he noted. Asked if he saw the influence of *Buffy* on other shows (*Smallville* was an example given), Whedon said that, sadly, he could. Finally, did Joss feel that Saddam Hussein might become a better person if he watched *Buffy*? 'It couldn't hurt,' he replied, adding that, 'Bush could probably use it, too.'

138
Storyteller

US Transmission Date: 24 Feb 2003
UK Transmission Date: 1 May 2003

Writer: Jane Espenson
Director: Marita Grabiak
Cast: Alan Loayza (Stressed Out Boy), Corin Amber Norton (Crying Girl),
Sujata DeChoudhury (Shy Girl), TW Leshner (Feral Teen),
Erik Betts (Vamp #2)[60]

Andrew creates *Buffy, Slayer of the Vampyres*, a video documentary describing the current situation in Sunnydale as a record for future generations. Meanwhile, the Seal of Danzalthar is causing outbreaks of manic violence and mystical occurrences at Sunnydale High. Buffy and Willow force Andrew to recall the circumstances that led to Jonathan's murder in an effort to find a way to close the seal and stop the madness.

Dreaming (As Blondie Once Said) is Free: Buffy tells Wood that she gets visions. He asks how she knows that they're not dreams. If you're running to catch the bus, naked, that's a dream, notes Buffy. She considers that an army of Über-Vamps is more likely to be a vision.

During Andrew and Jonathan's dream in Mexico, the Cheese Man from Buffy's dream in **78**, 'Restless', appears for a split second.

---

[60] Uncredited.

No Fat Chicks: Having managed to get the shy girl noticed and avoid a repeat of the infamous Marcie Ross incident (**11**, 'Out of Mind, Out of Sight'), Buffy is further troubled when another girl runs crying from the bathroom saying that a mirror told her she was fat (see **123**, 'Lessons').

Dudes and Babes: Andrew describes Anya as a feisty waif with a fiery temper and a vulnerable heart that she hides, even from herself. Wow, that's *deep*. Dawn, he adds, is a typical American teenager. Bubbly and sweet with a hunger for fun and a smile that lights up the room. Perceptive little cur, isn't he?

Willow and Kennedy have been in a bad place lately (subsequent to the events of **137**, 'Get It Done'). Kennedy pursued the reluctant Willow and won her broken heart, only to find herself frightened when she caught a glimpse of the darkness that still dwells within Willow's troubled mind. However, according to Andrew, things are now looking up.

Exposition!: Andrew, reasonably competently, explains the entire backstory vis-à-vis the First, the Bringers and the potential Slayers, with the visual aid of his Big Board (previously seen in **137**, 'Get it Done'). This is, presumably, just in case there are any casual viewers who have turned up and are having trouble following it all.

A Little Learning is a Dangerous Thing: All the Hellmouth's energy is trying to escape from one spot via the Seal of Danzalthar. Because of this, the hidden feelings of Sunnydale High's students are manifesting themselves. Buffy tells Principal Wood that if someone feels an emotion near to the Hellmouth, these are often made flesh. Buffy has seen such symptoms before, she notes, though never so many all at once. The students feel as though the teachers are out to get them, she adds. The chess club resents the French club for taking the activities room and *everyone* hates the cheerleaders. Being in high school can feel like being at war, Buffy concludes. In Mexico, Andrew told the First about a demon selling weapons, including a collapsible sword. In *Angel*: 'Spin The Bottle', Wesley bought and used just such a weapon. With hilarious consequences.

Denial, Thy Name is Andrew: Among the historical rewriting that Andrew indulges in – on camera – is his own, much less subordinate, position within the *troika*. (In his fantasy world, Andrew told Warren and Jonathan exactly what to do, and they did it.) And, also, his and Jonathan's confrontation with Dark Willow (see **121**, 'Two To Go'), which becomes a hilarious *The Lord of the Rings*-style battle between two massively powerful magicians.

The Conspiracy Starts at Home Time: When standing on the Seal of Danzalthar, Wood is temporarily possessed by the forces beneath. It's not a pretty sight.

It's a Designer Label!: Highlights include Andrew's velvet smoking jacket, Dawn's purple top and Willow's multicoloured blouse. Anya is a vision in red and white.

References: Books glimpsed in Andrew's imaginary room include *The Complete Works of William Shakespeare* and Friedrich Nietzsche's *Beyond Good and Evil*. There are vintage *Star Wars* posters on the walls. Also, the carol 'Good King Wensleslass' ('the wind was cruel') and 'La Cucaracha'. Visual references include *Planet of the Apes* and *The Usual Suspects* (Spike flicking his cigarette at the camera). Graffiti scrawled on the walls of Sunnydale High include 'No one gets out alive' (an allusion to the Doors' 'Five To One'; see **19**, 'Lie To Me'), 'Marching band rules!' and 'Die, cheerleaders, die.'

Awesome!: Andrew's Boris Karloff-style introduction and his ludicrous rewriting of both his own and the series' history (e.g. 'In my plan, we are *beltless*!'). The fantasy sequence relating to the heat between Buffy and, a shirtless, Spike. Plus, Anya eating grapes and winking at the camera. Andrew's observations on Buffy's motivational speeches (even Willow is looking bored, he notes). The beautiful completion of the Xander/Anya-circle that all viewers have been eagerly awaiting since **116**, 'Hell's Bells'. The *troika* 'living as *GODS*!' The exploding student. Andrew's tears closing the Seal and, thus, providing a kind of redemption for him after he has faced up to the terrible crime that he committed.

'You May Remember Me From Such Films and TV Series As . . .': Alan Loayza appeared in *Young McGyver* and *Candy*. Corin Norton's movies include *The Edge of the Midway*. TW Leshner was in *Judge Koan*.

Don't Give Up The Day Job: Erik Betts is a stuntman with credits on *Mr Deeds*, *Spy Hard*, *Alias* and *Martial Law*.

Cigarettes and Alcohol: Dawn loudly complains when Spike lights up in the kitchen. Note that, even in his fantasy, Andrew has problems smoking a pipe.

Sex and Drugs and Rock'n'Roll: Anya believes that Andrew videotaping himself in the toilet sounds like kinky business. Andrew films Xander and Anya in confessional mode; Xander believes that his decision not to marry Anya was the right one even though they still, clearly, love each other. Subsequently, the couple have fantastic sex (Anya considers that she's a spitfire in the bedroom). They then agree that it felt like a 'one last time'-style situation. And both are, actually, quite OK at such a positive closure to their relationship. (However, see **142**, 'Touched', for an utterly superb encore.)

'West Hollywood': After Andrew's memories of the *troika* at their most supervillain-y, he asks if his viewers considered Jonathan to be cute. Later, while Willow and Kennedy are, very visibly, making out on the couch, Andrew is much more interested in pointing his camera at the replacement windows which Xander fitted. And on observing what a good job Xander did on them and how talented he is.

Logic, Let Me Introduce You to This Window: Who's zooming the video camera in and out while Andrew is doing his exposition piece? When Buffy and Wood talk about the various mystical happenings, they do so with at least one secretary within earshot. Amanda has a mother (confirmed in **134**, 'Potential'). What sort of parent allows their daughter to stay overnight at someone else's house on a school night? How did Lissa open the Hellmouth seal with Xander's blood in **136**, 'First Date', when she was missing the third part of the ritual, the Tuaric blade? Also, what did the First use to make the markings on Spike's chest in **132**, 'Bring on the Night'? The blade was in Buffy's kitchen utensils drawer during this entire period. Andrew can read the language written on the dagger, but he had previously thought that the markings were merely symbols. That's all highly unlikely. Andrew asks why vampires show up on video (see **21**, 'What's My Line?' Part 1, and numerous other episodes). Good question and *still* unanswered in either *Buffy* or *Angel*. When the (non-corporeal) First, as Warren, appears to Andrew in Mexico, its footsteps can clearly be heard on the concrete floor.

Cruelty To Animals: The piglet that Andrew couldn't kill in **131**, 'Never Leave Me', is still running around in the school basement.

Quote/Unquote: Anya: 'You've been in there for thirty minutes. What are you doing?' Andrew: 'Entertaining and educating.' Anya: 'Why can't you just masturbate like the rest of us?'

Andrew, on Buffy: 'Honestly, gentle viewers, these motivating speeches of hers get a little long.'

Buffy: 'Willow did a search in the symbology databases. Turns out everyone loves goat's tongues. Rock groups, covens, Greek cookbooks.'

Andrew: 'Here's the thing. I killed my best friend. There's a big fight coming, and I don't . . . think I'm going to live through it. That's probably the way it should be.'

Notes: 'It's wonderful to get lost in a story, isn't it?' asks Andrew at the beginning of this extraordinary experiment in the complexities of narrative structure. A look into the elaborate fantasy world that Andrew Wells inhabits, 'Storyteller' is a riotous comedy episode of the kind that *Buffy* excels in. But it's a comedy which, even during its most absurd moments, never forgets the true darkness at its core. 'Life isn't a story,' says Buffy, bookending a tale in which Andrew attempts to film a video diary about the Slayer. His efforts bring, predictably, amusing results. Some of the Scoobies are quite flattered, and openly cooperate with him, mirroring the occasionally quasi-official nature of some unofficial works. Even Spike isn't immune to doing a retake if the video makes him look cool. Loaded with sexual tension, a plethora of continuity references, homoerotic overtones, numerous pithy TV industry jokes and constantly changing memories, 'Storyteller' is a voyeuristic study about voyeuristic needs. The fight sequences are mostly excellent too, but then you'd expect that in what is, essentially, a work of fiction within fiction. As with all of Jane Espenson's best work, however, redemption is the fist clutching at the beating heart of 'Storyteller', one of the lightest *Buffy* episodes in years. Yet, conceptually at least, it's easily the darkest too. This contradiction, fuelled by Tom Lenk's brilliant performance, make 'Storyteller' a highlight of season seven. Cherish this episode now that *Buffy* is no longer around. It, and stories like it, remain brilliant memories of a show that had, literally, everything.

'Storyteller' takes place exactly one year to the day after Xander left Anya at the altar (see **116**, 'Hell's Bells'). The episode contains numerous continuity references to episodes like **54**, 'The Prom'; **3**,

'The Witch' and **32**, 'Go Fish'. In **44**, 'Amends', the symbol made up from bones, rocks and candles by the Bringers looks rather like the symbol on the Seal of Danzalthar. Jonathan suffered from a shy bladder. Mr Hildebrand is the Sunnydale High maths teacher. The words written on the knife that Andrew used to kill Jonathan are in proto-Tawarick. Translated, they say 'the blood which I spill I consecrate to the oldest evil.'

Critique: 'This emerges as an above-par episode, with disparate storytelling styles fused, most entertainingly, thanks to more excellence from Jane Espenson,' wrote Mark Wyman. He also found time to admire the glimpses into Andrew's imagination – 'the sight of the toga-clad Trio playing at Gods in some Elysian fields: one of the funniest diversions from Sunnydale "normality" ever.'

'An outstanding blend of comedy and tragedy, as recurring character Andrew makes a Buffy "documentary" and also confronts his own demonic acts,' noted the *Chicago Tribune*'s Maureen Ryan. In *Xposé*, Paul Spragg added that 'as so often happens on *Buffy*, it's the conclusion that really makes this stand out, as the comedy disappears . . . A perfect *volte face*, well acted, and very effective storytelling.'

Did You Know?: The 'Grrr . . . Arrgh' at the end of the episode was replaced, brilliantly, with 'We are *GODS*.'

Cast and Crew Comments: Tom Lenk's favourite memory of his time on *Buffy* is 'When we were in our togas dancing on the hillside with the unicorn,' he told *E! Online*. 'I got to make such an ass of myself. I love that when I'm interviewing for acting jobs people think I'm really like my character. I say, "But I'm not really singing and dancing on a hillside in a toga. I only do that on TV for everyone to see!"'

Joss Whedon's Comments: 'A lot of shows – usually the more successful – are formula shows, where you know what is going to happen,' Joss told an online question and answer session. 'Jessica Fletcher is going to solve the murder. Sonny Crocket is going to be depressed. Scully [will] not believe it's a monster. That makes for hit shows, as opposed to cult shows. The problem is that really does get tiring. Those end up having a shelf life, because it's so difficult to find something new to say. So we have that advantage.'

139
Lies My Parents Told Me

US Transmission Date: 25 Mar 2003
UK Transmission Date: 8 May 2003

Writers: David Fury, Drew Goddard
Director: David Fury
Cast: Caroline Lagerfelt (Anne), Damani Roberts (Young Robin),
Ira Steck (New Vamp), Tom Williams (Vampire)[61]

Giles acquires a magical device which, it is hoped, will deactivate the First's ability to trigger Spike into acts against his will. When used, it causes Spike to remember the close relationship that he shared with his mother when he was still human. After he was sired, Spike attempted to save his dying mother by turning her into a vampire. But the demon within her rejected Spike's plans for them to spend an eternity together and he was forced to kill her yet again. This time, permanently. Meanwhile, with Buffy refusing to believe that Spike is a clear and present danger, Robin Wood asks Giles to help him gain his revenge upon the vampire who murdered his mother.

Dudes and Babes: Once, as Giles loudly protests, Buffy was prepared to sacrifice herself and everyone else in the world to protect Dawn from Glory (see **100**, 'The Gift'). Now, seemingly, the reverse of this is true and she will sacrifice everyone to save the world. This revelation partly supports a widely held fan theory: When Dawn was told by Joyce in **129**, 'Conversations With Dead People', that, when the time comes, Buffy would forsake her sister, it was really Joyce's ghost talking and not the First (however, see **143**, 'End of Days').

A Little Learning is a Dangerous Thing: Giles has a personal library at home in England which, he suggests, is complete enough to be used as an emergency school library. It is, presumably, filled mostly with the books that were saved from the Mayor's apocalyptic attack in **56**, 'Graduation Day' Part 2.

Mommy Dearest: Robin, seemingly, felt abandoned by his mother who always put her destiny and mission as the Slayer before him. As Spike tells Wood, Nikki clearly loved him as any mother

---

[61] Uncredited.

would. But seemingly not enough to give up her calling. Thus, Robin has spent his life seeking to avenge the loss of an idealised vision of a mother who, in reality, never existed.

Wood tells Buffy that she reminds him of his mother when he watches her patrol. Buffy notes that, usually, this is not something most girls would wish to hear. But that, in this particular case, she is grateful for the compliment.

Mommy Dearest, The Sequel: 'I'd like to know what he was like before being a vampire,' James Marsters said in 1999 concerning his alter ego. 'I have a feeling he was pretty much an asshole. I don't think being a vampire is what made him evil. Perhaps Mommy didn't love him enough!' In this episode we discover that, actually, nothing could be further from the truth. William's relationship with his mother, Anne, was a loving and caring one (if, perhaps, a touch suffocating, due in no small part to Anne's ill-health, apparently from consumption). Anne was, Spike tells Giles, a nice lady whom he loved deeply and who, apparently, reciprocated that love (William was always her little prince). After Drusilla sired Spike, enough of William's human compassion survived the transition for him to sire his mother so that she could join him as a vampire.

Denial, Thy Name is Spike: The newly vampirised Anne then cruelly tells Spike that she does not wish to accompany him in the afterlife. She will, on the contrary, be happy to metaphorically pry his greedy fingers from her apron strings. William, she suggests, always clung to her since the day that he first slithered from her, like a parasite, thus condemning her to a lifetime of tedium. Whatever he was as a human, Spike responds, that is not who he is now. That is, in fact, who he will *always* be, Anne replies with mock tenderness. A limp and sentimental fool. When Spike attempts to leave, Anne is at her most vicious, telling him to scamper off and cry to his new trollop, Drusilla. Does Spike think that he will be able to touch Drusilla, she asks, without thinking of his mother at the same time? All he ever wanted, Anne concludes, was to be back inside her and, when he sank his teeth into her and made her an unholy creature of the night, he achieved his life's purpose. Spike, tearfully, notes that he loved Anne. And, apologising to her, he stakes her, having realised that by turning her into a vampire, he had already killed the woman whom he wanted so much to save. This double matricide horror has clearly weighed on Spike during the subsequent years and may, indeed, explain some of his more psychotic tendencies as William the Bloody. (And, also, perhaps his quasi-Oedipal relationship with Drusilla, his surrogate mother/lover.) But, as Spike tells Wood, he now realises that, unlike Wood, he had a mother who not only loved him, but also had him at the centre of her world. When Spike sired Anne, he unleashed a demon. All the terrible things that it subsequently told him were the demon's thoughts and not Anne's.

Denial, Thy Name is Giles: Given what we know about Giles's previously established ends-justifying-the-means morality (his murder of the relatively innocent Ben for the greater good in **100**, 'The Gift', for example), it is not wholly surprising that he so readily agrees to Robin Wood's suggestion that they eliminate Spike. It's true that Spike has a soul now but, Giles rationalises, he is still not his own man due to the malevolent influence of the First. This makes him dangerous to everyone else. Furthermore, Giles has already seen the disastrous effects that the love of a vampire can have on his Slayer's decision-making abilities (he reminds Buffy, forcefully, that Angel had to leave Sunnydale because he saw their relationship as a potential liability to her). Thus, Giles decides to make a decision that, he feels, Buffy cannot – to destroy Spike. But this proves to be a disastrous mistake. By taking this decision out of Buffy's hands, Giles effectively uses exactly the sort of patriarchal authority that Buffy has spent so much of the last seven years rejecting (high school principals, her father, the Watcher's Council, the Shadow Men etc.). By doing this, Giles effectively betrays Buffy's faith in him and he loses her trust. (That he regains it, in **144**, 'Chosen', says much about the bond between the pair that adversity forges.)

Authority Sucks!: In marked contrast to her bewildered reaction when Giles first returned to England (see **109**, 'Smashed'), Buffy finally acknowledges, here, that it really isn't healthy for her to constantly live in his shadow. To enable herself to be a more effective if, it seems, a less caring leader, she overrules Giles's chosen strategy and, at the end of the episode, both literally and metaphorically, shuts him out of her life.

The Conspiracy Starts at Home Time: Since the closing of the Seal in the previous episode, things seem to have settled down somewhat in school (and, presumably, in the town at large). The marching band and the swing choir have gone back to their normal, healthy seething resentment.

Meanwhile, Giles notes that the coven's seers are certain that the First is continuing to gather its forces. The few potential Slayers left around the world are still being murdered before the Scoobies and their allies can get to them.

Work is a Four-Letter Word: The brain-matter that the school janitor is cleaning up at the beginning is probably from the boy who exploded in **138**, 'Storyteller'.

It's a Designer Label!: Highlights include Robin's royal-blue shirt, Buffy's black sweater and Dawn's pink jacket. However, what on earth is that thing on Anya's head?

References: The title comes from Bernice Kenner's 1996 novel. There's a witty allusion to *From Hell* (William asking his mother if he should get Dr Gull).[62] Buffy refers to Pink's 'Get This Party Started'. Also, numerous Jacobean revenge tragedies (Wood and Spike's virtual soliloquies to camera), Yul Brynner, *Star Trek II: The Wrath of Khan* ('for the greater good'), the Get Out of Jail Free card from Monopoly, *The X-Files*, *A Hard Day's Night* and *Hamlet* ('that's the rub'). Spike's sireing of his mother is a trait that he shares with Lestat in Anne Rice's *The Vampire Lestat*.

Bitch!: Anya: 'But, forgiveness makes us human. Bladeeblahdeeblah.'

Awesome!: The blood dripping from Robin Wood's hand as he watches Spike walk away from him. Wood's confusion at Buffy and Giles's discussion on Spike's soul/chip/trigger. Another glimpse of William, the sensitive-if-bloody-awful-poet. And, of his bloody awful poetry ('Hark. The lark!'). Even Anne considered it twaddle, but was far too polite to mention this until she was liberated from her strict Victorian manners by a demon. (There is, of course, the possibility that poor deluded Anne really did share William's fantasy world and thought his poetry was unappreciated

---

[62] A reference to William Withey Gull (1816–90), Queen Victoria's personal physician and a noted freemason. First proposed as a candidate for the Whitechapel murderer by Stephen Knight in the best-selling *Jack the Ripper: The Final Solution* (1976), Gull is the central character in Alan Moore and Eddie Campbell's 1990s comic masterpiece *From Hell*, subsequently filmed by the Hughes Brothers in 2002. Serious Ripperologists are said to scoff at this theory, which involves a complex high-ranking conspiracy, a liaison between the Duke of Clarence and a shopgirl and the impressionist painter Walter Sickert. But then, frankly, anyone who calls themselves a 'serious Ripperologist' deserves a bit of scoff in return.

genius. Some mothers are like that.) Wood's confrontation with Spike in his cross-filled garage, the juxtaposition of their subsequent fight with Spike's memories of killing his mother for a second time and the conclusion to this as Spike, apparently, kills Wood. Giles's attempts to rationalise to Buffy his actions, all couched in vastly unsubtle war metaphors. Buffy telling Robin that, if he carries his petty vendetta further, Spike will kill him and, more importantly, she will do nothing to stop Spike. Buffy shutting the door in Giles's face.

Self-awareness: Buffy asks if Giles has heard her motivational speeches lately. This appears to be a very conscious comment by the production team, making fun of the serious nature of many of Buffy's recent attempts to rally her troops. It's also, perhaps, an acknowledgement of criticism by some fans in the online community of this particular trend (see, also, Andrew's comments in **138**, 'Storyteller', on the same subject).

'You May Remember Me From Such Films and TV Series As . . .': Caroline Lagerfelt's CV includes *The X-Files*, *Minority Report*, *Glam* and *Nash Bridges*. Damani Roberts appeared in *Charmed*. Ira Steck was in *Thirsty*.

Don't Give Up the Day Job: Stuntman Thom Williams's CV includes *The Shield*, *Alias* and *Birds of Prey*.

Cigarettes and Alcohol: When he tells his mother that he has become a vampire, Anne asks Spike if he is drunk. He admits that, in fact, he is a little bit.

Logic, Let Me Introduce You to This Window: Giles says that the prokaryote creature will enter Spike's brain through the optic nerve. It enters his eye but then moves up his forehead and, therefore, away from the optic nerve. How were Spike and Dru able to enter William's home after he was sired? Spike tells Wood that he turned his mother into an uncaring demon. But Spike, himself, was also an uncaring demon at this point, so why did he try to save his mother by siring her in the first place? Unless, of course, everything that Anne said was true and he always *was* just parasite who needed her far more than she needed him. (However, for another theory, see **142**, 'Touched'.) The supposedly four-year-old Robin looks older than four. Anne gets the lyrics to 'Early One Morning' wrong at one point.

Quote/Unquote: Spike: 'Little tip, mate. The stake's your friend. Don't be afraid to use it.'

Spike: 'All the rubbish people keep sticking in my head, it's a wonder there's room for my brain.' Giles: 'I don't think it takes up that much space, do you?'

Wood: 'You took my childhood when you took her from me. She was my world.' Spike: 'And you weren't *hers*? Doesn't it piss you off?'

Buffy, to Giles: 'I think you've taught me everything I need to know.'

Notes: 'I don't give a piss about your mom. She was a Slayer, I was a vampire. That's the way the game's played.' From its credulity-stretching pre-title sequence to one of the most dramatically satisfying, if completely unexpected, closing lines in *Buffy* history, 'Lies My Parents Told Me' is an episode touched with a true sense of *magnificence*. A complex, introspective narrative, smeared with chunks of Oedipal shading, this focuses on the terrible insecurity that mother-loss produces in many young men and some older ones. In an effort to find more information about the trigger that the First has used to such shocking effect on Spike, Giles and Willow place a supernatural worm in the vampire's brain. This sends Spike off on a psychotic trip down memory lane and focuses on William the Poet's intense and almost incestuous relationship, both pre- and post-sireing, with his lovely, if rather smothering, Victorian mum. Spike has, as he tells Robin, killed many people's mothers, his own included as we subsequently discover. His reacquisition of a soul, however, means that he now regrets these acts and he's even grateful to Wood for giving him a valuable therapy lesson upon the nature of evil. That's, ultimately, why he allows Wood to live when he could so easily have killed him. Wood's agenda, by contrast, lies somewhere other than in Freudian psychoanalysis. He *understands* that Spike is a different person with and without a soul, but he still allies himself with a darkly suspicious Giles in a quest for closure by vengeance. Only the virtual absence of Willow, Xander, Dawn and Anya (all of whom get about ten lines of dialogue between them) detracts from this dramatic, visually stimulating and stylistically fascinating piece of work. With some beautifully direct metaphors and a couple of really shocking moments, this is, almost on its deathbed, yet another example of *Buffy* doing what it does best.

Apocalypses that Buffy actually survives, she considers to be the easy ones. She tells Wood about finding her own mother dead (see **94**, 'The Body'). Willow receives a telephone call from Los Angeles from Fred Burkle and leaves immediately afterwards (see *Angel*: 'Orpheus'). William reads poetry to his mother concerning his love for Cecily Underwood (see **85**, 'Fool For Love'). In 1977, he sought out Nikki the Vampire Slayer and travelled to New York to face her. Anya refers to the time when she slaughtered a fraternity house (**127**, 'Selfless'). The 1880 sequences would seem to take place sometime between William's introduction to his grand-sire, Angelus (see *Angel*: 'Destiny') and the initiation of the bloody reign of terror that gained Spike his new name and caused Angelus, Darla, Drusilla and Spike to flee London for Yorkshire some months later (see **85**, 'Fool For Love'; *Angel*: 'Darla'). Spike notes that he is not a great exponent of self-reflection. After his mother's death, Robin was raised by her former Watcher, Bernard Crowley. Giles knew of Crowley by his reputation – a New York-based Watcher who resigned after his Slayer was killed. It's only at this point that he realises Robin is Nikki Wood's son.

Soundtrack: Once again, 'Early One Morning' features prominently (see **130**, 'Sleeper'). The song's use, by the First, as a trigger to turn Spike into an instrument of evil is deactivated in this episode. It was seemingly used by the First due to its associations to Spike with his mother. The song was a favourite of Anne's and she often sang it to William when he was a child.

Critique: 'A study of parents and children hurting each other while meaning well that's straight out of Philip Larkin,' noted *Xposé*'s Kate Brown.

Did You Know?: Interviewed by *filmforce.ign.com*, Joss Whedon was asked about an extravaganza that he had once promised to fans. An all-gay, all-naked *Buffy* that, sadly, never materialised. '[That's] my biggest regret,' noted Whedon. 'But I'm sure there's a fanfic [of it on the Internet] somewhere.'

Cast and Crew Comments: Asked what it was like to film the infamous rape scene in **119**, 'Seeing Red', James Marsters described it as 'the hardest day of my life. I've turned roles down because they're rapists,' he told United Press's Karen Butler. 'The writers are fabulous, but that day I told them: "Sometimes you guys don't know what you're asking us to do." I'm proud of it artistically, but as a human being I never want to do a scene like that again.'

Marti Noxon's Comments: 'The whole genesis of Spike was that we just wanted a cool villain,' Marti told a US radio interview in 2003. 'For a long time he was good by default. But slowly you start to have moral questions. Is this a change in conditioning? I've always joked that he became attracted to Buffy because he liked to be abused. Then we discovered that there was a real heart to that storyline and they had a chemistry together. A lot of people see this as a grand design, an opera about good and evil. As we watched, eventually we found that Spike was a real romantic foil for Buffy. Also what we've seen is Buffy attracted to her own darkness, her own aggression, to sex without love, to sex where love is really subdued, all of the things that she can't permit, because she is a hero.'

Previously on *Angel*: 'Orpheus': Broken out of prison with the aid of her former Watcher, Wesley, Faith attempts to help Angel's friends and their battle with fearsome entity, the Beast. Spiked by Faith's drug-tainted blood, Angelus spirals back into the private hell of the last century of Angel's past. In this dose of psychic-psychedelia, however, he has a Slayer for company. Meanwhile, Fred seeks help in restoring Angel's lost soul. Willow arrives and, despite the sinister attentions of a now-evil Cordelia, is able to use the Orb of Thesula to bring Angel back. Together with a recovered Faith, she sets out to return to Sunnydale.

140
Dirty Girls

US Transmission Date: 15 Apr 2003
UK Transmission Date: 15 May 2003

Writer: Drew Goddard
Director: Michael Greshman
Cast: Rachel Bilson (Colleen), Carrie Southworth (Betty),
Christie Abbott (Helpless Girl), Miranda Kwok (Potential Slayer)[63]

Faith's arrival in Sunnydale brings much tension to established Scooby Gang dynamic. Meanwhile, there is another new arrival in town – Caleb, a violent Bible-thumping acolyte of the First with super-strength and a vicious line in white-hot misogyny. He sends

---

[63] Uncredited.

a message to Buffy in the form of a badly beaten girl, and says that he has something that belongs to the Slayer. But is this all just a trap?

Dreaming (As Blondie Once Said) is Free: Isn't it brilliant that, in the middle of the preparations for a coming apocalypse, Xander still finds time to have what amounts to a teenage wet dream? Buffy was seemingly correct in her suspicions in **52**, 'Earshot', sex *is* all Xander thinks about (see, also, **47**, 'The Zeppo'). In his dream, Xander comforts two beautiful young potentials, Caridad and Colleen, who tell him how scared they are about dying before they've had a chance to be with a man. And that neither of them *have*. Or, indeed, have they had the chance to be with *each other* in front of a man! The camera then reveals a slow motion pillow fight taking place next door with all the other girls scantily clad in bras, T-shirts and panties. Xander is abruptly pulled from this fantasy when he's woken by Rona telling him that Dominique has the stomach flu and the toilet is backed-up. Xander drowsily says that he will deal with the situation once his 'leg cramp' had subsided. Top comedy.

Dudes and Babes: In addition to blinding Xander in one eye, Caleb also injures several of the potentials (breaking Rona's arm, for instance) and kills two of them, including Molly.

Authority Sucks!: The first cracks in Buffy's authority over the potential Slayers appear with both Rona and Kennedy openly voicing discontent concerning her chosen methods of fighting the war. Xander manages to quell the rebellion with yet another inspiring moment of crystal clarity (see **57**, 'The Freshman'; **122**, 'Grave' etc.). However, the fact that Buffy's rash full-scale attack on Caleb's vineyard headquarters goes so disastrously wrong suggests that her stock among her young followers is rapidly falling (which the events of **141**, 'Empty Places', readily confirms).

A Little Learning is a Dangerous Thing: Wood tells Buffy that people are starting to leave town and that half the kids don't bother to show up for school any more. (By the following episode, the school has closed completely and the exodus is almost complete.)

The Conspiracy Starts at Home Time: The First appears to Caleb in the form of Buffy and also as a girl called Betty whom Caleb killed some time ago after she heard him preach. The First is seemingly happy to do requests for Caleb to relive memories of his past atrocities. Caleb says that he does not consider the First to be God.

Work is a Four-Letter Word: Principal Wood fires Buffy from her job at the school so that she can focus her energies on the potentials and the coming war.

It's a Designer Label!: Top items include Faith's extremely tight red T-shirt, Chao-Ahn's black dress, Dawn's miniskirt, Willow's gorgeous red top and Buffy's beige leather jacket.

References: The character of Caleb was probably influenced by the misogynist preacher in Davis Grubb's *The Night of the Hunter*. (Robert Mitchum played the role, brilliantly, in Charles Laughton's 1955 film adaptation.) Caleb refers to the Bringers as the Ray Charles brigade after the legendary blind R&B singer. His numerous Biblical allusions include Revelation 17 (the Whore of Babylon), 1 Corinthians 12 ('drink of this for it is my blood'), the last supper (Mark 14), Adam's rib (Genesis 2), Eve's original sin (Genesis 3), the story of Cain and Abel (Genesis 4), Matthew 6 ('the Kingdom the power and the glory') and the writings of St Paul. Also, paraphrases from Edwin Starr's 'War', Elton John's 'I'm Still Standing', *The Wild Ones*, William Cowper's *Olney Hymns* ('I move in mysterious ways'), Starbucks and visual references to *Spartacus*, *Almost Famous* and *King Lear*. The last movie that Faith saw while in prison was the disappointing Marian Carey vehicle *Glitter*. When someone refers to an evil vineyard, Spike alludes to the soap opera *Falcon Crest*.

Geek-Speak: Andrew seemingly believes that *Star Trek*'s Vulcans are real (confidently stating that it was, in fact, a blue-shirted Federation officer as opposed to a vulcanologist whom Faith murdered in **55**, 'Graduation Day' Part 1). He also alludes to Faith being seduced by the lure of the dark side (see **49**, 'Consequences'). When Amanda notes that Matthew Broderick killed Godzilla, Andrew and Xander are incandescent with rage. What Matthew Broderick killed, Xander notes, was actually a big dumb lizard that was *no*t the real Godzilla.

Bitch!: Spike is clearly concerned by Faith's assertion that, because he has a soul, he is like Angel. Angel's as dull as a table lamp, Spike notes. And the two vampires have *very* different colouring. (See also, *Angel*: 'In The Dark'; 'Just Rewards').

Awesome!: Faith's first meeting with Spike. Actually, the second one's pretty good too. The former is full of amusing misunderstandings and cool violence. The latter positively ripples with repressed sexual tension, especially when Buffy gets herself involved. Also, Andrew's fantasy-ridden history of Faith; Xander's erotic dream and Faith's tale involving a schoolgirl uniform. They really *should* film that and show it every Christmas (see **37**, 'Faith, Hope and Trick'). And, Molly gets killed. *Double bonus.*

'You May Remember Me From Such Films and TV Series As . . .': Nathan Fillion played Mal Reynolds in *Firefly* and the other James Ryan in *Saving Private Ryan*. He also appeared in *Two Guys, a Girl and a Pizza Place*. Daria Ramirez's movies include *Bayaning Third World*, *Sukdulan* and *Live Show*. Christie Abbott played Samantha in *Wishbone*. Rachel Bilson was Summer Roberts in *The OC*. Carrie Southworth appeared in *Soul Survivors*. Mary Wilcher's CV includes *Undressed*. Miranda Kwok appeared in *Jane Doe*, *ER* and *Earth: Final Conflict*.

Valley-Speak: Faith, on Dawn: 'Check it out. Brat's all woman-sized.'

Cigarettes and Alcohol: Spike bums a cigarette from Faith. She presumes that Spike can smoke as much as he wants since lung cancer isn't really an issue for him. On the contrary, Spike notes, over an eternity one's teeth can get yellow; a vampire has to watch things like that.

Sex and Drugs and Rock'n'Roll: A guy with whom Faith used to hang out liked to dress her up as a schoolgirl and have her brandish a bullwhip. Every guy has some whack fantasy, Faith adds. Scratch the surface of even the most respectable of men and you'll find dreams concerning naughty nurses and horny cheer-leaders. (Angelus had recently told Faith that she was still looking for someone to beat the badness out of her in *Angel*: 'Salvage'. See, also, Faith's acts of self-flagellation in the same episode – punching Wesley's bathroom wall – and in **72**, 'Who Are You?' Note, also, her knowledge of BDSM terminology in **49**, 'Consequences' and **51**, 'Enemies'. Compare this with Buffy's miserable self-loathing when she believes that she has abused her Slayer powers in **113**, 'Dead Things'.) Spike admits that he got somewhat dangerous for a while. Faith wonders if this was before he acquired his soul or afterwards. Spike is now over it, he continues, just in case Faith feels the need to kill the closest vampire to her after a long period of incarceration. Faith responds that, if Spike is feeling repentance, then she won't bother as that takes all of the fun out of slaying.

Logic, Let Me Introduce You to This Window: When we last saw Faith and Willow (*Angel*: 'Orpheus'), they were leaving Los Angeles to come directly to Sunnydale. At the beginning of this episode, Faith is wearing the same clothes that she wore at the end of 'Orpheus', but Willow wears something completely different. Technically, Faith reformed *way* before Spike did. At the time when she first recognised her crimes and sought redemption for them (*Angel*: 'Sanctuary'), Spike was allying himself with Adam in an attempt to destroy the Scoobies (see **76**, 'The Yoko Factor'). Is Caleb supposed to be a Catholic priest, or a minister from a Protestant denomination? There aren't a huge number of Catholic churches in the American South (certainly far less than there are Baptist churches), yet very few Protestant ministers wear a black outfit and white collar. Why are the people of Sunnydale leaving town? The First isn't doing anything overtly public. The only outward evidence of anything being amiss was the sporadic outbreak of insanity at the school (and, perhaps, a little beyond, geographically) and that ended when Andrew closed the Seal (see **138**, 'Storyteller'). If Sunnydale's citizens haven't left after previous much more wide-scale devastation – like the mayor becoming a giant snake, the events of **100**, 'The Gift', and biker demons attacking the town en masse in **101/102**, 'Bargaining' – then why would they suddenly evacuate now? (There is a partial explanation given in **141**, 'Empty Places', but it's not a very satisfactory one). Who is Buffy's most powerful weapon/warrior? She said it was Spike in **139**, 'Lies My Parents Told Me'. Now, apparently, it's Willow. When the doomed potential Slayer is fighting the Bringer, in the background another potential can be seen fighting another Bringer. Later in the fight, after Buffy is knocked out, the same shot of the same (anonymous) potential and the same Bringer is used.

Motors: Caleb drives a battered old Ford pickup.

Quote/Unquote: Buffy, on Spike: 'He's got a soul.' Faith: 'Like Angel?' Spike: 'I'm *nothing* like Angel.'

Andrew, on Faith: 'She wrapped evil around her like a large, evil Mexican serape.'

Xander, on Buffy: 'I've seen her heart . . . She cares more about your lives than you'll ever know. You gotta trust her, she's earned it.'

Caleb, to Xander: 'You're the one who sees everything, right? Let's see what we can't do about that.'

Notes: 'They don't truck with Satan, that was me just having fun. Satan is a *little* man.' Caleb turns up in Sunnydale to create a right load of havoc and mayhem. Nathan Fillion is the best thing to happen to this season so far, an effortlessly brilliant performance of controlled malevolence. And he remains the best thing until Eliza Dushku turns up about three minutes later, demanding a recount. A continuity-fest of obscene proportions, the many plus points of 'Dirty Girls' far outweigh a few negatives, particularly the episode's pointed pacifist message. Ultimately, this is a *Buffy* episode built around the concept of heroism. At the risk of stating the bleeding obvious yet again, it's increasingly evident that the most important character, from an audience perspective, in *Buffy* always has been, and remains, Xander. It's his speech that inspires the potential Slayers to action and it's his insight that provokes Caleb to one of the most shocking act of violence ever seen in the series. That's one in the eye for socio-realism.

Caleb refers to Xander as the one who sees things. This is similar to Dawn's observation in **134**, 'Potential'. Caleb was responsible for the explosion at the Watcher's HQ in **131**, 'Never Leave Me' (and, it is implied, various other acts of sabotage around the globe against the forces allied against the First). He's also the one controlling the Bringers. His other crimes include a series of murders of women while he was a, genuine, travelling preacher. One of those was a choirgirl in Knoxville. Faith tells Willow that she has spent too much time in hospital, referring to her period in a coma between **56**, 'Graduation Day' Part 2 and **71**, 'This Year's Girl'. She also mentions being attacked while in prison (see *Angel*: 'Release') and alludes to the events of *Angel*: 'Orpheus' in which she entered Angel's subconscious to battle Angelus. Faith reminds Spike that they have met before. Not that he would, necessarily, remember this as she was in Buffy's body at the time (**72**, 'Who Are You?'). Buffy seemingly did tell Spike about the body swap, but neglected to inform him of who, exactly, had replaced her. Spike tells Faith about Giles's foiled plan to kill him (**139**, 'Lies My Parents Told Me'). One of Xander's lava-lamps (see **107**, 'Once More, With Feeling') is briefly glimpsed.

Critique: Sometimes fans complain about the most bizarre aspects of their favourite show. 'Riley ruined an entire season [for me] by blocking the view of Spike. There's just no excuse for defending

his existence!' wrote Maria Berglund on *The Gutter* website. 'I
think that they should convince Marc Blucas to do a guest spot on
Angel so Riley, too, can get his ass kicked by Spike!'

Did You Know?: A Boston native of Albanian and Danish parents
(both are college professors), Eliza Dushku grew up in a strict
Mormon household and, consequently, suffered at school from
bullies. 'I don't care who you are, everyone has been through it –
the feeling where you'd like to be somewhere else,' she told *Shivers*.
'High school, with all those girls trying to be cool – they compare
it to prison and I'm with them all the way.'

Sharped-eared viewers may notice that Faith's voice seems
somewhat different from the last time that she appeared on *Buffy*.
This is because Eliza Dushku's voice was, according to the actress,
artificially 'broken'. Told by her doctors that her natural, raspy
tones was destroying her vocal cords, Eliza has since, as she
revealed on David Letterman's chat show, gone through voice
therapy to train herself to speak at a higher octave.

Cast and Crew Comments: 'Caleb is not a typical villain,' Nathan
Fillion told *DreamWatch*. 'He's soft, sweet and righteous. And yet
he's perverted and twisted.'

Joss Whedon's Comments: 'Every episode contains an attempt to
do something real, and at least one or two lines that crack me up,'
Joss told *TV Guide*. 'There are definitely ones where I scratch my
head and go, "This seemed a great idea on paper." But I never
singled one [episode] out [as] a total failure.'

141
Empty Places

US Transmission Date: 29 Apr 2003
UK Transmission Date: 22 May 2003
Writer: Drew Z Greenberg
Director: James A Contner
Cast: Dorian Missick (Young Police Officer), Larry Clarke (Monk),
Justin Shilton (Munroe), Nathan Brooks Burgess (Duncan),
David Grammer (Crazy Citizen)

Following the tragedy involving Xander, a guilty Buffy again
encounters Caleb, seeking revenge. Faith decides to take the
potential Slayers to the Bronze to relax, which leads to first a

brush with the law and then a furious argument between Faith and Buffy. This culminates in the potentials being forced to choose between their two leaders. Because of Buffy's recent series of rash decisions, the outcome is never in question. Meanwhile, Spike and Andrew investigate an abandoned mission and discover an important clue as to Caleb and the First's weakness.

Dudes and Babes: Faith alludes to Kennedy's privileged family background (previously mentioned in **133**, 'Showtime'), describing her as a boarding-school brat (see also **144**, 'Chosen').

A Little Learning is a Dangerous Thing: During her second confrontation with Caleb, Buffy pauses to wonder why she and her friends have spent all their time worrying about the Seal and the Hellmouth when Caleb and the First are, seemingly, guarding neither. Instead, Caleb is camped out at the Shadow Valley vineyard. The bad guys always go where the power is, Buffy tells her assembled forces. She believes that they should, therefore, attack the vineyard again. Faith disagrees and is backed by Robin and Giles, both of whom feel that Buffy does not have enough information to be certain that another attack will prove more effective than the last one.

Denial, Thy Name is Buffy: For seven years, Buffy notes angrily, she has been keeping everyone safe by making hard decisions. Now, suddenly, her friends are acting as though they do not trust her any more. Giles asks if Buffy didn't tell Giles earlier that *she* cannot trust *them*. Buffy suggests that this is why Giles sent Spike away, so that an ambush could take place. Rona angrily notes that this isn't about Spike. Rather, it's about Buffy's recklessness. She is so obsessed with beating Caleb that she's willing to jump into any plan without considering alternatives. Even Willow, pushed to speak by Kennedy's suggestion that she always stands up for Buffy even when Buffy is clearly wrong, notes that she is worried about Buffy's recent judgement calls.

Democracy Sucks!: I wish this could be a democracy, Buffy says. But democracies don't win wars. There has to be a single leading voice. Why is this voice automatically Buffy? asks Anya. In a virtual repeat of Buffy's argument with Giles in **1**, 'Welcome to the Hellmouth', Anya tells Buffy that she is not superior to everyone else just because she's a Slayer. She then goes on to make some observations concerning Buffy's apparently superiority complex, which are frighteningly similar to Buffy's own words during her conversation with Holden in **129**, 'Conversations With Dead People'. Buffy came into the world with certain advantages, Anya freely acknowledges. But she didn't earn them. That doesn't make her better than the rest of the world, just *luckier*. I've gotten us this far, Buffy argues. But not without a price, Xander adds, pointedly. Buffy notes that she is more than willing to discuss strategy but that it has to be clear that she is still in charge. Rona is the strongest voice of dissent, arguing that Faith is also a Slayer. Despite Faith's protestations that she isn't a leader, Kennedy suggests that they vote to see who wants Faith to be in charge.

Denial, Thy Name is Still Buffy: Buffy (incorrectly) sees Faith's earlier actions, taking the potentials to the Bronze, as a pre-emptive strike in a forthcoming popularity contest. Faith argues that she, at least, took the time to learn the potentials' names. At this point, Buffy loses it completely, accusing Faith of returning to Sunnydale simply to take away everything that Buffy has. She has done so before, Buffy adds (see **71**, 'This Year's Girl'). Faith says that she doesn't want to take anything from Buffy but that she has no intention of being Buffy's lapdog, either. She doesn't know if she *can* lead. But the real question is, she believes, can Buffy be a *follower*. When Buffy says that she had no intention of watching Faith lead the potentials to disaster, Dawn, who has been silent throughout the entire argument, tells her sister that, if this is the case, then Buffy must leave immediately.

The Conspiracy Starts at Home Time: While researching Caleb, Giles and Willow have collected information on various incidents of violence involving Californian religious institutions over the last decade. It's Dawn who subsequently spots that the disappearances of six members of a religious order at a mission in Gilroy, a town north of Sunnydale, are significantly different from the rest of the material gathered.

It's a Designer Label!: Highlights include Giles's black trenchcoat, Anya's flowing brown dress with flowers, Kennedy's pink top, Dawn's slinky red dress that she wears to the Bronze and Faith's rich blue blouse.

References: The best part of visual impairment, Xander notes, is never having to watch *Jaws 3D* again. Faith mentions Hogwarts, the school from the Harry Potter novels (see **80**, 'Real Me'). Giles alludes to Don Quixote and his obsession with windmills. Also, Bob Dylan's 'Just Like a Woman' and *The Wizard of Oz* (a really cruel reference to the Wicked Witch of the West, by Rona, at Buffy's expense). The final scene, where all of her friends turn on an increasingly paranoid and defensive Buffy, may have been inspired by the courtroom scenes in *The Caine Mutiny*. There's also a possible visual allusion to *Dogma* and an even more oblique one to *American Beauty*.

What a Shame They Dropped . . .: A line in which Anya noted that if Buffy needed to close the Seal of Danzalthar again, Andrew still has plenty of tears left. All they have to do is to tell Andrew that *Stargate SG-1* has been cancelled.

Bitch!: During Giles's angry confrontation with Buffy over how she sometimes endangers her friends, we realise something that many fans had suspected for several years; that Giles, at least partly, holds Buffy responsible for Jenny Calendar's untimely death (see **29**, 'Passion'). Faith has, apparently, told Anya that *she* had Xander, sexually, first (see **47**, 'The Zeppo'; **49**, 'Consequences'). Much to Anya's jealousy.

Awesome!: Willow's visit to Xander in the hospital – one of the most beautifully played, yet characteristically understated, bits of acting in *Buffy*'s entire seven years. Spike and Andrew's road trip – the oddest of odd couples. Particularly, their discussion about the onion blossom, which ends with Spike realising how ridiculous the entire conversation is and telling Andrew that if he ever reveals its contents to anyone, Spike will bite him. Also, Faith's fight with the cops.

Awful: Anybody else, besides Buffy and this author, want to see some serious injury done to Kennedy and, particularly, Rona during, or immediately after, the final sequences?

'You May Remember Me From Such Films and TV Series As . . .': Dorian Missick appeared in *Shaft*, *Two Weeks Notice* and *NYPD Blue*. Nathan Burgess's CV includes *Possums*. Larry Clarke was in *Law & Order*, *CSI* and *The Sopranos*. David Grammar appeared in *The Burkittsville 7*. Justin Shilton played Billy in *Angel* and was also in *Paper Cut* and *60 Seconds*.

The Drugs Don't Work: Buffy tells Xander that the doctors have noted the medication he has been given may cause him some stomach discomfort.

Cigarettes and Alcohol: Faith's lengthy journey towards responsible adulthood reaches something of a climax when she stops

Amanda from drinking beer in the Bronze, because Amanda is seventeen and, therefore, underage. Instead, Faith offers to get her a 7-UP.

Sex and Drugs and Rock'n'Roll: Andrew can be seen writing 'Breakup Sex' on his noteboard after Anya's lengthy description to the potentials of what she and Xander got up to in the basement in **138**, 'Storyteller'.

Within, literally, a moment of meeting Robin Wood for the first time, Faith is coming on to him. And not in a remotely subtle way either (see **142**, 'Touched').

Logic, Let Me Introduce You to This Window: At the beginning of the episode the exodus from Sunnydale has become a vast tidal wave of refugees. Yet when Faith and the potentials visit the Bronze, the club still seems quite full of punters. Would Caleb leave the rotting corpse of Molly and the other potential that he killed in the previous episode just lying around? When the potentials were taken from their homes, told about their destiny and relocated to Sunnydale, most of them, seemingly, had the time to pack some fashionable clothes in case of a night out at the Bronze. Vampires have stunning vision (they can, after all, see in the dark). So, why does Spike need a magnifying glass to look at the photograph that Giles shows him? How does Spike carry the candlesticks when they are cross-shaped? When Kennedy and Amanda are downstairs listening to Anya's speech, they have no scars on their faces. One scene later, both have visible scars. Later again, when Kennedy talks to Buffy, her marks have moved from her cheek to her forehead. When Rona attacks the police officers, she shows no obvious pain relating to her recently broken arm. Buffy clearly has a sore throat during the events of this episode. More worryingly, so does the First when it appears to Caleb as Buffy.

I Just *Love* Your Accent: Willow uses mind control to make a Sunnydale police officer believe that Giles is an inspector with Interpol.

Motors: The crash helmet that Andrew wears while riding pillion on Spike's motorcycle is the same one that Dawn wore in **102**, 'Bargaining' Part 2. Clem drives a red VW Beetle.

Cruelty To Animals: Clem tells Buffy that it has got so bad in Sunnydale one can't swing a cat without hitting some kind of demonic activity. Not that Clem swings cats, of course. Or eats them. Well, recently, anyway.

Quote/Unquote: Anya: 'I'd much rather be at the bedside of my one-eyed ex-fiancee than killing time ... And I would be, if not for a certain awkward discussion ... immediately following some exciting and unexpected break-up sex.'

Andrew: 'Mr Giles? Faith stole the last meatball-and-mozzarella-flavoured Hot Pocket out of the freezer even though I called dibs on it.' And: 'It's an onion. And it's a flower. I don't understand how such a thing is possible.'

Buffy: 'I can't stay here and watch [Faith] lead you into some disaster.' Dawn: 'Then you can't stay here.'

Notes: 'Folks work so hard at keeping the Lord out. Look what happens in return. He abandons *you*.' An expected lurch into the paranoia and loneliness that dogs great leadership, 'Empty Places' is a fundamental example of *Buffy*'s newly developed confidence in unexpected tangents. It may seem somewhat *faux-naïf* at this stage in the day for a series as established in the public psyche as *Buffy* to be trying new dramatic avenues, but this show didn't get as good as it is by standing still. At times achingly sad, 'Empty Places' also features much cutting humour, especially in those scenes that feature unusual characters pairings – Spike and Andrew, and Faith and Principal Wood, for instance. There's also Caleb's speech about historical context which is perched midway between genius and madness. All this, and an opportunity for Faith to beat the roaring crud out of a bunch of redneck cops. Best of all, though, there's poor Xander, lying in his hospital bed, in an incredibly touching and emotional scene with Willow. A patchwork quilt of *bravura* set pieces, 'Empty Places' features hard lessons for a hard world.

The photograph of Buffy, Xander and Willow that Buffy had in her office appears to be the same one that she looked at in **77**, 'Primeval'. It's also been previously seen in **18**, 'Halloween' and **36**, 'Dead Man's Party'. Spike and Andrew discuss the onion-blossom snack that used to be served at the Bronze. Spike had previously expressed his appreciation for this culinary delight in **89**, 'Triangle' and **92**, 'Crush'. Xander and Willow allude to the pirate costume that Xander wore at the Magic Box in **106**, 'All The Way'. Xander also notes that when there are parties at Buffy's house, he usually ends up having to rebuild something, a reference to the carnage caused by a demon's attack during **114**, 'Older, and

Far Away'. Caleb recently visited the Gilroy mission and killed the monks who worshipped there, except for one who survived by hiding. The Greek inscription on the mission's wall which so infuriated Caleb translates as 'It is not for thee. It is for her alone to wield.' Spike's ability to translate it suggests that he's nowhere near as thick as he often makes out (especially as the Greek is actually written in Latinate-style).

Much of the location filming for the final four episodes (including the opening sequence of this, featuring Buffy and Clem) was completed during one two-day block on 25 and 26 March 2003.

Soundtrack: What kind of band plays the Bronze during an apocalypse? Kennedy asks. Actually, they're series favourites Nerf Herder, who perform 'Rock City News' and 'Mr Spock'. Dawn is, seemingly, something of a fan.

Critique: According to former executive producer David Greenwalt, 'I think it's time for the show to end. Seven years is a great run by any standard. Get out while you're still good,' Greenwalt told *SciFi Wire*.

Cast and Crew Comments: 'I used to think I'd love to break into the West End, but I'm an American,' James Marsters told *Starburst* on a visit to London in early 2003. 'Now I'm one of those actors that I used to detest, who could get a stage job because he's on some TV show. Hell, I'll join the enemy!'

Joss Whedon's Comments: 'I gave up about a year ago trying to keep anything off the Internet,' Joss told the *New York Post*'s Don Kaplan. 'The one downside of [the Internet] is the destruction of surprise. However, a lot people don't go on it or deliberately avoid spoilers, so they're the people I'm talking to the most.'

142
Touched

US Transmission Date: 6 May 2003
UK Transmission Date: 29 May 2003
Writer: Rebecca Rand Kirshner
Director: David Solomon
Cast: Lance E Nichols (Middle-Aged Man), Bruno Gioiello (Captured Bringer)[64]

---

[64] Uncredited.

Spike and Andrew return to Sunnydale with news of Caleb's plans. But, when Spike discovers what has happened to Buffy in his absence, he is furious with the Scooby Gang. The First pays Faith a visit in the form of Mayor Wilkins. Meanwhile, Buffy goes to the vineyard, alone.

Authority Sucks!: Spike is outraged by the Scooby Gang's betrayal of Buffy: 'You sad, ungrateful traitors, who do you think you are?' he demands. Giles argues that Spike doesn't understand. On the contrary, replies Spike, he believes that he understands the situation all too well. Giles used to be the man in Buffy's life. Now she has surpassed Giles and, Spike suggests, Giles cannot handle this fact.

A Little Learning is a Dangerous Thing: At school, Amanda was involved with Sunnydale High's Model UN. She was Uruguay. Dawn can, seemingly, read Turkish.

Denial, Thy Name is Buffy: Buffy suggests that Spike only ever wanted her because she was unattainable. Spike is offended by this suggestion and, in one the series' finest moments, notes that he was alive longer than Buffy, and dead even longer than that. He has seen things that Buffy couldn't dream of and done things that he prefers she doesn't even try to imagine. He doesn't have a reputation for being a great thinker; rather, he follows his blood instincts. Thus, he has made many mistakes in his life. In over one hundred years, he notes, there is only one thing that he has ever been absolutely certain of, and that concerns Buffy herself. When Spike tells her that he loves her, it's not because he wants Buffy or because he can't, ultimately, have her. He loves what she is, he continues. What she does and how she tries. He has seen her kindness, strength and the best and the worst of her. And, he says, he understands with perfect clarity exactly what she is. A hell of a woman.

Denial, Thy Name is Faith: The First appears to Faith in the guise of Mayor Wilkins and messes with her head by telling her that, deep down, Faith always wanted Buffy to accept her (see **72**, 'Who Are You?'). Faith keeps looking for love and acceptance from these alleged friends of hers, the First continues, but she will never find it. The truth is that nobody will ever love Faith. Not the way that Wilkins loved her. Everyone else sees her as a killer. She subsequently admits to Robin that Wilkins was like a father to her.

The Conspiracy Starts at Home Time: There are the first references to the actual nuts and bolts of the First's plans, with allusions to an arsenal being built beneath the earth and to the First itself talking about its longing to have the ability to touch and feel as humans do.

Work is a Four-Letter Word: When all the lights go out, Faith speculates that the employees from the power company have joined the exodus from Sunnydale.

It's a Designer Label!: The best stuff on display includes Caradid's two-tone orange and sky-blue sweatshirt, Faith's sexy black top and Willow's gypsy-style skirt.

References: When Spike and Andrew are stuck in the mission during the hours of daylight they play (seemingly at Andrew's instigation) I-Spy. Andrew suggests a game of Rock Paper Scissors next. Giles alludes to the Plastic Ono Band's 'Power To The People'. The hive-like collective mind of the Bringers that Andrew describes when he's possessed by Willow's magic appears to be modelled on concepts drawn from *Star Trek*'s the Borg. Mayor Wilkins's favourite character in *Little Women* was Meg (as opposed to the more obvious Beth or Jo). Also, *Monty Python's Flying Circus* (Spike bemoaning having to sleep in a comfy chair), the Greek myth of Achilles' heel, the Rhodes scholarship (a scheme which places exceptional overseas students at Oxford University) and the parable of the Prodigal Son (as told by Christ in Luke 15). Buffy flipping backwards in slow motion to evade Caleb's attack was obviously influenced by Neo's manoeuvring in *The Matrix*. Other visual references and allusions include *Crouching Tiger, Hidden Dragon*, *Sleepy Hollow*, *High Fidelity*, *The Devil's Advocate*, *The Godfather III* and *Excaliber*.

Awesome!: The excellent use of dislocating and jerky camerawork during the opening debate scene. Ultimately, however, this is James Marsters's episode. His 'you're the one' speech to Buffy is a *real* choker – one of the series' finest moments, going to a particular emotional place and maintaining the impact for an astonishingly long time.

'You May Remember Me From Such Films and TV Series As . . .': Lisa Ann Cabasa's CV includes *Wild at Heart*, *Dark Angel* and *Twin Peaks*. Lane Nichols was in *Snake Eyes*, *Convicts*, *Cold Steel* and *The West Wing*. Bruno Gioiello appeared in *Days of Our Lives*, *Oxygen* and *Pulp Comedy*.

Valley-Speak: Andrew: 'Don't spazz out.'

Sex and Drugs and Rock'n'Roll: In a magnificent series of juxtapositions, Buffy and Spike, Faith and Robin, Willow and Kennedy and Anya and Xander all find solace, comfort and, perhaps, even a bit of pleasure in spending the night together. The actual interactions themselves range from the tender and touching to, in the particular case of Robin and Faith, the torrid and passionate. Kennedy and Willow get down to some necessary naughtiness and neck-licking and the noise they make (an a-cappella concert of people moaning and groaning, apparently) makes Anya jealous and ends with her and Xander writhing around on the kitchen floor. After spending the night with Robin, Faith seemingly reverts to old habits by casually blowing him off the next day, hurtfully telling him that she'll call him when she needs him again.

Logic, Let Me Introduce You to This Window: Kennedy doesn't have her scars from the fight in **140**, 'Dirty Girls', which appeared in **141**, 'Empty Places'. Yet this episode takes place immediately after the previous one and Buffy still has the wounds she had previously. How can a time bomb be used in a trap when the person setting it doesn't know exactly when the victims will be close to it? In **44**, 'Amends', the Bringers were shown chanting. How did they manage to do that if they have no tongues? Willow and Kennedy lie on the bed facing each other. Kennedy has her hand on Willow's side. When the angle subsequently changes, the hand moves with it. When Faith and Wood sit on the bed, a mike boom can briefly be glimpsed above Eliza Dushku's head. Where did Kennedy's tongue ring come from? She didn't have it in **135**, 'The Killer in Me'. Despite everyone's subsequent insistence on calling it a scythe, the weapon that Buffy finds beneath the vineyard basement in not a scythe at all. It's more like an axe.

Quote/Unquote: Anya: 'We're all on death's door repeatedly ringing the doorbell like maniacal girl scouts trying to make quota.'

Man: 'You can't just kick me out of my own house.' Buffy: 'Why not? It's what all the cool kids are doing these days.'

Andrew: 'I feel used and violated. And I need a lozenge.'

Caleb, to the First: 'You're the fire that makes people kill and hate. The fire that will cure the world of weakness. They're just sinners. You *are* sin.'

Notes: 'Nobody wants to be alone. We all want someone who cares, to be touched that way. The First deals in figments, but that wanting is real.' Democracy can prove to be a useless commodity. This is something that Faith quickly discovers when she finds leadership thrust upon her after Kennedy and Rona's *coup d'etat* at the climax of **141**, 'Empty Places'. Kennedy, for one, doesn't seem to like the new regime any more than the previous one. But it gives her, at least, the opportunity for a bit of role-play as a disgruntled minion. There's much that is laudable in Rebecca Rand Kirshner's final *Buffy* script: Spike and Andrew's coolly amusing little double act, for instance. Then Spike gets to be the one to inject a note of horrid reality into the situation, before he goes looking for the missing Slayer with his hormones on overload. There are great performances all round, from Tony Head (magnificent, as always), Alyson Hannigan (effortlessly witty and self-deprecating), Michelle Trachtenberg (who does so much with so few lines) and Nick Brendon, all in little cameos fitted in between major set-pieces. Good lines abound and there's also a fascinatingly juxtaposed sequence of various intimate encounters on the eve of war, with much nakedness, neck-licking and groin-thrusting therein. Weird alliances are formed (Faith and Robin Wood is a particularly interesting and unexpected one, packed with sexual tension and cunning wordplay). Plus, the return of the great Harry Groener. It sounds like this episode should be the highlight of the season, right? Well . . . it *should* have been. Unfortunately, some of the episode's messages are smothered in such bland construction and an overdose of the hurt/comfort fan-fiction principle that they're rendered less effective than required. Too much mush and not enough action, in short. A necessary bunching of plot-strands, 'Touched' almost fails to work on any level in spite of itself. But, finally, it succeeds through the sheer force of effort of the actors. A triumphant rabbit-out-of-hat-trick that even the signposted climax can't deny.

Caleb is said by the First to be the only man strong enough to be its vessel.

Soundtrack: 'It's Only Love' by Heather Nova accompanies the various sexual couplings.

Did You Know?: Asked by Jeff Jensen about her favourite episodes, Sarah Michelle Gellar expressed a particular fondness for **54**, 'The Prom' ('It stood for everything *Buffy* was about: the fact that she so badly wanted to be part of the other kids' lives'); **94**, 'The Body' and **72**, 'Who Are You?' ('Eliza was so great').

Cast and Crew Comments: 'One of the complaints about Spike was that [some fans] felt we were changing the whole vampire mythology, that Spike wasn't a vicious killer when he was a vampire. How come he was still like William?' David Fury noted during an online interview with the Succubus Club. 'What we've tried to [show is] that Spike is an anomaly in the vampire world. It's not a matter of bending the rules arbitrarily. We've tried to say from the Judge saying "You reek of humanity," and his mother saying to him "you will always be this," is that, for whatever reason, Spike is something special.'

Joss Whedon's Comments: *TV Guide* asked Joss how he felt about Sarah's decision to leave: 'It's a decision I support and respect and, in fact, imitate,' he replied. 'It's been seven years [and] a hell of a collaboration, but I completely understand. College was a lot of fun, but then I graduated, it's not like I stayed.'

Previously on *Angel*: 'Home': Having defeated the apocalyptic schemes of the Power That Was, Jasmine, Angel and his friends are offered the opportunity of a lifetime, to take over the running of Wolfram & Hart's Los Angeles branch. Angel accepts, so long as certain conditions are met.

143
End of Days

US Transmission Date: 13 May 2003
UK Transmission Date: 5 Jun 2003
105Writers: Douglas Petrie, Jane Espenson
Director: Marita Grabiak
Cast: Christine Healy (Guardian)

Buffy finds the weapon which the First has been attempting to hide from her: a mythical axe embedded in solid stone which Buffy removes, much to Caleb's dismay. Faith and the potential Slayers are caught in the explosion from Caleb's bomb. With Buffy's help, they escape from an attack by the Turok-Han, return to Revello

Drive and regroup for the final battle with the forces of the First Evil.

Authority Spanks!: In the aftermath of Faith's disastrous attack on the vineyard (see **142**, 'Touched'), Amanda tells Buffy that she believes, in some karmic way, the girls were being punished for following Faith instead of Buffy herself. Buffy notes that it was a trap and that it could just as easily have happened if she had been leading the group.

A Little Learning is a Dangerous Thing: Buffy and Spike have a lengthy debate on whether 'shirty' is a word or not.

Denial, Thy Name is Anya: Humanity is screwed up in a monumental way, Anya tells Andrew. They have no purpose that unites them so they just drift around, blundering through life until they all die. They know that death is coming, yet every single human is surprised when it actually arrives. And they have a nasty habit of killing each other, which is clearly insane. Yet, she notes, when something *really* matters, they fight for it. Andrew, perceptively, notes that Anya loves humanity – much to her, seeming, embarrassment.

The Conspiracy Starts at Home Time: Caleb's super-strength comes from a merging with the First. This was, Caleb notes, a spiritual experience for him. However, the effects are temporary and must be repeated occasionally. When the Hellmouth is opened and the Turok-Han armies sweep the world, the First intends to enter every man, woman and child on the Earth, just as it entered Caleb. The First appears to both Caleb and Spike in the form of Buffy.

The weapon was, the Guardian tells Buffy, forged in secrecy for one like her and kept hidden from the Shadow Men. This, presumably, means that it was created at the time of the first Slayer, seemingly in Africa at the very dawn of civilisation. The Shadow Men subsequently became Watchers. And the Watchers watched the Slayers. But the Guardians, women who wanted to protect future Slayers, were always there, watching *them*. The weapon was taken to the site of one of the Hellmouths to kill the last pure demon that walked the Earth. (See **2**, 'The Harvest'; this demon, before it died, bit a human and, thus, created the vampires who have been here ever since.) How is it possible that no one (Watchers, Slayers or, seemingly, anyone else) knew about the Guardians or of the weapon's existence? asks Buffy reasonably.

The answer she's given is somewhat unsatisfying – simply that the Guardians hid themselves.

Work is a Four-Letter Word: Xander tells Dawn that he has to take a driving test each year due to his loss of an eye. It's the state law; they no longer trust his depth perception.

It's a Designer Label!: Highlights include Buffy's brown leather jacket, Dawn's bright red sweater and Anya's black top with rose motif.

References: The title comes from Peter Hymes's 1999 Arnold Schwarzenegger vehicle. Buffy refers to King Arthur and the legend of his sword Excaliber which, like the Guardians weapon, was pulled from a stone. Xander wishes for some originality in any forthcoming eye-jokes pointed in his direction – with specific reference to the Greek hero Cyclops, the maxim 'beauty is in the eye of the beholder', Exodus 21 ('an eye for an eye') and *I, Claudius*. Spike mentions the Holy Hand Grenade of Antioch, a lethal weapon used to kill a particularly nasty rabbit in *Monty Python's Holy Grail*. Andrew alludes to Lipps Inc's 'Funky Town'. Also, David Bowie's 'Heroes', *I Love Lucy* and *Jaws*, with it's climactic scene involving Roy Scheider, a shark and an oxygen tank.

Awesome!: The explosive opening. Buffy telling Xander that he's her strength, the reason she's made it this far and that she trusts him with her life. Anya and Andrew's discussion on the idiosyncrasies of humanity. Spike's confession to Buffy. Xander's pre-kidnap scene with Dawn, which is touching and funny at the same time.

Lack of Surprise!: Unless you were reading certain spoiler sites on the Internet, then it really should have been Angel's appearance just before the episode's climax. Except, of course, that David Boreanaz's name appears in the opening credits of this episode. That's careless.

'You May Remember Me From Such Films and TV Series As . . .': Christine Healy's CV includes *ER*, *Don't Touch My Daughter*, *Sledge Hammer! Charmed* and *Star Trek: Deep Space Nine*.

The Drugs Don't Work: Buffy gives Xander the difficult task of getting Dawn away from Sunnydale, by force if necessary. He uses chloroform on her and drives off. When Dawn wakes up, needless to say, she's a bit pissed-off.

Cigarettes and Alcohol: Anya and Andrew use Giles's single malt whisky as an antiseptic to treat the wounded potentials. They also have a few sly drinks from it. When an angry Caleb throws a wine barrel to the floor of the vineyard, the First notes that Caleb is wasting a lot of robust, full-bodied merlot in his tantrum.

Sex and Drugs and Rock'n'Roll: Spike says that last night with Buffy (see **142**, 'Touched') was something special. He has done everything, he notes, including many things with Buffy that he can't even spell. But, he has never been so close to anyone. Least of all, her. All he did, he adds, was to hold her and watch her sleep. Yet it was still the best night of his life and that, frankly, terrifies him (see **144**, 'Chosen').

Logic, Let Me Introduce You to This Window: Can you actually *get* Jaffa Cakes in the US? You certainly couldn't in 2001 when this author was asked to import approximately ten boxes to various friends at a convention in Minneapolis. Perhaps Giles knows a specific importer. Several of the girls' hairstyles change radically during the course of the episode – notably Anya's. Is there a hairdresser still open in Sunnydale that we don't know about? If Buffy had left by the time that Willow got to the house where Buffy was staying, why didn't Willow merely recast the locator spell to see where she was now? When Buffy fights the Über-Vamps in the basement, one of the vampires bends over and the actor's skin can be seen beneath his costume. In the scene where Buffy fights Caleb, Buffy is thrown on to a cement block. When she gets up, viewers can see the (fake) block move a fraction. Despite the fact that the wall carving at the monastery in **141**, 'Empty Places' said, 'It is for her alone to wield,' Caleb seems to wield the weapon quite effectively when he grabs it from Buffy.

The Guardian says that she wants to help to protect Buffy. So where, exactly, has she been for the last seven years and various apocalyptic earth-shattering disasters? Where was she, for instance, when Buffy twice died? (See **12**, 'Prophecy Girl'; **100**, 'The Gift'.) Also, considering that the Guardian has been hidden since the time of the Shadow Men and the first Slayer (see **137**, 'Get It Done'), she speaks remarkably good English (complete with modern expressions like 'nope'). The weapon, she says, was forged centuries ago. Shouldn't that be millennia if it's pre-Christian? Of course, that brings up the question of when, exactly, the weapon was made and what it's made from. If its creation was at the dawn of civilisation – say 3,000 BC, approximately – then it's unlikely to be iron as no one knew how to forge such a metal at that time. Plus we have an artefact being created in the known ancient world (in the weapon's particular case, Egypt) and then, in some unexplained way, being transported to America, which wouldn't be discovered by the rest of the world for another four and a half thousand years. Who took it there? How did they know they wouldn't fall off the end of the world? Why, come to that, are the two Hellmouths that we know about both on a continent that, until 1492, only the indigenous population and, allegedly, a few lost Vikings had any knowledge of? Why did Buffy never notice that particular mausoleum previously in seven years of patrolling the cemetery near enough every night? And, how did she know where to go on this particular occasion?

Where on earth did Dawn have her tazer concealed? She's wearing extremely tight trousers and the tazer isn't, exactly, unobtrusive. Dawn uses the tazer on Xander who is driving the car. Let's ignore for a second just how insanely dangerous *that* is. Definitely don't try that one at home, kids. Next, we see an exterior shot of the car slowing, stopping, turning around and then immediately driving off back towards Sunnydale. Dawn simply has no time to get into the driving seat (leaving aside the fact that she's never been seen to drive in the series previously). Did she sit on Xander's lap all the way back? Actually, let's not go there . . .

Cruelty To Animals: Dawn remembers a seemingly tragic incident involving Miss Kitty Fantastico (see **76**, 'The Yoko Factor') and a loaded crossbow.

Quote/Unquote: Buffy, on the weapon: 'The only thing I know for sure is it made Caleb back off in a hurry.' Willow: 'So it's true. Scythe matters.'

Anya: 'I'll get Kennedy to watch the girls. She's tough, imminent death won't bother her.'

Buffy: 'I guess everyone's alone. But being a slayer? There's a burden we can't share.' Faith: 'And no one else can feel it. Thank God we're hot chicks with superpowers!'

Angel, as Buffy fights Caleb: 'God, I've missed watching this.'

Notes: 'Use it wisely and perhaps you can beat back the rising dark. One way or another, it can only mean an end is truly near.' 'End of Days' starts with a big bang. But, so does a puncture. It's a highly fragmented story, resembling a series of snapshots from someone else's photo album, or half-heard conversations between two strangers. It begins with a sense of overwhelming panic, and it completely blows it's *Big Surprise Ending* before the opening credits are even concluded. It's also, much more importantly, a truly *magnificent* episode. A conceptual sequel to **52**, 'Earshot' and, via a bunch of circular references, to **1**, 'Welcome To The Hellmouth' and **2**, 'The Harvest'. This means that we're ending *Buffy* right back where the series began, with the horror mythology and the series' own curveball from it, to the fore. Arthurian allusions, punishment metaphors and witty dialogue dominate the opening scenes. Thereafter, the episode settles down as a wonderful exercise in constructed characterisation. There's a great Giles/Willow exposition scene, which starts off as just another one of those "Oh, so that means . . ." conceits but one that builds and builds, reminding the audience exactly why both of these people are such important characters to the show. Anya and Andrew get drunk in the face of the coming apocalypse, yet they find time for a crucial discussion on the concept of humanity. Buffy and Faith engage in a stunning one-to-one that answers many questions about their complex, adversarial relationship. And, as so often in the past, it's Xander who gets to say all the right things at the right time. Given a specific task, by Buffy, with regard to Dawn, he tells the Slayer that he's reluctant to do it because it will mean leaving her alone in the face of the oncoming apocalypse. He always believed that he would be there with her when the end came. The audience, of course, knows fate will decree that he *will* be. They all will. It was foretold (see **78**, 'Restless'). The difference between this Slayer and all the others is that she has the strength of friends to help her. A week before it ended, *Buffy* continued to make its audience laugh, gasp and think in equal measure. Something that utterly befits the legacy it would leave behind.

Xander refers to his reviving Buffy from the dead (specifically in **12**, 'Prophecy Girl'). Anya mentions the occasion when she fled an apocalypse (**55**, 'Graduation Day' Part 1). The website that Willow accesses when researching the weapon is called *History of the Axe*. She refers to the Axe of Dekeron, said to have been forged in Hell and lost since the Children's Crusade. Giles mentions the Sword of Moskva and the Reaper of the Tigris. The website also mentions the Black Knight's Hatchet. Faith spends most of the episode off-screen in bed, recuperating. (This was due to Eliza Dushku filming the pilot for *Tru Calling* during this period.)

Did You Know?: Just as *Buffy* was ending – indeed, a matter of days after the production's wrap-party had taken place in a blaze of publicity at the Miauhaus studio – the British tabloid the *Daily Star* continued its impressive reputation for totally accurate reporting: it noted that ex-*Neighbours* actress and pop-wannabe Holly Valance was 'in discussions to replace Sarah Michelle Gellar in *Buffy*.' Yes, *of course* she was. Meanwhile, back in the real world . . .

Head On: Anthony Stewart Head told *Cinescape* that he, like James Marsters, had been approached about the possibility of appearing on *Angel*. 'I think maybe I will,' Tony noted happily. 'I talked to one of the writers about it. It's such an open book, and that's what makes it so exciting.'

Cast and Crew Comments: 'You always worry about being on a show for too long, especially when you're a cult hit,' Sarah Michelle Gellar told *Entertainment Weekly*. 'I was 18 when I started the show; I'm 26, married [and] I never see my husband. This has been the longest span of my life in one place. I want to try other things, live in different places.'

What was it like for David Boreanaz being back on *Buffy*? 'That was interesting,' David told the Los Angeles Comic Book and Science Fiction Convention in May. 'We shoot *Angel* on a sound stage in a big studio. Going back to *Buffy*, where they shoot in these warehouses, the biggest thing for me was the height of the ceiling, it's really low. As far as working with Sarah again, she's great. The characters picked up where they left off.'

Joss Whedon's Comments: The decision to end *Buffy* came about largely because, as Joss told CNN, 'Sarah's contract was up, and I knew that she wanted to branch out. She always gave her best but I knew that she was getting worn down by it, and so was I. Just physically, not mentally. I feel like the show could run forever in terms of the stories you could tell, but eventually the process grinds you down; you start letting things slip. I didn't want that to happen.'

'I'm glad I can say we did our best on every single episode', Joss told *zap2it.com*. 'We didn't always succeed, but we never slacked, and I'm immensely proud of my writers, actors and crew for that.'

144
Chosen

US Transmission Date: 20 May 2003
UK Transmission Date: 12 Jun 2003
Writer: Joss Whedon
Director: Joss Whedon
Cast: Dementer Raven (Girl at Bat), Katie Gray (Indian Girl),
Ally Matsumura (Japanese Girl), Kelli Wheeler (School Girl),
Jenna Edwards (Trailer Girl), Julia Ling (Potential with Power #2),
Ana Maria Lagasca (Potential Slayer)[65]

Buffy and Angel's reunion is rudely interrupted by Caleb, who is
ready for a final battle. So, Buffy kills him. Angel gives Buffy the
amulet to help her in the coming apocalypse. The First tells Buffy
that when the Turok-Han emerge from the Hellmouth, this will
upset the balance of nature, making the First itself corporeal. It
also says that the Slayer will always fight alone and upon hearing
this, Buffy realises what she must do. Willow creates a spell that
takes power from the Guardian's weapon and shares it equally
among every potential Slayer in the world. Buffy, Faith and their
newly acquired army of Slayers open the Seal of Danzalthar and
battle the armies of Hell. This leaves many dead, including Anya,
Amanda and Chao-Ahn. Spike allows the amulet to consume him
and the energy released from this devastates the Turok-Han
hoards. The First's plans lie in ruins as Sunnydale collapses in on
itself. Spike and Buffy share a final moment together before Spike
is seemingly destroyed by the amulet. Buffy runs after the speeding
school bus containing her friends and they make it out of town
just as Sunnydale disappears into a massive crater. As they look
back at where the town used to be, Buffy and the Scooby Gang
speculate on what the future holds.

Dudes and Babes: When Willow worries that she may not have the
strength to perform the required magics, Kennedy comforts her
and says that she will keep Willow grounded. Willow then suggests
that, if things get bad, Kennedy may have to kill her. The power
that she will unleash lies beyond the darkest place that she has ever
been to in the past (see **122,** 'Grave'). Buffy believes in Willow,
Kennedy notes. Buffy's a sweet girl but she's not that bright,
Willow replies. It may have escaped Willow's notice, Kennedy

---

[65] Uncredited.

continues, but Kennedy herself is kind of a brat. She has always got her own way in most aspects of life. So Willow is going to make it through this situation, no matter how dark it gets. Then, they kiss.

Before the final battle, Xander tells Anya that, if the worst happens she can always use Andrew as a human shield.

A Little Learning is a Dangerous Thing: Angel doesn't know exactly what the amulet is, or does, except that it's very powerful and dangerous. It has a purifying and cleansing power. The amulet bestows strength to the person who wears it, but it must be someone who is ensouled and stronger than a human. A champion in other words. Like Angel. Or Buffy. Or Spike.

Denial, Thy Names Are Buffy, Angel and Spike: Buffy rejects Angel's offer to stand with her during the final battle. She uses a fairly plausible excuse; that if she and her friends lose and the First gets past Sunnydale, then it will be days or maybe just hours before the rest of the world goes too. Buffy therefore needs a second front, presumably in Los Angeles, and she needs Angel to run it. Angel notes that's *one* reason why she wants him to leave Sunnydale, but he demands to know what the other one is. He notes that he can smell Spike on her. (Did anybody ever tell you the whole smelling people power that vampires possess is gross? Buffy asks.) Angel wants to know if Spike is her boyfriend. Buffy wonders if this is any of Angel's business. She then drops a bombshell on Angel by noting that Spike has a soul now. Angel, his bottom lip visibly trembling, notes that *everyone*'s got a soul now and that he had one first before it was cool to have one. 'I'm getting the brush-off for Captain Peroxide. It doesn't exactly bring out the champion in me,' he adds. Buffy says that Spike is not her boyfriend. But, he *is* in her heart. That'll end well, adds Angel, bitterly. Buffy is horrified by his attitude. What was the highlight of our relationship? she asks. When he broke up with her (**54**, 'The Prom'; **56**, 'Graduation Day' Part 2) or when she killed him (see **34**, 'Becoming' Part 2)? Buffy is aware of her stellar history with men, generally, and she doesn't see herself and Spike as a long-term couple. But, in this insanity, some things are starting to make sense to her and the guy thing is one of them. Buffy says that she always feared there was something wrong with her because she could never make a relationship work. But, she suggests, maybe she isn't supposed to. Because she is the Slayer? asks Angel. No, answers Buffy, because she's not ready yet for such a phase in her life. (She uses an amusing analogy concerning cookie dough that starts off well but gets silly after a while.) Angel accepts this and leaves but, before he does, Buffy tells him that sometimes she *does* think about the future and, although she isn't ready now, perhaps one day she will be. Angel says that he can wait for such an eventuality. (See *Angel*: 'The Girl in Question'.)

Later, Buffy visits Spike who tells her that he witnessed most of her meeting with Angel. Once they've discussed Angel's various attributes in some depth (see **Bitch!** and **Sex and Drugs and Rock'n'Roll**) Spike asks where the amulet is, believing that he must wear it during the final battle. Angel said that the amulet was meant to be worn by a champion, Buffy notes. Spike considers this and looks disappointed. Then Buffy hands it to him.

Denial, Thy Name is Faith: Faith apologises to Robin for blowing him off (see **142**, 'Touched'). It's nothing personal, she adds, just that after she has sex with a guy there's not that much more she needs to know about him. That's a bleak outlook, Robin notes, and also defensive, isolationist Slayer crap. There is a whole world out there that Faith doesn't even know about, and a lot of the men who are pretty decent guys, he continues. Faith is sceptical, noting that when a man looks at her, his priorities shift. Robin asks if this is because she's so hot, adding that, actually, he is much prettier than she is. And that, for the record, their little sexual encounter didn't exactly rock his world. It was nice enough in its own way considering how inexperienced Faith is, he concluded. Faith is outraged and starts to remove her pants, telling him that they're going to go again, right here, right now. Robin chuckles and asks Faith to make him a deal. If they both live through this, she has to give him the chance to surprise her. Faith agrees, although she suggests that *no way* is he prettier than her.

The Empowerment Starts at the Apocalypse: In every generation, one slayer is born. That's the way it has always been. This is because a bunch of Shadow Men who died thousands of years ago made that rule. They were powerful men, Buffy notes, but Willow is more powerful. So, Buffy decides to change the rules. Her power will become *their* power. Willow uses the essence of the Guardian's weapon to change destiny and create an entire generation of Slayers. Not just the potentials fighting with Faith and Buffy, but all around the world.

The Conspiracy Starts at Closing Time: The First appears to Buffy as, initially, Caleb and then as Buffy herself.

References: Willow's 'Oh My Goddess' is an allusion to the title of the contemporary season finale of *Charmed*. Buffy refers to Angel's jealousy of Spike in relation to *Dawson*'s *Creek*. Faith alludes to the toy Rock 'Em Sock 'Em Robots. Xander, Andrew, Giles and Amanda play *Dungeons and Dragons* in the hours before the final battle (Giles seems to be rather rubbish at it; his character, a dwarf, being badly wounded by Trogdor the Burninator). Also, *Little Red Riding Hood*, Elizabeth Taylor, *Raiders of the Lost Ark* ('very dangerous') and Alice Cooper's 'School's Out'. Among the establishments destroyed when the Sunnydale Mall disappeared into the ground along with the rest of the town were The Gap, Starbucks and Toys Я Us. There's an oblique allusion to *Hamlet*. Visually influences include *The West Wing*, *The Lord of the Rings*, *Raiders of the Lost Ark*, *Indiana Jones and the Last Crusade* and *Sleepy Hollow*.

Bitch!: Spike telling Buffy that Angel wears lifts in his shoes to make him look taller.

Awesome!: There's much to admire in this episode: The fact that most of the characters survive the series to fight another day in spin-off novels, fan-fiction and our dreams being not least among them. 'He had to split' and Buffy's little giggle after she says it – how we've missed such moments over the last couple of years. Dawn kicking Buffy as payback for her attempt to get Dawn away from danger. Spike's petulant jealousy over Angel (and, especially, his childishly incompetent drawing of Angel on his punch-bag – a definite series highlight). Giles's heart-warming reconciliation with Buffy. Faith and Robin in the cellar and Faith's discovery that not every man in the world is a worthless shit. The Mall discussion between four old friends and Giles's comment that the world is *definitely* doomed, a reminder of where we've come from. White Willow at her most awesome. Xander touching Buffy's hand as they part for what may be the final time. The sexual politics of Dawn saving Xander's life and Anya saving Andrew's, even at the cost of her own. The poetry of Spike's speech to Buffy. Vi keeping Rona awake and, as a consequence, alive. The Sunnydale sign falling into the crater, bringing a visual sense of closure. (It can also be seen, of course, as a signal to the unspoiled that Spike would be returning. He twice knocked that particular road sign over when he arrived in Sunnydale: see **15**, 'School Hard'; **42**, 'Lover's Walk'). Buffy's smile at the end.

What a Shame They Dropped . . .: A sequence in which, prior to the final battle, Giles and Wood share a 'hand-rolled cigarette' as Whedon identified it in the script. This scene was filmed but edited for timing reasons.

'You May Remember Me From Such Films and TV Series As . . .': Ally Matsumura appeared in *Rogues*. Jenna Edwards played Jane White in *Sick & Twisted*. Kelli Wheeler's movies include *Gabrielle*. Ana Maria Lagasca was in *The X-Files*.

Sex and Drugs and Rock'n'Roll: When Buffy sees Spike's Angel drawing on his punchbag she says that one of these days she's going put the two of them in a room and let them wrestle it out. Buffy actually seems quite excited by the prospect and asks if there could be oil of some kind involved. However, she assures Spike that when she kissed Angel, there were no tongues involved and Angel was merely saying hello.

Logic, Let Me Introduce You to This Window: Anya's rabbit-phobia remains unexplained. It *was* funny, though. The effect that the Slayer spell has on timid little Vi (turning her into a seriously ass-kicking Amazonian warrior) is one of the highlights of the episode, and a critical summation of the series' entire concept: I am woman, hear me roar. But, hang on, didn't Vi have a broken arm in **143**, 'End of Days'? We know Slayers heal quickly, but she's only been one for *seconds* before she's leading the charge against Hell's minions. Anya's hair is totally different to how it appeared in the last episode despite the fact that this one this takes places just hours afterwards. On a similar theme, Buffy's hair changes style after her night with Spike. Perhaps, in that case, it's best not to ask too many questions.

When Buffy jumps from building to building, the clouds in the sky appear and disappear between shots. Then the sky turns orange for no adequately explained reason. (Perhaps a whole town disappearing into a crater can cause this phenomena?) When Buffy escapes from the school, before she runs up the stairs she's holding the top of the weapon. But, when the angle changes, she's holding it in the middle. Buffy is stabbed and the First appears, saying that she has suffered a mortal injury. Not *that* mortal, seemingly, as Buffy is able to get up, continue fighting, tell Spike that she loves him and then jump over tall buildings within moments of this seemingly fatal wound. During the final scenes, she doesn't even show any sign of bleeding. When Andrew begins his little speech, he's on Anya's right. When she grabs him to walk away, he's on her left. When Buffy and the potentials first look into the Hellmouth just as the Über-Vamp army notice their presence, one of the vampires in the centre has his prosthetic headpiece in the process of peeling off. When Vi kicks a Turok-Han in mid-air, she's clearly on a harness. As Buffy jumps off the bus she is wearing flat-soled hiking boots, instead of the tan boots with pointed toes that she had on earlier. Where were all the demons and monsters from within the Hellmouth itself (like, for instance, the creature seen in **12**, 'Prophecy Girl', and **47**, 'The Zeppo')? It's established that Sunnydale is a coastal town (**32**, 'Go Fish'), with it's own docks (**25**, 'Surprise'; **49**, 'Consequences') and also at least one – possibly two – sizeable lakes (**107**, 'Once More, With Feeling'; **126**, 'Help'). So, when the town disappears into a massive crater, where does all the water go?

The whole business concerning the Guardian's weapon is never adequately explained. How does the weapon, which both Faith and Buffy feel power in but Willow, specifically, does not, allow Willow to change the future destiny of the Slayer line and of – presumably – thousands of teenage girls? There are an awful lot of cars in the car park opposite the school when one considers that Sunnydale is supposed to be abandoned. Plus, of course, there's an inevitable let down at the end. The First is not defeated, because it can't be. It is still free to initiate its plans all over again in Cleveland. Next week, if it wants to. Which is, in a series that has seldom counted ambiguity as one of it's virtues (unlike, say, *The X-Files*), a somewhat unsatisfying conclusion. And here's a question that has to be asked here even though, hopefully, it will be answered one day: who, subsequently, went into the Hellmouth crater, found the amulet in the ruins, and sent it to Angel in Los Angeles? (See *Angel*: 'Conviction'; 'You're Welcome'.)

The Big Issue: Taking the season as a whole, the production never fully resolved the question of what, specifically, Buffy did to allow the First its opportunity. It is, seemingly, something to do with Buffy having returned from the afterlife in **101**, 'Bargaining' Part 1. In the *Angel* episode 'Inside Out', the demon Skip alludes to the uniqueness of this situation when he tells Angel that no one has ever returned from paradise. Except for a Slayer, once. However, it's equally possible that events such as Buffy sending Angel to Hell (**34**, 'Becoming' Part 2; something that the Powers That Be specifically had to intervene to correct) or even Buffy sleeping with

Angel (**25**, 'Surprise', which, directly, led to the latter event) could
have caused the kind of cosmic ripples that the First needed here.
Note that the First only appeared in Buffy's life after Angel had
returned from Hell. Possibly the entity was able to hitch a ride into
this dimension in just this way. It's also notable that in **44**,
'Amends', the First's initial attempts to influence Angel were *not*
to have him kill himself (that came later) but, merely, to leave
Sunnydale and thus remove himself physically from Buffy. Presumably, the First knew all about the prophecy of the vampire
with a soul either stopping or, at least, having a significant part to
play in an apocalypse (see various *Angel* episodes including 'To
Shanshu in LA'; 'Blood Money'; 'Loyalty'; 'Hellbound'; 'Destiny';
'A Hole in the World' and 'Not Fade Away') and, therefore,
wanted him out of the picture.

The Future: We changed the world, Willow tells the others. All
over, Slayers are awakening everywhere. We have a lot of work
ahead of us, Giles suggests. Meanwhile, Buffy is no longer the sole
chosen one any more. What are we going to do now? asks Dawn.
Buffy merely smiles. (The *Angel* episode 'Just Rewards', which
features the return of Spike, takes place approximately three weeks
after the events of 'Chosen'. Angel tells Spike that Buffy is
currently in Europe. In a subsequent *Angel* episode, 'Damage',
Andrew reveals that Giles, together with several key Sunnydale
alumni, has reactivated the Council of Watchers. Buffy is based in
Rome, recruiting potential Slayers, while Dawn attends a boarding
school in Italy. Xander is in Africa and Willow and Kennedy in
Brazil.) See, also, *Angel*: 'The Girl in Question'.

Quote/Unquote: Angel: 'Everybody's got a soul now. I started it,
the whole "having a soul", before it was the cool new thing.' Buffy:
'Ohmigod, are you twelve?'
  Spike, when Buffy tells him that Angel has gone: 'Just popped
by for a quickie, then?' Buffy: 'Good. I haven't had quite enough
jealous vampire crap for one night.'
  Giles, on Buffy's plan: 'I think it's bloody brilliant . . . if you
want my opinion.'
  Buffy: 'I love you.' Spike: 'No, you don't. But thanks for saying
it.'

Notes: 'We're gonna win.' So we reach the end of a road, well
travelled. 'Chosen' is, from the outset, *Buffy*'s fitting finale to the
world. A dignified, thoughtful, controlled episode that gracefully

defines what this series was always about. Touching, without resorting to awkward mawkish gestures, brilliantly characterised to make the audience care about these people. Full of amusing, clever dialogue, witty allusions, *knowing* pop-culture references, featuring a dazzling use of metaphor, passionate sexuality, stunning visuals, thrilling action sequences and the *realpolitik* of informed social comment. That's 'Chosen'. It's also an accurate summation of *Buffy* itself. Relationships are the keys to the episode, just as they always were to the series as a whole. Faith, Spike, Andrew and Anya are all, in one way or another, redeemed through the power of their union with, or trust in, others. There's no room for betrayal or cynicism in Joss Whedon's vast final ambition. The series ends, as it began, with a wholly positive metaphor concerning the need for female empowerment and how we are all stronger when we have others to rely upon. So many TV series never achieve anything like their full potential – they either end before their time, or they carry on too long and masturbate to death on their own pretensions. *Buffy* did neither. It, like all great stories, had a beginning, a middle and an end. That end probably came at just the right moment, when the series was still aware of how to do all the right things – even if they weren't always the easy things. Most fans will, ultimately, agree that, as *Picnic At Hanging Rock* once suggested, everything begins and ends at exactly the right time. *Buffy* was a beautiful thing. The creation of a gifted auteur and his talented creative staff and truly special cast. And it remained beautiful right until the final shot of its final show, which says much about the qualities that the series always strived for. 'I wanna see how it ends,' says Spike, moments before the climax. It ended, as it was always going to end, with some tragedy, but with ultimate hope and much redemption. It ended with Sunnydale gone, but with many survivors to carry on the fight that the series always concerned itself with. It ended, in short, with a *future*. 'Did we make it?' asks Robin. They did, and they changed the world, as Willow notes. Maybe only a little bit, and only perhaps for those of us who surrendered our cultural and intellectual prejudices and saw beyond a silly title and an aesthetic that suggested teenage horror shenanigans with no depth, no poetry, no soul. *Buffy* had all of the above and more besides. They changed the world *and* they won.

The scene between Giles, Buffy, Xander and Willow immediately prior to the climactic events is a parody of the closing scene from **2**, 'The Harvest'. Giles mentions that there is another

Hellmouth beneath Cleveland (as vaguely alluded to in **43**, 'The Wish'). Xander says he needs a new look due to his eyepatch. Buffy thinks he looked good as a secret agent (see **60**, 'Fear Itself'). Willow suggests he could become a pirate (see **106**, 'All The Way'; **141**, 'Empty Places'). Andrew mentions his brother, Tucker (see **54**, 'The Prom'). When Buffy asks Xander what he wants to do tomorrow, he replies that mini-golf comes to mind (see **23**, 'Ted').

Some of Cassie Newton's predictions from **126**, 'Help', come true. For instance, Buffy does tell Spike that she loves him (even if, as Spike suggests, she doesn't really mean it). The climax takes place in a location that is dark and underground, just as Cassie said it would. And, ultimately, Buffy *does* make a significant difference. The amulet and the file that Angel brings to Buffy were given to him by Wolfram & Hart's Lilah Morgan in *Angel*: 'Home'. The source of the information, he notes, is not even remotely reliable.

Fan-fiction: Soon after this episode's broadcast a script appeared on the Internet that was alleged to be a genuine alternate version for 'Chosen'. There were many differences, including extended dialogue, Xander dying to save Dawn, Anya and Spike surviving, and a larger explanation as to why the First was able to act now.

Critique: According to Fay McFadden of the *Seattle Times*, *Buffy*'s legacy 'will outlive tonight's anticlimactic finale'. This view was shared by the *National Review*'s Thomas Hibbs who wrote that 'the multiple tensions Whedon set up in the weeks leading up to the final episode simply dissolve into thin air'. These, however, were lone voices compared to the avalanche of gushing reviews that accompanied the broadcast of the finale (see ***Buffy*: The Legacy**). Perhaps this was best summed up by one of the most consistently incisive commentators on the series, *TV Zone*'s Mark Wyman. He wrote of 'Chosen' that 'Spike's fate is undercut by casting news elsewhere,[66] yet is a radiant redemption in context,' and described the episode as 'a definitive, yet positive ending: not too tidy and not trite at all. Just very special. Thank you, *Buffy*.'

Did You Know?: Sarah Michelle Gellar's cast and crewmates were not sorry to see the back of her, according to a rather tawdry

---

[66] To the horror of Mutant Enemy, the WB chose the week of the *Buffy* finale to announce that James Marsters had been signed to reprise the role of Spike in the 2003–04 season of *Angel*, thus destroying much of the pathos that the character's self-sacrifice in 'Chosen' had achieved.

'exclusive' claimed by the US *Star* magazine. 'They felt like Sarah had sucked the life out of them,' noted one, anonymous, insider. Gellar was alleged to have infuriated the cast during the last week of filming by constantly harping on about the various films she was going to do next and they were said to be jubilant when she missed the show's wrap party (Sarah having left immediately after filming the finale to shoot *Scooby-Doo Too*.) 'There was such resentment toward her, they all agreed it was best that she say goodbye on the set,' continued the, still-anonymous, insider. Sarah's superiority complex, the article alleged, had earned her the onset nickname *The Duchess* from disgusted crew.

Cast and Crew Comments: Emma Caulfield told *SciFi Wire* that she was surprised to find herself in an emotional state after filming her last scenes. 'It was bittersweet,' Caulfield noted at the 29th annual Saturn Awards, where she was recognised as 'Female Face of the Future'. 'I wasn't prepared for how it was going to affect me. As soon as they announced [my final scene], I burst into tears.'

'It was very bittersweet, an emotional day for everyone,' added Alyson Hannigan.

For Sarah Michelle Gellar, as she told *Access Hollywood*, she had *Buffy*'s fans on her mind when the end came: 'I want to thank them all because without the fans, this show had no chance. We were a mid-season replacement on the WB based on an unsuccessful movie. People pitied me when I got this job, but I just knew there was something about this show. Then, all of the sudden, [it] became this huge success. It was because we had die-hard fans that supported our show.'

Joss Whedon's Comments: The last scene of this episode was written at the same time as the season opener by Joss. He noted that he knew all along how the season would end.

In what he announced would be his final posting to the Bronze message board on 20 May 2003, Joss revealed that, 'Now, at last, I can tell you guys what happens next Tuesday without lying. 1) I will probably have a beer. 2) Earth, more or less turning, pretty certain. 3) I might read. Now I get why everyone loves spoilers! I see that I was shackled by *Buffy* and now I'm free. Hope you liked [it].' I think it's safe to say we did, Joss.

Buffy: The Legacy: 'I truly believe that in years to come, people will look back and say, "That was a show that was on TV." Yessir. I truly do,' joked Joss Whedon to the press when the official announcement of *Buffy*'s conclusion came on 27 February 2003. Three months later, the outpouring of analysis and column inches across the Western media that greeted the US broadcast of *Buffy*'s final episode seemed, at first glance, somewhat ridiculous. Yes, it was a show on TV, all right. 'Without question, *Buffy* will live on for generations,' added Fox's president Dana Walden.

'No American series over the past decade – not even *The Simpsons* or *Friends* – captured the confident, post-modernist teenage Zeitgeist of the Nineties so unerringly well,' wrote Martin Sieff of Untied International Press. Describing *Buffy* as 'the most original, witty and provocative show of the past two decades', the *Independent* ran an obituary which concluded: 'With astonishing bravura, *Buffy* succeeded in blending the conventions of teenage soap-opera with smart, dialogue-driven comedy, a phantasmagoria of supernatural motifs and knotty theological debate.' The *Miami Herald* added: 'What should concern any TV fan is the end of a daring work of love and imagination, something born of passion instead of a fleeting, this-year's-flavour fame.' The *Toronto Star* lamented the end of a 'multi-dimensional, deeply recessed and densely layered mythology ... that could engage both supernatural escapism and earthly social constructs such as friendship, love, power, religion and free will'. The series was always smarter, funnier and more literate than almost anything on TV, but it was, for various reasons, always classified as a cult hit, wrote Rick Kushman. The truth, of course, is that *Buffy* was never a cult series in the accepted sense. 'Its fans,' noted Kushman, 'don't fit [into] one category, stretching from teens to midrange adults to, honestly, my mom. All it takes to appreciate this show is a developed sense of humor and some kind of brain.'

Such reactions were in accordance with the original strategy of Joss Whedon, who told the satirical US magazine *The Onion*: 'I designed Buffy to be an icon, to be loved in a way that other shows can't be. It's about adolescence, which is the most important thing people go through in their development.' *Buffy* 'mixed on-the-edge suspense, witty dialogue and heartbreaking drama in one show, often [all] at the same time', noted *ABC News*'s J Jennings Moss. 'Sometimes I've felt like a hostage to the show.' 'While *Buffy* takes its operatic themes and moral sensibility from comic books, its humor and lightness of touch are more akin to BBC fare,' added the *Daily Standard*'s Jonathan Last. 'And at every turn the show gives the audience what they need, not what they want.' Other press comments included: '*Buffy* has much to teach us about life' (the *Seattle Post-Intelligencer*); '*Buffy* gets a killer finale' (the *New York Daily News*); 'Forget about the world, *Buffy* saved television' (the *National Review*); 'eternal thanks go to [the] Slayer' (*Contra Costa Times*); and, perhaps inevitably, 'she saved the world, a lot' (the *Sydney Morning Herald*).

But, for many, even those within the media itself, *Buffy* always struck a far deeper chord than mere aesthetics. Like *The Simpsons*, wrote *The Globe and Mail*'s John Doyle, *Buffy* exists on several levels. 'It has a rare sense of humour about itself – an attribute that appeals to writers who like to think they can be knowing and ironic about pop-culture. It's been a heterosexual love story, a lesbian love story, a mother/daughter drama and a saga about high-school geeks.' Writing in *The Charlotte Observer*, Courtney Devores noted that she had become a *Buffy* addict in February 2001, directly as a consequence of watching **94**; 'The Body'. 'I loved the humor, drama, goth-spook factor and characters I'd much rather hang with than those from, say, *Friends*,' Devores noted. 'When my own father died a few weeks ago, I thought about *Buffy* losing her mom.' Another critic who supported the series throughout the years was Tim Goodman of the *San Francisco Chronicle*. He noted that 'the series was clever on many levels and never catered to simplicity or predictability'. *Buffy* was always, as Goodman added, smartly written, a wink to the intelligentsia who got past the title and embraced the concept. 'It led, not followed, the entire way. An amazing feat, although Whedon has missed out on the mainstream applause given to peers [like] Aaron Sorkin, David E Kelley and Steven Bochco.'

One aspect of the show's make-up that never received much press attention was that *Buffy* was always at its best when it was either skewering TV viewers' expectations or taking aim with pointed barbs at society's powerful elite, noted *Orange County Weekly*'s Victor Infante. '*Buffy*'s world was dangerous long before Sept 11. It's a place where violence at best draws a stalemate for the forces of good, and where everyone can be redeemed by love. A surprisingly charitable theme but, in a world [where] we're told to trust authority above individual conscience, also subversive.'

In an article celebrating his favourite episodes, the *Independent*'s Robert Hanks noted that: 'Dennis Potter once dared to stage such narrative coups on British TV. These days, we're encouraged to treat hammy drivel such as *Cambridge Spies* as the benchmark of our "quality" drama. Could that be a sepulchral laugh I hear through the Hellmouth?' According to the *Guardian*'s Gareth

McLean, *Buffy* was 'a collection of fairy tales that explore age-old concerns such as identity and redemption, as well as contemporary ones [like] moral panic and consumer culture. Whether showing lesbian kisses, tackling adult themes or prizing old fashioned romance, *Buffy* was a *brave* show.' 'It was the strength of the storytelling that made *Buffy* a hit,' noted *TV Zone*'s James Abery. 'The cast and the series grew with its fans.'

And still the plaudits continued: *Buffy* was 'one of the most ingenious and inventive TV shows of its era,' wrote Charles Shaar Murray in the *Evening Standard*. 'It combined and deconstructed a fistful of notionally incompatible genres, all served up with crackingly witty dialogue and Hong Kong-movie influenced martial-arts action.' '*Buffy* has always been the least guilty of TV pleasures,' noted Robert Bianco. 'As with all cultists, *Buffy* fans were often forced to defend themselves to the uninitiated. But, honestly, defending the show has never been particularly hard, or embarrassing.' The series, according to Kate O'Hare, turned 'an introspective screenwriter into a cult hero, a former soap-opera star into a pop icon, and a misunderstood and dismissed genre into fodder for everything from Internet mania to scholarly dissertations'.

The final word on *Buffy*'s legacy should, undoubtedly, go to Joss Whedon himself. The day after 'Chosen' was broadcast he was asked by *TV Guide* about what the future has in store. Today is the first day of life after *Buffy*, they noted with almost comic reverence. 'It's also Day 13 of trying to get my five-month-old to sleep, so I just go from one problem to the next,' Joss replied. 'Your sense of closure never comes when you think it's going to. It'll happen two weeks from Monday. I'll suddenly go, "Good Lord. My entire life has changed."'

Maybe *that*'s *Buffy*'s ultimate legacy, that it changed so many lives.

Buffy and the Internet

Buffy was, in many ways, TV's first *true* child of the Internet age. Even more than *The X-Files*, the other series to which such a term is frequently applied, *Buffy* not only saw its fans embrace new technology to spread the gospel, but the Net itself quickly became a vital part of the series' iconography.[67] Within weeks of *Buffy*'s debut, online fan-communities were spawned. As with most fandoms, much of what emerged was great, but a little was downright scary.

Newsgroups: alt.tv.buffy-v-slayer allows posters to discuss all aspects of the series. In the past it's been a stimulating forum with debate encouraged. However, it has also, occasionally, attracted an aggressive contingent and, that curse of usenet, 'trolls' (people who send offensive messages simply to stir up trouble). Hell hath no fury like overgrown schoolchildren with access to a computer. A case in point: when the last edition of *Slayer* was published in 2002, it was criticised by some newsgroup regulars because they regarded the above one-line description of trolling as a personal insult. This generated a heated thread with over 150 messages. All of which, kind of, proves my point: as with many fandoms the users of *a.t.b-v-s* like talking about *Buffy* but some of them actually prefer talking about themselves. uk.media.tv.buffy-v-slayer is, as the name suggests, a British equivalent and features, broadly, similar topics.

alt.fan.buffy-v-slayer.creative is a fan-fiction forum carrying a wide range of missing adventures, character vignettes, 'shipper (relationship-based erotica) and slash (same-sex erotica), some of it of a very high standard indeed. There are also lively newsgroups in Europe (alt.buffy.europe) and Australia (aus.tv.buffy) where *Buffy* has big followings and groups devoted to Sarah Michelle Gellar and Alyson Hannigan (alt.fan.sarah-m-gellar and alt.fan.hannigan respectively).

---

[67] 'More than any previous TV cult, *Buffy* sparked a state of creative synergy with the Internet generation,' wrote Boyd Tonkin in the *Independent*. Ironically, when asked about his own Internet usage in 1999, Joss Whedon told *DreamWatch*: 'I came to it late. I'm still: "What's download?"' The Internet was also, as Whedon told *filmforce.ign.com*, where 'we found out we had a fan base. They came together as a family on the Internet'.

Mailing Lists: More relaxed than usenet, at http://groups. yahoo.com/ you'll find access to numerous *Buffy*-lists. Simply type the name of your favourite character or actor into the 'search groups' box. Be warned, however. Mailing lists can be addictive, so resist the temptation to join too many. It's also worth noting how many members a group has. Some of the larger groups are *very* high volume; for example, *The Bloody Awful Poets Society* (motto: 'Spike HAS been redeemed, dammit!') has over 2,500 members and generates hundreds of messages every day. Especially recommended is the *JossBTVS* list, which features daily newsflashes on the activities of the cast and crew. *Buffy-Christian* are a group who pride themselves on being 'Christians who love *Buffy*' and reject small-minded bigotry in all its forms. If you're up for a lively debate, join the fun at *conversebuffyverse*. Fans of gossip can catch the latest media articles and news from other forums at *spoiler-crypt*.

Among the public lists are *BuffyScripts* (which provides a look at rarities such as early episode drafts), *skyonebuffythevampire slayer* and *BuffyWatchers*, which is basically a group of friends, including this author, who are happy for visitors to join us for after-dinner chats. A *Buffy* version of *The Algonquin*, if you will. In short there's a list for everything: each character, actor and writer will have a yahoo group somewhere. You will get the option of having posts sent to you or of checking the list via a web-link.

Posting Boards: The original official *Posting Board*, *The Bronze*, is sadly no more. But it's spirit lives on at www.bronzebeta.com. This includes occasional contributions from Joss Whedon and other members of the production team (Jane Espenson, David Fury and Steven DeKnight have all posted, for example). It's fast, cliquey and, to a newcomer, can seem bewildering with it's shout-out lists and in-jokes. But it's worth sticking around as you'll find yourself participating in some fascinating discussions. *All Things Philosophical On BtVS* (www.voy.com/14567/) is also well worth a visit.

Many fan-sites have their own posting boards like *http:// forums.morethanspike.com/*, a haven for all-things-Marsters, or the fascinating *http://pub165.ezboard.com/ftheducksversefrm1*, home to the Ducks, a loyal fan community devoted to 'classic *Buffy*' (for which read 'Buffy and Angel, tru-luv-4ever'). Fans of the Willow/ Tara relationship will be welcome at *http://froggyfrog.com/kitten/*, a friendly, welcoming place so long as you don't mention Warren.

An amusing diversion is to visit a number of 'shipper-sites and note the wildly differing reactions to the same episodes or events. What is nirvana to a Bangel (a Buffy/Angel 'shipper) will likely infuriate a Spuffy (Buffy/Spike 'shipper), while the Spanders (Spike/Xander) and Spangels (Spike/Angel) eagerly seize upon each 'West Hollywood' moment in *Buffy* and *Angel* where the subtext seems to become the text. Meanwhile, the Redemptionistas (see *www.tabularasa.com*) battle it out with the Ducks and the Evilistas in a never-ending game of 'my vampire's better than your vampire'. Fans argue, endlessly, about the amount of screen-time devoted to their objects of affections. Even those who've fallen out of love with the series have their own forums, known as 'ranting rooms'. If all of this sounds a bit silly then, yes, it probably is. But it's mostly good fun, especially if you remember to take most of what you read with a healthy pinch of salt. You will, however, be amazed that a television show can inspire such passion and devotion. And, within a few weeks, you'll probably wonder how you ever lived without knowing this world existed.

A good rule of thumb for newbies on *all* forums is to introduce yourself, read the rules, then lurk about for a few days watching what goes on. It's easy to make friends but certain issues can bring out an element of insane-troll-logic in everyone. So, don't be 'a Bezoar'. Or you'll get flamed. And, if you're feeling *really* brave, go and play hardball with the bitingly sarcastic (yet often, *very funny*) fans at *www.televisionwithoutpity.com*. They take absolutely no prisoners; their motto is 'spare the snark, spoil the networks'. You can, however, practice on somewhat gentler forums like *www.scoopme.com* first.

Websites: There are, literally, thousands of sites related to *Buffy*. What follows is a list of some of the author's favourites. Many of these are also part of webrings with links to related sites. An hour's surfing can get you to some bizarre places. Disclaimer: websites are, at best, transitory things and this information, though accurate when written, may be woefully out of date by publication.

UK Sites: The BBC's *Buffy Online* (www.bbc.co.uk/cult/buffy/ index.shtml) has become a breathtaking resource with one of the most up-to-date *Buffy* and *Angel* news services on the net. It also features numerous exclusive interviews and a plethora of other goodies. Check it daily and be secure in the knowledge that we still do something right in Great Britain!

US Sites: www.slayground.net (*Little Willow's Slayground*) is a delightful treasure-trove. It includes a VIP archive for the *Posting Board*, amusing subsections like 'The Xander Dance Club' and official webpages for both Danny Strong and Amber Benson. It's also a useful link to the *Keeper Sites* (www.stakeaclaim.net/), a webring with numerous associated pages. Leslie Remencus's beautiful *Buffy: The Music* (www.buffymusic.net) is devoted to the soundtracks on *Buffy*, including interviews, musical allusions, tour details etc. It's another absolute gem.

Suns – The Sunnydale Slayers (www.sunnydale-slayers/) was, according to the authors, started by 'a gang of people who wanted to talk about, lust after and discuss in depth *Buffy*'. It's great fun including fiction and well-written reviews. Love the *FAQ* where they answer the question: 'This isn't just a women's drool-fest over David Boreanaz, Anthony Stewart Head, Seth Green and Nicholas Brendon?' with 'Nope, we have male members too!' *The Complete Buffy the Vampire Slayer Episode Guide* (www.buffyguide.com/) was one of the best general review sites, with excellently written, intelligent episode summaries though it's now somewhat out of date. The legendary *Buffy Cross and Stake* (www.angelicslayer.com/tbcs/main.html) was one of the first major *Buffy* fansites and includes a huge range of material like character biographies, fiction, an extensive episode guide and an impressive links page.

Much Ado About Buffy (www.chosentwo.com/buffy/main/html) is another terrific site featuring extensive coverage of the *Buffy* comics. Fan-written transcripts and the shooting scripts of most *Buffy* and *Angel* episodes can be found at *www.psyche.kn-bremen.de*. Dan Erenberg's *Slayage* (www.slayage.com) is a media resource second to none. If you want to discover *anything* related to what's happening in the world of *Buffy* and *Angel* and those associated with the series, this should be your first port of call. The second ought to be *Whedonesque* (http://whedonesque.com/) which offers similar coverage plus a large and impressive message board.

Character- and actor-specific sites worth checking out include:

- *www.sarah-michelle-gellar.com* – the best of the, literally, hundreds of SMG sites.
- *Alyson Hannigan Appreciation Society* (www.network23.com/hub/ahas/default.htm).
- *David Boreanaz UK* (www.totallydavidboreanazuk.com/) – *the* resource for fans of the Broody one.

- *www.nicholas-brendon.com* – a frequently-updated Xander fan-site.
- *Be Back Before Dawn* (www.michelle-trachentberg.com) – for Dawnie-lovers.
- *www.JamesMartsers.com* – has an excellent archive from the, now-defunct, *Spike Spotting*.
- For up-to-date Marsters news, check out *www.morethanspike. com*
- If you're interested in James's music, go straight to *www.ghostoftherobot.com*
- Fans of Tony Head will love *www.angelfire.com/celeb2/anthony_head/MyHomePage.html*
- Info on everyone's favourite ex-vengeance-demon can be found at *www.ecaulfield.net/*
- Seth Green News (www.geocities.com/seth_green_news) – is the very place for Oz fans.
- Eliza Dushku's legion of followers should bookmark *Everlasting Eliza* (www.edushku.com).
- *Essence of Amber* (www.amberbenson.us) – features updates on Amber's flourishing career.
- *http://adam-busch.net* – includes links relating to Adam's band, Common Rotation.

Without the creator, and the writers, there would be no show. For more information, check out:

- Joss Whedon: *http://whedonesque.com/*
- Drew Goddard: *www.drewgoddard.com/*
- Jane Espenson: *www.pmcarlson.com/jane/*

www.slayerfanfic.com (*The Slayer Fanfic Archive*) is, as the name suggests, dedicated to *Buffy* fan-fiction with links to many related pages. www.buffysmut.com (*Bad Girls*) is a *must* for those adults yet to discover the joys of 'shipper and slash-fic. *The Darker Side of Sunnydale* (www.tdos.com), *Weetabix & Alcohol* (http://weetabixandalcohol.freewebtools.com) and *www.the-sandlot.com/* include fine examples of the various kinds of fan-fiction available. 'I love fanfic,' Jane Espenson told the *Posting Board*. 'I'm not really allowed to read *Buffy* [stories] but I do read other fandoms. There's some great stuff out there. Also some crappy stuff, but people should feel free to read/write that as well.' On the same forum, Joss commented: 'On the subject of fanfic I *am* aware that a good deal of it is naughty. My reaction to that is mixed; on the one hand, these are characters played by friends of mine, and the idea that someone is describing them in *full naughtitude* is a little creepy. On the other, eroticising the lives of fictional characters you care about is something we all do, if only in our heads, and it certainly shows that people care. So I'm not really against erotic-fic and I certainly don't mind the other kind. I wish I'd had this kind of forum when I was a kid.'

Marti Noxon, meanwhile, is full of praise for the genre. 'We're in a weird position,' she told *The Washington Post*. 'It's flattering because a universe you're part of has inspired people to continue imagining.' The writers, however, have to be careful, as a TV story with similarities to previously published fan-fiction could result in accusations of plagiarism. 'Because of legalities, we have to be judicious how much we read.'

Miscellaneous: Space prevents a detailed study of the vast array of *Buffy* websites around the world, but some demand to be highlighted: *Buffy*'s massive popularity in Australia is evidenced by the number of excellent Aussie domains. These include:

- *Buffy Down-Under* (www.buffydownunder.com/) – described as 'the ultimate Australian resource for *Buffy* and *Angel*'.
- Danny Sag's *Episode Title Explanations* (www.geocities.com/glpoj/buffy/) – a thoroughly fascinating site.
- *www.buffy.com.au/* – bang up-to-date and full of facty-goodness.

European readers, direct your search engines towards:

- *Buffy in Ireland* (www.//bite.to/Buffy).
- Numerous French sites including *Le Scooby Gang* (www.scoobygang.ht.st/), and
- *La Destinee de Buffy* (www. destinbuffy.ifrance.com/destinbuffy/Sommaire.htm).
- *Dutch Buffy* (http://members.tripod.lycos.nl.dutchbtvs).
- Germany's *SlayerWorld* (www,slayerworld.inf),
- and *Slayerweb* (www.buffy-tv.de/).
- The Italian site *Magic Shop* (http://digilander.libero/it/magicshop/).
- Iceland's *Blódsugubaninn Buffy* (http://oto.is/buffy/inngangur.htm).
- Portugal's *Buffy, a Caça Vampiros Page* (www.geocities/edilal/novaseries.htm).
- Sweden's *Totally Buffy* (http://medlem.spray.se/Totally_Buffy).

- And *Buffy in Israel* (www.geocities.com/TelevisionCity/Station/9409).

All of these offer impressive local coverage of the *Buffy* phenomena.

Band Candy (www.geocities.com/angeliklee/BandCandy.html) takes pride in being a site 'for *older Buffy* fans'. *Loaded* (www.dymphna.net/loaded) is the place for all Giles and Oz fans, whether your interest is their zen-like connection, a shared passion for high-quality rock'n'roll or just some slash-fic, there'll be something here for you.

http://pages/zoom/co/uk/kfantastico/frames/index.htm (*The Miss Kitty Fantastico Appreciation Society*) recognises the significant contribution to *Buffy* of Willow and Tara's sadly departed pussy. *The Buffy Body Count* (www.synapse.net/~dsample/BBC/) contains 'an ongoing count of the number of dead bodies on school property'. *You Thought YOU Were Obsessed with BtVS* (www.fortunecity.com/lavander/rampling/271/) assures readers that, no matter how much you love *Buffy*, someone out there *is* sadder than you. And, if you're searching for entertainment, head to *The Sunnydale Sock Puppet Theatre Company* (www.hellmouth.us/) a delightful mixture of role-play and fanfic.

At www.google.com a few clicks will take you from the useful and informative to the downright bizarre (ever wanted to know what would happen if Spike and Cap'n Jack Sparrow met? If so, you'll find it). Finally, there's *www.buffysearch.com* ('your portal to the *Buffy* and *Angel* community') a truly invaluable search engine that includes links to most of the above sites and, literally, hundreds more. Happy surfing.

'The Hellmouth is Officially Closed for Business'

One of the greatest, if least recognised, achievements of *Buffy* lay in it's ability to play textual games with many of life's truisms from within the series' fantasy framework. These subversions included: 'I had sex with my boyfriend and he turned into a monster,' 'nobody ever seems to notice me', 'redemption's a bitch' and, most obviously, one of the series' main recurring themes 'be careful what you wish for, it might come true'. In a deeper and more widespread context, however, one maxim that the series occasionally flirted with would, ultimately, come back to haunt those who watched *Buffy* to the end: 'You never know what you've got until it's gone.' And most of us realised the truth in this during the (metaphorically) dark days of June 2003 and beyond.

'Should [TV] producers try to determine what fans want?' asked SF author Peter David, rhetorically, in an article in *DreamWatch* around this time. No, he concluded, such second guessing is pointless because the fans themselves don't know. 'All they *do* know is that they want what they don't have and if they get it they don't want it any more. Until they don't have it. At which point they want it back.' He's right, you know. And we're *all* guilty of this to a greater or a lesser degree.

For seven years *Buffy* continued to work as a piece of satisfying dramatic artifice, on one level at least, directly *because* it challenged the hopes and expectations of the majority of its audience. Some of that audience reacted badly to such a conceptual slap in the face: they got all bolshy about constantly having to *think* about what they were watching and not simply being spoon-fed eye-candy set-pieces and painfully obvious dramatic situations. Some of these fans didn't like what they saw and said so, loudly and publicly, to anyone who would listen (and many who wouldn't). This was especially notable during *Buffy*'s sixth season. There were changes in the air and some of those changes were far from universally popular.

Now, here's a shocking revelation: TV fans, generally, are conservative people by nature and are usually resistant to change in their favourite shows. That's something of a universal constant. These people, however, are *not* idiots by any stretch of the imagination. They genuinely seem to care about the series that they follow – that's normally why they become fans in the first place. So it's probably worth acknowledging that there *are* occasions when there's a validity in such resistance of the inevitable. In one of his regular Internet postings during summer 2001, Joss Whedon indicated that the key theme of *Buffy*'s forthcoming sixth season would be, as he described it, 'Oh, grow up.' But some fans were never comfortable with the idea of Buffy, Xander and Willow growing up. They preferred them to be perpetual teenagers caught in a netherworld between the nightmares and nostalgia of childhood and the real-life, everyday horrors of the adult world. The boring stuff that *we* have to deal with every day: jobs, relationships, money problems. That's perfectly understandable – most people watch TV to escape the trivialities of life, not to *celebrate* them. I've always believed, however, that Joss Whedon and his writers had the ability to deal (either through metaphor or straight drama) with these characters as they grew up. To make such changes not only acceptable but, in fact, necessary. A revolution in evolution. In other words, to give the audience what we *needed* whether we wanted, or even *deserved*, it or not.

Critical acclaim was never far from *Buffy*'s doorstep. For example, in 2002 alone the series gained both Emmy and Golden Globe nominations and made the 10-Best lists of critics from such respected institutions as *Time*, *TV Guide* and *USA Today*. But fandom can be a far more difficult beast to tame. TV fandoms are strange places for the uninitiated. They grow up around a particular show primarily because of the quality of the product. But, by their inevitably incestuous and closed-bracketed nature, fandoms can sometimes become hypercritical seething pools of discontent if, in the consensus of a majority (or even a particularly vocal *minority*), whatever it was that made the show good in the first place has been lost or replaced. Of course, defining exactly what that 'whatever is was' *actually* consisted of is the hard part of such an equation.

The term 'jumping the shark' in Internet-speak refers to a single defining moment when a TV series reaches its critical (if not, necessarily, commercial) peak and that, from there on, it's all downhill. In other words, it's the point at which some of a particular show's fans start to use that old fandom standby, 'It's not as good as it used to be, is it?' There's actually a website that celebrates such moments and invites nominations at *www.jumptheshark.com* where, seemingly, cynicism and occasionally incisive critique can go hand-in-hand. The '*Buffy*'s jumped-the-shark' doomsayers were out in force during November 2001 around the time of the musical episode, **107**, 'Once More, With Feeling'. This was, a portion of *Buffy*'s fandom had apparently decided, *the* moment. Which, to this author, is not wholly dissimilar to those Harry Potter fans who are less interested in serious literary debate and more on whether Scooby Doo would belong to Gryffindor or Hufflepuff in bizarro-world.

The problem, in *Buffy*'s case, was always one of a consistent, almost unique, quality which set it apart from virtually everything else on television. A case of rank hyperbole? Not a bit of it. *Buffy* was, for most of the seven years of its existence, quite simply the best TV show in the world. OK, *maybe The Sopranos* or *The West Wing* or *24* are in the same league, but *that's* the extraordinary level at which *Buffy* always competed. Witty, inventive, dangerous and clever, the series use of teen-angst metaphor and media-referencing was an absolute revelation to cynical old hacks like myself. But this quality, it seemed, eventually jaded some viewers into expecting the unique every single week. After over 100 episodes, one could have been forgiven for thinking that it was OK for a show to settle for an if-it-ain't-broke-don't-fix-it formula. To, in effect, go down the Rolling Stones route and spend a year replaying the greatest hits to stadium audiences. That's exactly happened at *Star Trek: The Next Generation* around year six. It happened, too, on *The X-Files*. So, everybody had a bit of fun and got self-referential and a touch self-indulgent, and the ratings stayed relatively healthy. But in both cases a seven-year itch was just around the corner.

Was this an analogous situation with *Buffy*, then? Well, one can argue on relative quality issues all night – that's down to individuals. But the one thing that *Buffy* never did was to stand still and look backwards. Instead, there was, especially during its later seasons, not so much a gradual evolution in characterisation but rather an 'asteroid hitting earth and destroying all life'-style leap in focus and direction. It all really kicked-off at the end of season five. What are you gonna do now, we asked? Kill our lead character, they replied. OK, that's impressive. So, what do you do for an encore?

At least one rough year followed in the *Buffy*verse. We had storylines about addiction, betrayal and loneliness. We saw people whom we admired die, or leave, or suffer unbearable heartbreak.

We went to the brink of the apocalypse again and it was darkness and depression all the way. And, yet, we found that, ultimately, love redeems. Which always was and will remain, even now the series has ended, *Buffy*'s mission statement and what set it apart from its contemporaries. Because in *Buffy*, love conquered everything.

Of course fans, even the critical ones, knew *that* fact. The problem was in persuading others outside the Church of Slayer and All Her Minions to get with the programme. Many factors didn't help and one of the biggest was always the perception that *Buffy* was a cult series. Have readers noticed how often the word 'cult' is misused in connection with television? It's one of those dreadful, meaningless *NME* keywords like 'seminal' and 'postmodern' that, when you actually get down to it, nobody knows the true meaning of. When a television series is described as 'a cult show' that, in the past, has usually meant that about two men and their dog watch it, but that all three of those *really* like it. These days, it's somewhat different. When you hear about soap-operas, with their audiences of dozens of millions, being described in exactly these sort of esoteric terms, you realise that simple definitions no longer apply. The world has moved on and we, however reluctantly, have to move on with it.

Buffy, and *Angel*, both probably just about belonged in a category under the old definition of cult. It's certainly true that neither show ever had a massive audience in their country of origin, despite more than impressive worldwide sales and merchandising that *EastEnders* would kill for. Indeed, when *Buffy* made its controversial move from the WB to UPN in April 2001, some US media commentators – who were unfamiliar with the phenomenon – were forced to ask what, exactly, all the fuss was about. Let's remember, at that time *Buffy* was the 87th highest-rated show on American television. Those rating figures did rise, quite dramatically, during *Buffy*'s first season on UPN, but they went back down to roughly their former level during the seventh and final year.

People forget this now, and it's quite easy to because six and half years seems like ancient history to many, but there was a point when it looked as though Buffy Summers's legacy wouldn't be nearly so long-lasting. A flawed and not-even-particularly-interesting movie, and, four years later, 12 episodes of a TV show that merely dipped their toes into a magical world above the Hellmouth. A concept that promised, if it ever got the chance, to keep viewers entertained for years but which, due to the idiosyncrasies of US network TV, probably wouldn't. Rushed into production by Fox as a mid-season replacement for the emergent **WB**, *Buffy* burst on to the screens towards the end of the 1996–97 season and almost immediately gained a promising, if rather surprised, critical reaction. Those reviewers who weren't put off by the ridiculously over-the-top irony of the series' title, found themselves immersed in a show that used traditional horror clichés like vampires, witches and demons as a thoroughly sussed little metaphor for the very literal and realistic horrors of the high school years. A series with hip, knowing dialogue, observational comedy, aware pop-culture references and a sense of its own place in a genre that it was both a part of and a caustic reaction to. This wasn't, as most of the pre-publicity had led us to believe, some mildly amusing *The-X-Files*-meets-*Clueless*-at-Ridgemont-High. On the contrary, this was something that was brave and just a little bit dangerous. And you sensed, even at that early stage, that the people who were making the show *knew* this.

For all of these elements that *Buffy* had in its favour in those early days, the series' critical success (which had always been there and which, subsequently, grew stronger over the years) was, and remained, unmatched by any kind of audience-base to particularly write home about. An initial demographic of teenage girls was sought and, largely, gained by the network. Along the way, the series began to pick up converts: a devoted and literate fanbase among some of the more peripheral corners of SF and horror fandom, for instance. *Buffy* also acquired a big gay following; an element of upwardly mobile hipness as a name to drop in the right sort of circles (when *Rolling Stone* called the series 'the best in the world', you knew that was probably because *Buffy* was constantly being namechecked by many of the bands whom the magazine covered) as well as a certain following among the intelligentsia.

Yet, as late as 2002, during *Buffy*'s best-ever season in terms of ratings, it was *still* being described, by *TV Guide*'s Tim Appelo, as 'The least-watched great show on television,' and the series that was 'the most ridiculed by ignorati who think they're literati.' Like its peers which, Appelo continued, included such highbrow ratings favourites as *The West Wing*, *The Sopranos* and *ER*, *Buffy* was better than the average movie because the writer was the most important person on the set. Yet while all three of these top-rated series regularly won a shelf-load of awards, a 'lack of sameness is why *Buffy* is confined to tiny networks and snubbed by Emmys', the writer concluded. As many critics have noted, with distaste, television demands certain comforting rituals for its mass audience: safely contained and solvable crises; inelegant catch-phrases; overly familiar settings and static and bland everyman-type characterisation. All of these to comfort the average viewer that this is an unchanging world which will never let them down. A television of compromise, basically. *Buffy*, with its constant need to explore dark and unfamiliar spaces (both literal and emotional), to challenge conventions in terms of structure and, always, with the presence of mind to avoid being pigeonholed by inaccurate and superfluous labels, actually imperilled its own wider popularity, simply by daring to be different. The argument that a TV series is *too good* to find a mass audience is one that has been used by failed shows for as long as television has existed. In *Buffy*'s case, however, it may, just, have a grain of truth in it.

Or course, something being a critical success for exactly these reasons – that it refuses to dumb-down for the parts of its audience without an imagination – but not getting the viewers to match, is nothing new. Indeed, it's only a couple of years since the first season of *24* proved a textbook example. Nevertheless, at the end of its first, stunted, season, *Buffy* could be described as little more than a well-regarded and well-intentioned flop and it is perfectly possible that it would now be no more than a distant and hazy memory for the couple of million viewers that it initially picked up in the US had it been cancelled in June 1997. And it *very nearly was*. Tony Head came back to England to take a potentially recurring role in *Jonathan Creek*, and the Mutant Enemy production lot in Santa Monica was about to close its doors when, against all expectations, and very late in the day, the WB ordered a second season of *Buffy*.

Even then, with this show of support from the network, the viewers didn't come flocking. The only significant increase in the series' audience came halfway through season two when it was switched from an awkward, off-putting 9 p.m. Monday slot to 8 p.m. on Tuesday – where it would remain until the day it ended, despite a change of network. By the end of season two, *Buffy* had acquired, more or less, the bulk of the audience that it would retain for the next five years, and its long-term future was secure so long as it continued to be bold and daring and funny. Three things that it, thankfully, never stopped being. Indeed, towards the end of the second season, Joss Whedon was already in a position where he could suggest to the WB that they might like a spin-off series. And he followed this with the third season of *Buffy*, which remains, for many fans – this author included – the show's creative and imaginative zenith.

You know a series is comfortable and confident in its own abilities when it can afford to start experimenting. It's not, if it's well handled, a case of taking the audience for granted. Quite the opposite in fact. It shows that the production team have faith that their viewers will follow them through some baffling cul-de-sacs until they create something new and interesting. *Buffy* went through some peaks and troughs during season four. The idea of the Scooby Gang growing apart upset many fans, and the flowering of Willow's relationship with Tara lost the series a few viewers that it probably didn't want anyway. Things got worse before they got better, even in the, now critically lauded, fifth season. The Glory-arc took a while to get going, Dawn's introduction – these days seen as a conceptual masterstroke – confused many, and there was a really depressing period around the time that Riley left where it was difficult to work up much enthusiasm for any of the characters. This latter strand was even more obvious in *Buffy*'s sixth season which tried for minimalist realism at its core and, having for the most part succeeded, then faffed about playing annoying guessing games with the audience's tolerance for depressing storylines. It genuinely does say something that, during year six, *Buffy* got the worst critical mauling of its life at the very moment that it was getting its best viewing figures. You know what they say, you can please some of the people, some of the time . . .

So, after seven years and 144 episodes, the decision was taken to kill a groundbreaking television show *before* it jumped the shark – at least as far as most of the viewers were concerned. As fans, we should all be grateful for the past and look, expectantly, towards the future – whatever that may hold. 'Honestly, I hope the legacy [of *Buffy* is] there's a generation of girls who have the kind of hero lots of them didn't [previously] have and a lot of guys who are more comfortable with the idea of a girl with that much power,' Joss Whedon told the *Hollywood Reporter*.

Buffy ended, not because it particularly needed to, but because it was right that it should. There was, as Joss Whedon often noted, a vision involved in *Buffy*. This was tied in with various themes that the series has its heart – feminist empowerment; growing up; facing inner demons – and with the knowledge that, as each year passed, it was becoming harder to maintain the quality *and* maintain the ambition. The foundation on which *Buffy* was built, Whedon told the *Face*, was that 'if you make it through high school without becoming a monster, as some people did, then you are a hero'. *Buffy* could have continued for another year or two, just as *The X-Files* did. The question of whether it *should* was, thankfully, taken out of the fans' and the networks' hands by Joss Whedon's bravery in saying enough is enough.

'I don't have an ending in mind because I think of *Buffy* as life and I don't like to think about the end of that,' Joss had told *Horror Online* two years earlier. 'We know after the final frame of whatever episode ends the show that these lives will go on. Nothing is frozen in time. That's the whole point of the show, that we're always changing and growing.'

It was the right time to go and it was a beautiful ending. It provided closure and redemption and got a few laughs. And so *Buffy* ended with those of us who knew why it was so important filling magazine pages and the Internet with our perceptions on why it changed all our lives.

But, it *also* ended with those who simply never got it, still scratching their heads and wondering what the hell all this fuss was about. So, for them, here's the sitch: *Buffy the Vampire Slayer* was a TV show that concerned a teenage girl who, with her motley collection of friends, fought vampires on a school night and still found time to date and shop and do homework. And, together, they saved the world. A lot.

You *really* don't need to know any more than that. There's seven seasons of DVDs out there with your name on them. So buy them, watch them, and then wonder why you missed out the first time around.

Select Bibliography

The following books, articles, interviews and reviews were consulted in the preparation of this text:

Abery, James, 'Where Angel Fears to Tread', *Shivers*, issue 71, November 1999.

Acker, Amy, and Denisof, Alexis, 'Angel's Angels', interview by Jenny Cooney Carrillo, *DreamWatch*, issue 103, March 2003.

Adalin, Josef, '*Buffy* loss takes a bite of WB', *Variety*, 23 April 2001.

Adalin, Josef, 'Slayer shifts all the players', *Variety*, 10 July 2002.

Adalin, Josef, '*Buffy* creator mulls spinoff', Reuters, 27 February 2003.

Adalin, Josef, and Schneider, Michael, 'Plots are hot-spots for Net', *Daily Variety*, 23 September 2001.

Adams, Michael, *Slayer Slang: A Buffy the Vampire Slayer Lexicon*, Oxford University Press, 2003.

Amatangelo, Amy, 'Taming her inner demons: Outspoken *Buffy* star Emma Caulfield makes peace with acting profession', *Boston Globe*, 4 March 2002.

Amatangelo, Amy, 'Hits from the Hellmouth: The best and worst of *Buffy*', *Boston Herald*, 18 May 2003.

Andreeva, Nellie, '*Buffy*'s Brendon Takes Fox Pilot Dip', Reuters, 11 April 2003.

'Angel Restores Faith', *DreamWatch*, issue 68, April 2000.

'. . . and finally', *Metro*, 12 July 2001.

Anthony, Ted, '12 Weeks After Columbine, Delayed *Buffy* airs', *Associated Press*, 12 July 1999.

Appelo, Tim and Williams, Stephanie, 'Get Buffed Up – A Definitive Episode Guide', *TV Guide*, July 1999.

Appelo, Tim, 'Buffy Slays. Now What? The least-watched great show on TV grows up', *Slate*, 5 November 2001.

Appleyard, Bryan, 'A teenager to get your teeth into', *Sunday Times* (*Culture* section), 10 December 2000.

Atherton, Tony, 'Fantasy TV: The New Reality', *Ottawa Citizen*, 27 January 2000.

Atkins, Ian, 'Homecoming' to 'The Zeppo', *Shivers*, issues 70, 71, October, November 1999.

Atkins, Ian, 'Superstar' to 'New Moon Rising', *Shivers*, issue 81, September 2000.

Ausiello, Michael, '*Buffy* star dead again', *TV Guide*, 30 October 2002.

Ausiello, Michael '*Buffy* creator speaks!' *TV Guide*, 19 May 2003.

Ausiello, Michael, '*Angel* Mystery: Will Cordy Wake Up?' *TV Guide*, 26 May 2003.

Baldwin, Kristen, 'Green's Day', *Entertainment Weekly*, May 1999.

Baldwin, Kristen, Fretts, Bruce, Schilling, Mary Kaye, and Tucker, Ken, 'Slay Ride', *Entertainment Weekly*, issue 505, 1 October 1999.

Barrett, David V, 'Far more than a teenage fang club', *Independent*, 3 January 2002.

Battaglio, Stephen, '*Buffy*'s future is at stake', *New York Daily News*, 13 January 2003.

Behr, Jason, 'Behr Essentials', interview by Paul Simpson and Ruth Thomas, *DreamWatch*, issue 68, April 2000.

Beifuss, John, 'Empowerment at stake: *Buffy* phenomena strikes a blow for mythic adolescence', *Go Memphis*, 21 January 2003.

Benson, Amber, 'Every Little Thing She Does . . .' interview by Matt Springer, *Buffy the Vampire Slayer*, issue 8, Summer 2000.

Benson, Amber, 'Is there life after death on *Buffy*?' interview by Alec Harvey, *Birmingham News*, 25 July 2002.

Benson, Amber, 'What Amber Did Next', interview by Mark Wyman, *TV Zone*, issue 161, March 2003.

Benz, Julie, 'Little Miss Understood', interview by Ed Gross, *SFX Unofficial Buffy Collection*, 2000.

Benz, Julie, 'Princess of the Night', interview by Ian Spelling, *Starlog*, issue 14, June 2001.

Bergstrom, Cynthia, 'Slaying With Style', interview by Matt Springer, *Buffy the Vampire Slayer*, issue 3, Spring 1999.

Betts, Hannah, 'And now, ladies, just for yourselves . . . When Harry met Garry', *The Times*, 7 July 2001.

Bianco, Robert, 'Holiday Ghosts Haunt the Vampire Slayers: A *Buffy* with a *Christmas Carol* bite', ('Amends' review), *USA Today*, 15 December 1999.

Bianco, Robert, '*Buffy* finale slays its fans', *USA Today*, 21 May 2002.

Bianco, Robert, '*Buffy* will rise from graveness', *USA Today*, 16 July 2002.

Bianco, Robert, 'Buffy returns to chat up the dead', *USA Today*, 11 November 2002.

Bianco, Robert, 'The good, the bad and the ugly of 2002 TV', *USA Today*, 22 December 2002.

Bianco, Robert, 'Show creator takes stab at 10 favorite episodes', *USA Today*, 27 April 2003.

Bianco, Robert, 'The end of *Buffy* feels like a dagger to the heart', *USA Today*, 28 April 2003.

Bianco, Robert, 'Our Slayer won't go gently into the dark night', *USA Today*, 29 April 2003.

Bianculli, David, '*Buffy* Characters Follows Her Bliss', *New York Daily News*, 2 May 2000.

Bianculli, David, '*Buffy* fans to see more Giles', *New York Daily News*, 11 July 2002.

Bibo, Terry, 'Earth Needs New Slayer After Tonight', *Teen Hollywood*, 27 May 2003.

Bierly, Mandi, '*Buffy* 101', *TV Guide*, 19 October 2002.

Billings, Laura, ' "Like , Duh," says Gen Y', *St Paul Pioneer Press*, 10 October 2000.

Binns, John, 'No Place Like Home' to 'Shadow', *Xposé*, issue 52, January 2001.

Binns, John, 'Listening to Fear' to 'Into the Woods', *Xposé*, issue 53, February 2001.

Binns, John, 'Smashed', to 'Doublemeat Palace', *Xposé*, issue 66, April 2002.

Binns, John, 'Where Do We Go From Here?' *TV Zone*, issue 153, July 2002.

Binns, John, 'The Killer in Me' to 'Storyteller', *Xposé*, issue 79, July 2003.

Blakey, Bob, 'On *Buffy*'s Sunny Set', *Calgary Herald*, 16 July 2002.

'Blood-thirsty scholars gulp *Buffy*-related concoctions', *Chicago Tribune*, 7 November 2002.

Blucas, Marc, 'Slayer Layer', interview by Paul Simpson, *SFX*, issue 75, March 2001.

Boedeker, Hal, '*Buffy* to tap lighter vein, but be scarier too', *Orlando Sentinel*, 16 July 2002.

Bone, James, 'Declaration of Ignorance as American teenagers flunk July 4 Quiz', *The Times*, 4 July 2001.

Bonin, Liane, 'Ripper van Winkle', *Entertainment Weekly*, 4 July 2002.

Boreanaz, David, Landau, Juliet, and Marsters, James, 'Interview with the Vampires', by Tim Appelo, *TV Guide*, September 1998.

Boreanaz, David, 'Leaders of the Pack', interview (with Kerri Russell) by Janet Weeks, *TV Guide*, November 1998.

Boreanaz, David, 'City of Angel', interview by David Richardson, *Xposé*, issue 35, June 1999.

Boreanaz, David, 'Aurora Boreanaz', interview by Sue Schneider, *DreamWatch*, issue 69, May 2000.

Boreanaz, David, 'Good or Bad Angel?' interview by David Richardson, *Shivers*, issue 77, May 2000.

Boreanaz, David, 'Moving On Up', interview by Christina Radish, *DreamWatch*, issue 80, May 2001.

Boreanaz, David, 'Dead Man Talking', interview by Jenny Cooney Carrillo, *DreamWatch*, issue 96, September 2002.

Boreanaz, David, 'Voice of an Angel', interview by Jean Cummings, *Cult Times*, issue 86, November 2002.

Boreanaz, 'Reflections of the Undead', interview by Joe Nazzaro, *Starburst*, Special 57, March 2003.

Bottomley, Suzette, 'Conspiracy Theory', *Herald and Post*, 26 October 2000.

Bowers, Cynthia, 'Generation Lapse: The Problematic Parenting of Joyce Summers and Rupert Giles', in *Slayage: The Online Journal of Buffy Studies*, 2001.

Bradney, Anthony, 'Choosing Law, Choosing Family: Images of Law, Love and Authority in *Buffy the Vampire Slayer*', in *Web Journal of Current Legal Issues*, 2002.

'The Breeders Meet Buffy', *Rolling Stone*, 8 October 2002.

Brendon, Nicholas, 'Evolving Hero', interview by Paul Simpson, *DreamWatch*, issue 53, January 1999.

Brendon, Nicholas, 'Only Human', interview by Keith Austin, *Sydney Morning Herald*, 25 April 2002.

Brendon, Nicholas, 'Just a Normal Everyday Hero', interview by James Abery, *Shivers*, issue 98, August 2002.

Britt, Donna, 'The Truth About Teen TV', *TV Guide*, 28 October 2000.

Brown, Anthony, Brown, Kate, Spragg, Paul and Topping, Keith, 'Slay Goodbye! Seven Years in Sunnydale recalled', *Xposé*, Special #24, December 2003.

Brown, Kate, '*Buffy*: Season Seven', *TV Zone*, Special #54, December 2003.

'Buffy in love? Checkout girls are over the moon', *Toronto Star*, 11 December 2001.

'Buffy move will alter little, creator says', *Indianapolis Star*, 18 July 2001.

'*Buffy* producer knows dyke drama', *Advocate*, 4 December 2001.

'Buffy: The Animated Series', *Starlog*, issue 14, June 2001.

'Buffy lives. And she sings too', *Chicago Tribune*, 5 August 2001.

'Buffy's practical joke backfires', *National Enquirer*, 18 July 2002.

'*Buffy* goes back to school', *DreamWatch*, issue 96, September 2002.

'Buffy wants Bond role', *Teen Hollywood*, 13 December 2002.

'*Buffy* girl set to make her mark', *Grimsby Telegraph*, 13 January 2003.

'*Buffy* samples some of Head's home comforts', *Bristol Evening News*, 22 January 2003.

'Buffy roots out the adolescent demon in all of us', *This is Leicestershire*, 24 January 2003.

'Buffy passes on her powers', *Daily Star*, 21 May 2003.

Bunson, Matthew, *Vampire: The Encyclopaedia*, Thames and Hudson, 1993.

Butcher, David, 'Today's Choice', *Radio Times*, 13 December 2003.

Campagna, Suze, 'Bite Me: The History of Vampires on Television', *Intergalactic Enquirer*, October 2000.

Campagna, Suze, 'The World of Joss Whedon', *Intergalactic Enquirer*, February 2001.

Campagna, Suze, 'TV Tid Bits', *Intergalactic Enquirer*, June 2001.

Campbell, Angelique, 'Breeders on this weeks *Buffy*', *Dayton Daily News*, 1 November 2002.

Carpenter, Charisma, 'Charismatic', interview by Jim Boultier, *SFX* issue 40, July 1998.

Carpenter, Charisma, 'Femme Fatale', interview by Mike Peake, *FHM* issue 117, October 1999.

Carpenter, Charisma, 'Charisma Personified', interview by Jennifer Graham, *TV Guide*, 1 January 2000.

Carpenter, Charisma, 'In Step With ...' interview by James Brady, *Parade*, 5 March 2000.

Carpenter, Charisma, 'Charisma!' interview by Ed Gross, *SFX*, issue 75, March 2001.

Carpenter, Charisma, 'Heaven Sent', interview by Jenny Cooney Carrillo, *DreamWatch*, issue 103, March 2003.

Carrillo, Jenny, 'Buffy Round Table', *DreamWatch*, issue 80, May 2001.

Carter, Bill, '*Dawson's Clones*: Tapping into the youth market for all it is, or isn't, worth', *New York Times* 19 September 1999.

Caulfield, Emma, 'Insider: She Hath No Fury', interview by Michael Logan, *TV Guide*, 25 December 1999.

Caulfield, Emma, 'Anya Horribilis', interview by John Mosby, *DreamWatch* issue 70, June 2000.

Caulfield, Emma, interview, *Big Hit*, June 2001.

Caulfield, Emma, 'Hell Hath No Fury . . .' interview by Steven Eramo, *TV Zone*, issue 162, April 2003.

Caulfield, Emma, 'Demon at rest', interview by Neala Johnson, *Sydney Herald Sun*, 21 May 2003.

Cavallo, Jo, 'Buffy ready to give up her stake', *People*, 16 July 2002.

'Celebrity Shame', *Dolly*, October 2000.

Chan, Paul, '*Angel* faces do it all for laughs', *Huddersfield Daily Examiner*, 17 July 2002.

Chavez, Paul, 'Suspect's family "heartbroken" over son's role in UCSB deaths', *Los Angeles Daily News*, 28 February 2001.

'Cheers and Jeers' ('Hush' review), *TV Guide*, 1 January 2000.

'Cheers and Jeers' ('The Body' review), *TV Guide*, 17 March 2001.

Chin, Richard, 'Single-minded viewers: Some folks tune in to television for one – and only one – show. How do they do that?' *St Paul's Pioneer Press*, 22 April 2003.

Clapham, Mark and Smith, Jim, *Soul Searching: The Unofficial Guide to the Life & Trials of Ally McBeal*, Virgin Publishing, 2000.

Coleman, Maureen, 'Fans say fangs for the *Buffy* memories', *Belfast Telegraph*, 27 April 2003.

Collins, Scott, '*Buffy* star goes to the woodshed over remark about sticking with the WB', *Los Angeles Times*, 30 January 2001.

Collins, Scott, '*Buffy* deal goes to heart of new net economy', *Hollywood Reporter*, 11 July 2002.

Cornell, Paul, Day, Martin, and Topping, Keith, *Guinness Book of Classic British TV*, 2nd edition, Guinness Publishing, 1996.

Cornell, Paul, Day, Martin, and Topping, Keith, *X-Treme Possibilities: A Comprehensively Expanded Rummage Through the X-Files*, Virgin Publishing, 1998.

Cornell, Paul, 'Ally the Vampire Slayer', *SFX*, issue 60, January 2000.

Cornell, Paul, '20th Century Fox-Hunting', *SFX*, issue 63, April 2000.

Cornell, Paul, '*Buffy*: The Body', *SFX*, issue 80, July 2001.

Cortez, Carl, 'Bargaining Parts 1 and 2', *Cinescape*, 2 October 2001.

Danford, Natalie, 'Pop Goes Philosophy', *Publishers Weekly*, 3 February 2003.

Darley, Andy, 'Waiting for Willow', *Science Fiction World*, issue 3, August 2000.

Dauber, Jeremy, 'Talk about the end of girl power', *Christian Science Monitor*, 30 May 2003.

Dawson March, Catherine, 'Buffy unwrapped before her time', *Globe and Mail*. 22 January 2003.

Day, Julia, 'Teen website renews *Buffy* sponsorship', *Guardian*, 11 May 2001.

Day, Julia, 'Cheeky Kylie Goes Underground', *Guardian*, 24 July 2002.

DeCandido, Keith RA, *The Xander Years, Vol. 1*, Archway Paper Back Publishing, 1999.

DeKnight, Steven, 'DeKnight in Shining Armour', interview by Joe Nazzaro, *DreamWatch*, issue 103, March 2003.

Denisof, Alexis, 'A Revival of Spirit', interview by Simon Bacal, *Xposé*, issue 43, February 2000.

Denisof, Alexis, 'Vogue Demon Hunter', interview by Matt Springer, *Buffy the Vampire Slayer*, issue 7, Spring 2000.

Denisof, Alexis, 'Half Price', interview by Paul Spragg, *Xposé*, issue 65, March 2002.

Denisof, Alexis, 'The Right Pryce', interview by Steven Eramo, *TV Zone*, issue 150, April 2002.

Denisof, Alexis, 'Denisof On One', interview by Jean Cummings, *Cult Times*, issue 86, November 2002.

Devores, Courtney, 'Immortal *Buffy*', *Charlotte Observer*, 19 May 2003.

Donaldson, Andrew, 'Damsel in Distress', *Sunday Times* [South Africa], 30 June 2002.

Dougherty, Diana, 'Oh, Jonathan', *Intergalactic Enquirer*, April 2000.

Doyle, John, 'Buffy's secret: knowing right from wrong', *Globe and Mail*, 13 May 2003.

Dudley, Jennifer, 'Bye Bye Buffy', *Queensland Courier Mail*, 6 August 2003.

Duffy, Mike, 'All seems to be rotating perfectly on Planet *Buffy*', *TV Weekly*, October 1999.

Duffy, Mike, 'Brighter days ahead for Buffy and gang, creator promises', *Detroit Free Press*, 15 July 2002.

Dushku, Eliza, 'A Little Faith Goes a Long Way!' interview by James G Boultier, *Science Fiction World*, issue 3, August 2000.

Dushku, Eliza, 'Keeping Faith', interview by Ed Gross, *SFX Unofficial Buffy Collection*, 2000.

Ellis, Martin, 'Bad Girl Does Good', *Shivers*, issue 104, May 2003.

Elz, Amy, 'Five reason why *Buffy* may be the best thing on television', *STL Today*, 11 December 2001.

Espenson, Jane, 'Superstar Scribe', interview by Joe Nazzaro, *DreamWatch*, issue 74, November 2000.

Espenson, Jane, 'I Journalist, You Jane', interview by Lisa Kincaid, *Xposé* issue 58, August 2001.

Espenson, Jane, Petrie, Doug and DeKnight, Steven S, interview by Joe Nazzaro, *DreamWatch*, issue 103, April 2003.

Ewing, Charles Patrick, *Kids Who Kill: Juvenile Murder in America*, Mondo Publishing, 1993.

Fairly, Peter, 'Last Night's View' ('The Puppet Show' review), *Journal*, 4 March 1999.

Faraci, Daniel, '*Buffy* characters to live on', *Cinescape*, 5 April 2003.

Ferguson, Everett, *Backgrounds of Early Christianity* [second edition], William B. Eerdmans Publishing, 1993.

Fidgeon, Robert, 'Willow's witching hour', *Sydney Herald Sun*, 4 June 2003.

Fillion, Nathan, 'Lord of the Fly', interview by David Bassom, *DreamWatch*, issue 107, August 2003.

Fiore, Faye, 'Washington cast an eye on Hollywood', *Los Angeles Times*, 15 July 2001.

Fong, Kristina, 'Eternal thanks go to Slayer', *Contra Costa Times*, 20 May 2003.

Francis, Rob, '*Buffy the Vampire Slayer* Season 4', *Dream-Watch*, issue 71, August 2000.

Francis, Rob, 'TV Heroes', *TV Zone*, Special #45, March 2002.

Fretts, Bruce, 'City of Angel', *Entertainment Weekly*, April 1999.

Frutkin, AJ, 'Generation Next', *Media Week*, 3 February 2003.

Gabriel, Jan, *Meet the Stars of Buffy the Vampire Slayer: An Unauthorized Biography*, Scholastic Inc., 1998.

Gellar, Sarah Michelle, interview by Sue Schneider, *Dream-Watch*, issue 42, February 1998.

Gellar, Sarah Michelle, 'Star Struck Slayer', interview by Jenny Cooney Carrillo, *DreamWatch*. issue 55, March 1999.

Gellar, Sarah Michelle, interview by Jamie Diamond, *Mademoiselle*, March 1999.

Gellar, Sarah Michelle, 'Staking the Future', interview by John Mosby, *DreamWatch* issue 61, September 1999.

Gellar, Sarah Michelle, 'Sing when you're winning!'/'Buffy on Top', interview by Jenny Cooney Carrillo, *DreamWatch*, issue 89–90, February–March 2002.

Gellar, Sarah Michelle, 'Smile Sarah', interview by Linda Cardellini, *Seventeen*, July 2002.

Gellar, Sarah Michelle, 'Hearslay', interview by Jenny Cooney Carrillo, *DreamWatch*, issue 96, September 2002.

'Gellar Offered Big Bucks to Stay "Buffy"', *Teen Television*, 8 December 2002.

Giglione, Joan, 'Some Shows Aren't Big on TV', *Los Angeles Times*, 25 November 2000.

Gilbert, Matthew, 'Teenage Wasteland', *Boston Globe*, 7 December 2001.

Gill, AA, 'A Teeny Pain in the Neck', *Sunday Times*, 24 January 1999.

Gingerich, Danielle, 'Finding comfort in a TV Slayer: IU student has become "more" than the average viewer', *Indiana Daily Student*, 25 February 2003.

Glover, Kelly, 'Buffy: The Musical Ones – How LA's rock scene can raise the dead', *Impact*, issue 127, July 2002.

Goldberg, Jonah, 'Buffy, the UN Slayer', *Washington Times*, 25 September 2002.

Golden, Christopher, and Holder, Nancy (with Keith RA DeCandido), *Buffy the Vampire Slayer: The Watcher's Guide*, Pocket Books, 1998.

Golden, Christopher, Bissette, Stephen R, and Sniegoski, Thomas E, *Buffy the Vampire Slayer: The Monster Book*, Pocket Books, 2000.

'Good Deal for *Buffy* Fans', *NME*, 30 July 2002.

'Good Riddance, Buffy', *Star*, 6 May 2003.

Goodman, Tim, 'Standing ovation for singing *Buffy*', *San Francisco Chronicle*, 6 November 2001.

Goodman, Tim, '*Buffy*'s demise puts a stake in our hearts', *San Francisco Chronicle*, 19 May 2003.

Gottlieb, Allie, '*Buffy*'s Angels', *Silicon Valley Metro*, 2 October 2002.

Graham, Alyson, 'Today's Choice', *Radio Times*, 5 January 2002.

Gray, Ellen, 'The gay joke is becoming a staple of network TV', *Philadelphia Daily News*, 1 September 1999.

Gray, Ellen, 'There's nowhere that *Angel* star fears to tread', *Knight Ridder Newspapers*, 24 February 2002.

Green, Caralyn, '*Buffy* runs out of garlic; series to end in May', *Collegian*, 29 April 2003.

Green, Michelle Erica, 'Darla and Topolsky Are More Than Bad Girls', *Fandom Inc*, September 2000.

Green, Seth, 'In Step With ...' interview by James Brady, *Parade*, 17 December 2000.

Greenman, Jennifer, 'Witch love spells death', *News Review*, 6 June 2002.

Greenwalt, David, '*Angel* delivers a devil of a time', interview by Charlie Mason, *TV Guide*, 14 August 2001.

Greenwalt, David, 'Angel's Guardian', interview by James Abery, *Shivers*, issue 98, July 2002.

Greenwalt, David, 'Miracles Do Happen', interview by Davids Richardson, *Xposé*, issue 76, January 2003.

Groebner, Simon Peter, 'The Slayer bows out after seven seasons of wicked fun', *Star Tribune*, 6 May 2003.

Gross, Ed, 'Triangle' review, *SFX*, issue 75, March 2001.

Hallett, Andy, 'Angelic Host', interview by Pat Jankiewicz, *Starburst*, issue 272, April 2001.

Hallett, Andy, 'Smells Like Green Spirit', interview by Tom Mayo, *SFX*, issue 81, August 2001.

Hanks, Robert, 'Deconstructing Buffy', *Independent*, 1 July 2002.

Hanks, Robert, 'Farewell Buffy, and fangs for the memories', *Independent*, 21 May 2003.

Hann, Michael, '*Buffy*'s final slaying', *Guardian*, 27 May 2003.

Hannigan, Alyson, 'Slay Belle', interview by Sue Schneider, *DreamWatch*, issue 43, March 1998.

Hannigan, Alyson, 'Net Prophet', interview by Paul Simpson, *DreamWatch*, issue 55, March 1999.

Hannigan, Alyson, 'Willow Blossom', interview by John Mosby, *DreamWatch*, issue 73, October 2000.

Hannigan, Alyson, 'Alyson's Wonderland', interview by Jeffrey Epstein, *Out*, August 2001.

Hannigan, Alyson, 'Witchy Willow', interview by David Miller, *TV Zone*, issue 143, October 2001.

Hannigan, Alyson, 'Willow Pattern', interview by Kate O'Hare, *Sydney Herald News*, 1 February 2003.

Harrington, Richard, 'Unsung *Buffy*: Props for A Magical Musical Moment', *Washington Post*, 2 July 2002.

Harrington, Richard, 'Spike gives *Buffy* a darker, sexier tone', *Washington Post*, 11 August 2002.

Head, Anthony Stewart, 'Bewitched, Bothered & Bewildered', interview by Paul Simpson, *DreamWatch*, issue 54, February 1999.

Head, Anthony Stewart, 'Speaking Volumes', interview by David Richardson, *Xposé*, issue 39, October 1999.

Head, Anthony Stewart, 'Heads Or Tails', interview by Paul Simpson and Ruth Thomas, *DreamWatch*, issue 69, May 2000.

Head, Anthony Stewart, 'My Kind of Day', *Radio Times*, 30 September 2000.

Head, Anthony Stewart, 'Ripping Yarns', interview by Paul Simpson and Ruth Thomas, *SFX*, issue 80, July 2001.

'Hell is for Heroes', *Entertainment Weekly*, issue 505, 1 October 1999.

Hensley, Dennis, 'Sarah Michelle Gellar Vamps it Up', *Cosmopolitan*, June 1999.

Hibbs, Thomas S, 'Buffy's War: Good and Evil 101', *National Review*, 24 May 2002.

Hibbs, Thomas S', 'Forget about the world . . . *Buffy* saved TV', *National Review*, 22 May 2003.

Highley, John, 'Beer Bad' to 'Pangs', *Xposé*, issue 42, January 2000.

Holder, Nancy (with Jeff Mariotte and Maryelizabeth Hart), *Buffy the Vampire Slayer: The Watcher's Guide Volume 2*, Pocket Books, 2000.

Huff, Richard. 'WB Net Returns to Gender-Build on Initial Appeal Among Young Women', *New York Daily News* 14 September 1999.

Hughes, David, 'Slay Ride', *DreamWatch*, issue 42, February 1998.

Infante, Victor D, ' "She saved the world a lot": Buffy the vampire slayer and revolutionary', *Orange County Weekly*, 16 May 2003.

Innes, John, ' "Buffy" attackers escape jail term', *Scotsman*, 29 March 2002.

Jeckell, Barry A, 'Mann, Ladies, to rock *West Wing*', *Billboard*, 7 October 2002.

Jensen, Jeff, 'The Goodbye Girl', *Entertainment Weekly*, 7 March 2003.

Johnson, Allan, 'Willow's Soulful Visit Illuminates *Angel*', *Chicago Tribune*, 19 March 2003.

Johnson, Kevin V, 'Fans Sink Teeth into Bootlegged "Buffy"', *USA Today*, May 1999.

Johnson, Neala, 'Buffy had Danny in her spell', *Sydney Herald Sun*, 4 June 2003.

Johnson, RW, 'The Myth of the 20th Century', *New Society*, 9 December 1982.

Kaltenbach, Chris, 'Buffy is back, and she's training her replacement', *Baltimore Sun*, 24 September 2002.

Kaplan, Don, 'Inside the big *Buffy* finale', *New York Post*, 12 April 2003.

Kaplan, Don, 'Internet spoils fun as . . . Buffy bites dust', *New York Post*, 22 April 2003.

Katner, Bill, '*Buffy* ghost revisits old haunts', *TV Guide*, 12 November 2002.

Katner, Ben with Michael Ausiello, 'Is *Angel* Livin' On A Prayer?' *TV Guide*, 5 May 2003.

Katz, Paul S, 'Fans rally for their favorite vampire', *TV Guide*, 12 April 2003.

Kaveney, Roz [ed], *Reading the Vampire Slayer: An Unofficial Critical Companion to Buffy and Angel*, 2001.

Keveney, Bill, 'When it's quality vs. ratings, casualties abound', *Charlotte Observer*, 31 August 2000.

Kiesewetter, John, '*Angel, Buffy, Dawson* may end', *Cincinnati Enquirer*, 13 January 2003.

Kincaid, Lisa, 'Three's Company', *Xposé*, issue 67, May 2002.

King, Stephen, *Danse Macabre*, Futura Books, 1981.

Kramer, Clare, 'Glory Days', interview by Nick Joy, *Starlog*, issue 24, March 2002.

Kramer, Clare, 'Profile', interview by Paul Simpson, *SFX*, issue 90, April 2002

Kurtz, Frank, 'Whedon Talks *Buffy* Resurrection', *New York Daily News*, 17 July 2001.

Kushman, Rick, '*Buffy*'s last battle', *Sacramento Bee*, 20 May 2003.

Kuster, Elizabeth, 'Sarah Michelle Gellar', *Seventeen*, May 2003.

Lagos, Marisa, 'Dad wanted Attias to have "Normal Life"', *Santa Barbara Daily Nexus*, 29 May 2002.

Laight, Rupert, 'Demon Lover', *Starburst*, issue 284, March 2002.

Lambert, Brian, 'The WB network contemplates life after *Buffy*', *St Paul Pioneer Press*, 17 July 2001.

Lane, Andy, *The Babylon File*, Virgin Publishing, 1997.

Larbalestier, Justine, 'A Buffy Confession' in *Seven seasons of Buffy: Science Fiction and Fantasy Authors Discuss Their Favourite Television Show*, October 2003.

Last, Jonathan V, 'Where do we go from here?' *Daily Standard*, 20 May 2003.

Lenk, Tom, 'Follow the Leader', interview by Steven Eramo, *TV Zone*, Special 52, 2003.

Lenk, Tom, 'The Geek Makes Good', interview by Joe Nazzaro, *Starburst*, Special 60, November 2003.

Lewis, Randy, 'Musical *Buffy* finally lands in stores' *Los Angeles Times*, 23 September 2002.

Lewis, Scott D, 'Aimee Mann's World', *Oregonian*, 15 November 2002.

Lipson, Karin, and Lovece, Frank, 'High Stakes TV', *News York Newsday*, 27 February 2000.

Littlefield, Kinney, 'Avenging Angel', *Orange County Register*, October 1999.

Littleton, Cynthia, 'UPN sked has WB feel; Fox goes Conservative', *Hollywood Reporter*, 17 May 2001.

Lovinger, Rachel, 'Career Counseling', *Entertainment Weekly*, 17 October 2002.

Lowry, Brian, 'Actresses Turning Down Roles of Teens' Mothers', *Los Angeles Times*, 29 April 1999.

Lowry, Brian, 'WB Covers A Trend Too Well', *Los Angeles Times*, 29 June 2000.

MacDonald, Ian, *Revolution in the Head* – Second Edition, Fourth Estate Ltd, 1997.

MacKenzie, Kate, 'Last days of *Buffy* a kind of living death', *Australian*, 18 July 2002.

Madden, Michelle, 'Total Faith', *Mean*, July 2001.

Malcolm, Shawna, 'So Long, Slayer', *TV Guide*, 17 May 2003.

Mansfield, Sonia, 'Women on Top', *San Francisco Examiner*, 27 December 2001.

Mansfield, Sonia, 'Endgames', *San Francisco Examiner*, 27 May 2002.

Marsters, James, 'Sharp Spike', interview by Cynthia Boris, *Cult Times* Special 9, Spring 1999.

Marsters, James, and Caulfield, Emma, 'Vamping It Up', *Alloy*, Summer 2000.

Marster, James, 'I, Spike', interview by Ed Gross, *SFX Unofficial Buffy Collection*, 2000.

Marsters, James, 'It's Only Rock & Roll, But I Spike It!' interview (with Four Star Mary) by Tom Mayo, *SFX*, issue 81, August 2001.

Marsters, James, 'Loves Bites', interview by Abbie Bernstein, *DreamWatch*, issue 89, February 2002.

Marsters, James, 'Love in Vein', interview by Ian Spelling, *Starlog*, issue 24, March 2002.

Marsters, James, 'Demon Lover', interview by Rupert Laight, *Starburst*, issue 284, April 2002.

Marsters, James, 'Life at the Sharp End', interview by John Reading, *TV Zone*, issue 164, June 2003.

Marsters, James, 'Dead Man Talking', interview by Steve Dexter, *DreamWatch*, issue 107, August 2003.

Martino, John, 'Dead, Sexy', *Shivers*, issue 96, March 2002.

Mason, Charlie, '*Buffy* lowers its bawdy count', *TV Guide*, 10 July 2002.

Mason, Dave, 'When Bad Things Happen To Good Vampires', *Scripps Howard News Service*, 22 October 2002.

Mason, Dave, '*Buffy* producers plan for possible series finale', *Ventura County Star*, 26 January 2003.

Mason, Dave, 'The Big Goodbye', *Ventura County Star*, 20 April 2003.

Matthews, Richard, 'Boldly staying in with *Buffy* and *Friends*', *Daily Telegraph*, 4 July 2002.

Mauger, Anne-Marie, 'Staking their Claims', *Sky Customer Magazine*, January 2001.

May, Dominic and Spilsbury, Tom, 'Return to Sunnydale High for *Buffy* Season 7', *TV Zone*, issue 153, July 2002.

May, Dominic, 'It's a Wrap', *Cult Times*, issue 93, June 2003.

Maynard, Kevin, 'Hit Young Thing: Emma Caulfield', *Premiere*, January 2003.

Mayo, Tom, *SFX Presents Buffy the Vampire Slayer The Unofficial Episode Guide to the First Four Seasons*, Future Publishing, 2000.

McCarthy, David J, '*Buffy* staking out the seventh season: SMG fans ecstatic', *Pitt News*, 1 October 2002.

McCollum, Charlie, 'Joss Whedon gets so many ideas, he feels overwhelmed', *Mercury News*, 19 August 2002.

McDaniel, Mike, '*Buffy* Lauded for Gay Character', *Houston Chronicle*, 18 May 2000.

McDaniel, Mike, '*Buffy* will get back to basics for fall season says network chief', *Houston Chronicle*, 15 July 2002.

McFadden, Kay, '*Buffy* legacy will outlive tonight's anticlimactic finale', *Seattle Times*, 20 May 2003.

McFarland, Melanie, 'Musical *Buffy* could be a grave mistake for vampire slayer', *Seattle Times*, 6 November 2001.

McFarland, Melanie, '*Buffy* has much to teach us about life', *Seattle Post-Intelligencer*, 20 May 2003.

McIntee, David, *Delta Quadrant: The Unofficial Guide to Voyager*, Virgin Publishing, 2000.

McIntyre, Gina, 'Slay Anything', *Hollywood Reporter*, 21 May 2001.

McLean, Gareth, 'Last Night's TV: A real death in Buffyland', *Guardian*, 21 April 2001.

McLean, Gareth, 'Channel Surfing: Why *Buffy* is the best show ever', *Guardian*, 13 November 2002.

McNab, Mercedes, 'Vamping it Up!' interview by Steven Eramo, *Xposé*, issue 81, November 2003.

Meltzer, Dana, 'Raising the Stakes', *Guardian*, 5 January 2002.

Menon, Vinay, and Salem, Rob, 'Change is the only constant: Sitcoms aren't dying, they're just mutating again', *Toronto Star*, 30 December 2002.

Metcalf, Mark, 'Buffy's Master', interview by Mark Wyman, *Starburst*, issue 245, January 1999.

Miller, Anne, 'Bye-bye, *Buffy*: "Vampire Slayer" changed TV and gender roles, one vanquished vampire at a time', *Times Union*, 18 May 2003.

Miller, Craig, 'Xander the Survivor', *Spectrum*, issue 17, March 1999.

Miller, Craig, '*Buffy the Vampire Slayer* Fourth Season Episode Guide', *Spectrum*, issue 25, January 2001.

Millman, Joyce, 'Series finale is leaving *Buffy* fans in the lurch', *St Paul Pioneer Press*, 20 April 2003.

Millman, Joyce, 'Getting *Buffy*'s Last Rites Right', *New York Times*, 22 April 2003.

Mohan, Dominic, 'You're a Big Gell', *Sun*, 6 January 2003.

Monk, Katherine, 'Suddenly, all the singing and dancing is political: Once escapist fare, the modern musical is making tough points', *Vancouver Sun*, 1 October 2002.

Moore, Jennifer, 'Copyright Protection or Fan Loyalty – Must Entertainment Companies Choose? Addressing Internet Fan Sites', *North Carolina Journal of Law and Technology*, 2002.

Moore, Patrick, *New Guide to the Planets*, Sidgwick & Jackson, 1993.

Moore, Ronald D, 'Moore the Merrier', interview by Jim Swallow, *SFX*, issue 74, February 2001.

Mosby, John, 'UK-TV', *DreamWatch*, issue 71, August 2000.

Mosby, John, 'Last Writes', *Impact*, issue 127, July 2002.

Murray, Steve, 'Cracking the closet door: More visibility for gay characters on TV', *Miami Herald*, 9 July 2002.

Murray, Steve and Kloer, Phil, '*Buffy* lives . . . no more', *Atlanta Journal*, 29 April 2003.

Naughton, John, 'Buffy up on *Buffy*', *Radio Times*, 29 June 2002.

Nelson, Resa, 'Angel makes us ask: why do bad boys make us feel so good?' *Realms of Fantasy*, Feb 2000.

Nelson, Resa, 'To Live and Die in LA', *Science Fiction World*, issue 1, June 2000.

Nelson, Resa, 'Raising the stakes', *Sci-Fi Magazine*, August 2003.

Newman, Kim, *Nightmare Movies: A Critical History of the Horror Movie From 1968*, Bloomsbury Publishing, 1988.

'Nerf Herder: More than just vampire slayers', *Chart Attack*, 25 April 2003.

Norman, Matthew, 'Biological Warfare and the Buffy Paradigm', *Guardian*, 10 July 2002.

Norton, Phillip, 'Fang-tastic fans of *Buffy* question star', *Grimsby Telegraph*, 30 April 2003.

'No Sex Please, it's *Buffy*', *DreamWatch*, issue 89, February 2002.

Noxon, Marti, 'Soul Survivor', *DreamWatch*, issue 63, November 1999.

Noxon, Marti, ' "Nasty" Noxon', interview by Andy Mangels, *DreamWatch*, issue 90, March 2002.

Noxon, Marti, 'Blood Hound', interview by Kathie Huddleston, *Sci-Fi Magazine*, December 2002.

Noxon, Marti, 'The Undiscovered *Buffy*', interview by John Reading, *Starburst*, issue 300, July 2002.

Nussbaum, Emily, 'Confessions of a Spoiler Whore', *Slate*, 4 April 2002.

Ogle, Connie, 'Something's fangtastically wrong in Emmyland', *Miami Herald*, 23 July 2002.

O'Hare, Kate, 'Silent Buffy', *Ultimate TV*, 13 December 1999.

O'Hare, Kate, 'WB's Core Series *Buffy* and *Angel* Cross Time and Space', *TV Weekly*, 12 November 2000.

O'Hare, Kate, 'While *Buffy* Rages, *Angel* Still Flies', *St Paul Pioneer Press*, 15 April 2001.

O'Hare, Kate, '*Buffy* reaches end of run on the WB', *St Paul Pioneer Press*, 20 May 2001.

O'Hare, Kate, 'Fist of fury – TV's high-flying on-screen battles', *St Paul Pioneer Press*, 14 April 2002.

O'Hare, Kate, 'Willow pattern', *Sydney Herald Sun*, 1 February 2003.

O'Hare, Kate, 'The sun sets on *Buffy the Vampire Slayer*', *St Paul Pioneer Press*, 18 May 2003.

'Out with the old, in with the new – for *The Beano* turned *Buffy* fan', *This is Leicestershire*, 24 February 2003.

Owen, Rob, '*Pow! Bash! Bam!* WB, UPN trade barbs over *Buffy*', *Post-Gazette*, 17 July 2001.

Paulson, Kristen, '*Buffy* helps troupe slay stereotypes', *Boston Globe*, 13 December 2002.

Pearce, Gareth, 'Alyson Hannigan: She Shoots, She Scores', *The Times*, 13 July 2003.

Peary, Danny, *Guide For the Film Fanatic*, Simon & Schuster, 1986.

Pender, Patricia, '"I'm Buffy and You're ... History": The Postmodern Politics of Buffy', in Wilcox, Rhonda and Lavery, David [eds] *Fighting the Forces: What's at Stake in Buffy the Vampire Slayer*, Rowan & Littlefield Publishers Inc., 2002.

Perenson, Melissa J, 'Slay Time's Over', *Sci-Fi Magazine*, August 2003.

Petrozzello, Donna, '*Buffy* Exec Feels Slayed by "Insult"', *Daily News*, 19 March 2001.

Pierce, Scott D, '*Buffy* Sings!' *Deseret News*, 3 November 2001.

Pierce, Scott D, '*Buffy* will be going away, but that won't be the end', *Deseret News*, 30 April 2003.

Pierce, Scott D, 'Spike is in, Cordelia is out', *Deseret News*, 26 May 2003.

Pirie, David, *The Vampire Cinema*, Galley Press, 1977.

Plath, Sylvia, *Collected Poems*, Faber and Faber, 1981.

Poniewozik, James, 'How the *Buffy* coup could change television', *Time*, 23 April 2001.

'Potty About Paganism', *Alternative Metro*, 24 August 2000.

Pruitt, Jeff and Crawford, Sohpia: 'The Hitman and Her', *Science Fiction World*, issue 3, August 2000.

'Queen of the Damned', *FHM*, issue 114, July 1999.

Ramlow, Todd R, '"I Killed Tara": Desire and Death on *Buffy*', *Pop Matters*, 4 June 2002.

Richardson, David, 'Snyder Remarks', *Xposé*, issue 37, August 1999.

Robins, J Max, '*Buffy* Goes Too Far for the British', *TV Guide*, 17 March 2001.

Robins, J Max, 'UPN needs buffing', *TV Guide*, 7 December 2002.

Robson, Ian, 'Action Replay: Buffy's Show'll Slay You' ('The Freshman' review), *Sunday Sun*, 9 January 2000.

Roeper, Richard, 'Buffy Crackdown Won't Strike Heart of Problem', *Chicago Sun-Times*, 27 May 1999.

'Role Offers New Blend', *Evening Chronicle*, 12 February 2001.

Rose, Lloyd, 'Outcast Buffy Embodies Teen Angst', *Washington Post*, October 1998.

Rosen, Lisa, 'RIP *Buffy*: You drove a stake through convention', *Los Angeles Times*, 20 May 2003.

Rosenthal, Phil, '*Buffy* boss: It's not over when it's over', *Chicago Sun-Times*, 29 April 2003.

Roush, Matt, 'The Roush Review', *TV Guide*, 3 April 1999.

Roush, Matt, 'The Roush Review – Buffy Rocks: Better Late Than Never', *TV Guide*, 10 July 1999.

Roush, Matt, 'Shows of the Year '99', *TV Guide*, 25 December 1999.

Roush, Matt, 'The Roush Review', *TV Guide*, 1 April 2000.

Roush, Matt, 'The Roush Review: End Games', *TV Guide*, 16 June 2001.

Roush, Matt, 'Spaced Out – *Roswell* Beams to UPN with *Buffy*', *TV Guide*, 7 July 2001.

Roush, Matt, 'Great Performances: Emma Caulfield', *TV Guide*, 27 October 2001.

Roush, Matt, '*Buffy* Reborn: Slayer is full of life – and song', *TV Guide*, 24 November 2001.

Roush, Matt, 'So Good It's Scary', *TV Guide*, 3 May 2003.

Rubinstein, Julian, 'Politically Correct', *US Magazine*, October 1999.

Rutenberg, Jim, '*Buffy* Moving to UPN, Tries to be WB Slayer', *New York Times*, 21 April 2000.

Rutenberg, Jim, 'Media Talk: Hold the Tears in Vampire Slayer's Death', *New York Times*, 29 May 2001.

Rutenberg, Jim, 'Expletives? More coming on fall TV', *New York Times*, 3 September 2001.

Ryan, Maureen, 'Bye-bye *Buffy*', *Chicago Tribune*, 18 May 2003.

Sachs, Robin, 'The Eyes Have It', interview by Paul Simpson and Ruth Thomas, *DreamWatch*, issue 68, April 2000.

Sansing, Dina, 'Secrets of Sarah', *Seventeen*, August 2001.

Sangster, Jim and Bailey, David, *Friends Like Us: The Unofficial Guide to Friends* [revised edition], Virgin Publishing, 2000.

'Sarah gets a spanking: *Buffy* star forced to eat humble-pie after "Quit" gaff', *Daily News*, 30 January 2001.

'Sarah Michelle Gellar: American Beauty', *FHM*, issue 128, September 2000.

Schneider, Michael, '*Roswell* Joins *Buffy* for UPN Fall Lineup', *Variety*, 16 May 2001.

Scott, Melissa, 'The slayer is slayed: Seven years of fighting vampires ends tonight', *Mansfield News Journal*, 20 May 2003.

Sellers, John, 'Slay You!' *Maxim*, March 2002.

Sepinwall, Alan, 'Delaying episode could make *Buffy* target of witchhunt', *Network Star-Ledger*, May 1999.

Sepinwall, Alan, '*Buffy* network switch could slay TV industry practices', *St Paul Pioneer Press*, 29 April 2001.

Shaar Murray, Charles, 'Bon Voyage *Buffy*', *Evening Standard*, 6 March 2003.

Shaar Murray, Chalres, 'A passionately perverse sexiness', *Word*, issue 4, June 2003.

Shuttleworth, Ian, 'Bite me, professor', *Financial Times*, 11 September 2003.

Sieff, Martin, 'Analysis: Bye-bye *Buffy*', United International Press, 22 May 2003.

Simpson, Paul, 'Red Shirt Robia', *DreamWatch*, issue 59, Summer 1999.

Simpson, Paul and Thomas, Ruth, 'Interview With The Vampire', *DreamWatch*, issue 62, October 1999.

Simpson, Paul and Thomas, Ruth, 'The Lizard King', *SFX*, issue 80, July 2001.

Simpson, Paul, *CSI: The Files – An Unofficial and Unauthorised Guide to the Hit Crime Scene Investigation Shows*, Virgin Books, 2003.

Simpson, Richard, '*Buffy* bites the dust', *Evening Standard*, 25 May 2001.

'Single Women: If The She Fits, Air It', *St Paul Pioneer Press*, 6 January 2000.

Silverman, Steven S, ' "Buffy" on Big Move: Nervous', *People*, 17 July 2001.

'SMG going out with a bang', *Cult Times*, issue 82, July 2002.

Smith, Jim, 'This Hollywood Life', *Starburst*, issue 283, February 2002.

Speck, Rebecca, 'Farcical end to worst kept secrét of century', *Daily News*, 28 May 2003.

Spelling, Ian, 'Biting Talent – An Interview With Charisma Carpenter', *Starlog*, May 2000.

Spines, Christine, 'Getting Buffed!' *Glamour*, October 2000.

Spragg, Paul, 'Welcome to the Hellmouth', *Cult Times* Special 9, Spring 1999.

Springer, Matt, 'Cruisin' Sunnydale', *Buffy the Vampire Slayer*, issue 3, Spring 1999.

Springer, Matt, 'The Evil That Geeks Do', *Entertainment Weekly*, 20 May 2002.

Strachan, Alex, 'If you like Buffy you'll love her sister', *Vancouver Sun*, 24 September 2002.

Stanley, John, *Revenge of the Creature Feature Movie Guide*, Creatures Press, 1988.

Stanley, TL, 'Buffy the Rules Slayer', *Los Angeles Times*, 20 May 2001.

Stanley, TL, 'Is it the end of the road for *Buffy-Angel* connection? *Los Angeles Times*, 21 May 2001.

Steel, Bill, 'Beautiful Buffy's Back, Big Boy' ('Anne' review), *Journal*, 31 March 2000.

Streisand, Betsy, 'Young, hip and no-longer-watching-Fox', *US News & World Report*, 15 Nov 1999.

Strong, Danny, 'Big Man on Campus', interview by Matt Springer, *Buffy the Vampire Slayer*, Fall Special 1999.

Strong, Danny, 'Strong Enough', interview by Michael Logan, *TV Guide*, 30 September 2002.

Strong, Danny, 'The Force is Strong with this one', interview by Ian Spelling, *Starburst*, Special 60, November 2003.

Strong, Danny, 'Lonely Among Us', interview by Steven Eramo, *Xposé*, Special #24, December 2003.

Summers, Montague, *The Vampire, His Kith and Kin*, Kegan Paul, Trench, Truber & Co., 1928.

Sutherland, Kristine, 'Source of Denial', interview by Paul Simpson, *DreamWatch*, issue 58, July 1999.

Sutherland, Kristine, 'Mommy Dearest', interview by Steven Eramo, *Xposé*, Special #24, December 2003.

'The Boo Crew', *Entertainment Weekly*, issue 505, 1 October 1999.

'Today's Trout' ('Earshot'/'Bad Girls' preview), *St Paul Pioneer Press*, 27 April 1999.

Tonkin, Boyd, 'Farewell, *Buffy* and fangs for the memories', *Independent*, 21 May 2003.

'The Top Fifty SF TV Shows of All Time!' *SFX*, issue 50, April 1999.

Topping, Keith, *Hollywood Vampire: A Revised and Updated Unofficial and Unauthorised Guide to Angel*, Virgin Books, 2004.

Topping, Keith, *High Times: An Unofficial and Unauthorised Guide to Roswell*, Virgin Books, 2001.

Topping, Keith, *Inside Bartlet's White House: A revised and Updated Unofficial and Unauthorised Guide to The West Wing*, Virgin Books, 2004.

Topping, Keith, *Beyond the Gate: An Unofficial Guide to Stargate SG-1*, Telos Publishing, 2002.

Topping, Keith, *A Day in the Life: The Unofficial and Unauthorised Guide to 24*, Telos Publishing, 2003.

Topping, Keith, '*Buffy the Vampire Slayer* Season One', *Dream-Watch*, issue 55, March 1999.

Topping, Keith, '*Buffy the Vampire Slayer* Season Two', *Dream-Watch*, issues 57, 58, May, July 1999.

Topping, Keith, '*Buffy the Vampire Slayer* Season Three', *DreamWatch*, issues 60, 61, August, September 1999.

Topping, Keith, 'The Way We Were', *DreamWatch*, issue 58, July 1999.

Topping, Keith, 'Body Rock', *Intergalactic Enquirer*, March 2001.

Topping, Keith, 'Teenage Kicks', *Intergalactic Enquirer*, April 2001.

Topping, Keith, '*Sed Quis Custodiet Ipsos Custodes?*' *Intergalactic Enquirer*, May 2001.

Topping, Keith, 'Changing Channels', *Intergalactic Enquirer*, August 2001.

Topping, Keith, 'Has *Buffy* jumped the shark?' *Shivers*, issue 97, May 2002.

Topping, Keith, 'TV Reviews: season six', *Shivers*, issues 94–98, 2002.

Topping, Keith, '*Les Cirque des Vampires*', *Shivers*, issue 100, September 2002.

Topping, Keith, 'Back Where It All Began', *Shivers*, issue 101, November 2002.

Topping, Keith, 'So Let Me Rest in Peace', *TV Zone*, issue 158, December 2002.

Topping, Keith, 'TV Reviews: season seven', *Shivers*, issues 102–105, 2003.

Topping, Keith, 'Do You Know This Man?' *TV Zone*, issue 160, February 2003.

Trachtenberg, Michelle, 'Summer's Dawn' interview by Ian Spelling, *Starburst*, issue 272, April 2001.

Trachtenberg, Michelle, 'Dawn Tomorrow', interview by David Miller, *TV Zone*, issue 143, October 2001.

Trachtenberg, Michelle, 'Fast Times at Sunnydale High', interview by Nick Joy, *Starburst*, issue 289, August 2002.

Tsai, Michael, 'Slaying stereotypes, one fan risks ridicule to defend *Buffy*', *Honolulu Advertiser*, 26 May 2003.

Tucker, Ken, 'High Stakes Poker', *Entertainment Weekly*, issue 505, 1 October 1999.

Tucker, Ken, 'What's At Stake? Five reasons *Buffy* gets snubbed at the Emmys', *Entertainment Weekly*, 13 September 2002.

Udovitch, Mim, 'What Makes *Buffy* Slay?' *Rolling Stone*, issue 840, 11 May 2000.

Udovitch, Mim, 'We Like Spike', *New York Magazine*, 9 December 2002.

van Beek, Anton, 'Bite Me!', *Total DVD*, issue 21, January 2001.

Verma, Sonia, 'Did *Buffy* character inspire PC's "reptilian kitten eater" insult?' *Toronto Star*, 13 September 2003.

Wagner, Chuck, 'Punk Shocks', *SFX*, issue 49, March 1999.

Waldon, David, 'Rest in Peace, *Buffy*', *TV Zone*, issue 163, May 2003.

Waxman, Sharon, 'Hollywood pleads its case', *Washington Post*, 7 May 2000.

Weir, William, 'Wesleyan Mafia Racks Up Credits: New Center For Film Studies Is Evidence Of A College Program Building On Success', *Hartford Courant*, 30 December 2002.

Weinstein, Farrah, 'Boffo *Buffy*', *New York Post*, 28 April 2003.

'What Girls Learn', *Entertainment Tonight Online*, 11 October 2001.

Whedon, Joss, interview by AJ Jacobs, *Entertainment Weekly*, 25 April 1997.

Whedon, Joss, 'How I Got To Do What I Do', interview by Wolf Schneider, *teen movieline*, issue 1, March 2000.

Whedon, Joss, 'Whedon, Writing and Arithmetic', interview by Joe Mauceri, *Shivers*, issue 77, May 2000.

Whedon, Joss, 'Blood Lust', interview by Rob Francis, *DreamWatch*, issues 71–72, August/ September 2000.

Whedon, Joss, 'Prophecy Boy', interview by Matt Springer with Mike Stokes, *Buffy the Vampire Slayer*, issue 20, May 2001.

Whedon, Joss, interview by Gina McIntyre, *Hollywood Reporter*, 21 May 2001.

Whedon, Joss, 'Buffy RIP?' interview by John Mosby, *DreamWatch*, issue 84, September 2001.

Whedon, Joss, interview by Tasha Robinson, *Onion*, 5 September 2001.

Whedon, Joss, 'The Wonderful World of Whedon', interview by Ian Spelling, *Cult Times*, issue 79, April 2002.

Whedon, Joss, 'TV's Cult Hero', interview by Mike McDaniel, *Houston Chronicle*, 11 November 2002.

Whedon, Joss, 'Tales from the Crypt', interview by Ian Spelling, *Starburst*, Special 60, November 2003.

Whedon, Joss, 'Life after *Buffy*', interview by Camilla and Neil, *Face*, issue 84, January 2004.

'Whedon Reflects Post-*Buffy*', *TV Zone*, issue 164, June 2003.

Wigmore, Gareth, 'Powers That Be Wanted Us Here', *TV Zone*, issue 154, August 2002.

Wilcox, Rhonda V and Lavery, David [eds], *Fighting the Forces: What's at Stake in Buffy the Vampire Slayer*, Rowan & Littlefield Publishers Inc., 2002.

Wilde, MJ, 'The TV Queen', *Albuquerque Tribune*, 1 October 2002.

Williams, Zoe, 'The lady and the vamp – a buff's guide to *Buffy*,' *Guardian*, 17 November 2001.

Williamson, Kevin, '*Buffy* still slays 'em', *Calgary Sun*, 24 September 2002.

Wilson, Steve, 'Web Sucks TV's Blood – *Buffy* Fans Bite Back', *Village Voice*, May 1999.

Wright, Matthew, 'Endings and New Beginnings', *Science Fiction World*, issue 2, July 2000.

Wurtzel, Elizabeth, *Bitch*, Quartet Books, 1998.

Wyman, Mark, 'The *Buffy* Guide Season Two', *Xposé*, issue 29, December 1999.

Wyman, Mark, 'Anno I', *Cult Times* Special 9, Spring 1999.

Wyman, Mark, '*Buffy* Joins The Banned – A Fable For The Internet Age', *Shivers*, issue 68, August 1999.

Wyman, Mark, 'Crush' to 'The Body', *TV Zone*, issue 140, July 2001.

Wyman, Mark, 'Who's The Daddy?' *TV Zone*, issue 150, April 2002.

Wyman, Mark, 'Entropy' to 'Grave', *TV Zone*, issue 152, July 2002.

Wyman, Mark, 'Selfless', *TV Zone*, issue 157, November 2002.

Wyman, Mark, 'Potential', *TV Zone*, issue 160, February 2003.

Wyman, Mark, 'Storyteller', *TV Zone*, issue 162, April 2003.

Wyman, Mark, 'End of Days' to 'Chosen' *TV Zone*, issue 165, July 2003.

Wyman, Mark, '*Buffy* and *Angel* in 2003', *Xposé*, Special #24, December 2003.

Zinn, Howard, *A People's History of the United States*, Harper & Row, 1980.

Grrr! Arrrgh!

Like so many aspects of the *Buffy*-world, one is terrified to put a full stop at the end of any sentence that attempts to draw the story to a conclusion. Because you can guarantee that the second you do, some major new development will happen.

For example, on the day that part of this manuscript was due to be delivered to the publishers, I received a lengthy Joss Whedon interview in which he talked with passion and integrity about the liberal politics that had infused *Buffy* and how out of step such ideals seemed in today's television, full of loathsome reality shows and the macho isolationist posturing inherent in much dramatic storytelling. How Whedon's ideas on feminism were, largely, shaped by his remarkable mother, Lee Stearns, a radical feminist teacher who ran an artists' commune in upstate New York during Joss's youth. And how painful Whedon finds America's current place in the world. 'We're the scrappy kid who got beat up in the playground and then had a huge growth spurt and hasn't realised he's become a disgusting bully,' Joss noted, sadly. Whedon is a thoughtful, intelligent and impressively humane man who wanted to make the world a better place by creating television shows that spoke to people's hearts, not their wallets or their testosterone levels. He achieved that with *Buffy* and *Angel* and may have done so again with *Firefly* had short-sighted executives at Fox not cancelled the series before it had the time to register on the viewing public's psyche.

Nevertheless, in April 2003, Joss told *Sci-Fi Wire* that most of his *Buffy*-related projects were either dead or on hold. 'No spinoff [is] in the works right now,' Whedon noted. 'We just want to relax.' The postponed or abandoned projects included an animated *Buffy* series for Fox,[68] a BBC co-production, *Ripper*, based on the

---

[68] 'I still like the idea,' Whedon told *Sci-Fi Wire*, regarding *Buffy: The Animated Series*. 'But right now I'm not planning it.' A cartoon version of *Buffy* seemed to dismay the less broad-minded elements within the series' fandom. But for fans like this author, who grew up on *Scooby Doo*, DC and Marvel, it seemed such an obvious idea that one wondered why nobody had thought of it sooner. Whedon told the *New York Daily News* that producing an animated show would provide 'an opportunity to take our characters back to the beginning of their adulthood and tell the stories we never got to tell'. Another name associated with the proposed series was Jeph Loeb, writer of superhero comics like *Batman*, *Superman* and *Daredevil*. 'I got a call asking whether I was a *Buffy* fan,' Loeb told Susan Kuhn. 'I think both Joss and I [wanted] to meet each other as

character of Giles,[69] and a proposed *Buffy* spin-off series for UPN (or another network) involving Faith and Spike. There were other rumours, of course – *Dawn the Vampire Slayer* or a series focusing on Willow – but whether these were simply the inventions of overexcited fan groups, or were genuine formats that were discussed within Mutant Enemy during the final months of *Buffy's* existence we will, perhaps, never know. Having spent much of the winter of 2002 fighting a losing battle to keep *Firefly* on the air, Whedon was, he admitted, exhausted and looking forward to a period of reflection. One can forgive Joss for taking a little time to rest on his laurels. At San Diego's ComicCon in July 2003, he spoke proudly about the impact of *Buffy* on the general portrayal of young women in the media and the show's influence on concepts as disparate as television shows like *Alias* and *Dark Angel*, Tarantino's *Kill Bill* and the Keira Knightley character in *Pirates of the Caribbean*: 'We were trying to make a statement about women. Where they are in society and where they could be. We don't need heroes so much as recognising ourselves as heroes.'

'I feel that I wrote the perfect ending for *Buffy* and wrapped up everything exactly as it should be,' Joss told *Cinefantastique*. 'That, unfortunately, was in season five. With season seven, the weight

---

fanboys.' Loeb and Whedon's visions meshed immediately. 'I was asked "How do I see the show?"' noted Loeb. 'I thought, "Is this a trick question?" I [said] "you guys have 100 episodes of some of the best television on the air. Why wouldn't the cartoon reflect that?"' The concept of the series was to be *Buffy: Year One*, as David Fury excitedly commented: 'It's all those episodes you didn't see when Oz, Angel and Cordelia were there.' 'Stories that work in terms of Buffy aged 15 or 16, you couldn't do [once] she graduated high school,' added Loeb. 'Willow's first babysitting job, Buffy going for her driver's licence – those kind of teen-angst moments.' As an additional twist, however, history would have been rewritten with the inclusion in the Sunnydale of 1997–98 of a 10-year-old Dawn Summers. A number of scripts were written, including two by Jane Espenson that greatly impressed those who read them. 'I never understood why the series wasn't produced,' a disappointed Espenson told an online interview. 'We still have a bunch of really good scripts,' noted Whedon in 2003. 'But I won't do it at a cut-price. That show had to look wonderful.'.

[69] Joss Whedon's vision for *Ripper*, as he told the *Los Angeles Times*, was 'a grown-up show about a cool, non-teenage man solving ghost stories'. Compared to *Buffy*, he added, the intention was to make something 'slower. More like the series already on TV in Britain.' 'I've asked Joss to talk to the BBC about setting it in the West Country,' Tony Head told Paul Simpson. 'It's got an incredible amount to draw on: Wells, Glastonbury Tor, Bath has a huge wealth of history relating to the English Civil War.' Joss was clearly excited by the project, telling the *Bronze Posting Board*, 'One of my writers was like, "He could just walk into a room, make a drink, sit down and think. That can be a scene!" I said, "That's

was crushing me. I was terrified. But I also, specifically, knew what I needed to say.' He wanted *Buffy* to be remembered, Whedon continued, as a consistently funny, intelligent and emotionally involving show that, subtly, changed the world. 'I'm gonna miss the writers,' Joss Whedon told *TV Zone* at the *Buffy* wrap-party. 'I love filming, but [that] has so much going on. It's not like being in a room with the writers, where it's just us and the characters.'

So, *Buffy* is over. But can a format that inspired such a following ever, truly, die? Tony Head, for one, believes that there *is* a future in the *Buffy* franchise. 'There might be a movie,' he told *Radio Times*. 'If it happens, three years from now, there'll still be an audience for it. Ultimately, it's all about the availability of Joss Whedon. But the guy really needs to make some movies.'

The *Buffy* franchise, inevitably, will live and die with its audience. As long as there is interest in the characters that Joss Whedon and his team created, there will be calls for more tales from the same universe. The fans, at the end of the day, were probably the reason that *Buffy* lasted longer that just those 12 initial episodes in 1997. Six years later, the show ended with a devoted fanbase that had followed the events of 144 *Buffy* episodes (not to mention 110 *Angel* ones). Just in case you're as *sad* as this author, that's approximately 10,000 minutes of our lives that we've spent watching these characters. Becoming emotionally involved in their lives as they tried to do what's right in the face of sometimes overwhelming odds.

We witnessed a natural evolution in the lives of these people as *Buffy* remained, to the final moment, what it had been for the previous seven years – the most unique TV series in the world.

---

just the kind of show I want to do.'" In 2002, Joss told the audience at the N3K convention in London that discussions were progressing and that Jane Root, Controller of BBC2, had told him the BBC envisioned a series of six or more episodes. 'One of the chief greatnesses of *Buffy*,' Tony acknowledged, 'is that it can make you laugh – with witty, sardonic humour – and the next moment, scare the living-Jesus out of you.' Describing *Ripper* as '*Cracker* with ghosts' to *Dream-Watch*, Tony even gave *SFX* a list of British actors with whom he'd like to work. (These included Eddie Izzard, Michael Briant, Phil Daniels, Ray Winstone and Michael Kitchen.) However, by 2003, Whedon told *Sci-Fi Wire*: 'I wanted to do something on the BBC. We talked about a two-hour movie. But the one conclusion I've come to, if I do something, I'll do it not as a set-up so much as a story about Giles. What I'm interested in is the character that Tony plays, not some mystery [that] he might solve.'